# MISSION POSSIBLE

## INTRODUCING JESUS TO THE UNREACHED

## Dr. Richard Charlick

# CONTENTS

# FORWARD

This book is an account of how God has used me in helping change the lives of thousands of people by just saying "Yes, Lord."

I have had the privilege of leading 35 healthcare mission teams into many remote parts of the world, where there was little or no healthcare, and where the people have never heard of Jesus. This book shares the fantastic workings of the Holy Spirit, and many exciting, unusual and unique experiences I have witnessed.

Some names have been changed to protect certain individuals from embarrassment or possible persecution. All stories are true, as accurately as I can recall them.

After traveling on short-term missions to extremely remote areas of our world over the last thirty years, I can truly say, my Lord has always been with me, and has blessed me "real good."

My wife, Dora May, has gone on most mission trips. Each of our four children, a son-in-law, and a granddaughter, has also accompanied us on one or more missions. I have never been sick one day and have experienced many different living conditions and cultures. I have had the joy of helping and seeing many thousands of people accept Jesus into their lives, and become Christians. Life just doesn't get any better.

My life is literally bursting at the seams with joy and happiness. I feel I need to share these experiences with others, hoping they too may surrender their lives to serve our Lord, and be blessed with the same joy and happiness.

# ACKNOWLEDGEMENTS

This book would have never been printed without the help of a lot of people.

The Lord has allowed me to have many years of interesting, unusual, rewarding experiences about which I have written. It has only been through patient and tireless help of many friends that my crude writings have been put in a more proper and readable form.

The most important person who has helped me from beginning to end as my chief editor and proofreader has been my dear friend, Shirley Chiles Humphreys. She lives hundreds of miles away but with the help of e-mail, fax, U.S. mail, telephone and UPS we have communicated regularly over a 3-year period.

Many others have helped me with corrections, editing and proofreading some of the chapters. These friends include Dr. Roger Youmans, Edward and Charlotte Pedley, Ruth Belleville, Allan Sayle and Vernon and Elizabeth Jones. All these friends have been a great encouragement to me.

My wife, Dora May, has helped me in many ways with ideas, typing, editing, proofreading and being patient during the hundreds of hours that it has taken to prepare this book.

I have thoroughly enjoyed reliving and preparing these experiences shared in this book, but I sincerely need to thank all my friends who have helped me make this possible.

# CHAPTER 1

# WHO AM I

I was blessed from the beginning to be born to loving Christian parents in Southeast Michigan, U.S.A. My one brother, 4 grandparents, lots of aunts, uncles and cousins were all solid Evangelical Christians.

I accepted Christ into my life and was baptized at a young age. As I grew up my entire family and I were very active in our nearby rural Baptist Church. Today, some 75 years later I am still worshipping and serving in the same wonderful church.

My formal education was in the Detroit public schools followed by 2 ½ years at Michigan State University. After that I had 7 years of education at the University of Michigan where I received a D.D.S., Doctor of Dental Surgery, and a M.S., Masters of Science in Restorative Dentistry. In the time between acquiring those two degrees, I served 3 years as a U.S. Naval Dental Officer, during which the Navy provided me one year of advanced training in a Dental Internship program.

I married Dora May Briggs in 1955, the summer before I started dental school. We have been happily married for over 55 years. We have 4 wonderful children. All are married to great Christian spouses and live within 10-15 minutes from our home. Mark, Karen and Todd have 2 children each while Beth has 3.

Mark and Todd are both dentists and have practiced with me for over 23 years. We have never had a cross word. Karen has worked with me for over 30 years and is currently our office manager. Beth is a dental hygienist and works in a dental office near her home. All our children, spouses and grandchildren are devoted Christians and attend and/or work regularly in their churches.

After I was discharged from the Navy we returned to Brighton, Michigan where I set up a private practice in dentistry. In part, because of my excellent academic record at the U of M, I was asked to teach in the Dental School 20 hours a week, which I thoroughly enjoyed. I retired in 1992 after 30 years, as an Associate Professor Emeritus.

My dental practice grew from 1 dentist, 1 assistant and 1 operating room, to a large new office of 8 dentists, 13 hygienists and over 35 various assistants with 16 operating rooms. Mark and Todd joined me in the mid 1980's after graduating from U of M. They now own and operate the office. Currently I am working for and with them a couple of days a week and still enjoy it, even at the age of 75. I have been practicing dentistry in Brighton for 47 years, and I have thoroughly enjoyed every minute of it.

My hobbies have been coaching and playing softball for over 50 years and traveling. We have traveled over 137 different countries, and have learned that by our living in the United States we have much for which to be thankful.

The Lord has blessed me with a loving and faithful wife, 4 wonderful children and 9 beautiful grandchildren who all live close to us. I have a wonderful profession with a terrific dental practice which I enjoy, a beautiful home, a great church, and many friends. I have had almost perfect health, and an unusual and fantastic opportunity to serve my Lord through Dentistry. What else could a person ever want? I am truly a blessed man.

# CHAPTER 2

# MY FIRST MISSION TRIP
# HAITI

In 1979 Dora May and I were high school youth leaders at our church. The youth group included 3 of our own teenage children. Edward Pedley was Youth Pastor and also a respected cousin of mine. Ed had the challenging idea that it would be a valuable experience if we could take our young people on a mission trip to Haiti.

Our church supported several missionaries in Haiti. Ed contacted them and they encouraged him to bring the young people and come. It could be beneficial for three reasons. One, it would be a valuable learning experience. Two, we could help with some simple construction projects, and three, we could bring some much needed supplies.

We discussed the potential mission trip to Haiti with our young people and received an enthusiastic positive response, so we started planning. We had special meetings with parents and interested youth. We planned several major fund raising projects that included car washes, garage sales, etc., because this could be expensive. Several of our church members hired our youth to do work in or around their houses.

It took almost a year, but we finally raised the money, and completed our planning. We left our church in Michigan in mid-June 1980 with 14 young people, with Ed, his wife Charlotte, Dora May and me as sponsors.

I drove our large motor home and Ed drove the church bus. We had 36 large suitcases and 18 fully packed carryon bags. With all that, we still could not take all the donated used clothes we had wanted to take for the children. We packed in our suitcases a disassembled wagon, two tricycles, many durable toys, lots of medications, and all the used clothes we could carry for the mission hospital and orphanage in Limbe, of which Dr. Hodges was the director. He also was one of the missionaries our church had supported for many years.

We drove the first day to Jim and Deb Cartwright's, who were also missionaries from our church who were working with Wycliffe Bible Translators. They were stationed at the

JARRS Aviation Headquarters in Waxhaw, South Carolina. We set up our tents in their front yard, had a good meal, and visited with them. The next day we drove to Jellystone RV Park in Orlando, Florida. Our third day we left our campsite early, and had a full day at the Magic Kingdom in Disney World.

Day four we headed to the Miami airport where we took a flight to Port-Au-Prince, the capital of Haiti. Most of our 14 youth had never been out of the State of Michigan and most had never flown in an airplane, and none of them had been to a foreign country.

When we arrived at the Port-Au-Prince airport we were greeted by a missionary couple, Kent and Linda Ragsdale. It took a long time to get through customs with our 54 bags. The officials went through everything. We had a broken bottle of medicine. They wanted to know what it was. We told them it was aspirin and indeed it was. Kent suggested that they help themselves to some if they wanted. They did, and after that, we sailed rapidly the rest of the way through customs.

Kent and Linda Ragsdale had been missionaries in Haiti for 25 years, and they knew the traditions necessary to get through customs. One of our youth was a nephew of theirs.

Kent and Linda arranged for us, and our luggage, to be transported to a small hotel near their home. Dora May kept telling me she thought she knew Linda, but couldn't remember from where. When we arrived at the hotel Linda came up to Dora May and said, "Are you Dora May?", and instantly they both remembered. Dora May and Linda had gone to grade school in Hartland, Michigan, together from K through 6th grade, then Linda moved away. They had not seen or heard from each other for over 30 years. It's sometimes a small world.

The next morning Kent and Linda transported all 18 of us and our 54 pieces of luggage to the city dump. The city had been dumping there for many years, and they still were. They had leveled and packed down a large area where several 1 ½ and 2 ½-ton trucks were scattered around in no particular order. Kent informed us this was the bus station. The smell from the freshly dumped garbage was very strong and foul. There were no buses. They called these trucks buses.

Kent kept driving from truck to truck and talking to the drivers in their native language of Creole. Finally he found a larger empty truck that was going to Cap-Haitien, our destination, a large city on the far north shore of the country. He bargained with the driver, and told him which hotel we were staying in, and signaled us that this was our bus. The truck was empty. In the back of the truck were wooden benches that went from side to side. About every 12 to 14 inches there was a number painted on the boards. We were each given a seat number. Metal poles went up the sides of the truck which supported a durable top.

We helped hoist our luggage to the top of the truck where they were piled high. We then got in the back of the truck, out of the hot sun, found our seat and bid a thank you and farewell to Kent and Linda. We sat and sat, all the time smelling this pungent odor of rotting garbage. It got hotter and hotter. Slowly other people came and started putting their baggage on top of ours and climbed into the back of the truck. Some people brought live chickens and little pigs into the back of the truck, which they didn't want to put on top with the luggage.

They put a canvas over all the baggage on top, and tied it down securely. They could pile the baggage as high as they wanted because there were no bridges to drive under. The truck looked a little top heavy to me. Finally about 2 ½ hours later our truck was fully loaded and we started to move. Our truck was a fairly new Mercedes Benz with a big diesel engine that was needed to power heavy loads up the steep mountain roads.

The trip was about 4 ½ hours, stopping anywhere people wanted to get on or off. Usually each stop required the driver and his helper to go on top, take the canvas off, and find the person's baggage. We traveled along the coast for a while which had small mountains that went out to the ocean, followed by big populated valleys. The truck slowed and labored intensively going up these coastal hills or small mountains but when it reached the top, it picked up speed as it descended.

I sat in the middle of the truck and could see the road ahead through the back window of the truck. We were driving on the country's main north-south road. It was the only paved road we saw. In the bottom of each valley, where a river would usually be, there was a village. I could see the road ahead and it was packed with bicycles, carts, animals and was thick with a mass of humanity.

As the truck continued to pick up more and more speed, the thought ran through my mind, that the driver would never be able to stop this truck. About that time he started laying on his horn. It was a horn the likes of which I had never heard on a truck before. It sounded like a large boat horn. He continued picking up speed, with his pedal to the metal. He blasted through the center of town doing 70 to 80 miles an hour, like a train. I couldn't believe it, but everything moved out of our way. The chickens were the last thing to fly out of the way. Several times I was certain we would collect some chickens. The driver's great speed gave him a good start up the mountain range on the other side of the valley.

We repeated this scenario several times. Each time I held my breath and watched in great amazement to see the enormous mass of humanity clear off the road at the very last minute, only shortly before we blasted through the town with the horn blaring continuously. This was a scary experience, and one I will never forget.

When we arrived at our hotel the bus stopped in the road. There was no shoulder, so the 18 of us, and our 54 pieces of luggage, unloaded right in the middle of the road. The hotel was across the road and down an embankment several hundred yards. We struggled with our luggage, dragging it over to the hotel, then registered, and found our rooms. The hotel was single story, very old, poorly maintained, and spread out in separate sections. It was very hot with no air-conditioning. They had a swimming pool but it was empty as it had a big crack through the concrete in the bottom.

15

Ed and I were on our own most of this day. We were not sure where we were going, and could not speak any of the language. 100% of the people were black and we were responsible for 14 teenagers. Needless to say, we were really happy and relieved when our missionary host showed up to welcome us and to take charge.

Some of the highlights of our stay in Cap-Haitian included a few days of a work construction project. We cleaned and repainted a church youth camp. Ed and a couple of our boys took a very old, leaky, rusty sheet metal roof off the outhouse and put on a new one. I remember when they threw down the old rotten sheet metal roofing that the local natives were waiting, fought over the pieces, and disappeared into the underbrush. You would have thought we were throwing down hundred dollar bills the way they excitedly grabbed those pieces and ran.

After a hot day of painting and construction we were very dirty and tired. There wasn't much to clean up with at the hotel, so we walked a short distance to a beautiful ocean beach. We were on the leeward side of the island where there were no waves. The sand was white, the water was very shallow for a long way out, and the sun was very hot. I will never forget the feeling I had when stepping into this ocean water. It was actually warm, just like my bath water. We all enjoyed it, cleaned up and felt refreshed.

I was swimming in a little deeper water near one of our youth named Mike. All of a sudden Mike started screaming loudly and thrashing around in the water. I thought that maybe he had been attacked by a shark, but I instinctively swam over to him. He yelled that something got his leg, and when he popped it out of the water I could see it was bleeding. We headed toward shore, as did everyone else. One of the English speaking local natives that had been helping us with our construction project came quickly to see what was causing all the noise.

He immediately knew what the problem was. "You bumped into a spiny sea urchin, it's nothing serious," he informed Mike. Mike's leg kept stinging severely. Our native friend said, "Come with me," and he hurried Mike into some dense foliage out of the view of the rest of us. He told Mike "If you want to stop the sting, do as we natives do, just pee on it." Mike took little time soaking his wound with his own urine, and instantly the stinging went away. On our next day's swim everyone kept a lookout for these spiny sea urchins, which were rare, and we didn't have any more problems.

One day we traveled 45 minutes to visit another of our church supported missionaries, Dr. Hodges. He had founded and was running a large general hospital of several hundred beds, in the smaller town of Limbe. We took our wagons, tricycles, medications and lots of clothes to give to Dr. Hodges and his hospital. The hospital staff took the wagons and tricycles to a paved area outside the children's wards. It was rewarding to see the children pour out of the wards and start riding the tricycles, and pulling each other around in the wagons. Most of them had never seen a tricycle and we actually had to show them how it worked. It was just like Christmas. They were happy and so were we.

We had lunch with Dr. Hodges and his wife. After lunch Dr. Hodges talked to our group for about an hour, telling us about the hospital and life in Haiti. The one significant thing I recall was Dr. Hodges telling us that the hardest part of his job was to go out to the waiting shelters at the end of the day, and go through the 50 to 100 patients who had been waiting, but had not yet been seen. They would wait in the tent until the next day in hopes of being seen. Dr. Hodges' job was to pick out those he did not think would still be alive the next morning, and take them into the hospital and treat them after hours. He shared that, unfortunately, he would not always recognize the seriousness of some patient's illness, only to find the person dead the next morning. How would you like that job?

We toured the hospital as well as his infant orphanage. It seemed that when a newborn was deformed or got seriously sick shortly after birth, the parents would bring the child to the hospital and just abandon it on Dr. Hodges' doorstep. They had 10 to 20 infants, and several were only a few days old. After they got stronger and healthier other natives would adopt them.

One day we went to the Bible Seminary which our church helped to support. We were ushered into a lecture room and the founder, Dr. Hennessy, who had been there over 25 years, came into the room, walked over to the lectern, and told us all about the Bible Seminary, and many other interesting things. He was an older man. He informed us that his son was now taking over the leadership of the seminary. When he finished he walked out of the room before any of us had a chance to greet or talk to him. It was at this time our host told us Dr. Hennessey had been totally blind for several years. He knew the school by heart, and was determined not to let his blindness stop his ministry. We were all surprised because no one had detected any signs of his being blind. We were all very impressed by the training of the native Haitian pastors that was taking place at this seminary.

On Sunday we went to a local church in Cap-Haitian which was started by our host missionary, who was also partly supported by our church. They had reserved front row seats for their guests from America. We were the only white people around anywhere. The church was packed with people sitting on the floor, standing around the walls, hanging in the windows, standing in the doorways, and actually surrounding the whole church 3 or 4 people deep. There was a lot of singing, and it was singing like I had never heard before. When these people sang they clapped and sang at the top of their voices with rhythm and enthusiasm.

After church and lunch we took a hike to the top of a mountain where the Haitians had built a great fort that they called the Citadel. After the Haitians had kicked the French out of their country in the 1800's they expected the French to return in large numbers to recapture their land. They built this great Citadel as a defense, and it still stands on top of the mountain today. Fortunately it never was used.

We had a jolly black pastor that spoke English well, who led us up a small dry river bed to the fort. As some of the young people spread out along the way, the pastor turned to me and said, "We need to keep together, because I cannot keep track of everybody." Then he made a statement which really hit home to me. He said, "All you white people look alike."

In the Miami airport a week earlier, we had a porter who wanted to handle our bags. When I asked him how much, he told me $50.00. Our youth were young and strong and had been sitting on a bus for several hours so I decided against it. When we were checking in, the porter's fee came up in our conversation. The check-in attendant got very upset, and went and got his supervisor. The supervisor informed me that it was strictly against policy for those porters to take any money. He asked me to identify the porter, and he would fire him on the spot. Ed and I went with the supervisor to where the porters were, and he asked us to identify the porter. We were having trouble deciding which one, so the supervisor lined them all up against the wall, 6 or 8 of them, and again impatiently asked us which one. I couldn't tell which one, and finally turned to Ed and said, "I can't tell, all these black people look alike."

When it was time to return to Port-a-Prince and go home, a truck actually pulled into the hotel parking area and loaded us up. This time we had a smaller truck, but we had it all to ourselves. Two memorable instances happened on this trip. Mike got motion sickness and vomited extensively. He was very neat about it as he caught everything in his new, souvenir straw hat. We tried to get him to throw his hat away, but nothing doing. He took it to the hotel, washed it, and was wearing it the next day.

The second incident was when Ed and Charlotte took advantage of the empty, soft front seat, and asked the driver if they could ride up front with him. The driver evidently hadn't had much sleep, and started to fall asleep while driving over the narrow, winding mountain roads. He started wandering all over the road. Ed and Charlotte quickly picked up on this, and spent a good hour trying to keep the driver awake. First they tried talking to him, but there was the language barrier. Then they began singing songs and clapping. Several times during their clapping they actually had to purposely slip and hit the driver to wake him up. God was with us, and we made it safely to our hotel in Port-a-Prince.

That evening was June 25, 1980, a moment to remember. It was Dora May's and my 25th wedding anniversary. We had supper in the hotel so I contacted the kitchen early and surprised my wife with an anniversary cake big enough for the whole group. Then she took her girls to their rooms and I took my boys to our rooms.

We had one day to shop and look around in Port-a-Prince. Kent asked us if our group would like to go with him to an evangelistic service that evening. Ed and I said, "Sure." He picked us all up, (we always stayed together as a group,) around 6 p.m., and we traveled to the outskirts of Port-a-Prince. We turned down a small dirt road that was lined with tar paper shacks as far as we could see, and children were everywhere. There were no electric lines anywhere.

There was a native pastor with us that was trying to reach these people and share Jesus with them. He had asked Kent to furnish a generator, movie projector, screen, sound, and lights, so they could show the Jesus film. Kent's ministry in Haiti was furnishing a generator, movie projector, lights and especially sound systems for pastors and churches for special events in areas where such equipment was not available. He had done this for over 25 years. Twenty eight years later Dora May and I personally still support them and their mission.

When we came to a small fork in the road, we stopped and started setting up. First they set up and started the public address system playing loud Christian music. Then they set up the movie projector and screen just as it was getting dark. It gets dark quickly the closer you get to the equator with very little evening twilight. There was no electricity in the entire area so Kent had brought his generator.

People started gathering quickly. They showed a short movie first and then the Jesus Film in their own language of Creole. All movies in Haiti were in French, the official language of the country. Unfortunately 90% of these people did not understand French. Television was not available to these poor people. Most people had never seen a movie, and if they had, they would not have understood it because it was in French. No one had ever seen a movie in Creole, and no one had ever seen a movie on the life of Jesus.

When it got dark, it was as dark as ink. There was no moon or reflected light from anywhere. It was so dark you couldn't see your hand in front of your face. I was standing when all of a sudden something hit me in the back of the knees, and someone put their hand on my shoulder and sat me down on a chair. The people had brought us chairs from their tar paper shacks. Evidently they could see more than I could. Eventually we were all given a chair, while everyone else stood.

All during the film there was lightning and thunder all over the sky, but we never got a drop of rain. When the film ended the lightning and thunder ended, and Kent turned on several big spotlights that lit up the whole area. The open field was packed with hundreds and hundreds of people.

The native pastor quickly got up on a makeshift platform, and started talking to the people over Kent's excellent loud speaker system. After the pastor had talked with the people for 30 minutes, he gave an invitation, while Kent played some soft music over the sound system. Many people came forward and stood in a little open area in front of the pastor. He helped them pray for their sins to be forgiven and for Christ to come into their heart. It was a very thrilling and touching moment.

It was absolutely amazing that with a little drive and determination of that native pastor, combined with the technical help from Kent, they turned a small, dirty, dusty, open field in the middle of a slum shanty town, in the black of a stormy night, into a great evangelistic theater where hundreds heard about Jesus. Probably for many this was the first time, and there were many people who turned their lives over to Jesus and were saved. Praise the Lord!

The next morning we boarded a plane with lots of empty suitcases, and had an uneventful trip back to Miami. We then boarded our church bus and motor home and were home in 2 days. It is great to go away, but always better to come home.

I was thinking on our way home, about what a culture shock this had to have been for our young people. One day we were in Disney World with all the latest technology, including the fantastic automation of the Hall of Presidents, and the very next day we were in Haiti, the western hemisphere's poorest country.

It was rewarding to hear each one of our students share one or two of their experiences in front of our total church congregation. They were so excited that it was difficult to get them to stop talking. Time has proved that this was an experience none of them will ever forget, and you can be sure it was an experience I will never forget. I pen you these details 28 years after the fact.

# CHAPTER 3

# MY CALL TO MISSIONS

We were surprised one Sunday to see Jim Cartwright in church. He was a missionary in Colombia, South America. In talking with him he explained that he needed to come home for a family emergency and would be home for a week or so. I asked if he had a free evening to come over to our house for supper. He agreed, so we set a date.

Jim was raised in the same church as I, and was just a couple of years younger. We played on the same church softball team. His mother and dad were very active in our church. His mother taught Dora May's and my Sunday school class for many years.

After high school graduation Jim went to Moody Bible Institute. He met his wife, Debbie, got married and graduated. He had always been interested in flying and felt a call to mission aviation. He and Deb went to a small town in eastern Tennessee to the Moody Aviation School. Jim was not eligible to be a pilot, so he worked and graduated in aviation mechanics.

After raising their financial support of which a large part came from our church, he and Deb were accepted into the Wycliffe Bible Translators Mission Program, with Jim as an aviation mechanic. After significant mission training by Wycliffe, they were assigned to Bogotá, the capital of Colombia. His job was to maintain an old World War II twin engine DC-3 airplane, and keep it flying safely. This was a significant sized plane that could carry 30 to 40 passengers plus baggage, or it could be just used as a cargo plane. It usually did both.

The DC-3 was the main source of transportation between Bogotá, located on a large high plateau in the Andes Mountains and Wycliffe's Headquarters at Lomalinda, east of the Andes in the Amazon River Basin. During the rainy season, the DC-3 was the only source of transportation, because the roads became impassable.

During dinner that evening, with all our family present, Jim told us many details of his mission activities in Colombia. Then he told us an unusual and very interesting story.

There was a Wycliffe pilot that flew a small plane out of Lomalinda into the massive Colombian Amazon Jungle Basin to small airstrips carved out of the jungle by the Wycliffe missionaries and the native Indians they were helping. There were many native tribes with various spoken, but unwritten languages. The Wycliffe Bible Translators were working to take their spoken language and develop it into a written language. Then they taught them how to read and write. They also translated the Bible into their local language, so they could read it for themselves. This resulted in many people becoming Christians.

This pilot's job was to regularly take supplies to the missionaries spread throughout the Amazon Basin, as well as to transport people. On one airstrip there was a young man who always rushed to the airstrip when he heard the plane coming, in order to help the pilot unload the plane and guard it if the pilot went into the village.

Although they could not speak the same language, one day this young man got the pilot's attention, by pointing to a black, broken off front tooth. The pilot just shrugged his shoulders. Every time the pilot landed at this village, the same young man would get the pilot's attention and point to his front tooth. Finally the pilot, out of frustration went to the small tool box on the plane, got out an ordinary pair of mechanic's pliers, grabbed the young man's tooth and yanked it out. The young man yelled and ran off. The pilot thought probably that would be the last time he would ever see that young man.

The next time the pilot landed at that village, the young man was back and before he could get the engine shut off, he noticed a long line of natives lining up behind the plane. It turned out they were lining up to get their aching teeth pulled, just like the young man had on his last trip there. At this point the pilot realized the severity of pain these people must be experiencing.

When the pilot got back to headquarters at Lomalinda he went to the small empty dental clinic and found the book, "Where There is No Dentist". This book explained to a lay person how to extract a tooth when there is no dentist available. This was just what he needed.

The pilot borrowed several surgical extraction forceps from the clinic. When he returned to that village he was better prepared to help the people by extracting their teeth, and that is what he did.

Soon the word of his tooth extraction services spread from jungle village to village and he was being requested to extract teeth in many places where he landed. This was all being done without any anesthesia. If a root broke off, he had no way of removing it, so he just left it.

As we sat at the dinner table we were all fascinated by Jim's story. Todd was a freshman and Mark was a sophomore in dental school. Mark had just finished learning how to give local dental anesthesia.

Mark was sitting across from Jim and next to me. He turned to me and really surprised me by saying, "Dad, we could do better than that, we could use anesthesia." Jim then commented "Well, why don't you come down and help us?" A million things raced through my mind. How could the Lord speak to me any clearer than through Jim's invitation? The Lord has given me skills in a wonderful profession to serve the physical needs of people. I also have the ability to regulate my income and to take time off any time I want. What reason could I justify for saying no? I felt in my heart, that if I said no, I wasn't saying no to Jim, I was saying no to my Lord.

I turned to Mark and asked, "Will you go with me?" He promptly replied "Yes." My decision that evening changed the future direction of my life. Today I have now led 35 short-term health care missions, doing dental work in 16 different countries all around the world. I have spent a total of one year and four months, over the last 25 years, on various missions.

This decision to serve my Lord has turned out to be one of the greatest joys of my life. I am continually looking ahead and cannot wait for my next mission trip.

# CHAPTER 4

# COLOMBIA 1
# FIRST DENTAL MISSION

After committing to Jim Cartwright that Mark and I would come down and help him, it was time for an extensive first time dental mission preparation. We needed to decide when we were going and exactly where we were going. I needed to find out what type of dental services they were expecting, what type of instruments and materials needed to be taken, where I was going to get them, and if they would all fit into our suitcases.

How long were we going to stay? What type of vaccinations and medications would we need? Mark would need to get a passport. What about visas? We needed to get airline reservations. Who was going to meet us at the airport? What type of clothes would we need? How much money would I need to take? The list just went on and on.

This was all new to me, and a rather enjoyable, exciting challenge. Mark wasn't much help. He was up to his neck in dental school work. It actually took several months, including lots of slow international communications to put all the detailed preparations together.

Finally in late June 1984, after Mark had successfully finished his sophomore year of dental school, and had started his summer break, we bid our families farewell and departed. We flew to Miami, and then took an Eastern Airlines flight to Bogotá, Colombia.

We had to pass through immigrations and customs by ourselves, but fortunately we had no difficulties. I always travel in a suit, white shirt and tie. Right or wrong, there is no question that it creates respect, and seems to help in getting through customs.

After clearing customs we found Jim waiting for us. His mechanics office, workshop and the DC-3 plane for which he was responsible was in a different area at the same airport. He took us and our 350 to 400 lbs. of luggage to his home where we joined Deb, his wife, and their 3 children, Gabriel, Naomi and Benjamin.

Jim's children had attended our church academy a few years earlier when they were home on furlough. My, how they had grown! After Deb fixed us a great supper, we talked late into the night. We stayed overnight with Jim and his family.

The next morning we went to the airport where Jim needed to prepare the DC-3 for flight. A few people started gathering with all types of baggage. Finally it was time to load and leave. Jim always flew with the plane and acted as the flight attendant, but more importantly he traveled with the plane in case of any mechanical problems. Jim related to us that the plane often landed in very remote locations, and sometimes had mechanical problems that he had to fix before the plane could return to Bogotá.

The high, cool, large plateau where Bogota was located was between 2 ranges of the Andes Mountains, at about 8,000 feet elevation. It was very populated and very fertile with a lot of agriculture. After we took off, we noticed out our windows, huge greenhouses which occupied several acres each. Jim told us the greenhouses raised almost 90% of all the long stem roses that was available for purchase in the United States.

After flying along the plateau and gaining altitude, we started up and over the eastern portion of the Andes Mountain Range. The passenger cabin of the plane was not pressurized. Jim instructed us to suck on a small oxygen hose found near our seats when we reached the higher altitudes that would be needed to cross the Andes.

Once over the mountains they ended very abruptly. There were no foothills. The Amazon River started on the eastern slopes of the Andes and only had about a 600-foot drop from central Colombia all the way to the mouth of the Amazon in eastern Brazil. This was several thousand miles. I guess this is one of the reasons the Amazon River if so navigable. There are no waterfalls and few rapids, except in the small tributaries.

We traveled about another hour east with a thick green jungle canopy below us. As we started to descend, a child passenger grabbed his ears and started to scream. Jim went up to the child, talked to him, and then went up and talked to the pilots. Remember, the passenger cabin was not pressurized. This child was having problems equalizing the pressure in his ears. The pilots pulled the plane up, and circled around, and descended much slower. That solved the problem.

We landed on a bumpy grass landing strip and taxied up to a small building. This was Lomalinda, Wycliffe's main headquarters for their large translation work in Colombia.

Twenty years earlier Wycliffe had received permission from the ninety percent plus Catholic government to contact the 50 to 55 native Indian tribes, properly called indigenous people, isolated in the mountains or jungle. Wycliffe offered to translate their verbal language into a written language, and to teach them how to read and write in their own native language. They also obtained permission to translate the Bible into their language, and use it in teaching them to read. In twenty years they had been able to start work in 42 of the 50 or more indigenous people groups.

The government granted Wycliffe several hundred acres of semi-jungle land to use as their headquarters. This land was at the edge of the large isolated eastern jungle, just a couple of miles from where all roads ended at a large river. It was as close as they could get to the jungle where they could fly personnel and supplies into the various indigenous people groups located deep in the jungle.

Wycliffe had built some 25 to 30 houses in the area. They had their own large generators that supplied electricity 24 hours a day. The local government village had electricity only two hours a day. Lomalinda had stores, a school (K-12), print shop, libraries, computer and office center, medical clinic, church, electronic center, flight control tower, radio communications center; a lake with swimming and fishing, a motel-like guest center, and an airport with several special airplanes. This was a small city where about 150 to 200 missionaries and support personnel lived. They even had their own form of government with elected officials.

After everything was unloaded and the plane was secured, Jim, the 2 pilots, Mark and I went to the guest house that was hosted by Gary and Char Shingledecker. They fed us a great lunch. After lunch Jim and the pilots went back to the plane, loaded it with passengers, luggage and supplies, and returned to Bogotá before nightfall.

Gary and Char were our hosts while we were in Lomalinda, and they took care of our every need. Since their 2 teenage daughters had gone back to the states for the summer, they had us stay in their own personal home with them rather then put us in the guest house. In addition to running the base guest house, Char was a high school teacher in their school and Gary was a general handyman.

The next morning Gary took Mark and me on his small motorbike to the medical clinic; three adults on one small motorcycle WOW!!! Motorcycles constituted 90% of Lomalinda's transportation. The medical clinic building had about 10 rooms in it including a crudely equipped dental room.

Lomalinda had not had any dentist, even a part time one, for over 5 years. We had just started to look things over when our first patient arrived. Word of a dentist coming had spread quickly. Mark had completed all his basic dental school training. He had been taught how to give anesthesia and how to put in fillings in artificial teeth, but he had not started working on patients yet. He was scheduled to start working on patients in the fall. Well, he got an early start.

It didn't take long before we got things up and running. We were soon cleaning teeth, anesthetizing and putting in fillings. I even needed to extract several teeth. Mark had not had any surgical training yet. We worked long and hard for several days. Mark got along fine. No one really knew, and we didn't say anything. I watched him more closely than he would have been supervised at the dental school. It got warm in the clinic and we did sweat a lot.

There was no medical doctor at Lomalinda and there hadn't been for a long time. Occasionally one of the missionaries, who had also been trained as a nurse, came to the clinic and saw patients.

In the evening we were invited to different missionaries' homes for supper. This gave us a unique opportunity to see how they lived, and find out what part of the mission work with which they were involved. It was a pleasant way to get acquainted with a variety of missionaries.

Sunday we went to a very unique worship service in a nice but a very simply constructed church. The church was close to Shingledeckers' house, so we walked. I remember as I was approaching the church I observed no cars, but 20 to 30 motorcycles parked around the church. That surely was a unique sight. They had a wonderful and very touching worship service, with many different people participating.

The church service taught me a very important lesson that I will always remember. We had some 150 people at the service and the interesting thing was that they were from many protestant denominations, and from several different countries, but they all worshipped in perfect harmony. This taught me that it can be done, particularly when people keep their eyes focused on Jesus, and not on man. When people have a common objective of sharing Jesus with other people, it is easier to bond.

After church we had dinner with Gary and Char. After dinner Gary gave us the ores to his row boat. We went exploring on the lake. We rowed up the river that came into the lake as well as down the river that went out of the lake. It was strange because both the inlet and outlet rivers, which were 20 to 30 feet wide at the mouth of the lake, had a moderate current, and after a half a mile, suddenly it just seemed to stop and spread out into the jungle and disappear.

On the river we saw a lot of wild orchids, colorful parrots, and many monkeys swinging high in the trees. It was very different, to say the least, than cruising down a river on a Sunday afternoon in the U.S. On our way back to the dock we passed a row boat that had 8 people in it. They were stopped and were fishing. They had so many people in the boat that the water was only 2 inches from the top of the boat. We stopped and asked if they were catching anything and they held up a big stringer full of piranha. This seemed to be a dangerous adventure. Either they could catch the piranha, or if they tipped the boat slightly, they could fall into the lake, and the piranha could catch them. We didn't do any fishing.

A few days later when the DC-3 made one of its tri-weekly flights to Lomalinda, we packed, said goodbye to our many new friends, and headed back to Bogotá. Many of our new friends begged us to return next year to continue to help them with their dental needs. All we could say at that time was, "We will try". It turned out I returned 6 years in a row. I'll describe more about that later.

We returned to Jim and Deb's house where we began to repack. Jim, along with the Wycliffe leaders, had arranged for us to go out to Ron and Mary Jane Michael's indigenous Chami village of Buena Vista, located high in the western Andes Mountains.

Jim took this opportunity to go with us. This was the first time he had ever had a chance to get away from his DC-3 responsibilities, and travel to one of the remote indigenous villages.

There was a young lady, Kay, in her late 20's that went with us also. Kay was a trained translator, but was waiting for a partner to join her so she could go and start translation in one of the ten to twelve indigenous groups that Wycliffe had not started working with yet. She had been waiting a couple of years for a partner. Wycliffe requires all translators to work in pairs of two or more when in isolated indigenous villages. Kay operated the flight control tower that kept radio contact with all Wycliffe's planes when on flights, and she maintained daily radio contact with all of the missionaries that were in their remote jungle villages. The missionary translators had established a village base in each of the 42 remote tribal areas where they were working. Kay also had never had an opportunity to go out into an indigenous village.

Colombia has been in a 3-way Civil War for many years. They have the official Spanish immigrant-based government that is in control of 90% of the population, and about 50% of the land. They also have a Communist Guerrilla group that is in control of the other half of the land area. The Guerrillas control mainly the sparsely populated jungles and mountains. The third group is the cocaine cartel that is always fighting against the government troops. The Communist Guerrillas have actually been hired by the rich cocaine cartel to help protect them. They both occupy the same remote, less occupied parts of the land, which is basically only accessible by foot, and they both have the same enemy, the government.

Out of the 42 indigenous people groups that Wycliffe translators were working with, there was only one group that the Wycliffe administration felt was safe from potential Communist attack, at the present time, and that was Ron and Mary Jane's village.

Jim, Kay, Mark and I got all packed and took a commercial flight from Bogotá to Cali, a large city on the western slopes of the Andes. From there we hired a station wagon taxi to take us further west to a small town where Ron and Mary Jane had agreed to come and meet us.

There were two interesting things about our taxi ride, besides it's being a very old beat up station wagon. As we left town the driver pulled into an isolated gas station and filled up with gas. Then he came to Jim, shrugged his shoulders, pulled his empty pockets inside out, and explained he had no money. He asked Jim if we could pay part of our fare up front. We were packed very tight, and were out in the middle of nowhere, so needless to say we paid some up front.

The trip took about three hours. After we had been driving a while we came to a fork in the road with a sign pointing each way. The taxi driver stopped and asked Jim if he would read the signs for him, so he would know which way to go.

Near sundown we reached our rendezvous hotel in the designated village we had been trying to find. Ron and Mary Jane were out front looking for us, wondering if we would make it before dark. They indicated it was not safe to be on the roads in this part of the country after dark.

After supper and lots of good conversation, we all got a good night's sleep. After an early breakfast, we were asked to pack so we could hit the road again. This time there were six of us plus a driver and our entire luggage, including several big bags of dental instruments and supplies. What showed up to transport us for the next half day further into the remote western Andes Mountains, was a small World War II army jeep. I laughed and said, "No way!" They started packing anyway.

They packed most of the luggage on top and tied it down. It must have been six feet high. The driver and Ron got in front while Mary Jane, Kay and I squeezed into the back along with some luggage. Jim and Mark stood on the rear bumper, and we took off.

We traveled about four hours on smaller and smaller roads until there was grass growing between the two tracks as we headed higher up and over a mountain pass. It was interesting, because on the eastern slopes of the mountains it was dry, with lots of cacti. As we went over the dividing pass and started down the western or Pacific side of the mountains, the vegetation rapidly turned green and dense. First thing we knew we were in a mountainous jungle. There was very little civilization along this entire four-hour drive. We finally came to a small village where the road ended. We stopped, unloaded and had lunch.

I wondered where we would go from here. We couldn't possibly carry all this baggage ourselves. Just then, a string of mules and horses appeared, and they started loading our baggage onto them. Finally they loaded us on the animals too, and we started out of the village single file into the dense jungle undergrowth on a small trail. We didn't have to rein the horses or mules because there wasn't any other place for them to go, and it was obvious they had done this many times before. This part of our trip took about five hours.

In some areas the vegetation cleared, and we could see we were on a narrow path on the side of a very steep mountain. It was obvious that if the horse took one step to the side it would be like going over a cliff. Sometimes there were six to eight-inch wide washouts that cut through the path. I was concerned that my mule might step into one of those and stumble, but he never did.

I was on a mule in the middle of the pack. Mark followed me on a horse. There was a young boy ten years old that walked in between us carrying a big machete. Every now and then he would swing his machete and chop at the ground. We didn't give that much thought then. Later we found out he was there to clear the snakes off the path, if the mules ahead of him hadn't scared them away. We were told snakes don't bother mules, but a horse gets easily spooked when it sees a snake and may jump over the side. I think it was probably the first time Mark had ever put his life in the control of a ten year old Indian boy and not even knew it.

The afternoon sun was getting very hot. After two or three hours, we came to our first dwellings. We got off our animals for a rest break. Some children brought us some coke, and wanted to sell them to us. They were warm but wet. We were very dry. I don't usually drink coke but it was so good. The thing that really amazed me was that it only cost twenty five cents a bottle out in this jungle wilderness. This was considerably less than we pay for coke back home.

While we were stopped, Ron pointed down the valley to a village where he and the chief lived. It was on the opposite side of this very steep mountain valley. I wondered how we were ever going to get down the side of this steep mountain and up the other side.

We continued along the high mountain trail that we had been on for a little longer, then turned off on a small cleared area, and started to zigzag back and forth down the side of this very steep mountain.

Upon reaching the bottom there was a very rapid river about 40 feet wide. They picked the widest, swiftest area, and walked the mules and horses across in just one or two feet of water. It was very rocky and they stumbled a bit but we all got across ok.

We then started to climb on a very zigzag path. The animals started breathing heavily and snorting a lot. Jim's horse got so sweaty that his saddle just slid sideways and he took a dive into the mud.

I was accustomed to the Rocky Mountains in the U.S., but on the western slope of these Andes there were no rocks, everything was dirt. Because of the numerous daily showers the western slopes received, this area got wet every day, the vegetation was heavy, and the soil was saturated. The animals were sinking into mud several inches with each step.

Well, Jim got up, a little messy but unhurt because his fall was into deep, soft mud. He wiped himself off the best he could, tightened up the horse's saddle cinch, and climbed back on, and we continued.

When we approached the village there was a small flat area cleared of heavy vegetation that actually protruded from the side of the mountain. The view up and down the valley was spectacular. The view is where the name of the village got its name, Buena Vista, meaning beautiful view. It was a good place for the chief to live and rule because he could see up and down the valley a long way.

As we approached the village we met a large, long-horned bull that stood right in the path staring at us. At first we just slowed down, but when the bull started snorting and pawing at the dirt, we stopped and waited and waited some more. We were only a hundred yards or so from the village, so we thought someone from the village would come out and rescue us, but they didn't, so we continued to wait. Finally the bull wandered off to the side of the trail and we proceeded as he stood there and watched us. We found out later that the bull belonged to the chief. No cows were around, just one big, frisky bull wandering around loose. We also found out he had never attacked or hurt anyone.

Upon arrival we proceeded directly to Ron's house where a crowd started to gather. There were about 20 to 25 small houses on this small, flat clearing on the side of the mountain and most of them were attached, but Ron's house was separate and larger.

Ron told us how he got his house. He and Mary Jane discussed with the Colombian Wycliffe Administration that they felt called to the Chami Indigenous people.

They heard about Buena Vista where the chief lived and felt this would be a good place to start. Upon reaching Buena Vista they had supper and spent the evening with the chief. They explained their objective to translate their verbal language into a written language and to teach them how to read and write. They asked for his permission, which they heartily got. The chief could speak and understand Spanish. They also asked if they could live in his beautiful village. They received no response.

After sleeping that night in the chief's home, or better described as a hut, they were awakened in the morning with banging and other types of loud noises. They hurried out of the hut as there were no windows to see what the commotion was. They found a large number of villagers starting to build a large building. The chief joined them and informed them that this was to be their house. Everything was done by hand. Even the boards that they used for the floor were totally sawed by hand.

We received a lot of help from the villagers unloading our animals at Ron and Mary Jane's Buena Vista home. When we first arrived it was so hot, so primitive, and such a long way from home that I started asking, "Lord, what am I doing here?"

On our first night after a candlelight supper, Ron wanted to have devotions and prayer. He got out a "Secret Place" devotional booklet, turned to that days devotion, dated July 12, 1984 and read this scripture, starting at James 2:14; "Dear brothers, what is the use of saying you have faith and are Christians if you aren't proving it by your helping others? Will that kind of faith save anyone? If you have a friend who is in need of food and clothing, and you say to him, "Well, good-bye and God bless you; stay warm and eat hearty," and then don't give him clothes or food, what good does that do? So you see, it isn't enough just to have faith. You must also do good to prove that you have it. Faith that doesn't show itself by good works is no faith at all, it is dead and useless."

When I heard these scriptures I immediately interpreted it this way. If you have a brother or sister who is sick and in pain and you say, well goodbye, hope you feel better and get well, but you don't give that person any treatment or medication, what good does that do? So you see it isn't just enough to have faith. Faith that does not show itself by good deeds is no faith at all, it is dead and useless.

This answered my question as to why I was there. I will never forget that night and that scripture. They have become key motivational verses in my life, and have helped power me to 36 additional mission trips so far, and I'm still going at 75 years of age as I am writing these memoirs.

We slept under a large mosquito net that Ron had told us about at supper. He said it wasn't for the mosquitoes which were few, but rather to protect against the large jungle spiders which grew up to six inches in diameter, and had a very painful bite.

Jim ended up sleeping out on the porch in a hammock that had a solid blanket top over it. He woke up the next morning hearing a strange noise that sounded very close to him. He slowly lifted the top covering and peeked out. The chief's bull was standing on the porch about six inches from him, staring straight at him. The noise he was hearing was the breathing of the bull. Jim slowly closed his peep hole, laid very still and waited. In a little while the noise went away, and so did the bull.

I have used an electric razor all my life, and was dreading to have to learn to use a safety razor for the first time. As I got my safety razor out Ron said, "Here, use my electric razor." It looked exactly like the one I had at home, but it was battery operated. I didn't know such a thing existed. It worked great. When I got home I found and bought a battery operated electric razor. It will shave me for over three weeks without recharging. To this day I still have never used a safety razor.

After breakfast the next morning, we looked the village over and decided to set up our dental clinic in an uninhabited, one room building made of poles, palm leaf siding and a thatched roof. This building had some large window openings in the wall which we needed for light for our dental work. It had a dirt floor, as most homes did.

We were told that this building, approximately 12 by 25 feet in size, was used occasionally for village and tribal meetings. It normally rained several times a day, so it was good to have a roof over our heads. Also visitors from other villages could sleep in it as a guest house.

We found a table which we moved into our newly formed dental clinic, and we put our dental instruments on it. We brought a heavy plastic shower curtain to put over the table. We sprayed it well with a sterilizing solution, before we put our instruments on it.

The big, tough-looking chief requested to be our first patient. After examining him, I found a large, tender abscessed lower molar which he requested me to remove. With a little fear and trembling, I numbed him down using a little extra local anesthesia, waited several minutes longer than normal, before starting to work. Mark held the flashlight and watched intently. The tooth came out with great difficulty, but eventually it all came out.

The chief stood up and announced something to the many villagers that were watching. I was anxious to find out what he said, so I asked Ron, who had already learned the Chami language. Ron said, "He told them there was no pain, you didn't hurt him at all, and if they had any aching or bad teeth they needed to let us take them out." What a relief that was.

Immediately a large line formed. At first I had Mark numb them up, and I extracted the teeth. Then I started thinking, there is no reason I can't teach him to extract teeth. There were no dental laws in Colombia, and there was no possibility that these people would ever get to a dentist.

Mark had all the dental basics in his first two years of dental school, so he learned very quickly. By later the first day Mark was giving the anesthesia, and extracting teeth almost as fast as I was. This almost doubled the number of patients we could see.

That evening the six of us had supper by candlelight again around a small wooden table, about the size of a card table. It was in a very small room which served as both the kitchen and dining room. Kay was sitting next to me. All of a sudden someone across the table said, "There is one of the giant spiders," and pointed to the wall close behind Kay and me. Kay turned around, took one look at the spider, screamed, got up and ran right across the middle of the table, with dishes flying everywhere.

After her initial fright reaction, she sheepishly apologized, and started to help pick up things. At this point Jim asked, "Kay, what are you going to do when you eventually go out into an indigenous people's village to live if you are that frightened by a simple spider?" I well remember Kay's answer, and have applied it to aspects of my life many times. Kay said, "When I go out into my own tribal village the Holy Spirit will give me power to overcome such things as this." Kay came right over and sat down next to me with the spider still on the same spot on the wall behind us. It was at this point I took my shoe off and swatted the spider.

Kay was exactly right. When we are asked to do something for our Lord, He gives us his Holy Spirit which can and will give us power to overcome many obstacles. Since then I have asked and received power from the Holy Spirit to overcome many things in my life that I personally wouldn't have had the power to do, such as overcoming fear.

That night as we were sleeping, we were awakened by voices of a lot of excited people talking near the outside of our house. I guess we were too tired to get up and see what was going on, even though it continued for quite a while. The next morning I asked Ron, "What was the racket in the middle of the night?" He told us one of the night hunters had killed a moderately sized jungle animal with his blow gun. I never did find out exactly what kind of animal it was. He indicated that without any refrigeration or preservatives it was their custom to cook it immediately and to share all the meat with the whole village.

Our dental clinic continued without any problems. About the third day the chief came back into the clinic with a cloth tied around the top of his head down to and extending under his jaw. He was complaining of pain. I examined him and found a dry socket where I had extracted the lower molar.

A dry socket occurs when the bacteria that normally live in the mouth eat up the blood clot, leaving a raw hole in the jaw bone. It slows down the healing and is very painful. It is not an infection and heals normally in 7 – 10 days. We gave him pain tablets to reduce the pain, but he continued to wear the head bandage all the time we were there. This is the only dry socket I have seen in all my mission trips. Thankfully this didn't slow our number of patients. Word was spreading quickly. We had people coming in from many other villages.

We had four children who came into the clinic late one afternoon. The oldest was a twelve year old girl, and the youngest was four. They didn't look like Chami. They had more Spanish features. Then I remembered where we had seen the older children. It was across the valley at our rest stop where the young people had offered us the refreshing coke.

They had lots of abscessed teeth. We extracted several teeth from each of them. I took a picture of Mark extracting teeth from the young boy, with Jim holding the flashlight well after dark. We extracted all we felt we should at one appointment, and told them if they wanted the rest of the bad ones extracted they would have to come back another day.

It was now night and pitch black. You couldn't see your hand in front of your face, and these four kids had to go all the way down the side of that steep muddy mountain, across the river, and up the other side to go home. It took us two hours to do that on horseback. I thought to myself, no way, this was impossible. I tried to get the oldest girl, who was obviously the leader, to agree to stay all night in the dental clinic. Her answer was, "No, our parents are expecting us home. They will worry about us, and probably come looking for us." She said, "We have to go home tonight." I looked at Ron and he just shrugged his shoulders and said, "We can't keep them here against their will." So off they went into the black of the night, and disappeared into the thick jungle vegetation. I felt badly and very concerned.

Early the next morning when we were setting up the dental clinic we were surprised to see these same four children come up over the edge of the embankment right where they had disappeared the night before with a big smile on their faces.

I asked them if they made it home all right last night, and they said, "No problem." They had come back to get the rest of their abscessed teeth out. It was then that I saw something that blew my mind. They were wearing small white canvas tennis shoes, and there was not a spot of dirt on them. They looked brand new. How could that be?

Ron had taken us for a hike down the valley a day or so earlier, and he had furnished us with high boots to wear. I can remember how hard it was to walk almost anywhere we went outside without sinking several inches into the muddy, reddish soil, and these kid's tennis shoes were perfectly white. I asked Ron, "How come?" He just shrugged his shoulders, and to this day I do not know how these kids' shoes stayed so spotless.

Late one afternoon the chief came to Ron, who spent most of his time with us doing translating, and asked Ron if we could go over to the other side of the valley where he had an important member of his tribe that had a big fire. No one was hurt, but he owned and ran a sugar cane press which squeezed the sugary juice out of sugar cane stalks that grew abundantly in the area. They were able to save his little gasoline generator, but the motor that ran the rollers of his press had burned up, and he didn't know how to fix it. The Chief knew

Jim was a mechanic, and thought he could help him fix his motor. Ron asked me what I thought. We had a long line of patients waiting, and it was getting late in the day. Mornings were usually slower, so I suggested we go early in the morning. When Ron told this to the chief he started laughing. After they talked, I asked Ron what was so funny. Ron explained that the customs of their culture is to plan just one day at a time, and let tomorrow take care of itself. The chief thought my plan to do something tomorrow was really funny.

Nevertheless, we got up early the next morning, picked up the chief, walked down the mountain, across the river, and up the mountain on the other side to the high trail that went down the valley near the top of the mountain. After walking down this trail a while, we came to a clearing that was all charred black. It must have been a big fire, because it was all black right up to the green dense jungle perimeter.

We met the owner, and he took us over to a large blackened motor. Jim unscrewed the cover to look inside. Jim quickly determined that the fire had been so hot the main shaft had melted and was bent. There was no fixing that without a new shaft, but everything else was so badly charred he just told the man it was not fixable.

As we were on our way back to the village we crossed the large rapid river at the bottom of the valley. Jim commented that this river could furnish all the power needed to run his sugar press with just a simple water wheel. He just wished we had a few weeks to help him build it. Unfortunately, it never happened.

The young 10 year old boy that walked between the mules and horses when we first came, and cleared the trail of snakes in front of Mark, got to be a close friend of Mark's. Every place we went he walked quietly beside Mark with his big machete hanging on his waist almost to the ground. He went with us to the burned sugar cane mill. We couldn't talk with him and didn't know his name, so we nicknamed him "Me Too".

There were coffee plants planted and cultivated all over the sides of these mountains. They were one of the Chami's main sources of income. When we were walking on the main trail we passed several groups of burros with large sacks of coffee beans tied to their backs. They were hauling them up and out of the mountain valley to sell at the nearest village which had access to a road.

Near dusk one night, a very pregnant woman came up the side of the mountain and into our village. She was carrying one child and pulling along another small child. I knew she wasn't from our village because she was very pregnant and close to delivery. I hadn't seen anyone in Buena Vista like that.

The next morning I asked Ron, "What happened to the pregnant lady that came into the village last evening?" He told me, "The chief's older wife (he had an old wife and a young one) was a midwife. The lady had her child during the night, and had taken her children and left, and was walking back home."

One evening after supper I asked Ron how he met his wife, Mary Jane. He told me this very interesting story. After he graduated from college he felt called into missions. He went back to Bible School for 3 more years. When he graduated he still hadn't found the right girl who shared his interest in becoming a missionary. He got a nominal job in Chicago and continued to search. He decided that there were no potential prospects in the small church he was attending, so he started attending a much larger church. Again he was disappointed to find no eligible ladies who shared his enthusiasm for missions, and worse yet he didn't feel he was being adequately spiritually fed in this new church. So he returned to his smaller home church and prayed, "Lord, if you want me to find a wife to go to the mission field with me, I guess you are going to have to bring her here to me."

A few weeks later they had a missionary and his wife who worked with Wycliffe Bible Translators in Mexico visit their church, and put on a slide program of their work. At the close of the service he went up and talked to the missionary. In the course of conversation he expressed his interest in being a missionary. At this point the missionary turned to his wife and asked her, "Where is Mary Jane?" His wife looked around and then left. Shortly she returned with a beautiful young lady. The father introduced his daughter, Mary Jane, to Ron with the comment, "She wants to be a missionary also."

Mary Jane had been raised in a remote group of indigenous people in Mexico. Her goal in life was to become a Wycliffe Bible Translator like her mother, dad and brother. Ron said in his heart, thank you, thank you Lord, and the rest is history. I thought to myself, how many people have been introduced to their future wife by her father?

Ron related to us another story, told to him by the Chief. The Chami Indians, like our American Indians, had warring disagreements with the invading Spanish. Finally the Spaniards made peace with the Indians, and gave the Chami people this mountainous jungle area as a reservation, much like the Americans did with their Indians. They signed a treaty, and in the treaty the Spanish government gave the Indians some self rule, and promised never to bring their government troops into their reservation again.

One day a group of 10 heavily armed military men came into the reservation, and walked the path we had used. They marched into a Chami village much further down the valley, and arrested a young man whom they charged with murder. They claimed the man had been off the reservation, and killed a man in a bar fight. So they took him and started marching out.

The problem was that all of the villagers knew they must have the wrong man, because the man they arrested and took had never been off the reservation, so the men decided to rescue their innocent fellow villager. They also believed the government had broken their truce by sending armed militia men into their reservation.

Several of the men took their blow guns with a quiver of fresh poison tipped darts, and went up near the place where the trail exited the reservation. They hid themselves well in the dense foliage, and waited. When the lead man passed a certain point on the trail, they each took a designated man and *puff*, off went the swift poison darts. All 10 militia men hit the ground, and were dead in a few minutes. Not a shot was fired. The Chami have never had an armed government man come back into their reservation since.

I became quite intrigued with these blow guns. The Chiefs brother offered to sell me his blowgun, with a full bamboo quiver of nonpoisonous darts, for $20. I bought it. The blowgun was 9 feet long.

When we got back to Bogotá, Jim suggested we find a stiff hollow cardboard tube, like they rolled new carpet on. We found one, put the blowgun inside, and shipped it home on the airplane with no problem.

At home I found a large cardboard box, and put a large archery type target on it. When I am asked to speak and show my slides, I often take my target and blowgun along with me as a demonstration. People are absolutely fascinated to see how quickly, silently, and accurately the dart will penetrate deeply into the target on the box, with just one short puff of breath. I have taught a five-year-old child how to shoot it fairly accurately.

I felt a little guilty buying the Chief's brother's blowgun. I thought, what would he use when he hunts? The chief said, "Don't worry; he can make himself another one anytime he wants." In a couple of days we noticed chickens running around the village. We were told that the Chiefs brother had gone to town, and bought some chickens with my $20. He told the chief that the jungle was getting quite depleted, and there were not a lot of edible animals left out there. He felt he would get a lot more food from these chickens than he could from hunting. It sounded logical to me. I felt better.

One day we had many of the adult villagers gathered around in a circle in our makeshift dental clinic. I planned to give them a lecture, with Ron's help with translation, about the basics of dental hygiene. I went around the circle and handed each of them a toothbrush that I brought with me. By the time I got back around the circle to where I started, the first two people were busy scrubbing their toenails with the toothbrush. No one ever wore shoes, and they had no idea what the toothbrush was for. Ron said later, "They had never seen a toothbrush before."

Ron and Mary Jane's front porch was large, about 18 feet square. From their front porch you could see many miles down the valley. We often had short showers two or three times a day. It was interesting to watch the rain showers move up the valley from the Pacific Ocean. You could rather accurately tell when the rain was going to start.

On the porch there were benches around three sides, except for where the door was. Frequently the villagers would come and sit on the porch in the evenings, and talk to us. One evening the Chief's younger wife gave me a beautiful 8-inch tightly woven basket that had a good tight fitting top. She gave it to me while we were talking on the porch, as a thank you for coming to help them. Twenty five years later, the basket is still in my home and in great shape.

One day while we were sitting around on the porch, a lady had a young child in her lap who decided to urinate. After she got a little wet, she just held the child out in front of her and it made a puddle on the dirty floor. Diapers were nonexistent.

Mark gave a couple of 10-year-old boys some bubblegum, and he was trying to teach them how to blow bubbles. They were having difficulty as obviously they had never had bubblegum before. Suddenly one of the boy's bubblegum popped out of his mouth, and landed right in the puddle of dirty muddy urine still on the floor. Before anyone could blink an eye, the boy scooped up the gum and popped it back into his mouth. No one seemed to be the least bit concerned, and yes, the boys finally did learn how to blow bubbles.

On our last day we finished a few extractions in the morning, and then packed everything so we could leave right after lunch. The horses and mules arrived around noon. We were just about ready to start loading the animals, when a woman walked into the village carrying a baby, and holding a small boy by his hand. She told Ron she had walked for two days over two mountain ranges to get her badly aching teeth removed. Ron turned to me and asked, "What do you want to do?"

We had a full half day's trip on our mules and horses to get out of the reservation, and back into the small village. We didn't want to be on the trail after dark. With Ron's permission, I quickly unpacked the instruments I needed, and numbed up several abscessed teeth. The young boy sat on the floor in front of me, while the mother held the baby. As I started to extract her teeth, the baby in her arms started to cry, wiggle, and kick. I didn't let it slow me down. I just concentrated on getting those teeth out quickly. Suddenly the baby stopped crying and I completed her extractions. When I was finished I stepped back and saw what had happened. The mother had pulled down the front of her dress, and was breast-feeding the baby. That's why he stopped crying so suddenly. I have frequently worked on nursing mothers, but this was the first time that I've ever worked on a mother while she was nursing. Mark took a very memorable photo.

During the commotion, Mary Jane had picked up the young boy off the floor who had been sitting in front of me. She noticed the child was very warm and coughing. She quickly took his temperature, and found it was very high. Ron and Mary Jane had basic medical training, and often treated sick people in the area.

Mary Jane got her stethoscope and listened to the child's lungs. They were very congested. She quickly concluded the child had pneumonia. After I finished, she consulted with the mother, and gave the child an injection of a long-acting antibiotic. She then gave the mother several follow-up capsules that she would need to get into the child's stomach during the next few days.

I had relieved the mother of pain, but more importantly, Mary Jane felt that she may have saved the young child's life.

We quickly loaded up with all the villagers gathering around to bid us farewell. "Me Too" assumed his position in front of Mark, and walked with us all the way out, with his machete in his hand. We arrived at the village just before dark. Ron and Mary Jane came with us.

That evening after supper, Ron told us a story of how God instantly answered one of his prayers in a very unusual way. He told us "Earlier when Mary Jane and I had been at Buena Vista learning the Chami language, we both became ill and developed very high temperatures. The symptoms matched those of hepatitis for which there was little treatment in those days, except rest. We felt we were too weak and sick to try to make the trip out of the reservation. After several weeks of not getting any better, we decided we had to try to get out somehow. Buena Vista is one of the few Wycliffe based villages that did not have an airstrip to use for emergency evacuation. They couldn't even get a helicopter in there for us."

"Finally we radioed for some horses to come and get us. We were helped into the saddle, and we left. We traveled the same narrow trail near the top, and on the side of the steep mountain. My temperature was very high, and I was groggy, weak, and sleepy. I caught myself a couple of times starting to fall asleep. I knew if I fell asleep I would probably fall off the horse, and I would surely be killed falling down the side of the mountain."

"I cried out to God, "God help me keep awake." I got an answer instantly. Suddenly the horse in front of me stopped, and my horse walked up and bumped into the back of the horse. The horse in front gave a big kick, which just happened to hit me right in the shin. It caused excruciating pain, and guess what, I wasn't sleepy anymore."

We returned to Bogotá the next day, basically the same way we came. We stayed overnight with Jim and family, and flew the rest of the way home the following day. We had been gone 16 days.

Mark certainly had a unique experience. He had the opportunity to extract several hundred teeth. I personally had a great sense of peace and satisfaction. We had been treated great by everyone we met, almost like a king sometimes. We had been able to relieve many people of infection and pain, and yes, we used anesthesia.

My life has been full of leadership positions, but on this trip I was reduced to a missionary's helper, and I was totally dependent on them. It was a fantastically humbling experience, and I couldn't have felt happier.

## And Now the Rest of the Story

This very positive first dental health mission changed the direction of my serving my Lord, in demonstrating my faith by doing good works in relieving otherwise helpless people from their pain and suffering. As you will read in the following chapters, this was just the beginning. It did much more. Eventually it saved hundreds of people's lives, for an eternity in heaven.

# CHAPTER 5

# COLOMBIA 2

We received many letters of appreciation after we got home from our first Colombia mission trip. We also received a written invitation from Jim Cartwright asking us to return the following summer. Something came up and Mark couldn't go back. Todd was one year behind Mark in dental school, and the next year he would be between his sophomore and junior years just like Mark had been. Todd had heard the exciting stories from Mark about his experiences, so when I asked him if he would like to go to Colombia with me next summer, he quickly said, "Yes". Of course it made it easier to say yes, when dad paid all the expenses, which I was glad to do.

A friend from our church, Cindy Sherwood, asked if she could join us on our next Colombia mission. She had heard all about our first trip during one of our services when I had been asked to speak and show my slides. She and her family had been friends of ours through church. She also knew Jim and Deb Cartwright rather well since they were originally from our church.

Cindy was no ordinary young lady. She was a nurse in her late 20s with special training in midwifery. She had been a missionary in the hills of Kentucky, where she practiced nursing and midwifery for several years. Recently she had gone to London, England, and took the world-famous Tropical Medicine Course. She had applied for a visa to be a missionary in a remote area of Irian Jaya. She was just waiting for her visa to be granted, and thought she might be of some help to us on our trip. We gladly added her to our team.

We set a late June departure date, and started all our preparation again. Preparation was much simpler this time, having been through it the year before. Shortly before we departed, an Eastern Airlines flight from Miami to Bogotá had crashed into the side of a Mountain in the Andes, killing everyone on board. I often wondered if the lawsuits arising from this crash helped to put Eastern Airlines into bankruptcy. I liked flying Eastern, and the crash didn't particularly frighten us. We packed our supplies, bid farewell to our families, and took off in June 1985 on the same Eastern flight path on which the crash had occurred a few weeks earlier. Jim met us at the airport in Bogotá and he transferred us to his home.

When Jim and Deb first came to Colombia they rented a home that a previous missionary couple had vacated. The only catch was that they inherited a young German shepherd. Deb hated dogs with a passion. They quickly trained the dog to stay on the wooden floor in the front narthex, and not to come into the carpeted part of the house. Todd loved dogs and played with it a lot, but no way would that dog step beyond the wooden floor and onto the carpet.

Actually Jim and Deb found the dog to be a good babysitter. When their three children were 8, 10, and 12 years old, they felt much better about leaving them home alone for short periods of time with the dog there. Their inside front door was solid and had no windows. It opened into a small hallway that led to an outer door constructed of heavy steel bars. They kept both doors locked. At that time Bogotá was known as the most violent city in the world, which included regular criminals, and the combatants in Colombia's civil war with the Communist guerrillas and the cocaine cartels. This short hallway allowed them to open the solid door and look to see who was at the steel-barred front door before they opened it. Jim's neighborhood hired 24-hour armed guards to patrol it.

Jim and Deb observed something rather unusual about their dog. When a Colombian person rang the doorbell, the dog that was on the inside of the solid front door, would start to growl and bark. When an American rang the doorbell, the dog would just sit and wag his tail. How he could tell who was at the front door, we will never know. We're guessing it must have been his sense of smell.

The front yard was surrounded by an eight foot fence made of iron rods about 8 inches apart. One day the family went away, and left the dog in the front yard as usual. A small Colombian infant crawled through the fence and started playing with the dog. The parents tried to coax the baby to come out, but no deal. He was having too much fun with the dog. The father of the baby started climbing over the fence and the dog barked and started to attack him. They remembered the story about the dog not liking Colombians, but it seemed to like Americans. After waiting a while, one of the parents walked down the block to where some Americans lived, and asked if they would help. An American came, climbed over the fence, got the baby, and handed it to its parents. The dog just sat there and wagged his tail, and never barked once. I don't know how a dog could be trained to do that.

Deb and her family fell in love with their new German shepherd. Several years later when they left Colombia, it had become part of the family. They had to bring the dog back to the U.S. where it lived with them the rest of its life.

In a day or so, Todd, Cindy, and I, with our entire luggage, took the flight on the DC-3 with Jim to Lomalinda. There were numerous people that had gathered to meet the plane. It was obvious that they were very happy to see, we thought us, but instead, they ran right past us and started hugging the couple behind. Oh well! They were returning to Lomalinda after a one-year furlough.

After they unloaded the plane, Jim, the pilots, Todd, Cindy, and I went up to the guest house where Gary and Char fed us a nice lunch. After lunch, Jim and the pilots flew back to Bogotá. Todd, Cindy, and I settled into a separate guest house about 100 yards from Gary and Char's house. We ate breakfast and lunch with them, and were usually invited out to different missionaries' homes for supper in the evening.

The next day we went to the medical clinic. Todd and I set up in the small partially-equipped dental room, and started to work. It had an old dental chair, a fairly good light, and a counter behind the chair. This year a short-term medical doctor was present. He had retired from the U.S. military service. Cindy got acquainted and started working with him.

Todd had training in anesthesia and fillings, but hadn't worked on any patients yet. He caught on quickly and started filling teeth almost as fast as I. No dentist had visited Lomalinda in several years except the few days that Mark and I were there last year. A very pretty high school girl, a missionary's daughter, came into the clinic. She had a very big beautiful smile, but it was dotted with black spots of decay. Over several days, Todd restored her smile to health and beauty by putting in over 20 fillings. This was a great confidence builder for him.

Early one morning when we had just started working, Todd reached behind him to get an instrument from a small box on the counter. He jumped with surprise. A 12-inch snake had curled up inside the box. Todd's patient happened to be a 14-year-old boy who had grown up at Lomalinda. He took one look at the snake and said, "Oh, that's one of our 1-2-3-snakes." Todd asked, "What is a 1-2-3 snake?" He said, "It is a very poisonous snake, and if it bites you, you'll only get 1, 2, or 3 steps before you're dead." He said, "I'll take care of him."

The boy got a long stick, and coaxed the snake out of the box, but it crawled into one of the drawers, and then behind it. The boy took out all the drawers and teased the snake onto the floor. He finally pinned the snake's head firmly to the concrete floor with his stick. He asked, "Do you have a knife?" We didn't, but I asked, "Is a scalpel okay?" He said, "Yes," and he cut off the snake's head. After a little reorganizing, Todd went ahead and finished putting in the young boy's fillings.

As if that weren't enough excitement, a few moments later, several people burst into the clinic carrying an Indian with a badly bleeding foot. The doctor and Cindy took him immediately into the operating room. It seemed he had been riding barefoot on the back of a motorcycle and caught his heel in the chain. It had torn a 4-inch flap of skin down the back of his heel right to the bone. They reduced the bleeding, cleaned the wound, disinfected it, and the doctor started to suture it up. After a couple of stitches he turned to Cindy and said,

"You suture it." He said, "I haven't sutured a wound in 30 years. In the military the medical corpsmen did that." So Cindy put in 20 to 30 stitches, with the doctor's assistance.

Cindy also experienced other interesting cases. One afternoon an Indian woman came into the clinic crying quite hard. She had a towel wrapped around her foot. She had been sitting on the dock, down at the lake, with her feet dangling in the water. All of a sudden she felt a severe pain in her foot. She pulled it out of the water and found a clean dime-sized hole in the back of her heel about a quarter of an inch deep. It was bleeding heavily. A piranha had just taken a bite out of her heel. There wasn't anything to sew up. It was a nice clean hole. Cindy stopped the bleeding, put disinfectant on it, bandaged it, and gave her some antibiotics and pain medication.

Another afternoon when the doctor wasn't in, one of the pilots came in not feeling very well. Cindy diagnosed the symptoms as malaria. She drew some blood, prepared a slide with it, and looked through the microscope for the malaria parasite. That is the only way to positively diagnose malaria, by actually seeing the parasite under a microscope. These parasites are frequently very difficult to find. Cindy's London Tropical Medicine training came in handy. She found the malaria parasite, and let us all take a look at this rare find. Having confirmed the diagnosis, she was able to give the pilot the appropriate medication with confidence that it would relieve his symptoms.

Al Meehan, the head pilot, and currently the Chief Administrator of Wycliffe Translators in Colombia, came to us one evening and asked if we would be willing to go out to the Kogi Indian tribe. Two Wycliffe women translators, who were living in the area, had radioed him and asked if we could come and help them, particularly with extracting teeth. He said, "The area should be safe." I said, "Why not, that's why we came, to help where needed."

Al promised that he would personally fly us, because it was a long and difficult flight, and he wasn't sure if the other pilots were capable of it. Early the next morning we packed our gear and went to the hangar. We were flying in the new super-charged single engine, Helio Courier. These planes had been developed and produced especially for the U.S. military. Wycliffe was granted special permission by the military to purchase these planes. They could idle down to 35 mph and still stay in the air, and could land on a very short landing strip, not much longer than a football field. After Al weighed both us and our luggage, he personally packed the plane to the maximum. Everyone at the hangar gathered around in a circle and held hands while Al prayed for God to form a hedge of protection around us, and keep us safe from all problems. This was the first time I had ever flown in a single engine plane. We took off, started to climb and headed toward the high Andes Mountains. Al's wife was on the radio in the control tower, and continually talked with him.

I sat in front with Al, while Todd and Cindy sat in the back. We flew up a mountain valley gaining altitude all the time, between tall mountains. Suddenly we flew into a cloud bank and couldn't see anything. These planes had no special navigational instruments and were flown visually.

I knew the mountains on both sides were higher than we were but had no idea what was in front of the plane. My mind flashed back to the Eastern Airlines plane, with all of its precision navigation instruments, and that it had crashed into one of these mountains. I don't remember ever being more frightened in my life. We stayed in the clouds for what seemed like forever. My adrenal glands worked overtime and my heart pounded. I prayed, "O Lord, not now," and held my breath for an instantaneous departure from planet Earth.

Suddenly, we popped out above the clouds. I could see no mountain tops around us. What a relief, but then the thought struck me, about how we were going to get back down. While we were gaining altitude in the clouds, Al reached under his seat and turned on an oxygen tank. He put a hose in his mouth and started to breathe oxygen. He told us later, that without oxygen at high altitudes, a pilot could get lightheaded and disoriented. All we got were pounding headaches, but he assured us they would go right away when we came down, and they did. He apologized for not having enough oxygen for all of us.

Shortly the clouds disappeared, and we flew over some flat inhabited agricultural land. We started to lose altitude, and an airport came into view. We landed and taxied to an area away from the terminal. Al shut the engine off, got out, and said he was going to see if we could get some fuel. He asked us to stay in the plane.

Al was gone a long time, and we started to get concerned. Finally he came back, taxied over to a fuel tank, and they fueled our plane. He told us the government was very careful to whom they sold aviation fuel, because it was necessary to use to process cocaine leaves into the white refined addicting powder. There was a lot of red tape he had to go through before they agreed to give us the fuel.

We took off and flew another hour over rich fertile agricultural land. I could see a tall snowcapped mountain in the distance rising near the ocean, with no other mountains around it. We approached it and started to skirt around it. Finally Al turned and flew up one of the valleys toward the top of the mountain. Shortly he shook his head and said, "Wrong valley," and banked the plane 180° and headed down out of the valley. We flew a little further around the mountain, and headed up another valley. Soon he pointed down, smiled and said, "There it is." All I could see was a light green rectangular patch in the dark green jungle canopy. Al banked the plane 180° but this time kept turning sharper and sharper and going down fast, in a corkscrew pattern. The more we descended, the more the valley walls closed in on us. Suddenly, he straightened the plane and headed for the little green patch, which I could now see was a grassy runway chopped out of the jungle.

Just before we landed, a sharp wind hit the side of the plane and blew us 15 feet sideways. We landed on the side of the runway with the tips of the wings clipping a little vegetation. Al got out of the plane and grabbed the pulse in his neck and said, "My adrenal glands are working real well, how about yours?" I said, "I emptied all my adrenaline from my glands back in those clouds." We both laughed.

The two women translators Al had talked to earlier on the radio were not there to meet us. As we unloaded the plane, some of the indigenous Kogi Indians started to gather around us. I smiled and said "Hi," and put my hand out to shake theirs, but they neither extended their hands nor smiled. They just stood there and stared at us with sober faces. This was a little scary. I always thought that a smile was a sign of international friendship, but I smiled and smiled to no avail.

Shortly the two missionaries, Linda and Grace, came from underneath the jungle canopy to greet us. They had observed the dangerous noontime wind shear, and they were hurrying back to their radio to warn us about the strong crosswinds. After they heard us land, they turned around and came back.

After our greetings and introductions, I asked Linda why the natives appeared so unfriendly. She said, "They are really very friendly, but the Kogi culture forbids them from showing any emotion in public. They are not allowed to smile, frown, cry, or shake hands."

Each man had a brown waist-length striped cloth like purse hanging around his neck. Linda said, "These are called Kogi bags. They contain cocaine leaves." Linda said that their customary form of greeting was to walk up to another Kogi, reach into the other persons Kogi bag, take a pinch of cocaine leaves, and put it in their bag, while the other person did the same.

These dried cocaine leaves had no addictive or hallucinogenic properties. Kogies chewed the leaves for two important reasons. They were a potent appetite suppressant, which allowed them to travel for days without having to carry food, and they were a stimulant similar to caffeine that would keep them awake late into the night. Oftentimes their group village council meetings would last into the wee hours of the morning, and the cocaine kept them awake.

Linda spoke to the men and they brought a mule. We loaded some of our heavier equipment, such as our generator, and our heavy suitcases onto the mule. Some of the Kogies picked up the rest of our belongings and carried them up a path, which I assumed led to Linda's and Grace's house.

We stopped at the end of the runway, and observed what looked like a little village of about 20 round huts. All were empty, and no one was around. The Kogies made their huts with poles, thatching and mud. They made a circle of 4 inch poles, 5 feet high, with one end firmly buried in the ground. The roof poles went from the sides to a high point in the center and were tied together with vines. They tied thatched leaves to the roof which extended two feet beyond the side walls. The side walls were made of grass and mud which had dried as hard as brick. This was a very simple house constructed entirely of all natural materials.

I asked Linda where all the people were. She told me that they lived up in the mountains in various isolated areas, and gathered in this village for a few days once or twice a month for council meetings or celebrations.

We walked about a mile, crossed a small primitive bridge, through more dense vegetation, and alongside a big clearing. When we arrived at Linda and Grace's house, our baggage was sitting outside the front door. It was a fairly large and rather nice house. It had seven rooms, each with a window without glass. It had two doors, a dirt floor, and a nice tin roof. The outside walls were made of sticks, dry grass, and mud. Inside the house they had three bedrooms, all with beds, and a kitchen with a small table, chairs, cupboards, a counter, and a sink with a faucet and running water. They got their running water by hooking a small plastic PVC pipe to their faucets and running it up a hill behind their house to a small mountain stream.

I asked Linda how they ever got the supplies here to build their house. I knew they would never fit in the plane. She said, "We had a large commercial helicopter drop them in the clearing. Then Bonnie and I, along with some of the Kogies, built it ourselves."

After lunch Al headed back to the plane and took off. He didn't have enough daylight or fuel to get back to Lomalinda. He decided to stay in the surrounding area, to visit other Wycliffe missionaries, and do some public relations work with the government officials in the area, until we were ready to go back.

We spent the rest of the afternoon getting organized. We set up our dental clinic in a small corner room with a big window and a door for light. We set our small Honda generator just outside the window, to power our dental drill.

Grace cooked dinner for us. I don't remember what we had to eat. One thing I do remember, and will never forget. I laid my spoon down on the small table as we ate. Linda reached over and pushed my spoon off onto the dirt floor. I was a little surprised and didn't know what to say. Linda said, "Can't you see that table is red? Anything that is red contains germs that can make you sick. All of our food is either boiled or peeled, and our metal bowl and silverware have been well-boiled to kill all germs. From now on you need to keep your silverware in your metal bowl at all times!" That was a lesson well learned!

After dinner I asked Linda, "How did you become involved with the Kogies?" She then told me a most interesting story: To begin with, you must understand a little bit about the Kogi Indians. The Kogies, like many of the American Indians, fought against the Europeans that were taking their land. In Colombia the Europeans were primarily Spaniards. Finally they agreed upon a peace treaty and the Kogies were given this whole snowcapped mountain with all of its valleys as a reservation. The Spaniards kept all the fertile farmland. This is similar to what happened in the U.S. When we made peace with our Indians we gave them reservations consisting of deserts, badlands, and forests. The Kogies got self-rule with the promise that the Spanish government would never bother them again.

The Kogies sealed off their borders. They didn't let any outsiders enter their reservation. The chief made a law that forbade anyone from teaching their language to an outsider, or for a Kogi to learn another language. The penalty was death. When a measles epidemic swept through the tribe and many people were dying, the government sent a doctor with medicine to help them. The Kogies captured the doctor and locked him in one of their jails for three days until he agreed to leave. Nobody was allowed into the Kogi reservation.

Linda said, when my original partner Bonnie and I felt called to come to the Kogies, we put on backpacks and walked deep into the reservation before we were discovered. Near sundown one evening some of the Kogies spotted us, and took us to their chief.

You need to understand, the Kogies are very small people who are only approximately four feet tall. They have dark brown Indian skin. All the men and women have very long black hair. They are often referred to as South American pygmies.

We have fair, white skin, blond hair, and are over six feet tall. The chief had never seen anyone like us before, and didn't know what to think. He wasn't afraid of us because we were women, in a strongly male dominated culture. The chief decided we were goddesses sent by some god to help them, so he made everyone get down on their hands and knees and worship us.

We were both nurses as well as Wycliffe Bible Translators, and we had brought anti-biotics and other medicines in our backpacks. We treated very sick people, even dying people, and suddenly with the help of the antibiotics, they got better. Then the chief knew for sure that we were goddesses. He let us stay and learn their language, with the promise that we would never teach anyone else.

Bonnie was currently in Bogotá, doing other Kogi related work. Grace had joined Bonnie and Linda about a year ago. Wycliffe had a policy that a single woman was not allowed into the Indian tribes by herself. They always had to have a partner, so Grace was currently working with Linda. It had been three years since Linda and Bonnie first walked into the Kogi reservation. During that time they had built the airstrip, constructed their house, learned their language, and were starting to translate their verbal language into a written language. They had only one convert to Christianity in their first three years.

Before Todd, Cindy, and I were allowed to go into the Kogi reservation, Linda had to get both the lesser chief's and the big chief's permission. Al had to get both the local and central government's permission also. The Kogies had never seen a white Caucasian male before we came.

Linda, Bonnie and Grace were spending a lot of time caring for the sick, and it was reducing the time they wanted to spend on translation. One evening the wife of a lesser chief came to Linda and Grace's house, and wanted Linda to extract a badly aching tooth. Linda didn't know anything about extracting teeth, and didn't have any equipment. She really didn't want to start taking teeth out or they would have so much work they would never have time to work on translation.

The lesser chief's wife was determined to get that tooth out, so she sat down in the middle of Linda's kitchen floor, and dug and pried at her tooth with a machete until she was sitting in a big pool of blood. She finally passed out and became unconscious, because of the large loss of blood. Linda stopped the bleeding, and then started an IV, and other medications. Linda brought her back around, but the tooth never got out.

Linda heard that there were visiting dentists at Lomalinda, so she called Al on their shortwave radio, and asked if we could come and help them. Al then asked us if we would be willing to help.

Early the first morning, just as it was getting daylight, we heard voices outside our window. Upon inquiring we found there were patients starting to gather, to get their aching teeth removed. Todd and I got up, had a quick breakfast, and started to work. I think that was the earliest I have ever started doing dentistry in my life. It was barely 6 a.m. These people had no electricity, so they went to bed when the sun went down, and they got up when the sun came up or seemingly a little earlier.

Since the Kogies didn't have any money or currency they frequently brought us food as a way of saying thank you. Often they would bring us different sized and colored eggs. We frequently had eggs for breakfast. I asked Linda how she knew if the eggs were fertilized or ready to hatch. She said they had been taught in their jungle orientation training to put the eggs in a pan of water, and if they remained flat they were good to eat, but if they turned up on their end, they were too far developed to eat.

Todd had not been taught how to extract teeth yet in his dental classes, so I gave him a personalized crash course, and he caught on quickly. The Kogies grew sugarcane, and had lots of sugar in their diet, with zero dental hygiene. The result was a lot of advanced decayed and abscessed teeth. I taught Todd how to remove teeth when they were decayed level with the gum, and he got lots of good experience. Today most dentists in our area would not remove a tooth if it were decayed off near the gum; they would refer the patient to an oral surgeon. Not Todd, he's not afraid of them. He removes them just like we remove them with the Kogies.

One afternoon I had a six or seven-year-old boy sit down in my chair, maybe I should say stool, because it had no back. All four of his lower molars were abscessed. After I numbed him, I stood behind him and cradled him in my arms. It was hot. I proceeded to remove all four of his molars. He never moved, and in fact, he closed his eyes. When I finished I stepped back, and he slowly started to tip over, and was about to fall on the floor, when I grabbed him. He had fallen asleep. He awakened with a start, and promptly stood up. We gave him his postoperative instructions, pain pills and he left. I have worked on people who have occasionally gotten tired or relaxed, and dozed a little while I was filling their teeth, but in my 54 years in dentistry, this is the only person that has ever fallen asleep while I was extracting his teeth.

I had taken a National Geographic magazine with me, and I placed it in the small room where our patients were waiting. One time when I went to get another patient, I noticed a lady looking at my National Geographic, but something strange caught my eye. She was holding the magazine upside down, and looking at a large picture of a car. I said to Grace,

"Why is she looking at that upside down?" She shrugged her shoulders and said, "Well, if you had never seen a car, and if you had never seen a magazine, and no one had told you what side was up, you wouldn't know either."

The Kogies were friendly people, but very primitive. They not only had no written language, but the people didn't know how old they were, because they had no concept of time, such as a week or a year. They just knew the sun came up in the morning and went down at night. All their names were totally secret, because they didn't want anyone to be able to cast an evil spell on them. This would be hard to do if you didn't know the person's name. They had never seen concrete, blacktop, multi-story buildings, motorized vehicles, and they didn't know what money was. They had absolutely no form of currency.

The Kogies all wore the same type of clothing. It was a dirty white loose sack-like garment that had a hole in it for their head and two holes in it for their arms. Their one-piece garment was made from the fibers they pulled out of the leaves of a certain type of cactus plant. They then hung them up to dry, and when dry, they hand-rolled them on their thighs into a coarse thread. From these threads they wove their gowns. The gowns all hung very close to the ground, which they said helped keep the mosquitoes and bugs off their legs.

There was one difference between the dress of men and mothers. The mothers had a hole in their garment big enough so that it left one of their shoulders and arms bare. This made it easier for the mothers to breast-feed their infants, which they normally carried on their backs. The women were not modest. They breast-fed their babies anytime and anyplace.

When a dentist needs to extract an upper tooth he has to inject anesthesia into the roof of the mouth. This often is momentarily very painful, and usually makes an adult flinch or squirm. When we do this to young children in the U.S. they normally scream bloody murder. I first noticed when I had to inject the adult Kogies in the roof of the mouth that they never flinched at all. Then I noticed every time I injected a child, even as young as three or four years old, they also never flinched or complained one bit. This puzzled me. I asked Grace, who was working as our translator, three different times, "Doesn't this injection hurt these young children." She talked with the child a while, and came back with the same answer three different times, so I stopped asking. She said, "Yes it's painful, but it was very minor in comparison to the pain they were used to feeling." I guess even pain is relative in relation to whatever it's being compared.

One morning just before daybreak, a man came to the door and excitedly called for Linda. Linda was a nurse and frequently treated many of their illnesses. Linda went outside and talked with the man for a while. When she came back inside we were up and dressed. Linda explained to us. The man had married the big chief's daughter. In the Kogi culture the women are expected to have a minimum of 10 children, and the husband is responsible for delivering the babies. This man had helped his wife deliver a baby during the night, but it was stillborn. The Kogies had not experienced stillborn babies before, and furthermore his wife was still bleeding quite a lot. This was the big chief's daughter, and he was scared. He had run two hours down the mountain in the pitch black of the night to get Linda to help him. How he could see at night to travel in these mountains, I'll never know. Their eyes must be a lot different from mine.

Linda was hesitant and not sure what to do. The women always had to travel in pairs, according to Wycliffe policy, and if she and Grace both were to leave, there wouldn't be any translator, and we would have to close the dental clinic. It would probably take a full day to trek up and then back down the mountain where this man lived. Cindy then said, "I'm a R.N. midwife, why don't you let me go with you, Linda, and let Grace stay home and keep the dental clinic operating?" Linda agreed that this was a great idea, so she and Cindy packed a few things and disappeared into the dense green undergrowth, and headed up the mountain.

Todd and I had a very busy and productive day. We only did two fillings using the generator the entire time we were there. There were so many people waiting to have their infected, aching, abscessed teeth removed, that we had little time to stop and do fillings. We could extract 8 or 10 teeth in the same amount of time it would take to do one filling.

One day we extracted a tooth from a very pretty 14 year old young lady. It turned out she was the lesser chief's daughter. The lesser chiefs are like our governors, under the big chief's authority which would be like our president. The next day she came back and asked if she could help us. There were a few things that she could do, like scrubbing and sterilizing instruments, so we put her to work. Grace explained to us, that this girl was considered one of the most beautiful young ladies in the tribe, primarily because she was a little plump. Linda and Grace had named her Anita. Being slightly overweight was considered to be of great beauty in the Kogi tribe. We never saw another Kogi that was the slightest overweight. Linda thought the Kogies obsession with being overweight comes from the fact that before Kogies die, they usually become very skinny, and a little extra weight is a good sign of a long and healthy life. Anita was a few years past the usual marrying age, but her lesser chief father was waiting for just the right man. We met Anita again on our fifth Colombian mission, along with her husband and two children. We will describe more about Anita and her family in chapter 8.

One man brought in 12 children which were all very similar in age. When I asked Grace why he had so many children that were all the same age, she told me this story: This man married and started having children. His wife's sister's husband suddenly died, and she had several small children and no one to take care of her and her children. So he took the sister into his household, married her, and she continued to have more children. The first wife had a third sister whose husband died, and she was left with several small children. Again the man took her and her children into his household, and married her, and she continued to have more children. He currently had 3 wives and 35 children. Grace then said, "The

Kogies don't have any sort of welfare or Social Security, so they just have to make do the best they can."

It was getting late in the afternoon, and we hadn't heard from Linda or Cindy. Near sunset they came popping out of the thick underbrush. Cindy said, "The chief's daughter's bleeding was because the afterbirth had not come out." Cindy indicated that she had sat on the ground, in the dark smoky hut, put the mother's legs up on her shoulders and attempted to remove the afterbirth, but was unsuccessful. But in defense, she indicated she didn't have anything with which to work. It was dark, and all the smoke from the inside cooking was burning her eyes and making them water.

Cindy finally asked the man if there were any way they could bring his wife down to Linda's house. After a short conversation with his wife, he said, "OK." Linda and Cindy started back down the mountain. On their way they observed their patient walking with her husband on a parallel path not far away from them. They were walking considerably faster than Linda and Cindy, and passed them and went out of sight.

When Linda and Cindy got back to the house, the husband and wife were sitting in our waiting room. Cindy made an instrument out of a coat hanger and boiled it well to sterilize it. They prepared a place in one of the bedrooms to work on the lady. With no smoke, a good flashlight, and a crude instrument, they proceeded to attempt to do a D&C, trying to remove the afterbirth. Although Cindy had done many D&C's with proper instruments, and with more favorable conditions, including a D&C back at Lomalinda a week earlier, she was not successful in removing this woman's afterbirth, and had to stop because of excessive bleeding.

The situation was discouraging. If the afterbirth were not removed, there would be a high probability of infection, bleeding, and death. Linda got on the solar powered shortwave radio, and contacted Al Meehan, our pilot, who was in a nearby town. She asked Al if he would be available for an emergency medical evacuation early the next morning. Al said, "I'll be there." Linda explained the options to the lady, and asked her if she would go to a hospital with her in the morning to get a simple operation that would save her life. Her comment was, "Whatever my husband says." Linda asked the husband if they could evacuate his wife on our plane in the morning to a hospital where they could get treatment, otherwise she would probably die. He wouldn't say yes, and he wouldn't say no.

Linda and Cindy started an IV on the patient, and prayed her bleeding would stop, or at least slow down. They also prayed infection would not start, and that she would still be alive in the morning. They had the patient and her husband stay in the house overnight, and asked her to lie very still.

The next morning the husband was gone, and they couldn't find him anywhere. He hadn't given Linda permission to take his wife to the hospital. No one from the Kogi tribe had ever left the reservation to go to a hospital, and no Kogi had ever flown in an airplane.

Linda asked the patient what they should do, and all the patient would say was, "I don't want to die." By this time Al was in the air and on his way.

Linda thought about what she should do. If Linda did take her and something happened, or she died, it would be her entire fault. This could greatly harm or even terminate their ministry of three years of hard work with the Kogies, because it was the big chief's daughter. Linda also started to realize why the husband disappeared without giving his permission. If he had said it was okay, and something happened, it would be his fault. This way if something happened, it would be all Linda's fault.

Linda finally got peace that God would protect her, and the patient would be okay. We started hearing the distant purr of the plane. Linda asked the lady if she could walk, and she said, "Yes," so they started walking toward the landing strip. It wasn't long before we saw the plane circling to land. It also wasn't long before we saw and heard the plane leaving. It flew down the valley and out of sight.

We had dental patients accumulating, so Todd and I set up our clinic and started to work. All the time we were working extracting teeth, Cindy was helping medical patients. Grace was kept busy translating for all three of us. Linda had told Cindy one of the common problems of the Kogies was that beetles would crawl into their ears at night when they were sleeping on the ground. Sometimes these beetles would get stuck in their ears and couldn't get out. The beetles would die and the decaying ones would cause such a bad ear infection that sometimes the patient would die. Fortunately Cindy had brought the right instruments, and reported removing several beetles from patients' ears.

One time I had a straight surgical instrument slip off the tray behind me. When I finished the patient, and bent to pick up the instrument off the floor, it had landed just right, one end was stuck in the dirt floor and the other stood straight up vertically. Again this is something that never happened to me before or since.

As it got into mid-afternoon the radio remained silent. We had heard nothing. Their shortwave radio was Linda's and Grace's only link to the outside world. It was powered by a car battery, which was continually recharged by a solar panel on the roof. Every day Linda and Grace were responsible to report to Kay at Lomalinda, and let her know how everything was progressing, and that everything was okay.

Mid-afternoon the wife's husband showed up, and wanted to know where his wife was, as if he didn't know. Then the big chief's elderly wife came, who was the patient's mother. Then 10 to 15 other relatives showed up. Todd and I just kept on extracting teeth.

I had a 16-year-old very active young man sit down in my chair with a request that I remove the worms that were eating his teeth. When I looked in his mouth I found several large holes in his front teeth as a result of dental decay. They were totally filled with soft dental plaque. He was in no pain and didn't want any of them removed. He just wanted me to get out the worms.

My first thought was how ignorant, how stupid. Then I got to thinking, you know this illiterate Kogi was exactly right. There were worms in his teeth and they were eating and destroying them. The worms were very small, as a matter of fact microscopic in size, and we call them bacteria. They didn't directly eat his teeth, but their waste products were very acidic, and the acid dissolves the minerals in teeth. I gave him a toothbrush, showed him how to use it, and told him it was his responsibility to keep the worms out of his teeth by daily brushing.

As the afternoon went on it was obvious that Grace was starting to get quite nervous. She repeatedly tried to contact Al on the plane's radio, but with no success. She tried about every 15 minutes. Then the magic hour passed. It was 30 minutes before sunset, and Wycliffe's policy was that all planes were to be on the ground 30 minutes before sunset. Grace was beside herself, and the waiting relatives were getting restless.

Just then as the sun was starting to set, we heard the distant purr of the plane coming up the valley. All the relatives left and headed toward the airstrip. The plane landed and the chief's daughter got out and said. "I feel great, everything is okay." She had a successful D&C and all was well. The whole group came back to the house. Grace knew that all the relatives were far from home and had to eat, regardless of what happened, so she had put on a large pot of rice.

There was much celebrating as the group arrived at the house. The custom of not showing any emotion seemed to break down. Maybe this was not considered public since they were all family. They had supper, stayed overnight, and then headed back up the mountain.

Linda explained the next morning, that even though the Colombian Government was technically responsible for the healthcare of all indigenous people, she had an extremely hard time getting someone to do the needed D&C. She said, "I just would not accept a no answer, and ended up going all the way to the head hospital administrator before they agreed to do it late in the afternoon."

The next morning the number of patients slowed, so Linda and Grace took us on a hike for a few hours. First we visited the lesser chief's compound. There were several huts close together in a small area. As we talked with the lesser chief, our beautiful dental assistant, Anita, came out of one of the small round huts. She had not been at the clinic the previous day, so we inquired why, and she said her mother just had a baby, and she was needed to help around the house.

We continued walking up the side of the mountain on a path. I noticed the path we were walking on was only about five or 6 inches wide, at least where the dirt was. It was a little difficult walking because your feet always seemed to land on one side of the path or the other. I commented to Linda about this just as a Kogi was approaching us on the trail. Linda said, "Stop, and watch the way the Kogies walk." I watched, and to my amazement, even though they were walking quite rapidly, they placed one foot exactly in front of the other. Try doing that sometimes as you walk. I tried and found it was very awkward. This explains why the paths were so narrow. I have never observed any other people in the world who walk this way.

We came to one set of buildings where they had a sugarcane press. I found it most interesting. The press was made entirely out of wood. There wasn't one nail or any piece of metal in it anywhere. It was obviously all hand carved, even the several sets of wooden gears. The source of power was two mules that continually walked around the press in a circle. It reminded me of the description of the threshing floors as described thousands of years ago in the Bible. It surely was skillful, creative and very primitive, but it worked.

We came to an area in the path that entered into the dense jungle foliage. It was obvious they had cut this path with a machete. You could see the sharp cuts on the wooden stalks of the foliage. If you didn't stay in the middle of the trail you could bump into the sharp wooden stalks and they could be very uncomfortable. It was actually like a tunnel through the foliage for about a half mile. I noticed that I was getting a stiff neck. I then realized that I had been walking stooped over, because the path through the vegetation had been cut to about four and a half feet high, because that's the height of the Kogies.

We spent the afternoon working in the clinic. That afternoon a Kogi man brought his young teenage daughter into the clinic, and sat her in my chair. I examined her and found several abscessed molar teeth on both sides of her lower jaw. I asked the father if he wanted me to remove these bad teeth, and he had an unusual reply. He asked, "Will this stop her from eating?" I thought, well, she's going to have a pretty sore jaw for a few days, so I simply answered, "Yes." He quickly grabbed the girl, pulled her out of my chair, and went out the door. I had no idea what was happening, so I asked Grace, "What's going on with them?"

Grace said, "You have to understand the Kogi culture. Kogi customs are very similar to Old Testament customs back in the days of Jacob, with a very strong male dominated society. One of the Kogies' customs was that a young man, who wishes to marry a girl, must agree to care for his wife's father and mother for the rest of their life, particularly in old age. The Kogi society had no taxes, retirement, or Social Security. Grace indicated it also helped to know the background about this particular man. He had many sons, but this was his only daughter and his only ticket to Social Security, or a chance for help in his old age. The other thing that is helpful to know is that before a Kogi dies, one of the first symptoms is they stop eating. He wasn't taking any chances, by doing anything that would cause her to stop eating.

That evening Linda told us a mystery story. After Bonnie and I had been with the Kogies for a year or so, and had learned their language, the big chief, called us to the top of the mountain and requested we read to him out of our great book, that he had been told we had. We hiked almost to the top of the mountain to his house, and after our greetings, I started reading to him out of the Bible. I started reading the story about Moses. The chief stopped me and said, "Do you have a different story? We know all about that one." I asked, "What do you know about this story?" The chief rather accurately told us the whole story. I then started reading the story about Noah and the flood. Again the chief stopped me and said, "We know all about that one also," and he again proceeded to tell about Noah and the flood.

I asked the chief, "Where did you learn these stories?" The chief told me, "We used to have a great book with all these stories in it, but our ancestors got lazy and lost the book. Since then these stories have been handed down verbally from generation to generation." I quickly discovered he knew nothing about the New Testament. We were puzzled over the chief's loss of their great book, because the Kogies didn't have a written language, and there was no evidence they had ever had a written language. So I shared the story about Jesus as found in the New Testament and he was greatly interested. How the chief learned these Old Testament stories remains a mystery to this day.

The morning that Al had been scheduled to come and pick us up finally arrived. We packed up early and with the help of some Kogies we carried our baggage down to the airstrip. The Kogies showed great appreciation, and repeatedly thanked us for coming and helping them.

When Al landed, he told us we had too much weight for him to take off in one load. It was because of the steep surrounding mountains and the shortness of the airstrip. He said, "I'll take Todd and Doc out on the first load." We said farewell to our new friends, which we had started to get quite attached to in just a little over a week. The thought struck me we probably would never get to see any of these people again. It turned out to be a permanent farewell, because we have never been able to get back.

We took off with no problem. We flew down the valley and out over the densely covered jungle foothills. Al spotted a runway clearing carved out of the jungle ahead, and he put our plane down. He requested that we absolutely not try to get out of the plane. He got out and walked over to a small building, and talked with some men near the building.

Finally he came back and said, "You can get out now." He walked us over to the side of the runway and asked us to sit down on a log, and he told us this story: "I was low on fuel, so I landed at the first airstrip I spotted. Actually this airstrip is not even on the map. This airstrip is operated by the cocaine cartel, and is used to transport cocaine. For the right price, they agreed to sell me some fuel, so I am going to refuel, and go back and get Cindy and your luggage. The agreement is that you are to sit on this log and not get up. Do not even look around, just sit here very still." He refueled and took off.

This was the longest hour and a half of our whole trip. We sat there virtually motionless, and didn't dare to move anything except our eyeballs. Al finally returned, taxied up to us, and motioned for us to get into the plane, which we did. He immediately took off. The rest of our trip back to Lomalinda, and then back to Bogotá, was uneventful.

We had planned one day in Bogotá with Jim and his family to rest, shop, and look around before flying home. When we arrived Jim told me the Central Government Intelligence Agency wanted to talk with us. I started getting a little apprehensive, but Jim said, "Don't worry." We went downtown to one of the large government buildings and found the correct office. They wanted to ask us many simple questions about the Kogies. Apparently it turned out that Todd and I were the first male outsiders to be allowed into the Kogi reservation. The interviewers were very pleasant. They were just interested in knowing what was happening on the reservation. We had a friendly and informative chat.

After our first mission to Colombia I thought no trip could top that one, but as I look back on our second mission trip, it was even more exciting and adventurous. Todd received a tremendous amount of experience giving anesthesia, putting in fillings, and in extracting hundreds of teeth. I guess you could call this a certain type of home schooling.

My wife and I took a cruise earlier that spring, and I remember the feeling I had returning home after being waited on hand and foot for over a week. I am used to being the server, and having somebody serve me all the time just left me with an empty feeling. But returning home from this mission trip I felt tremendously fulfilled, excited and rewarded. I had a good feeling that I had been proving my faith through my good works, by helping others in need as the Bible commands us.

## Now for the Rest of the Story

I have been in regular communication with Linda ever since we got home, primarily through her newsletters, and this is what has been happening to Linda and the Kogies.

Just a few days after we left, two women excitedly came running into Linda's and Grace's house crying and said, "You have to leave immediately. The Communist guerrillas are coming down the mountain valley." They quickly gathered a few items, and fled with the two women down a jungle path away from the guerrillas. Linda asked, "Where have these guerrillas been staying?" The women said, "They were just two hours away over the mountain ridge in the neighboring valley." Linda asked, "Why didn't you tell us sooner?" They replied, "Because if we had, you and the dentists would have left, and we wouldn't have received any treatment." They said, "Don't worry we'll get you safely out of here." The women walked for three days, until they reached the Kogi reservation border, where they could see a small village in the distance. Linda and Grace made the women promise they would meet them in a certain small hotel in this village in exactly 30 days. They thanked them, and departed, traveling the remainder of the way to the village on their own.

Linda and Grace had no problem getting back to Lomalinda. In 30 days they returned to the designated hotel, with the hopes that the two women would show up. Surprisingly enough, they did come. The women reported that the Communist guerrillas had stopped and set up their new headquarters in Linda's and Grace's house. After all, it was much larger than any of the small round Kogi huts, and it had a good tin roof, running water, and several good beds. It was unoccupied, there was a nearby stream, and it had a nice clearing in which their troops could make camp. The guerrillas had treated all of the Kogies very well because they were trying to win their friendship and support.

It was obvious that it certainly would not be safe for Linda and Grace to return anytime soon. The guerrillas treated white people or foreigners as if they were the enemy. They often kidnapped foreigners, killed them or held them for a big ransom, to help finance their cause.

This was the beginning of a new phase of Linda, Bonnie, and Grace's translation work. They had been successful in getting two Kogi women to come outside the reservation. Maybe they could get more Kogies to come out and help them with their translation work. Linda, Bonnie, and Grace rented a small apartment in this village and made it worthwhile for some of the Kogies to come out and stay with them for short periods, to help them in their language translation work. Eventually they got some Kogies to go back to Lomalinda with them for longer periods. There they had better living conditions, access to computers, and help from other missionaries.

After a couple of years, Linda was told by some of the Kogies that the guerrillas had left, and it was now safe for them to return. Linda and Grace asked Al to take them back. Al waited while they checked out the situation. On the walk up to the house, some women came out of the dense underbrush, and told them that the guerrillas had returned. They had heard the plane, and they were at the house waiting for them. They told Linda and Grace that the guerrillas would do them great harm and they needed to leave as quickly as possible. The women also told them the guerrillas had told them if they warned Linda and Grace of their presence that they would kill them, but they just had to warn them. Linda and Grace ran back to the plane, and quickly took off. Neither Linda, Bonnie, nor Grace has been able to return to their jungle-based home since we left 25 years ago. Today the translation work has been completed by having the Kogies come out of the reservation and help them.

Today Linda is the only one of the three women left working with the Kogies. She has a large home in Bogotá where she houses several Kogi young people who have become Christians, and are going to school, and even college. Several of them have graduated and returned to the Kogi tribe as pastors, teachers, and missionaries. The Communist influence on the Kogi reservation has been greatly reduced. Many of the Kogies have learned to read and write their own language, and they now have the Bible in their own language. Many have become Christians.

A few years back, Linda was diagnosed with a terminal illness. With good treatment and God's help she has been able to overcome the disease. She continues to work for the Lord by acting as a mother and counselor to help train many young Kogi Christians, so that they may go back and teach, and help lead their people. I thank the Lord for the small part we had in helping the Kogies, not only with their dental problems, but to learn to trust and respect Linda, Bonnie, and Grace, so that they in turn could help them.

# CHAPTER 6

# COLOMBIA 3

A year after returning from my second mission trip to Colombia, I had a dental student named Tim, come up to me in one of my dental laboratory classes that I was teaching, and asked, "Any chance I could go with you to Colombia next summer?" He obviously had been talking with either Mark or Todd. I didn't even know at that time if I were going back to Colombia. We agreed on a time when we could have lunch and talk.

At lunch I found out Tim was single and engaged to be married in late August next summer. He had a good solid active Christian faith and was anxious to serve the Lord. We discussed Colombia, and I only promised him I would consider his request, and keep him informed. I already knew that neither Mark nor Todd would be able to go.

A couple of months later, I received an official written invitation to return to Colombia the next summer. Jim and Deb, our Colombian hosts, had been home on furlough in 1986. Again, I didn't have any good reason to tell them, or the Lord, no. The Lord had been blessing my family and me really well. After talking with Mark and Todd about Tim, I told Tim if he were still interested, I would be happy to take him to Colombia with me. His tremendous show of enthusiasm was a real encouragement to me.

I did nearly all of the planning and packing. Tim and I bid farewell to our families in late June 1987, and left for Colombia. Upon arriving in Colombia, we had a problem getting through customs. In fact, customs took away all of our luggage. They said they needed to keep it for further inspection.

Jim met us and we stayed overnight with his family. The next morning we went with Jim back to the airport where he normally worked every day. After Jim talked with the customs officials, in Spanish, for quite awhile, they released our luggage. I asked Jim, "Why did they keep it?" He said, "They didn't say why, and when they said take it and go, I didn't ask any questions."

On my first two mission trips I took new toothbrushes and distributed them to each of my patients. I also gave them a small red rose that stuck to their clothes rather well. They seemed quite excited and happy to get gifts from us, even if they seemed small to us.

I was brushing my teeth shortly after I had returned from my second missionary trip to Colombia, when I noticed it was time to change my toothbrush, because it was getting a little old. I started to throw it into the wastebasket, but then the thought struck me, there is really a lot of use left in this brush, especially for the indigenous people in Colombia who have absolutely nothing. So I saved it, took it to the office, cleaned it, and completely sterilized it. It looked pretty good.

I asked my wife, friends, family, church members, and employees to start saving their used toothbrushes. Our hygienists at the office routinely give each patient a new tooth-brush. One of the hygienists suggested we ask our patients to bring their used toothbrushes back, so we could sterilize them and give them to people who had no toothbrush.

Our local newspaper, serving several hundred thousand people, asked if they could do a story on our mission trip to the Kogies. They used several of my photos, and did a major full-page article on our trip. They also mentioned that I was saving used toothbrushes to be sterilized to take back to the indigenous people in Colombia. Suddenly school teachers were putting on used toothbrushes drives, along with Cub Scouts, Boy Scouts, churches, and vacation Bible schools. They were all collecting used toothbrushes.

When a child is asked to give to missions, parents frequently give them some change to put in the collection plate. When a child is asked to give his own toothbrush to a needy child who doesn't have a toothbrush, that is something he can give that belongs to him. It is probably the first thing he ever gave to missions that belonged to him. I think this is a valuable way to start teaching children the meaning of giving.

Suddenly I was getting hundreds, and soon thousands of used toothbrushes. I don't know why, but they started coming in the mail from all over the country. I was reluctant to tell people to stop, because oftentimes it's hard to get something like this started again, so I just said, "Thank you." I started taking larger quantities of toothbrushes on my mission trips, and handing them out to family groups and sometimes small villages. I started sup-plying other dental mission teams that were going on similar Christian missions. Today I have over 30,000 used toothbrushes in my basement all sterilized and ready to go. The only problem in taking toothbrushes is their weight. The weight quickly adds up. We are only allowed so many pounds of luggage on the airlines and our dental supplies and equipment are first priority. We always maximize the weight of our luggage by adding toothbrushes.

I had been told that some countries wouldn't allow a large supply of new products to be brought into the country because distributing them might undermine their local economy and manufacturing. Used toothbrushes and clothes are allowed in any quantities. We learned that when we have new toothbrushes donated to us on occasion, we take them out of their wrappers or packages, mix them together with the used toothbrushes, and pack 30 or 40 of them together in a bundle with rubber bands around them so they look used. The thought struck me that on this particular mission trip I had brought a large number of new toothbrushes in their original new boxes, and that may have been the reason that triggered the customs investigation. We will never know, but I haven't done it again.

The same morning that we recovered our luggage, Tim and I flew with Jim on Wycliffe's DC 3 out of Bogotá, east over the Andes mountains and down onto the plateau of the Amazon River basin to Lomalinda. We stayed in the guest house, with Gary and Char being our hosts again. Tim and I worked in the Lomalinda dental clinic for a few days.

Joel and Nancy Stolte invited Tim and me over to their house for supper on our first night. Joel asked us if we were interested in flying out to his jungle village where we could do dental work on his indigenous people for whom he was doing translation work. Of course we said "Yes."

Joel had been recently elected chairman of all Wycliffe operations in Columbia for the current year. The translators took turns each year sharing this responsibility. He gave us some forms, and asked us to sign them. It was actually Wycliffe standard regulations, and we should have signed them on our first two trips. The form simply stated that we give Wycliffe permission to bury us within 24 hours if we should die while in Columbia. It was a national law in Colombia that all people had to be buried within 24 hours after they died, and Joel said there was no way they could get a body out of the country in 24 hours. Everyone in Lomalinda had signed this form, so we reluctantly signed it. I didn't tell my wife about this until many years later. It is called faith in action.

A couple of days later, Tim and I met Joel at the hangar early in the morning with our dental supplies and personal gear. After packing the plane, we gathered together and Joel prayed, asking God to build a hedge of protection around us and keep us safe. We took off in one of Wycliffe's Helio Courier airplanes, with Don as our pilot. We flew directly east over the vast Amazon jungle. We saw no roads, trails, or any sign of life below, just the green vegetation of tree tops, which looked much like broccoli from the air. Don said, "There are 3000 miles of jungle straight ahead of us, and that is a lot farther than our plane has fuel to fly."

We flew for about two hours and finally we saw a light green patch in the dark green jungle canopy ahead. We circled and landed on the small grassy landing strip carved out of the jungle. I didn't see any small huts as we landed, but I did see one very large thatch-roofed building.

After landing we taxied up to a rectangular wooden building with a tin roof and a nice front porch. It was right at the end of the runway. We parked just 10 feet in front of the house with the plane headed straight down the runway.

This was Joel's house. Joel had been a construction supervisor before he became a Wycliffe Bible Translator. He had slowly and gradually brought all the building supplies out on the plane over the last 20 years, and built this rather nice house. I'm not sure how he did it. With Don, Joel, Tim, and me and five pieces of luggage our plane was full. We found out later that the other missionaries referred to Joel's house as the castle in the jungle.

As we were unloading, I went back to the plane to get our last piece of luggage, and I noticed Don leaning against the front of the plane with his hands in his face. I said to him, "Is everything all right?" As he turned, I could see he had been crying. He said, "Yes," and smiled. He then told me this story: "I am one of Wycliffe's new pilots, and have been training for some time. This was my first solo flight out into the jungle. There are no landmarks to follow out here, and I was lost, and didn't know where I was. I just kept my compass on the setting that I was told. I thought we would get here much sooner, and I was really getting worried." It was a good thing we didn't know all of this earlier, but we were here safe and that's all that counts right now.

Just then we heard the purr of another plane. I wondered what another plane was doing way out here. The plane flew low and right over us at treetop level. I was puzzled. Then the plane circled and landed. It was Wycliffe's current senior pilot who had been following us just to be sure that Don made it safely without getting lost. He taxied up next to our plane, got out and congratulated Don. Don had no idea that he was following us. Both were smiling and happy.

That afternoon and the next day, the senior pilot took Don up on training flights. He took him to several of the other villages in the surrounding jungle where Wycliffe translators were often living.

Communist Guerrillas were regularly moving around in the jungle. They liked to kidnap foreigners and hold them for ransom. To prevent a plane from landing in a village where the Guerrillas were present and waiting for them, the Wycliffe missionaries had made previous arrangements with indigenous village people. The village people always hurried to the runway when they heard the plane coming. If the Guerrillas were present they would force the villagers to go to the runway as usual to welcome the Wycliffe plane. The plane usually flew over the runway fairly low once and then circled before landing. The signal was, if all the people along the runway were waving, it meant it was safe to land. If the people didn't wave, that meant don't land, because the Guerrillas were in the village. This signal worked well.

We had lunch with Joel, and then set up our two-chair dental clinic in Joel's large living room. In dental school, Tim had completed training in anesthesia but had no training in extractions, so I demonstrated for him a few times, giving him some personal instructions. It wasn't long before Tim was ready to do his first extraction. I have a picture of him with a huge smile on his face, as he held up the bloody tooth from his first extraction. He caught on quickly, and we got a lot of infected abscessed teeth removed that afternoon.

After supper that evening, just before dark, Joel took us over to what he called the Big House. It was only a few hundred yards away, but it was through some tall dense jungle, so we couldn't see it from Joel's house. On our way, we passed several clumps of sugarcane that were growing along the path. I thought to myself, that's the reason we see so many decayed and abscessed teeth.

The Big House was very big. It was about 75 feet tall, almost as tall as the surrounding jungle trees. It reminded me of the size of two or three gymnasiums all put together. It was round and teepee style with the center going up to a point. Joel told us the entire village of almost 200 people lived in this one house.

I thought to myself, this is a good example that neighbors can live together peacefully. Joel said, "They are very passive people, and I have never heard of any fighting."

Joel indicated that in translating their language, which he had almost completed, he found no words in their language for winner or loser. Can you imagine what our society would be like if we had no winners or losers?

Inside the Big House there were groups of people with small wooden cooking fires gathered around the outer edge where families were cooking their suppers. There were no windows. It was quite dark except for the light of the small fires. Surprisingly, it didn't seem to be too smoky. Both the walls and the very high roof were constructed out of palm leaves and thatching. I guess the smoke just went up and through the thatched roof.

I asked Joel, "Where do they all sleep?" He pointed to the bundles of cloth tied to the poles that supported the roof. He said, "These are hammocks. They just pull them out and tie them to another pole at night before they go to bed." These hammocks were sometimes stacked three and four high, one on top of the other. I didn't see any closets or cupboards. There were no tables, but I did see several small stools, each carved out of one piece of wood. They were about 6 or 8 inches high, but most of the people were just sitting on the dirt floor.

In the morning Tim took a shower. Yes, Joel had built a shower. He had taken a barrel and put it under the eaves trough just under the roof to catch rainwater. He hooked up a shower head in the bottom of the barrel with a rope attached to it that you pulled when you wanted water. The shortcoming was you needed to shower outside under the eaves, so you needed to wear your shorts. The water wasn't warm, but it really wasn't cold either, and the amount was limited. This barrel also supplied running water to the kitchen sink faucet. The shower worked well, and Tim was happy.

As we were eating breakfast, a couple of men came across the airstrip carrying an electric generator. Joel said, "Finally!" He had the men put the generator in a room in the center of the house that had no windows and only one door with a lock on it. The room was constructed completely out of wood boards.

As the men were putting the generator back into Joel's safe room, Joel told us this story: "When we arrived I unlocked my middle safe room door for which no one has a key, except me. I noticed my generator was missing, just gone. The door or the lock had not been tampered with, and I couldn't see any way someone could have gotten inside and removed this big generator.

I talked with some of the head men from the big house, and I was told that while I was gone they received advance information that the Guerrillas were coming down the river that ran near the Big House. They were afraid the Guerrillas would break into my house and take the generator, and then I would not be able to show them any more movies in their Big House."

"I left a key to my house with a couple of the men, but never the key to my locked room. One of the men told me, "We came into your house, and very carefully removed several of the boards in the side of your locked room, took your generator out, and carefully replaced them. We then took your generator out into the jungle and hid it. Don't worry, we kept it safe. You will show us more movies, won't you?" Joel said to us, "A lot of good my secure locked room is. This is the first time that this has ever happened, and I still can't see where they removed the boards."

Patients started coming, so we set up our dental clinic in Joel's living room and started to work. Don and the senior pilot took off for more jungle flight training. The day was long and hot, but we accomplished a lot. It was a little dark in Joel's living room. We selected a couple of curious teenagers that were watching, and asked them to hold flashlights so we could see better. They were very excited, and did an excellent job.

Joel told us that the villagers currently had look-outs posted both up and down the river. In case the Guerrillas came again they would have time to come and warn us. He told us that was the reason the planes were parked close in front of the house and headed down the runway. If we needed, we could jump into the plane and take off very quickly. Rivers were the normal route of transportation in the jungle. We never had any problem.

Joel did some emergency extractions without anesthesia when he had a request. Sometimes their teeth were hard to grab hold of with forceps, because there was so much decay, and there wasn't much tooth to get a hold of. Joel had a unique philosophy he used when he extracted teeth. He said, "When I get a good grip on a tooth, I never let go until the tooth is out." It sounded a little barbaric, but I have often remembered his philosophy when I've had a good grip on a tooth to remove and after wiggling it for a while, I have gotten tired and I stopped to rest. Sometimes I found that when I went to get another grip on the tooth the second time, I couldn't get a grip on it no matter how hard I tried. At that point I wished I had followed Joel's philosophy.

One afternoon in our makeshift dental clinic, I looked up to find an eight-year-old girl deeply engrossed in one of Joel's magazines. Actually it was a medical journal, with no pictures. It was dated 1984 and on the front cover it had a big title on it that said AIDs. I thought, no pictures, she can't read, but she has her nose buried in this magazine and never moved. What an irony, particularly concerning the subject matter.

Joel told us that most of these people were born in the Big House, lived there their entire life without going more than 25 miles away from home, grew old, and died there.

That night Joel showed a Jesus type of movie to a large number of very enthusiastic people. Most of them had already become Christians.

After staying only three days, we started to catch up on the people who needed aching teeth removed. So early in the morning, Don, who had stayed with us, loaded us up and we took off and returned to Lomalinda. In some areas the clouds were low, so Don had to fly low and stay between the treetops and the clouds, and sometimes we got pretty close to the treetops.

When we got back to Lomalinda, Vick Kondo, another translator, asked us if we would go out and help his indigenous people. We were there to help, so naturally we said, "Yes."

Vick had been a veterinarian before he became a translator. He and his wife, Riena, had been working with a large group of Guahibo Indians for 20 years. They had their verbal language translated into writing, and had the Bible translated, printed, and distributed to the people. They had taught many people how to read and write. They were currently working on a dictionary for the people, which was part of Wycliffe's agreement with the government. The Colombian government was solidly Roman Catholic, but they allowed the Wycliffe Bible translators to work with 60 indigenous Indian groups that didn't have a written language, but under certain conditions. Writing a dictionary for the people was one of the requirements.

Vick and Riena had lived in their jungle home most of the 20 years. They had trained teachers and opened numerous schools. They had trained people to be nurses and had set up several medical clinics. They had converted most of the people to Christianity, trained pastors, and opened many village churches.

Unfortunately the Communist Guerrillas had moved into Vick's village where he and Riena lived. Fortunately they escaped, but they had not been able to go back in over a year. Vick had been in contact with Jack Cain and his family who were living in a different area but with the same Guahibo Indians. Jack was with New Tribes Missions, which were involved primarily with evangelism. The Cains had been living there several years, and hadn't been bothered by the Guerrillas. They had a short landing strip, and they invited Vick to come and bring us to help the people with their painful dental problems.

The very next morning we repacked and went to the landing strip and met George DeVoucalla who was going to be our pilot. After prayer, George loaded Vick, Tim and me, along with our luggage, into the Helio Courier. We took off and headed northeast over the seemingly uninhabited jungle for 2 1/2 hours. Finally we spotted a light green grassy landing strip. There were a large number of indigenous people who came running to the landing strip to welcome us.

Jack Cain was there to meet us. Vick had never personally met Jack. They only knew each other by their contact over the shortwave radio. Jack had heard a lot about Vick and his work with the Guahibos. Vick was well known by most of these native people. He was the first outsider to ever move in and live with them. He and Riena had done so much for the people. Vick was sort of a hero to these people, somewhat like a George Washington.

Jack walked us to his house, where we met his wife and two children, and had lunch. After lunch, Jack, Vick and the village chief talked for quite a while discussing plans for our stay. We didn't understand anything they were saying, so we just sat and observed. Finally it was decided. They agreed that first we needed to go down river to a very isolated village, that neither Jack nor Vick had ever been able to visit, and try to help them.

Jack had a boat and an outboard motor, but no fuel. George, our pilot, agreed that he could spare some fuel, so he took some fuel from the plane and gave it to Jack to run his boat motor.

Jack's house was on a hill with a large meadow gradually sloping down to the river, which was about a half mile away. Jack told us that the Guahibo's Reservation was on this side of the river. The other side of the river was controlled by the Communist Guerrillas and they could sometimes see them walking around on the other side. Jack said, "The Guerrillas know we are living here, but they're not supposed to go onto the Reservation, and so far they haven't bothered us." Jack radioed their New Tribes headquarters daily to report on their safety, but everything they said was in code, so the Guerrillas, who could monitor their radio, didn't know what they were saying.

With the help of some of the villagers, we took the motor, our fuel, and all of our supplies down to the river. On the banks of the river, hidden in a clump of trees and bushes, was a large dugout canoe. It was about 25 feet long and it was actually a half of a log from which chunks of wood had been obviously chiseled out by hand. They had boards wedged between the sides on which we could sit. The front was pointed, while the back was flat to accommodate a place to attach a motor. A real strong, husky young man hooked up the motor, while we loaded our gear into the canoe.

The Cain family and the villagers bid us farewell, as the young man started the motor and backed us out into the river. Evidently he was going to be our captain and guide on this trip. We headed down the river with Tim, Vick, and me, and all of our gear in this hollowed out log. One of the things that concerned me was that we were loaded so heavily that there were only about two inches of the side of the log that stayed above the water. We sat very still.

We saw alligators sliding down the banks and into the river on both sides. It was an Amazon tributary and most likely the river was full of piranha. The river was about 30 to 50 feet wide, and a long way from any civilization. We had Communist Guerrillas on one side, and native Guahibo Indians on the other. Then I saw white-water ahead, and we started picking up speed, dodging around rocks and logs.

I figured I had over $5,000 of valuables in this hollow log. My adrenal glands started working overtime, and I couldn't help but cry out to God asking, "Lord, Lord, what am I doing here? Yes, I know, Lord, we are here to serve you. Please keep us safe. Lord, Jesus promised us in the great commission that He would be with us always, even to the end of the earth, and Lord, I think we're just about there."

We made it safely through about a quarter of a mile of rapids, and continued on quiet water for at least another hour. We then turned off the main river and headed up a small tributary on the reservation side of the river. This river was only 10 to 20 feet wide and was very crooked. The jungle canopy often hung over the entire river in places. After a half hour, our boat captain pulled alongside a muddy bank where there was a clearing in the vegetation. We got out, stretched our legs, and said, "Thank you, Lord!"

We unloaded our gear. Our young guide and boat captain removed the motor and went into the surrounding jungle thicket and hid it. We pulled our log, or probably more properly called our dugout canoe, well up onto the bank. We divided up our gear and started carrying it on a dense jungle path away from the river. We soon emerged from the jungle vegetation that was near the river, into a large meadow. Our path went up a long gradual hill. We saw no village or any signs of people, so we just kept following the path. For some reason Vick found communication with our boat captain a little difficult, so it was just like playing follow the leader. Where he went we followed, but we weren't sure where we were going. It was starting to get dark. I decided it was time to put my faith to work. This time I needed to stop worrying, and have faith that our guide knew where he was going.

Shortly we saw a lone figure coming down the path toward us. As he got closer we could see it was a young teenage boy. He stopped about 20 feet from us, and asked, "Who goes there? What do you want?" Vick answered, "I'm Vick Kondo, and we have come to visit and help you." The boy immediately turned around and ran back up the hill. We continued walking.

It was almost dark as we approached the top of the hill. We could see a couple dozen huts and then we saw about 40 or 50 people gathered at the edge of the village. As we reached the group of people, an older man, the chief, stepped forward. Vick went up to him and introduced himself as Vick Kondo. This was one of the villages that Vick had never had a chance to visit before, but obviously the people had heard of Vick, because they started cheering and chanting Vick, Vick.

The chief and Vick shook hands, and Tim and I were introduced. The chief invited us into his larger thatched hut. Some women appeared and offered us a very hot drink. Vick motioned to us that it was okay for us to drink. "It has been boiled," he said. There was a lot of conversation between Vick and the chief. We didn't understand a word.

Finally the chief led us to the only other room in his hut, and Vick said, "This is where we will sleep." We put all of our baggage in there, and Vick and Tim got busy hanging their hammocks in which they planned to sleep.

Since I normally sleep on my stomach, I don't sleep well in a hammock. We had brought a lightweight cot with us to serve as a table for our dental instruments. Thankfully, I was able to use it for my bed. We had each brought lightweight sleeping bags since it did cool down at night.

I slept very well. Just before daybreak I was awakened by a high-pitched screeching noise. I looked up and saw dozens of bats flying around inside our room near the roof. They came in the openings for the doors and windows and flew up to the roof and disappeared into the thatching. No one else was awake, so I just watched and waited. When Vick woke up, I asked him about the bats, and he commented, "Don't worry, they never bother humans. They live in most all thatched roofs. They are good because they help keep the mosquito population down."

We had some hard biscuits that Vick had brought along for breakfast. I saw Vick get out a small plastic bottle, and put a drop or two into our drinking water container. I asked him, "What's that?" He said, "Clorox, we needed to sterilize our water."

I found out later that we were sleeping in the chief's bedroom. While we were having our hot drink the evening before, which was much like tea, someone moved all of the chief's belongings out the back door, so we could use his bedroom. I never did find out where the chief was staying.

I asked Vick, "Where do we go to the bathroom?" He said, "Follow me." He grabbed some toilet paper, and a small collapsible shovel which he had brought, and headed down the side of the hill. When we got 100 yards or so down the hill, in waist high grass, but still in the wide open meadow, he stopped and dug two shallow holes. We went to the bathroom in the holes, covered them up, and headed back to the chief's hut. Vick said, "I have been trying to teach sanitary hygiene to the Guahibo's for years and certainly we need to set an example."

Tim and I started setting up our instruments on my cot, right in the center of the village, with the small round huts in a circle around us. At least we were out in the open where we had good light. The morning was cool and refreshing, probably about 65 ° F.

My first patient was the chief. He had some aching molars, which he wanted removed. By this time, most of the villagers had gathered around us in a big circle. I gave the chief lots of anesthesia. When I turned around, I was startled by a man wearing a big straw hat, and with a big bow and arrow with a sharp stone tip drawn back and pointed right at me. He said something in the local dialect which I didn't understand. Needless to say, I was a little concerned. I asked Vick, "What did he say?" Vick smiled and answered, "He said you better take good care of the chief, he is my brother."

Just then a big smile came over the man's face, and he took his bow and arrow down. Vick said, "Don't worry, he is just joking." Later on I got to be good friends with him. I not only bought his straw hat, but I bought his bow and arrow and brought them home with me. I still have them over 22 years later. Vick said, "He was delighted with the sale, because he can easily make more, but sales are few and far between out here in the jungle."

I got along fine with the chief. When he was finished, he stood up and he said something to the people, and they quickly started lining up. By midmorning it was getting rather hot out in the sun, so we moved under a small shade tree.

One of the things I will never understand is that early the first morning, just at daybreak, several people came up the hill on the same path we had used to enter the village the night before. When I inquired, I was told, they were from a neighboring village two hours away. They came to see the dentists.

There were two things that puzzled me. First, how did they know we were here? We arrived at the village at almost dark the night before, and no one knew that we were coming. I didn't hear any drums beating in the night. Secondly, how could they walk through the jungle for two hours in the pitch black of the night? We were told that they even had to cross two rivers. I had commented when we turned our flashlights off the night before, "Boy, it is dark." I couldn't even see my hand in front of my face. This continues to remain a mystery to me to this day.

That evening the chief told us, "Two weeks before you arrived, a group of heavily armed Communist Guerrillas came up the same path you did from the river. They looked around the village quite thoroughly. I didn't know what they were looking for. I told them that they were not welcome on our reservation, and asked them to leave. We just had sticks and bows and arrow. They had big automatic guns. They didn't hurt anyone, and finally left, but we were pretty scared." That is probably why the young boy came down the path to find out who we were the night we arrived.

That evening the chief invited us to go to their evening church service. We had started to hear some singing. We went to a rectangular thatched building they used as a church. There were a lot of people packed into this building. One man was playing a guitar, and everyone was enthusiastically singing and clapping. There were several of the hymns which we recognized the melody, but the words were in their native language.

After singing, a man read from the Bible. This was a copy of one of the Bibles that Vick and Riena had spent many years translating. Wycliffe had printed the Bibles, and Vick and Riena distributed most of them. After the Bible reading, another man talked for a few moments, then had prayer, and it was over. We were told that they had a church service like this every evening.

The next morning, Tim showed the women that had fixed us breakfast a picture of his fiancée that he was going to marry in just a little over a month. The women giggled, laughed, blushed, turned their heads and covered their eyes. I asked Vick, "What's going on?" He said "In the picture, Tim has his arm around his fiancée, and in their culture men and women never touch in public. This is considered indecent."

I noticed that each hut had a patch of dirt surrounding the hut where no vegetation grew. It was about 10 feet wide. I didn't think much about it until I saw several chickens that were patrolling this bare ground. Every time a bug came out of the grass and started running toward the hut, a chicken nailed it, and had his breakfast. There were no bugs in their houses. Actually the main reason for keeping the dirt surrounding the hut was to keep the snakes out, and it did a good job of that also.

We set up our morning dental clinic, and this time we started out under the shade tree, after our scorching sun experience the day before. One of my most memorable observations was the very excessive amount of decay that we found, especially in young people. I saw two very pretty young girls. One was 12 and the other was 13 years old. Their permanent upper front teeth were black with decay and were half gone, and they were in pain. The other thing that I had never seen before, was their first premolars, that normally come in at age 12, were decaying level with the gum as fast as they were coming in.

The children really liked Tim. He laughed and smiled and played with them. He would let them come and sit on his lap. Sometimes he would have 10 to 15 children sitting around him.

That night we were dirty and tired. We asked Vick if there were any way that we could wash or clean up. He asked around, and then said, "Okay, but after dark." There was a little moon underneath the clouds, so we could just see a little bit. We walked two or 300 yards down the side of the hill until we came to a water hole. We undressed down to our shorts, and then slipped down a muddy bank of about a foot into some rather warm water. I'm guessing the water hole was about 20 feet wide, but it was really so dark we could hardly see. The water came a little above our knees. We squatted down, but didn't sit down because our feet were in 2 or 3 inches of mud on the bottom. After being hot and sweaty all day, splashing the water on us felt refreshing in the cool of the evening.

On our way back up to the village, I said to Vick, "Thanks, that really felt good. I would like to see the waterhole we bathed in sometime in the daylight." Vick said abruptly, "No you wouldn't," and we never did. Since we never really saw much that night, this left a lot to my curious imagination.

That night we didn't go to the church service since we were dead tired, and couldn't understand anything anyway. I can still remember lying in my sleeping bag, and listening to them singing hymns to melodies that were very familiar.

The third morning we were fairly well caught up with our extractions, so Vick decided we needed to start back to Cains' village.

Before we left, we got everyone in the village together for a photo. After Tim and I took pictures on our cameras, Tim got out a Polaroid camera and took several pictures of the group, and then a single picture of the chief. He gave the pictures to the chief and everyone huddled around and watched them develop. You can't imagine the excitement that it created. This experience resulted in my purchasing a Polaroid camera and using it on many future mission trips.

When we tried to say goodbye, the chief and many of the people started begging and begging us to stay. They promised us they would build us a big house. They promised they would take good care of us, and even build us an airstrip for our plane. They just couldn't understand why we had to go. Then the chief asked, "If we build an airstrip, will you at least come back and visit us sometime?" They were just very insistent. In the 35 mission trips I have taken, this was by far the most difficult farewell we ever had.

Many of the villagers followed us down to the river carrying our bags, and helped us load our canoe, all the time saying thank you, thank you. We finally got away and headed down the small river until it joined the big river. Then we headed upstream. All the time I was thinking, how are we going to get through those rapids? Our captain solved that very simply. We didn't go up the rapids, we went around them.

Actually, what happened was the old river was meandering a lot and was very crooked. One of the big loops had gotten so big that some of the water started to break through at the isthmus. That created the rapids, but the big loop was still there, and although it was a much longer way around, we took that route, thank goodness.

After we safely arrived back at the Cains, we had lunch, and set up our dental clinic out in a clearing in front of their house. It was cloudy that afternoon. While we were gone, an American couple arrived to stay long-term with the Cains. The man was Bob, and he seemed quite interested in what we were doing, and watched intently.

After supper, Bob asked me, "Would you teach me how to extract teeth, I have a nursing background." I said, "Sure, why not? Let's get started right now." I spent well into the night going over basic dental anatomy of the teeth, including the size and shape and number of the roots. We discussed the nerves and the blood supply to the teeth, and where, when, and how much anesthesia to give each tooth.

The next day I gave Bob one on one instruction and demonstrations. Then I had him give anesthesia, and extract some teeth while I was watching him closely, almost holding his hand. I talked to him and gave him instructions continuously. It was nice that the patients couldn't understand what we were saying. Rarely have I had this type of teaching opportunity. This made the teaching fast, although it initially slowed our extraction production. By afternoon Bob was doing so well that I set up a third dental chair, and just stopped and consulted with him when he had a question, so our speed actually increased. This is the first person outside dental school that I have ever taught to extract teeth.

That evening the chief, who was rather an old man, came up the path from the river carrying a big fish. It was probably two feet long and weighed several pounds. He had shot it down in the river with his bow and arrow which he was also carrying. On the tip of his arrow he had an inch and a half long, very sharp bone which had a lot of barbs in it. He also had fishing line tied to the end of his arrow. Jack said, "That's how they do all their fishing in the river because the water is so clear."

There was also a young man that had shot a big bird with his bow and arrow that day. They cooked both the fish and the bird at the chief's house, and most all the village went over to the chief's house for supper. Jack said, "That's what they do when anyone catches a big fish, bird or animal. They share with the rest of the village, because there's no way of keeping leftovers in this hot climate without it spoiling." Thank goodness, we had our own supper at the Cains' house.

That night when we went to bed we were all very tired. It had been a long hot day and we worked until dark. Tim was especially tired. He commented to me, "I don't think I've ever worked this hard or been this tired in my entire life." This made my mind wander. I could just imagine Tim making this comment to his classmates when he got back to school. Then the rumor would get started that Dr. Charlick takes students down to the jungle, where they can't get away, and then he works them to the bone until they're ready to drop. His comment made me a little uncomfortable.

The next morning before we started working, one of the village men came to me and asked if I would come to his house and check his sick daughter. I got Bob and Vick with their nursing backgrounds to go with me. This man led us to his house, which was one of the round thatched huts. He told us to wait outside while he went inside. He and his wife came out slowly helping their 18-year-old daughter. She was stunningly the most beautiful native young lady I had ever seen. She smiled faintly at us, while her dad told us this story: "She has been sick for two years. Her main problem is she just has no energy. She lies there in her bed day and night, and hardly has enough energy to get up or to go to the bathroom. We have taken her to several people for treatment, and although they all gave her medicine, nothing has helped. She has just stayed the same." He and his wife just begged us to help her.

Vick, Bob, and I talked together, but didn't come up with any diagnosis, treatment, or solution. We talked about tuberculosis, malaria, worms, and other things, but we couldn't positively diagnose anything, or treat anything. We didn't even have those types of medications with us.

I got a sick feeling in my stomach when I had to tell the father that we were sorry we couldn't do anything to help his daughter. I felt like I just wanted to take her home with me, so we could find out what her problem was, and get her cured. As I thought about it for a moment, I realized my idea was impossible. I just felt helpless. I will never forget this girl. Her image is burned into my mind.

This experience probably helped lead me to take MDs on all of the trips we possibly could, and certainly 100% of the last 20 trips I have led. I asked myself, where is Cindy when we need her, but I knew she was currently in Irian Jaya.

After returning, we set up our clinic with three dental chairs. Just as we started to work, we heard the distant purr of a plane. That couldn't be our plane. It wasn't due until tomorrow. But it circled and landed. We continued working, and shortly George came into our clinic. He announced, "We have thirty minutes to get out of here. There is a big storm front moving in which could ground us for several days."

Tim and I had our international flights back to the U.S. scheduled in three days. We didn't want to get caught in bad weather and miss our flight back home. We had a long line of people waiting. Bob encouraged us to go. He said, "I can finish up the patients." It was at that moment I realized he didn't have any dental supplies or equipment. I brought all my supplies and equipment from my personal dental office back home.

I made a quick decision. Bob would need anesthetic, needles, syringes, gauze, and several forceps, to continue to extract teeth, not only to finish up the current patients, but to continue to meet the people's needs after we left. I decided to leave him four forceps as well as the needed supplies. I decided I would just buy new forceps when I returned home.

We hurriedly packed up, and literally ran down to the runway. As we were packing the plane, the villagers gathered around us. Tim then announced to Bob, the Cain family, and the village chief, "Never fear, I shall return." The first thing I thought of was General Douglas Macarthur's famous World War II quotation. Tim's statement surprised me a little, but at the same time gave me a sense of peace that maybe Tim wasn't that unhappy about my working him so hard, and maybe he really did feel appreciated. He certainly received more surgical experience during these last two weeks than he will receive in his last two years of dental school.

We could see dark clouds moving in from the east, with a lot of lightning and thunder. We hurriedly got in the plane, taxied to the end of the runway, and George gave it full throttle for takeoff. I will always remember the hundred of villagers, standing strung out along the side of the grassy runway, waving enthusiastically as we left.

We immediately turned west, and headed away from the storm, and easily beat it back to Lomalinda. We flew to Bogotá, Miami, and Detroit and returned home safely.

In Summary: This has been another mission of great excitement and adventure, but more importantly, I felt greatly needed and appreciated. We not only relieved many helpless people from their pain and infection, but helped our missionaries develop better relationships with their people, which would enable them to better share the Gospel. I taught Tim many things, and gave him some valuable experiences, not only of dental skills, but in trusting God in times of need. We worked well together, to the point of exhaustion, in trying to fulfill Jesus' great commission.

I also had my first opportunity to teach a non-dentist how to extract teeth, so that when we left there would be someone to help as needs arose. This has become a goal, and a reality of several of my future mission trips, to teach people, and leave somebody behind to help. Not only had we helped many people, but I felt I was blessed the most, with a great sense of peace and satisfaction that I had worthily served my Lord using the skills with which He has blessed me.

# And Now the Rest of the Story

Neither Tim nor I have had the opportunity to return to the Guahibo villages. After Tim graduated I lost contact with him. Twenty two years later I met Tim at a dental convention. He is married, has a family, and a nice dental practice in the central area of Michigan. He said he thinks of me every day, because he has a picture on his desk of me with the village group of Guahibo Indians, taken on the day we had such a hard time saying goodbye. Tim indicated his goal is to return to short-term dental missions someday.

One of the hidden benefits of this and most of my mission trips is I lose five to ten pounds of weight. I lost ten pounds on this trip.

There were several experiences I had on this mission that significantly influenced many of my future missions.

My faith was tested on this mission and greatly strengthened, and it was needed for some of my future missions.

Having had such a positive experience in teaching Bob, it has encouraged me to do a lot more mission teaching, as you will read about in later chapters.

What a shock I experienced when I got home. It had been a long time since I had bought any new forceps. The four forceps I left Bob cost me between $100 and $150 each to replace. Yes, I was shocked, but didn't really feel bad, because I knew it would help eliminate a lot of pain and infection for many people who otherwise would have no one to help them.

The beautiful young sick girl that we couldn't help caused me to take physicians on many of my future mission trips.

This was my first introduction to the value of a Polaroid camera on a mission trip. I bought one, and have taken it and used it several hundred times on future mission trips.

# CHAPTER 7

# COLOMBIA 4

B efore I came home from our third Colombian mission, I was given a solid invitation to return the following summer. I immediately started planning. I knew Mark, Todd, or Tim was not available to go. One day I had a patient at the office that was a pastor. I shared some of my Colombian experiences with him, and he said, "I have a young dentist in my church that wants to go on a short-term dental mission. Would you like to talk to him?" "Sure," I said.

That evening the dentist, Jim McHenry, called me and expressed his interest in going on a short-term dental mission. We talked for a long time. I determined he was a solid Christian, recently married, and a recent graduate from dental school.

I shared with him some of the experiences we had on our last three trips, and he said, "That's exactly what I am looking for. Is there any chance I could go with you next summer?" I agreed, and we started planning.

We went the same time of year, in late June 1988. We traveled the same route, Detroit, Miami, Bogotá. We stayed with Jim Cartwright overnight in Bogotá, and then we flew on to Lomalinda on Wycliffe's DC-3. Jim and I stayed at the guest house with Char and Gary being our hosts again. The Wycliffe administration had our schedule completely planned for us, before we arrived. We spent two days in the dental clinic at Lomalinda, working on the dental needs of the 150 to 200 people that were currently living there.

This time they had planned for us to visit four jungle villages, in four different tribal areas. Stan Showers was our missionary host, who was going to be traveling with us. Stan and his wife, Junia, had been with Wycliffe for over 20 years, since the founding of Lomalinda.

Stan was somewhat a self-made dentist with no formal training, but he had thoroughly read the book, "Where There Is No Dentist." He was a very intelligent man and was often asked to help with dental problems by his indigenous people in the jungle, which frequently required extractions. His reputation had spread, and since he was the only one at Lomalinda that knew anything about dentistry, when the people got a dental problem, they would ask him for help. He actually was doing simple fillings. He was a great man to work with us.

When we were scheduled to fly out into the jungle, the weather turned bad, and we were grounded for two days. During that time Stan asked if I would train a sharp young man from his tribe, named Danielle, how to be a dentist. He was currently at Lomalinda. Well! I was a professor at the University of Michigan, and spent all school year teaching young people how to become a dentist, but this wasn't exactly what I had planned. I knew I was here to help the missionaries, and if this were the best way I could help, then okay, I would do it. I was told that there were no dental practice laws in Colombia.

I got started early the next morning, with Stan translating every word. Stan was somewhat familiar with dental terminology and that was helpful. We spent some very concentrated time going over the basics of dentistry with Danielle. He listened intently. I then demonstrated to him oral hygiene techniques, examining patients, giving anesthesia injections, cleaning and scaling teeth, drilling out small areas of decay, filling the teeth with silver fillings, and extracting teeth. He was an unusual student and listened to every word without ever getting distracted. He asked good questions. While I was teaching Danielle, Jim continued to work on Lomalinda personnel.

Later the same afternoon, Danielle started doing many of the procedures I had been teaching him, on patients. I watched him carefully and was amazed at how well he did.

Lomalinda currently had a full-time nurse, Joanne Forsberg, at the medical clinic. She invited us over for supper. It happened to be that time of year when there was a short-term population explosion of May fly type of bugs, except they were a little smaller. They were everywhere. Thankfully, they didn't bite. We walked over to Joanne's house and were invited inside. She was busy preparing dinner in a dimly lit kitchen. We started to go into the living room, where there was a bright light. There was a cloud of these bugs around the light and everywhere in the living room. Joanne said, "I keep the bright light at the other end of the house, trying to draw the bugs away from the kitchen and dining room. You might want to stay here in the dining room until dinner's ready. There is no way I can keep them out of the house. Fortunately, they don't hurt anything, and they will be gone in a couple of days."

We had a pleasant enjoyable dinner and conversation, with little problem from the bugs in our darkened dining room, until time for dessert. Then for some reason, the bugs invaded us. They were crawling all over us, the food left on the table, our plates, and in our desserts. Joanne, without any concern, just picked the bugs out of her dessert, and continued eating, so we did the same. There were hundreds of these bugs, so many that it was impractical to shoo them away, or try to kill them. We just joked about them and continued eating our dessert.

We didn't stay around very long after dinner. We learned something important that evening. Life on the mission field can be quite different than what we are used to, but it isn't always bad, unless you voluntarily decide to make it bad. This was a good time to apply the principles of Norman Vincent Peale's, "Power of Positive Thinking." Nothing hurt us at all, it was just different.

The next day, as our weather delay continued, I worked hard teaching Danielle. He really did amazingly well. Near the end of the day we had a young indigenous Indian teenager come into the clinic. I examined her, and found her to be a good test candidate. So I said to Danielle, "This patient is going to be your final examination. You need to find a small decayed area in her teeth, remove the decay, and put in a silver filling. You also need to identify an abscessed tooth, anesthetize it, and extract it, without any help from me."

He did an excellent job with both the filling and extraction, as I watched him very closely. When he finished, I told him, "You did an excellent job. Congratulations, you are now a dentist." Stan said to me, "I think it would be good if we could give him some type of diploma. Diplomas are really an important thing to these people, and I could print one on my computer." I said, "Great."

That evening I thought to myself, at the University of Michigan Dental School we start teaching students after they have had four years of college, and then we teach them for four more concentrated years, before they become a dentist. With Danielle, who had never gone to school one day in his life, and couldn't read or write, I spent two days training him, and now he is a dentist. Stan told me, "My people may be uneducated and illiterate, but they're not stupid by any means." Danielle proved that to me, but I still had some mixed feelings.

The next morning we were told that we could fly, so we packed our gear and took everything to the hangar. Stan had made arrangements for Danielle to meet us there. Stan had created an amazingly nice diploma for Danielle, stating that he had passed his dental training, and was now a dentist. Stan had me sign it as a professor from the University of Michigan. I hoped my dean never heard about this, but I guess I really wasn't worried. Stan had arranged for a little ceremony with picture taking and everything. Needless to say, Danielle was delighted.

We loaded our small single engine Helio Courier, had our time of prayer, and departed. Our first stop was going to be Stan's village, which was one of the furthest from Lomalinda. It was in the southeast corner of Colombia near the Brazilian and Peruvian borders. The plane couldn't make it there and back on one tank of fuel, so we headed straight east to the town of Mitu, which is home to several hundred people. Mitu is near the Brazilian border and is several hundred miles from the nearest road.

The Colombian government helps to support Mitu, and supplies it with two DC-3 planes that fly needed supplies into the town most every day. The government also had a military outpost in this town, trying to prevent Brazil from accessing the land and claiming it to be theirs. There was sort of a minor border dispute that was ongoing. There were no border markers in the jungle.

We arrived at Mitu in the middle of the afternoon. Our pilot, George DeVoucalla, was able to fill up with aviation fuel. George was an interesting person. He had been flying with Wycliffe for over 20 years. When he started flying over the jungle, he found there were no aerial maps of the area at all. He then decided to make his own, and in 1988 his maps were still the only ones available of this vast jungle area. His maps have been adopted as the official government maps of the area.

There were a few pickup trucks in Mitu. Stan told us that the first pickup was the only one in town for over a year. There were city streets, but no roads left town. When the second pickup arrived, it was only in town four hours before it crashed into the first one, leaving the town without any vehicles for a while.

We walked several blocks to a house where Stan knew the owner. We knocked and a man came to the door and invited us to come in. Stan had been there many times. This man and his family offered the only overnight lodging in town. They showed Jim and me to a small bedroom where we took our sleeping bags. We shared a small bathroom with Stan and George. It had cold running water, and even a showerhead with a pull rope. The interesting thing was that the shower was directly over the toilet stool. In order to take a shower, I guess you had to sit on the pot. We weren't in need of a shower, yet.

We ate supper with the man, his wife and children, around their personal family dining room table. There was a telephone sitting on a small end table near me. I noticed it had no wires coming from it. I laughed to myself, and thought, I'm sure this works, 500 miles in the jungle. I knew Lomalinda had no phones, and they were on the edge of civilization. I thought it was just decoration, and I made some sort of comment about the phone, that evidently didn't please the owner. Remember this was in the year 1988.

The man of the house got up, came over and picked up the phone, and sat it down by me. He picked up the receiver and handed it to me and said, "You can call anywhere in the world you want." He told me four numbers that were necessary to dial before the regular number. I listened and heard a dial tone. I'll have to admit, I was shocked. I was tempted to call my wife back home, but we had agreed, no news was good news. I asked him with great curiosity, "How does this work?" He answered, "This is a satellite phone. The signals are bounced off a satellite." I guess it's good for me to be dead wrong about something occasionally, because it helps keep me humble.

The next morning after breakfast, we walked to the airport. On the way we passed a small store that had some beautiful delicious apples out front on display. It surprised me and I found myself picking the apple up and looking at it. I was even more surprised to read the little sticker on it. It said Washington State Apple.

We packed our plane and took off for Stan's village. We arrived at noon with no problems. We had to walk a mile or so to get to Stan's house. His house was made of the traditional poles and thatching, but it was up off the ground on poles about 8 feet high. We had to climb a ladder to get in. It had a large porch with a bouncing bamboo floor, a big table and benches, and a roof over it. We set up our dental clinic on the porch, using the table for our instruments and supplies.

We had a busy and productive afternoon. That evening I asked Stan, "How did you ever find these Yucuna Indians so far out in the jungle?" He told us this story: "The main village is actually located on the banks of a fairly large river. We heard about the Yucunas from some natives who traveled the river. They indicated the Yucunas were totally isolated and untouched by western society. Twenty years ago Junia and I felt we needed to contact these people to see if they wanted our help. It took us one month traveling mainly by river to finally find these Yucuna Indians."

"Junia was actually more accustomed to jungle life and jungle travel than I. Her mother and father were traveling interim pastors in the jungles of Brazil as she was growing up. Brazilians speak Portuguese. Junia learned English on the back of a donkey. Her parents, although American missionaries, they normally spoke Portuguese at home, but when they traveled from village to village on their donkeys, they purposely spoke English to teach Junia."

"When we first arrived, the Yucunas were very receptive to our coming to live with them, and to help them. As proof of their good faith, they helped us build a house. They also helped me cut down a small section of jungle, so it could be used as a runway for our Helio Couriers, and it was purposely made short so other planes couldn't land. Then Junia and I spent another month getting back to Lomalinda."

"The next time we went to the Yucuna's village we flew on one of Wycliffe's Helio Couriers. We went first to Mitu, stayed overnight, refueled, and then the next morning we left for our village. As I mentioned earlier, there were no aviation maps of the jungle area at this time, so our pilot followed the river where he though the village and runway was located. The runway didn't show up, and didn't show up, and suddenly the pilot realized that he had just used up over half of his fuel, and he didn't have enough to get back to Mitu, or anywhere else. We continued on, hoping the runway would pop up at any moment. When our fuel got very low, the pilot0 spotted a sand bar in the middle of the river. He circled and it looked rather solid, so he put the plane down on the sand bar without any problem."

"We tried to radio Lomalinda, but we were too far away and couldn't get contact. Occasionally a commercial airplane would fly over high above us, and we would try to radio an SOS to them, but to no avail. Then on the third day we finally got a response from a commercial plane flying overhead. Our pilot asked the commercial pilot to try to radio Lomalinda, and tell them about our situation, and give them our location. The commercial pilot radioed back that he was successful in contacting Lomalinda, and gave them the message. So we waited."

"Around noon on the fourth day, we heard music to our ears, a low-flying single engine plane. It was one of Wycliffe's Helio Courier's, which circled and landed safely. The pilot didn't have any extra passengers, only a lot of extra fuel. We refueled our planes, and returned to Lomalinda without any problem"

"George flew over the same area one month later, while mapping the jungle, and reported there was no sandbar in the river. It was gone. I am convinced that the sandbars present at our time of need was purely and simply an act of God. He must not have been finished with us yet."

The next morning Stan showed us one of his inventions. He had a bicycle frame. He took the chain sprocket off the pedal area, and replaced it with a V-belt sprocket. He ran a V-belt from the bike sprocket to a small air compressor. If you pumped the bike fast enough it would power the air compressor, and build up enough air pressure to run a high-speed air turbine dental drill. So if a patient needed a filling, he was required to bring someone to pump the bike. It actually worked very well. Stan had been putting in fillings when they were here, but they had almost finished their translation, and didn't live there much anymore. That's why he was glad that Danielle had learned to put in fillings and do extractions, so that he could take over Stan's job using his equipment that he left at his house.

The next morning, a couple of men came from a neighboring village. Stan had been teaching them how to extract teeth. He asked if I would continue to teach them more about extracting teeth. I spent much of the day working with these two men, helping them give anesthesia and extracting teeth. We actually started catching up on the number of waiting patients.

I saw my first albino person that evening, when Stan took us for a walk around the village. He was very light-skinned, had white hair and pink eyes. Stan said, "He is at a big disadvantage in this hot sunny jungle. He needs to keep himself completely covered when he is in the sun or he will burn severely."

Stan told us that when he first came to the main village on the river, there was a Catholic Priest who had a small mission church. He also had the only store in the village, and he sold a few of the basic essentials, such as soap and fishhooks. With his store, he basically controlled the town. If you didn't obey him you couldn't get any supplies.

Stan and Junia's purpose was to analyze the Yucuna language, translate it from a verbal language into a written language, teach them how to read and write, and translate the Bible, so they could read it themselves. They had fairly well completed this project during the 20 years before we arrived.

Some of the Yucunas became evangelical Christians. The priest became very jealous and angry. He told several of the new Christians that if they wanted to become evangelical Christians that they would need to leave, because they were no longer welcome in his village. This is one of the reasons why Stan built his current house a mile out of town.

Fortunately a different Catholic priest came to the village, and Stan was able to reason with him, and they got along fine.

Our pilot, George, stayed with us. The next morning we flew to another village of different indigenous Indians. When we landed, the plane suddenly turned to the left and stopped very quickly. We got out to see what had happened, and found that the left front wheel was completely buried in mud. They had had a lot of rain recently, and the runway had become soft. The right front wheel was on fairly solid ground. We unloaded everything, and dug some of the mud away from behind the wheel with a machete. George directed us to push the tail of the plane sideways. This turned the plane sideways, and pulled the left wheel out of the mud and onto solid ground.

After we turned the plane around straight, George left to go back to Stan's village to get the rest of our supplies. It was less than an hour away. The runway at Stan's village was so short that George couldn't take off with all of us and all of our gear at the same time.

We walked into the village along with the many children and well-wishers that had come to the plane to greet us. When we arrived in the village we went first to visit the chief. Stan had a friendly smiling conversation with him, but we didn't understand one word. The chief led us to an empty small thatched hut that was to be our living quarters. Most villages in the jungle have a guest house for visitors. The missionary couple that was translating for this group of indigenous Indians was not in the village at present. They had asked Stan to stop for a day or two and help the people with their dental problems, which they had been complaining about frequently.

We waited, and waited, and waited some more for the plane to return with our supplies. Finally Stan said, "George must have a problem. It is now too late for him to return tonight. Let's see what we have for supper." Stan had been caught like this before, so he was prepared. He had some dried hamburger, rice and onions in his personal overnight bag. We had about half of our dental instruments.

Stan, Jim, and I went over to visit the chief. We told him our plane didn't come back with our supplies, and asked if he could help us. We needed a pot in which to cook our supper and three hammocks and blankets for the night. The chief had his wife give us a pot and utensils, but said he would have to work on the hammocks and blankets. We observed that the chief had a 4 - foot alligator slowly roasting over his fire pit. I was glad we weren't invited to the chief's hut for supper.

We started a fire, boiled our water vigorously, and added our dried hamburger, rice and onions. Believe it or not, it was really good, and actually one of the best meals we had anywhere in the jungle. After supper the chief and some men came with our hammocks and blankets. It seemed that he had to go around to his villagers and borrow the hammocks and blankets from different families. We thanked him, and tied them up, and climbed in.

All the natives in the Colombian jungle normally slept in hammocks. Some were large enough to hold 3 or 4 people. This was my first and only time in my life that I attempted to sleep overnight in a hammock. I usually sleep on my stomach, and hammocks aren't designed for stomach sleepers. Needless to say, I didn't sleep very well.

The next morning we set up our dental clinic with the equipment we had, outside in a clearing. It had rained during the night. When we set up our clinic, it was cloudy and misty. The temperature was probably about 70 to72°F, with a moderate wind. It really felt good to us. I had several people sit down on the tree stump that I was using for my dental chair, and they were physically shaking. One child sat in her mother's lap, with her mother's arms around her because she was shaking so badly that I didn't think I would be able to work on her. I said to Stan, "Boy, these people are really frightened of the dentist." He laughed and said, "I don't think so. They are just shivering because they are so cold."

This was the first of July, and it was the time of the year that they traditionally got cool Antarctic winds. It felt good to us, but this was as cold as it got there. They were accustomed to 90 to 100°F temperatures every day, and suddenly when they got wet, and were out in the open with a 70°F wind, they were cold and shivering. They had no warm clothes.

Ironically, this village was almost exactly on the equator, and in July the people were cold. Back in Michigan near the 45th parallel, we were later told, they had 10 days in a row around the first of July, where the temperature was over 100°F. It broke records in Michigan, and they were cold at the equator. It was hard for me to comprehend that phenomena.

Suddenly the children started screaming and running all in the same direction. I couldn't figure out what was going on, for about one minute, and then I, along with Stan and Jim, started hearing the purr of the plane. There was no question that those kids' hearing was far superior to ours.

We kept on working, and soon George and his many young helpers brought the remainder of our gear to our cool clinic. We asked George what the problem was, and he said, "I had bad weather set in on me, so I had to wait until this morning."

We worked two days there, and got the majority of the aching teeth extracted. We would usually numb two or three patients at a time, then go back and extract teeth on each patient. This way we didn't have any waiting time for our patients to get numb. This method was quite efficient.

On our third morning we bid everyone farewell, and started for our next village, which was about 30 minutes away by air. When we landed, there was no village, and not one person in sight. We unloaded the luggage that we brought, and George took off to go back and get the rest of our supplies. I assumed the runway was too short again to take off with a full load.

There was a little open thatched shelter at the edge of the runway, so Stan said, "Let's put our gear by the shelter, and we'll wait." This was Bev and Clay Strom's jungle base, where they had been translating for the Retuara Indian tribe. They were not in the village at this time, but they knew we were in the area, and that their people had many dental problems. They had asked Stan if we could stop for a couple of days, and help their people.

Stan had never been to Bev and Clay's jungle home, and he didn't speak the Retuara language. Stan had phlebitis in his legs, which sometimes became painful. His legs were bothering him, so he laid down in the shelter, put his legs up, and fell asleep.

Jim and I were bored, and the uniqueness of the tropical jungle fascinated us. We decided to walk into the jungle and look around. We agreed before we entered, that we would stay in sight of each other, and not go any further than we could still see the runway. The jungle was mature, with a lot of tall trees, and not much undergrowth. We walked slowly about ten feet apart, watching and listening to the sounds of the jungle, mainly the birds.

Then I spotted a small native woman, about 50 to 75 feet away, with one of our suitcases containing our dental equipment on her head, and she was trucking right past us, going deeper into the jungle. I didn't know what to say, and she wouldn't understand me anyway. I turned to tell Jim, and I noticed another woman about 50 yards away on the other side with another one of our suitcases on her head, and she was moving rapidly into the jungle also. We had already gone into the jungle as far as we dared, and could just barely see the light of the runway. We quickly decided not to run after our suitcases, because these women were a fair distance away and moving fast and going deeper into the jungle.

Jim and I walked rapidly back to the shelter where we had left Stan. He was still there, thank goodness, and still sleeping, but all of our suitcases were gone. We woke him up and told him, "Our suitcases are all gone. We saw some women carrying them deep into the jungle." Stan nonchalantly shrugged his shoulders, and said, "There's not much I can do about it. We'll just have to wait." So we waited, but stuck together this time.

After an hour or so, two men came out of the jungle near the end of the runway. They walked up to us. Stan greeted them, and they motioned for us to follow them. We walked to the end of the runway, and then off onto a small jungle trail. We went down a hill until we came to a river about 30 to 40 feet wide. They had a small hollowed out log on the bank, about one foot wide and ten feet long. One man got in the back and motioned for one of us to get in. One by one, he paddled us across the river.

On the other side there was a trail going up and away from the river, and then through the dense jungle. We walked for about 40 minutes. It was an interesting walk but we really didn't know where we were going. We came to a clearing. There was a very large round thatched hut. It looked much like the Big House I had seen at Joel Stoltie's village. It turned out that was exactly what it was, a Big House where the entire village lived.

At one end of the clearing there was a rectangular thatched building. The two men led us straight to this building. The building was up on stilts four feet high. It had a nice big porch. We climbed up on the porch, and surprise, our suitcases were there.

Stan fairly quickly found a lady named Maria that spoke his tribe's Yucuna language, as well as the local Retuara language. Maria acted as our interpreter.

The strict custom of the jungle was that a young man never marries a girl from his own language or people group. He needed to travel to a different people group, seeking a girl with a completely different language, marry her, and bring her home to live with his people. This is what happened to Maria. She was originally from Stan's Yucuna tribe and she married a man from the Retuara tribe and he brought her home with him.

We found out that the building where we were staying was Bev and Clay's home. Maria showed us a hand-pumped well a few yards away, that Clay had hand-drilled for the people, so they didn't have to walk over a mile down to the river. It was much cleaner and healthier water. Maria also told us the delay we had at the runway was caused by the two men who needed to carry the log boat from the Big House back to the river so we could cross. Evidently there was no boat there at the time we arrived. Our luggage was carried by the women who arrived at the runway before the men. The women took our luggage upstream where they could wade across the river with our suitcases on their heads, and they beat us back to the house.

Near dusk, George buzzed over the top of the Big House, and several men took off on the path to the runway. Stan got busy and cooked us some more hamburger, rice and onions. George joined us shortly for supper.

As we ate I noticed that it was so dark outside that you couldn't see anything. We turned our lantern off, and you couldn't see your hand in front of your nose. It never gets this dark at home because there's always reflected light from somewhere. But here there was no reflected light from anywhere, and at the moment, no moon.

Just then we had one of the native men stop by and greet us. He was headed down the path toward the runway. He said he had to go to the neighboring village. I knew it was over 40 minutes away. He had to cross the river, and it was totally pitch black. He didn't seem to be concerned about the darkness. Stan found a very short candle and lit it and gave it to him to take with him. He seemed happy as he left us.

The inside of Clay and Bev's house was hot and stuffy, so we elected to put up my cot and their hammocks on the porch, even though it didn't have any screens. The interesting thing was, we didn't see any mosquitoes, and we were right in the middle of the jungle. I suspect the main reason was that we were far enough away from the river and any water source that were necessary for the breeding of mosquitoes. Stan indicated this was actually the reason why the Retuaras located their village over a mile away from the river.

In Michigan, I get more mosquito bites walking out to my mail box, than I did sleeping in the open all night, in the middle of the jungle. There are a lot of things about the jungle that I just don't understand.

Our morning started early, about 3:30 A.M. to be exact. The roosters started crowing right under the house just about three feet under our bamboo porch floor. I didn't get up then, but I surely didn't get any more sleep.

We set up our clinic between Bev and Clay's house and the Big House. It was cloudy and not too hot. Stan had asked Maria to translate the Retuara language into her native Yucuna language, which Stan understood, and then Stan translated Yucuna into English. This was a double translation, which slowed us down a little bit, but we got a lot of extractions done anyway.

I couldn't help observing an unusual situation. The women's teeth were extremely decayed, with many abscesses. I removed 21 abscessed teeth from one lady in one sitting. The men had no decay. Their teeth had an ugly greenish gray slime that completely covered their teeth. It looked terrible, but they had no cavities. I thought for a moment, I had made a great jungle discovery, but then on second thought, the appearance would not be acceptable in the U.S.

We had the opportunity to visit inside the Big House several times. It was very similar to the Big House I described in Joel's tribe last year. The one thing different here was the men pounded dried cocaine leaves into a powder. They used a long round-headed stick, which they pounded into the end of a one foot high log in which the end was hollowed out. After they pounded the leaves into powder, they added some ashes from a certain type of wood. They pounded it together until the ashes mixed completely with the leaves. This made a greenish gray powder which the men chewed. Only men were allowed to chew this mixture. Obviously this explained why their teeth had the greenish gray slimy appearance, but it didn't tell me why they had no decay. The only reason I could conclude was that cavities are caused by bacteria, and ashes are a strong bacteria killer. A mixture of ashes and cocaine would not go over very big in the U.S. for decay prevention.

Why did these men go to all this trouble to do this? There were two reasons. This mixture was a strong stimulant, much like caffeine which we have in our coffee. They can't grow coffee in the jungle. It made them feel alert, sharp, and kept them from getting sleepy for long periods. Secondly, it suppressed their appetite, so they didn't have to carry a lot of food when they traveled. It was light to carry, and they could travel long distances without getting hungry or sleepy. If they tried to sleep in the open jungle they would be easy prey for wild animals. I thought this appetite suppressant quality would be the perfect solution for the massive American weight-loss industry. But again on second thought, because it was made from cocaine leaves, it might not go over too well. Cocaine leaves by themselves, are not hallucinogenic or addicting.

On the second day we finished the patients early in the afternoon. Maria asked if she could go home, and invited us to come with her. She didn't live in this Big House. She just happened to be visiting when we came. She lived in another Big House with her husband and children which was an hour away.

Jim and I were up for a jungle walk, so we packed our dental instruments into our suitcases and put them in the house. Stan joined us and we took some people from the local Big House, so that when Maria stayed at her home, we would have someone to lead us back.

Early in our walk we came to a clearing in the jungle, where the jungle had been cut down and burned. This was their farm. They planted their food crops in the ashes of the big trees. They said the ashes acted as a fertilizer that was necessary to raise their food, because the soil was so sandy and poor. They also showed us where they raised their cocaine. They had a couple of acres of cocaine bushes, about 3 feet high, with green leaves about the size of a quarter.

Stan told us that one of the biggest advantages of Wycliffe's Helio Courier airplanes is that they could land on short runways. The Cessna and Piper airplanes that the cocaine cartel used required a much longer runway. These indigenous Indians didn't have to worry about the cocaine cartel coming and getting their cocaine leaves, because they couldn't land on their short runway.

After two hours of walking, including our stops, and our slow walking speed, we finally came to Maria's Big House. We went inside and met her husband, children, and many others. There was no furniture in the Big House except stools. I was fascinated by some of the stools they sat on. They were short, only 8 to 10 inches high, but they weren't flat. They were contoured to the shape of your bottom, when it is 8 to 10 inches off the floor. The stools were carved out of one piece of wood. I sat on one and was surprised that they were so comfortable. After I admired the stools, Maria asked me if I wanted to buy one for a few dollars. I felt bad about buying their furniture, because that was the only furniture they had. They were very excited to sell it to me, and indicated it was no problem, because they could make another one tomorrow. I bought it and have it in my home today. Maria's Big House was very interesting; with over a hundred people living under one roof.

We walked home more rapidly and made it back just before dark. The next morning we packed and walked to the runway. George had stayed with us again. This time we were able to get all of our gear in the plane in one load, and we had no problem taking off.

Our next stop was Joel Stoltie's jungle mansion. We stopped there for one day, even though Joel and his wife were not there. It was on our way home. Joel had a reserve of aviation fuel so we could refuel and make it back to Lomalinda without going out of our way to Mitu. It was fine with Jim and me, because we enjoyed helping people. Wycliffe furnished the plane and the pilot without any cost to us, but we paid for the fuel.

Stan, George, Jim, and I were having breakfast the next morning at Joel's house, when George pulled a small container out of his pocket, the size of a 35mm film container. He dumped out several small irregular white objects. He took two and popped them into his mouth, and chewed them. I asked him what they were. He told me they were garlic cloves. He then offered some to Jim and me. We were a little hesitant, so he told us about his garlic. He said, "I have been flying these jungles for over 20 years, and I've always taken my garlic with me. Two or three of these garlic cloves each day will kill any parasites or bugs that enter your gastrointestinal tract." He swore it worked every time. So Jim and I took a couple of the garlic cloves, and chewed and swallowed them. We were surprised.

They weren't that bad tasting at all. This was the one and only time in my life that I have eaten pure garlic cloves. We didn't get sick, but we were also taking a variety of short-term prophylactic medications.

George also told us that when he and several other Wycliffe pilots started flying in the Colombian jungle over 20 years ago, they decided it was a fairly difficult and stressful job. They all agreed that they should plan to retire at age 45. When the group of pilots approached the age of 45, they started rethinking the age limit. They concluded that age 45 is still young. They still felt great and they decided they could probably fly until age 50. So they made new rules, and changed the age limit to 50. When they got near 50, they changed it to 55. When nearing 55, they changed it to 60. George said, "I am now 59, so this may be my last year, because even the commercial pilots have to retire at age 60, even though I still feel great." It's easy for me to identify with the pilots' progressive thinking about age, because I have been down the same aging road also, and I still feel great at 75.

The day of extractions at Joel's house went uneventfully. The next morning we headed back to Lomalinda. We purposely arrived back there a day early, just in case we were delayed by bad flying weather. We didn't want to miss our international flights home.

We worked in the dental clinic at Lomalinda the following morning, and in the afternoon Stan took us three miles into the neighboring town. It was on the river bank where all roads ended. From that point there were over a thousand miles of jungle before the next road.

We observed several interesting things in town. They had both cats and dogs skinned, cleaned, and hanging in the open meat market, to be sold. We visited the pharmacy where you could buy any medication you wanted without a prescription.

I remember Jim Cartwright telling us the story of when he first came to Colombia. He got sick and went to the doctor. The doctor gave him a prescription, and when he went to pick it up, the pharmacist gave him a vial of liquid, along with a syringe and needle. Jim asked, "What am I supposed to do with this?" The pharmacist said, "Just fill up the syringe and give yourself an injection. That's the way we do it in Colombia." Jim found a nurse translator who gave him the injection.

While visiting the pharmacy, Stan ran into the one and only dentist in town. Stan introduced Jim and me to him. He was a tall well-built young man, age 25 or so, good looking, well dressed, and had a big friendly smile. He asked us, "Would you like to see my office?" We naturally said, "Yes."

We walked a few blocks, and entered a door where there was a small waiting room big enough for two people. The waiting room consisted of two chairs and bare concrete walls with no windows or decorations. He took us into his operatory, the room where he did his dental work. It was about 8 by 10 feet in size. He had a dental chair that I recognized as the type that had been in our old dental school in the 1930s. He had a dental light and air compressor in the corner. He said that the light and the air compressor only worked from 4 to 6 P.M., when the village generator was turned on, and electricity was available. He had a drill which he pumped with his foot, when he didn't have electricity. He had a small sink, with no faucet, in the corner of the room where the drain emptied into a bucket under the sink. He had a small wooden bench about 18 inches square, where he was in the process of making someone a denture. He had one small cabinet with a few instruments and forceps in it. He had a bowl with instruments in it, covered with a liquid. I asked him, "What is the liquid?" He said, "Benzalkonium Chloride," a liquid which we used in U.S. dentistry 50 years ago, until it was proved to be very poor in sterilizing instruments.

I asked him, "Where did you go to dental school?" He said, "My dad was a dentist." I asked, "Did your dad train you?" He answered, "When you're young, you're not really interested in what your dad is doing. My dad was unexpectedly murdered a few years ago, so I just decided to take over his office." Then he said something I will never forget. He put his arms around me, squeezed me, and said, with a great big smile on his face, "It's not really necessary to get training to be a dentist. It is not that hard. Anybody can be a dentist." He was completely serious about it, too.

In the evening, Stan asked if we could remove a couple of teeth from one of the translator's pet monkey. It seemed the monkey's canine teeth were sharp, and they often scratched his owner when they were playing. Vick Kondo, being a former veterinarian, put the monkey to sleep, and filed his teeth down several months earlier. The only problem was, he filed the teeth into the nerves and the teeth abscessed. The monkey wasn't eating well, and had big red abscesses under both eyes, which had pus coming out and it wouldn't heal.

Vick put the monkey to sleep and they carried him to the dental clinic. Jim and I put him in the dental chair. I extracted one of the canines, and Jim extracted the other one. The roots were much bigger around than those in human teeth, and they were three times longer. It took me about 15 minutes to remove it, and it took all the strength I had. I have never extracted a harder tooth in my life. I guess that is what you call, an evening of "monkey business."

Our return trip home was uneventful. On the way home, Jim told me he had been reading a book which was a true story, about a pilot named Smokey, who had flown for Wycliffe in the Colombian jungles several years ago. The story primarily dealt with Smokey's crash into the top of the trees in the jungle. It didn't kill him, or any of his passengers, but injured them seriously. Much of the book described the difficulties of their rescue. The only problem was, Jim forgot and left the book on his pregnant wife's bed stand before coming. He just hoped she didn't pick it up and read it, and get worried about him. Fortunately, she didn't.

In summary: This was a unique, interesting and valuable experience, which again left me with a wonderful feeling of peace and fulfillment.

# And Now the Rest of the Story

This was Jim's first mission trip. Like me, he felt great satisfaction, and caught the mission bug. He has a missionary friend from their church working in the remote areas in Guatemala. Jim has gone and eventually took his wife and four children down to Guatemala for several years, doing missionary dentistry. Praise the Lord.

Three months after I got home, I received a letter from Stan. He indicated Danielle was getting along great. He was working out of his house, and he had started his own Dental School, and was teaching 5 native students how to become dentists. Wow! This was hard to believe. What could happen next?

I wrote Stan back and said, "I'm supposed to be the Dental Professor. I have all the supplies, equipment, and teaching aids. If they really want to be taught dentistry, maybe we should set up a school and I will come down and teach them." I received a return letter from Stan, and he said, "That was exactly my thoughts. Let's plan tentatively to teach some of our indigenous Indians dentistry here at Lomalinda next April."

# CHAPTER 8

# COLOMBIA 5
# DENTAL SCHOOL

After Danielle started his dental school, Stan and I agreed that we needed to start our own dental school to train more indigenous Indians. Stan received approval from Wycliffe's administrators. He also discussed the idea with various translators, and their responses were very positive.

This is what they planned. Each translator would ask their own indigenous Indian chief if he would like Wycliffe to train one of his people to become a dentist. If so, the Indians were to select an individual, and Wycliffe would come and pick him up in one of their planes, and bring him to Lomalinda for a two-week course next spring. The response was so positive that Stan had to limit the number of students to 25. When I heard about the plans, I was excited too.

I realized there would be no purpose in training them, if they didn't have any instruments or equipment with which to work when the training was completed. So I started a nationwide search for instruments and supplies. I got great support from many sources. The American Dental Association sent me hundreds of excellent training slides. I called World Medical Relief, which is a charitable Christian organization in Detroit that collects used medical and dental equipment, supplies, and new medicines. Contributing doctors and pharmaceutical companies can be given a tax deductible write-off for their donations. A lot of dental and medical offices that buy new equipment, or move, or retire, often donate their old equipment to them. World Medical Relief in turn donates and ships the supplies, equipment, and medications to mission hospitals and clinics in third world countries all over the world.

I talked to the director of World Medical Relief by phone. She invited me to come and see if they had any dental supplies or equipment that I could use. Their huge warehouse was a large former moving company warehouse, right in the middle of Detroit's downtown ghetto. I was more frightened going there, than I was going to Colombia. When I arrived, there were two armed guards with big dogs that opened the gate. They let me into a parking area that was surrounded by a tall barbed wire fence. The guards had been told that I was coming, and they knew what type of car I would be driving. I met with the director. She called into her office the volunteer dentist that was in charge of the dental section, and told him I could have anything I wanted. She knew I had to carry everything in my suitcases, so I couldn't take a lot.

The thing I needed most was extraction forceps. I had recently discovered that forceps cost $100 to $150 each when purchased new. They were made of stainless steel, would never rust, and were almost indestructible with a lifetime guarantee.

To my pleasant surprise I was shown two bushel baskets filled with forceps. There were several hundred of them. I figured I would need six different forceps for each of the 25 students, so I selected 150 different forceps, which would have been worth $20,000 if they had been new. I also selected a variety of other supplies, equipment, and medication.

Another big and unusual donation came from a supplier at the Michigan Dental Convention. Astra, a leading supplier of dental anesthetic and syringes, was offering $50 off the purchase of any new syringe, if the dentist returned an old syringe. Syringes are essential to giving anesthesia, and can be sterilized and reused since they are all stainless steel. They also cost about $100 each, and each student would need at least three.

I told the Astra representative what I was planning to do, and asked if I could have the used ones, that were being turned in. I knew they would just throw them away. The representative said, "No, absolutely not." I was surprised and didn't understand, so I asked him why. He said, "Their liability insurance would not cover his company selling or dispensing any used equipment." I was disappointed because I thought I had discovered a gold mine.

Then the representative gave me a big smile and said, "See this box full of used syringes behind and underneath the counter?" I looked and said, "Yes." "I'm going to lunch at noon, and if this box is removed by a non-authorized person while I am gone, I would be very happy, because I wouldn't have to haul them back to the factory for disposal." I could tell by his smile, and the twinkle in his eyes, that I had unofficially just received over a hundred anesthetic syringes. The Lord works in mysterious ways sometime. I received needed supplies and equipment in smaller amounts from all over the country. My used toothbrush collection was in high gear also.

Now all I had to do was to convince some dentists to come to Colombia and help me. I phoned and talked with many dentists. Many of them said, "Yes I would love to do that." This was the period of time when the news media was reporting daily about Colombia's Cocaine Cartel, and all the fighting, murders, and various types of violent things taking place in Colombia.

When the wives of the dentists that had already agreed to go with me, found out their husbands were going to Colombia, they just said, "No way!" Every single dentist had to cancel and say, "Sorry." I was discouraged.

One Sunday my daughter, Beth, was home from Ferris State University, where she was a senior in the Dental Hygiene School, president of her class, and doing well. She heard me mention to my wife, Dora May, that every single dentist that had promised to go to Colombia with me had canceled. I told Dora May, "I guess you will have to go and help me teach hygiene." At this point, Beth spoke up rather forcefully, and said, "Dad, Mom can't do that; she doesn't know anything about dentistry." That was true. Then she surprised me by saying, "I'll go and help you."

Stan had asked me to come the first part of April. Beth would be in the last month and a half of her senior year. I said, "That would be great, but I doubt if you could get out of Hygiene School for two weeks at this point." So I basically put it out of my mind.

Beth, our youngest, had just gotten married the previous summer, so Dora May was free to go with me. She had never gone with me on any of my previous four Colombian missions, because she believed it was her duty as a mother to stay home and be with Beth, while she was still a high school teenager, and I agreed. Now our nest was empty.

Jim Cartwright's mother and dad surprised me by asking if they could go to Colombia with me to visit Jim and Deb and their three grandchildren, which they hadn't seen in a long time. They had never traveled outside the U.S., and only felt safe if they could go with me. They were not supposed to help teach, but their request to go, helped to encourage Dora May to go.

A week or 10 days later, I got a phone call from a very excited Beth. She exclaimed, "I can go!" Actually Beth had received permission in a most unusual way. She had discussed her opportunity to go to Colombia to teach hygiene to the native Indians with one of her most approachable instructors. Her instructor thought it would be a great opportunity and encouraged her, but said, "You need to get permission from the Dental Hygiene School Dean." So Beth went to the Dean, and explained the opportunity to her. Her answer was, "Absolutely, no!" Then Beth received a lecture on how stupid the idea was. Beth didn't have a degree or license. It was illegal. There was no way she could miss two weeks of school and so on. She belittled Beth, and made her feel really terrible.

When Beth told her instructor what the Dean had said, and how she had belittled her, the instructor got upset also. Beth gave up and thought it was impossible. Her instructor then went to the President of the University and explained the situation. The president agreed that it was an opportunity of a lifetime. He called Beth's Dean and instructed her to make arrangements for Beth to go. Suddenly Beth received a call from the Dean, who wanted to talk to her. Beth didn't know any of these things had been transpiring, and after her last encounter with the Dean, she was anxious and afraid. When Beth went to see the

Dean, she told her, "The President wanted me to make arrangements for you to go, and I have done that. You are free to go." This was another unusual answer to prayer.

With Beth, Dora May, Jim's parents, and me, that made five of us going. That meant with two suitcases at 70 pounds each and one carry-on which they didn't weigh, I figured we could take 950 pounds of total weight. I figured a maximum of 50 pounds for light tropical clothes and toiletries per person. That left 700 pounds for dental equipment for our 25 students. That was over twice as much weight as I had ever been able to take before.

My son Mark and his wife, Vivian, came over one Saturday for most of the day, and we sorted through all of our donations. We had well over 2000 pounds of donations, so we had to select the most essential ones to take.

The 700 pounds that I calculated for our supplies and equipment turned out to be not enough for the essentials. We were close, but had to pack one extra 70 pound suitcase, and I expected that we would have to pay an overweight fee to the airlines. 1989 was before the Airlines limited luggage to 50 pounds, and before all the security concerns about what we could put in our carry-on. I weighed every suitcase to the exact pound on our bathroom scales.

The five of us left for the airport in early April 1989, with 16 pieces of luggage, including our carry-ons, weighing 1020 pounds. When the airline clerk had weighed eight suitcases at exactly 70 pounds each, he looked at me and said, "You've done this before haven't you?" I said, "Yes", and started talking about the purpose of our mission. When it came to the 11th suitcase, which I figured would probably cost $100 extra, he just tagged it and said, "God bless your mission." He didn't charge us a penny.

Our luggage was checked straight through to Colombia. As we were transferring planes in Miami we observed our luggage being loaded onto our plane, but just before they called us to board, they took off most of the luggage including ours, loaded it onto carts, and took it back into the terminal. Without our luggage we didn't have much purpose for going, so I stood in the doorway of the loading ramp, and refused to get on the plane until they put our luggage back on the plane. After a lot of discussion, they finally convinced me that if I didn't get on the plane they would put a standby passenger in my seat. They reassured me I didn't have to worry about my luggage. It would be put back on the plane. So I reluctantly gave in and went on board and found my seat. I have had luggage that didn't arrive several times in the past, so I was apprehensive.

Shortly after I was seated, two uniformed police boarded the plane and went to the back. They then escorted a male passenger off in handcuffs. Then I began to understand why they removed the luggage from the plane. They had to find and remove this man's luggage. We were delayed a little, and arrived in Bogotá slightly late, but thankfully all 16 pieces of our luggage arrived. We had no problem getting through customs. I suspected we looked like a non-threatening three-generation family.

We met Jim, and after our greetings, he introduced me to a man whom he identified as a representative of the Colombian Government Department of Health. Jim told me that the government had heard about our plan to teach the native Indians from the jungle how to become dentists. He said the government representative was here to tell me that the government totally forbids it. My heart sank. Jim said, "I've invited him to dinner so we can talk about it."

Jim knew a well respected dental professor from the University of Colombia Dental School who was a good Christian friend, and a member of his church. Jim secretly invited him to dinner also, and filled him in on our problem. Jim, the government representative, and the professor talked throughout supper and into the evening in Spanish. We just sat there, listened and tried to look concerned.

Finally Jim filled us in on what was transpiring. The government representative told them, "The government is responsible for the dental health of the natives, and we will take care of them." The government had been called in two emergency situations. One was when a native Indian had given a small girl too much fluoride. She became sick and almost died. In another case, an Indian tried to reline a denture. The plastic hardened in the patient's mouth, and they couldn't remove it. A government dentist had to literally cut the denture out of his mouth.

I asked the government representative if he had ever been out in the jungle to check on the indigenous peoples' teeth. He said, "No." I told him that I had been at eight different indigenous Indian villages, for a total of two months, and most all of the Indians had terribly infected and painful teeth. They had never seen or heard of any government help. I said, "The least we should be able to do would be to teach them how to control pain and infection in an emergency. There was no way any native could get out of the jungle and find a government dentist to treat them."

The Colombian Dental School professor strongly agreed. The government official finally compromised and said, "You can teach hygiene, prevention, and emergency treatment for pain and infection." I was pleased, because the only emergency treatment for an infected, painful, abscessed tooth, in my mind, was extraction.

The next morning, we packed and went with Jim in the DC-3 to Lomalinda. Jim's parents went along for the ride, and returned to Bogotá the same day with Jim. Stan met us at the runway and took us to a nice house. The translators that had built and lived in this house were home on furlough, so Stan asked permission for us to live in their house for two weeks. We usually ate a light breakfast in the house, had lunch in the cafeteria, and were invited out for supper.

Stan was aware of our government problem. In fact, two of the passengers on the DC-3 were dentists that were sent by the government to monitor our teaching, and make sure everything was as we had agreed. They were essentially government spies.

Stan explained to us how the government received knowledge of our teaching plans. The government had briefly taught a few indigenous Indians basic health care in a few of the tribes. When the tribes elected who they wanted to send to Lomalinda for dental training, some of the native Indian healthcare workers were not elected, and they became jealous and angry and went to the government, and told them what we planned to do. They warned the government that there could be big trouble, and they made up a variety of false stories.

Lomalinda had a small farm on the road going toward town and it had the best facilities for our course. You could either walk through the fields a quarter of a mile, or you could drive by the road which was about three quarters of a mile. I went by the road with the truck so we could carry our supplies and equipment. Our dental course started the day after we arrived.

It was obvious that there had been a lot of preparation. They had a classroom with tables and benches for 25 students and their interpreters. They had a large blackboard, a Kodak 35mm slide projector, with remote control, and a screen.

An interesting observation occurred just before class began, when all the students were gathering together for the first time. Stan had placed a large map near the door, with a pin in the location from which each student had come. Many were dressed in their native clothes, which often was quite different. A few spoke Spanish, in addition to their native tongue. They were introducing themselves to each other, and showing where they had come from on the map. There were smiles and laughter and they showed a lot of excitement.

There were two students that I had met before. Professor Danielle was there from Stan's Yucuna tribe and Anita from Linda's Kogie tribe. Stan introduced me to Anita again, and I met her husband. They had two children, whom I met later. Stan also introduced me to the two government dentists.

We had 25 students, who spoke 18 different languages. Their missionary translators sat next to them, and verbally translated for them. I was asked to speak in phrases, and to wait for their translation. I had practice doing that last year when I taught Danielle, and Stan translated.

I had made a course outline of the material I wanted to cover. We started with Stan introducing Beth, Dora May, and me. He then said a prayer. I started with some dramatic slides of various severe dental diseases. The slides were particularly exciting to them, because most of them had never seen a projected slide before. We discussed dental anatomy, and other dental basics.

Beth then taught the hygiene class, which included at this point, prevention by diet, brushing and flossing. We showed them how to make a toothbrush out of a stick, by fraying the ends. We also showed them how to make dental floss, by pulling the fibers out of cactus leaves and letting them dry. Then we gave them a homework assignment to make a stick toothbrush and some dental floss, and to bring them back to class the next morning. They did amazingly well. We had them brush and floss their own teeth in class, using small mirrors which we had brought with us.

It was obvious that the two government dentists were bored out of their minds. One of the government dentists was a middle-aged married man, and the other was a pretty young single girl. It was rumored that they had some nighttime personal disagreements at the guest house. Between their being bored and having personal disagreements, they both left after three days on the next DC-3 flight back to Bogotá. This was another answer to prayer because we were just starting the part of the course about how to give anesthesia and extract teeth. I didn't know if they would agree with my definition of emergency treatment. I was concerned that they might stop me, but the Lord answered our prayers, and they disappeared.

We started to teach them how to give anesthesia. We first injected anesthesia into an orange, and then into a pig's jaw, that Stan had picked up from the local butcher. After sterilizing everything, we had them give anesthesia to each other. They found this quite exciting and memorable.

Beth taught them how to clean and scale calculus, or hard deposits, off of extracted teeth. I had brought a couple of quarts of extracted teeth from the University, which had been kept moist in glycerin. The teeth had a lot of calculus on them, so they had a chance to remove the calculus while holding a tooth in their hands, using the scaling instruments I had brought.

I carried these teeth in my carry-on in clear plastic quart bottles when we came. The security officer at the airport requested to look into my carry-on. When she unwrapped one of the quart bottles of extracted teeth and took one look at them, she immediately put it down, turned white, placed her hands over her face, and turned her head to the side. I thought for sure she was going to throw up. She just waved me on.

After a week of class, slides, lectures, demonstrations, lab work, and working on each other, we were ready for patients. Wycliffe had very thoroughly cleaned out a former chicken coop, disinfected it, and divided it up into five rooms. We used the largest room as a waiting room, where they had the Jesus film running in Spanish on a screen most of the time. We had two rooms for teaching dental hygiene, which Beth supervised. We had two rooms for extractions, which I supervised, with the help of Stan and Danielle.

There had been some excellent communication with the local people who were primarily poor people of Spanish descent, because we had more than enough of all types of patients. If you had a toothache, no money, and were offered free treatment at a U.S. supervised dental clinic, I suppose it would be an easy choice to make.

Before starting our extraction clinic, I thought I would do a demonstration. One of our students had several abscessed lower molars that were bothering him a lot, and he had asked earlier if I would extract them. I gave him anesthesia, and removed five molar teeth, while the students watched closely. He got along fine. Several hours later one of the students came to me and said, "The student for whom you did extractions is still bleeding." I sat him down, cleaned him up, examined him, and yes, he was still bleeding quite a little. I put gauze over the bleeding area and put pressure on it for several minutes. This normally stops 99% of the bleeding, but it didn't stop his bleeding at all.

I stopped each of the clinics, got all the students together, and explained the problem to them. I then asked them for a solution. "What would you do?" We hadn't really discussed this in our lectures, so I wasn't surprised when I didn't get any answers. I told the class, "He will probably bleed to death by morning if we don't get the bleeding stopped." But the students still didn't offer any suggestions. I then told them, "I will show you how to stop the bleeding and you better never forget it!" I numbed him, and put in 10 good tight sutures and the bleeding immediately stopped.

That evening back at the house, I found the heavy felt cloth which I had brought, and I nailed it to a wooden board about a foot square. I then put one inch cuts through the felt in several areas. I reminded Dora May, "You are good at sewing." She used to make all of our kids clothes. I told her, "I'm going to teach you how to sew up these cuts in the felt using a hemostat and sutures, so you can teach the students." I spent an hour or two teaching her how to suture. The hardest part was holding the needle with a hemostat. A hemostat is a small surgical pair of pliers that allows you to control the needle when you need to reach into the back of the mouth. She learned rapidly.

Dora May was left-handed, which turned out to be a big advantage. She could sit with the board in front of her, and place the students across from her. She then asked the students in front of her to do exactly the same thing as she did, because they usually did it with their right hand. Dora May ended up spending one hour or more with each student, one-on-one, teaching them how to put in sutures. After our one student's bleeding problem, all the students were highly motivated, and couldn't wait for their turn to put in sutures. The thick felt cloth was very close to the texture of tissue in the mouth. The following year when we came back, several of the students told us of all the unusual situations they were called upon to put in sutures for their people, most of the time outside of the mouth. I'll share the details with you in the next chapter.

One evening when Dora May, Beth, and I were walking to one of the translator's house for supper, it was still light, and we had to walk on a path that went through a short jungle thicket. As we entered the thicket, suddenly something heavy hit me on the top of my back and shoulders. Quickly I felt a fuzzy arm slide around my neck. I was so startled I must have jumped three feet in the air hollering at the same time. Then suddenly it was gone. I turned to see what had happened, and saw a monkey running down the path behind me. Dora May and Beth were laughing so hard that I just laughed with them. We found out later the monkey was a friendly pet of one of the translators, and it just wanted to play. I suspected that I probably scared the monkey as much as he scared me. Talk about having a monkey on your back, I sure had one!

When we got to our host's house, supper was not quite ready, so we waited in the living room and sat on the couch. We observed bugs running all over the place. When one big bug ran right in front of Beth, she stuck her foot out and squashed it. Just at that time our host came into the living room, and she said, "Now you pick it up." The tone of her voice indicated she was not happy. She then said, "If we killed all the bugs running around here, I would spend my whole life picking up dead bugs. They don't bother us, so we don't bother them." Dora May gave Beth a Kleenex and she picked up the bug and put it in the wastebasket.

We then enjoyed a nice supper, good conversation, and ignored the bugs running around us. As we got ready to leave I noticed a four foot boa constrictor snake on a single bed in an adjacent room. I made some type of comment. Their youngest son who was about 8 years old, stated, "That's my pet boa. He sleeps with me at night." First we had a monkey and now a boa. I guess pets are quite different at Lomalinda.

Our clinics were very busy. Each student had the experience of scaling several people's teeth, teaching hygiene, giving anesthesia, suturing, extracting several teeth, and even taking out some broken roots.

Stan said this was a real amazing cultural breakthrough. The Spanish people were actually coming and allowing the indigenous Indians to clean and extract their teeth. Native Indians had been classified by the Spaniards as dumb, stupid, ignorant, and people that had very little value. Stan compared it to a white southern landlord in the early 1800s going into town, and letting a black dentist fix his teeth. It would have never happened. But here for the first time that anyone could remember, the native Indians were treating the Spaniards, teeth. Stan said, "This is truly a cultural breakthrough."

The night before graduation was a busy night. Stan and the other translators prepared the diplomas, planned a graduation ceremony, and a celebration party. Dora May, Beth, and I had to sterilize all the instruments. We then divided them into 25 equal packages. We also had to give them supplies such as anesthesia, gauze, sutures, toothbrushes, etc.

Graduation day started with a formal graduation ceremony and the handing out of diplomas. We then gave each student a package with all the instruments and supplies they would need, to do what we had taught them, when they returned to their jungle villages. This added up to over $1000 per student, if everything had been bought new. A party time and celebration followed, with a variety of snacks and punch. We had a group of very proud, happy, and excited new dentists from all parts of the jungle. What a joyous time that was.

Anita's husband graduated and received a diploma, but Anita did not. She had to drop out of the class because her two children became very ill. Her husband was 17 years old, married, had two children, and was a Kogie schoolteacher, a pastor, and now the only dentist for several thousand Kogies. That's what I call, "living on the fast track."

Stan instructed the graduates that they would need to charge their people a small fee, so they could purchase new supplies. He would make sure they received new supplies when needed.

Beth mentioned one day that she sure would like to call and talk to her husband, even though she knew there were no telephones at Lomalinda. She had been married eight months, and had been away almost two weeks. Stan overheard her and said, "I'll see what I can do." Stan came to Beth that evening and said, "Come with me and we will see if you can talk with your husband, if we are lucky."

We went to a translator's house, whose hobby was using a shortwave radio. He got on his shortwave radio, and radioed for someone to answer who lived in Michigan. He finally got a ham radio operator near Grand Rapids, Michigan to answer. He told his contact the situation and asked if he would call Beth's home, collect, and patch the phone call through on his shortwave radio. He called Beth's husband, Ed, who accepted the charges, and Beth got to talk with him over the shortwave radio. It was a little different, because they could only talk one way at a time, but this made Beth happy.

Beth had an experience she will never forget. One week she was a student listening to lectures. The next week she was the lecturer, teaching her own students. One week she was a lowly student being told by everyone what to do, and the next week she was honored professor telling her students what to do. She was looked up to, almost as a goddess, as the students showed her great respect, continually asking her questions, and forever thanking her. It was a quick, pleasant, turnaround of events and a super self-confidence builder. It was truly a life-changing experience.

We returned to Bogotá with much lighter luggage than we had brought. We picked up Jim's mom and dad, who had a great time with their family, and we all returned home safely.

In summary: Although we had a disappointing reception upon arriving in Colombia this year, I feel we had a very successful Dental School. We taught 25 indigenous Indians, who spoke 18 different languages from all over the jungle, good dental hygiene and how to safely and painlessly, extract an aching, infected tooth. We supplied the students with a total of over $2500 worth of necessary equipment and supplies. We made arrangements for them to continue to receive supplies when needed. Beth had a fantastic experience and gained a lot of self-confidence. I personally felt that teaching these Indians would result in the relief of more pain and suffering than I could ever provide. Again this was a help to our missionary translators to increase their respect and friendship with the Indians they were serving, in hopes that they would be more receptive to the Good News of Jesus.

# And Now the Rest of the Story

This was the first mission that Dora May was able to join me. She felt the same satisfaction and fulfillment in helping these people that I did. She has continued to go on most of my future missions and has been a most valuable helper.

Communication from Stan shortly after our fifth mission trip to Colombia indicated Wycliffe's Administrators were concerned that our confrontation with the government officials concerning the teaching of dentistry to the indigenous people may have harmed their fragile relationship with the Catholic dominated, ever-changing, Colombian Government. Wycliffe had worked hard and long to maintain good government relationships. There was a concern that if I returned, it might create more hostile relationships. I was greatly disappointed and felt my missions to Columbia were probably ended.

Shortly thereafter I received an invitation from Cindy Sherwood for Dora May and me to come to Zimbabwe, where she was currently serving, so we could teach nursing students how to extract teeth. She offered to be our host in Nov. 1989 at a remote TEAM mission hospital. We gladly accepted.

Stan who had a great love for the indigenous people and a concern for their dental problems was bothered by Wycliffe's decision. He went to Bogotá to see the Government's new Head Dental Officer, Dr. Casta Neda. Stan said, "I understand your government is responsible for the dental healthcare of all of Colombia's indigenous people, even in remote jungle villages." Dr. Neda said, "That's correct." Stan asked, "Have you personally ever had the opportunity to survey the dental needs of any of the indigenous Indians in the jungle?" He said, "Well, no!"

Stan said, "I am planning to visit several remote jungle villages using one of our Helio Courier airplanes, to do some surveying. Would you like to come with me, free of charge, and check these people's dental needs? You can also check on some of the indigenous Indians that we trained last summer, and make sure there are no problems." Much to Stan's surprise, Dr. Neda said, "Yes, I would like to do that." If you think about it, there was no other way in the world he could personally have done such a survey.

Stan took Dr. Neda with him for almost 2 weeks. They traveled to several indigenous Indian villages, including some that had a dentist that we had trained and equipped.

Dr. Neda was shocked by the amount of decay, pain, infection, and abscessed teeth that he saw, due in part to a lack of oral hygiene, and to the sugarcane they consumed. This was particularly bad in those villages where they had no trained dentist. In the areas where we had one of our trained dentists, he noticed that the dental conditions were much better.

He was impressed by the number of dental forceps, instruments, and supplies that the native dentists had. He questioned them about sterilization, and they assured him they boiled all of their instruments every time they used them. He saw no problems that had occurred, and was impressed by their knowledge when he questioned them.

The last small village he visited was a village where we had trained a native Indian named John Fredy. Fredy was a small young man who was very intelligent and had a big broad charming smile. He had complained to Stan, at the end of the course, that it would be hard for him to charge his people any money for his services, because he loved them so much, and they were all just like family.

After Dr. Neda met Fredy, and was talking to him, Fredy told him this story: "A couple of months ago a government dentist came to visit our village for the very first time. He sat my villagers down, checked their teeth, and extracted teeth he thought were bad. He didn't give my people enough anesthesia and they were screaming and crying with pain. He stopped in the middle of the afternoon and left our village. He left many people bleeding, and I was up well into the night trying to stop the bleeding by suturing. Your government dentist broke a lot of teeth off, and just left the roots. It took me almost 2 weeks to go back and get all the roots out. Your dentist doesn't love my people. He hates us and he hates you for sending him here. I love my people very much, and I would never treat them that way."

Yes, Dr. Neda realized that they had a big problem trying to get government trained dentists to go into the jungle, and oftentimes they had to threaten and force them to go. He also observed that the dental needs were much greater than he had ever expected.

After talking to Fredy, the light finally popped on in his head. These native people that had been trained as dentists were good, and they hadn't hurt anyone. They lived in their villages, and were always available to handle dental problems in an emergency. They loved their people and would never intentionally hurt them.

Then Dr. Neda turned to Stan and said, "These native dentists that you have trained are doing a good job. I am convinced that this is the way our government can best care for our country's indigenous people, by training native dentists to take care of their own people. They love their people and they are doing a great job caring for them." He then said to Stan, "See if you can get that American Professor, to come to Columbia again, and we will train more natives to be dentists. I will arrange for several Colombian dentists to help him." Wow! What an unexpected turnaround that was. The Lord is good.

# CHAPTER 9

# ZIMBABWE

Over a year passed before I received another invitation to help with a short-term dental mission. Cindy Sherwood, a highly trained nurse from our church invited Dora May and me to help in Zimbabwe.

Cindy had gone to Colombia with Todd and me in 1985 while waiting for a visa to Irian Jaya. When she finally received her visa it was only good for six months. She went to Irian Jaya hoping to either extend it, or get a more permanent one, but was unsuccessful and had to return home after her six months.

After looking for a new mission location, she joined TEAM, The Evangelical Alliance Mission. There was a need for a person with her tropical medicine and midwife training, in a remote TEAM hospital in Zimbabwe. Cindy answered the call, and went to Krunda Hospital in rural Zimbabwe. She worked there as a nurse and also trained nursing students. Zimbabwe had only five dentists in the entire country of over 8 million people. That meant 99% of the people never had an opportunity to see a dentist. She had heard of my training of the indigenous people in Colombia and invited me to come and to train their nursing students in some basics in dentistry, including extracting painful infected abscessed teeth.

I had no difficulty accepting this challenge. Cindy indicated Dora May and I would be all that was needed to accomplish their teaching objective, and all that she could accommodate.

Dora May and I packed the dental supplies that we thought we would need and left in November of 1989. This was our first time to go to this part of the world. The only way our travel agent, Jill, could get us to Harare, the capital of Zimbabwe, was through Johannesburg, South Africa. We thought that on our way home it would be nice to take a few extra days and tour South Africa. Jill suggested we go to Cape Town and that we fly from Johannesburg and return by the world-famous blue train. Since I didn't know anything about South Africa, I gladly accepted her suggestion. The mind-boggling thing to me was to see her, in 1989, sit at her desk and make airline reservations from Johannesburg to Cape Town, and then to see her make reservations for our return on the blue train, even including the number of our onboard stateroom. She did all of this on her computer in just a few minutes, halfway around the world.

We flew from Detroit to New York, to Brussels, then onward to Johannesburg, South Africa, and finally to Harare, Zimbabwe, without any overnight layover. This was a very long trip. Cindy met us in Harare and took us to the TEAM guest house where we stayed overnight. The next morning after looking around the city a little bit, we started driving north toward Krunda Hospital. The road quickly turned to gravel, then to dirt, then a single lane, then a two track with grass growing in the middle and brush scraping the sides of our vehicle. When we came to a small river we just drove through it with our four-wheel vehicle. Finally toward evening we arrived at the Krunda Hospital compound, which was built, owned, and operated by TEAM. There were about 15 to 20 buildings, one of which was a small house in which Cindy lived. She had an extra bedroom so we stayed with her for two weeks.

The next morning we walked over to the hospital and met Dr. Drake, who was in charge of the 200 bed hospital, and his wife, who was in charge of the nursing school of 40 students. Dr. Drake had been the only M. D. at the hospital for over 28 years. That being the situation, he rarely had a chance to leave. He met his wife when she came to teach the nursing students. They got married and had two children, a boy and a girl who were now 8 and 10 years old.

I asked Dr. Drake how I could best help. He indicated that I would have to wait until afternoon to teach the nursing students, because they were needed in the hospital for essential duties in the morning hours. He asked if in the mornings I could examine the nurses' teeth, and see how their teeth were. He gave me a small empty private hospital room with a single bed to use as my dental office. We pushed the bed to the back wall and unpacked all of our dental gear, stacking it on the bed until it was 2 feet high. We borrowed a straight-backed wooden chair to use as our dental chair and placed it near the window to help get additional light. We used a small bedside table for our instruments. This setup worked fairly well.

I examined the nursing students' teeth in the mornings, and started my lectures in the basics of dentistry in the afternoons. I used numerous slides as well as the blackboard. After a couple of days, Dr. Drake came to me and asked how I was getting along. I told him fine, and that I was almost finished examining each of the nursing students. He asked me for the results of the examinations. I told him that the students had beautiful teeth but quite a few of them had small cavities starting in the tops of their molars. He asked me, "Can you fix them?" I told Dr. Drake, "I did bring along equipment to fill teeth, but I need air pressure to run my drill." I asked him, "Do you have somewhere I can get air pressure to run my drill?" He said, "No problem, we have lots of compressed air." He took me to three different sources of compressed air in the hospital, but all were too weak to run my drill. He then said, "Let's check the air compressor in the repair barn that we use to inflate our vehicle tires." This compressor was powerful enough to run my drill, but it was very large, heavy, noisy, dirty, and bolted to a concrete slab in a filthy barn. It had a long hose that could be taken outside to put air into the vehicle tires.

I looked around and there was a good shade tree nearby, so I suggested to Dr. Drake, that if I could get a chair and a table, I could put it under the shade tree and work right here. He said, "Good." After we had finished the nurses' examinations, Dr. Drake assigned one of the nursing teachers to help me. His name was Stephen. He asked Stephen to schedule the nursing students that needed fillings. We first took the students out to the barn and under the shade tree to drill out the decay in their teeth. Then we took them 300 yards back to the hospital, where I filled their teeth in our makeshift dental clinic. I used both white fillings in front and silver fillings in the back. I taught Dora May how to mix the silver by hand, using a mortar and pestle. She then handed it to me and I filled the tops of the back molars. It worked well.

The nursing students were between 20 and 25 years old, mostly female, and could speak good English. Zimbabwe was formerly the country of Rhodesia, a British colony before it was given its independence. The nursing students knew from my lectures that decayed teeth would only get worse, and lead to infection, abscesses, and pain. They also knew they would never have a chance to get their teeth filled, so they were extremely grateful for all we did for them. I even filled several of Dr. Drake's teeth.

Dr. Drake received his medical training at New York University, and served his internship at Cook County Hospital in downtown Chicago. He took the medical licensing board exam three times and failed it all three times. He felt the Lord was telling him something. When he discovered TEAM had a hospital in Zimbabwe with no doctor and that no medical license was required, he accepted the challenge. At that time he had no wife or family and he found himself the only doctor in this isolated hospital in the middle of nowhere.

Originally TEAM had asked three different neighboring tribal chiefs where they would like a hospital to be built in their area. They couldn't agree, so finally they compromised and had TEAM build the hospital between the three tribes' villages. This ended up being in the middle of nowhere.

One of the nursing students was a very pretty and popular young lady. Her two upper front teeth were almost black and had been all of her life, as a result of a developmental growth problem. She asked me to fix them. Fortunately, I brought the right material, so I put on a layer of white bonded filling material and, *"Presto!"* they were white and beautiful.

This got the rest of the nurses excited. In fact, there were so many nurses that were anxious to get their teeth filled, that I could easily see we were not going to get them all done. I needed to change tactics. I said to Dora May, "Why don't I go to the barn and drill the decay out, and send them back to the hospital and you can fill the teeth? I'll teach

Stephen how to mix the silver and assist you." Of course she said, "I can't do that! I don't know how! I don't have a license!" I told her, "No license is required here. I have taught freshman dental students who knew nothing about dentistry to fill teeth at the dental school for many years, and I can teach you too. The fillings we are doing here are a very simple type." She reluctantly agreed, so I taught her. I showed her, helped her, watched her, and within a couple of hours she was doing great. That was certainly a lot better than not getting any fillings at all, and that's exactly what would have happened if she hadn't helped. In that way we doubled our production. I would go to the barn and drill out the decay, send them to the hospital dental clinic, then Stephen would mix the silver, hand it to Dora May, and she would fill the teeth. When we got home, Dora May told our two sons that she had placed a lot of silver fillings while in Zimbabwe. At first they would not believe her, but eventually we convinced them it was really true.

## A Day to Remember

We awoke early in the morning, had breakfast, and headed to the hospital. Every morning at 7 Dr. Drake had a chapel service in their small church. This morning Dr. Drake asked me to speak at the chapel service and I did. The hospital had an outpatient clinic of which Cindy was in charge. The surrounding village people with medical problems, sometimes very serious, started lining up at daybreak. Chapel was not required, but any patient who elected to go to chapel service was given a number that put the patient at the head of the line. The chapel was full.

At this particular time Dr. Drake had two female TEAM missionary MDs from Germany who had come to help temporarily. After chapel, the doctors, Cindy, Dora May and I had a daily strategy planning meeting for about 10 to 15 minutes. We attempted to coordinate our daily schedules.

Dora May, Stephen and I had perfected our drill and fill routine quite well. We filled 30 to 40 teeth that morning. In the afternoon in my class with the nurses, we reached the point where we needed to practice giving anesthesia. Each student had to practice giving anesthesia to one of the other students in both the upper and lower jaws. Then they in turn had to be the patient and let someone else give them anesthesia. Needless to say, this was by far the most exciting and memorable day for the students.

Actually, I couldn't supervise all 40 students at one time, so I selected six of the best students, and spent a couple of hours in the evening instructing them on the next day's projects. Then I appointed them as junior instructors to help with such projects as giving anesthesia. They were a big help, and it worked well.

That evening Dora May, Cindy, and I were invited to the home of the Smiths for supper. The Smiths were a retired American couple who had volunteered to work with TEAM at the Krunda Hospital doing odd jobs and handyman work of general repairs. This particular day, November 23, was Dora May's birthday, and it was also Thanksgiving in the U.S. It was a double celebration. We had a special meat for supper. Since turkey was unheard of in this part of the world, we had roast kudu, a large deer-like animal which Mr. Smith had shot on a recent game hunt. It was actually very good.

Our host told us a story about their cat. They had a tight board fence around the back-yard so they could raise a garden without animals destroying their crops. One day they looked out in the garden and saw a big snake trying to get out of a knothole in one of the boards of the fence. There was a big lump in the snake that wouldn't go through the hole. They looked around for their cat and couldn't find it. They ran out to the fence with a big knife and cut the snake in two, just in front of the big lump. Out popped their cat, a little sluggish, but it recovered and returned to normal.

In the middle of supper the electricity went off, so we finished by candlelight. They said the electricity often went off in the evening and they were accustomed to it. As we were fin-ishing dessert, their hand-cranked phone rang. It was Dr. Drake. He wanted to speak to me. When I answered, he said, "Dick, I need your help. My scrub nurse has gone and I can't find him. I have an emergency C-section, and I want you to scrub in with me." I said, "Are you sure? I have never even seen a C-section." He said, "Yes, you know surgical technique, and that's all you need to know, so come right over and help me."

My heart started beating fast as I headed through the dark night toward the hospital. I thought to myself, "What am I getting into?" Once in the hospital, I went straight to the operating room, where Dr. Drake was waiting for me. I scrubbed, gowned, and gloved, with memories of my hospital experiences during my naval dental internship. We went into the operating room where Dr. Drake had already given the patient spinal anesthesia, although I didn't know that. We finished gowning the patient so that all that was exposed was a very large protruding abdomen. Dr. Drake picked up a scalpel and, "*swish*," he made a 16 to 18 inch incision from top to bottom in one single stroke. I gasped! He handed me some gauze and I started blotting the bleeding. He then cut more slowly until he got through the uterus, and we could see the baby's head. When he thought he had the uterus open far enough, he gave one big push, and the baby popped out. After he tied the cord, he handed it to his nursing students. The baby started crying as they cleaned it. Dr. Drake talked to the patient much of the time while we were working. My job of blotting the seeping blood was not very difficult until he pushed and the baby popped out. Then there was blood everywhere, but just for a moment or two. He had me help tie off a couple of large bleeders, and then he started doing the internal suturing. By the time he finished the internal suturing, the bleeding had nearly stopped. He then reached behind him and got a big instrument. In about 30 seconds he placed 15 wide silver staples in the skin surface of the incision. I had never seen anything like this before, and it greatly surprised me. It looked so barbaric with all those big wide silver staples covering the length of her belly, but I found out later this is standard procedure in many U.S. hospitals, even today.

When we finished, Dr. Drake walked back with me to Cindy's house. The Smiths were with Cindy and Dora May. When they saw our flashlights coming across the yard, Cindy came to the screen door and called out, "Don't come up on the porch. There's a big snake up here." Dr. Drake said, "Well, throw me a broom or something!" I was already backing up. Cindy threw out a broom and Dr. Drake cautiously went up on the porch, moved some of the furniture, found the snake, and killed it with the broom handle. It turned out to be a very poisonous puff adder snake.

We went into Cindy's house, and she had fixed tea and cookies for us. It was around midnight. As we were enjoying the snack, the phone rang. Cindy answered and said, "Dr. Drake, it's for you." Dr. Drake talked for a moment and then turned to me and asked, "You up for another one?" What could I say, as if I hadn't had a full day already! "I'm ready," I said. So we both took off back to the hospital. The nurses already had the patient on the operating table. Dr. Drake stepped in and gave the spinal anesthesia and then we scrubbed, gowned, and gloved up for C-section number two. The C-section went just like the first one, a carbon copy. Only one thing different happened. When we were about halfway through the procedure, a nurse came in and reported that a 13-year-old girl, who had been in labor for three days, was experiencing her baby's heart rate starting to drop rapidly. Dr. Drake instructed, "Put her on oxygen and prepare her for an immediate C-section as soon as we finish here." He didn't even ask me this time.

When we finished, the students hurriedly scrubbed the operating room, and brought in this 13-year-old crying girl. We scrubbed, gowned, gloved and started all over again. This time two different things happened. There were a couple of bugs flying around, and one of them decided to go into my ear, and go "*buzz, buzz*." There was absolutely nothing I could do about it, or I would have broken the sterile technique, and Dr. Drake would have been left by himself. The bug wasn't biting or hurting, it was just buzzing, so I endured it for another hour or so.

When Dr. Drake finally popped the baby out, he handed it to the nursing students and said, "I want to hear the baby cry." It didn't start crying like the first two. He said again louder, "I want to hear the baby cry!" At that point he looked at me, and said, "You finish up!" He took off his gloves, threw them on the floor, went to the corner of the room where the baby was, and started giving it mouth to mouth resuscitation. In a moment the baby was crying.

It all happened so fast. I just closed the incision, blotted the bleeding, and watched what was happening. After the baby was responding normally, Dr. Drake came back over to me and said, "You're not finished yet. Don't you know the law of the jungle? You see one, you do one, you teach one. This is your third one tonight. You should be teaching by now." He wasn't smiling either. He went back out and scrubbed, gowned, and gloved again, and came back in and finished closing the incision. As we walked back to the house, the sky in the East was starting to lighten, and the roosters were crowing. I know for me, this was unquestionably one of the most memorable "Days of My Life."

For Dr. Drake this was just another day in his 28 years at Krunda Hospital. Cindy said he often worked 18 to 20 hours a day. I don't know how he did it. Oftentimes in the evening, a flatbed truck would arrive with 10 to 20 wounded soldiers and victims from Mozambique, where there was an ugly civil war raging. Dr. Drake often worked late into the night trying to save their lives. Dr. Drake probably saved more lives in one day than the average U.S. doctor did in six months, and he didn't even have a license to practice medicine.

One day as we continued our morning clinics, Stephen asked me, "Will you teach me how to be a dentist? After you leave we won't have anyone to help us with our dental problems." I checked with Dr. Drake and he said, "Great!" So I concentrated more and more on teaching Stephen prevention, hygiene, scaling, anesthesia, and extractions. I didn't teach him fillings because he wouldn't have a drill or supplies, and it was much more complicated. He was a great student and learned quickly.

The doctors occasionally brought us patients from the hospital. Oftentimes they just ended up being an extraction, but sometimes they turned out to be some of the most unusual dental problems I have ever seen. One time I had to cut the gum open and pull it back, to locate an infected root. I then had to chisel the bone away with a surgical hammer and chisel to take the root out, then sutured up the gum. Stephen watched closely and helped me through the whole surgery.

Classes in the afternoon went very well. We found lots of patients for the students to get experience extracting teeth. The tradition in much of Africa is that when a patient is put in the hospital, the family comes and helps care for the patient, including cooking and feeding them three meals a day. There was a large building for the families to live in and cook their meals. When they heard we were offering to extract aching teeth for free, we had more patients than the nursing students could treat. Each student received experience in extracting many teeth.

We didn't have a special graduation for the nursing students. Dr. Drake said their dental training would be part of their nursing training, and would be included in their nursing diploma.

Cindy had one of the biggest and toughest jobs in the hospital. She was responsible for caring for 100 to 150 out-patients every day. She had nursing students to help her, but she was responsible for teaching them how to help. Cindy was also responsible for prescribing and dispensing the needed medication. Again, she had to teach the nursing students how to help her in this area. As a nurse Cindy was well trained with comprehensive additional courses in midwifery and tropical medicine. She had many years of experience, and did an excellent job.

Dr. Drake spent much of his day in the operating room. When Cindy got a serious, urgent, or complicated patient, she would send for Dr. Drake. He would drop by and check those patients. Sometimes it would require hospitalization, and occasionally it resulted in emergency surgery.

At Cindy's house I noticed in her kitchen there were small red ants everywhere, including on her counter and in her sink. There were not just a few, but sometimes many hundreds of them. They didn't bother Cindy. When she needed to work in the kitchen, she just brushed them off the counter, washed it off, and did her thing. She said, "It's totally impossible to eliminate the ants, so I keep everything tightly sealed, and don't let them bother me."

One night we had an invasion of beetles. They were just like June bugs, but only about one-third the size. They covered the screens completely about two or three deep. Cindy said, "Don't worry, they won't bite or hurt you. They will be gone in a couple of days." In the middle of the night I had to get up and go to the bathroom. As I walked across the floor in my bare feet it was crunch, "*crunch, and crunch.*" They had gotten inside and they completely covered the floor. I got a flashlight and checked our bed, and although they covered the floor, none of them were on our bed. Why they were not, I will never understand. I just said, "Thank you, Lord."

Dora May had a new and unusual experience in the dental clinic, not only putting in fillings, including fillings in third molars, but in receiving very abundant expressions of appreciation from the nursing students. She gave them toothbrushes and floss, and they just couldn't stop thanking her. She began to understand better why I enjoyed my work, and why I came home from work late and tired some evenings. It was because I enjoyed helping people out of their problems.

A few of the female nurses invited Cindy, Dora May, and me over for dinner one night to show their appreciation. It was a most unusual meal. First of all, we ate on a mat on the concrete floor like they normally did. We had a lot of food which we had never eaten before, including rape. Rape was a green leaf vegetable they grew in their gardens, which they picked and ate like lettuce or spinach. I can't really say the meal was good, but it was different and appreciated.

What really topped off the evening was, after supper the four young ladies stood around and sang to us. They had wonderful voices and sang in beautiful harmony, in their native language. The last song they dedicated to us, and sang it in English with great feeling. They sang Bill Gaither's, "Because He Lives." This caused tingles to run up and down my spine, and tears to come to my eyes. I will never forget it.

When we finished teaching the nursing students, Dr. Drake asked, "Would you go with me to visit some of TEAM's rural clinics, and help teach the nurses out there how to extract teeth?" My response was, "Fine, whatever you say." The last day before Dr. Drake and I left, I gave Stephen a final exam, hoping I could announce him as the new hospital dentist. We had a lady come into the clinic with a sore, aching, swollen jaw. She told us this story: "I had a very bad toothache, so I went to Harare, and was lucky enough to get one of the country's five dentists to pull out my lower back tooth. I never got better, and it still hurts and is swollen."

I looked in her mouth and saw an open wound in the lower third molar area. She said, "It has been three weeks since the surgery." I knew there must be part of the tooth still in there. I took one of my instruments and put it into the hole in her gum, and could feel the tooth. A tooth feels completely different from bone, to a sharp delicate instrument. I didn't say a word. I turned to Stephen and said, "If you were the dentist, what would you do? If you can solve this problem I will appoint you as the new hospital dentist." I really didn't think he could do it, but it was the only challenge of our last morning that I found.

He gave the woman anesthesia, and took a scalpel and opened the gum wide, to see what was there. The dentist had removed the third molar crown but left the entire root broken off level with the bone. No question, this was one of the most difficult extraction problems in the mouth. 90% of the U.S. dentists would not have tackled this problem.

Stephen had watched me closely on a similar case a few days earlier and he learned fast. He picked up the bone chisel, pulled the tissue back, and asked me to swing the surgical mallet or hammer. He chiseled quite a little bone away from around the root, until he could get an instrument wedged between the bone and the root, and then he pried the root out. It came out with great difficulty, but he removed it all in one piece. He then cleaned the wound and sutured the gum nicely back together.

I guess Dr. Drake's law of the jungle was working. Stephen saw me do it one time, and he did it himself the second time, and I believe he could have taught someone the third time. He did a very nice job. I'm not sure I could have done any better. He surely did a lot better job than the so-called dentist in Harare who botched the job. With Dr. Drake's permission, I appointed Stephen as the new hospital dentist. He was one happy man, smiling from ear to ear.

Early the next morning Dr. Drake and I loaded a four-wheel drive land rover with our needed personal belongings, my dental equipment, and a few nursing students that were going out to one of TEAM's rural clinics to do their nursing school rotation. We dropped the students off at a remote rural clinic. After Dr. Drake checked out the clinic, we continued to drive northeast toward the Zambezi River and Mozambique. We traveled all day on a two-track road, with grass between the tracks, never seeing another vehicle. Occasionally we would see small round mud huts with thatched roofs. We also saw baobab trees, zebras, and giraffes along the road.

Near evening we pulled into a small group of buildings at the edge of a small village. It was the base of another American TEAM missionary and his wife. They had a small church and school, where they taught the local people. Dr. Drake and I stayed in their home overnight. As we were finishing supper we witnessed a phenomenon that no one in this area had ever seen before. A storm came up and it rained hard, and then it started to hail. The hail was about the size of marbles and it totally covered the ground. As soon as it stopped, everyone ran outside and picked up the hail. They couldn't understand why it was so cold. Eventually they started throwing it at each other.

Dr. Drake had called in advance and told them that we were coming. They asked him to bring needed supplies. They were about 7 hours from Krunda hospital, and about 10 hours from Harare, the country's only major city.

The next morning we went to a rural TEAM clinic in the neighboring village that was operated by a lone middle-aged nurse. She had been there for a while and had things pretty well under control. She had numerous very interesting medical emergency stories to tell us. I started extracting teeth for the many patients that had gathered. After the nurse finished talking with Dr. Drake, she asked me to show her how to extract teeth. She said, "The people here have lots of toothaches, and all I can treat them with is aspirin. If it's swollen very much I give them antibiotics. It is impossible for anybody to attempt to travel to Harare to get their tooth out." Dr. Drake needed to go and visit another TEAM clinic. He told me, "You have two hours to teach her how to extract teeth." She spoke English, so I immediately started teaching her. Two hours later when he returned, she had already given anesthesia and extracted numerous teeth.

Dr. Drake then drove down alongside a row of buildings located on the banks of the great Zambezi River, which looked dried up to me. He stopped at a military outpost, and we got out and went inside. He talked with the head officer for a while, and then the head officer asked to talk with Dr. Drake in private. After a few moments Dr. Drake came out. We took some packages out of the land rover, and started to walk across the dry sand of the Zambezi riverbed, with two armed soldiers accompanying us. The riverbed was about a mile wide in this area. Dr. Drake didn't always discuss with me in advance what he was planning to do, so I asked him, "Where are we going and why is the river dry?" He indicated that this was the end of the dry season, and there were large dams up-river that held the water in reservoirs. I also asked Dr. Drake, "What was the private talk all about with the head officer?" He said, "The officer was concerned that he might have the symptoms of AIDS, but I didn't think so." Dr. Drake continued, "The way they recruit for the Army is to just kidnap a young man off the street, and ship him to a different part of the country for his two years of duty. As a result, currently over 90% of all men in Zimbabwe's Army is infected with AIDS." Wow! How could anyone deal with an army like that?

It was very hot in the middle of the afternoon, with the full sun on the sand. When we finally reached the other side we were in Mozambique. We walked a couple of blocks to a small building with a red cross on the outside. Once inside, Dr. Drake greeted a nurse who had been long time friend. They talked for a bit, and then Dr. Drake gave him the supplies we had brought. They primarily consisted of medications.

This nurse was very grateful, and said, "I am totally out of everything, and don't even have an aspirin." Mozambique was in the middle of a very bloody civil war, and the nurse couldn't go anywhere in the country to get supplies, and often the wounded would come to him for help.

We didn't stay long before we headed back, and again walked across the hot dry Zambezi riverbed. We returned to the missionary's home for supper and overnight. The next morning we drove back to Krunda. Early the following morning we packed our suitcases and loaded them into Cindy's vehicle. Several people gathered to say goodbye, including Stephen who again and again thanked us. I can still remember his great big smile.

Cindy explained to us that one time when her financial support was getting low, she borrowed money from her parents, and had the money sent to a bank in South Africa. Then she went to South Africa, bought a pickup truck, brought it back to Zimbabwe, paid the import duty tax, and sold it in Zimbabwe for considerably more than what she paid for it. The government wouldn't let any of its citizens send money out of the country, or leave the country with more than $20 on their person. The country didn't make cars, and this was the only way anybody could buy a new car or truck, so the prices were high. This was legal and worked well for Cindy. It helped to furnish her needed financial support. The buyer of the car was very happy also. The government was happy. This was their way of keep money coming into the country, and not leaving it. None of the country's remaining rich British landowners and merchants could take their money and leave the country.

When we finally arrived in Harare, we stayed again in TEAM's guest house. We met a missionary whom Cindy knew, and he invited me to go on a wild game hunt with him. He would furnish the guns and make all the arrangements. Cindy had previously arranged to take us for a couple of days to one of Zimbabwe's wild game parks. Upon learning that, he indicated we could go as soon as I returned. He said I would most likely be able to shoot a zebra, and probably several other types of game. He also said I could get the animal skins dried and shipped back home. I then could get a taxidermist to mount them. Since I already had several trophies of wild game mounted and on display in our basement, this got me extremely excited.

We took off for the wild game park the next morning. While driving in the game park, heading toward the lodge where we were going to stay, we came over a slight hill and Cindy stopped very suddenly. There was a big rhino standing right in the middle of the road looking at us. Cindy said, "We don't mess around with rhinos", so we waited 5 or 10 minutes for it to walk away before we continued.

We stayed overnight in a very nice lodge. Early the next morning, we mounted horses and rode into the game park. They told us that humans on foot frequently spooked the animals, but if we were on a horse and stayed quiet, hopefully we could almost walk right up to them. Our best memory was when we came over a little knoll just at sunrise, and in front of us were many various wild animals that had come to a watering hole for their morning drink. There were zebras, giraffes, warthogs, various types of African deer, and several animals we didn't even recognize. We rode slowly up to them and around them, getting lots of good pictures. The horses didn't seem to spook them at all. We saw a variety of animals scattered throughout the park during the rest of the day.

The next morning we headed back to the TEAM guest house in Harare. I was ready for my big game hunt. When we arrived, Cindy's friend told us he couldn't arrange the hunt, because it was mating season, and hunting was not allowed at that time of the year. He said, "You come back in a month or two and I'll take you then." It didn't happen. I was disappointed, but Cindy said, "Why don't we hop a plane in the morning and fly over to see Victoria Falls?" That certainly helped take some of the disappointment away.

The next morning we flew to Victoria, and walked all around the world-famous Victoria Falls. They said because it was the end of the dry season, there was little water coming over the falls. There sure seemed to be a lot of water to me. When I saw all that water coming over the falls and running down the Zambezi River, I remembered we had walked across the dry Zambezi riverbed a few days earlier. We had a pleasant visit, did some souvenir shopping, stayed overnight, and flew back to Harare the next morning.

The following day we left Harare and flew to Johannesburg, and then on to Cape Town. On our flight to Cape Town, we met a young white Dutch South African high school teacher, who had been coaching a sports team out of the country, and was just returning. She said, "I have a few days off before I have to go back to teaching, and I would be happy to come to your hotel, pick you up and show you around." This sounded too good to be true, so we accepted her offer.

She picked us up the next morning and took us to the top of the famous Table Top Mountain. She then drove us to the very tip of the Cape of Good Hope, where the Atlantic and Indian Oceans meet. We stopped at an oceanfront restaurant, and had a fresh lobster lunch. Lobster is not one of my favorites, but this was the best lobster I had ever eaten.

The next day she picked us up and drove us to a very large fertile agricultural valley, and then to her parents' plantation house. We met her parents, and had lunch with them. The most interesting part of our visits was stories and information they told us about their history, and the big changes that were occurring as a result of their racial problems. Their explanation of their racial problems was certainly nothing like the information we receive from our media back home, and it was enough to fill a book.

We took the world-famous blue train back to Johannesburg. This train was originally built to honor the Queen of England. This was about a 24-hour train ride which cost about the same as our airfare. It was the most luxurious and memorable train ride that you could ever imagine.

One of our good friends in our church back home had a sister and brother-in-law that were full-time missionaries in Johannesburg. They had arranged for them to meet us at the train, host us for a few days, and show us around the Johannesburg area.

As we approached Johannesburg, it suddenly struck me as to how we would recognize each other because we had never met. I got a big piece of paper and wrote our names on it.

When we got off the train we walked down the train platform holding our sign. When we got to the end, we just stood there with our luggage and our sign feeling very alone and a long way from home. It seemed like we stood there forever, before a couple came up to us and said, "Hello, Dr. Charlick, we have been looking for you." We relaxed, and had a very nice time with these wonderful people. They showed us all around, and told us a great deal about South Africa's history, and what was currently happening there, again nothing like we hear from our news media back home.

We then took the long flight back home, through Europe, New York, and finally to Detroit. It's always nice to go away, but always better to come home, especially after having been gone for almost a month. Again this was a very rewarding mission trip, during which we were able to help a lot of people, as well as teach, supply, and equip a lot of them, who in turn would help others, all in the name of JESUS.

## And now the rest of the story

Cindy told us a couple of years later that Stephen did very well as the hospital dentist. Dora May and I got several letters from Stephen after we got home. One letter announced that he was going to get married, and he asked us if we could send him a suit for his wedding. Dora May and I went to the Salvation Army and bought Stephen a nice suit, and mailed it to him. He thanked us for it later.

# CHAPTER 10

# COLOMBIA 6
# DENTAL SCHOOL 2

Stan phoned me from Bogotá immediately upon returning from his survey in the jungle with Dr. Neda; the Colombian Government's Head Dental Officer. He informed me that Dr. Neda had requested that I come back and teach more indigenous Indians to be dentists. I wasn't aware of what Stan had been doing, so as a result I was greatly shocked, but also pleased. Stan asked "When can you come down again?" His phone call came in March 1990, so I suggested, "How about June?" He said, "Great! Could you come for four weeks this time so we could teach two classes of students, and this time we could teach them how to put in fillings also." I gladly agreed.

This gave me a little less than three months to put a team together, and get all supplies and equipment for twice as many students. I had some leftover supplies from our last trip, and I had developed several good contacts. I believed God would somehow help me to accomplish this task.

The biggest challenge was how we were going to furnish the natives in the jungle with drills, when they had no electricity. Also the way we normally mix our silver filling material is with a heavy expensive electrical mixing machine. This presented another big challenge!

I tried to find the old foot pump type drill, like the dentist near Lomalinda was using, but no one had been manufacturing those for many years. I couldn't even find any used ones to buy. They were only found in dental museums. I remembered seeing, at a Dental Convention, a battery operated dental drill that the U.S. military was using in remote field operations. It was fairly light and compact. The drill was not much bigger than a cigar, and the battery was about the size of a package of cigarettes. I checked the cost and it was about $300, which was very cheap for a dental drill, and it was available through a Japanese company.

I remembered how Linda and Grace recharged their radio batteries with solar panels. I found an expert in the solar panel business in Ann Arbor, near the University of Michigan. I made an appointment and went to visit him, taking along one of my portable electronic dental drills and the battery. I explained to him what I needed and why. Much to my surprise, his answer was, "No problem, I can easily make you a cheap solar panel with all the proper connections." He showed me a solar panel that was similar to what he planned to make for me. Its size was 6 x 12 inches, and was as thin as cardboard. That was an amazing answer to prayer. I really didn't think it was going to be possible.

A fully charged battery would run the drill for eight hours, at 20,000 RPMs, fast enough to drill teeth. He made one solar panel for me in just a few days, and put the proper connections on it so that I could connect it to my battery and check it out. I ran the battery completely down, hooked it up to the solar panel, and fully recharged the battery in one day of sunshine. The neat thing about the solar panel was that it was small, light, and cheap. He only charged $28 to make it. Needless to say, I was happy. For $328 I could get a solar rechargeable electric drill which would be adequate for doing fillings out in the jungle.

I named this procedure, "Filling teeth with sunshine." I started a campaign to raise money to purchase the solar panels and drills. I communicated with Stan, and told him what I had found, and the campaign I had started to raise money. Several of the translators were excited about the solar powered drills, and they started fundraising from their supporters also. I ended up purchasing and taking 18 solar panels and drills.

The other challenge was how to mix silver for the fillings without electricity. I thought this would be a simple problem because I remembered when I started dental school in the mid-1950s; we used a small mortar and pestle with finely ground silver filling to mix with mercury for our fillings. I would just go back to the old method. It wasn't that simple. The silver had not been manufactured in filling form for several years. It was currently pressed into hard tablets, to be used in our electric mixers. If that weren't enough, the small dental mortar and pestles hadn't been manufactured for 20 years.

I had one in my old student dental kit, which I had stored for some reason in my basement for 30 years. I thought maybe some other dentists might have their old ones also. I searched and searched, and only received one dental mortar and pestle from a dentist named Von Chapman. He was a dentist from Washington State, who ran a fairly large used dental equipment and supply mission, along with a large active dental mission organization. He sent one mortar and pestle to me with a note, "I don't think you'll find many, but good luck."

One day I was impressed with the idea that surely the University of Michigan's chemistry and pharmacy departments must use mortar and pestles. I went to the University's large chemistry store where staff and students could buy chemicals and related equipment. I explained my dilemma. The clerk said, "No problem," and he went and got their smallest mortar and pestle that they had available. It was about three to four times the size that we used in dentistry, but I bought it anyway, just to check it out. It was relatively cheap.

I took it home, and found a silver tablet, and put it in the mortar and found that it broke into a fine powder with just a little effort with the pestle. I then added the mercury to the powder, and it looked totally lost in this big mortar. I thought, no way, but I gave it a hearty try and to my surprise it worked perfectly. When I went to get more mortars and pestles they had to special order them. I ordered 25. They were made of thick rough glass, which could break, so I purchased several extras. They arrived in time with no problem.

The collection of forceps was my next biggest challenge. My source at the World Medical Relief was a little reluctant to give me as many forceps as I needed, because I was depleting their inventory, but I did get quite a few. A local oral surgeon heard of my need, and one day he brought about 40 old forceps to my office and said, "I don't use these much anymore, and thought you could get better use out of them." With a few others that I collected, it put me over the top of what I needed.

As far as recruiting a team, it was the same problem as last year. The daily news was full of the killings and violence surrounding Colombia's Cocaine Cartel, No way would the wives consider letting their husbands go to such a place.

I asked Beth if she would go with me again, and she excitedly said, "Yes," and asked if her husband, Ed, could come with us? I thought, why not? Dora May was excited about going again, so basically we had the same team, with a promise from Dr. Neda to send some Colombian dentists to help.

I took a lot of supplies and equipment to Colombia last year, with the hope of teaching fillings. We didn't use them, because we just didn't have time, and because of the government restrictions of only teaching emergency treatment. So we already had a lot of our needed equipment and supplies there, and we were able to get the rest of our supplies and equipment in our eight suitcases and four carry-ons.

The four of us left for our first month-long mission in the middle of June, 1990. We had no problems with customs, which is always a concern. Jim met us, hosted us overnight, and took us on the DC-3 to Lomalinda the next morning.

Stan met us, and again he had arranged for us to stay in an empty house of someone who was on furlough. Stan and his helpers had done a lot of preparation, and had 25 students at Lomalinda ready to start. For this course, the government requested that they be allowed to send six non-Indian female government trained healthcare providers to our course, and assured us we would not need to give them any equipment or supplies.

The first morning of our course, I met Dr. Miguel, a dentist the government promised to send to help with the course. Dr. Miguel was single, and only had been out of dental school two years. He was in this remote area because when the government helps pay for your education, you become obligated to work for them, wherever they assign you, for a certain number of years. Our U.S. Armed Forces have similar programs with the same set of rules.

Miguel was a new Christian, which was a surprise, and an added bonus. He had a very friendly, lovable, expressive personality, with a lot of humor. The students immediately fell in love with him. He could speak both English and Spanish. Most of our students this year understood Spanish.

Beth did most of the lecturing in prevention, hygiene, and scaling. After I lectured for several hours, with Dr. Miguel interpreting for me, I had a bright idea. Why don't I have Dr. Miguel do some of my lectures? He was delighted with the idea, so I had him over to the house in the evenings, and we went through my slides, and outlined exactly what I planned to cover in my lectures.

He was spectacular. He held the students' attention excellently, and had them laughing and learning at the same time, without any delay for translation. He was a natural. He did so well that I got him to do a lot of the lecturing. The students loved it. The second week, our students received their clinical experience, and all went well. We had many patients, and every student got a lot of valuable experience.

Stan indicated that we had several Communist Guerrillas, that put away their guns, dressed in civilian clothes, sneaked across the river at night, and we extracted their aching teeth. He didn't tell us this until after the fact, but I guess it wouldn't have made much difference, because we didn't have much choice.

Ten of our students had been in our class the previous year. They came back for a review, but mainly to concentrate on learning how to put in fillings. Dora May taught suturing again to all the students, including a review to our second-year students. It was interesting to hear how the second-year students had used their suturing skills over the last year. Not only did they use their suturing occasionally to stop bleeding after extractions, but more commonly they were called upon to sew up people's heads, arms, and legs after accidents, especially cuts from their machetes.

Beth supervised the hygiene clinic, Dr. Miguel supervised the extraction clinic, and Stan and I taught the 10 second-year students in an advanced course of how to put in silver fillings. I had special lectures on drilling teeth, mixing the silver amalgam, and putting in fillings. Each of the 10 students received a drill, battery, and solar panel. After my lectures and demonstrations, the students first removed decay and filled extracted teeth out in their hands. Danielle returned again, and he did a nice demonstration for the class on a patient. He then helped Stan and I supervise the students. Each student had the opportunity to drill and fill several teeth on patients.

Graduation Day again was very exciting. The students not only got their diplomas, but they all received the equipment, instruments, and supplies needed for doing dentistry out in their native jungle villages. This is something they would never have been able to buy in their entire lifetime. The 10 students that learned to do fillings were able to keep their drills and solar panels.

Shortly after graduation, Stan and I, with all of our remaining supplies and equipment, took off by plane to go and teach another course. This time we were going to teach the course deep in the heart of the jungle at one of the larger villages. Wycliffe had determined that it would be much cheaper to transport the native students who lived deep in the jungle near the Brazilian border to this large village, rather than to bring each of them all the way back to Lomalinda. There were also lots of needy patients in this village. This all seemed to make good sense, but I was concerned, because I wouldn't have Beth, Dora May, Danielle, or Miguel to help me.

When we landed I noticed another Helio Courier already at the end of the runway, and then as we started to unload, another one landed. They were bringing students in for the course. Shortly the planes took off to get more students. There were a large number of people on the side of the runway, especially children, because of all the planes that were coming and going. We had no problem getting help to carry our equipment and supplies a quarter of a mile down to the village, which was located on the banks of a fairly large tributary of the Amazon River.

This village had a Catholic priest, a church, and an elementary school. The Catholic priest had been working with and supporting the Wycliffe translators in the translation of their verbal language into a written language, teaching them how to read and write, and in translating the whole Bible into their language. The translation had now been completed, and the Bible was available in the church, or from the priest, for anyone who wanted it.

There were a lot of people speaking languages that I didn't understand. It was a little intimidating. I stuck very close to Stan, who was the only person with whom I could communicate. I was a long way from home, and was feeling a little uncomfortable.

We ate supper with the priest, in a small room at the mission school. Most all the students were from surrounding jungle villages, so they had to room and board at the school. Some of these elementary students had walked for several days alone through the jungle to come to school. We heard a lot of stories of their adventures which occurred on their trips to and from school.

One thing unusual I noticed when we ate supper was that each leg of the table was sitting in the middle of a tuna fish type can, which was half full of oil. Naturally, I had to ask, "Why?" "Simple," the priest said, "It keeps the ants and other crawling bugs off the table. They can't swim through the oil." That made good sense. Why didn't I think of that?

After supper the priest asked Stan if he would like to accompany him to the big guest house, because the villagers were gathering there tonight. That day had been a special day, where the village men all gathered together to work on a common community project. On these special days when they did that, the women would get together and prepare a drink for them, which the priest said was a home-brewed alcohol.

Stan told the priest, "Sure, we would like to go," so I followed closely behind them. When we entered this large, somewhat dark guest house, the women were sitting on one side with their containers of home brew, and the men sat on the other side. There must have been over 50 people.

The priest started on the women's side, slowly shaking hands with each of them, and saying a little something to each one. It seemed obvious that he knew them all. Stan followed along and shook hands with each one also, and said something to them. I felt awkward, but I followed Stan, shaking hands with each of the women, but not saying anything to them, because I didn't speak their language. I just nodded and smiled.

As I got almost to the end of the line, when one young woman looked up at me, smiled broadly, and said in very good English, "Hello, Dr. Charlick." I almost dropped dead in my tracks. I thought I was near the end of the earth, and suddenly I was greeted by name by this unknown Indian woman deep in the middle of the Amazon jungle. I trust you can understand why I was flabbergasted. After I got over the shock, I asked her how she knew my name. She just shrugged her shoulders and smiled. I asked her two or three other questions, but she didn't answer. Stan recognized my situation, and he said to me, "Don't you recognize her? She was in your dental class last year." Sorry, I didn't recognize her. Stan said, "Remember when Beth taught the class to say, "Hello, Dr. Charlick," when you came to class each morning. That's the only English she knows." Well, yes, I did remember Beth teaching them that, but you can be sure, I will better remember the shock and surprise that this gal gave me that evening.

That night we stayed in the Wycliffe translators' home. They were not in the village at this time, and they had given Stan an invitation to stay in their home. Their house was like all the other native houses, made of sticks, mud, and thatching. As we climbed into our sleeping bags, and turned off our flashlight, I remarked to Stan, "Boy, it is dark." You couldn't see your hand in front of your nose. There were all types of strange sounds coming from the village and the jungle. I just pulled my sleeping bag over my head and finally went to sleep.

I was awakened in the middle of the night by a strange rustling and squeaking noise. It sounded close. I got my flashlight and peeked out of my sleeping bag. I rather quickly located the noisy ruckus. There were two big rats, and I mean big rats, on the rafter pole directly above my head, and they were fighting. The dirt and dust they were stirring up was falling down in my eyes. I thought about what would happen if one of them fell while they were fighting. They would land directly on my head. I quickly turned off my flashlight, pulled my sleeping bag as far as I could over my head, and squirmed down deep into my sleeping bag. I said a little prayer, "Lord, Lord, help!" Shortly the noise disappeared and I got back to sleep, but I stayed well down inside my sleeping bag. That was just another memory I will never forget.

Next morning at breakfast, I was introduced to a government dentist, who had been requested to come in from the jungle and help me. He was also a recent graduate working off his dental school debt to the government. His instructions to help me were not very clear. At first he was very reluctant to help, for fear he might get caught teaching natives dentistry, and lose his dental license. Stan talked to him for quite a while, explaining what Dr. Neda had told us, and explained how Dr. Miguel had helped us so well the week before. Finally, he started to relax, and when I asked him if he would like to do some of the lecturing he said, "Yes." He proceeded to give the students a short lecture on AIDS.

My lectures and slides went well. Just before we were ready to start working on patients, a beautiful young Spanish looking girl, walked in from the jungle with a backpack on, and introduced herself as Susie, a government dentist who had been instructed to come and help us. She didn't hesitate to help us at all.

As we started working on patients, I put Susie in charge of two dental chairs, teaching prevention, hygiene, and cleaning teeth. She was enthusiastic, and her happiness rubbed off on the students. She did a great job. She could talk directly to them in Spanish. The male dentist I put in charge of two dental chairs doing extractions. Stan and I took the second-year dental students and taught them how to put in fillings. I had eight students, and eight drills, batteries, and solar panels.

After we had used the drills extensively one morning, removing decay on extracted teeth, I hooked them up to their solar panels, and set them out in the sun during lunch. I was pleasantly surprised to see how much the speed of the drills increased in just an hour recharging in the hot noontime sun.

The priest wanted us to check and treat his school students. After they had their morning assembly, they all lined up on an outside grassy clearing. We three dentists, using only tongue blades, rapidly examined the one hundred students, and had the teachers record which ones would need treatment. Along with the other villagers, we had more than enough patients.

I expressed my concern as to how we were going to teach suturing to the students. There was a little older student by the name of Kato and he was really sharp. He and his wife had been in our class last year, and he was also a government trained healthcare promoter, from a village on the Brazilian border. Kato spoke up, and said, "I'll teach suturing." He was a very nice man, who had good self-confidence, and easily had the respect of the students. He taught outside of regular class time, because he didn't want to miss learning how to put in fillings. I watched him, and he did a fantastic job, and could speak directly in Spanish to the students.

One evening the priest started the generator so Stan could show "The Jesus Film." The area was packed, with people sitting and standing everywhere. Their attention and concentration on the film was amazingly good.

On Sunday we all went to the Catholic Church, where the priest preached a sermon. Just as he started to preach his sermon, it started raining very hard. The church had a tin roof, and the noise was very loud. The priest came down from the pulpit and walked up and down the central aisle screaming loudly due to the noise of the rain on the roof. Another thing different was there were three women sitting close to me who openly breast-fed their babies during the sermon, to keep them quiet.

After the service the priest showed us the Bibles that the natives had in their own language, and told us about the big celebration they had when they first received their Bibles. Then the priest said, "I don't know why it has to rain so hard every time I have an especially good sermon, oh well."

There were several mature young ladies walking around outside the church after the service. They were obviously different from the rest of the natives. They were dressed very nicely. I asked Stan about these girls, and he told me they were eligible young ladies just waiting for some young man to come from another native Indian tribe with a different language, and ask one of them to marry him. Then he would take her back home with him.

There was a large sturdy walking rope bridge over the river. I was surprised to hear that it was a gift from the people in Sweden. They brought all the materials and built the bridge for the people. As I was walking near the bridge, I was pleased to observe two of the school students sitting on a rock by the edge of the river diligently brushing their teeth with their new toothbrushes which we had just given them the day before.

I walked by the students dormitory. The windows were open so I looked in. There was one large empty room with not one bed or piece of furniture in it. I was startled. Then I saw the hammocks tied up to the posts. I remembered the sleeping arrangements that I had observed in the Big Houses. All these jungle natives sleep in hammocks and take them down and tie them up to one of the posts during the day. I guess I was shocked because it was just not what I expected a dormitory bedroom to look like.

Both our classes and our clinics went well, and I believe that every student received a lot of good practice working on patients. Soon it was time for graduation. The one thing that was different at this graduation that made it special was, as I gave a special thank you to Kato for teaching our suturing class, he motioned that he wanted to speak. He thanked me, and all those who taught him and his wife. He really appreciated it, but something more important had happened to him. He told the students how he had found Jesus, and had invited Him into his heart and his life, and he was now a changed man and a happier person. During the graduation another student spoke and he said that Kato had told him about Jesus and he had invited Jesus into his life also. It truly was a time of great celebration.

I guess I didn't notice or remember Stan videotaping the course and Kato's testimony, but sometime later I had another dentist come up to me and say, "What a great work you are doing in Colombia!" I asked him how he knew about it and he said, "I saw a video of the class you taught in Colombia at the American Dental Association Convention last year

122

in Seattle, Washington." Later Stan sent me a copy of the video, documenting my teaching dentistry in the Colombian jungle, and it included Kato's testimony.

When it was time to leave, and we started loading the plane, there was a group of about a hundred people that had gathered around the plane thanking us and singing to us. I usually gave each patient I treated a cloth red rose sticker which had become very popular. I even had one patient come to me and ask me to pull a good tooth, so he could get a rose sticker. I had a few left so I started handing them out to the people gathered around the plane. That was a mistake. I quickly started a stampede of people all trying to get a rose. I began to get a little concerned that the pilot wouldn't be able to start the plane, because there were so many people so near. Finally the pilot gave out a loud yell, and started the engine. The people quickly backed away and we were able to take off and return to Lomalinda.

Dora May, Beth, and Ed, had been helping out in various ways at Lomalinda, but after a month we were all ready to head home. The next morning we went to the airstrip to fly back to Bogotá. The DC-3 was not available, so they decided to take us in the Helio Couriers to the fairly large town of Villavicencio, on the eastern edge of the Andes Mountains. From there we could get a taxi to take us to Bogotá, which involved driving up a steep winding road about 10,000 feet.

The four of us couldn't all fit in one plane. There was also a family that was going home on furlough that needed to get to Bogotá. I got in the front seat of the plane with the pilot, and Dora May and a 12-year-old boy, from the family going on furlough, climbed into the back seat. After we had been airborne for about a half hour, the boy pulled a sock out of his pocket, and untied a knot in the end of it, and pulled out a baby boa constrictor about 2 feet long. Dora May, thankfully, kept her cool even though she has a fear of snakes. She didn't jump out or scream. She just suggested that the boy put the snake back in his sock. I was proud of her, although she really didn't have much choice. As he put it back, he said, "I just wanted to check and make sure it was okay." He was taking it to the U.S. to sell. I saw one later in a pet shop for sale for $350.

Our plane left first and as we were approaching Villavicencio our pilot observed an unusual and unexpected break in the clouds over the Andes, so he was able to fly us all the way to Bogotá. Beth and Ed, and the mother that was going home on furlough, took the next plane out, and followed us by about 30 minutes. When they arrived at Villavicencio the clouds were back, and they were forced to land. At Villavicencio the mother helped Beth and Ed get a taxi to take them up 10,000 feet and over the eastern ridge of the Andes Mountains and down onto the plateau where Bogotá was located, and directly to Wycliffe's guest house, where we were staying. Jim, Deb and family were out of the area at this time. The road up the mountain, known as the suicide highway, was the only road east out of Bogotá. It was very steep and treacherous, oftentimes with no guard rails, and lots of crosses along the side of the road where people had been killed. The taxi driver drove fast and wild. It was a scary thrilling five-hour ride.

Dora May and I were at the guest house, and didn't know what happened to Beth and Ed, or where they were. It started to get dark, so Dora May and I decided to get some supper. There was a small pizza restaurant just a half block away, so we told our host in the guest house where we were going. We were half finished eating supper, when in walked Beth and Ed. I made a big mistake by asking Beth, "Where have you been?" Beth ran over to me, put her arms around me, and started to sob hard. She had so much tension and apprehension built up in her that she was just about ready to burst.

After things settled down, she explained their harrowing experience coming up the mountain. We ate and went back to the guest house. I asked our host to help us reconfirm our flights back to Miami. By this time Eastern airlines had gone bankrupt, and we were flying Avianca Airlines, Colombia's National Airlines. Dora May's and my reservations were fine, but they couldn't find Beth's and Ed's reservations. I had the tickets right in my hand. Translation slowed our communication. Finally, they said they found their reservations, and they had been bumped off this flight. But how could that be? We had reservations for over a month. We had connecting domestic flights in Miami to reach Detroit, and both Beth and Ed had to work the next day. We were told, "Sorry, there is no way. They are off this flight, and that's final." After we hung up, I told our host about the stressful day that Beth and Ed had. I didn't think they were going to handle this very well.

Our host said, "Let me call Avianca, and see if I can work something else out." He called and talked and talked and talked. Finally he turned to me and said, "They can put all four of you on a local domestic plane to Cali, which is the country's second-largest city. From Cali you can get a direct flight to Miami, and if the flight is on time, you can catch your domestic flight from Miami to Detroit." With a big sigh of relief, I said, "Book it." He did, and we got home on schedule with no further problems.

## And Now the Rest of the Story

Stan wrote me a couple of months later, and said, "Miguel came to me and said he likes working with the native Indians and with Wycliffe. He said his obligation with the government was completed, and he asked if there were any way he could work full time with Wycliffe. His monthly salary was $40 a month." Stan thought that was a great idea, so several of the translators got together and raised the needed funds for Miguel, primarily from a Canadian source.

Miguel offered to teach future classes. I offered to give him copies of my audiovisual materials. He agreed to keep the native Indians which we had trained as dentists, supplied. He also offered to go out to the jungle locations where we had trained native dentists, and to work with them, and help train them further. It really sounded great, and it actually worked out very well.

Miguel's Christian faith grew stronger, and he fell in love with one of the translator's daughters. She had graduated from high school at Lomalinda, and had gone to college in the U.S., and had received a teaching degree. She returned to Lomalinda and was teaching at their school. She and Miguel got married and things worked out very well. At one point Miguel and his wife had to return to the U.S. and both get jobs to pay off her school loans. Miguel couldn't work as a dentist, so he worked in a Pizza Hut. As soon as they had her school loans paid they returned to Colombia, and continued to work for Wycliffe.

I was happy and disappointed. I work myself out of a job, and they didn't need me anymore in Colombia. I guess it's a sign of a good missionary, when a person can train the locals to do the work themselves, so that he can move on to another mission field. I just thanked and praised the Lord. Where to next, Lord? I personally have no idea, but I'm sure He knows. I just need to be patient and continue to put my trust and faith in Him.

# CHAPTER 11

# ZAIRE-CONGO

Shortly after returning from Zimbabwe, our church had a visit from Jack and Trissie Rumohr. They had been American Baptist Missionaries in Zaire, (now named Democratic Republic of Congo), for 30 years. Our church had financially supported them for many years. They were on furlough and were reporting to the churches that supported them. In addition to Jack's many missionary duties, he had his own airplane, which our church helped him buy many years ago. He provided transportation to the remote central areas in Zaire.

After Jack's and Trissie's Sunday morning report, our church sponsored a dinner in their honor. We only have the opportunity to personally see them once every five years when they come home on furlough. After dinner I had a chance to talk with Jack, and discuss my dental missions to Colombia and Zimbabwe. He said, "That is something we could really use in Zaire. Any chance you and Dora May could come to Zaire and help us?" I thought, why not? We don't have any other mission trips planned, so I said, "Sure."

As always, there was a lot of planning. I needed to work through the International Ministries Office of the American Baptist Churches/USA. Tourists were not welcomed in Zaire. You were required to have an invitation which needed to be approved by their government. The American Baptist International Ministries office helped Dora May and me to obtain the needed invitation, approval and documents.

We reserved our airline tickets, and assembled our equipment and supplies, primarily from my private dental office. We finished packing our luggage to the maximum weight limit a few days early. The day before we were to leave, a United Parcel Service truck delivered a package to our front porch. I thought, we haven't ordered anything. I went to pick it up and discovered it was unusually heavy. I brought it into the house, opened it, and found a large oversized car battery. This puzzled me because I knew we hadn't ordered any battery, I was unsure what to do or who to call.

Shortly the phone rang, and a man on the other end said, "Jack Rumohr ordered an airplane battery, and asked me to send it to you. He said it's very important that you bring it to him." While that explained where the battery had come from, how was I going to carry it? It was too big to fit into my suitcase, and it would take up most of my weight allowance. It would probably break in the suitcase if it got thrown around. Besides, my suitcase was filled to the limit with supplies and equipment. What was I going to do with my supplies? I finally decided to put it in my carry-on. This was before I had one with wheels. It was also before they x-rayed carry-ons. Mine was a leather bag with two handles. I tried it and it fit ok, but it was so heavy. I packed a few things around it, put some things in other bags, and took out a number of my used toothbrushes. It looked like it might work.

The airlines usually weigh suitcases carefully, and all of our suitcases were exactly 70 pounds. Carrying the battery was the only practical option. When I picked up my leather bag, I could see the stitching on the handles straining, so I carried it close to the floor in case the threads would break. Thankfully, the airlines didn't usually weigh carry-ons. I did well carrying it with regular rest stops, except when I had to put it in the overhead carry-on compartment on the plane. This took all the muscle I had. I was hoping that the stewardess didn't see my face turning red or she might have become suspicious.

Shortly before we were scheduled to leave, the Desert Storm Gulf War began. When we arrived at the airport there were armed national guards stationed outside. You had to have an airline ticket to go inside the airport. Once inside, I could have shot a cannon through the lobby without hitting anyone. The lobby was empty, and it created a rather eerie feeling. Our luggage got an unusual inspection. I had to do some fast talking when they opened our suitcases and found several thousand used toothbrushes, but they finally accepted my reasons, and let them go.

We took off for Kinshasa, Zaire, in early February 1991. We had no flight problems, and were met at the airport by Glen Chapman. He met us after immigrations, but before customs. He had a young man load our luggage onto a cart. We went around customs without even slowing down, and went directly to Glen's pickup. We loaded up, and were gone in no time. I commented to Glen, "This is the easiest we have ever gotten through customs." He said, "You saw me pay him, didn't you?" I commented, "I thought that was just a normal porter's tip." Glen smiled and said, "No one gets through customs in Zaire without paying." I had never in my life had to pay to get through customs. Oh well! I guess there's a first time for everything.

We went directly to the American Baptist Headquarters Compound in Kinshasa. The American Baptists have concentrated their mission efforts in Zaire for over 125 years. They have many mission outposts, churches, schools, and hospitals all over the country.

Kinshasa is the capital of Zaire with a population of several million, and it contains the country's main International Airport. The American Baptist Compound consisted of about 10 acres, with many different buildings. We stayed in the guest quarters.

I asked Glen if I could exchange some American money into the Zairian currency since we were scheduled to stay for a month. Glen's comment was, "Are you sure you want to? I doubt that you will need it." I answered, "Yes, I'm sure. I always carry some local currency for emergencies, shopping, etc." I gave Glen a $100 bill, and he came back with a stack of bills several inches high, all 100,000 denominations. Glen commented, "The country has been experiencing a big problem with inflation."

We went to the grocery store the next morning with Glen, and noticed a big sign in the front window. All I could read was 20%. Upon inquiring Glen told us, "The sign says, sorry our prices increased 20% overnight. We are used to that, since it occurs two or three times a week these days." I thought to myself, this is unbelievable.

Glen was born to missionary parents, and raised in Zaire. He had returned to the U.S. for college. After college he came back to Zaire as an American Baptist Missionary, and was currently stationed at the Headquarters in Kinshasa, before being transferred to a mission station.

Zaire used to be called Belgium Congo, as it was a Belgian Colony. When Congolese violently overthrew the Belgian regime, the country received its independence, after which the country was renamed Zaire. The Belgian people left the country, which included all the educated and technology experts. It was a massive brain drain. That happened about 30 years before we arrived. Since that time, when something became broken there wasn't anyone to fix it. Their phone system was 90% broken. We went by a relatively nice unoccupied 20 story glass office building. When I inquired, Glen told me that the elevators were broken, and no one knew how to fix them. The air conditioners were also not working with no one to fix them. Kinshasa was normally very hot and the windows wouldn't open, so it sat empty.

We saw garbage piled in the center of the residential streets as high as the houses, with large dead rats around the base. Glen said, "There has not been a garbage pickup in some areas in 30 years, since the Belgian people left."

The government, when we arrived, was a military dictatorship under President Mobutu. There were soldiers with rifles everywhere. Glen told us, "President Mobutu does not allow any of the soldiers to have bullets for their guns. Only his personal guards have live ammunition." I had no idea the country was in such dangerous chaos.

The second day after we arrived, Glen took us early in the morning to a small private airport. We loaded our luggage onto a single engine plane, operated by MAF, (Missionary Aviation Fellowship). We met a chunky black Zairian pilot, who spoke good English and was very pleasant. He indicated that Jack Rumohr had requested that he fly us out to his village. This surprised me a little because I assumed Jack would pick us up in his plane. We learned that MAF had to go out near Jack's area to pick up other passengers, and it made more sense to have passengers flying both directions.

It was a beautiful morning. We took off and left the big capital city of Kinshasa, and flew out over beautiful green rolling hills. The thing that puzzled me was there was nothing on these beautiful green hills, no cattle, sheep, villages or any signs of life. We flew for several hours crossing numerous deep river valleys, and finally we landed on a small grassy runway out in the middle of nowhere.

Because of good radio communications, Jack was there to meet us. We loaded our gear into a Land Rover and headed down a grassy trail as the plane left. We were soon in dense vegetation, where thick heavy sharp leaves towered 5 to 10 feet over our Land Rover. The vegetation bent into our path, and almost totally closed it. Sometimes you couldn't see 5 feet in front of the vehicle. Jack continued to plow through this vegetation until suddenly we popped out into a large clearing, with lots of buildings around the edge, and with a church in the middle.

We drove to the far side of the clearing across the grass. There were no signs of a path or trail in the grass anywhere. It turned out this was the only vehicle in the whole area. We came to one of the nicer houses in the corner of the clearing, and found out this was Jack and Trissie Rumohr's home for the last 30 years. We greeted Trissie, unloaded our gear, and had lunch.

Jack spent the afternoon showing us around the mission complex, which was called Moanza. When Jack came here 30 years ago, this was just a level clearing, that he, the American Baptist leaders, and the local native leaders thought would make a nice place for their mission outpost. Several other missionaries came, and with their help and some of the local people, they built a church, school, hospital, and several homes. Many of the local natives moved to the surrounding area. If they had a child in the mission school, the child would need a place to stay and eat, so the family moved to the area. It was impressive how Moanza had been developed with the church in the middle, surrounded by several acres of grass, and then on the outside of the clearing, in the shade of the trees was the school, hospital, several missionaries' houses, and many of the local natives' houses.

Behind Jack's house was a runway. It was not flat. It had a little dip in the middle, but Jack thought it worked just fine. Evidently the MAF pilot didn't think so, because he wouldn't land on it, and that's why we went to the other landing strip. About 20 feet in back of Jack's house, and just a little to the side, was a concrete slab with a roof over it where Jack's plane was tied down.

I asked Jack, "Why didn't I see any cattle, sheep, or any signs of life on the beautiful green hills we flew over coming from Kinshasa?" Jack answered, "Do you remember the tall vegetation we drove through coming here? That's what covers those hills. It is 10 to 15 feet tall, and so dense you couldn't walk through it. If you even tried, the sharp leaves would cut you to ribbons." Ok! Now I understand.

Jack expressed great appreciation for the battery we brought him. He said, "My airplane battery went bad, and I had to replace it with my spare. If I had ordered a new one, it would take six to nine months for it to get here, and sometimes it might never arrive, because things were often stolen on the way."

The next morning when Jack, Trissie, Dora May, and I were sitting around the table eating breakfast, Jack suddenly jumped up and ran quickly out to his plane. I was right behind him. He went to the tail of the plane, and knelt down next to a puddle of fluid on the concrete slab. He put his finger in the liquid, and lightly touched it to his tongue. His comment was, "Oh, no!" Without another word he went to his tool box, and got a screwdriver and started taking a panel off the side of the plane near the tail. Guess what? Inside was the battery. It was split right down the middle, and cracked wide open. The puddle on the concrete was the acid from the battery. Jack turned to me and said, "Good thing you brought me a battery, or you might have been here for a long time."

There was one medical doctor, a general physician named Dr. Mulembakani Mongombo, who was in charge of the hospital at the mission station. He was a young Zairian with a wife and three year old twin girls. The American Baptists couldn't get a medical missionary to come to this rather primitive and remote mission station, and if they did, they only stayed for a short time.

Jack and some of the other missionaries thought of an idea to solve this problem. They would take one of their brightest students from the mission school and personally pay his way to go to college, and to medical school in Europe, if he would promise to come back and run the hospital. This is exactly what they did, and Dr. Mongombo had been there five years and was doing a great job. Not only did Dr. Mongombo run the hospital, and a nursing school, but he was responsible for the health of over one million people in the surrounding area. Moanza was located near the geographic center of Zaire.

Jack had discussed with Dr. Mongombo ahead of time how I might best help. Jack had warned me that I probably would be doing some teaching, so I brought some of my teaching materials that I used in Colombia and Zimbabwe. Dr. Mongombo decided to bring back to the hospital 40 nurses he had trained and sent to remote health clinics, so I could give them dental training. They were all males. I used a large room at the school, and Jack furnished me with a primitive slide projector. Dora May projected the slides while I lectured. We covered the causes of dental diseases, prevention, and some treatments.

The local natives had very little decay in their teeth, probably because they had very little sugar in their diets. Their main complaint and problem was gum infection, with swollen, painful, and bleeding gums. There was little value for me to tell them to brush and floss their teeth, and develop good hygiene, unless I could convince them of the reason why it was necessary. I had many slides which showed red, swollen, infected gums, which were treated only by brushing and flossing. The results as indicated by follow-up slides, showed almost totally healed gums with no more redness, swelling, or infection after a few months of only brushing and flossing. These were actually true cases from the university, and this greatly impressed and motivated the nurses.

Now they knew how and why to treat their patients that were complaining of painful, swollen, bleeding gums. The nurses were very attentive, and got excited when I gave them each two bundles containing 40 or 50 toothbrushes each at the end of the course. I had brought two suitcases full, 140 pounds, of good sterile used toothbrushes. You would have thought that I had given them gold. Jack told me that a toothbrush would normally cost about one week's wages, but the even bigger problem was, they weren't available to buy. They were extremely happy to get these brushes.

I taught them how to make a stick toothbrush and dental floss from the fibers in a common cactus leaf, like I did in Colombia. I then taught them how to brush and floss properly. They practiced brushing and flossing on themselves using mirrors, and then on each other. Most of them had never seen or heard of a toothbrush or floss before, and they previously had no oral hygiene. Most of them had never seen slides before. They were a very excited and an appreciative group. I truly had fun teaching them.

A 23-year-old American Oriental male, Steve, was working in the area as a Peace Corps Volunteer. He had graduated from Harvard, and had been accepted into the Harvard Medical School, but he wanted a break from school. He decided to do something different, yet worthwhile, for one year, so he joined the Peace Corps. Steve's father was a prominent surgeon in the U.S., and was disappointed with his son's decision, but Steve promised his dad, he would come back next year and pursue his medical degree. Steve volunteered to work as my translator, during the time I was teaching the nursing students. He was a great help.

Dr. Mongombo and the missionaries had been requesting a Peace Corps volunteer for some time to come and help them with their water problem. Dr. Mongombo said he felt he was wasting a lot of his time, because he was treating patients with infections caused by contaminated water. After he got them healed using antibiotics, they were right back in a few weeks with the same water contaminated infection. This was a continuous cycle for which he could see no end. Dr. Mongombo threatened to stop practicing medicine to develop a safe water supply to prevent these diseases, thinking it might be a more valuable use of his time, but he was kept very busy with other medical problems. Hernias were a very common problem and frequently resulted in death if not treated. He usually did several hernia operations each day.

When Steve first checked with the Peace Corps administrators, they explained Dr. Mongombo's problem with the contaminated water. Steve offered to come for a year, and try to solve this water problem. When he arrived, Dr. Mongombo and Steve sat down and created a plan to develop safe drinking water.

The Belgian authorities, when the Congo was still a Belgian Colony, had persuaded the natives to move their villages from the river banks to the high plateaus, because of malaria and numerous other insect transmitted diseases that were causing great health problems. There were few, if any, of these insects present in the higher dry plateaus. In order for the natives to get water, they had to walk over a mile down a dense jungle path to the river. Then they had to carry it back up to the plateau, usually on their heads. Water was very precious, but even then the river water was frequently contaminated and caused infections.

There were springs where water trickled out of the side of the hill, about one third of the way down toward the river. We went with Steve one day, down to where he had made this spring water available and safe for drinking. He had dug a trench 10 to 15 feet back into the hill in the area of the spring. He built a 5 foot dam at the lower end with a pipe through the dam about 3 feet off the ground. The seeping spring water collected in this dugout trench, and when it got high enough to reach the pipe, the water ran out of the pipe at a fairly good rate. In order to make the water safe he had covered the pool of water with poles, palm branches, and a foot of dirt. This kept all the bugs, and airborne bacteria out of the water, and the water came out of the pipe directly from underground. It was clear, clean, safe spring water. It was actually very simple and it worked well.

Steve had tested the water and found it to be safe. The natives didn't have to walk all the way down to the river to get the infected water, and risk getting infected from insect bites in the process. They only had to walk one third of the way down, where they could get safe spring water. Dr. Mongombo quickly noticed a significant drop in infections related to contaminated water.

Steve had been there almost a year. One time when Dr. Mongombo was away from the hospital, Steve developed a severe case of malaria. It was so severe that he became delirious with fever. He was living a short distance from Moanza. When the missionaries heard about the severity of his condition, they went and brought him back to their house. They treated him intensively 24 hours a day for several days, until he recovered. Steve said that he would have probably died, if the missionaries hadn't taken him in and treated him so aggressively. He felt he owed his life to the missionaries, so he and the missionaries had become close friends.

We had an opportunity to visit where Steve lived one Sunday afternoon. He elected to live in one of the nearby villages, in the same type of primitive mud and thatched roof huts as the natives. He was greatly respected by the natives. On our way back from his house, there was a group of children that gathered along the side of the path. I couldn't help but observe the condition of their clothing. One boy in particular had on a T-shirt that was literally torn to shreds with numerous large holes in it. I commented to Steve that his shirt looked pretty well used. He said, "Most of them only have one set of clothes." I asked him, "Where do they get their clothes? I didn't see any stores in the area." Steve admitted, "There are no stores anywhere, and if there were, these people don't have any money anyway. Jack brings bundles of used clothes that he picks up in Kinshasa. They are sent to Zaire by charitable organizations in the U.S., like the Salvation Army."

One young boy, 4 or5 years old, who sat there smiling and waving at us, had a problem with one of his eyes. It was swollen, red, and had something white over the pupil, with pus running out of the corner of his eye. I took a close-up picture of his eye, and as a result of seeing it repeatedly, it is permanently embedded in my memory. I felt so sorry for him, and wished there were something I could do, but I guess I had more than I could handle, just treating infections in the mouth.

I taught the nursing students each morning and early afternoon. In the late afternoon Dr. Mongombo had me set up my dental extraction clinic in a small room in the front part of his private office. The first patient I saw was a very beautiful, well-dressed young lady that had a badly decayed and infected lower first molar. She said, "This tooth has been aching for two years." The tooth was so painful I could hardly touch it with my finger without causing severe pain. I anesthetized it while Dr. Mongombo watched closely. In about five minutes, after it got numb, I simply got hold of it with the proper forceps, and removed it in about 30 seconds without causing any pain.

Dr. Mongombo was absolutely astonished. He then told me this story: "This young lady is my sister, and she lives with me. I have observed how much pain she has endured for the last two years, because many times it was so painful it disabled her to the point she could hardly do anything, even around the house. I didn't have any local anesthesia, but I tried to remove the tooth on several occasions at her request, and had always been unsuccessful, and just made it worse." Then he said to me, "Will you teach me how to do that?" Again my answer was, "Sure, however I can help."

We started that very evening with the basics of dental anatomy, including the number, size, and shape of the roots, location of the nerves and blood vessels, where to put the local anesthesia, how much anesthesia to use, which instruments to use, how to get hold of the tooth, which way to rock or to twist it, etc. The next day I went over everything again while working on patients, and he watched carefully and asked many good questions. He learned very fast. Within a couple of afternoons Dr. Mongombo was giving anesthesia and extracting teeth himself. He usually was treating patients and doing general surgery until late afternoon. Our teaching and practice was limited to late afternoon and early evening. Dr. Mongombo was very happy and excited to learn how to extract teeth. He got his head nurse, and asked if I would start teaching him how to extract teeth also. I left Dr Mongombo a good supply of anesthesia and several good forceps when we left Moanza.

Jack and Trissie were great hosts. We ate well, and they took care of our every need. Jack had a tin roof on his house, and he carefully collected rainwater into several barrels. Water was precious. For our evening bath we were given a few quarts of water in a small bucket with a washcloth and soap. It worked well, and felt good because the weather was very hot and humid. At night when we went to bed, I perspired so much that after a while, the sheets would be soaking wet. When I turned over, the wet sheets, for a few moments, felt cool. I can never remember sweating that much at night in my whole life.

One day Jack had a big palm tree cut down next to his house. It was getting old, and he was afraid it would fall on the house. That evening we had a very special treat for supper.

We ate the heart from the top center of the palm tree, where the new palm leaves were just starting to form. This was considered a great delicacy. It was the consistency of potatoes, and the taste was actually pretty good. We were glad that Trissie didn't feed us one of their other native delicacies. She had a couple of gallons of dried brown fuzzy caterpillars, which she saved and gave to the natives that did a special good deed for her. She said, "It is like giving them ice cream to eat." Yuck!

One night we were invited next door to Bob and Anelise Smith's for supper. They were both teachers in the school, and had helped start it many years ago, but they had currently turned the management and most of the teaching over to the Zairians. They acted mainly as advisers. The Smiths were born and raised in northern Indiana, not too far from where we live.

There are two things I remember about that evening. We had hamburger gravy for supper, which tasted exactly like my mother used to make. It was one of my favorites, and I complimented our host, Anelise, accordingly. The second thing I will never forget. I went to the bathroom and urinated in a regular U.S.-type bathroom stool, and flushed it as usual. Anelise promptly and rather firmly informed me that water was precious, and the rule in their house was, "If it's brown, you flush it down, but if it's yellow, you let it mellow." This was a good philosophy that I've never forgotten, and have actually used it on several occasions.

One evening Dr. Mongombo invited Dora May and me over to his house for supper with him and his wife. His sister would take care of their young twin daughters, who were sick with malaria. She was feeling much better. I asked Jack what we should do. He talked with the doctor and told us it was ok to go. He assured me that all of your food would be cooked thoroughly, so it would be safe. We had a nice supper and good conversation. They both spoke excellent English.

The main staple of the African diet is called manioc. It is a big root tuber, similar to potatoes but much larger. The plant grows 6 to 8 feet tall in dry sandy poor soil. Originally it was imported from South America where they called it yucca. In Zimbabwe they called it sosa. Of course, we had to have manioc for supper. No African meal would be complete without it. It was prepared like mashed potatoes, but had a little bitter taste. It was the first and only time we ever ate manioc. It was full of sand. I had never eaten anything full of sterile sand in all my life, but we never said a word. It was an unusual and different experience. We didn't get sick. Jack told us later that it was difficult to get the sand out of the manioc unless it would be peeled like potatoes, and that would waste a lot of valuable food. It was normal for them to have a little sand in their manioc.

On Sunday we went to church. Jack didn't usually preach, but he did that day. He had an unusual method of preaching. About every fourth or fifth sentence he would ask the congregation a question, and they would all answer in unison. We didn't understand what they were saying but you can be sure, no one went to sleep. The church was packed. For the collection everyone filed up to the table in front of the pulpit and put their money in a Joshua chest, while the congregation sang lively spirited songs. Two men removed the money almost as fast as it was put in the collection plate, and counted it. At the end of the collection, they stopped singing, and the native pastor announced the amount, and said it wasn't enough, so they started singing again, and took up another collection, which was enough that time.

After church, people stood out in front of the church talking. It was a lovely cool sunny morning, and the bright colored, long dresses on the women sparkled with beautiful bright colors. Women had their hair braided in unique designs like I had never seen, and not two of them were alike. I took several pictures of their dresses and hair designs. They were beautiful.

At the end of the week we had a graduation ceremony for the nurses. We gave each of them a special diploma for completing their dental training. Diplomas were rare and a real big deal in remote third world areas. The doctor encouraged all the nurses to return home to their native villages, because he said, "Your people are going to be waiting for you to treat them." Many of them had several days of walking to get home. The nursing students from the hospital returned to work at the hospital.

There was not one store in or around Moanza. You couldn't buy anything. When we left Zaire one month later, we had not spent one bill of the several inch stack that Glen had exchanged for us. It was then that we understood why he was reluctant to exchange our money in the first place.

One day Jack offered to take us to a waterfall using the mission station's only vehicle, the four-wheel drive Land Rover. It turned out to be almost a whole day's trip. Jack indicated that it was impractical, and frequently impossible to drive to Kinshasa. It depended on if the rivers were high or low, whether the ferries were working, and if it had rained a lot, which could make the roads muddy and impassable. It still would take several days. It was only a few hours by plane.

We drove for two or three hours through tall grass, across the plains, through the heart of several heavily populated villages, on a two-track grassy trail, where sometimes you could hardly see the trail. The people were curious and lined the road when we came into a village. In one village a man along the side of the road wanted to sell us a couple of cute playful baby leopards.

We came to a river, where there was no bridge. There was a crude log raft along the shore, so using our 4-wheel drive, and with some difficulty, we drove onto it. Using poles, we pushed our way across the river. Fortunately the raft was guided by a cable, so we didn't float down river.

We finally arrived at a very pretty waterfall, and ate our picnic lunch. Before we headed back, Jack showed us how the natives cross the river. In a nearby wooded area the trees hung over the river, where you could actually cross the river by climbing through the trees.

I tried it a little, and felt like a monkey. I got scared and returned to shore, because the water was running very rapidly, and it looked dangerous if I were to slip and fall. I was a long way from home to have an unnecessary accident.

We returned on the same two-track path. Jack indicated that this path was the main road, if we did try to go to Kinshasa. The rivers and the rafts were a significant problem, he said, because sometimes they were broken or nonexistent because they had been washed down the river. As we were returning, we went through the village where the man was still trying to sell the two leopard cubs. Steve was with us, and requested that we stop. After petting the cubs, he fell in love with them, and had to take them home with him. He kept them in his small round mud hut, by making bars for the door. One day while he was away, they dug a hole through the side of the mud hut and escaped. No one ever saw them again. We returned to the mission having had a very unique experience crossing through part of rural Central Africa.

Jack said he would like to fly us to the village of Tonu. He and Trissie had adopted the people of Tonu as a personal evangelistic mission project. They had built a little house in this village, and they tried to visit it every few months, to help teach and encourage the pastor, and the many new Christians they had been able to win to the Lord.

Jack, Dora May, and I took off one beautiful sunny morning, and flew one hour and a half directly south. I sat in front with Jack, and he pointed out the rivers, villages, and landmarks as we flew. Trissie was on the radio back home, as always, when Jack was flying, following his progress.

Evidently Jack had radioed the pastor ahead of time and told him he was coming and bringing a dentist, because when we touched down on the little grassy runway, there were over a hundred people on the side of the runway waiting for us. They cheered as we got out of the plane. After our greetings and introductions, we started down a slight hill toward the village.

The natives had built a pathway several hundred yards long, leading toward the village, by sticking 4 to 6 foot palm branches into the ground on either side of the path, and putting palm branches on the ground in the middle of the path. The natives excitedly gathered around us as we walked down this palm lined path. I said to Jack, "I almost feel like Jesus on Palm Sunday." Jack did admit this was special.

The natives took us directly to the house that Jack built. Over the years, Jack and Trissie had brought building supplies in their plane and built a nice little house in which they lived whenever they came. Jack unlocked the house and we went inside. It was dark, hot, and stuffy. Jack opened the shutters to let in some breeze and light. There was no electricity in this village. Jack had put screens over the window openings but all of them had very neat 6-inch perfectly round holes cut out of the screens. Upon inquiring about the holes, Jack said, "The natives have a fine strainer or sieve that they use to clean the twigs, stones, and bugs out of their manioc that they had pounded into powder. When the screen breaks they needed to replace it."

Jack had left them an extra roll of screen, but evidently they had used it all. He wasn't the least bit upset, and just said, "I guess I will have to bring some more screen next time."

We had a nice lunch at the native Zairian pastor's house, where we ate all of our meals. Jack brought food supplies for the pastor. After lunch I was introduced to my interpreter who was going to work with Dora May and me. He was the only one in the village who could speak English. His name was Tad, and he was the English teacher in their small village school. I asked him why anyone way out here would want to learn English, and he said, "If you don't know English, you are a nobody."

We walked about a quarter of a mile through the village, to a three-room medical clinic. We met a very friendly and pleasant middle-aged gentleman they called Nurse, who was in charge of the clinic. Nurse had us set up our dental clinic in one of the three rooms, and shortly we were extracting aching, abscessed teeth.

Nurse watched very carefully, and finally asked, "Would you teach me how to extract teeth?" I was a little reluctant without Jack's and Dr. Mongombo's permission, and furthermore, I didn't have any supplies or forceps to leave with him, so I just encouraged him to watch for now.

We were there three days. Jack kept very busy in the village, counseling with the pastor and church leaders. He led a Bible study in the church twice a day. We hardly saw him except at meal times and at night.

One afternoon Nurse brought a lady patient to me with several localized swellings under her jaw and in her neck. I examined her teeth and couldn't find any dental problems. I said to Nurse, "Her teeth look good, and the swellings weren't caused by any dental infection." He said, "Yes, I know that. The swellings are caused by very advanced TB (tuberculosis). I don't have any medicine to treat her, and I hoped you might have some medicine for her," but I didn't.

In the U.S. we are warned not even to be in the same room with a TB patient, and never to do anything in their mouth because TB is transmitted by airborne bacteria, and it is very contagious. In the U.S., TB patients are treated for dental problems under very special hospital conditions. Well, I had just been exposed big time, but the Lord protected us, because neither Dora May or I have ever had any TB problems.

Dora May worked closely with me and we made a great team. Together we extracted many infected painful teeth. With Dora May working with me it doubled the number of teeth that I was able to extract. We saw a lot of unusual dental conditions. At one point Nurse disappeared for an hour or so. When he returned he was smiling and said, "It was a boy." He had been in the next room where he had helped deliver a baby.

One teenage boy came to me with nice looking teeth but he had a fat lip. All his teeth were normal except he had two extra pointed teeth that grew straight out of his gums right in front, underneath his upper lip. They were distorting his appearance and making the inside of his lips sore. He was the only patient we treated that wasn't infected. It only took a couple of minutes to numb him and slide out those two extra teeth. He was most appreciative and couldn't stop thanking us.

I had a female school teacher come in complaining of an aching lower molar. Upon examination I found an infected impacted third molar. I have always been careful not to do surgery on things that were beyond my training and abilities. This looked like it could be very difficult. I told the lady I couldn't help her. She started crying and explained this had been aching for several years. I told her that she would need to go to a hospital where they were equipped to do that type of surgery. She explained to me that was impossible and started crying again. She started begging me. I really felt sorry for the lady. I finally said, "I will try to take it out but I will probably have to take the good molar out in front of it so I can get to the impacted tooth." She said, "Fine, do whatever you have to do, but get it out."

I didn't have an electric drill, special chisels, good lighting, suction or other things that oral surgeons had when they cut impacted third molars into pieces, before they take them out. She insisted I try and just do my best. I numbed her real good, and asked God for help. I took a scalpel and cut the tissue over the top of the tooth and opened it up so I could see it. There it was laying flat in the jaw bone, but at least I could see it now. I took one of my instruments and started to pry it, and surprise, it popped completely out all in one piece without touching the good molar in front of it. Boy was I happy. All I could say was, "Thank you, Lord."

When we packed up our dental clinic the last afternoon, Nurse came to me shaking a quart-sized empty plastic bottle. Tad said, "Nurse doesn't have even one aspirin. He wants to know if you have any extra aspirins that he could have." We gave all of our patients who had extractions either aspirin or Tylenol for their post-extraction discomfort. Nurse had seen my big aspirin bottle, and was begging me to spare some. I did have an extra bottle of a thousand aspirin tablets, so I gladly left it with him.

Nurse repeatedly asked me over and over if I would come back again with extra supplies and instruments, and teach him how to extract teeth. I felt this would be a tremendous service, and I told him I would try. But because a massive civil war broke out shortly after we left, I never got back, and to this day, it has bothered me.

The last night as we were walking back to the pastor's house, Tad showed us his school where he taught English. A memorable moment occurred when I saw a high school student, right in the middle of Africa, in this very remote village, walk by wearing a maize and blue University of Michigan T-shirt. It had the University of Michigan lettering on both the front and the back of the shirt. I asked Tad, "Where would he have ever gotten that shirt?" He said, "Occasionally Jack brings us a bale of used clothes and gives it to the village. It comes from the Salvation Army, or some other U.S. charitable organization. Actually that is where most all of our villagers' clothes come from."

Thankfully, we were able to care for everyone who came to us with aching teeth. I think we were able to accomplish a lot of good in a very short time. The next morning we had a large group of villagers accompany us to the landing strip, where we loaded the plane, said good bye, and took off. I can still see the many people that lined the runway waving to us as we took off; it surely made us feel appreciated.

We returned to the runway in back of Jack's house that had the dip in the middle. We had no trouble landing and taxied right up to the back door of his house. Jack had been on the radio with Trissie, and there was a small group of people waiting for us, including a couple of the nurses from the hospital, and a mother holding a young child. The nurses quickly explained to Jack, that Dr. Mongombo had gone with the Land Rover to try to get some medical supplies. This young child had a strangulated hernia, and unless he had an operation very soon, he would die.

Jack didn't even go into the house. He loaded the mother and child, and one of the nurses into the plane and immediately took off. Trissie said, "They are headed to Vanga, where there is a large mission hospital." Jack dropped the mother, child, and nurse off at Vanga, and he returned home. Jack received a radio message the next morning to come and pick up the mother, child and nurse. When he returned home, the family had gathered to meet the plane. When the mother got out of the plane she was crying, and the child was all covered up. The child didn't make it in time. He had died during the night shortly after surgery. There was a lot of crying and wailing as they walked away heading home.

I have always felt a little sad and actually guilty about that child's death, thinking that if we hadn't gone away with the plane, the child might have lived. Jack said, "Every time the doctor goes away there are always people who die because he isn't here, but if he doesn't have medicine, he can't help many people even if he stays here."

We could see across a big river valley from where Jack lived. Jack said it would take two days to cross that valley on foot, and 20 minutes to cross it by plane. You can see why his plane was so valuable in this remote area.

Jack had made arrangements for us to go to Kikongo for our last 10 days, and to help them with their dental needs. Our hosts were to be Orval Chapman and his wife, Jenny, both longtime American Baptist Missionaries, and good friends of Jack and Trissie. The American Baptists had built a Bible School at Kikongo to teach native young men how to be pastors and evangelists. Orval was currently teaching in the Bible school.

The next morning we packed and flew straight north for about two hours. We landed on a grassy landing strip alongside the fairly good sized village of Kikongo. As a result of good missionary radios, Orval was there to meet us. Jack introduced us. We then bid Jack farewell and he took off to fly back home. Orval took us to his home where we met his wife, Jenny, and unpacked our personal belongings in their guest bedroom.

After lunch Orval took us to meet the medical doctor, Dr. Zoko, who was in charge of their mission hospital. He was also a Zairian. Dr. Zoko indicated his people had a great number of dental problems, and he asked us to set up our clinic in one of the empty hospital rooms. Dora May and I set up and started extracting teeth. Dr. Zoko was one of our first patients. He had an abscessed, aching tooth which we numbed and took out for him quickly, with no pain. He was impressed, and immediately asked me to teach him how to do that.

Early the next morning we were up at 6 A.M. ready for breakfast. Orval was listening to the BBC on a small shortwave radio. He called to me and said, "Dick, come and listen to this." The news on the BBC was announcing that at 12 P.M. midnight, Washington, DC time, President Bush had just announced a U.S. victory in the Desert Storm Gulf War. He had ordered his troops to stop fighting in Kuwait, and the Iraqi soldiers were leaving the country and returning home. We celebrated the moment of good news.

Orval said, "At the start of the war, the Zairian government-operated newspaper came out with a front page story telling the Zairian people not to worry, because there was not one known Moslem in the entire country." I was amused at the thought that we, in the middle of the jungle in Africa, had heard about the end of the war before any of our family did in the U.S. It was 6 A.M. here in Zaire, but 12 midnight in the U.S. when President Bush made the announcement and all of our family was probably sleeping.

Our second morning of clinic Dr. Zoko came into the clinic ready to learn. I explained to him a lot of the basics as he watched me give anesthesia and extract teeth. By the end of the day I had him giving anesthesia and extracting teeth. He came back the third day and extracted a few more teeth, but finally said, "I need to get back to the hospital and catch up on some of my medical responsibilities." We left him some supplies and equipment. With Dora May's help, we became very efficient, and extracted a lot of aching teeth in this little temporary dental clinic.

Dr. Zoko also had called his nurses in from their remote surrounding village clinics, the same as Dr, Mongombo had done. He had me teach them the cause, prevention, and treatment of dental diseases. The class went well and the students were very attentive and enthusiastic. When we finished the classes, I gave each of the nurses a bundle of toothbrushes and a certificate at our little graduation ceremony. This was a big deal for these nurses because they never had any formal training or a certificate. They were just trained on the job by Dr. Zoko.

One special patient I saw in the dental clinic was an older white-haired Zairian man who was a professor at the Bible school. He spoke excellent English. He was an exceptionally nice man. He had a lower abscessed molar that had been aching for several years, and had been draining pus from a pimple-like opening under his chin. I anesthetized him, and had it removed in just a few minutes. A few days later, he invited Dora May and me, as a thank you, over for supper. After checking with Orval, we went and had an excellent meal and fellowship with him and his wife.

Sunday we went to church with Orval and Jenny. Needless to say, Zairian church services are very different from ours. It lasted two and one half hours. The singing was out of this world. They sang with great gusto and excitement. Every seat in this fairly large church of 300 to 400 was packed. The children were exceptionally well behaved. They had seven choirs in this church, but only three sang at this service. The adult women's choir sang just before the sermon. After they had sung a long time, the pastor finally got up, went to the pulpit, and started preaching by shouting over the singing. Slowly and gradually the women stopped singing. Orval said later, "That happens every Sunday. Unless the pastor gets up and starts preaching the women would never stop singing."

Sometimes when they prayed, they all prayed out loud at the same time. The part of the service that was most unique was the offering, which took over half an hour. Again, each person, one at a time, went forward and put their money in the Joshua chest, while the congregation sang. They just didn't sing ordinary hymns. They had a brass band that played very loudly, and they sang very fast high-spirited songs, with all the people shouting at the top of their voices, while clapping and dancing in their places or in the aisles. The offering was the last part of the service.

There was a lady sitting in front of me, about 30 years old, with two small children. The children had sat very patiently and quietly during the two-hour service before the offering. During the offering she and her children were singing, clapping, dancing, and shouting at the top of their voices. After I finished going up front with my offering, and as I was returning to my seat, I passed right in front of this formerly docile lady. She screamed at the top of her lungs just as my ear was passing inches in front of her mouth. I thought for sure I was going to be permanently deaf. I have never had a louder human sound hit my ear before or since.

The other thing that was unique about this collection was that once a year they gave the farmers and others who didn't have any money, the opportunity to give something from their gardens or crops as part of their offering. There were piles and piles of corn, wheat, coconuts, manioc, garden vegetables, peanuts, as well as several live chickens and pigs with their feet tied. There was a full pickup load of food products piled in front of the pulpit.

Sunday afternoon Orval took me down the side of the valley toward the river. This village again was built on a high plateau two miles away from the river, to avoid mosquitoes and infections that came from the river area. Kikongo had an agricultural missionary, and one of the projects he had accomplished was to secure and install a water pump. This had to be one of the most unique engineering marvels I had ever seen.

Halfway down the valley there was a large pump that made an extremely loud noise. There was no electricity available. This was a water-powered water pump. After the pump had been primed with water, the water ran sharply downhill inside a pipe for about 30 feet. This water running down the hill created enough energy to pump water one mile up from the river. 90% of the water was used to operate the pump and was eventually lost onto the ground after it powered the pump. The pump was strong enough to pump 10% of the remaining water another mile up the valley to the village of Kikongo.

When we got back to the top of the plateau, and into the village, there were several women waiting to put their open pail containers under a water spigot that was gushing water out of it like a fast running faucet. What a fantastic time and energy-saving piece of equipment that was. This unique, noisy, water-powered water pump was the first and only one I have ever heard about or seen.

One day Jenny said, "I bet you are getting hungry for a salad." We had learned early that you don't eat anything that is not boiled, baked, or peeled when in third world countries, and this principle certainly eliminated salads. Jenny took a few tiny black seeds and put them in a jar, and added a half inch of water, and said, "In a few days, we will have salad." In two days the jar was full with 6 inch high sprouts. She said, "These will be safe for you," and she fixed us a nice green sprout salad. It was good.

Orval and Jenny told us about raising their children on the mission field, and the unusual experiences they had. We found out that Glen Chapman who had picked us up at the airport in Kinshasa and was our host in Kinshasa, was their son.

On our last evening with Orval and Jenny, the men's choir from church, who hadn't had a chance to sing on Sunday, asked Orval if they could come and sing for Dora May and me, as a thank you for coming and helping them? This was the same evening that we went to the professor's house for dinner. Orval told the choir to come to his house about seven o'clock, when he thought we would be back from dinner.

The choir got there about 15 minutes early, and since it happened to be my birthday, Orval thought he would try to teach the choir how to sing "Happy Birthday" to me in English. There were about 20 men from the age of 15 to 40, with a super dynamic director. When we arrived back at Orval's house, they started to sing. They stood in a semi-circle in front of us with their director in front of them. They sang the most beautiful four-part men's harmony I have ever heard. They watched their director intently, as he directed them with great feeling with varying volumes and tempos. They sang for 45 minutes, and in five different languages. Many of the hymns they sang had the same melody as our hymns, but the words were different. They never had any music or words in front of them. There was no instrument to accompany them. They sang completely acappella. Then to finish, they sang "Happy Birthday" to me in English with great feeling and beautiful harmony.

None of these men spoke English or could read music. I will never understand how they learned the tune of "Happy Birthday," which they had never heard before, learned it in a foreign language, which they didn't speak, learned it in 15 minutes, and sang it in beautiful harmony with no written music.

Some people think these African jungle natives are dumb or stupid because they can't read or write. They live in mud huts with thatched roofs and dirt floors, and they have no money, or skilled occupation. After hearing these men sing for 45 minutes in perfect four-part harmony, without any music, acappella, in five different languages, and having learned to sing "Happy Birthday" to me in 15 minutes, I can guarantee one thing for sure, they are not stupid people! Their IQ is just measured differently from ours. There's no way I could do what they did in a hundred years even after my 24 years of school. Orval recorded the whole evening of singing on a tape which he gave to me. This is the only country in over 137 countries that we have visited that we never bought one souvenir. This tape was better than any souvenir that we could have bought. We have replayed the tape many times, and repeatedly relived those precious memories.

Jack had MAF pick us up and fly us back to Kinshasa. We paid all of our own expenses, and Jack recommended that this was the cheapest and best way.

While we were at Jack's and Trissie's we met a man named Bill. Bill had been a pilot for Delta Airlines, and had flown a 747 jumbo jet round trip from Salt Lake City to Honolulu, Hawaii, for many years as the senior pilot. When he turned 60 years old, federal law required commercial pilots to retire. He wasn't ready to retire, and wanted to serve the Lord, so he and his wife volunteered for one year to help Jack fly his plane. It was amusing to see last year's pilot of a Boeing 747, hand-cranking the propeller of the small single-engine plane. He flew Jack's plane several times while we were there.

One evening Bill and his wife had Dora May and me over for supper, while we were staying with Jack. In the process of our conversation, Bill indicated one of his solar panels wasn't working and he needed a special part. He asked when I got back to Kinshasa if I would ask Glen to purchase the broken part for him.

After flying back to Kinshasa, I gave Bill's request for the solar panel part to Glen. He got the phone to work enough to find the part at a store. When he asked the price they told him the price, and said it would be good until 4 P.M. After that they wouldn't guarantee the price because of the rising inflation. Glen quickly went and purchased the part.

On our last evening in Kinshasa we got a knock on our guest room door, and a gentleman introduced himself as Dan Fountain. He asked if he could come in and talk with us a little. He was very nice and friendly. He was interested in knowing how we got along, and all the things that we had done. He was just passing through Kinshasa and thought he would take a few moments to meet us.

# And Now the Rest of the Story

After we returned home, I found out that Dr. Dan Fountain was one of the most famous African medical missionaries of modern times. He had been in Zaire as an American Baptist medical missionary for well over 30 years. He founded, worked in, developed and managed a mission hospital in the village of Vanga. He developed it into one of the most important and respected hospitals in Zaire, outside of Kinshasa. Today he has retired, and is a professor at a Bible college. He is a highly respected medical missionary speaker, and speaks all over the world. I feel honored he took the time to seek us out and become acquainted with us.

Shortly after we returned home we received a nice thank you letter from Dr. Mongombo. He invited us, and pleaded with us strongly, to come back again and help him. Dr. Mongombo told me that he had trained three nurses to extract teeth, and now he had the only dental clinic in a Central Africa area that was responsible for the health of over a million people. Jack and Trissie also sent us a thank you letter with an invitation to come back.

After we left Zaire, inflation continued to rise, until it became totally out of control. Some of the people who lived there told me some of the events that followed. You won't find any of these descriptions in a history book. President Mobutu could see his power slipping with this runaway inflation, so he became increasingly brutal in an attempt to maintain control. Mobutu's military got paid by check, and when the government couldn't print money fast enough for the banks to be able to cash the soldier's checks for over five months, they started rioting. The soldiers tore the city apart and totally destroyed the down-town area of Kinshasa. They terminated Mobutu's many years of military dictatorship, and the whole country broke into chaos, with civil warring factions occurring all over the country. Zaire has 250 ethnic people groups speaking over 700 different languages.

Mobutu had become one of the richest men in the world and had deposited several billions of dollars in his Swiss bank accounts. He escaped the country only to die of cancer four months later.

All foreigners, including missionaries, tried to rapidly evacuate the country. Kinshasa was the area where the rioting started, and it was the country's main airport, so people had to try to find other ways to leave.

Jack was kept very busy for several weeks flying missionaries out of the country to safe havens. Finally Jack and Trissie evacuated their own home of 32 years, and have never returned. They were well over retirement age, so rather than start all over again somewhere else, they retired back to their quiet hometown in Central Michigan.

The civil war raged on for several years with many thousands of innocent people being killed. Finally in 2005- 2006 it started quieting down and under the UN's largest ever peace keeping forces, they had elections. They elected a somewhat democratic government, which changed the name of the country to the Democratic Republic of Congo. There are still sporadic areas of violence in 2009, and we are not sure when it will be safe to return.

We thank the Lord for our month-long experience we had in Zaire. We hope that we were able to teach the Zairians how to prevent and treat dental pain while showing them genuine Christian love. We still hope to go back someday.

# CHAPTER 12

# BELIZE

After my experiences in Colombia, Zimbabwe, and Zaire, (Congo), I became extremely excited about being able to help people in remote Third World countries, by teaching and treating those who had acute dental disease, but I didn't have any place to go, and no requests for my help. The Lord had greatly blessed my family and me, and I was anxious to show my faith by my good works in helping others who couldn't help themselves, and to share the love of Jesus.

I went to the American Dental Association's National Convention in the fall of 1992. I observed an exhibitor's booth that had a big sign that read, "Health Teams International," and under it was printed, "Helping Evangelize the Unreached." I stopped and talked with Dr. Robert Miller and his wife Jan who were founders of this organization. Dr. Miller described Health Teams International (HTI) as a loose knit group of evangelical interdenominational Christian healthcare providers, whose common purpose was to help evangelize unreached people groups of the world, through the ministration of short-term Christian healthcare teams. He described unreached people groups as any group of people with their own unique culture and language, who had never heard the Gospel of Jesus Christ, or was comprised of less than 2% Christians.

It felt like somebody had just hit me between the eyes with a hammer and woke me up. Yes! Yes! That's exactly what I wanted to do! I could share my dental skills while at the same time sharing the Gospel with people who had never heard the Good News of Jesus.

Dr. Miller told me that HTI had many invitations for dentists. He also explained some nice added benefits of HTI. They would make the necessary arrangements, and furnish all the needed dental supplies and equipment, packed and ready to go. This sounded too good to be true.

I asked him, "Where does HTI go?" Dr. Miller showed me a list of 40 countries in which HTI groups had served. I asked him, "What countries do you currently have invitations from?" He named several countries, but said, "The most urgent need is in Belize." He said, "I had a team of two dentists and helpers committed to go there next spring, but one dentist had to cancel because of personal health problems, and his helpers decided not to go without him. The other dentist has no mission experience. I really need another dentist, some helpers, and someone with mission experience to lead the team."

Then Dr. Miller asked me, point blank, "Is there any chance you could go and lead the team for one week next spring? All the plans have already been made." I had been praying fervently for God to give me an invitation, and here it was. I said, "Sounds great, but I need to pray about it, and talk with my wife. I will give you my answer in the morning."

As Dora May and I talked about it, we realized that the Belize mission was the same week we had invited my cousin, Ed Pedley, and his wife, Charlotte, to go on a vacation with us to Cancun, Mexico. We had planned this many months ago. It was planned this specific week because it was spring break at the University of Michigan and I could get off that week.

Ed had been the youth pastor at our church, while Dora May and I were serving as senior high youth sponsors during the years when our four children were teenagers. We worked very closely together with him for years. Ed introduced me to my first mission trip to Haiti. He had recently started as senior pastor in a church 60 miles away. I knew they couldn't afford much of a vacation, so Dora May and I offered to pay for their vacation to Cancun with us. I knew they were looking forward to it. In some ways it was a "thank you" for the good years we worked together, and also for Ed's marrying our four children.

What should I do? I made a promise to Ed and Charlotte, and at the same time the Lord had given me an answer to my prayers by furnishing me with a great mission opportunity that same week. I telephoned Ed and told him my situation. I gave him two options. One, I would honor my promise to him and Charlotte and take them on the Cancun vacation, or two, he and Charlotte could go on the mission trip to Belize with Dora May and me this year, and I would take them on the same Cancun vacation next year. Ed and Charlotte had heard about my exciting mission trips. In fact, I had presented a mission program in his new church with a full slide show just a few weeks earlier, trying to interest his congregation in missions. It didn't take Ed or Charlotte long to decide to delay Cancun and go to Belize with Dora May and me. I told Dr. Miller the good news. He was happy, Ed and Charlotte were happy, and Dora May and I were happy. What looked like a difficult road block turned out to be a win-win situation for everyone.

Planning for this mission trip was much easier. We were planning just for one week, instead of four like my last three missions. Dr. Miller was well experienced in planning mission trips, and that helped me a lot. Our dental supplies and equipment were all pre-packed and sent to me by HTI.

We left in March, 1993. Our flight to Belize was only six hours with one transfer, rather than 25 to 30 hours of traveling, as with our former mission trips to Africa. In addition to Dora May, Ed and Charlotte, I took a young dentist from the Chicago area, Dr. Kevin Wegrzyn. It was his first mission trip. We landed at Belize City, and were met by our host, Reverend Charles Williams.

Reverend Williams was a Southern Baptist missionary who had been working in Belize for several years. One of his evangelistic outreaches was working with a group of former West Indian slaves, whose ancestors escaped from the West Indies by building rafts and floating westward to Belize over a hundred years ago. They continued to live in this remote coastal island-like area that was separated from the mainland by a 5 mile wide swamp. They had little contact with the outside world until a crude road was built through the swamp giving them access to the mainland.

Rev. Williams, who preferred to be called Charlie, had worked with this group of Africans on numerous occasions over several years. He started a church in the area and trained a young local man to be the pastor. He knew they had dental problems, because the locals would frequently ask him for help. He wasn't able to help, but when he heard of Health Teams International, he contacted Dr. Miller, and asked him to send a dental team, and we were it. It's interesting how we get invited to these isolated people groups. Most of the people in this island like area, had never heard about Jesus, so we had an opportunity to help them both physically and spiritually.

After Charlie met the five of us at the airport, he took us to his home. He lived in Belmopan, a fairly large city about 50 miles inland from Belize City and the Gulf Coast. Charlie had a beautiful wife, Judy, and two boys, 8 and 10 years old. We stayed in their home and ate our meals with them.

The next day was Sunday, so we went to church with Charlie and his family. Belize was a former British colony and most people spoke English. Church was uneventful for a foreign country. After noon dinner, Charlie showed us around the area. He was in charge of starting a Christian school in his church. This was something that I had done in our church 20 years before, and I had been President of the school board most of the time since, so we had much in common to discuss. That evening on Charlie's TV, in central Belize, we watched the University of Michigan basketball team win the National Basketball Championship.

Early Monday morning we climbed into Charlie's church minivan, and headed for the village of Hopkin, which was home for the descendents of the escaped African slaves. It was a trip of several hours. We finally turned off the main road and the last five miles we drove on a crude, bumpy, dirt road, built through a large coastal swamp. In the village of Hopkin there were several hundred people living on a sandy strip of land about 2 miles long and a quarter-mile wide. I don't think there was any area on the island that was over 20 feet above sea level. Most of the houses had thatched siding and either a thatched or tin roof. Hopkin was in the center of hurricane alley. A hurricane would probably destroy all their homes, but if the people went far enough inland to survive, they would just come back and rebuild. I suspect that is why the homes were built so simply, because they were cheap and easy to rebuild.

One of the larger buildings in the village was used as a guest house. It had two fairly sizeable rooms in it. We stayed in one of the rooms, and slept on the concrete floor in our sleeping bags. There was an outhouse located 20 to 30 yards behind our building. One day Charlotte went out to the outhouse and came back twice as fast as she had gone out there. She said, "I'm not going out there! There's a scorpion on the wall behind the seat." We all went out and checked, from a distance, of course, and she was right, so we looked for a different outhouse.

We met the young pastor that Charlie had trained, and saw the little church building they had built. The pastor had arranged for us to set up clinic in Hopkin's Community Center. The natives had built it in the center of their village. This building had one room 20 x 40 feet. It had heavy doors with locks, so we could lock our equipment up each night, and not have to setup and breakdown each day.

We set up clinic, and started to work that very afternoon. HTI had packed portable drills and filling materials, so we not only extracted teeth, but filled them as well. Dora May assisted me, while Charlotte assisted Dr. Kevin. Ed was in charge of patient flow and crowd control. He gave the patients numbers and kept them in order. We also taught Ed how to do fluoride treatments on children, so he was kept really busy.

For lunch we often would go out to the end of a long dock where there was a little gazebo, and would eat our sandwiches out there, because it was quiet, peaceful, and there was a nice ocean breeze. It got very hot during the day, but cooled off comfortably at night.

Wednesday evening we went to prayer meeting in the small church Charlie had helped build. There were 15 to 20 people present. One evening we stopped and visited an older retired couple that had, without question, the nicest home in Hopkin. They had built a two-story concrete house on the highest spot on the beach. They lived on the second floor. Most of the first floor was just supporting posts and a little storage.

Their story as to how and why they were there was interesting. They had been born and raised in Hopkin but left and went inland to school. Both of them were accepted into a U.S. college and earned their master's degrees, and the husband had received a Ph.D. They became U.S. citizens and worked in the Chicago area. At 65 they retired and having no family they moved back home to their childhood village. They became well-respected leaders in their community. They were able to persuade the government to bring electricity into the area, and they had the only TV in Hopkin. We had a good conversation with them. You could tell they were pleased to talk with educated people from the U.S. This was not a place visited by tourists.

Charlie took us to the only store on the island. It was a one-room hut, where you stood out front at a counter, and the owner would get what you wanted off the shelves which surrounded the room. He probably had 50 to 75 items on his shelves. Charlie said, "These people have something that I'll bet you don't have in the U.S." He asked the owner to get a small bottle off of the back shelf. It was a treatment for babies with colic. Charlie commented, "The people say it really works well." It was about a half pint of clear liquid. He handed it to me and said, "Read the label." I looked it over. I had never heard of the name. I saw that it was made in London, England. Then Charlie said, "Read the ingredients." It was made of 99% ethyl alcohol. Maybe a couple of teaspoons would make a baby happy, I chuckled. I had to come all this way to this remote island in Belize to find a cure for colic.

We saw lots of patients with very bad teeth. We extracted a lot of teeth, but also filled a large number of them. The people were very kind, patient, and appreciative. We taught a lot of hygiene and gave out many toothbrushes. One time when I was trying to diagnose a tooth problem, I asked the patient if his tooth was sensitive to cold. The patient looked right back at me and asked, "What is cold?" Charlie heard us talking and commented, "They never have experienced anything cold."

Saturday morning we packed up and headed back to Charlie's house in Belmopan. We got there about noon, and our flight home wasn't until Sunday morning. After lunch Charlie asked if we wanted to drive an hour to near the Guatemalan border where there were some interesting Mayan ruins. Why not, we thought. We loaded up and took off. The Mayan ruins indeed were very interesting. They were quite an advanced civilization of builders several hundred years ago. Another interesting sight to see was that of the many mounds covered with vegetation in this Mayan village that had not begun to be uncovered. Everyone speculates as to why this great Mayan civilization disappeared, but I don't think anyone will really ever know. Even the few living Mayan descendents don't know.

Sunday morning we bid farewell, and Charlie took us back to the airport in Belize City. Charlie and his family were wonderful hosts and we were very appreciative. We boarded a nice Boeing 727 American Airlines plane and headed home. They served us a nice lunch and it was so good to have a nice lettuce salad again. We had carefully avoided eating salads, or anything that wasn't boiled, baked or peeled for the whole last week. Ed, Charlotte, and I ate the salad, but for some unknown reason, Dora May didn't eat a bite of it.

The day after we got home, Ed, Charlotte, and I were all sick, with gastrointestinal problems. Ed became so sick he was put in the hospital. Dora May had no problem, so we started to put the puzzle together. I called American Airlines, and found out the flight's origin was in Costa Rica where the meals had been prepared and loaded. American Airlines only response was, "Sorry!" This taught me another important lesson, which I have never forgotten, and I have never had gastrointestinal problems like that again.

# And Now the Rest of the Story

Ed and Charlotte enjoyed the trip immensely. Charlotte really enjoyed dental assisting with Dr. Kevin. When Ed had some health concerns, Charlotte realized that she had no marketable skills to earn a living if anything ever happened to Ed. Since she had enjoyed her dental assisting, she decided to go to college and study to be a dental assistant. She did just that. She graduated and became a Certified Dental Assistant. Since their three children were nearly grown, she got a job as a dental assistant and did very well. She joined the Dental Assistant's Association and became its president. She has worked happily as a dental assistant for several years. The following March, Ed, Charlotte, Dora May, and I enjoyed our week's vacation in Cancun.

# CHAPTER 13

# GHANA

After returning from our short mission to Belize in March, Dr. Miller asked if I would lead a team to Ghana, West Africa, in August. He explained that Dr. Roger Youmans, an M.D. and General Surgeon, one of Health Teams International's (HTI) founders, and a member of the HTI Board of Directors, was currently living and working in Ghana. The previous year, Dr. Youmans hosted a HTI team that had outstanding success, both physically and spiritually. He requested HTI to send another team. Dr. Youmans wanted to go into the northern part of the country, to work with the Hausa tribe, an unreached group of people. He had a pastor from that area who was begging him to come, and told him he would host the team and make all arrangements. Dora May and I had no good reason not to go, so we cheerfully said, "Yes."

One evening a Christian friend of mine, Steve Morgan, called and said, "I have a 16-year-old daughter, Kim, who thinks she wants to become a missionary, and she would like to go on a mission trip to see what it is like." He asked, "Is there any chance you could take her on a mission trip with you sometime?"

I told him about my upcoming Ghana mission. After Steve talked with his daughter, he called back and said that they were very interested. I made an appointment with mom, dad, and Kim, and I sat down and talked with them, filling them in on all the details that I knew about the trip. Kim was an exceptionally mature young lady for a 16 year old. She was very excited about the mission, and strongly wanted to go. I said, "Ok," and we made arrangements to take her with us.

Dr. Gorden Bentson, a dentist from Minnesota, called and asked if he and his dental assistant, Joanne Flannigan, could go on the mission trip to Ghana. After a phone interview, we added them to our team also.

In August of 1993 we packed and left for Ghana. We flew to London and transferred to a plane destined for Accra, Ghana. The plane made one stop in Lagos, Nigeria. The Captain came on the PA system and announced, "We have a one hour layover in Lagos, but if this is not your final destination, I advise you to stay on the plane." He said, "There often are robberies and violence right in the airport terminal, and I don't want any of my passengers to get hurt." Needless to say, we didn't deplane. This was the only time in my life I had ever been told anything like this by a pilot. It was most unusual!

When we got to Accra, Dr. Roger Youmans was at the airport to meet us, but our luggage did not arrive. We put in a lost luggage claim and were told it would probably arrive on the next flight, which was in three days.

Dr. Youmans took us to his house, where we met his wife, Mary. Dora May and I stayed as guests in Dr. Youmans' home. Dr. Bentson, Joanne, and Kim stayed at the Manna Mission Guest House near Manna Mission Hospital. Kim met a 20 year old girl named Sally from the U.S., who had been there for six months getting acquainted with the mission field. Kim and Sally immediately became friends and Kim roomed with her. They stayed close together for the entire trip.

Dr. Youmans showed us around, including Manna Mission Hospital, where he routinely did surgery. We met Dr. Seth Ablorh who had founded Manna Mission Hospital and was in charge of operating it. Dr. Ablorh was a black native Ghanaian. He had been given a scholarship by Reverend Oral Roberts, to come to the U.S. and attend Oral Roberts University in Tulsa, Oklahoma.

After Dr. Ablorh graduated from Oral Roberts Medical School with an M.D. degree, he took a three year Family Practice residency in Chicago. He returned to Accra to help his people physically and spiritually. Within a few years he had opened and was running Manna Mission Hospital. He started a church, which was attached to the hospital, and had around 600 people attending. He also started and was overseeing a Bible school, which trained young people to be pastors and evangelists. Sunday afternoon we also visited a large area where he was in the process of building, with help from U.S. contributors, a permanent concrete multi-story hospital with initially 30 beds with room to expand to 60 beds. Dr. Ablorh was a big success, and people and organizations like to support winners.

Sunday morning we went to Dr. Ablorh's church around 9 A.M., and were treated as special guests. The service had already begun, and the sanctuary was about half full. It continued to fill as they sang hymns with much clapping and great rhythm. They had prayer, scripture reading, and short talks between hymns. About 11 A.M. the place was packed and overflowing. Dr. Ablorh then preached a powerful evangelistic sermon. Everything was in English.

I witnessed something I had never seen before or since. In the middle of Dr. Ablorh's sermon, a lady in the congregation stood up and started shouting very loudly in tongues, or an unknown language. Dr. Ablorh paused. When she finished, a man stood up and interpreted what she had said. His interpretation made good sense. Dr. Ablorh then continued his sermon just like nothing had ever happened.

After the service I asked Dr. Youmans why the service was so long and why the people kept coming in for two hours. He said, "These people don't have watches or clocks. They just go by the position of the sun which isn't always accurate.

Ghana was a former British colony, and the new government continued many of the former British policies. One of the policies required that we go to the Central Government Health Office in Accra, and apply for a Temporary Dental License. This was the only country in some 20 countries in which I had done mission work, that anyone had even asked to see my license, let alone required me to get a temporary dental license.

On Monday Dr. Youmans took us to the required office. He had advised us about the government's red tape before we came, and had asked us to bring a notarized copy of our U.S. dental license, and two letters of recommendation, which I had done. I was called into the office of the Health Officer first. Dr. Youmans told him what we planned to do, and I presented him with my notarized copy of my license and my letters of recommendation. He quickly granted a temporary dental license. Dr. Bentson was called in and presented his papers to the officer but he wouldn't accept them. Dr. Bentson had not bothered to get his dental license notarized. After about 20 minutes of intense discussion, mainly between Dr. Youmans and the officer, he reluctantly gave him a temporary dental license. In 35 mission trips, I had never been questioned about my qualifications or license, but ever since, I have always taken copies of everything with me.

Dr. Youmans had planned to take us north on Tuesday, but our departure was delayed because we hadn't received our dental supplies and equipment. If our luggage didn't arrive on the plane Tuesday, Dr. Youmans said he would have to cancel our trip north completely, because the next plane wasn't due until Saturday.

Tuesday morning, Mary, Dr. Youmans wife, took us souvenir shopping, because if we left a day late for the North Country we would probably come back a day late, and there might not be any time for shopping. We went to the airport Tuesday afternoon when the plane was due, and all of our luggage was on board. Praise the Lord.

After we brought our luggage back to the house, Dr. Youmans needed to make a house call on a sick patient, and he asked me if I would like to go. We had to drive across town during the five o'clock rush hour. It was wild. Suddenly I heard Dr. Youmans talking. I turned to see what he was saying to me, and found he wasn't talking to me. He was talking to God, thanking him for the arrival of our luggage, asking for safety in this wild traffic, and praying for the patient we were about to see. He was doing this while he was driving through this horrible traffic. I always thought you had to bow your head and close your eyes when you prayed. That day I was a witness to something that I should have known. God hears us just as well when our eyes are open and our head isn't bowed. It's scary, but He even knows our thoughts.

Tuesday evening we packed everything we thought we would need for the next 10 days, but left it in our locked house. Dr. Youmans routinely hired an armed guard to watch his house at night to keep out intruders. Early the next morning before we left, the guard came to Dr. Youmans very agitated. After their conversation ended, I asked Dr. Youmans, "What was that discussion all about?" Dr. Youmans said, "It seemed the guard fell asleep last night, and a burglar cut a hole in the fence, and stole the guard's bicycle." What a sad irony that was.

The potential for burglary was the main reason we waited to pack our van until morning. Dr. Youmans had bought a nice new 12-passenger white Ford Van, had it painted with Manna Mission Hospital, a cross, and Christian slogans on it, and had it shipped to Dr. Ablorh six months before he came to Ghana. Dr. Youmans hoped to be able to use it while he was in Ghana, and then he would leave it for Dr. Ablorh and the Manna Mission Hospital when he left.

Dr. Youmans drove. We had 10 people, all of our luggage, and medical and dental equipment and supplies. The passengers in the van were Dr. Youmans, Dora May, Dr. Bentson, Joanne, Kim and Sally, three native Ghanaians and me. We were packed "to the max" with most of our baggage on top. We left Accra around 8 A.M. It turned out to be a 15-hour drive, and we were packed so tightly that we could hardly move. We ate a packed lunch and supper while driving. I'm glad we didn't stop to eat at any of the restaurants we saw along the way. They didn't look to be very sanitary.

The last two hours was through a huge swamp, which contained a lot of water during the rainy season and for a month or two after. Basically, it was the only road north in that area. The road was dirt, and often mud, with huge 8 to 10 foot wide holes filled with water, and we couldn't tell how deep they were. The swamp separated 90% of southern Ghana from the 10% of northern Ghana, which occupied a 40 to 50 mile band of good land between the swamp to the south, and the border of the country of Burkina Faso to the north. The people of this area were very primitive, and untouched by much of the civilization of Southern Ghana.

We had three young Ghanaians with us, who were originally from this area, and they were currently studying in Dr. Ablorh's Bible school. They helped Dr. Youmans with driving directions, did translation for us, and even guided Dr. Youmans to the pastor's house when we finally got through the big swamp. It was late in the evening before we arrived, and we were all very tired. It had been the longest, hottest, bumpiest, most difficult ride of my life, but an experience I wouldn't trade for anything.

After the long-awaited celebration of our arrival, the pastor took us to a place where we quickly unpacked and went to bed. The next morning the pastor took us about 10 miles to a neighboring village. Our first order of business was to meet the chief, which is the custom in most African villages. The village consisted of about two hundred mud huts with thatched roofs. Many of these houses were attached and all of them were surrounded by a huge mud wall, with only a few entrances. The pastor led us into the village, and then through a long maze, around and in between the mud huts until we got to the chief's house.

Upon arrival, the chief came out of his house and greeted us with a big smile, and we went through the greeting formalities.

There was no room to set up our clinics inside the village, so we went outside the village and were led to a small unoccupied building under a shade tree. I set up our dental clinic outside underneath the shade tree to get better light and a breeze. Medical needed to set up inside the building because of the occasional need to see patients privately.

We had taken our drills and air compressors to do fillings, but there were so many aching abscessed teeth that needed extracting for relief of pain, that I think we only put in two or three fillings in the 10 days we were there. This was the last mission trip that I hauled 125 pounds of equipment with me to do fillings. We had no way of drying a tooth before we put in a filling, and as a result, the fillings we placed were of a very poor quality. Our compressed air had water vapor in it which damaged our drills. We could remove 8 to10 aching teeth in the same amount of time it took to put in one poor filling in a tooth that wasn't even aching.

The patients couldn't understand why we would put a filling in a tooth that didn't hurt. They wanted us to fill the very large holes in the abscessed teeth, to make them stop aching. They didn't understand that putting a filling in a tooth that had already abscessed would just make it hurt worse. They frequently got upset when we told them we couldn't fill an abscessed tooth. We wanted to be friends and make them happy, not to make them angry and upset.

Dora May assisted me, and Joanne assisted Dr. Bentson. Kim scrubbed and sterilized our instruments and that kept her quite busy. We had one translator for each doctor. Sally assisted Dr. Youmans, especially in dispensing medications. We treated a large number of patients. The pastor and some of his church leaders did spiritual counseling with each patient.

Every day we went to a different village. School wasn't in session at this time of year, so we often set up our clinic in their primitive village school building, if they had one. One school was in an open field outside of town. It consisted of poles that supported a thatched roof. It was about 70 feet long and 20 feet wide. It had no front or back walls, but it did have 6-foot mud walls every 10 to 15 feet inside that separated the classrooms. The floor was dirt, and there were no blackboards, chairs, desks, or any furniture.

At this particular school I learned another good lesson. At the end of the day I had quite a few toothbrushes leftover. We usually gave one to each of our dental patients, but I decided to give the rest of the toothbrushes to the people who were standing around watching. I started handing them out at random, and immediately a stampede occurred. I was literally crushed and feared for my safety. I was about to get trampled when our three translators came shouting and running to my rescue. I have never done that again.

Each day I tried to set our dental clinic up outside in the open, where we could get better light, and often a breeze, in an otherwise very hot humid climate. This allowed for large crowds to gather all around and watch. I didn't mind this at all. I thought it was good to show the people that were watching that we weren't hurting our patients. Most of them had never seen a dentist before. Oftentimes I would have 20 to 40 people gathered around me watching, and getting closer and closer. I would frequently pick one of the teenage observers to hold the flashlight for me. It was an exciting privilege and usually the selected teenager did an excellent job.

One day on the way home from our clinic we found a 12-foot crocodile alongside our road. Dr. Youmans came down with all the symptoms of malaria, but he kept working every day, and treated himself just like he treated many of his patients that had the same symptoms. It is not contagious.

We slept in a building that had five or six big rooms with a double bed in each room. They had us spray a bug killer around the room before we went to supper. The first time I did this, I thought, it was silly because I didn't see any bugs. We then had to vacate the room for about an hour, and the vapors were supposed to kill the bugs. When we came back after supper to the room we had sprayed, I was shocked to see 50 to 100 dead bugs of all kinds on the floor and even on our bed. It worked like nothing I had ever seen, before or since.

Joanne was asked to room with our black female Ghanaian translators. No one thought anything about it. I found out later that Joanne who was from Minnesota, had never had any contact with black people before, and even though she knew better, she was very frightened. She didn't sleep much at all the first few nights. By the end of our time there, they had become the best of friends. That was another lesson well learned.

Every night the pastor had a special service at his church. All our team was requested to sit on the platform. We didn't understand the language. The services were very upbeat and emotional. For the first and only time in my life, I witnessed several people who were "Slain by the Spirit." People would come forward and the pastor would pray for them very loudly in a shouting emotional voice, one at a time. He then put his finger lightly on their forehead and many of the people would pass out and fall to the floor. Some just fell over backwards. Oftentimes the ushers would catch them in a blanket, so they didn't hurt themselves. Most of them recovered and returned to consciousness in a minute or two, while the pastor was praying for the next person. If they didn't wake up in a reasonable time, the ushers picked them up by their arms and dragged them down the aisle and out the door of the church.

I didn't understand this "Slaying by the Spirit" part of the service, but just because it was different didn't mean that it was right or wrong. I refused to judge the way they worshipped. I just worship in the way I am comfortable worshiping, and that's exactly what they do also. It was very obvious that they had a deep, emotional, and a very sincere love for the same Lord I did.

On Sunday after church, we had a big dinner at the pastor's house, with a lot of guests present. Chicken was the rarest and most expensive type of meat. The pastor had killed some of his chickens that ran around the outside of their house. It was considered a very special treat. When the chicken was passed to me, I took a drumstick. When I took a bite, the meat was as hard as bone. I couldn't bite it at all without fear of breaking my teeth, so I quietly laid it down on my plate. After a little while, a young Ghanaian man that was sitting next to me asked if I were going to eat my chicken. I sheepishly shook my head, no. He said, "Can I have it.?" I shook my head, yes. He picked it up and ate the whole thing, bone and all. I made some sort of comment, and he said, "We always eat the bones of chickens. They are soft." I was told later that usually the Ghanaians crack the long bones with their teeth and suck out the marrow, but most don't really eat the bones.

The last day, the pastor had us work at his church. He had been telling the people we were coming, and they had been waiting for us. We were swamped, with the biggest crowds and longest lines ever. We stopped for a short lunch, and decided we would try to finish before supper.

It was hot. I had brought along a plastic water bottle, with a built-in straw. I placed it on the ground by my dental chair. I had put some Tang in the water to improve the taste. One time in the late afternoon I tried to take a drink, and there didn't seem to be much coming up the straw. I could feel that it was still half full. I unscrewed the top, and will never forget what I saw. There were about 10 to 15 red bugs in there, about twice the size of a giant ant, moving around very fast. I popped the top back on, screwed it up, pinched off the straw, and had a very sick feeling in my stomach. I never had any physical problem, but mentally it took me a while to recover. The only way they could have gotten in there was down the straw, when it was sitting on the ground. I only thank the Lord that one of them didn't come up the straw and pop into my mouth when I was trying to drink. I never have seen bugs like that before or since. They are etched permanently in my mind. Twenty years later, I still have a hard time laughing about that experience.

On the last afternoon, I had a patient come to me with a swelling under her eye and alongside her nose. It was about the size of a tennis ball. I checked her teeth and she had no visible tooth problems. The swelling was hard, and not painful. Infections are usually soft, red, and painful. I had never seen anything like this before. The woman was in her 30s, and she told me she had gone to a lot of doctors and dentists, and had even gone to the capital of Accra, and no one had been able to help her. She started to cry, and begged me to help her. My heart was full of compassion for her.

I took her to Dr. Youmans for consultation. He confirmed what I was starting to think. He said, "It is a cancerous growth." I asked, "Why can't they do surgery, chemotherapy, radiation, or something to help her?" Dr. Youmans, who was a general surgeon himself, said, "There is no chemotherapy, or radiation available in this entire country of Ghana, and it's simply too big to do surgery." Fortunately she couldn't understand any of our discussion. It broke my heart, but I had to tell this lady, "I'm sorry but there's nothing we can do for you." She hung her head, and walked away.

We were determined to finish all the patients before we quit, because there was no tomorrow. Everyone had been so good and kind to us, but it seemed the faster and harder we worked, our lines didn't get any shorter. Finally at 12 o'clock midnight, Dr. Youmans said, "We have to be on the road at 6 A.M., and we have a big day ahead of us tomorrow, so I guess we will have to quit." Dr. Youmans had about 20 patients waiting to see him and so did dental. We gave all the waiting patients a package of Tylenol and a toothbrush, which seemed to make them happy, and I think they understood.

The pastor's church attendance had doubled in size since we had been there. We said our goodbyes at midnight, and at 6 A.M. we started our long, hot, bumpy, road trip back to Accra. On our way through the great swamp, we met a bus that had broken down with passengers all standing out in the muddy road. There was very little traffic, and not a building of any kind for 20 miles in either direction. We slowed down, but there was no use stopping, because we were loaded to capacity.

We got back to Accra in the early evening all very tired, even though we hadn't worked all day. We just sat around and bounced as we traveled. Dr. Youmans gave Dora May and me some medicine to take home in case we experienced any of the signs or symptoms of malaria. We gave the medication to Kim for her to take home. The next day was Saturday. The five of us caught an early evening flight back to Europe, and then Sunday back to the U.S. and home.

In Summary: This was my first mission trip where we had a medical doctor available. Most missions I have led since that time have had both dental and medical team members, and later trips, optical also. We learned a lot and were greatly blessed. I believe we showed genuine Christian love to many people. We certainly encouraged our host pastor and his church, and their evangelistic efforts were highly successful. Our team was able to relieve a lot of pain and suffering for many of the people, who otherwise would never have been able to receive help.

## And Now the Rest of the Story

Dr. Ablorh completed his hospital, which is now currently ranked as one of the best in Ghana. Dora May developed all the classical signs and symptoms of malaria the day after we arrived home. I retrieved the medicine from Kim that Dr. Youmans had given us, and two days later Dora May was back to normal.

Dr. Youmans brought his wife, Mary, back to the University of Oklahoma Medical School the week after we left. He had been professor of surgery there for many years. She had some abdominal symptoms, which they did not have the equipment to diagnose in Ghana. She was diagnosed with advanced abdominal cancer and had radical resection of the ovary and part of the colon with colostomy. She elected not to be treated with chemo-therapy and died about nine months after surgery. She was able to make a short visit back to Ghana four months before her death.

A few years later Dr. Youmans married a widow of an M.D., Bev, and they both returned to Ghana, and served there for several more years. Eventually they returned to the U.S. and Dr. Youmans retired. Recently Bev was diagnosed with ovarian cancer also. She had rad-ical surgery and chemotherapy and lived five years before she died. Dr. Youmans moved to Arkansas to be near his children and grandchildren. He is still a valued HTI board member and adviser. In talking with him recently he said, "My heart is still in missions and I hope to return to the Democratic Republic of Congo soon."

Dr. Youmans is planning to go back to Africa for an international meeting on River Blindness. He is vice president of a NGO (United Front Against River Blindness), which works in eastern Congo in the Kosongo District of over one million Congolese to try to control or eliminate the disease.

Dr. Youmans served in Africa as a medical doctor for many years. He wrote a book titled, "When the Bull Elephants Fight," about his Congo experiences. After reading his book, it inspired me to write my own memoirs of my 35 mission trips. His book was the inspiration for this book.

Kim determined she wanted to continue preparation to become a missionary. She graduated from high school and went to a Christian college where she received a nursing degree. She married a young man who had committed his life to full-time Christian service. They started a family. Her husband is serving as an assistant pastor of a church while he is finishing an advanced degree.

# CHAPTER 14

# CAMBODIA

Cambodia has had a long history of violence. In 1975 the Khmer Rouge forcefully took over the country. They tortured and killed almost as many people as the Germans killed Jews in the late 1930s and 40s. They kept extensive records and took photos of all the prisoners, and many of their torturing methods. They killed all government officials, their families, and all the police and military. They arrested, tortured, and killed anyone with more than a sixth-grade education, anyone who wore glasses, anyone who had a business or property, and anyone who had a religion. It is estimated they killed 50,000 Buddhist Monks. They totally emptied the cities and put everyone to work in hard hand labored agriculture. Pul Pot was their leader. There is a movie named "The Killing Fields" (1984), which is a reasonably accurate account of what happened. Finally with the help of the Armies of South Vietnam, ASEAN, the Association of South East Asian Nations, and the United Nations, a cease-fire was agreed upon, and a gradual fragile peace was accomplished.

The UN sent the largest number of peacekeeping troops in its history into Cambodia, to stabilize the country, remove as many of the 9 million land mines as they could, and eventually supervise an election to establish a democratic government. It had been less than a year since the elections in that country. The Khmer Rouge Party had several members elected to the government. After the elections, the UN removed all of its peacekeeping troops from the country. The British and the U.S. embassies were reestablished, and missionaries started to return to the country. Things seemed to be going well.

Lee Wiggins, a HTI director, led a team into Cambodia in the fall of 1993. He reported a very successful mission. He also reported that they desperately needed another dental team to come and help them as soon as possible. Dr. Miller asked if I could go. Again I thought why not? Because of the recent violent history, and since it had only been eight months since the elections and the UN peacekeeping troops had gone, I couldn't find another dentist to go with Dora May and me.

I had a hygienist named Karen, and a dental assistant named Denise, who came to me together one day at the dental office and asked if they could go to Cambodia with me. I was delighted. They were long-term excellent employees, and had a lot of advanced dental training and experience, and both were Christians.

That made four of us; Karen, Denise, Dora May and me. Our communication in those days was by fax. After I had a lot of communication with a missionary named Norbert Bauer, at the missionary headquarters in the capital city of Phnom Penh, we set a date for April 1994. We ordered and received all of our dental equipment and supplies from HTI, received all of our immunizations, made our airline reservations, and completed a million and one other details.

Ten days before we were scheduled to leave, I started passing a kidney stone. I told my urologist about our mission, and he said he would mechanically remove the stone for me. The next day I went into the hospital, they put me to sleep, and he attempted to remove the stone. When I awakened in a hospital bed, the doctor came in and said, "I wasn't able to get a grip on the stone to remove it, so instead I pushed it back up into your kidney". He told me he had put a straw-like stint in my ureter. The ureter is the tube that connects the kidneys to the bladder where a kidney stone can cause a great deal of pain. He assured me it should be okay. The stint should keep the stone in the kidney until I could get home.

I told my doctor there was no medical treatment available in Cambodia. They had killed all the doctors. He gave me some Vicodin for pain, and a strong antibiotic in case I started developing a fever, which could be a sign of infection. I felt good, so he just kept me overnight in the hospital. I went home, back to work, and finished my packing.

It was a cool crisp morning when we left home for the long trip to Phnom Penh, Cambodia. We flew from Detroit to Los Angeles, to Tokyo, and on to Bangkok, Thailand, where we stayed six hours overnight in the airport hotel. The next morning we continued to Phnom Penh.

Our host, Norbet Bauer, with whom I had been in communication, was at the small, somewhat primitive airport to meet us. We had no problems with customs. After our introductions and greetings, the first thing Norbet said to us was, "I guess, I should have faxed you and told you not to come. Things have changed here. The Khmer Rouge has gotten upset and pulled out of the government. They have threatened to take over the capital of Phnom Penh again by force at our New Year. This is our New Year's time." The Khmer Rouge currently occupied and controlled two thirds of the country, including most of its wealth, timber, gem mines, and rice production.

Norbet continued, "The Khmer Rouge has started kidnapping foreigners throughout the country. Both the U.S. and the British embassies have declared a curfew which recommends that foreigners not go out at night, and to not leave the city". Then he said, "I have checked and you can't fly out of the country for two weeks, until your ticket reservations come up, because all planes leaving the country are full. I guess we'll just have to make the best of it." What a warm and wonderful welcome that was, not exactly what we were expecting.

We loaded up and headed for the mission compound, which was right in the middle of downtown, one block from the central market. When the Khmer Rouge invaded the city, in 1975, they forced all two million people out of Phnom Penh, and into rural village agricultural communes. Several million people were killed. When peace occurred, people started returning to the city. Since everything was empty, and they didn't know who was still alive, they just started settling into anything they wanted. Some people came back to find that someone else was living in their house.

An evangelistic Christian Cambodian preacher, named Chen, had escaped the country just before the Khmer Rouge invaded Phnom Penh, and he was one of the first people to return to the country after the cease-fire and peace was established. There was a large old multi-story former French boarding school downtown that no one wanted to claim or inhabit. It covered an entire square block and was five stories high. It had been used as one of the torturing and killing locations when the Khmer Rouge captured the city in 1975. There were large blood stains on the floor, which couldn't be removed, so no one wanted this huge building.

When Chen returned and saw this large, unoccupied, centrally located building, he asked the government to let him use it, and he would establish an orphanage, and a Christian Mission. Permission was granted and several missionary couples and families came from Sweden, Germany, and Switzerland. Norbet, his wife, and several children came from Switzerland to help Chen, and had been there for less than a year. Norbet had been assigned to be our host.

When we arrived at the mission compound, Norbet got out and unlocked and opened the gate. We drove through a tunnel-like opening in the outer wall of the building, into a fairly large central court. The old school building, now the mission headquarters, completely surrounded this central opening with this four-story building.

We unloaded, met Norbet's family and others, and then Norbet showed us to our quarters. It was on the second floor, and consisted of a moderate-sized living room with a table and chairs, a bathroom with a western-style stool and sink, and two small bedrooms, each with a double bed. It had a window type air-conditioner which really helped because it was extremely hot.

Norbet said he didn't have any clinic scheduled for us that afternoon, and asked if we would like to look around the city. He took us to a large building that had been turned into a museum. This was one of the main locations where the Khmer Rouge tortured their victims, trying to get information, such as names and locations of other people that they needed to capture and kill. Their methods of torture were extremely horrible. They actually took photos of each victim, and the various methods used in torturing them. One method of torture especially sticks in my mind. They took an inner tube from a car tire, and made it into a large slingshot. They would put babies into the slingshot, and project them up into the air, and practice shooting them, like we shoot skeet.

After we visited the torture chambers, we went to the actual killing fields, where they took the prisoners and killed them. They didn't want to waste their bullets, so they just hit them in the head with an ax, and split their head open. They buried them in mass graves, several hundred at a time.

Many of the graves had been dug up, and they had piles of human skulls as big as a small house, all with the skulls split open. There were jawbones, and other types of human bones lying all over the ground where we walked. The bones were similar to sea shells on the beach. This was all unbelievable, depressing, and gave me a sick feeling in my stomach.

We returned to the mission compound, and had supper in the dining room with 40 orphaned children. The missionaries had just taken them off the street. They had no parents or relatives, and were just subsisting on any garbage that they could find. The mission gave them food, a bed to sleep in, security, friends, clothes, sent them to school, medicine if they needed it, and a meaning for living with a Christian faith. Our supper was 90% rice, with a little topping of papaya fruit. It had been a long, hot, and depressing day, so we went to bed early. Thankfully our room was a little cool.

At 4 a.m. we were suddenly awakened by machine gun fire. The entire city erupted in machine gun fire. We could hear the machine guns right outside our window. We huddled together and asked ourselves what we should do. We decided to stay in our rooms, keep the lights off, and keep the door locked. Actually Karen and Denise got dressed in the clothes they planned to be buried in. Needless to say, we thought the Khmer Rouge was attacking the city again, and our end was near.

Personally, I was in severe pain, just like I was passing a kidney stone again. I took some Vicodin and went back to bed. I did a lot of praying as the machine guns continued. I asked the Lord for his protection over us, but I also told him, if He was calling me home, I was ready. I actually fell asleep. I awoke about 7 a.m. feeling much better. Everything was quiet and everyone was lying down, but not sleeping.

I got dressed and peeked out the window. All seemed quiet. Then I looked out the door, and all was quiet there. Then I quietly crept over to the dining room where I thought I could hear voices. All the children were in the dining room eating breakfast.

Norbet was in the dining room, so I went over to him and asked, "What was all the noise about last night?" He said, "It was a little scary wasn't it? It scared us a lot also, but we finally figured it out. Four a.m. this morning was the exact moment of their New Year. They didn't have any firecrackers, which were the tradition in celebrating an Oriental New

Year, but everyone had an AK-47 Russian machine gun with lots of bullets. They simply were just out celebrating." WOW! What a relief.

I went back to the room and explained to the girls. They laughed about it, and were greatly relieved. We all went to breakfast. After breakfast we loaded our dental supplies and equipment into the mission's van, and headed toward our first clinic. Norbet told us that they had several locations outside the city to which they had planned to take us, but because of the embassy's restrictions, we would be forced to stay in or very near the city.

The first place we went was actually on the edge of the city. We took the main road out of the city, which eventually went to Saigon, Vietnam, and at the edge of the city we turned down a dirt road, and proceeded a couple of miles. We came to a small cluster of primitive thatched huts. We pulled our van into a clearing in the center of these huts, and started unloading. A nicely dressed middle-aged man came to us and introduced himself in rather good English, as Pastor Bob. He did not have white skin. He was definitely a tan-skinned Cambodian. Norbet knew him and had worked with him before.

We set up our clinic under a big shade tree, which was right in the middle of the village. Pastor Bob got us a table from his house on which we put our instruments. People started lining up before we finished getting ready. We had two dental chairs. I planned to use one for extractions, and the other one for Karen, our hygienist, to clean teeth.

Shortly after we started working, it became very obvious to me that I wasn't going to get all the peoples' teeth extracted that were in line. I changed my tactics by asking Karen and Denise if they would help me extract some of the teeth. They both had worked for years with oral surgeons and assisted in extracting thousands of teeth, but they had never actually extracted any teeth themselves. They were both excited about the opportunity. My thinking was, either I get these girls to help me, or there would be a lot of painful abscessed teeth that never got extracted.

The Khmer Rouge had killed all the dentists in the country almost 20 years ago, and to Norbet's knowledge, there wasn't one trained dentist in the entire country at that time. There were no licensing laws to cause any concern, and it didn't take much training. Within 30 minutes Karen and Denise were taking turns giving anesthesia and extracting teeth, just about as fast as I. The thing that surprised me most was neither Karen nor Denise ever asked me for help when roots broke off, or the going got tough. They just jumped right in and dug out the roots, and took care of all the problems themselves. I guess they had seen it done so many times that they knew exactly what to do.

Pastor Bob's wife prepared a wonderful lunch. She served it on a table right under our big shade tree. Pastor Bob explained how he and the people of this village had recently moved to this area. All of the people in this village had been refugees in one of Thailand's refugee camps, during the years of the Khmer Rouge killings. When the UN peacekeepers came, and peace was established, they closed the Thailand refugee camps, and brought the Cambodians back home. The UN arranged for them to have a section of land on which to live. Each individual was given a 100-pound bag of rice, which would be enough to feed one person for a year, until they could start raising food for themselves. Pastor had been the leader of this group. He had led these people to Christ in the refugee camp, and they all worshipped together. There were probably about 200 people. They had been there about eight months. They had built their houses with natural building materials. Their gardens were doing well and they had even built a building large enough for a church.

Karen ask Reverend Bob if he could get as many people as possible together in the church, and she would give them a hygiene lecture, and give out toothbrushes. Pastor Bob got about 75 people assembled, and Karen lectured while he interpreted. None of them had toothbrushes so Karen made sure everyone got one.

The restrooms were typically third world. The outhouse had a hole dug in the ground with some boards over it except for a small opening. They had palm leaves stuck in the ground around the hole for privacy. One time when Dora May was using the outhouse, she took her scrubs down and bent over, and her fancy electronic mosquito repeller, which was clipped to her scrubs, fell off and went right down the hole. Needless to say we didn't attempt to retrieve it.

In the middle of the afternoon a middle-aged lady whom I will never forget, came rolling up to our clinic in an obviously homemade wheelchair. She had both of her legs missing right up to her trunk. She struggled through the sandy soil, but had a great big smile on her face. She had several aching abscessed infected teeth. Denise examined her and treated her right in her wheelchair. This lady had the most positive joyful attitude of anyone. She was always smiling, and very cooperative and appreciative. Her cheerfulness and positive thankful personality was very strikingly different from anyone we treated. After Denise had extracted several teeth, she not only thanked and thanked her, but she asked what she could do to help.

Pastor Bob walked by us about that time. I couldn't help asking him, "What's with this happy lady in the wheelchair." Pastor Bob told me this story: This lady, her husband, and three children were trying to escape from the Khmer Rouge. They were walking in the woods at night, on their way to the Thailand border, when they stepped on a landmine. It killed her husband and three children, and blew both of her legs off. Someone nearby who was also trying to escape, heard the explosion, and came over. He saw she was still alive, so he tied ropes around both of her legs to help stop the bleeding. Since he couldn't carry her, and she was unconscious, he dragged her by her hair into the Thailand refugee camp.

American doctors finished amputating both of her legs, and saved her life. Here she was, lying in a hospital bed with no legs, no family, or relatives, in a foreign country. Pastor Bob said, "We visited her regularly and brought her food, and when she was able to get out of the hospital, we took her into our home, and adopted her into our family." I asked him, "How many do you have in your family." He said, "45," and then he added, "All are adopted except our own two children. This lady has found the peace and joy that only Jesus can give, if they will have faith and believe in Him."

I thought to myself, if this lady can be happy after all she has gone through, I certainly should be twice as happy every moment of my life. When I get a headache, a little discouraged, depressed or down, all I have to do is to think about this lady's example, and immediately it lifts my spirits. For me, this lady's example has been a life-changing experience.

That evening we had supper in the dining room with the orphans. The next morning all four of us had varying degrees of diarrhea. After breakfast I went back to the kitchen to fill our water bottles for the day. The missionaries had installed an ultraviolet water purifier in the kitchen, and had it hooked to the water pipe. They assured us it was the best way to get pure water.

You have to understand the way the water system in Phnom Penh works. They pump the water out of the Mekong River to a higher level in the city, and then they let the water run back into the river through narrow 6-inch wide open ditches, which run down the sidewalks in front of the buildings. If you wanted water, you put a little electric pump about the size of a football, next to the water ditch, and put a hose into the water, then run the hose from this pump to a water tank mounted on the highest point of your building. From this water tank you had pipes to all your sinks and toilets using gravity pressure.

The Mekong River runs thousands of miles through Vietnam, Cambodia, Thailand, Laos, Burma and China, with millions of people dumping their sewage into the river, and with all types of animals drinking and going to the bathroom in this river. To look at the river, it was so dirty you couldn't see one-half inch into it. It was a gray brown color. I couldn't think of a more contaminated river.

The purified water ran out of this ultraviolet purifier very slowly, so I had to wait a good 10 minutes to fill our water bottles. While I was waiting I observed a lady who was supervising 4 or 5 orphans who were washing dishes and doing the breakfast cleanup. They were washing dishes in a big sink of soapy water, using the water that came directly from the Mekong River. They didn't rinse the dishes, but just set them on a big counter to dry. I didn't like what I was seeing at all. Then I observed something even worse. There were two big baskets of leftover rice. We had rice for every meal, as it was their main food. There were around two gallons of this rice in the baskets. When the dishes were finished, the lady supervisor took the baskets of leftover rice, and dipped them in the dirty soapy Mekong River dishwater and swished them up and down several times and set them on the counter to drain. I asked her, "What are you going to do with them?" The supervisor said, "We never let any food go to waste. We will have this rice for lunch."

Then I knew why we were all having diarrhea. This was the last meal we ate in the dining room. Fortunately we had brought along a fairly good supply of snacks, including raisins, nuts, cheese crackers, M&Ms, power bars, and various dried fruits. We made our snacks last for all three meals, for 12 days. Our diarrhea cleared up in a few days. We all lost a little weight, which we probably all needed anyway.

The next morning we went to a small hospital in the city. It was totally financed by a U.S. charitable organization and had just been open a few months. The entire country had no dental services and very little medical services. We set up our clinic on a large outside porch, hoping to get better light and a breeze. Immediately we had large numbers of people starting to form lines.

The doctor, who was the Chief of Staff of the Hospital, asked if I would look at his wife. She had been having several bad toothaches. When I looked in her mouth, I found several badly abscessed teeth. I numbed her down, and while waiting for the anesthesia, I asked the doctor where he received his medical training. He said, "Actually I'm a dentist." I asked, "How could you let your wife suffer with such pain without taking her aching teeth out?" He said "I have never extracted a tooth." I asked him again, "Where did you say you got your training?" He commented, "Oh! I read a book once."

He was Chief of Staff of the Hospital, the big man in charge of the whole hospital, and his qualifications for the job was that he had read a dental book once. I thought to myself, this is unbelievable, but then I also thought, he is risking his life in taking this job, and admitting that he could read. The Khmer Rouge was threatening to invade Phnom Penh, and take the city over again. Last time they did that, people like him were tortured and killed.

Here, we actually ran three dental chairs; one for me, one for Denise, my dental assistant, and one for Karen, my hygienist. Together we extracted hundreds of teeth. Even then, there was still a long line waiting when it started to get dark, and we had to stop and pack and go home.

One day we went to the edge of the city on the banks, or a flood plain, of the Mekong River. There was a large shanty town of hundreds and hundreds of dwellings, made out of cardboard boxes, and scraps of anything that could be used for building material. We walked a long way down an alley-like street, which was often so narrow there was just room for one person to walk. Most of the houses were attached together which seemed to help hold them upright.

After a long walk, we came to a dwelling where Norbet knew the occupants. They came to the mission church, and Norbet had made arrangements for us to set up our clinic in their small dwelling. There wasn't enough room to set up in the street which had no shade and was directly in the sun. They had cleared out one small room and even though it was dark, we set up inside, and got out our flashlights. It was extremely cozy trying to work in this very small room. It was extremely hot. I was sometimes embarrassed because the sweat from my face would occasionally drip right into the patient's face, eyes, or mouth. It was salty, and they would often stop and spit it out, or they would blink their eyes many times.

The last patient of the day had a lower third molar in which the roots broke off, when I tried to extract it. I have never before left a root in a patient's mouth, and I was determined I wouldn't let this be the first time. I was hot and tired, but I was determined to remove all the roots. I worked on the patient for over 40 minutes, but finally got out all the roots. I knew if I left them, there would be a good possibility of endless infection and pain. Generally speaking, their teeth came out quite easy, but not this one.

Again we saw a lot of people, and extracted many teeth, but we also left a lot of people untreated when we had to pack up at the end of the day and leave. On our way out of this cardboard jungle, we walked along the bank of the Mekong River, which actually had a foul odor, and was extremely dirty.

We observed a large island in the middle of the river. Norbet told us the government had given this island to the amputees that had lost legs or limbs from landmines during their civil war. He indicated that Cambodia had over 9 million landmines put in the ground, more than any other country in the history of the world. There were still many landmines that had not been discovered, and many areas where people wouldn't walk. Cambodia had 35,000 amputees, which figured out to be 1 out of every 250 people in the population. Norbet said that there were several thousand amputees living on the island, and we were not allowed out there.

On Sunday they had a church service in the largest room in the mission. It was on the fifth floor. People from the city were welcome to come to the church services. As we were going up several long flights of stairs to the fifth floor, I noticed several wet spots on the marble stairs. It looked like someone had been leaking large drops of water. When I mentioned this to Norbet he said, "They are drops of sweat." It was very hot, and the drops increased in frequency as we got nearer the top. I could begin to understand this, because I was sweating myself by the time I got to the top.

I wondered how many people we would have in church on Sunday morning in the U.S., if they had to walk up five long flights of stairs in a hot temperature, which would cause them to sweat like that. Then when we got to church it would be 90° to 100°, with no air-conditioning or breeze.

Reverend Chen conducted the morning service, which was about two hours long, none of which we could understand. There were several hundred people in the congregation. The lady immediately in front of us had a young girl, one or two year's old sitting on her lap. In the middle of Reverend Chen's sermon, the girl started to urinate on the mother's dress. The mother then held the girl out in front of her, and she created a puddle on the floor. The mother put her back in her lap without saying a word, and at the end of the service, she just got up and walked away. This incident caused me to look at the floor around me, and I could see several large bloodstains that were permanently in the floor.

On Sunday afternoon we walked to a park on the Mekong riverbank. I observed several unusual things. First of all, it was so hot, that after I walked one block, my sport shirt was totally soaked with sweat. I can't remember any place in this world that I have felt this hot. We were told that April is Cambodia's hottest month of the year. I expect the very high humidity contributed to our hot feeling.

I observed some construction workers, busy building a multi-story building along the street on which we were walking, even on a Sunday afternoon. There was a continuous line of people picking up baskets of bricks, and baskets of mortar, putting them on their heads, and walking up a three-story bamboo ramp to the top area where they were laying the bricks. The most interesting thing to me was that neither the men nor women doing this manual hauling of this heavy material, were breathing hard, or sweating one bit. I was sweating just standing there watching them.

We observed a teenage boy sitting along the road with 10 or 15 quart-sized wine type bottles sitting on a small table, with a light reddish brown liquid in them. I asked Norbet, "What's he selling?" Norbet said, "That's a gas station. He is selling gasoline." Sure enough, a motorcycle pulled over, and bought two bottles of gas. The biggest irony of this primitive gas station was the teenage boy while sitting there waiting for customers, was playing a hand-held Game Boy.

A little further down the street, near the park, there were vendors with portable bird cages, selling small yellow sparrow-sized live birds. Their singing created quite pleasant music. I watched people buying them. The vendor put a rubber band around their wings. The people would go to the next vendor booth, where the vendor took the live birds, and dipped them into boiling water for a couple of minutes, then pulled them out, and plucked off the feathers. Then he put them into boiling deep frying oil, and after a few moments he would pull the deep-fried bird out and give it to the customer. Holding it by its legs, the person ate the whole bird, like a hot dog on a stick. At no time did they clean the entrails out of the bird. We passed on that one. In some places people were buying the birds and just letting them go free.

We went to the central Buddhist temple, which used to be the king's temple. It was covered with millions and millions of dollars worth of gold and jewels. I couldn't help but think what a fantastic waste of natural resources and wealth, when within a mile there was the island of amputees, and the big slum area we had been the day before.

We also observed several vendors with hand-cranked sugarcane presses. They were pressing the sugarcane into a liquid, pouring it into glasses, and selling it to customers, who were drinking it like we would drink a Coke. You could also buy sugarcane that had the outer skin peeled off, with a toothpick stuck in it. People were eating and sucking on this like suckers. With no toothbrushes, and zero dental hygiene, it was easy to understand why we were seeing so many decayed and abscessed teeth. They just didn't know any better.

The taxis in town were mainly three-wheeled bicycle rickshaws that usually held two people. We rented some of these taxis to take us back to the mission compound. Even though the city was relatively flat, I felt uncomfortable, and somewhat guilty, watching this man straining in the heat, as he peddled us back to the mission. I guess he was just happy to have a fare.

On Monday we went to another church member's house with whom Norbet had made previous arrangements. They lived in a small concrete house, on a side street just a few houses from the main street. They had set up a tarp over the sidewalk in front of their house for our clinic. It worked well. We set up three chairs in the shade of the tarp. We gathered a big crowd in a semi-circle around us, so deep that it extended across the road and completely blocked traffic. We had no waiting line and little control over who was next. When one person got up out of our chair, two or three people would try to sit down in the chair at the same time.

There was a man standing beside me holding a cute three year old little girl. After a bit, Denise walked up to them and asked the little girl to open her mouth. In a flash Denise reached up and extracted the little girl's four front teeth. The little girl never complained or squirmed at all, as her dad was holding her in his arms. I was rather surprised, and asked Denise, "What are you doing?" She told me, the little girl was in her chair earlier, and she determined her front teeth were all decayed and abscessed, and that they needed to be removed. She gave the little girl anesthesia, and she got back in her dad's arms. People were pushing so much to get into the chair that the little girl couldn't get back into her chair. She felt a good place to extract these previously numbed teeth, was right in her daddy's arms. I congratulated her. She was right, and did a good job.

Some days like this day in the street, it was impossible to stop for lunch, so we just worked through lunch and ate our snacks after we returned to our rooms at night. Again we extracted hundreds of teeth. These people hadn't had a dentist available to them in almost 20 years, and even then, most of them probably could not have afforded to go to a dentist anyway. They were desperate, and you could see the feelings of desperation on their faces. It was difficult to stop. When it finally got dark enough that we were having trouble seeing, we felt comfortable closing the clinic. At that time of day, I think the masses of waiting patients understood.

We had brought a 5-gallon water filter with us. We put water in the top, and it filtered through some ceramic filters, and collected in the bottom container. You could filter up to 10 gallons of water in 24 hours. The sides of the filter container were somewhat transparent, and it was interesting to see the water in the top before it was filtered. It was a dark gray color, whereas the water in the bottom after filtering was crystal clear.

It was interesting to read the directions that came with this filter. It said that the U.S. Department of Agriculture guaranteed that the ceramic filters would filter out 100% of all micro-organisms. That meant that we could put swamp water in there and filter it into pure drinkable water. It sounded too good to be true. We all felt good when we were drinking the water from of the mission's ultraviolet water purifier so we kept using that for our drinking water. We used the water from our filter for the large quantities of water we needed to wash and sterilize our dental instruments.

In one of the places that we worked there was a young missionary couple with two small children. When they heard about our water filter, they begged and begged us to leave it with them, or sell it to them. They only had a small hand-pumped ceramic water filter that they had to pump by hand for 5 or 10 minutes just to get a quart of drinkable water. They couldn't buy anything like ours in Cambodia. Unfortunately the water filter didn't belong to me. I borrowed it from HTI with the agreement that I would return it when we returned. I felt very guilty telling them, "I'm sorry, I can't leave it with you."

We had an opportunity to walk one block to the city's main central market. They sold just about everything you would have expected a hundred years ago. They were selling mostly food and clothing, but nothing that interested us. They did have some interesting types of protein, which included baskets full of black beetles, grasshoppers, worms, caterpillars, and other types of unusual insects.

I asked Norbet, "Can we take you and your family out for a good steak dinner some evening?" He started to laugh. I asked, "What's so funny?" He said, "You couldn't find a piece of meat in this whole city bigger than a green pea." He continued, "They take all meat, along with most food, and chop it up on wooden blocks with a big meat cleaver into small pieces." I asked, "Why do they do that?" He said, "I thought you would know quicker than anyone. Their teeth are so bad that most people couldn't chew meat or anything much at all, so they chop everything up into small chunks so that the people can swallow it without chewing."

Dr. Craig Mallow contacted us and invited us out for supper one evening. Dr. Mallow was a former student of Dr. Miller's at Oral Roberts University Dental School. Dr. Miller had contacted Dr. Morrow and asked him to look us up. On our way to supper we stopped at a small grocery store. This was toward the end of our stay and we were running low on snack foods. We found some U.S. Ritz crackers and bought them, but they were so stale and musty tasting that we were afraid to eat them.

Dr. Mallow had been in Cambodia for almost a year, working with a different mission organization. One of his goals was to help start a dental school in Phnom Penh. We had a good supper and everyone enjoyed the good conversation with Dr. Mallow. He invited us to visit their dental school which they had just started with 20 students.

The next day during our lunch hour, we were able to get away and visit the building where they were starting the dental school. They had some very old U.S. type dental equipment. The dentist in charge of the school was a very energetic, hundred-pound Philippine female, who spoke perfect English. She showed us all around the school. When we came to the library, it had only about 25 books in it, which drew an apology from the Philippine dentist. As I was glancing at the books, I noticed they were all in English. Suddenly my eyes caught a familiar book. It was a workbook in dental anatomy that I had written when I was teaching at the University of Michigan. I asked her how she got my book, and she just shrugged her shoulders and said she didn't know. It is a small world sometimes.

We had a clinic in several other areas, all within the city. The last day we had a clinic at the mission compound, in the large room where we had church, the one with all the blood stains on the floor. We treated the orphans, the mission staff and their family, and many of the church people. Norbet told us that Pul Pot, who had led the killing of several million Cambodian people, came back to Phnom Penh a few weeks after the election. He said, "It's a good wonder the people didn't riot and kill him. The prevailing philosophy concerning his visit was, to let the past be the past, and to not start any more killings, because the people just wanted to live in peace."

When we got ready to leave the country our snacks were gone, but we were all feeling fine. We said our farewells and went to the airport. While waiting at the airport I observed another unusual situation. When we went into the bathroom we found a western type toilet stool, with a seat and toilet paper. We had never seen this once in Cambodia, except at the mission. The Cambodian people squat when going to the bathroom, as do most Southeast Asians. We noticed that the paint was off both sides of the toilet seat. When we asked Norbet to explain what we observed he said, "Simple, this is where the Cambodian people stand and squat when going to the bathroom. They don't know how to use a toilet seat."

We flew to Bangkok, Thailand, where we stayed and toured for three days. None of us had ever been in Thailand before. Our faithful travel agent, Jill, pointed out to us, that a Northwest Airlines Vacation Package to Bangkok included our airfare, two nights in a first-class hotel, and three days of touring, was cheaper to buy than just the airfare alone. Needless to say, we took it and everybody enjoyed our stay in Bangkok on our way home.

I felt very good about our Cambodian mission. We relieved over a thousand people of pain and infection. They had no other possible way to get treatment. We were able to show the love of Jesus in us by our example. Our presence and work gave the missionaries greater respect among the people, and it enabled them to better share Jesus with the Cambodian people.

## And Now the Rest of the Story

My kidney stone pain was quite severe the first night in Cambodia. After that it died down a little but was always there to some degree. One of the most uncomfortable parts was the intense urge to urinate. When I got busy I tended to forget about it. I developed a fever about halfway through the mission trip, so I took the antibiotics and kept going. I didn't miss any part of the mission trip, or post trip.

We got home late Sunday evening. Monday morning I went to my Urologist's office without an appointment. I told him I was extremely uncomfortable, and would he please remove the stint. He took an x-ray and found the stone had come half way down the ureter, between the stint and the ureter wall. He had assured me that it wouldn't do that, but it did. That was the reason for all the discomfort and even the infection and fever. In about 60 seconds he went in and grabbed the stint, and with a big memorable yank, he pulled the foot-long stint out. The stint had enlarged the ureter, so the stone passed out by itself the next day, with no further discomfort. Fortunately I have had no significant problems since. Praise the Lord!

Dr. Lee Wiggins has taken a team back to Cambodia many years since, and he has worked with the same mission people. He believes they are making good progress in not only helping people physically, but in introducing them directly or indirectly, to salvation through Jesus Christ.

# CHAPTER 15

# CHINA MANCHURIA

China always seemed to me, to be an ancient, forbidden and somewhat mystical country that I really knew little about.

Dr. Miller had a friend, Mary Lou Smith, who was formerly from his hometown of Tulsa, Oklahoma. She had been an undercover missionary in northeastern China for over 10 years. She worked as a health adviser, and her office happened to be across the hall from the government's Director of Health, Dr. Chang. She was responsible for the health of several million people in the northeast part of the country, called Manchuria.

Mary Lou became friends with Dr. Chang. One day Mary Lou asked her, "What would you think if I could bring a team of U.S. dentists to visit and to treat your people, in one of your isolated areas that don't have a dentist?" Mary Lou was surprised when after a few days Dr. Chang said to her, "I like your idea." She told Mary Lou to make arrangements to bring a dental team. This team could go to the remote farming village of Sue Nu, which had been surveyed as one of the poorest areas in China. Dr. Chang said that this type of help for the isolated rural poor people had never been tried.

Mary Lou was excited, and immediately contacted Dr. Miller, her HTI friend, for help. Dr. Miller would have liked to have made the trip, since he had always wanted go to China; however, he was 74 years old, and recovering from a massive stroke. Dr. Miller called me and asked if I would lead the team to China. My response was "Why not?" Dr. Miller provided me with the name of a dentist in the Seattle, Washington, area that he thought might be interested in joining me. I phoned Dr. William Pratt. I explained our invitation, and both he and his wife Peggy wanted to join Dora May and me.

Bill and Peggy had been going to Guatemala, Central America, as short-term missionaries for several years. Bill had recently retired from private practice, and was currently teaching a national men's Bible study. They met every Monday night for nine months of the year. He was very committed to these 200 men, and could only go after May, when the Bible study was completed for the year. We planned to go in June so this worked well for him. The area in northern Manchuria where we were going was located at the same latitude as North Dakota or Lake Superior. In June, the weather would just be starting to get nice.

Karen, my dental hygienist, who went to Cambodia with us, asked if she could go. That sounded good to me, and Mary Lou authorized the five of us to come.

Dr. Pratt had put much of his retirement investments into a charitable trust, to be used for mission trips. He had planned that after his retirement from private practice, he would spend much of his time doing mission trips. His responsibility to his Bible study teaching was limiting his availability to go. Dr. Pratt had personally purchased a complete set of portable dental equipment, from his charitable trust. It included the newest and most modern portable equipment to do fillings. He enjoyed doing fillings. So we made an agreement; he and Peggy would do fillings, while Dora May and I would do extractions. I planned for Karen to do hygiene work, such as cleaning, scaling and patient education.

In June 1995, Karen, Dora May, and I boarded one of the first direct flights from the U.S. to China. It was a Northwest flight from Detroit, non-stop to Beijing, a total of 14 hours in the air. We met Bill and Peggy in Beijing. Our flights arrived at almost the same time. They had to fly from Seattle to Tokyo, and then to Beijing. Mary Lou had a travel agent friend, Chin, who met us at the airport, and transferred us to the Friendship Hotel, the main tourist hotel right in downtown Beijing.

We went three days early so we could visit the sites in and around Beijing. Chin did an excellent job of arranging good tours for us. We had an opportunity to visit Tiananmen Square, the Forbidden City, the Temple to Heaven, the Great Wall, the Silk Market, the Summer Palace, and several other interesting places.

Early in the morning on our fourth day, Chin took us to the train station, for an all day train ride to Shenyang, the capital of Liaoning Province. We noticed that the countryside was uniquely different, as we looked out the train windows. We saw many primitive houses and a lot of people everywhere. All available land was planted into crops, even to the banks of the railroad tracks.

Shenyang was a very large city of several million people, and it was heavily industrialized with steel mills and heavy manufacturing. We could see the city from a distance, with many tall smokestacks billowing out black smoke, which hung over the city like smog.

Late in the afternoon Mary Lou met us at the train, thank God, because we were a long way from home, and none of us spoke any Chinese. She took us to a small overnight hotel. Early the next morning we packed into two small minibuses and headed north. Mary Lou had brought two young Christian evangelist translators, Beth and Sheila. Surprisingly, Dr. Chang and her secretary also came with us.

The trip was long, bumpy, and dusty. The farther we went, the smaller the road became. We went through many small villages. About 1 p.m., we arrived at the small village of

Sue Nu. We pulled between two large official looking buildings, and into a big courtyard. Immediately about 20 government officials, all dressed in their finest uniforms, surrounded our bus and welcomed us as if we were royalty. Obviously there had been a great deal of advanced planning done by the big boss, Dr. Chang. It turned out that we were the first foreigners that anyone could remember, to have come to their small village.

After extensive greetings and introductions, we were taken into a large room, where a banquet was set for us. A lot of toasting and welcoming speeches were made by many of the officials. I was also asked to make a speech. Since no one understood English, I trusted Mary Lou who translated for me, would take the liberty to say the culturally correct comments. Finally, we had a very nice lunch.

After lunch we drove a few blocks down Main Street to the health clinic, where we were met by several white-jacketed healthcare providers. The building was long and narrow and faced Main Street. It had a sizable central vestibule with halls extending both ways to small rooms. They took us and our baggage straight through the clinic to a small building 40 or 50 feet behind the clinic. This also had a central vestibule with halls going both ways to small rooms. These rooms were to be our sleeping quarters.

Upon entering our room, I was impressed by the beautifully colored hand embroidery on the pillowcases. After setting our suitcases on the bed, I noticed a white substance on them. Upon investigating, I found it was wet paint. It is still on my suitcases today. The beds were made special for us out of wooden two by fours. They had been recently painted, and while most of the paint was dry, in some areas the paint had pooled and thickened and was still a little wet. Chipped corn cobs, 2 or 3 inches thick, were placed on the bed frame. A heavy linoleum cloth was tacked over it for a mattress.

We were told later that this building was a very dirty old storehouse shed that they totally cleaned out and repainted for us to stay in. The town had no rooms for guests, since no guests had ever been there. Actually, even the villagers were not allowed to travel outside their own villages without special complex government permits. Military road checkpoints were placed between each village. We were stopped many times in our travel to Sue Nu.

We walked about three buildings down Main Street from the medical clinic for our meals. The officials had arranged for a family that lived in a house with a big room to cook all of our meals. There were no restraints in the village. About six or eight of the government officials ate with us every evening. Their hospitality and kindness could not have been better. I assumed they were just trying to impress Dr. Chang, because she was a very important top government official. I found out on several later trips to China, that this very enthusiastic and warm hospitality was common in China, wherever we went.

All of our meals consisted of rice with vegetable toppings, and most meals had roasted peanuts. The peanuts kept me alive for two weeks. I love peanuts. We had no silverware, and I actually became pretty good picking up the peanuts with my chopsticks, after a little practice, of course. We brought a large quantity of bottled water with us from Shenyang, which was our only drink, except for hot tea. The government officials brought their alcoholic drinks with them each evening, and drank fairly heavily.

It was quite easy to see some of the fallacies, and potential corruption, in the 30 to 40 year old ideas of the Communist philosophy that everyone needed to be treated equally. In this very poor farming community, where most houses were made of mud and corn stalks, the government officials drove to supper in the evening in their highly polished, chauffeur driven Mercedes. What a dramatic contrast that created. One does not have to be a genius to see through this fallacy.

The next morning we set up our dental clinic. We decided to all work in one room. Even though it was a little cozy, we were all together in this strange and unusual place. We set up three dental chairs; one for Dr. Pratt and Peggy to do fillings, one for Dora May and me to do extractions, and one for Karen to do her hygiene work. We started quickly because many patients were waiting. The medical personnel had hung a large sign in front of the clinic announcing our arrival.

These villagers had no dental services available to them. There was no such thing as private dental practice. The government owned and operated all dental clinics. The only dental clinics available were in large hospitals in big cities. It was difficult to get a pass to travel through the roadblocks to the big city. Needless to say, the dental care of these people had been totally neglected for a long time.

Dr. Chang observed the dental health of these villagers very closely for the first few days, and she watched how we were treating them. As time went by, she seemed to lose interest, and would wander in and out of the clinic occasionally. Mary Lou tried to organize and supervise the waiting patients. Her big problem was with the government officials and their families, who came in and insisted that they didn't need to wait in line. The villagers seemed to understand this inequity better than we did. Fortunately, there were only a few such patients.

I quickly observed that I was getting far behind because many people were requesting extractions. Karen had extracted a lot of teeth successfully in Cambodia a few years previously, so I asked her to help me. She did, and soon we doubled the number of patients we were helping. Occasionally Karen would get pressured into scaling and polishing the teeth of a government official or his wife.

One day Karen actually extracted a tooth that I couldn't, or I refused to extract. A mother walked and carried her four year old girl from a neighboring village about two and a half hours away. She walked through the fields so she would not get stopped at the roadblocks. The child screamed hysterically every time the mother tried to put her into my dental chair and the child absolutely refused to open her mouth. The mother was very patient and determined. She refused to go away. She would take the screaming child outside, talk to her, calm her, and then bring her back. The same problem recurred. This happened several times, so I gave up on the child. It was time to go to lunch, when Karen said, "Let me try her."

Most of the patients had left for a lunch break. Karen then set the little girl down on her mother's lap, and the mother held her head very tightly while the child continued to scream and thrash. Finally, the child stopped crying, and fell asleep in her mother's arms, totally exhausted. At that time, Karen propped the child's mouth open, numbed the area, and extracted the tooth before the child awoke.

I am suspicious that without any dental services in the area that the mother had probably tried to extract the tooth previously without any anesthesia. A child will not forget this type of trauma for the rest of its life. An early unpleasant childhood experience results in more complete dentures than any other cause. Regardless of how intelligent a person may be, if hurt as a child, many adults will not go back to a dentist until it is too late to fix their teeth. Generally, most of our child patients were excellent, and much better than the average child in the United States.

At lunch, I couldn't help but notice the cornfield growing close to our window. I also observed with amazement, a man who had a donkey pulling a cultivator. He was cultivating the weeds out of the corn. I watched my uncle do this for many hours at a time back on the farm, with a tractor of course, when I was growing up. It required a lot of skill, because one wrong movement and you could remove the corn rather than the weeds.

Sue Nu was corn country. Corn fields stretched as far as you could see in all directions. I assumed either their soil was unusually fertile, or they just had not heard of crop rotations. They used the corncobs and corn stalks for cooking and winter heating fuel. There were very few trees in the area for firewood.

Karen was a jogger. Very early on the first morning, she got up and started jogging down the center of Main Street. She happened to glance behind her, and noticed a uniformed soldier with a rifle jogging a short distance behind her. As she continued, the soldier continued to follow her. She became a little uncomfortable, so she stopped alongside the road at a fruit stand. The soldier stopped also. After a few minutes she started jogging back toward the clinic. The soldier waited until she passed, and he then jogged behind her all the way back to the clinic.

Karen asked Mary Lou, and Mary Lou in turn asked Dr. Chang, why the soldier was following her that morning. Dr. Chang explained, "We have two soldiers living in the other end of our housing unit. Their responsibility is to protect us and keep us safe. These villagers have been taught all their life that Americans are bad, and they were taught to hate them. We weren't sure how strong this hatred might still be, and if anyone would try to harm you. We thought we would play it safe and keep you well protected." That seemed both alarming and comforting to us. The next morning when Karen got up and started jogging down Main Street, she looked behind her to see if the soldier were following. He was coming, but this time he was riding a bicycle.

We found out that the medical clinic had six doctors and ten nurses, but they didn't have any supplies or medications. They didn't have a bandage, an aspirin, a scalpel blade, sutures, or any type of pills. They had absolutely nothing, which I am sure disturbed Dr. Chang. The doctors would come in at 11 a.m., have some lunch and tea, and go home about 1:30 p.m. Usually they never saw one patient all day. We had long lines of patients, and we were treating many people.

One young physician kept hanging around our clinic, and watching everything we were doing, especially extractions. Beth was my translator. Finally this physician told Beth that he was a trained surgeon and he would like to learn to extract teeth. I thought about his request for a while, and concluded he had absolutely no equipment with which to extract teeth. If the clinic could not buy an aspirin, they certainly couldn't buy dental anesthesia and extraction forceps. Besides, if I took time to teach him, this would significantly slow my work, and there would be a lot of patients with toothaches that I wouldn't be able to help. So I decided not to teach him.

He kept hanging around and watching. He was exceptionally nice and courteous. He asked Beth if we would like to come and visit his house some evening. This sounded interesting to me. Beth indicated we would have to develop a plan where we could sneak away from our two soldier guards, because she didn't think a home visit would be officially allowed. After dinner that evening, we waited until the half drunken government officials left. Then half of our group got up as we had previously planned, and started walking back to the clinic, while some of us stayed behind and talked. We were fortunate because the two soldiers got up and went with the first group.

Mary Lou, Beth, Dora May and I sneaked out the back door and headed down the alley in the opposite direction. The surgeon's house was only a block or two away. We knocked and he came to the door and let us inside. He introduced himself as Pul and then introduced his pretty wife, and proudly showed us his two month old baby daughter.

The doctor's house was nothing like I expected. It was concrete instead of mud, like most of the other houses in town. It was attached to several other houses, similar to apartments. His house consisted of one room about 25 feet square with a concrete floor, walls and ceiling, and one big bed of concrete on the side of the room. The family had a small fire going under a big wok in which they did all of their cooking. They had no stove, refrigerator, heater, furnace, TV, nor any electrical appliances. They had a few chairs and a table. They also had a hood over their fire, which had a chimney pipe that curved around, and went the full length underneath their concrete bed, and went up a wall on the other side of the room. They used this to heat their home in the winter. Their winter temperature drops to zero degrees, with lots of snow. They had several thick blankets that they put under them for a mattress, and over them to keep warm. We were told that the nearest telephone was one hour away by car.

I was astonished at the primitiveness of Pul's home. After all, he was a doctor, and he had a family. He wasn't complaining. He seemed proud of what he had. After a while Pul got us into a small circle in the middle of the room, and whispered to us in a low voice, that he and his wife were Christians. We were shocked. I asked him how he became a Christian, and he told us this story. "During my surgery training at the University I had an American professor that was very nice and different from my other professors. When I asked him why he was so different, he told me that he was a Christian. I asked him if I could be a Christian like he was, and he told me all about Jesus. Then he told me how to become a Christian, and I did. I then told my wife about Jesus and she became a Christian too. This professor helped us in our early Christian growth, but when I graduated, the government assigned me to this clinic in Sue Nu, where there are no Christians."

I asked Pul if he had a Bible, and he said "No." Mary Lou said, "I will get you one." She had brought six Bibles with her, even though people had been getting six-year prison terms for handing out Bibles.

Pul said, "No one knows that I am a Christian. Please promise not to tell anyone. If anyone knew that I am a Christian, I would lose my job, and be thrown out of my government house. I probably couldn't leave the area, and my family would starve or freeze in the winter." He was obviously very concerned about this.

I asked him how he was fed spiritually. He told me he had a small illegal short-wave radio, and that he and his wife listened to a Christian broadcast out of Hong Kong at 6 a.m. each morning. Interestingly, Dr. Luke Sheng, a Chinese Christian acupuncture medical doctor in my hometown of Brighton, owns and operates a Christian radio station in Hong Kong that continuously broadcasts Christian messages into the mainland of China every day.

Pul asked me again, "Is there any way you could teach me how to extract teeth?" I explained to Mary Lou what I had decided and why. She said, "We can buy instruments and supplies when we get back to Shenyang, and I will personally see that he receives them." She really knew how to change my mind. She then said. "After you leave, the people will be able to continue to get dental treatment, if you teach him."

She totally convinced me, so I said, "Let's get started at daybreak. I need to go over many basics with him first."

Beth said, "I will get up and translate for you, but do you know what time it gets light here this time of year? 3:30 A.M." The entire country of China is on one time zone, and we were in Eastern China near the end of June.

We met in the clinic at 3:30 A.M. It was light, so we got started. He was partially trained and smart, so he learned quickly. During the day in the clinic, I talked to him continuously, and demonstrated a lot of procedures to him. The next morning we got up at 3:30 A.M. again and continued teaching basics.

When starting the clinic the afternoon of Pul's second day, I felt he was ready to begin extracting teeth. My first patient was a pleasant, docile little old lady that came in and sat down in my chair with a big smile on her face. I said to Pul, "This is your first patient. I want you to identify the tooth that is causing the pain, numb it well, and extract it."

He immediately had big drops of sweat appear on his forehead. I thought this was a little unusual for a surgeon. He diagnosed the problem, numbed the abscessed tooth, and extracted it. He did a nice job. When the patient got up, she gave him a big hug and a kiss. I thought, "I've never gotten a hug or kiss from anyone." Then he told me, "That was my mother-in-law." No wonder he was sweating! I supervised him closely and he learned very quickly.

While I was spending time teaching Pul, Mary Lou had asked Karen if she would teach her how to extract teeth. Karen became busy teaching Mary Lou. I was happy, but couldn't help but think how ironic it was for a hygienist to be teaching someone how to extract teeth. In the U.S. it is illegal for a hygienist to extract teeth, and she had never received any formal training. I had taught Karen how to extract teeth, when she went with me to Cambodia. Now she was teaching someone else. It was exciting to see this progression.

We saw several very unusual dental conditions which we would never have seen in the U.S. in a lifetime. One lady had a very primitive bridge, replacing her upper two front teeth. She was very happy with it, even though she had large silver bands on the two teeth next to the front teeth, to hold it in place. It was tight and doing the job. Her complaint was the pain above the bridge. Upon examining the situation, I concluded that the dentist who made this primitive bridge did not remove the roots of the two front teeth. The two roots were still underneath this permanently fixed bridge, and the roots were abscessed. The gums were red, swollen, infected, full of pus and very painful. I knew the patient wouldn't be very happy if I removed her bridge in order to get access to the roots, so I did something that I had never done before or since. I cut a hole in her gum, removed some bone, removed the roots out of the hole in the bone, and then sutured the gums. We didn't disturb her bridge at all, the roots were out, and she was happy.

I only saw about ten fillings in teeth during the two weeks we were in Sue Nu. Interestingly enough, every single restored tooth had an abscess, so I had to remove the tooth that contained the filling. The restorations were so poorly done, that I am convinced that the patients would have been much better off if they had never had the tooth filled in the first place.

On Sunday afternoon, we asked if we could walk around the village, and we were granted permission. The two armed soldiers came with us. We saw the man who cooked our food at the vegetable market, buying our food for supper. We were told that he bought fresh food every day. They didn't have refrigerators or even ice boxes.

In one area, while we stopped and talked, a lady came out of her house and invited us to visit her home. Their three room house was made completely of mud with cornstalk reinforcement. A big wooden block was near their wok with a meat cleaver sitting on top of it. Beth told us all of their food was chopped thoroughly before being put into the wok. This was routine in most Chinese houses. Their wok was heated by an open fire, fueled by cornstalks, which was also used to heat their house in the winter. There were poles between the dried mud walls, which supported a grassy thatched roof. This was typical of the construction of most village houses. They had a nice garden behind their house, which was fenced in by a 5-foot tall mud wall. They had a hand-pumped well, for drinking and for watering their garden. Their garden looked really great. They had two 10-year-old boys that helped with the garden. This was the only family that we saw with two children, but their family was accepted, because they were twins. The Communist government has been very strict on their policy of one child per family.

We saw an old man sitting along the side of the road. Beth, our most aggressive evangelist, asked him if he had ever heard of Jesus. He said "No, he had never heard of anyone called Jesus." Then he asked, "Who is Jesus?" Today we have over 2 billion people in the world who have never heard the name of Jesus. It is hard for us in the United States to understand how this could possibly be true, but it is.

We have a cuckoo clock at home that cuckoos every half hour. During our walk I heard a rather loud and clear cuckoo, just like our cuckoo clock. I asked, "What's that?" Beth answered, "It's a cuckoo bird." I asked, "Where is it? I want to see it." She said, "Don't bother to look. They are real easy to hear, but almost impossible to find." She continued, "They are really bad birds. They eat the eggs out of other birds' nests." I was just surprised to know that there was a real cuckoo bird.

When we got back to our rooms, Dr. Bill Pratt decided to take a bath. He put on his bathing suit, took his soap and towel, and went out to the hand pump in front of our quarters. He pumped a bucket of water into a pail. It must have been a deep well because the water was very cold. He took the pail, poured water over his head and used soap. Then he pumped more pails of water and poured them over his head to rinse. We watched him flinch every time he poured water on himself, because it was so cold. The rest of us chose to continue our sponge baths.

The bathroom was something else. It was a concrete outhouse building big enough for two or three people. There were several holes in the floor, along with a lot of moisture on the floor. The floor was covered with slimy bloodsucker type organisms that piled up a couple of inches deep. This was in addition to the wonderful smell. I usually manage fairly well with outhouses, but this one was the worst I have ever experienced.

One evening we started to get a heavy wind. We thought a rainstorm was coming, so we closed our shutters. Our windows had no glass or screens. Thank goodness we were in the dry season, because we had very few bugs. The next morning there were little piles of sand all around the cracks in the shutters. We learned that we were in the middle of a sandstorm blowing from the great Gobi Desert that was not far away. The sandstorm kept up all day, so we had to keep the shutters of our clinic closed also.

The chipped corncobs that were supposed to be our mattress didn't work too well. The slats in the bottom of the bed were too far apart, and after a couple of nights, a pile of corncob chips was on the floor under our bed, and we slept on the boards.

One afternoon we had three schoolteachers come to the clinic. They asked for us to explain to them what Christmas meant. Beth, our evangelist, spent quite a little time explaining to them the real meaning of Christmas. Pul told us that on two occasions before we came, the authorities had distributed fliers around town warning people not to be influenced by false philosophies that the foreigners might bring. We had to be careful as to when and to whom we talked to about Christianity, but we did have numerous good conversations with some of our patients about Jesus. We didn't force anything on them, but just informed them what Christians in America believe.

The main street in town was made of dirt. How many main streets in U.S. towns are dirt today? The following description of their method of paving Main Street will give you some idea as to how far behind their society was. While we were there, we observed the paving of Main Street. Some trucks came and dumped gravel all along both sides of the road. Then bags of concrete were thrown from a truck onto the piles of gravel. Several hundred men came along with shovels and thoroughly mixed the dry cement with the dry gravel, and threw the mixture out on the road. The mixture was raked until smooth. Then a water truck came along and sprayed water on the road, thoroughly wetting it. We were told that when it dried it would turn into concrete. They did several blocks in the downtown area like this while we were there. We didn't stay long enough to see it turn into concrete.

The last evening, they had a big banquet for us. They held it outside in the backyard of the house where we had been eating. About 20 officials came. They had decorated the area nicely and everybody was laughing and having a good time. The officials were drinking alcohol, and they must have made 10 or 15 different toasts. One of the top officials that had been eating with us regularly decided it was time I had a drink, so he offered a toast. Then he stood up and brought a glass over to me and put it up to my lips. Everyone started to chant and clap. They knew I didn't drink alcohol. I didn't open my mouth, and after awhile, I just turned my head to the side. After the banquet, the official came over to me and apologized. I can't remember feeling a stronger temptation in my life to give in to pressure, but I stood my ground, and I believe it was well worth it.

We wanted to leave some things with Pul, so we asked him to come to Mary Lou's room after the dinner. We gave him some of our leftover supplies, and then each of us took turns praying for him and his family. While we were praying, there was a knock at the door. It was one of the important local officials. Immediately Pul hid under the bed. He was visibly frightened. Mary Lou and Beth went to the door, and went out into the hall and talked with him, and slowly walked away from the room. After they were gone, Pul slipped out the back door and went safely home.

Near the end of our stay, Beth had several long conversations with Dr. Chang about our Christian faith. She seemed surprisingly quite receptive. At the end of our stay, Beth asked Dr. Chang directly if she would like to become a Christian, and her answer was interesting. She said, "If I were to say that I were a Christian, I would lose my important job that I have worked for all my life, and I would be publicly disgraced. But if God looks at what you believe in your heart, nobody can control that, but yourself, and no one needs to know what you believe in your heart."

Early the next morning all the medical staff arrived dressed in their best whites to bid us farewell. We all had our pictures taken in front of the clinic. Our two minibuses came, and while we were loading, two armored trucks rolled up with several armed soldiers in them. Then three cars with the local officials came. All types of thoughts were flashing through my mind.

We loaded and took off like a convoy but headed down a different road from the one on which we had come. We went along for about 5 miles. I wondered where we were going. Finally we came to a military road checkpoint, and everything came to a stop. The local officials quickly got out of the cars, and came up to our minibuses smiling. They commented that they couldn't go any further because of the road checkpoint. They just wanted to give us one final thank you for coming and helping them. They shook hands with all of us and stood in the road and waved as we drove out of sight. I have never had a farewell like that before, or since.

We had only one day back in Shenyang to do our dental shopping for Pul. In the morning we did personal shopping at one of the biggest and busiest markets that I have ever seen. It was an open air market that covered more than ten acres. It was packed so tightly with people that we could hardly get up or down any of the aisles between the vendors.

In the afternoon Beth helped us shop for dental supplies and equipment. Dr. Pratt was excited about getting equipment for Pul, and offered to split the cost with me. We shopped all afternoon, and went to five or six dental supply stores. We could get only a few instruments or supplies from each store, because none of them had very much. In one of the stores we got about 10 items. Beth busily added up all the prices on her hand calculator. One of the clerks picked up her abacus and started moving beads back and forth, and finished adding everything well before Beth. They both had the same total. I was astonished at how fast the clerk added on her abacus.

We finally got all the supplies and instruments we thought that Pul would need to operate an adequate dental clinic. When we added up all of our cost, it came to only one hundred and twenty dollars. I couldn't believe the price. One extraction forceps at home cost one hundred and fifty dollars. The same forceps in China cost nine dollars. I bought a couple of small delicate instruments to bring home to see how they stood up under the test of time. They did well, so we have bought Chinese forceps on several of our subsequent trips to expand our HTI warehouse equipment.

We used our taxi for about three hours while we were going around town. When we went to pay the driver we were shocked, because the total cost was $3.50. Mary Lou was delighted with our purchases, and said she would get all the instruments and supplies to Pul quickly.

One thing I had never seen before was people riding bikes and walking down the streets wearing surgical face masks, like we wear in the dental office. The people were obviously aware of the heavy air pollution from the local factories. It actually left a black cloudy haze over the city. I guess they were just wisely trying to protect their lungs.

Beth was a very personable, beautiful, and well educated single Christian young lady about 25 years old. She was beautiful, that is, until she smiled. She had the worst case of tetracycline stained teeth I have ever seen. All of her teeth were a very dark gray, and she had a big broad smile. She had this condition since childhood, so she was not self-conscious about it at all.

For a dentist this was a super challenge. I knew we could make her teeth beautiful and white, but it would take time and technology, which was not available in China. Many crowns would be required. I knew she wouldn't be able to afford it, even if China did have the technology. Dr. Pratt and I talked about it, and agreed that we could do this for Beth, if she could just come to the United States for a little while.

We discussed this with Mary Lou, and her comments surprised me. Mary Lou said, "In the past I have sent helpers to the U.S., primarily for medical operations, and not one of them has returned. Beth is my best helper, and is a fantastic evangelist. She has brought many Chinese people to Christ. If Beth went to the U.S. and stayed, like all of the others, a lot of Chinese people would end up going to hell, because she wasn't here to lead them to Christ." She also said, "Beth is a very happy person. Her teeth are strong and healthy and they don't bother her at all." We understood, and withdrew our request. Nothing was said to Beth. She was truly a happy evangelical Christian sweetheart. We bid our farewells, took the train back to Beijing, and flew on to Tokyo.

We stayed a couple of days in Tokyo to look around. We wanted to take a taxi one mile to an arts and crafts store. The driver wanted $45 one way. What a change in the economy from two days before! Our travel agent, Jill, said that she sends very few people to Japan, because the exchange rate makes Japan one of the most expensive countries in the world to visit.

In summary, I felt good about showing the Chinese people that Americans weren't bad, that we loved them, and were willing to help them. I was disappointed that we could not share more about Jesus and our Christian faith, but we definitely did what we could. I think we were a big help and encouragement to Pul. We were able to relieve a lot of people of their pain that previously had absolutely no chance of getting help. We also trained, supplied and equipped Pul to continue to help the people. Because we were the first American healthcare team of this type, and were successful, we opened the future for many other teams to follow.

## And Now the Rest of the Story

Dr. Bill Pratt joined the HTI Board of Directors, and was put in charge of all HTI's China mission trips. He retired from his Bible study teaching, and he now leads four or five mission trips a year, and has led many teams back to China.

Dr. Chang was very favorably impressed with how we helped the people of Sue Nu. She has since allowed and actually encouraged Mary Lou to host over one hundred teams to come to Shenyang and the surrounding area.

Mary Lou took all the instruments and supplies to Pul, and you will find out in chapter 17 what happened next.

# CHAPTER 16

# INDIA
# MADRAS

My next challenge was India, a diverse multi-cultural country which has the second largest population in the world. Shortly after I returned from China, Dr. Miller asked if I would be interested in going to India. So I continued to ask myself the question, "Why not?" I had no good reason. Dr. Miller was aware that it often took the best part of a year for all the preparations.

Dr. Miller knew an important pastor in Madras, India, now renamed Chennai. The pastor, whose son had recently graduated from dental school, had requested HTI to send two dentists to help his son with a short-term dental mission project. His son's name was Philip. Philip would be our host. Dr. Miller had a HTI dentist from Scotland, who had indicated he wanted to go to India, but he was inexperienced and didn't want to go alone. Dr. Miller always liked to have an experienced team leader on all of HTI's missions.

Dora May and I left in February 1996. We stopped in London, picked up our Scottish dentist, and then flew directly to Madras. Philip met us at the airport and took us to a small, but nice hotel.

The next morning Philip picked us up in his dad's church van. We traveled through the morning traffic for about an hour to a suburban village. We went to a church and set up our clinic in the sanctuary. Instead of church pews there were folding chairs, which they had taken down for us. I asked Philip where our missionary outreach was, because most of the patients we first started seeing were from the church. He indicated that after we finished the few church people, 90% of the patients would be Hindus, and they were.

Hindus normally would never enter a Christian church, but this was different because they were in pain. They would find that the people were really friendly and nothing bad would happen to them by entering a Christian Church. The pastor and many of the church people stayed around and tried to make friends with the Hindus, and invited them back to church, or shared with them what Christians believed, if they wanted to know. This made good sense to me, and I felt a lot better.

We called our Scottish dentist, "Scotty." Although Philip was a licensed Indian dentist, he didn't do any dental work with us. He helped with organization, translation, and many other details. He was a very recent graduate, and hadn't started practicing dentistry regularly. He helped other dentists from time to time for short periods. We were doing mainly extractions, and I'm not sure he had extracted many teeth.

The bone structure of the Indian people was not as hard as the Africans, and as a result the teeth came out quite easily. We saw several patients whose abscessed infection resulted in a chronic drainage of pus out the side of their face or underneath their chin. These draining abscesses often relieved the pressure, and greatly reduced the pain, but it wouldn't heal until a tooth was removed. Some of these patients told us these draining abscesses had been present for several years. It took 5 to 10 minutes to remove these teeth, which would then allow the infection and draining pus to quickly heal.

Once tooth decay gets large enough that bacteria enters the nerve, the tooth abscesses. The abscessed tooth acts much like a wooden sliver would in the skin. As soon as you remove the sliver, it heals right up. Scotty and I extracted many, many teeth. We kept Dora May busy assisting, as well as sterilizing our instruments. Philip interpreted for both Scotty and me.

During our evening drive back to downtown Madras, we were caught in the middle of the evening rush hour traffic. In India, car production had grown much faster than road construction. Traffic was extremely heavy, often bumper-to-bumper. The rules of the road were quite different in India. Philip was an excellent driver, but he wove in and out of traffic unbelievably fast and very close to other vehicles.

When we got back to the hotel, Scotty said to me, "I'm going home! I have a wife and family back home, and I plan to get home alive. I'll take a taxi to the airport. I'm not getting back in that van again." The concern to me was that he meant every word of it. He had been scared nearly to death on our drive home.

We talked for a long time. I tried to tease with him and said, "I can see you're not used to third-world driving. Did you see any accidents?" Nothing was funny to him. He was dead serious. Finally we reached a compromise. We would bring Philip into the hotel, sit down with him and tell him exactly our concerns. If he couldn't slow down and drive carefully and safely, then Scotty was on his way home. That talk solved the problem. Philip drove safely and slowly and Scotty was happy.

We went to a different church each day, and repeated our clinics similar to the first day. Early one morning Scotty had a patient whom he evidently didn't numb enough. He proceeded to extract the tooth anyway, while the patient screamed bloody murder very loudly. Our waiting line suddenly disappeared, and we saw very few patients the rest of the morning. I have never in 50 years of practice had to extract a tooth from a person while they were in pain. I tried to talk to Scotty and all he would say was, "I gave her anesthesia, and she should have been numb."

I think the real problem stems from the difference between capitalism and socialism. In socialized healthcare, such as in Great Britain, everything is basically under the control of the government. People don't have choices. If you don't like your treatment, that's just tough. In capitalism, if you don't treat your patients kindly, they will go someplace else, and you will personally lose income, and eventually go broke. The only way you get away with that in the United States would be if you work for the government, or work for a union, HMO, PPO, or other restrictive insurance companies where you have few or no choices. Fortunately in the past, that has been a small minority, but unfortunately it's growing.

Another day Scotty broke an upper cuspid tooth off level with the bone. He cut the gum and moved it back away from the bone, chiseled the bone away, and finally after 45 minutes he got the root out, and sutured the patient's gum back together. He didn't ask me for any help. He was a middle-aged man with many years of experience, so I didn't interfere. The patient happened to be the pastor's wife. She became so emotionally stressed that she became very weak and dizzy, and when he finished she was too weak to stand. They made a makeshift bed in the sanctuary, which was our clinic and waiting room, and someone came and started an IV on her. She was there for two or three hours. This wasn't the greatest advertisement for our dental clinic, but we still kept busy. At least we didn't have any blood curdling screams.

A little later that day I heard Scotty say, "Oh no." This time I checked, and he had broken the same tooth off level with the bone again. The upper cuspid or canine has the longest and strongest root of any tooth in the entire mouth. I didn't wait for him to ask this time. He was pretty well exhausted anyway. I said, "Let me show you a little trick." I gently pushed the gum back a little from the bone, without cutting the gum. I slipped my favorite forceps, which Dora May has nicknamed, "Super Ronie," down under the gum, and over the bone that was around the root. This forceps is a bone cutting forceps. I squeezed the forceps firmly, and it cut through the bone, and grasped the root. I rotated the root, and within a matter of seconds it came right out. The entire procedure took less than two minutes, with no cutting of the gum, hammering or chiseling the bone, or suturing.

Scotty's mouth dropped open, and he said, "How'd you do that?" I showed him again exactly what I had done. He said, "WOW! That's really neat." I was forced to learn this procedure many years ago on the mission field, where most of the teeth we needed to extract were decayed off level with the gum, and you couldn't get hold of them any other way.

On Sunday we went to Philip's father's church in Madras. It was a very large church holding over a thousand people. I was surprised that the entire service was in English. They had a guest speaker for the sermon. He was a Gideon, who shared stories of how Gideon Bibles had resulted in salvation and changed lives for people. I was surprised because I didn't know that the Gideons were an international organization. They speak in our church at least once a year to tell us about the results that occur when people read the Bibles that the Gideons make available.

Sunday afternoon Philip took us on a tour. Traffic was much lighter. It was very hot. I commented to Philip about the heat, and he said, "This is why we invited you to come in the middle of our winter. In the summer the temperature reaches 125°F in the shade, and we were afraid you northerners might melt and disappear in the cracks in the sidewalk."

Philip took us to the area where the apostle Thomas landed in India, and where he preached and taught for several years. He showed us the church he started, where he had been martyred, and explained why, and where he was buried. It was very interesting to me, because I'd never known that the apostle Thomas came to India, preached, and died there. Philip said, "As a result of the apostle Thomas starting Christianity in India, today 15 to 20% of the people in southern India are Christians." Unfortunately, this only amounted to less than 3% of the entire country of India being Christians.

A taxi driver we had one day in Madras complained bitterly to us that all his friends were abandoning Hinduism and becoming Christians. Our comment to him was, "Why don't you try it? I think you'd like it."

Phillip's dad asked us if we would go to Bangalore, where he pastored another large church. Bangalore is a large city in south-central India. Philip took us by train. The train station was something else. It was a very large ornate old British structure. Trains were still the major source of transportation for most people in India. We got there early in the morning, and the station was very crowded. It was an all-day trip. I kept waiting for us to leave Madras, and get out into the country, but it seemed to stay heavily populated all the way.

We got to Bangalore early Saturday evening. Phillip's dad met us and transferred us to a hotel within walking distance of his church. The hotel was a fairly large five or six-story building. It didn't seem busy. After we checked in at the reception desk, the hotel bellman took us to our rooms. We walked up three flights of stairs, with the bellman going ahead of us, turning on lights as we went. It was obvious that we were the only ones in this part of the hotel.

When we arrived at our room we couldn't find the bathroom. The room had a balcony, so we checked it out. To our surprise, there was the bathroom. It was on a balcony that was in full view of several other multi-story buildings around us. Oh well, we just kept our clothes close to our body when sitting down. But there was no toilet paper. I went back downstairs to the front desk and asked for toilet paper. The clerk said, "Oh yes." He then located a key and unlocked a cabinet behind the counter. He got out one roll of toilet paper and gave it to me. When we went to check out of the hotel later, there was a $.10 charge added to our bill for toilet paper. This is the only time in my life I have ever been charged for toilet paper at a hotel. Different!

It was getting a little late, but we thought we should get a little something for supper since we hadn't eaten since noon. We went down to the hotel restaurant, and we were the only ones in that rather large restaurant. We looked at the menu, and weren't tempted by any of the Indian entrées, but at the bottom they had banana split. We ordered two banana splits. In Madras we had almost lived on banana splits in our hotel, along with watermelon juice. We never had watermelon juice before, but it was actually very good. The prices in the restaurants were very cheap, as most things were in India.

We waited and waited for over an hour, and were starting to get a little restless. No one had come to say anything to us. Finally our waiter came back, all sweaty and out of breath. He said, "Sorry, I can't get you a banana split. All the stores in town are closed." By that time we just said, "Thank you, anyway," and we got up and went to our room.

Sunday morning Philip came and walked with us to his dad's church. It was a couple of blocks away and in a rough looking part of town. Phillip's dad had started the church in an old empty warehouse. He had lots of room, and there were over 500 people in attendance. Phillip's dad preached.

After church they asked Scotty and me to set up our dental clinic in the front of the church, to help the needy people of the church. The only dental service anywhere in the area was at a large general government hospital nearby.

We set up our clinic and started to work. There were a lot of patients waiting to see us. As we were working, a well-dressed man entered and started talking to Phillip's dad. Finally Phillip's dad came over and introduced him to us. He was Director of the Dental Services at the large Government Hospital. Immediately all types of things flashed through my mind. He's going to want to see our license. He's going to shut us down. We're taking paying customers away from his clinic, and treating people for free.

His first comment was, "Boy, you really have a good selection of instruments," as he was inspecting them closely. Then he said, "You have twice as many instruments as our whole Hospital Dental Clinic." I figured he wanted our instruments. I thought he was going to close us down and take our instruments.

Finally he smiled, for the first time, and said, "You're really doing a good and kind service for these needy people. You are to be congratulated." Then he shook our hands, smiled, and left. Thank you, Lord.

The next day we went to a large orphanage that Phillip's dad had started and was supervising. We took care of several children's dental problems there, and then went to small churches and set up clinics like we had been doing in Madras.

Finally it came time for us to start heading home. First was our train ride back to Madras. This trip was an all-night trip this time, so Philip got us Pullman berths so we could lie down and sleep. Our bed turned out to be a wooden board stacked up alongside the aisle, like a bookshelf, four berths high. They were about 2 feet wide and 5 feet long, and had a curtain you could pull over the opening. Dora May had the second from the bottom, and

I had the third, which was up about 4 or 5 feet high. We had no mattress, no pillow, or no blanket. We just crawled in with our clothes on, curled up, and hoped we wouldn't fall out, as the train was rocking back and forth. After I had been in there a while, I peeked out from behind the curtain, just in time to see a huge 2-inch long cockroach running up the wall about 2 feet from me. My first thought was, "I hope Dora May doesn't see it, because there isn't room in here for both of us." Believe it or not, I didn't sleep very much that night.

I had noticed earlier, as we drove around Madras, large billboard signs offering 30% interest for bank savings accounts. I thought to myself, this is unreal. I could make a lot of money just by putting my savings and investments in one of these accounts. But here's the rest of that story. The Indian people didn't trust the banks because of previous bank problems, bankruptcies, and losses. These bank savings were not insured by the government, like U.S. banks. The Indian currency, the Indian Rupee, is a dead currency. You couldn't exchange the Indian Rupee into money of any other country. All the money I put in the bank or would take out of the bank, I'd never be able to get out of the country.

One of the reasons the Rupee is dead, is because of India's extreme poverty and overpopulation. It is expected that India will be the most populated country in the world, passing up China, in a few years. Almost everyone in India has one goal in life and that is to get out of India, sometime, somehow, to somewhere. For the majority of people in India, life is very hard, and they are very poor. If you are an educated person, such as a doctor or an engineer, you could make 10 times more money in many countries of the world, and have a much better standard of living. But if you can't take out one single Rupee with you when you leave, it makes it much harder to leave. If this weren't true, the country would immediately have a massive brain drain, with all the educated people leaving.

One day as we were driving through Madras, I saw a line of people on the sidewalk for about a whole block. I asked Philip, "What's going on there?" He told me they were waiting in line to get into the U.S. Embassy to apply for a visa. He indicated that it usually took three days in line to get into the U.S. Embassy just to apply for a visa, and very rarely did anyone ever get one. I know people from India, who are living and working in the U.S. at near minimum wage, while back in India they own lands, houses, and have significant wealth. They gave up all of it, just to get out of India.

I was happy with the experience and the time that we spent in India. We helped a lot of people out of pain and suffering. When I think of India there are two things that come to my mind. First, there are the beautiful bright colorful saris that the women wear. Indian women have to be some of the most beautifully dressed women in the world. Secondly, I remembered India as wall to wall people. I have never seen so many people living so compactly anywhere in the world.

## And Now for the Rest of the Story

Philip wrote me several times after I got home, asking me to help him come to the United States. I didn't answer because I didn't know how to help him. I frequently receive letters after we get home from mission trips, and that is one of the most common requests that everyone has. They want to come to the U.S. I even had one black African male whom we had met on one of our missions, write and ask me if I had a daughter. He said that he would be happy to come to the U.S. and marry her.

One day several years later I got a phone call from Philip. He was in Toronto, Canada. After a few months, I got another phone call from Philip. He was happily settled in the state of New York.

# CHAPTER 17

# CHINA
# INNER MONGOLIA

Inner Mongolia is in the north-central region of China. It borders on and includes the great Gobi Desert. The Great Wall of China was built to keep the Mongolians out, but it didn't and today the vast desert and grasslands of Inner Mongolia are a part of China.

In 1996 visitors were not usually allowed in much of Inner Mongolia, and tourist facilities were few. You might wonder how an evangelistic Christian dental team got invited into Inner Mongolia.

It all began after Mary Lou delivered the dental supplies and equipment to Pul at Sue Nu. Pul then started the only dental clinic covering a large area. One day a Mongolian physician was traveling through Sue Nu and stopped at the medical clinic. The only one with patients was Pul's dental extraction clinic. This interested him and he became friends with Pul, and asked Pul to teach him how to extract teeth.

Pul spent a great deal of time teaching him and gave him some of his supplies and equipment to take back to Inner Mongolia, where they had no dentists. After returning, he started to extract teeth and quickly became very popular.

The government's Minister of Health heard about this physician who was extracting teeth, and asked him to come to his office. He wanted to know where he had learned to extract teeth because several other physicians wanted to learn also. The physician reported that he had learned from Pul, a physician in Sue Nu.

The Minister of Health contacted Pul and asked where he had learned to extract teeth. Pul reported that he had been taught by a U.S. dentist whom Dr. Chang, the Minister of Health from Shenyang, had brought to Sue Nu. He then contacted Dr. Chang, and she in turn contacted Mary Lou, who gave him my name and address.

The next thing that happened was that I received a long letter from the Minister of Health of Inner Mongolia, which was sent through Mary Lou who translated it. He invited me to bring a team to Tongliao, Inner Mongolia, to teach 50 physicians how to extract teeth. He indicated there were no dentists in the vast grasslands of Inner Mongolia. He offered to take our team to the National Mongolian Festival, to treat us to a fresh lamb dinner, and to let us sleep in a Mongolian yurt. A yurt is a collapsible round tent made of poles and skins, often brightly decorated. The Mongolians use a yurt as their home, when they move from place to place as they migrate across the grasslands.

I immediately consulted with Mary Lou, who was fully aware of the invitation, and she encouraged me to accept. Mary Lou indicated that she, Beth, and others of her team would go with us and support us in any way they could.

I immediately contacted Dr. Miller, and informed him about this unique invitation. His first comment was, "My wife Jan and I want to go too." Dr. Miller had a complete recovery from his massive stroke, even though the doctors in the beginning didn't give him much chance to survive. I thought it would be great to get Dr. Miller, the founder of Health Teams International, to lead the team. He had led a great many teams, and I could learn from him.

When I suggested this to Dr. Miller, he said, "I just wanted to be a team member and for you to lead the team." I thought it would be rather awkward for me to tell the boss what to do, but it worked out fine.

Dr. Miller asked to bring along Larry Gonzales. Larry was a dynamic lay evangelist who had traveled with him on previous missions. Dr. Miller was in his mid-seventies and not as strong as he once was. Larry offered to care for any of Dr. Miller's special needs.

A former dental school classmate, Dr. George Eastman, contacted me about that time to ask about my mission trips. When I told him I had been invited to go to Inner Mongolia, he immediately said he would like to go. Dr. Eastman had a son who was a young lawyer, and he was between jobs at the time we were going. Dr. Eastman asked if his son, Brad, could come along and be his dental assistant. That sounded good to me.

Mary Lou contacted me and said she had a charitable organization that contributed $5,000 to buy the needed dental supplies and equipment for our 50 physician students.

One of the problems to be solved was that the dental supply houses in Shenyang wouldn't have that sizable amount of supplies and equipment in stock. I also wondered how I could describe to Mary Lou what instruments and forceps I needed. The Chinese names are all different from ours in the United States. I took numerous U.S. dental supply catalogs and cut out pictures of the needed instruments and forceps. I mailed a detailed list, with the pictures, of every item I would need for one good $100 dental kit. I then asked Mary Lou to order 50 kits and to make sure they all arrived before the class began. We gave the supply dealers four months lead time. It was no simple task, but she did it, and got all the requested supplies and equipment for our 50 students.

I visited the Dean at the University of Michigan Dental School, and I told him that I had been invited to teach 50 physicians how to extract teeth. He interrupted me with a loud astonished, "WHAT?!" Then I told him the rest of the story. It was in Inner Mongolia, where they had no dentists. He then became very excited and he gave me the authority to copy and use any of the teaching materials belonging to the Dental School. This turned out to be very useful, as I copied several important videos and hundreds of slides.

I wrote the Minister of Health of Inner Mongolia and said, "I have a team of three dentists and four dental assistants, and I accept your invitation." I requested that he furnish a 35 mm slide projector, and a method to show my videotapes. I asked him to confirm the date.

I received a response with dates for early August, because that was the date of the National Mongolian Festival. He also said the 35mm projector and video player would be available for me to use. I was really surprised that he could come up with the video player and slide projector, but I figured it wouldn't hurt to ask. He said I would have seven days to teach the course.

I thought my preparation and planning was a big job on my previous trips. This time I had all the usual preparations, plus I had to prepare 25 hours of lecture outlines, and sort and set up almost 1000 slides to go along with my lectures. I like challenges, and I was truly excited about this great and unusual opportunity.

Shortly before we left, Dr. Eastman received a personal letter from his U.S. congressman which stated, that proselytizing by foreigners was against Chinese law. He also said religious activities could be perceived as subversive.

We left in late July 1996, and flew directly from Detroit to Beijing. We were met at the airport by Chin, Mary Lou's travel agent friend, and he took us to the Friendship Hotel again. We went three days early so that the Millers, Eastmans and Larry could tour Beijing and the surrounding area. Dora May and I toured again with them. We always tried to stay together when traveling as a team. We saw basically the same sites that we had on our Manchuria trip and Dr. Miller had his life-long dream fulfilled.

On our fourth morning, Chin took us to the train station, where we boarded a train for our 24-hour trip to Tongliao, Inner Mongolia. Upon arrival, Mary Lou, Beth, and Sheila were there to meet us. Mary Lou introduced us to Dr. Su. He was our Inner Mongolian host physician who was in charge of our stay, and the school. Mary Lou also introduced us to Dr. Samuel, a physician, who was part of her team that she had brought with her from Shenyang. All of Mary Lou's team spoke excellent English, were great translators, and good evangelistic Christians.

Dr. Su took us to a multi-story building. We were assigned rooms with a bed, table, washbasin, and a pitcher of water. The room was much like those in Manchuria, but the mattresses were better. The bathrooms were inside, down the hall, still with holes in the floor, but with no bugs. It was a big improvement over Su Nu.

We checked out our lecture room. It had several narrow tables, with 60 chairs. It had a video player with a good sized TV and a slide projector. Big signs and slogans were all over the walls. I asked Beth, "What do they say?" She said they were Communist slogans. She told us that this lecture hall was normally used to indoctrinate young Chinese men into the Communist Party, and that one of the slogans said, "There is no God." The bedrooms to which we were assigned were usually used by students that were being indoctrinated.

Our afternoon was free, so we walked around town. Tongliao is one of the bigger cities in Inner Mongolia, located on the side of a fairly large river, on the edge of the vast grasslands. It had a population of several hundred thousand people. We didn't observe any hotels, restaurants, doctors' or dentists' offices, churches, pharmacies, car dealerships, or drive-in anything. Very few cars were seen. Most of the taxis were bicycle rickshaws. We observed several sidewalk vendors selling meat cleavers. Beth told us everything put into their woks for cooking was traditionally chopped with these big cleavers. Several cows were along the sidewalks with men actually milking them. People lined up with containers, waiting to get the freshest milk I have ever seen sold.

The next morning, Dr. Su had us load into a small bus with our overnight bags packed, and we headed north to the National Mongolian Festival. We drove through some very fertile agricultural land on the flood plain of the river. I was surprised to see a couple of very large new harvesting combines driving down the road. I was also surprised to see what appeared to be a large nuclear energy plant alongside the river. It was truly a land of contrasts.

Traffic picked up as we approached the festival. The grounds were similar to a fair-ground. Many vendors' booths, several brightly colored permanent buildings, and a very large oval horse track made up the bulk of the grounds. The biggest part of the Mongolian competitions was centered on their horses. We spent the remainder of the day walking around the grounds. Early in the evening we were invited to a private dining room, where we were served a wonderful fresh lamb dinner. We sat on the floor in front of our short tables. It happened to be Dr. Miller's birthday, so we got a little extra, including some entertainment.

We were then directed to our overnight quarters, which consisted of a big colorful Mongolian yurt, made of collapsible poles and skins. The women were in one yurt, and the men in another. We were given sleeping bags, so we crawled in with our shoes off, but with our clothes on. The floor was grass. I had a good night's sleep. Dora May did also, except when, in the middle of the night, some type of animal ran across the middle of her sleeping bag. She didn't know what it was, and decided she didn't want to know.

In the morning we were given a nice breakfast, after which we headed back to Tongliao to get our class started. The class began with a formal opening program. A variety of officials spoke to the class of 50 physicians. Originally I was told that the students would be medical students, but when word got around, a great competition occurred as to who was going to be in the class. Instead of medical students, the most important physicians from a very large area were present. These doctors were famous physicians that had written textbooks, or had developed new Chinese medical treatments, also university professors, Chiefs of Staffs of hospitals, and physicians that had good political clout. Several of them were over 50 years old.

Lecturing was a slow process, because I had to wait after each phrase or sentence for Beth to interpret for me. Beth was a university English teacher before giving her life to Christ. Trying to make physicians into dentists in seven days was a big undertaking. I started class at seven in the morning and went until nine at night. After a couple of days, Dr. Su came to me, and said the students were getting sleepy before I finished at nine. He asked if I could shorten the day. I shortened it an hour at each end, and only went from eight to eight.

An extra student monitored the class, a female physician, named Mi Mi. She repeatedly told us that she didn't want any instruments or credit, but that she just wanted to know more about oral health. It became evident fairly quickly, that she was a Communist spy, planted in the class to report any Christian philosophies that we might express. One example was when one of us sneezed, and another said, "God bless you." Immediately she ran to Dr. Su and reported, "I overheard them talking about God again."

When the time came to get clinical experience, we divided the group into three sections. Dr. Miller, Dr. Eastman, and I each demonstrated on patients before we allowed the class members to start to extract teeth. Usually our demonstrations were on our student physicians, who themselves had abscessed teeth that needed to be extracted. They wanted one of the instructors to take them out, rather than have their fellow physicians practice on them. One of the physicians for whom I extracted a big molar, was 60 years old, and was a very famous author and inventor of a special type of Chinese medical treatment. All of the other students respected him as a great legend in Chinese medicine.

I am not sure where our extraction patients came from, but we had a great many. Dr. Miller, Dr. Eastman, and I supervised three chairs each. The physicians used these chairs in which to place their patients while they worked on them. Dora May and Jan worked as chair-side assistants, while Brad and Larry were kept very busy sterilizing the instruments. Each of the physicians had an opportunity to extract numerous teeth. They learned very quickly. They were able to check out the medical history of the patients prior to surgery much better than we could.

Interestingly enough, the small talk in the clinic, as we worked on patients, helped us to develop personal relationships with these physicians. The professional and international barriers seemed to break down. There were really some interesting individuals in the class. We showed each other pictures of our families, and in general, developed significant friendships and respect for each other.

As the friendships developed, we started to be a little more open about our faith. This started driving Mi Mi crazy. We asked Dr. Su several days in advance, if it would be possible for our team to go to church on Sunday. He said, "I'll see." The Communists were proud that they had totally wiped out all Christian influences in China, but they only worked six days a week and rested on the seventh. They still had one active Christian church in Tongliao.

Mary Lou and Beth felt we had developed enough respect and friendship, that we could start witnessing our faith, one-on-one, in the evenings. Generally, Communist teaching does not object to one-on-one personal discussion of philosophy and religion. So when our courage grew stronger, we went out to witness one evening. Guess who the first person was that we encountered? It was Mi Mi. We first engaged her in small talk, which eventually led to the question; do you really know what Christians believe? She said, "No," but she was interested in knowing. Guess who our first Christian convert was. It was Mi Mi. She had never heard because no one had ever told her. She was very excited. She ran home and brought back her physician husband, and he accepted Christ also. Then both of them went home, and got several of their neighbors, and brought them back, and they accepted Christ. Mi Mi and her husband started a church in their home before we left. Several other physicians that we talked to accepted Christ as well.

Eventually, Dr. Su came to us and reported he had made arrangements for us to go to church on Sunday. We immediately started to invite our student physicians, one-on-one, to come to church with us. I guess the word got out, because one of Dr. Su's bosses required a meeting of all students at eight on Sunday morning.

On Sunday morning, after breakfast, we left at eight and walked to the church which was about a mile through town. When we approached the one-room church, it was surrounded by masses of people. Dr. Su led the way, and created a path through all the people right up to the front door. As we entered the church, we observed that it was totally packed with people. They were sitting in the aisles and standing around all the outside walls. A couple of empty pews toward the back of the church were roped off and the ushers took us and seated us in them. In the U.S., a sanctuary this size would probably seat 150 people, but there were a good 300 people packed into this church. People were leaning in the open windows, and completely surrounding the outside of the church, as many as three or four people deep. Finally about 8:30 we were seated.

We were told that this church was the only one in town. When we arrived, there was a lady in front of the congregation singing a phrase of a song, and then the congregation would repeat it. They had neither hymn books nor musical instruments. They continued on to 9:00, 9:30, and 10:00. I finally asked Beth "When is the church service going to start?" I was informed that it was an 11:00 o'clock service. I mentioned to Beth, "I wonder if the physician's 8 A.M. mandatory meeting is over. Several of the physicians indicated they would like to go to church with us. They might be free now to come." Immediately Beth and Sheila got up, left the church and went back to check. About 10:45 A.M. Beth and Sheila came back with about 20 of the physicians.

I could not believe what I saw next. The ushers came up, and asked the people sitting around us, if they would give up their seats for some special guests that had just arrived. I don't know how long before we arrived that these people had been sitting and waiting, but immediately they got up and went outside. This continued to occur until all the physicians were seated around us. Could you imagine this happening in a U.S. church? I don't think so.

Bibles were being sold in the narthex of the church. Mary Lou and Beth both said they had never heard of this being done before. We pooled our money, bought and gave every physician a Bible just before the service started. Many people in China have been imprisoned for giving Bibles to people, but for some unknown reason this was being allowed.

At 11 A.M., the service started. Everything was in Chinese, so we didn't understand anything, but I am convinced that our example was valuable. Another unusual thing that happened was that the female pastor preached on the second coming of Jesus. Mary Lou was astonished. She had been in China for 18 years, and had never before heard the subject of the second coming preached. She had been told that it was forbidden in China. Mary Lou told us "The pastors are employees of the Communist government, and they are paid by the government and controlled by the government. The government tells them what they can preach, and what they can't preach." No collection was taken. Mary Lou said "The physicians got a good sermon about Christ's return." We continued to witness to our physician students, one-on-one, at every possible opportunity we had.

On the last afternoon we had a graduation ceremony in our lecture hall. Several short speeches were given by government officials, then Mary Lou and each of us doctors were given an opportunity to speak. Mary Lou went first, and she gave a short testimony of her faith, and no one said a thing. Along with our praise for the physicians learning so quickly and well, both Dr. Miller and I expanded on our Christian testimonies, and again, no one said a thing.

After the speeches, we handed out the kits of supplies and equipment. Each of the physicians immediately looked through the kits in detail to see what they had received. They seemed to be very happy, with our gift that we had given to them. It was in fact, $100 worth of supplies and equipment which included all things necessary to extract teeth.

Each of the seven of us that came from the U.S. had brought along a good supply of snacks which included raisins, M & Ms, hard candies, crackers, nuts, soft candies, etc. We had been fed so well that we didn't need to eat any of our snacks. We put all of our snacks in dishes on a big table at the back of the lecture room for the students to eat. I am sure they never saw snacks like that before, because they dug right in and quickly ate everything. They seemed to enjoy all our snacks. We had a good opportunity to just stand around and talk with them for about an hour.

That evening, a special graduation banquet was held for the physicians and us. One of the customs, which we weren't aware of, was that after supper one of the physicians or a group of physicians got up and entertained us by singing or playing an instrument. They expected us to return the entertainment, and do something for them. Many of the physicians had surprisingly good talents. All we did was to sing Christian songs that we all knew, such as, "Jesus Loves Me," or "This is the Day." It was too bad they couldn't understand the words. A great time was had by all.

The morning after our banquet, and before we left, was memorable. It was a cool, calm, sunny morning. The physicians all turned out for a planned photo session. They sat all the U.S. team in front, and then the physicians stood behind us. We got some great photos. After the photos, many of the physicians came up to each of us, thanked us personally, and gave us a hug. Many wanted an individual picture with us. Mi Mi was there, and she just couldn't stop thanking us and hugging us. It was a very emotional and touching time. We all knew that when we parted, we would probably never see each other again, and we haven't. We had a total of 43 out of the 50 physicians that became Christians. Beth said that if we had more time we could have converted all 50 of them. We never had one with whom we shared the Good News that did not want to become a Christian.

An interesting observation was that on this trip, God used us to bring the top leaders of the local society to Jesus Christ, rather than the average people. These physicians would spread into the small villages throughout the Mongolian grasslands, as respected leaders of their community, and their influence for Christianity could be powerful. The members of HTI consider themselves as seed planters of the Gospel. We just pray that some of these seeds landed on fertile ground.

We still had four days before our ticketed train ride back to Beijing. Dr. Su had arranged for us to go north to do dentistry in a small village hospital.

We bused two or three hours north alongside the river, and the fertile flood plain. The plain didn't extend very far away from the river, before it turned sharply into sandy desert like grassland. After reaching the small village of She Bai Du, we stopped in front of a building next to the hospital. This was to serve as our living quarters for three days. It became quickly obvious that a lot of work had been done to this building to change it from storage and office space into living quarters. We had no running water, but each room had a water basin with a pitcher of water. It was very adequate, and we could see a lot of time and effort had been spent to prepare it for us. The outhouse was very similar to the one at Sue Nu.

We ate our meals around a large round table. Meals took a long time. Supper frequently lasted two hours. Rice was always served with six or eight toppings. There was a 10-minute wait between each hot topping dish. We later learned that the whole meal was cooked in one wok, one dish at a time.

We set up a clinic in a room at the hospital that had been cleared out for us. The room was small and cramped, but we made it work. To our surprise, one of the physicians that had just graduated from our class turned up in the clinic to help us. Dental services had never been available in this village. Very quickly the news spread about our clinic, and we were swamped with patients. We had four dental chairs operating at the same time, just doing extractions, and we certainly did a lot of them. We were able to help our new physician graduate with many advanced techniques, such as removing broken roots, and unusual things that we couldn't really teach in the class.

In talking with our newly trained physician, we found out he had a home, a wife and two children in the village. He invited us to stop and visit him some evening. We took him up on his offer, and we walked through town to his small but nice house that very evening. He introduced us to his wife and family, and then he turned on the television. The national news had an extensive story and videos of our team teaching the class of physicians in Tongliao.

Beth recognized our host as one of the physicians that had accepted Christ while at school. Beth quietly and privately asked him if he had had a chance to tell his family about Jesus, and he said, "No." Beth asked if he would like for us to tell his family about Jesus, and he very happily said, "Yes." After sharing the good news of Jesus Christ for the best part of an hour, his wife and two teenage children very excitedly accepted Jesus. Praise the Lord! We made sure they had a Bible.

One of the unusual and puzzling things we observed while working in the clinic was that almost every patient we saw had a significant notch in one of their upper front teeth. I asked our local physician dentist, "Why the notches?" He explained that most people hand-filed this notch purposely into their tooth to help them crack sunflower seeds faster. Many times in the winter, sunflower seeds became their main food, and they had to crack a lot of seeds to get very much nutrition. That notch really helped them.

At the end of our three-day clinic, we had a final banquet, with several government officials present to thank us. The most surprising comment came from the Chief of Staff of the hospital, who after thanking us said, "I don't know how you men can work so hard and such long hours at your age. Our physicians would have been well-retired before your age, and when they did work, their hours normally would have been only six hours a day." Dr. Miller was in his mid-seventies, and Dr. Eastman and I were in our mid-sixties. We had been working 10 and 11 hours a day, which was not unusual for us. The comment was both flattering and surprising. Everybody seemed happy with our efforts.

We returned to Tongliao by bus and stayed overnight. The next morning our ever-present chaperone host, Dr. Su, took us to the train station. When the train came in, and I had one foot on the step to go up into the train, Dr. Su came to me privately, and said in a soft voice, "Thank you for sharing Jesus with my people. I have been a Christian for six years, but as a member of the Communist Party, I can't tell anyone, or I would lose everything."

Now I understood why he never did or said anything when Mi Mi would run to him earlier during the course, and tattle that we were talking about God. That also explained why at the end of our course, we were given the freedom to share our Christian testimonies. As a team we had prayed together every morning, that God would give us the courage and opportunity to share the Gospel. God was way ahead of us. He gave us a Christian host before we ever arrived.

On our 24-hour train ride back to Beijing, something happened that I will never forget. We rode in a nice West German-made Pullman car. Each compartment contained four beds and four people. Dr. Samuel came with us to help us transfer to the airport and see us off. Samuel and Larry were assigned to a compartment which they shared with a very high-ranking uniformed military officer and his wife. His wife was carried in on a stretcher and placed in one of the beds. He was taking her to Beijing hoping to get treatment for her severe back problem. They were not able to get any help in Tongliao. She was obviously in severe pain because she was verbally moaning and groaning loudly.

Larry took compassion on her and told her we had an all-powerful God that could help her. She was interested, and so he continued to tell her about Jesus and how He healed so many sick people. She begged to be healed.

The first that I knew about this lady and her back problem was when she and Larry walked into our compartment. The lady was smiling and told us this story. She said "Larry told me his God could heal me. He put his hand on my back and started to pray. I felt a warm tingling sensation in my back and the pain let up and went completely away. I was afraid to move but eventually I sat up, then stood up, and finally started walking, and there is no pain. Larry's God, who is now my God, has completely healed me."

Her husband, who had observed everything, was greatly puzzled and astonished at what he had witnessed. Being a high military officer and a member of the Communist Party, he wouldn't make any comment. The next morning when we arrived at Beijing, his wife walked off the train by herself, smiling and feeling no pain.

I never doubted that our God, who created the whole universe, had the power to heal anyone He wanted to heal. I personally had never witnessed anything as exciting as this lady's healing. We all praised the Lord for His great witness in a land that so desperately needs Him.

## Now the Rest of the Story

After returning home I received a thank you letter from the head doctor at She Bai Du Hospital. He stated that our team was a good example to his medical staff because we worked hard and long even though we were old. We were diligent in sterilization, and were cheerful in spirit when treating patients. He said, "May our friendship last forever." Rarely do we get a written thank you for our efforts. This was an unexpected, pleasant reward.

A few months after I got home, Dr. Miller called, and asked if I would consider joining the HTI Board of Directors. My answer was, yes. The following year I was elected vice-president. In 2000 I was elected President and CEO, which I have been for ten years now. HTI has seen well over 80,000 totally unreached people come to Christ in the last 23 years. I just pray that I can be worthy of the great responsibility with which I have been entrusted.

After returning home, I received an invitation from Mary Lou asking HTI to send another team back to China and she would sponsor and work with us. Dr. Pratt had joined the HTI Board of Directors and had been put in charge of our China Missions. I turned the invitation over to him. He has returned to China with several teams in the following years. I had the pleasure and unique experience of going with him to Western China and Tibet which is reported in chapters 24 and 26.

# CHAPTER 18

# CAMEROON 1

Cameroon is a West African country of 16 million people including over 250 ethnic cultural people groups, speaking over 420 different languages. Oftentimes you can travel 20 or 30 miles in any direction, and be in an area where the people speak a different language. Cameroon consists of dense tropical rain forests or jungle in the south, to a very hot Sub-Sahara Desert in the northeast, with a variety in between.

Originally Cameroon was a German colony, but after World War I it was divided in half by the French and the British. Today Cameroon has received its independence, with half of the country speaking English, and the other half speaking French. Cameroon is truly a land of contrasts, with some fairly modern cities, buildings and technology, while some remote areas are often living 2000 years or more in the past.

Dr. Miller had a friend in Tulsa named, John Ngoh. John was born and raised in Cameroon. Being an excellent student in school, Reverend Oral Roberts, granted him a scholarship to come to the U. S. and study at Oral Roberts University. He worked part time as a nurses-aid while attending the University. It was here he met his wife, Kathy. They got married and had two children. John felt the call to return to Cameroon as a full-time missionary, and Kathy supported him 100%. They raised their needed financial support, visited Cameroon, and were ready to move permanently to Cameroon.

John's mission goal was to reach the unreached with the Gospel, the same goal as HTI. John knew the dental and medical needs of the Cameroon people were great. He also concurred with what HTI had experienced; that treating health care needs was a wonderful way to show God's love to people, which in turn often opened their hearts and minds to accept the Gospel.

John asked Dr. Miller if he could send a team of medical and dental providers to Cameroon shortly after he and his family had arrived, to help him jumpstart his mission work. He wanted to begin in the area where he had been born and raised, and where he had family and friends to help him.

Dr. Miller called me and asked if I would lead a team to Cameroon. He offered to help me assemble a team. I accepted the challenge. Dr. Miller gave me the name and phone number of a physician that somebody had given him, who had said he might be interested in going on a mission trip. I called one evening and reached Dr. John Hibbert. I introduced myself and Health Teams International, and told him I was putting together a team of Christian health care providers to go on a mission trip to Cameroon for two weeks, and I would like to invite him to join us. Dr. Hibbert said, "My wife and I were discussing how we might be able to better serve our Lord just two evenings ago. We came to the conclusion that the best way would be to use our skills in medicine that the Lord has given to us, but we didn't know how. Then two days later, you call me out of the clear blue sky, and invite me for the first time in my life to serve as a physician on a short-term Christian mission. I think the Lord has just answered my prayer, Yes, I will go."

Dr. Hibbert was a general surgeon, a colonel in the U.S. Air Force, stationed in Tampa, Florida. His commanding officer encouraged him to go, and indicated that the Air Force would pay him his regular salary, and not charge him leave or vacation time. Dr. Hibbert had never been on a Christian mission before.

Dr. Miller contacted a former Oral Roberts medical student named Nick Cardinale, MD, who was serving in the Navy in Spain, and made arrangements for him to join us. Another name and phone number that Dr. Miller gave me was Dr. Donald Kuenzi, a physician in Kansas City. I called him, and both he and his wife Martha agreed to join us. Dr. Kuenzi reported that just a couple of months earlier, he felt a call to medical missions. He discussed this with his pastor and they both prayed earnestly for the Lord's guidance in this matter. In part, because of the timing of my call, he felt the Holy Spirit was answering his prayer request.

Dr. Miller called David and Bonnie Anderson in Seattle, Washington, and asked if they would like to join us. Dr. Miller had never talked with them before, and how he got their name and phone number, I will never know. Bonnie was a nurse and both she and her husband agreed to join us.

I was able to persuade a dentist, Sam, from Alabama, and an orthodontist, Dr. Bill Ziegler, and his assistant, Pam, from Philadelphia to join our team. Perry Sherwood and his wife Penny from our church asked to join us. Penny is a nurse, while Perry is the brother of Cindy Sherwood. Cindy went with Todd and me to Colombia, and she hosted Dora May and me on our Zimbabwe Mission.

This made a team of 13, which was comprised of three physicians, two nurses, three dentists, two dental assistants, and three spouses. This was by far the largest team I had ever led. Each of the team members was responsible for their own finances. Since none of our team members had ever been on a mission trip before, I had to help them with getting their inoculations, visas, airline tickets and much more. I also had to figure out what supplies, equipment, and medications we needed plus a million more details.

After many months of preparation, we left in April 1997. We met in New York, and flew on Sabina, the Belgium National Airways. We met Dr. Nick, who was coming from Spain, in Brussels, Belgium, and we all flew together to Douala, Cameroon. John met us at the airport. John had attempted to get a pre-customs clearance for us, but the government officials didn't get the letter to the customs agents in time, so we spent two hours getting through customs.

It was very hot and humid, and even worse inside the airport since it had no air-conditioning. We all had been up for over 40 hours, so needless to say we were very tired. John had a small bus waiting to transfer us to a rather nice air-conditioned hotel. It was about 10 P.M. when we finally arrived at the hotel. We quickly got our rooms and went to bed.

The next day was a planned day of rest, orientation, and recovery from jet lag. It was also a day planned to recover any lost luggage. Fortunately, all of our luggage came as scheduled. John took us out to lunch at a nice little downtown restaurant. We then went to the city central market, and to an arts and handicraft market. There were people everywhere. We observed several women sitting naked on the sidewalk and a man walking naked down the street. What a mass of humanity that was!

The next morning we packed, and headed for the town of Kumba, John's childhood home. We drove through banana, rubber, and coconut plantations. For lunch, we stopped at a nice resort restaurant, that was a short distance up the side of Mount Cameroon, the tallest mountain in West Africa. John had arranged for an officer from the Minister of Health to join us, to answer questions, and brief us on typical tropical diseases we would likely encounter. The official warned us that the most common disease we would find would be malaria. She estimated that 70% to 90% of the people that we would see in the area where we were going would be infected with malaria. We had anticipated before we came that malaria would be a major problem. I tried to get malaria medication in the U.S. before we left, but because malaria is not a problem in the U.S., we couldn't find malaria treatment medication anywhere. All our team was taking their personal anti-malarial prevention medicine. The day we were in Douala, we bought 1800 treatment doses of malarial medication. It cost us $2000, but we had planned for that and were prepared.

We arrived at Kumba in the late afternoon. Kumba was located in the English speaking half of the country. We went to a small 12-room hotel on the edge of town, which was called Hotel Metropole. John had rented the entire hotel, and we were their only guests for 11 days.

John had planned to bring all of his family permanently to Cameroon a couple of months before we came. As it turned out, John came two months early by himself, and made all of our advance arrangements. He brought Kathy and his two children to Cameroon one week before we arrived. Kathy and their two children, along with three helpers came to Kumba with us. In addition to all the other team responsibilities John had, he also needed to help Kathy, and particularly the children, deal with the cultural shock and moving adjustments that they were experiencing.

The hotel had room air-conditioning and running water, but otherwise it was quite primitive. John had one of his relatives cook our food, being sure to boil everything well for our safety, and then bring it to the hotel. We ate in a special room. The hotel itself had no food service.

The next morning we drove to a grassy park in the center of town. John had several large tents with tables and chairs set up to help us organize our clinic. Everything worked quite well once we set up our supplies and equipment. The word had been spread that we were coming, so we had patients lining up before we were ready.

It was very hot, but the shade, along with a gentle breeze, kept us going. One time I looked down and my thigh areas on my scrubs were soaking wet. I then realized that my hands were sweating under my gloves, and it was running down my arms, and dripping off my elbows onto my scrubs, when I worked sitting down. I also had the problem of sweat dripping off of my forehead right into the patient's mouth, when I worked standing directly over them. The patients could detect the saltiness of my sweat, but since I had sterile gloves on, I couldn't stop and wipe my brow.

After we had worked for a while, Dr. Kuenzi came to me, upset and frustrated. He was a perfectionist type of person, and he was having difficulty being sure of his diagnosis without any lab tests or x-rays. He said, as an example, "I think this patient has anemia, but I can't tell for sure without a simple blood test." Then there were patients whom he suspected had TB, diabetes, high blood pressure, and heart problems, which he just was not equipped to treat, because they required long-term supervised treatment. I had to tell Dr. Kuenzi, "Yes, there will be some diagnoses we will just have to make an educated guess at, and yes, there are some people we just can't treat, but there are many people we can treat, and we need to concentrate on them. There are so many people that we can treat, we probably won't be able to treat all of them anyway." He accepted the reality of the situation, and felt better as he returned to work, treating patients the best way he possibly could under the circumstances. We treated a lot of patients successfully that first day.

There were several churches of various Christian denominations in Kumba. The city had a population of over 100,000 people. John had arranged for them to all work together, so we could have, for the first time ever, citywide evangelistic meetings in the central park every evening for a week. Actually, in order to get official permission, John had come to Kumba a month earlier and called a meeting of all the local pastors. He told them what he planned to do and asked for their help, and they agreed. He asked each of them to sign a request letter addressed to the central government Minister of Health, requesting permission to hold our health clinics as well as outdoor evening evangelistic services. Their request was granted.

After supper we returned to the park for our evening meeting. They had a sizable platform built for the speakers and guests. John rented and set up a powerful amplification system which could be heard for a long way around the city. They had a 10-piece band, with a 30-voice combined choir from many churches. They furnished excellent lively music with a bouncy beat. There were a few chairs on the platform for the speakers, which included many of the local pastors as well as John and Kathy. Our team also had some guest chairs down off the platform and along the side.

The Cameroon government had been very paranoid about conflicts, fighting, or a potential government overthrow, for the first 20 years of its existence as a new independent nation. As a result they had forbidden all types of teams like ours from coming into the country. We were told we were the first dental medical team to be allowed into the country since its independence. The open-air revival meeting in the central park was the first type of meeting like this that anyone could remember, because of the government's previous ban on all outdoor assemblies. As a result, we had a massive turnout. There were around two thousand people that stood up for the full two-hour service, the first evening. It grew in size each evening.

Our host Reverend John Ngoh was the primary speaker for the first service, and he gave an excellent evangelical message with a very challenging invitation. There were several hundred people that came forward, and prayed for salvation. Each church had trained numerous people to be counselors, but I don't think they had prepared enough people for the several hundred that came forward. The music and the PA system all worked great. It was a very exciting evening.

The remainder of the week we followed the same schedule. We had clinic during the day and a tremendous open air evangelistic meeting in the evening, with many people giving their hearts to Christ.

Sam, the dentist from Alabama, didn't blend in well with the team. He didn't come to our morning devotions and prayer time. He didn't go to the evening evangelistic services either. He stayed back in the hotel, smoked cigars, and drank beer. Before he came, he had professed to be a Christian, and agreed with HTI's purpose for coming.

Sunday John divided the team up, and we went in small groups to different churches. We were each asked to give a small speech or testimony. Dora May and I went to a large church, and they asked me to speak. I asked how long, and they said between forty-five minutes to one hour. Although the service was in English, my Western English was so confusing to those who spoke Pidgin English that they asked for me to have a translator, to translate my English into Pidgin English. I managed to speak forty-five minutes, with the help of my translator. My speaking was only a small portion of the five-hour plus service. When we arrived there at 8 A.M., the pastor was disappointed that we were late. We left at 1 P.M. when John came to pick us up for lunch, but the service was still ongoing. They were getting ready to have communion where everybody in the congregation drank out of the same cup.

Sam didn't go to church with us. He was picked up by a local female who had been working with him. Our two minibus drivers had become Christians a few days earlier. One of the drivers came to John and me, and reported that Sam had requested him to go and pick up his female helper at 1 A.M. He then requested the driver to take her home at 4 A.M. This was heartbreaking news. I got all the male team members together after Sunday lunch, and asked for their advice. One of the team members reported he had observed Sam making inappropriate gestures to this woman during clinic. John reported he had visited Sam in Alabama several months before coming, and Sam had asked him to help him smuggle items into the country that were illegal, which could have landed John in jail for several years. Of course, John refused. Working in the dental clinic, Sam continually complained about everything.

The consensus of the team was we needed to confront Sam as a group, and get his side of the story about the visit of this woman during the night. This type of activity could destroy our entire Christian witness if it became public. That evening the team met privately with Sam. I confronted him with the driver's report. He totally denied all charges, which made it even more difficult than it already was. Why would the driver make up such a story? We explained to Sam how this could destroy the team's whole purpose for coming. Finally, Sam offered to leave the team and go home. The whole team felt that this would be good.

The next morning he left the hotel in my presence about 6 A.M. in a taxi, continually denying all charges made against him. We will never know, but in my heart considering all his other non-Christian activities, I am convinced leaving the team was the best solution. This is the only team member I have ever had to send home from any of my 35 missions. This was certainly the most emotionally difficult problem I have ever encountered as a team leader on any of my mission trips.

I learned something important from this experience. I need to carefully check out our future team members' Christian commitment, and to explain to them in detail, what is expected of them. HTI probably accepts one out of every ten people who inquire about joining us on a mission. A couple of other HTI directors have had similar problems, so we developed a "Code of Conduct," which we require each team member to sign before being accepted. This describes in writing, the Christian conduct that we expect each team member to follow while on a HTI mission trip. I have had no problem since.

Sunday afternoon we walked up to the rim of a nearby volcano. We then climbed down inside the volcano using some very old metal ladders, installed by the Germans before World War I. We then proceeded down to a very large lake which filled most of the crater. We walked around the water's edge until we came to a break in the rim, where a small stream flowed out of the lake. There was a young man at the mouth of the stream loading some items into a small dugout canoe, and getting ready to paddle across the lake.

We started talking to him, and learned that he was one of the leaders of a very remote and totally isolated village on the other side of the lake. We told him who we were and what we were doing and he started begging us to come to his village and help his people. There were no roads into his village, and the only access to his village was across this huge lake.

We asked John about our schedule, and he indicated we were totally committed. He had planned a few hours in the morning of our last day for us to go to the market and shop, before returning to Douala in the afternoon. All the team agreed that they would rather go to this man's village, and help his people on our free morning, rather than go shopping.

The young man was very excited and happy. He agreed to have two longboats with operators at the mouth of the creek at daybreak on our last morning. We were all excited, too. We started walking out of the crater along a path on the side of the creek. It was a good mile and a half downhill before we came to the nearest road. This meant all supplies and equipment we planned to take across the lake, we would have to carry back up this path. Oh well! We were still very excited.

For our second week John had planned for us to visit remote villages which surrounded Kumba that we could reach by dirt roads. Each day we started early, and drove about an hour to different villages. Our first order of business was always a courtesy call to the chief. After getting the blessing of the chief, we started setting up our canopies in an open area in the middle of the village. This unusual activity created a crowd. John had visited all these villages earlier and had prearranged our visit with the chief.

While we were setting up our clinics, John used a portable battery operated PA system, which I brought him from the U.S., to play Christian music. After the crowd grew large, he turned the music off and using the PA system, he told them why we had come, and gave an evangelistic message with an invitation. Many people responded.

John then tried to get them in line for registration. This was not an easy task because there was such a large group of people all wanting to be seen by the doctors. Some just wanted to watch what was going on, and they were hard to control. Generally they were a very kind and gentle people, which responded to authority quite well. It just took time and patience.

Dr. Rambo, our enforcer, then took charge. Perry Sherwood had a physical physique similar to Rambo, so we labeled him Dr. Rambo. He moved the people back from crushing the doctors, and he roped off the clinic areas. He got people put in the correct lines. He quickly learned to hand out numbers to the waiting patients, on pink or green paper that couldn't be counterfeited. He spent much of his time just maintaining order, which allowed us much more time to treat patients.

John and his team stayed very busy doing one-on-one spiritual counseling with each patient, which gave us more time to treat patients. We certainly treated a lot of them. I let Perry extract a few teeth that were so loose from gum disease that they were ready to fall out. Dr. Bill, my only remaining dentist, was an orthodontist, and didn't usually extract teeth. He saw me allowing Perry to extract teeth, so he started to do so also. Much later, Perry told me that Dr. Bill called him to extract teeth that were so hard to take out that he was having difficulty muscling them out.

There is no question that these black Cameroonians had the hardest teeth that I have ever extracted in my life. Many times I had Dora May swinging the hammer, as I retracted the soft tissue, and held the bone chisel in place, to remove enough jawbone so that we could get the tooth out. Oftentimes when I applied the forceps to a tooth and tried to wiggle it, it felt like it was anchored in concrete. But with a little sweat and extra effort, we got all the needed teeth completely removed.

Late Monday afternoon the pastor of the church that I had spoken in on Sunday, came to our clinic and wanted to talk to me. I stopped working, and he told me this story: "Last night about 3 A.M., I was awakened by someone in the house. When I went to check, I was confronted by three armed bandits. They wanted to know where the rich American was, that had spoken at church on Sunday. I tried to tell them that you were not staying with us. They got mad, and when my 19 year old son who had been awakened and had joined me, stepped forward, they hit him in the head with their gun, causing a big cut in his head. They looked around the house, and finally left. I just wanted to let you know they're looking for you." I thanked him and asked him to talk to John.

When we got back to the hotel that evening, there were half a dozen men from different churches there to greet us. They had heard about the problem, and they came to stay up all night and protect us. There was a little old man that had a primitive bow and arrow. I asked him if he were going to use that to protect us, and he said, "Yes." He then loaded the arrow into the bow. The only problem was he loaded it backwards, so that the tip of the arrow was pointing toward him. We all laughed, and he quickly turned it around the other way. We all gave him an A for effort. One of the young men was a tailor, and as we got better acquainted, one of our team members asked if he could make her an outfit. He was delighted, and took her measurements, and made her exactly what she wanted the very next day.

The next morning Perry went out to the village early with some of John's team, and helped set up the canopies for our clinic, while John and I went to the local army military office. The army was the police. Finally we got to see the highest officer, and explained to him what had happened, and that we needed special protection. He indicated he couldn't do that. After some discussion, John took out approximately $60 in Cameroon bills, and handed it to the officer. He quickly put it in his pocket, and informed us we would have two armed soldiers at the hotel each night to protect us. We then got the rest of our team together, and headed to our new village.

In the afternoon we had a young man about 20 to 25 years of age come up to one of the busiest physicians, and want to talk to him about a personal non-medical problem. The physician brought him to see me. The young man told me this story: He had been to our evening evangelistic meetings, and realized his life was not good, so he came forward and gave his life to Christ. He counseled with someone and decided that he wanted to give his life totally to Christ. He wanted us to tell him where he could go to school and study to be a pastor or a missionary like John. Praise the Lord! But there were some complicating factors. This young man confessed to having been a member of a violent gang of men, who had raped, robbed many homes, and he personally had killed two people. He was very afraid, that if his gang members knew about his becoming a Christian, and if he were to quit the gang, they would hunt him down and kill him. Then he asked me, "What should I do?"

That was a difficult question. I know Jesus would forgive him, and I know the Bible tells us that we need to forgive him also. But does forgiveness mean that he doesn't have to pay for his crimes against society? Should we harbor or protect him, knowing that he is a murderer? I asked John to counsel with him, and he did for over an hour. When I asked John what the result had been, he said he really didn't know. We never saw the young man again. What would you have told him? If he had gone to the authorities and turned himself in, his gang would have immediately killed him. That was one of the most complicated questions that I've ever had to try to figure out, and in my mind I'm still searching for the right answer, and wondering whatever happened to that young man.

That afternoon we had a 50 year-old man come into our clinic with his foot and leg all bandaged up. When the doctors removed the bandages, they found part of his lower leg and his foot was full of gangrene. Part of his foot was already missing. He indicated that this had been progressing for a long time. The doctors could do nothing. He needed an amputation to save his life. They encouraged him to go to the Kumba hospital, and he said, "No." The doctors offered to pay for his treatment, and he still said "No." They told him he was going to die without treatment, and asked why he wouldn't go to the hospital. His answer was, "I'm not ready to die yet."

John told us that the general thinking of most people was that hospitals were a place you went to die. John said the vast majority of the time, that's exactly what happened. The doctors bandaged this man's leg up, and he hobbled away, but only after receiving Christ into his life. We had a chance to briefly stop and visit the local hospital, and most of the patients had very advanced and terminal conditions. It was a very depressing sight.

When we got back to the hotel that evening we had two uniformed army soldiers there, both with AK-47 machine guns. They stayed all night, and watched over our hotel. We never did have any problems, but the last night it was reported that the soldiers heard people in the bushes 50 feet in front of the hotel. They shouted for them to come out, so that they could use their machine guns, but nothing ever happened.

The first night when we thought a robbery might occur we took all of our valuables and money and hid them in various places. Two years later Perry reported that he found some of his money hidden under the insole of his boot. He had forgotten that he had hidden it there.

We usually plan a day or two on our mission trips for R & R or sightseeing. There weren't a lot of sites in Cameroon to see. One evening when discussing our options for our two open days in Douala at the end of our trip, Dr. Bill inquired about an African game park. John said Cameroon's Wasa Game Park was the best one in all of West Africa. It was in the northeast part of the country, and only accessible by plane. The team all agreed they would like to go to this game park, even if it cost a little extra. Several of them were concerned that they might never get back to Africa to see the wild animals. Making reservations was not simple, because Kumba did not have a travel agent, or a working telephone. We had to send someone back to Douala to make the arrangements. It was an all-day project. Pastor Moses and Dave went and they were successful in making all the arrangements.

We took turns doing a short testimony or devotion along with prayer each morning, at 6 A.M. before breakfast. When it came Dr. Bill's turn, he said, "Before I start devotions this morning, I want everyone to witness this." He went over in front of his dental assistant, Pam, got down on his knees, took a small box out of his pocket, opened it, and there was a diamond ring. He then asked Pam, "Will you marry me?" Her face lit up like a Christmas tree and said, "Yes, yes!" This was the first, and only time in my life I ever witnessed a marriage proposal.

We had clinics in several different villages. The visit to the chief's house in each village was uniquely different. Not only were the chiefs' clothes unique and colorfully different, but they had the most unusual decorations in their guest reception rooms in their mud huts.

One day a young teenage boy walked into the clinic. He said he wasn't in any pain, but he had a problem. He opened his moisture-soaked gown, and from his neck to his groin there was one mass of knobby, wet, raw, foamy, red growth of irregular cancerous tissue. I don't know, for the life of me, how this boy was still alive. The only thing medically we could do for him was to give him antibiotics, when infection came, and pain pills, when the pain would come. It was truly sad, but most importantly we introduced him to Jesus. The Africans call cancer, the white man's disease, because they rarely get it.

One afternoon we had a rather new car drive up to the clinic. A man with a white shirt, coat and tie got out, along with a very pretty well dressed seven year-old girl. The little girl wasn't feeling well. They had been to several doctors, and none of them had been able to help her, and they wanted to see if the American doctors could help. Sadly when the doctors finished examining her, they had to say they couldn't help either, and told the father it didn't look good. What they didn't tell the father, because they weren't sure, was that they thought the girl would probably die within a month. It was an untreatable terminal disease. We just couldn't help everyone, and it was sometimes heartbreaking. On the other hand, most of the people we could help, and we did help many of them.

Our last day finally came. This was the day we decided to give up our half-day of shopping, so that we could go across the Crater Lake to the isolated village. We got up very early and packed all that we figured we might need, and that we could carry. Actually our supplies were running low, because our clinics were supposed to be finished. We drove to the trailhead, and started the mile and a half hike alongside the stream up to Crater Lake. John told us this stream was where Kumba received all of its freshwater supply. Our two bus drivers and Kathy came with us.

The young man we had met earlier was at the mouth of the stream with a friend, and they had two long dugout canoes. There was some water in the bottom of the canoes, so they had laid some rough 2 x 4 planks on edge in the bottom of the canoes, so that we and our supplies wouldn't get wet. We all had to sit in the bottom of the canoes with our supplies. We loaded up. The boats were so heavily loaded that they sank in the water, so that only about two or three inches of the sides of the boat were above the water. It was a sunny, cool, quiet morning, and the surface of the water was as calm as glass.

Sitting on the edge of the sharp boards soon became extremely uncomfortable, but we had no choice. We decided that we could handle it for a short ride. After our boat drivers pushed off, they started paddling from the rear of our boats across this huge volcanic lake. Our boat drivers as well as the bus drivers that were with us started talking about how no one had ever been able to find the bottom of this lake, because it was so deep. They talked about burying their dead in the lake, and how they were sure that they were still alive and well, at a village, at the bottom of the lake. Africans have many such fantasies concerning their dead. Ancestor worship is quite common in Africa.

We saw crocodiles splashing into the lake at a distance around the edge. Near the middle of the lake, Kathy started having a panic attack. She started screaming at the top of her voice, and crying, that we were all going to die, and she wanted to go back. They held her tight, and talked her down, so that within five or ten minutes, her problem was just limited to crying, as we continued to proceed. None of us were wearing life jackets and the canoe was a little unstable.

As the sun came up further, it became warmer. The lake was a lot larger than it looked. We found out that it was three miles across and it took us an hour and a half to paddle across. When we arrived on the other side, there was a crowd of people on the shore to welcome us. We weren't sure we were going to be able to move because of the pain in our bottoms, but we finally all got out and the villagers helped us carry our gear. We hiked another mile or so to the village. We called on the chief, set up our clinics, and got to work. We only planned a half day. Some of the people were far out of the village tending their gardens because they were sure we would never come. They had many promises of help in the past, but no one had ever come.

The village was not very big, probably about 150 to 200 people. They truly lived in the Stone Age. They had no electricity, communications, or anything that represented civilization, except they had steel machetes.

Dr. Kuenzi reported that he and his medical colleagues had experienced an interesting and unusual tropical disease, called Bilharziasis, which they had never seen before. This disease was caused by a blood fluke which was contracted by drinking contaminated water, and it caused bleeding in the urine. A surprising number of people in the village had this disease and fortunately, they had enough of the right medicine left to treat them.

I had an experience that day that I have only read about in textbooks. We were kept moderately busy extracting what they called their shaking teeth. The people had zero oral hygiene, and their teeth had advanced periodontal infection. When the periodontal infection got bad enough, their teeth would get loose, and become painful when they tried to bite or chew. We took a lot of these types of teeth out. They came out easily. The thing that I had never seen before, or since, and have only read about, was that there was absolutely not one single decayed tooth that we saw in the whole village, even though the teeth were covered in white bacterial plaque.

We had always been taught that it took three things to cause decay; a susceptible tooth, bacteria, and sugar. We in the U.S. tried to make the teeth less susceptible to decay, by using fluoride. We try to control bacteria by brushing and flossing, and we try to eat fewer sugars, particularly less frequently. In this village they had no fluoride, which made their teeth very susceptible to decay. They had lots of bacterial plaque, but they were lacking the third essential ingredient totally. They had 100% no sugar in their village, and as a result they had 100% no decay.

We had hoped to finish and start back by noon, but it was 1 P.M. before medical finished their last patient. We quickly packed and were on our way. Our return trip across the lake was uneventful. We arranged the bottom of the boat so that the boards were a little more comfortable, because we all had sore bottoms. Several of the team members got sunburned on the way over, so they took precautions to cover up on our return.

When we finally got back to our minibuses, two hours late, we loaded up and immediately headed for Douala. John didn't like for us to be on the road at night, for safety reasons. It was just a little after dark when we arrived at our hotel. I think everyone felt good, that we had been able to help a lot of otherwise helpless people, and John and his team had good results in sharing the Gospel.

By 8 A.M. the next morning, we had our overnight bags packed, and we were on a plane flying directly to Maroua, the capital of the northeastern province of Cameroon. A small bus met us at the airport, and we were off on a four-hour bus ride to an overnight resort, near the entrance to Cameroon's Wasa Game Park. This area of Cameroon was a dry sunny Sub-Sahara Desert. I had a new experience during this ride. I found it was hotter and more uncomfortable to open the window and let the blast of hot air blow on us than it was to close the window. We didn't have air-conditioning, but the wind coming in the window felt like a giant hairdryer blowing on us.

Our overnight resort was on a big rocky outcropping, in an otherwise flat dry desert. There were several small cabins spread between the huge boulders. The office was at the very top, which had a fantastic view over many miles of flat desert. They had an outdoor restaurant where we had supper. During supper, I met the European owner of the resort, and I commented on how hot it was. I well remember his comment. He said, "What do you expect, this is part of the Sahara Desert."

When we went to our cabins that evening, we were pleased that we had running water, but the electricity was not working, and as a result the air-conditioning didn't work. We had observed the water pipes running over the top of the huge boulders. When we turned on the water, it was hot, very hot, having been in the hot sun all day on top of the rocks.

Perry and Penny left their non-screened window wide open trying to get a little breeze. At dusk they observed the silhouette of a large four-legged animal crossing in front of their window, and it had the outline and movements of a mountain lion. This got Perry's adrenaline pumping, and he ended up sitting up all night waiting to see if the animal would return and try to come into their room. Nothing happened.

The next morning the resort loaded us into a couple of their small minibuses, in which they routinely took their guests into the game park. The game park was very large and went for over 50 miles. The drivers followed a maze of two-track trails, trying to spot the big elephant herd. We saw warthogs, a variety of antelope, and a large group of graceful giraffes very close up, as well as baboons and jackals. We went to the watering holes and looked all over for the elephants, but didn't find them. There was plenty of evidence of the presence of elephants. Much of our two-track minibus trails had potholes made by their big footprints, which sank two to four inches into the ground, giving us a very rough ride.

The sky started to get dark, and when our driver saw lightening, he started heading very rapidly for the exit. The rains of their rainy season weren't supposed to start for several weeks, but they came early. Before we got to the exit the sky opened up, and the rain poured down, and the ground started soaking up the moisture. Our tires kept leaving deeper and deeper ruts. The driver didn't slow down, thank goodness. He kept the minibus rolling quite fast. By the time we got to the entrance we were leaving six-inch deep ruts. I'm sure if we had ever stopped, we would have never started moving again.

That afternoon we headed back to Maroua, where we planned to overnight in a hotel. We had a flight scheduled out around noon the next day. We planned to get back into Douala about 4 P.M. and then catch our international flight home at 11:30 P.M.

That evening, John went over the finances with me. He had paid for all of our expenses inside the country. HTI's goal was to not be a financial burden to our missionary host.

This was John's first time hosting a team. He had estimated $1200 a person, which we had already paid him, but when he got all the expenses added, it came to $1300 per person. With 13 team members, he was $1300 short. He felt bad and so did I. We had paid extra for our game park trip, and I knew most of the team members were broke. Dr. Kinsey sat in on our financial conference with John, and he suggested that he and I split the $1300 shortfall, and not even discuss it with the rest of the team. That's what we did, but we advised John for any future HTI teams, he should charge $1500 for the in-country expenses and give any surplus as a refund at the end of the trip. This is exactly what he has done on our 14 subsequent trips, and we've never had a problem again. Most of the time any surplus he attempted to return, the team members just told him to keep as a thank you for a job well done.

We arrived at the airport about 10 A.M., and saw the morning plane leave for Douala. We checked in for our flight and then waited. Then an announcement came. The noon flight to Douala had been canceled. How could they do that? Didn't they know we had 13 international flights to catch that night? John went and talked to the airport manager, and they called the Cameroon Airlines head office in Douala and explained our dilemma. They said there were not enough passengers on the afternoon flight to warrant sending a plane to get us, and they would book us on the morning flight the next day. After two hours of intense negotiation, John came back and told us there was no way we were going to get out of Maroua, or make our international flights. Then he sat down and put his hand over his face and sobbed like a baby. He was exhausted, and had tried so hard to make our first HTI mission trip successful, so he could have more HTI teams come and work with him in the future. He thought he saw his mission dream crumbling.

The Cameroon Airlines did put us in a hotel overnight, and paid for our supper and breakfast. That evening at the hotel, Dr. Bill, the orthodontist, tried desperately to call or fax home to let someone know he wouldn't be in his office on Monday. He had over 40 orthodontic patients scheduled, that had been waiting more than two weeks to get their braces adjusted. After a couple of hours of trying, he finally got a phone call through, and felt a little better. I got a phone call through to Dr. Miller, and asked him to notify all the team's families that we would be delayed.

The next morning we got to the airport early and took the morning flight to Douala with no problems. There were normally only two flights a day out of this airport. We arrived at Douala about noon, and took the team to a hotel, and got a day room in which they could relax and wait, while John and I tried to solve the dilemma involving our missed international flights.

We collected all the tickets, and headed to the Cameroon Airlines central office. It was Sunday and they were closed, so we went to the airport to the Cameroon Airlines office. They couldn't do anything for us, and sent us somewhere else. Each place we went we had a long wait to be seen. They couldn't do anything for us either. Our team had nonrefundable international group tickets, that were about one third the normal prices, but you couldn't change anything.

Around 5 P.M. we drove by a Sabina Airlines office that was open. Our international tickets were with Sabina, but the problem was not really theirs since they had not caused the problem in the first place. We stopped anyway. We had run into a dead end everywhere else. After waiting, we finally got to the desk, and the young man asked us how he could help us. I told him our long sad story, and how we had spent two weeks helping his people, and how we were tired, and needed to go home. He said somewhat sharply, "Sit over there!" and he pointed to the back of the room. He continued to help other customers. We waited and waited. Finally at 6 P.M. he got up and locked the front door. After everyone left, he called us back to his desk, and said, "Let's see what I can do." He took all of our tickets and started working on his computer and made some phone calls. In one hour's time he had all 45 flights from Douala to New York and from New York to each of our homes in the U.S., completely rewritten. He handed me a stack of 45 new tickets all the way home for everyone. I knew the tickets couldn't be changed, and I was expecting him to say, this will be $20,000. But all he said was, "I am sorry for your trouble, and I'm glad I was able to help. Have a good flight home." This was truly another answer to our prayers.

It was about 7 P.M. when we left his office. He had scheduled us out on an 11:30 P.M. Cameroon Airline which was already full, but he had made space for us. Sabina didn't have a flight that day.

We hurried back to the hotel, and got the team and rushed to the airport. We just made it in time. We thanked John and Kathy for everything, and left Douala at 11:30 P.M. I had no problem falling asleep on the plane. I was emotionally exhausted. We flew to London, and then back to Paris. We transferred to a Sabina flight in Paris, and flew to Brussels, Belgium, where we caught our Sabina international flight to New York. We arrived in New York in the early evening. Everyone had a scheduled flight home that evening, except Perry, Penny, Dora May, and me. Our flight was scheduled the next morning. We checked and there was no available flight out that night to Detroit. We found a hotel for the night, and finally returned home Tuesday morning, rather than Sunday afternoon, as we were originally scheduled. It is nice to go away, but always better to come home.

In summary: John reported that we treated a little over 3000 patients, and that over 2200 people accepted Jesus, and became Christians. I don't know how you could possibly call that a bad mission. It was great, and we even had some extra, unusual, unique, and memorable experiences. I felt we broke a couple of important barriers in Cameroon, by being the first health care mission to enter the country since its independence, and having the first large outside public gathering with our evening evangelistic meetings.

# And Now for the Rest of the Story

Dr. John Hibbert took his wife, Amelda, a nurse, on seven additional mission trips with HTI to Cameroon. Dr. Hibbert has now retired from the Air Force, and he and Amelda have moved to Cameroon to be full-time medical missionaries. He has started a school and he is training students how to be advanced Christian medical nurses to work in remote areas where medical treatment is not available.

Dr. Kuenzi has become a valuable HTI board member and has gone on many more HTI mission trips.

Reverend John and Kathy Ngoh have started a church, and three Bible schools, that are graduating 25 to 35 students each year, fully equipped to be pastors and evangelists. John and Kathy have continued to be active evangelists, and have hosted 14 successful HTI teams. We have seen well over 30,000 unreached people come to Christ in Cameroon, resulting from our HTI partnership with John and Kathy. We have seen more unreached people come to Christ in Cameroon than in any other country that HTI has ever served. Praise the Lord!

# CHAPTER 19

# CAMEROON 2 PYGMIES

Pygmies are generally thought of as a primitive black African tribe of people, known to be the shortest and smallest humans in the world. The majority of Pygmies live deep in the rain forest or jungles of Africa, far away from roads or civilization. It is because of their isolation that not a lot of details are known about their culture.

With the results of our rather difficult, but safe and very successful first HTI mission to Cameroon, Reverend John Ngoh immediately e-mailed me and requested me to bring another team back the following spring. He planned to target the mysterious Pygmies. I happily accepted his invitation.

With John's and his team's great evangelistic skills, we had more unreached people accept Christ during our first mission trip than I had in all my previous 15 mission trips combined. I felt the fields in Cameroon were ripe unto harvest, and John and his team were committed and organized to accomplish that task. I was very excited about the opportunity.

I was able to assemble a 9 member team. The team included Dr. Donald Kuenzi and his wife Martha, Perry and Penny Sherwood, Dora May and me, all whom had gone the previous year. Dr. Reid McCullough, a dentist, and Connie, his wife and dental assistant, from Oklahoma, also agreed to join us. Both were previous experienced HTI team members. I had a former dental assistant, Lisa Hussan, who contacted me and asked if she could go. Therefore, we had one physician, one nurse, two dentists, three dental assistants, Dr. Rambo (Perry), and Martha who planned to act as our pharmacist.

John planned our trip for March rather than April, hoping to get farther away from the rainy season, and possibly we could have a little cooler weather. After our lengthy preparation we packed and left in March 1998. We met in New York and flew Sabina Airlines through Brussels. Because of a delay, we arrived in Douala at 9 P.M. instead of 5 P.M., and because of lost luggage and customs difficulties, we didn't get out of the airport until 10:30 P.M. We all had been up over 40 hours and were dead tired.

Expecting that we would arrive at 5 P.M. as we were scheduled, John had rented an entire restaurant, for 7 P.M., and planned a big welcoming banquet, with the mayor of Douala, several health officials, some prominent physicians, and dentists, which were all patiently waiting for us. All the food had been prepared and was ready. There was no canceling.

Everyone groaned a little, but we left the airport and arrived at the restaurant at 11 P.M. We were given a wonderful welcome by the officials and dignitaries. We also had a nice buffet dinner. Somehow we all managed to stay awake and smile. We got to our hotel and into our beds around 1 A.M. It was a very kind gesture of John's, but because of the unreliability of the flight schedules, luggage, customs, and the number of hours it took to travel to Cameroon, John promised never to do that again, and he hasn't.

The first day was a day of rest, to overcome jet lag, orientation, shopping, and recovering our lost essential luggage before we left town for two weeks. We didn't need to purchase any malaria medication in Cameroon because a Christian charitable organization called MAP started carrying the medication in the U.S. I purchased enough malaria medication to be able to treat 3000 patients. It only cost $150 from MAP. It would have cost us over $3000 to buy it in Cameroon, and much more if ordered from a U.S. pharmacy.

Early on our second day, John gathered together his team of translators and evangelists, along with our team, and we all loaded into a large Land Rover, and a small Volkswagen truck, and headed for Yaounde, the capital of Cameroon.

After the First World War, when the French and British took Cameroon away from Germany, they divided their occupation of the country in half. Douala, the largest and only port city in the country, had been the capital. The French and British agreed to move the capital to Yaounde which was inland quite a ways. Yaounde was cooler, less humid, less rain, and most of all, less mosquitoes, which frequently caused malaria.

We arrived at Yaounde in the early afternoon. We went to John's sister's home, and had a nice buffet lunch, which she had prepared especially for us. John was well aware that we could easily get sick from improper food or drink, and he supervised all of our meals very carefully to keep us healthy. We never had any serious problems caused by food or drink on the entire trip. It was difficult for John to supervise a restaurant. In our truck, John had packed enough bottled water and pop to last the whole team for two weeks in this very hot Cameroon weather.

Our lunch stop was good, but short, and we continued inland to the east. The road from Douala to Yaounde was the best road in the country, but it got progressively worse as we traveled inland and away from the capital. There were huge logging trucks which traveled these roads, all carrying large mahogany logs out of the rain forests to the docks in Douala, for shipment to Europe. Mahogany was Cameroon's main export, and it was all owned and controlled by the government.

The road quickly turned to gravel and became very rough, greatly slowing our progress. We drove on this road for a good three hours. About 6 p.m., near sunset, we turned onto a small logging road with grass growing between the tracks, and headed directly south into the rain forests. There were really no roads going south except for the logging roads made by loggers. We drove for eight hours in the pitch black of night, and only went 100 miles over this rough, narrow, winding, logging road. This was an average of 13 miles an hour. We never stopped once. Occasionally, our headlights would show the whites of someone's eyes standing alongside the road.

It was about 3 A.M. when we finally got to the place where we were going to stay for two weeks. John had rented an entire small motel-like facility. Lisa was the only single person, so she was assigned a room by herself. When we started unpacking, she came to me and said, "Dr. Charlick. there's a critter in my room." I went and looked, and on the floor I saw what looked like a millipede, but it was about 6 inches long and one inch wide. Brave me, I went and got Emanuel, our driver, and had him look at the beast. He said, "It's friendly, and won't hurt you." He leaned down and carefully picked it up, took it outside and let it go in the grass. We all quickly went to bed to get some much needed sleep.

In the morning we evaluated our surroundings. Our rooms were small all-concrete bunkers, even the ceilings. We learned that termites were a big problem in this area, so they didn't use any wood. There were about 10 rooms, all attached. We had one small window in our room which had bars on it, a shutter, and a screen with lots of holes in it. We had a bed that occupied 80% of the room. There was no place to open up our suitcases except on the bed. There was a small 3' x 4' attached room that had a small porcelain stool in it with no seat cover, and a bucket of water alongside to be used to flush the toilet. We observed a hand-pump well about two hundred yards away. The owner had filled several large barrels with water and placed them in front of our rooms, so that we would have water handy for washing and flushing our toilets.

Dora May and I had brought a mosquito net, so we put it over our bed. It worked well. The first morning we both noticed we had several small red welts on our bodies which were a little itchy and were on the side of our bodies that lay on the bed. We had brought a sheet, so we took the owner's sheet off the bed, and spread a couple of plastic raincoats over the mattress, and then put our sheet over them. We had no more red spot problems. It was so hot that we didn't need a top sheet.

One of John's team members was named Ruth, and she was a single female. Lisa asked John if they could room together, and he agreed. I assumed that Lisa was feeling a little apprehensive about rooming by herself, and she was located several rooms away from us. Lisa and Ruth moved into a room right next to us.

The concrete roof and walls heated up during the day in the hot tropical sun. We were located very near the equator. When we got home at night, our rooms felt like a sauna. The concrete held the heat well into the night.

On our first morning John showed us our dining room. Our eating facilities consisted of a separate small room with a concrete roof and 2 open sides. There were two crude tables with benches. We watched them scramble our eggs for breakfast over an outside wooden fire. John supervised them to make sure everything was well cooked to kill any bacteria.

Reid had brought along a bottle of hot Tabasco sauce. Any time our food didn't taste particularly good, we would put a couple of drops of his hot sauce on it, and it took away the taste of the food. All you could taste was the hot Tabasco sauce. Reid and his hot sauce were very popular. We used the entire bottle by the end of our 2 weeks.

As we were sitting at our crudely made tables, watching our eggs being scrambled, Dr. Kuenzi, bless his heart, set the mood for our entire stay by announcing, "Martha and I have talked about our living conditions here, and have decided if these people can live in these conditions their entire lives, we can survive for two weeks. You won't hear Martha or me complaining one bit about our living conditions," and we didn't. Dr. Kuenzi was our only physician, probably in his mid 70s, and was well respected by all. His example was followed by everyone, and I didn't hear one complaint from anyone all week.

The first morning we all got up late, because of the late hour we went to bed. John had planned our first day as a day for getting organized and looking over the area. Our accommodations were actually located on the edge of a small town, called Lomie. We drove a mile or so into town where we observed 50 to 75 primitive houses, and one small general store. We looked around the store and I purchased a 30 foot heavy wire cable that I thought might be nice to have in case one of our vehicles got stuck, or for any other emergency.

An interesting observation that I made at the store was looking at a big bag of rice that was probably 100 pounds. There was a large English label on this bag. It said a product of Vietnam. Lomie was certainly a long way from Vietnam. I couldn't help but wonder how a bag of rice from Vietnam could end up this deep in the rain forest in Cameroon, Africa. I guess I'll never know.

We made the customary courtesy call to the governor who ruled this whole rain forest area in which we were staying. We also visited a small Catholic church on the edge of town. The priest wasn't there, but we looked into the small sanctuary. They had unique stained glass windows made of clear, green, and brown glass that made the design of a cross and other designs. Interestingly, all the glass consisted of the bottoms of beer bottles. It looked surprisingly nice.

Early the next morning, we packed and headed further south on the logging road, deeper into the rain forest. Occasionally we would have to find a place to move off the one-lane trail, so that the huge logging trucks could pass. We came to a group of huts, where John had previously visited, and had received permission from the chief for us to set up our clinic. Actually, John had visited all the villages in which we worked, prior to our arrival, and had secured permission for us to come and help them.

Perry had unique foresight, because he purchased and brought a large used parachute from the Army Navy store. All the ropes had been removed. Perry got some sticks out of the rain forest, and put the parachute up to shield us from the hot sun. It worked great. We saw many medical and dental patients. The pygmies are small people averaging about 4 feet tall. We had to have double translation, from Pygmy to French, and then French to English. We were in the French speaking southern half of the country.

We were disappointed to have several of our patients tell us that the Catholic priest had visited them earlier and told them to stay away from the American doctors, because they were evil, and they would tell them about a false religion. They must not have had much respect for the priest, because they came to our clinics for treatment in great numbers, and many listened to the Gospel and became Christians. That afternoon we moved further down the logging trail, and set up another roadside clinic next to a group of huts. We had a successful afternoon clinic there also.

Every day we went to a different pygmy village. The villages were located anywhere from 30 minutes to an hour and a half drive away. Rather than describing each village clinic individually, I will combine the highlights. The custom was to meet with the village chief first. We always had a very warm welcome. The villages ranged in size from 20 huts to 200 huts. Pygmies were often mobile people, and frequently moved from place to place in the rain forest.

In one village I was assigned a 15-year old pygmy girl to translate from Pygmy to French, and then Emanuel, our driver, would translate from French to English. The 15-year-old girl was a school teacher, teaching children how to speak French. She was nice-looking with a big smile. She had a design of scars on her forehead and cheeks, which she said was to identify the particular tribe of pygmies to which she belonged. She also had her two central incisors filed to a point. She indicated this was a mark of beauty, and it also helped tear her food better. The only problem was they had filed her teeth into the nerve, and the nerve had died and both teeth were abscessed and painful. I was told that the filing process was done with a small stone. Filing her two front teeth right into the nerve, without anesthesia, must have been extremely painful.

For some reason I happened to ask her if she were married, and she surprised me by saying yes, and even surprised me more by saying she had two children. After lunch her mother brought her two children to the clinic for us to see, and they were old enough to be running around. This is what I call living on the fast track; married, two children, and a school teacher by the age of 15.

In one of the villages the chief insisted at the end of the day that we stay and watch his villagers put on a ceremonial dance. They got dressed in costumes and brought out their jungle drums and put on a half-hour performance for us. The drums had a wild African beat and had an unusually deep hollow sound. They sure liked beating on those drums. This was the way the chief had to say thank you for coming to his village and helping his people.

This was also the same chief that personally gave me a set of African antelope horns. I still have them, but have never learned what type of antelope they came from, and furthermore none of my hunting buddies around here have been much help.

In the largest village we visited, there was a man who ran a health clinic of sorts. We visited him and found he had little or no medications of any kind. We left him some of ours that we thought would be extra. He also had a crude pair of pliers that he said he sometimes used to extract teeth. He was fascinated by our anesthesia. He had never seen or heard of it before, so we gave him some and showed him how to use it.

We saw patients that brought their pet monkeys with them to the clinic. We saw a young girl whose face and body had been severely scarred, because she had fallen into the fire when she was very young. Dr. Kuenzi said, "90% of the patients I examined have symptoms of malaria, so I just automatically treated everyone." He also indicated that 70% of the patients had signs or symptoms of worms, so again he treated everyone. Martha handed the patients a glass of water along with their medication and had them take it right in front of her. In one village we saw a child size two wheel bicycle, without the chain or sprockets, all very uniquely made out of wood. A child was riding it around the area. Their creative ingenuity was most fascinating.

We were told that a pygmy woman's job was to build the house and maintain it. Their houses were built of sticks and leaves, and they said that they could build a house in one day. The houses were round and about 15 feet in diameter much like a teepee. The women planted the gardens, cared for the gardens, gathered and cooked the food, bore the children, and raised them. The man's job was to father the children, and to hunt. We were told that 50% of the children died before the age of three.

People have often thought of the pygmies as being warlike or ferocious. We found them to be extremely docile, laid-back, passive, and very friendly. If you stop to think about it, if you lived where the temperature was 110° to 125° each day, you were malnourished, had malaria, worms, and a variety of other physical ailments, how ferocious do you think you would be?

Outhouses were nonexistent. We often saw some of the giant mahogany trees that loggers had not cut down. The trees were extremely large and very tall, and said to be hundreds of years old. Some people were concerned that the Government loggers were denuding the rain forest of Cameroon's most precious natural resource. When talking to the loggers they claimed they were just cutting the old and diseased trees to give the smaller trees a better chance to grow. It was difficult to know who to believe.

One day we got a few light showers. Perry's overhead parachute worked well in keeping us dry and working. On our way back to our overnight quarters, we got into a very heavy rain, and when our Land Rover hit an area of wet clay on a downhill slope, the vehicle slid just as if it were on ice. Emanuel had never driven on slippery surfaces or icy roads, and he didn't know how to handle it. He turned the wrong way, and we ended up in a small ditch alongside the road. We were going so slow that no one was hurt. The front wheel got buried in mud almost to the top of the tire. The vehicle wouldn't move. We all got out and stood in the pouring rain in the middle of the road. The rain actually felt good because we had all been so hot and sweaty all day.

Again Dr. Rambo took control. Perry determined that the four-wheel Land Rover was only in 2-wheel drive. The way that this vehicle engaged the front wheels, was to turn a knob on the axle of the front wheels. He turned one easily but the other one was buried in the mud. He dug it out with his bare hands, until he could find and turn the knob. With all four wheels engaged, and all the passengers out, he backed it out into the middle of the road with no problem.

When we got back to our quarters, we gave Perry a shower, which involved taking water out of the barrels with a small pail and pouring it over his head. At least the rain had cooled our concrete bedrooms, or "hot boxes," as we called them, down to a more tolerable temperature.

We spent two days holding clinic under a big shade tree in the center of Lomie. The grass had grown up waist high under the tree, so John, our forward thinking host, made special advance arrangements. When we arrived, there were eight prisoners from the local prison under the tree with machetes cutting down the high grass. There were also armed guards watching them.

When we started to set up our clinic, two people came and asked the doctor if he would come to the governor's house. It seemed the governor, who was not a pygmy, and had been appointed by the central government, had a drinking problem. He was 6 feet tall and weighed 250 to 300 pounds. He was an intimidating monster in comparison to the pygmies. Evidently the governor had gotten so drunk the night before that he had fallen down a flight of stone stairs. He had been unconscious or sleeping all night, and he was just beginning to awaken. They wanted the doctor to come and examine him. Emanuel, Dr. Kuenzi, and I went, while John was sharing the Gospel with the crowd that had gathered.

Dr. Kuenzi examined the governor fairly thoroughly, and beside a few bumps and bruises, he checked out okay. Dr. Kuenzi warned him to stop drinking alcohol. They were all appreciative and we left. We had a very busy day under the shade tree, but there were many people we didn't get to see, so we planned to return the next day to try to finish the rest of the patients.

The next morning when we arrived, and before we even started to set up our clinic, two people came running and very excitedly asked Dr. Kuenzi to come quickly as the governor had become unconscious and was thrashing violently. Emanuel, Dr. Kuenzi, and I immediately went while John again shared the Gospel with the waiting crowd.

Dr. Kuenzi said to me, "It sounds like he may have fractured his skull, and has intracranial pressure and bleeding. If that is the case, we probably can't get him out of here to the nearest hospital, which is in Yaounde, about 11 hours away, before he would be dead." Dr. Kuenzi was concerned that he might have missed this diagnosis the day before.

When we got to the house, the big man was violently thrashing around and was unconscious. There were about six men trying to hold him down but with limited success. A person that had some medical knowledge was there, and he told Dr. Kuenzi that he had just given the governor a shot of Valium. Dr. Kinsey tried to examine him, but he was thrashing so much that it was impossible. After a few minutes his thrashing started to lessen and in 10 minutes he lay totally relaxed but still unconscious.

Dr. Kuenzi felt a big relief. If he had been bleeding in his skull from the fall the day before, the Valium would not have worked. Dr. Kuenzi asked the family if the governor had any alcohol since his fall, and they proudly told him, not a drop. That was the problem. Dr. Kuenzi quickly determined that the problem was DTs, delirium tremors, a condition resulting from his sudden withdrawal from alcohol.

We went back to the clinic and finished all the patients that were waiting. At the end of the day we returned to the governor's house and he was up and walking around. John went with us, and shared the Gospel with him. He made no commitment, but he listened intently. We didn't push anything, because the governor had great power. He did promise us that he would try to stop drinking.

On Sunday John indicated we had been invited to attend a small house church. There usually were six people that met in the living room of a young pastor's house. There had been many people during the week that had accepted Christ at our clinic, and John had invited all of them to church. Guess what? We had a multitude of people. We had to hold the service outside on the front porch area.

We had a great Sunday morning service. This was the young pastor who had originally invited John to come to this area, and he helped John with many of our arrangements. He promised he would follow up on all our new converts. He was extremely happy and excited. He had been in town for a year and had only six converts. Then all of a sudden since we had our clinic in town, he had almost 100 people at his service. After church the people stood around in front of the house and talked and they were still talking when we finally left for lunch about 30 minutes later.

One of the new Christians asked if we wanted to visit a new pygmy village that had just moved into an area on the outskirts of town. We had nothing planned Sunday afternoon, so I said, "Yes". We met him after lunch and he went with us and showed us the way.

Thinking ahead, Dr. Kuenzi packed some medicines in our backpacks. We walked down a narrow jungle path for about 30 to 40 minutes, and finally came to a clearing with 10 to 12 pygmy huts around the outside edges. We greeted the people and talked with them, through our interpreters of course. Dr. Kuenzi consulted with a few patients and handed out some medications.

Back in Douala on our first day, Dr. Kuenzi had purchased one hundred one-pound jars of peanut butter. He said last year he had seen many children with red hair and pot bellies, which was a simple sign of severe protein deficiency, and the best treatment for them was to eat protein. Peanut butter was cheap, and rich in protein. We had taken several jars of peanut butter with us on our afternoon walk. We had enough to give each family one jar. They were excited to receive it.

Just as we had finished giving out our peanut butter handouts, a sudden storm came, and with a flash of lightning, it started to pour. Several of us were standing near one of their huts. I looked inside, and it was pitch black, but I couldn't see anyone in there so we stepped inside. The hut was made by putting flexible sticks 1 or 2 inches in diameter and about 10 feet long, into the dirt in a 12 to 15 foot circle, and then bending all the sticks into the center and tying them together. Leaves were then put on the top and sides like shingles, leaving a small opening for the door. There were no windows and it was as black as ink in there. The center of the hut was just barely tall enough for us to stand upright. It was amazingly waterproof. It rained hard and there was no water leaking anywhere in that hut.

Our eyes slowly became accustomed to the dark as we stood there for a while. Then a very spooky thing happened. As we started looking around the outer wall, on the inside of the hut, we could see the whites of people's eyes looking at us. There were six people sitting around the inside walls of this dark hut all this time just staring at us. Fortunately, the rain let up about that time, and we all scrambled out, wondering what they were thinking about our having invaded their home. After we gave out a few other little gifts, we started our walk back. They were very friendly people. I kept watching but we never saw anyone come out of the hut where we had been standing during the storm. I guess either we scared them to death, or they were children.

Just as we started back, we met a hunter from town, who was returning from his day of hunting. He had a very crude single-shot rifle, which we were told was very rare, and a bulging burlap bag. We stopped and asked him how his day of hunting had been. He immediately reached into his bag and pulled out a good-sized monkey that he had shot. He was very proud of his kill. We understood that monkey was the choice meat of all game to be hunted. At first it made us a little sick and angry, but then we had to remember where we were. It turned out to be one of the most interesting Sunday afternoons I have had in a long time.

When we returned we were informed that one of the patients from whom I had extracted teeth two days earlier was in pain, and she had run out of her pain pills. John indicated that we would be going past her house on the outside of town the next morning, as we drove to another remote pygmy village. He suggested that would be a good time to stop and give her more medication.

As we drove out of town the next morning we stopped at the woman's house. She was sitting on the ground in front of her house, about 20 feet from the road, with a bunch of children running around her. We all got out of the vehicles, and I checked her mouth, and found that it was healing fine, but there was still some soreness, so I gave her some more pain pills. This was one of the women who had become a Christian. We asked her if these were all of her children, and she said, "Yes, all 10 of them." Her husband wasn't there. John asked if we could look inside her house and she said, "Yes."

Her house was about 10 feet wide and 20 feet long. It was made of sticks, palm branches, and leaves. It had just one room with a dirt floor with a pile of live wood coals glowing in one corner, where she must have been doing her cooking. The kids seemed healthy and were very lively and energetic. There were no beds or any furniture in the house. There was one woven reed mat on the floor about 3' x 6' in size. I looked at the size of the house and tried to figure how 12 people could lie on the floor to sleep at night if it were raining outside. There was a doorway, but no door. There was one window opening, but nothing to cover it if it rained. I thought to myself, this looks like the way people in the jungle would have lived 2000 years ago. There had been very little change. She seemed very happy that we stopped and we continued on our way.

Perry had bought on the Internet before we came some MRE's, Meals Ready to Eat. He brought almost 100 of them with him. They were made by the company that used to make the old army K-rations, but these were improved and made for civilian use. When we were out in the villages this was our lunch, along with some warm water or pop.

These MRE's came in brown foil-sealed bags and they didn't look very appetizing. The memory of the stories of the old army K-rations was not very exciting either. But surprisingly, these meals were very tasty, nutritious, and filling. The meals were so large that often we couldn't eat everything. There were 12 different types including beef stew, chicken and rice, and frank and beans. They all had crackers, jelly, a beverage powder, and various desserts. If I had spaghetti, and I wanted it warm, I would just lay it out in the sun on a rock, and at lunchtime it was nice and warm. Surprisingly, they were good cold also. The cost was about two dollars per meal, and they weighed about 1 pound each. It was a lot of weight to carry 100 MRE's all the way from the U.S. to supply lunches for our 9 team members, but it worked, and it worked great. The MRE's were certainly a lot tastier, and safer meals than we ever had back at our living quarters.

One evening shortly after supper a man came to us and said his neck was swelling, and he was having a hard time breathing. Upon examination Dr. Kuenzi and I found that he had a badly infected tooth, and that some of the infection had spread into his neck. His neck was so swollen that it had starting closing off his trachea. Personally, I had never seen a swelling this large that actually endangered a person's breathing. I was a little scared. Dr. Kinsey said, "We've got to get the pus out, or it could close his trachea completely." I got out my dental surgery instruments and we put a little anesthesia into his neck. Dr. Kuenzi then made a one-inch incision in the skin of his neck over the area where the swelling was the greatest. He then gently separated the tissues down into the swelling. Suddenly we got a large discharge of pus. The man's breathing immediately became easier. After draining the area thoroughly, we sutured the incision closed, extracted his tooth, and put him on antibiotics and pain medication. We checked him daily for several days, and his recovery was amazingly good.

One day Dr. Kuenzi had a pygmy come to see him that had a hole in the center of his forehead that had pus coming out of it. Dr. Kuenzi asked, "How long has this been there?" and the pygmy said, "Several years." Dr. Kuenzi injected a little of our dental anesthesia around the area. He then took one of our small dental spoons, and scooped out a small stone about the size of a small green pea. The patient didn't know how it got there. We thought that possibly he might have slept on it one night while sleeping on the ground. Dr. Kuenzi said, "There's a good chance now that it will heal." Penny sat next to Dr. Kuenzi in our clinics, and also treated patients, asking Dr. Kuenzi for advice whenever there was something of which she was uncertain.

Lisa worked with me, and on several occasions I let her give anesthesia, and extract teeth under my close supervision, almost holding her hand. She was very pleased and did a good job. She also became anxious when some small red welts appeared on her face, like small insect bites or something. She asked me if I thought they would go away before she got home. Currently Lisa was working for a modeling agency in Chicago, and earning up to $250 per hour when she had work. Thankfully they were all gone before we went home. Lisa had also been financially sponsored on this trip by the largest Cadillac auto dealer in the United States. She requested that I take her picture surrounded by 25 smiling black children while she held up a sign of the Cadillac dealership. She had it enlarged and framed and gave it to the owner of the dealership as a thank you gift.

One morning, about a week into our stay with the pygmies, we were driving to a village when the Volkswagen truck stopped behind us. We waited a bit, and then turned around and went back to see what the problem was. It was just a minor problem. The entire engine which was in the rear of the vehicle, was sitting on the ground behind the truck. The heavy mounting brackets that held the motor in place had just broken off completely. I went to the Land Rover and got out the cable I had purchased in case of emergency. It was under the seat. I thought we would have to tow the truck.

They slid the motor back under the rear of the truck, then took some rocks and pounded a small hole in the back of the wooden bed of the truck. They put my cable under the engine and tied the other end around a 4-foot pole on top of the wooden floor of the truck bed. They then turned the pole in circles which twisted the cable and shortened it, and gradually lifted the motor back up in place. They lined the gears of the motor up with the gears of the drive shaft. They then put the rest of the cable around the motor in several directions to firmly secure it into place. They reattached the gas and electric lines.

They started the engine and believe it or not, it worked. In about an hour and a half we were on our way again. When we got back to Lomie that night the driver went to a shop that the logging trucks had in town, and tried to get the motor brackets welded back in place, but it was a metal that could not be welded. We were 11 hours away from the nearest telephone. They bought more cable and secured the motor tighter into place. We drove for another week in the rain forest, and then all the way back to Douala, and never had one single problem.

The driver and his main helper only had a grade school education, but they had a lot of common sense, and they just used what they had. I'm not sure if they had had a Ph.D. degree in engineering they could have done any better. The truck was much lighter going home after our two weeks of drinks were consumed, our 100 pounds of peanut butter were given away, and the 100 lbs of MRE's were eaten.

The evening of our last day in Lomie, the owners of our accommodations prepared a large exotic buffet, and invited many of the local town people. By this time we were out of Tabasco sauce, and John hadn't supervised the preparation of all of this food, so we tried to be nice, but we didn't eat much, only the items that appeared well cooked. This was their way of saying thank you to us.

The morning we left, a young American man came to the place where we had been staying. Actually, the night we arrived, he had been sleeping in one of the rooms of our little motel, but he left early the next morning before we had a chance to meet him. He told us a most interesting story. He was a graduate student from the University of Southern California, and was working on his Ph.D. thesis by evaluating certain aspects of the pygmy culture. He had been there about a month before we came. He had developed severe diarrhea, which was red with blood. He quickly left and went to the hospital in Yaounde, where he was hospitalized and treated for two weeks. He was better now and had returned.

He told us the doctors called his disease red diarrhea. It was caused by bacteria, which was spread when people wiped themselves with their hand, then shook hands with someone else, and then that person ate something using their fingers. Hygiene was almost nonexistent in the rain forest among the pygmies.

On our way back to Douala, we stopped at the ocean resort town of Kribi, and spent our last day at the beach. We ate the last of our MRE's for lunch and had an enjoyable and relaxing day. Our return home to the U.S. was noneventful.

In summary: Our living conditions were the poorest, and most primitive, of any of my 35 mission trips, but no one got sick, no one complained, and it really didn't hurt anyone. As I look back I don't regret one moment of this valuable, fantastic, and memorable experience. We were able to treat 1800 pygmies medically and dentally. These pygmies were totally helpless when it came to medical and dental problems.

The pygmies were very responsive to the Gospel, and John's team led over 1000 people to the Lord. We left a big job for the young pastor and his church leaders to follow-up and disciple all these new Christians. I had a very satisfied feeling in my heart when I returned home. It was truly one of the most unusual and rewarding experiences of my life.

# And Now the Rest of the Story

John e-mailed me a month after we got home and told us that the newspapers reported every day on an epidemic of red diarrhea that had broken out amongst the pygmies, around Lomie, in the exact area where we had been. It also was reported that several hundred pygmies had died, and that the government was mobilizing a major emergency health effort to stop the epidemic, which they finally did. We were glad that our whole team used a generous amount of hand sanitizer before each meal. We had no problems.

Lisa had started to work for me as my chair side dental assistant when she was just 19 years old. She was a tall and beautiful girl. She had been taking karate lessons for many years, and in the process she had been kicked in the mouth, and one of her front teeth had been broken. She had a very ugly looking crown placed on her tooth before she came to work for me. She had a very big, otherwise beautiful smile. After working for me for a little over a year, I got tired of looking at that ugly front tooth, and said, "Lisa, how about my putting a better crown on your front tooth?" She agreed, and I constructed a very beautiful crown for her front tooth. It blended perfectly with her natural teeth and gave her a fantastic smile.

A few months later Lisa informed me that she had won a major beauty pageant which made her eligible to enter the Miss Michigan Beauty Pageant. She was runner-up in the Miss Michigan Beauty Pageant and was designated as the most photogenic contestant. After this happened, General Motors approached her and asked her if she would be a model at their auto shows. She was happy working with me, but the difference between $8 an hour, and $250 an hour was something that she couldn't refuse. She continued in a very successful modeling career.

Lisa knew she wouldn't be young and beautiful forever, and that her modeling career wasn't very permanent. As a result of her happiness working with me, both in the dental office and on this mission trip, she decided to go into dentistry as a career. She graduated from a four year degree program at the University of Michigan as a dental hygienist, and is currently practicing dental hygiene, while still modeling part -time at the auto shows.

# CHAPTER 20

# BOLIVIA 1

Bolivia is a landlocked moderate-sized country, right in the middle of South America. It is a relatively poor country. The capital is La Paz, one of the highest capitals in the world, located on a treeless plateau high in the Andes Mountains. The people of the La Paz area have unique appearance, dress, and cultural traditions. As a result, they are often easy to identify wherever they go.

The largest city in Bolivia is Santa Cruz, located near the center of the country, on the flat plains, east of the Andes. The city was founded and developed about two hundred years ago, along the side of a major river, so it is relatively new in comparison to the thousands of years of history of the native Indian people. Bolivia has had seven major wars with its neighbors, and has lost all seven times. Each time they have lost some of their valuable land to their victories neighbors.

Ken and Diana Krestan were friends which we knew from church. I played softball with Ken on our church softball team. Ken was interested in aviation. After college he trained to be a pilot and a small airplane mechanic. Eventually they felt the call to the mission field. They went to Santa Cruz, Bolivia, with SAM, (South American Missions). Ken was appointed head pilot and put in charge of SAM's aviation program.

Our church helped to support them financially, and we kept in contact. One day I received an interesting e-mail from Ken. He invited me to come to Bolivia, and bring a physician, to help them in their ministry. He planned to fly us to remote jungle villages, where they were doing mission work, so we could help their people with their medical and dental problems. Those areas had no health services available, and they had many health problems.

Of course, I said, "Yes." I found a recently retired physician in Florida, Dr. Jack Rathgeb, who was a dedicated Christian and was willing to accept the challenge. Dora May was not invited, primarily because of the limited space on their single engine planes. We planned our mission for May, 1999.

SAM had a retired missionary, Don Elmore, who acted as their short-term mission facilitator. He did what I had been doing for our HTI mission trips, which was making airline reservations, working out the schedule, and all of the little details. It seemed nice, for a change, to have someone else do much of the detail work for me. I was surprised to find out when all the planning was done, that it came with a bill for two thousand dollars. No one ever told me that bit of information, or I would have been glad to do it myself. It certainly wasn't that big a project. I was still responsible for securing and packing all of our medications, dental supplies and equipment.

I left on May 14, 1999, and flew to Miami where I picked up Dr. Jack Rathgeb, who I will refer to as just Jack. We continued on American Airlines, on an overnight flight. We had one stop in La Paz, and then continued to Santa Cruz, Bolivia. Ken met us at the airport and took us to his home. We met Ken's wife Diana, and their three children; Rachel (13), Hendra (9), and Kenny (3). Jack and I put all of our supplies and equipment into the girls' bedroom, where we were to stay. I guess the girls got displaced temporarily to somewhere else in the house.

This being Sunday morning, we went with Ken and family to a small local church. Ken and Diana chose this church because it had been struggling and needed their help and encouragement. The service was all in Spanish, the national language.

After church we had lunch at a local restaurant, then stopped and visited the SAM headquarters. Upon returning to Ken's house, we met Placido and Toni Mercado. They were both young medical physicians who had been working part- time with SAM. Dave Simmons, a SAM pilot, and his wife Marilyn were also there. Together, they planned for Jack and me to do three different missions. We sorted all our supplies, equipment and clothes into three different sets of duffel bags, because it was not possible to take every- thing on the plane all at once due to weight restrictions.

Monday morning we got up early and went to a small private airport right in town near Ken's home. It was raining hard and after Ken got the weather report, he decided we could not fly at all that day. Since we could not fly, Placido asked if Jack and I could go to Barrio Bolivar with Toni and him. Ken agreed that would be a good alternative.

Barrio Bolivar is an Ayore Indian slum settlement on the outskirts of Santa Cruz. The Ayores are a nomadic tribe that moves from place to place. Placido and Toni had adopted the Ayores as their primary mission outreach. They learned their language and built a prim- itive church with a one-room medical clinic in it. Their goal was to bring the Ayores to Christ, as well as to help them with their medical needs

We drove in pouring down rain over dirt roads with huge water filled potholes. The Ayore Indians lived in extremely poor conditions, with no electricity, no running water, no bathrooms, and dwellings made out of cardboard and various scrap pieces of material.

It was truly one of the poorest shantytowns I had ever seen. When we arrived, they were cooking their food in front of their dwellings, in pots over open fires, which consisted of burning weeds, paper, cardboard, twigs, and scraps of wood. There were several hundred dwelling shacks.

They were very excited to see Placido and Toni and ran to welcome them. Placido and Toni had built the church and clinic out of cement blocks and with a metal roof. It looked like the only real waterproof building in the community. As quickly as we unloaded, the building was filled with people.

The Ayores had no dental service and only the limited medical help that Placido and Toni could give them on two half-days a month. Needless to say, we had a very busy clinic day. I worked with very little translating help from Placido or Toni, as they were busy with medical patients. My patients would point to an obviously abscessed tooth and I would numb it and remove it. I removed over sixty teeth.

I think Jack suffered a little culture shock that day. It was his first mission trip. He just couldn't believe how those people were staying alive with all these serious diseases they had. He reported their bodies were covered with mud, with multiple infected skin sores, worms, malaria, scabies, lice, TB, heart murmurs, liver problems, painful arthritis, kidney infections, and serious respiratory infections, hypertension, and numerous other problems. He concluded that in the U.S., half these people would be in the hospital. He said he had feelings of sadness and hopelessness. We returned to Ken's and Diana's home very tired that night.

The next morning the sun was shining, so we arose early and went to the airport again. Dr. Placido arrived with his gear. Ken weighed each of us and all of our supplies and equipment, before carefully packing the plane. He was our pilot. We took off in a Cessna in which he had recently rebuilt the engine, and put a super turbo charged booster on the engine.

The first village we planned to visit was Zapico, an Ayores Indian village deep in the jungle with no road near it. We flew an hour over beautiful Mennonite farms, recently cleared out of the jungle, and then another hour over dense tropical jungle. I sat up front with Ken. Finally we spotted a rectangular clearing in the jungle. Ken lowered the plane and buzzed over the top of the runway, circled around, and put the plane down on the bumpy grass runway. Ken told us he always buzzed the runway first, to check it out and to scare off any animals that often like to graze on the nice grassy runway.

By the time we landed and taxied back to the middle of the runway, there was a crowd of 50 to 75 people there to meet us. We unloaded, and the people carried our supplies several hundred yards to an empty building at the edge of the village. As we walked into the village we went past a big two-story wooden house that was boarded up, and quite run-down. Ken explained that this was the home of Bill Pencil, an American missionary and his family who had lived there and served the Ayore Indians of Zapaco for over 30 years. They also built a church, school, and a clinic in the village. When they got older and needed to return to the states to retire, SAM couldn't find any missionaries to replace them. Ken said that this was a worldwide general trend. When the older 20th-century missionaries retired, there was great difficulty in finding younger generation missionaries to replace them.

The primary mission of the aviation division of SAM was to support the many missionaries scattered throughout the jungle villages with transportation of personnel, supplies, and emergencies. With many of these villages no longer having foreign missionaries, SAM set up a school at their Santa Cruz headquarters to train native Bolivian Christians to carry on the mission leadership in those villages.

This village had a SAM trained missionary, Pedro, who lived in the village with his wife and family. Ken knew him well, and they worked out the details for our clinic. They opened the old boarded up clinic that Bill Pencil had built that had fallen into disuse. Ken and Pedro served as translators for Jack and me. Placido knew the language. Ken translated for me. He asked if I would teach him how to extract teeth, so I did, and let him remove several. He said "You never know when this experience could come in handy someday."

A memorable moment occurred when I sat down on a beautiful ornamental old style English dining room chair, left by the retired American missionaries. As I sat down, there was a crackling noise, and then I suddenly crashed to the floor, with the chair breaking into a million splintered pieces. I felt badly because it was a beautiful irreplaceable chair, and it did not look reparable. As I quickly got up, everyone, including all the waiting patients, had a good laugh.

It got warm and I perspired a lot, but it was not nearly as hot as in Cameroon or Cambodia. At noon we took a break, and quickly ate the lunches that Diana had packed for us. Placido's hobby was fishing. He wanted to check out the local stream with his fishing pole. We walked through the village, which was very interesting. We saw all the jungle-type houses, and the people involved in their daily activities. We went by the one-room school house, which was in session. It had one teacher, an older man, who had been trained by Bill Pencil. Around 25 students were sitting on the dirt floor, and he was teaching all grades in this one room at the same time. We walked down a sloping path to the river. It was memorable because of the hundreds of beautiful butterflies of all different sizes and colors. I had never seen so many beautiful butterflies in my entire life.

We continued clinic in the afternoon until around 3 P.M. We had caught up on all the patients that were waiting. We packed up, said our farewells, thanked Pedro and his family, and headed for the plane. Ken got after Pedro a little bit, because the runway was not being maintained adequately. The grass was 8 to10 inches high, and there was an area 50 feet from the end of the runway where rainwater had run across the runway and created a little gully.

We loaded the plane, sang a song, and prayed with the 75 people who had come to see us leave. Ken taxied back to the gully in the runway, which was about 50 feet short of the end of the runway, turned around, and gunned it for take off. It was a little scary seeing the trees at the end of the runway coming up, and still being on the ground. Finally at the last minute we picked up, just high enough to clear the trees, with the wheels just touching the leaves on the top of the trees, as we lifted into the air. Ken turned to me and said, "WOW! That was close." Ken glanced at his gas gauge and then said, "I told the boys back in Santa Cruz to only fill my gas tank half-full, and they filled it completely. The plane was heavier than I thought." I was just thankful that we were flying in the plane Ken had just rebuilt and added the special super turbo charged booster. In my heart I said, "Thank you, Lord," as we sailed off over the dense green jungle.

We landed at the small commercial airport in San Ignacio, which had a good long dirt runway. Ken had radioed ahead and Steve White, an American SAM missionary met us with his pickup. Steve took us to his home where his wife, Buffy, had a nice dinner for us. We had a pleasant time talking and getting acquainted with their two children, Sam and Sarah. We stayed in Steve's home overnight.

San Ignacio (population 15,000) had a crude dirt road by which you could access Santa Cruz, but it was a long, difficult, full day's trip. Steve was an agronomist (organic agriculturist) who had a large garden which he used to teach classes and sell seeds. He was also in the final phases of finishing a new Christian school at his church.

The next morning Steve drove us an hour to the remote village of Villa Cruz, (population 200). They had one-room adobe homes with tile roofs. Steve had been ministering there and was trying to start a church. We worked in the building they were using for their church. Jack and Placido worked inside because of the need for privacy. I set up my dental clinic out under a shade tree where I had good light and a nice breeze. We had lots of patients with all kinds of problems. There were essentially no medical or dental services available to these people. Jack and Placido worked well together and often consulted back-and-forth. I removed over 100 teeth while Jack and Placido saw even more patients than I.

When we returned to Steve's home, Dave Simmons was there. He had flown in that afternoon with a full load of extra fuel which he put in SAM's storage reserve for future SAM flight needs. Dave came to relieve Ken, as planned, so Ken could return to Santa Cruz the next morning. We had dinner and stayed overnight with Steve's family again.

Early the next morning Dave flew us to Las Petros, near the Brazilian border, where there was a small military outpost. The landing strip was right down the center of the village, almost like a main street. When we landed, the military was there to check our passports and visas. They were very nice and helped us to carry our supplies to the village medical clinic. We met the male nurse who didn't know we were coming, but was happy to see us. He said it had been a long time since a medical doctor had come to his village, and he was low on medications.

SAM did not have a mission presently in this village, but planned to start a major outreach in a couple of weeks. It was hoped we would generate a favorable impression on the people that would help SAM's forthcoming outreach.

Word spread fast, and shortly we had many patients forming a line. We quickly got our clinic set up and started seeing patients. At noon we were invited to a local widow's home. She just loved to cook and feed strangers that were passing through. It was great for us because there were no restaurants or hotels in the village. We had supper and breakfast there also. It was an interesting experience watching her cook everything over an open fire. She even baked great bread in a wood-fired clay oven. Her meals were good.

At supper time we still had a long line of patients. Since we planned to stay overnight, we agreed to see the rest of the patients after supper. Some of the patients had been in line since early morning. We worked until late that night and finished all the patients.

We got our sleeping bags out of the plane, and slept on the floor of the clinic. Shortly after we got to sleep, Jack started singing and talking in his sleep. We knew he was very tired, so we did not wake him. The next morning when I told him about his singing and talking, he was concerned. He then admitted that he was not feeling well and had a temperature and had taken some medication. He said, "I must have been hallucinating."

When we took our supplies to the plane early in the morning we were surprised to find an armed soldier asleep under the plane. At first I thought we might be in some kind of trouble. He was nice and explained that he had been sent to guard our plane overnight and to keep it safe.

Dave flew us to a much smaller village of Natiodad (population 200). There were cattle on the runway and Dave had to buzz the runway twice before we could land. It was very isolated, as it was located many miles from the nearest road. They took our bags to a small two-room adobe school house. Again I set up outside under a shade tree and started extracting infected, painful teeth.

Jack and Placido worked inside the hot school house. Jack said that he thought over half the people in the village had hepatitis, and most children had parasites. A mother and father brought in a two year old boy with a swollen painful abdomen. He had a fever, was crying and had been vomiting. The mother said she had been standing by the river and a cow pushed her and the child into the river. She was concerned that the child might have swallowed some of the water, which could have made him sick.

Jack was more concerned about peritonitis from a ruptured appendix. Jack consulted with Dave and Dave said, "You use your own judgment and if it is necessary we can fly him out of here to the nearest hospital." Jack gave him a large dose of two different antibiotics and asked the parents to bring him back after lunch.

We ate lunch at one of the villager's houses. Mid afternoon the parents brought the child back to see Jack. Things were getting worse. His temperature was higher, his respiration was shallow and rapid, and he was less responsive. His abdomen was more swollen and tender and he continued to cry. Jack consulted with Placido and they agreed and told Dave, "We need to get this child to a hospital, fast."

Dave discussed this with the parents, who had great reservations about leaving the village. Finally Dave had to tell them, "If we don't take him to a hospital fast, he will die very soon." They finally agreed, if the mother could go with him. Dave agreed and said, "Let's go immediately".

We hurried and packed and headed for the plane. I was a little concerned about a four passenger plane taking five people and the baby. Dave calculated, we had used up a lot of our dental and medical supplies as well as our airplane fuel. The runway was longer, and the mother was a very small person. After we loaded the plane, we waited for the mother and the child to show up. We were ready, but no mother or child. Maybe she changed her mind. Then down near the end of the runway, came a crowd of people, I think, about half the people in the village. They all walked slowly toward the plane. Finally the mother and the child appeared from within the midst of the crowd. They said their goodbyes, with lots of emotional crying and tears, and got into the plane. The mother sat between Jack and me in the back seat of the plane, holding her baby in her lap. Some men ran down the runway and drove the cattle off. We took off with no problem.

The mother had never been in a motorized vehicle, let alone an airplane. As we took off, she shut her eyes, and grabbed hold of my arm, and squeezed it like there was no tomorrow. The closest hospital was in San Ignacio, Steve's village. Dave radioed Steve and he met us at the airport. Steve, Placido, the mother and child left immediately for the hospital.

Shortly Steve and Placido returned and we took off for Santa Cruz. We had planned to return to Santa Cruz that afternoon, but not by this route. We landed just before dark. There were no lights on this runway, so we were glad to be on the ground.

Ken was there to meet us and took us to his home. Ken's family had been invited to a local Bolivian friend's wedding that evening. They asked Jack and me if we would like to join them. I said, "Sure," but Jack declined and said he was still not feeling well and thought he should stay home, take some medication, and go to bed. The wedding was beautiful, interesting and different.

Saturday morning Jack was feeling better. We both went with Diana and Rachel to the large downtown central market. Diana shopped there once a week for most all of her food supplies. After Diana got her supplies, she wanted to go home. Jack and I wanted to stay and look around this large sprawling market and possibly buy some souvenirs. Thirteen year old Rachel offered to stay and help us. She showed us all around, translated for us and even bargained hard for us, as we bought a few small souvenirs. When we finished, she flagged down a taxi and had to direct the driver at every turn to get us to her home.

When we arrived home I began to realize the irony of this situation. Here we were, two mature doctors with 25 years of education each, head of our families, owners of our private practices with numerous employees, and many patients that depended on us, and the two of us had been led around for hours, almost helpless, by a thirteen year old girl. I observed Rachel and she seemed to have had a boost in her self-confidence, and she deserved it.

In the afternoon Dave and Marilyn took us to a big souvenir store. While shopping we observed a big parade with lots of people going by on the street. Dave told us it was a Jesus parade. They expected 60,000 people to march in it. It was being held by the Christian Evangelical Churches in Santa Cruz to demonstrate the strength and enthusiasm of the Protestant movement in a country which had been predominately Roman Catholic which often discriminated against Evangelical Christians.

As we watched the floats and marchers go by, Dave pointed out one float that had Jesus talking to his disciples. Dave said to me, "See Jesus on that float? That is Steve Cubas. He is going to be your translator next week." That was a rather unique way to first see your new translator.

The parade was expected to last for several hours. Dave and Marilyn took us to a restaurant where we met Ken and Diana, and a native Bolivian, Chi Chi. Ken introduced us to Chi Chi as our pilot for our next week of travels. Ken explained that he had personally trained Chi Chi, and that he had been flying for SAM successfully for several years.

Early Sunday morning we all met at the airport. Chi Chi was there early getting the plane ready. Placido was not available that week. We officially met Steve Cubas. Steve was a MK (missionary kid), 20 years old, who was born and raised on the mission field. He had just finished his second year of pre-med studies at John Brown University, and was home on summer vacation. He was anxious to work with a doctor in the villages to see what a missionary doctor was really like. We also were taking a missionary student, John Vaca, home for the summer. He was a student in SAM's Missionary School, and he lived in the first town where we were scheduled to stop.

It was a beautiful day. After Chi Chi checked our weight closely, he loaded up and we took off. We flew directly east, right into the rising sun. The first hour we flew over large fertile flat jungle land which had 100 acre fields that had been cleared by bulldozers for farming. Chi Chi informed us that they were Mennonite farmers that had immigrated to Bolivia from the U.S. That sounded different. Usually you don't hear of people emigrating from the U.S. All we hear about is that masses of people who want to immigrate to the U.S. It appeared they were quite prosperous, with nice homes, barns, roads, and vehicles. Chi Chi said the only crop they grew was soybeans.

At one time I owned 460 acres of farmland in Missouri, which my cousin, David, farmed for me. Our primary crop was soybeans. When we started farming, the price for soybeans was $7-$8 a bushel. As time progressed the prices fell gradually to about $3 a bushel. The reason given was because of all the South American soybeans that were flooding the market. After flying over these vast areas of clearings in the jungle, I can understand what they were talking about. I can also understand the concern some people had about reducing the size of the jungles. There were hundreds of miles of jungle, cleared for soybean farming. Today the pendulum has swung the other direction, and we do not have enough food to feed the world's expanding population. Currently food prices are increasing, while many people are dying of starvation. It seems you can't win either way.

As we left the farmland, we flew for two more hours over the green jungle. Suddenly there was a huge cliff where the land dropped over 1000 feet. This cliff ran north and south as far as you could see. Eastern Bolivia was also flat jungle land, but a lot lower in elevation than central Bolivia.

We finally circled and landed on a small dirt runway, at a commercial airstrip at the edge of Robore, a moderate sized town (population 8000). Robore was near the Argentina border and on the main road from Santa Cruz to Argentina. The road was dirt and in poor condition. This was one of Bolivia's main routes to and through Argentina to the ocean for its exports and imports.

This was the town where Chi Chi had been born and raised, so he knew his way around town well. There was no one at the airport. We taxied the plane to a building at the side of the runway, where SAM had stored extra aviation fuel. John Vaca took his bags, said thanks, and took off for home. We left our medical and dental supplies in the plane and locked it.

The four of us carried our overnight luggage, in the hot afternoon sun, and walked a mile into town, to a small motel- type complex. Chi Chi informed us that this was a hotel, not a motel, because in Bolivia motels were considered the red light district. We registered, settled in and unpacked.

We had our Sunday noon dinner in the hotel dining area. They had a large nice buffet. While we were eating, a pretty fair-skinned blond came up to us and asked if we were Americans. Her husband was with her. After introductions, we found out they were Milton and Kathy Whittiker and were American missionaries who had often worked with SAM on special projects. They had known Steve since he was a little boy but had not seen him in several years, so they did not recognize him. We had a nice conversation until Chi Chi returned with a three-quarter-ton stake truck and wanted us to go swimming with him at the hot springs.

Chi Chi drove around town picking up numerous friends that wanted to go also. We left town and drove on a dirt path through the jungle for an hour. It was one of the poorest and roughest trails I had ever experienced. Everyone else seemed to accept it as normal.

Finally Chi Chi pulled off the side of the trail and stopped. We got out and walked through the jungle until we came to a small river about 20 to 30 feet wide. It was only two feet deep. It was very clear with a sandy bottom. What a surprise I had when I stepped into the river. It was as hot as a Jacuzzi. We walked a short distance up-river until we came to several bubbling springs where the river started.

As I was walking around the bubbling spring area, I stepped into an area of very soft sand and started to sink. I could not stop or get out, and it was sucking me down. I panicked. All I could think about was the movies I had seen where the bad guy stepped into some quicksand, and he was slowly pulled down under the mud. I started yelling, but the natives around me, including Chi Chi, just started laughing. I kept going slowly down and down. Finally I hit solid bottom. I started in 1 foot of water, and now I was up to my chest. With my feet on a solid bottom, I could feel the warm spring water coming up on the bottom of my feet. The sand was swirling in such a way that it just kept holding me down and I could not move. This spring was probably a foot and a half in diameter. Finally Chi Chi and a couple of his friends came over and pulled me out. He laughed and said, "Quite a sinking feeling wasn't it?" He told me, "You can step back into it, and experience it again if you want." I didn't want! That one sinking feeling will last me a lifetime.

We walked down the river several hundred yards to where the river emptied into a moderate-sized lake. It was probably 20 to 30 acres in area, and it was the same temperature as the river. There were no beaches, people, or cottages on the shores of this very warm lake, just jungle. I thought, if I could just transport this natural phenomenon home, I'd be a multimillionaire. We returned to town, had supper and went to two different church services, where we were asked to give our testimonies.

Early the next morning we walked to the airport and flew to the village of Santa Corazon, as preplanned by Ken. When we landed, I didn't see any village. We unpacked the plane and waited. There was no sign of life. Chi Chi had never flown into this village. While waiting, I observed the largest mass of dragonflies, flying all around us that I had ever seen. There were hundreds of them. I had been told that dragonflies keep the mosquitoes away, so I guess that was a good thing.

After a little while, an old beat-up pickup truck came out of the jungle, and onto the runway where we were waiting. We packed our baggage in the truck, and climbed up on top. We had a mile or two of rough riding on a small trail through very dense jungle. We finally came to a clearing on a little hill where a number of round mud and thatched huts were. On the top of the hill was a moderately large and very beautifully decorated Catholic church.

We pulled up to one of the buildings that was just in front, and to the side of the church. A 30-year-old white Caucasian lady dressed in a white nurse's uniform came out and welcomed us. She was Mary Jane, a nun who was a nurse, who was from Spain. She had been there for about a year trying to help the people with their medical problems. She had a number of patients that were beyond her ability to diagnose or treat. She had few medications, and there never had been any dental services in this area. Mary Jane had contacted SAM and asked for help. That's why Ken had arranged for us to go to this village.

When Mary Jane first came, there were a couple of evangelical Protestant Christian missionaries who had come to this village. They upset the Catholic priest so much that he physically drove them out of the village. He had made a statement in church which had become well-known, that he would personally kill the next evangelical Christian that came into his village. Guess what! We were the next evangelical Christians that came into his village. Mary Jane assured us that the priest had approved our few-hour stay, especially since there were several very sick people in the village that Mary Jane couldn't treat. Mary Jane also said that the priest had arranged to be out of the village on the day we came. That way he would have an excuse for not keeping his promise.

We set up clinic and started to work. After things were running smoothly, Mary Jane asked Jack if he would come with her and visit several sick people who were too sick to come to the clinic. Jack agreed to go during lunch hour, because he had many people waiting. I set up my dental clinic in the backyard of the building under a shade tree that wasn't very large. We had to move as the shade moved, with the movement of the sun.

Jack and Mary Jane went and made the house calls just before lunch. Upon returning Jack reported that he was able to diagnose and treat three bedridden patients. He reported one older lady was inside a dark mud hut with no breeze, and was totally wrapped in several layers of blankets, which had been soaked with some kind of herbs, oils and spices, which had been prescribed by the witch doctor. She had a high fever. The first thing he had to do was to get her cooled down, by getting all the blankets off of her, and taking her outside in the shade where there was a breeze. This proved to be no easy task, because it broke with tradition, but he finally succeeded. He diagnosed and treated her with appropriate medications. He returned and checked on her later, and she was doing much better.

Mary Jane had arranged for us to have lunch with a local evangelical Christian family. The food was different, but adequate. The conversation and stories of the host family was most interesting. Our host showed us where they had partially built an Evangelical Christian Church, before the priest blew up, and drove the missionary couple out of town, and made his threat. No one had dared to work on it since. On our walk back to the clinic, Mary Jane showed us a large well-built sundial clock which was outside, in front of the church, which she said actually worked quite well. The time was very close to the time on our watches. She said the priest adjusted it once a month to the sun's movement. No one had watches or clocks, so it was a big thing in town.

Our afternoon clinic went well. At four o'clock we had to stop, even though there were still patients waiting. We loaded into the truck and headed back to the airstrip. The old truck was the only vehicle in the village. We knew we had to get out of the village well before dark, because we did not want a confrontation with the priest.

We flew to the village of Ricon Del Tigre where Ken had made arrangements for us to stay overnight. We arrived at dusk, to the cheers and screaming of 50 children, mostly under 10 years of age who surrounded our plane. The airstrip was next to a densely populated group of primitive native huts.

A fluent English-speaking white man with a pickup came and took us about a quarter of a mile to a nice complex of buildings. We were taken to a cottage, where we were shown a nice bedroom to use for overnight. Our host pointed to a fairly large building where he indicated we were to meet shortly for supper.

This turned out to be the most unique and fascinating village that I had ever visited in any of my mission trips. When we went to supper, we met a spry elderly white lady in her mid-80s, called Ruth. She had left Latvia to be a Christian missionary at the age of 17 and she had never gone back. She had come to Brazil where she kept working deeper and deeper into the jungle. She finally crossed into Bolivia, without realizing it, as the borders in the jungles weren't marked. Her goal was to bring the Gospel to a remote group of native Ayore Indians living on a large island. The island was a flat fertile piece of dry ground many square miles in diameter, which was totally surrounded by the large Panpanal swamps. She was successful in gaining the respect of the native Indians, and then she converted them to Christianity.

Some passing adventure explorers were surprised to find this lovely young pretty white gal living permanently on this island with all these Ayroe Indians. They took many photos, and wrote an accounting of her and her work, which was published and circulated widely in both U.S. newspapers and magazines.

Christian organizations saw the need, and sent missionaries and money to help Ruth. She met her husband when he came as a missionary to help. They married and had a family. She learned a lot about medicine and helped her people greatly. She started a school, using some of the missionaries who were sent to help her. That was the reason for so many houses along the side of the runway. Most families who wanted their children to go to school, just moved there, so they could feed and house their children, although she did have some dormitories. Currently her school had 400 students, of which 150 lived in dormitories. She had six other schools throughout the island, all K-12. She had 26 teachers, most of whom were former students who had received their bachelors and masters degrees by correspondence. Each student was fed three meals a day. There was no charge for anything. The school was self- supporting from livestock, gardens, fields and groves.

Ruth had the Indians help her by clearing a runway, so a plane could land. Various organizations sent medications and supplies to her by plane. Her oldest son eventually became a pilot, and some U.S. churches helped them purchase a plane. Her son married, had a family, and was living there and helping his aging mother greatly. He was the one that picked us up from the runway when we arrived.

She had taught the people how to farm. The mission had over a thousand head of cattle, of which her son was in charge. They sold some of the cattle each year to help support the school and mission. One year they had an extreme drought and one section of the swamp dried-up enough that they were able, with great effort, to drag an electric generator along with a boiler removed from an old railroad steam engine locomotive, to the mission. They actually pulled them over logs which they continually placed in front of them.

When we were there, they had electricity in the entire area. They showed us the old locomotive boiler that they were feeding with logs of wood. The steam from it turned a large wheel which was hooked by a belt to the electric generator. It also powered a saw mill, which allowed them to saw lumber for their buildings. Ruth had been there continuously for almost 60 years, directing the mission. Ruth was still spry and going strong, giving advice and orders to people all around her. They had extensive gardens, which provided most of their food.

After a good supper Ruth came to Jack and asked if he would please see a few emergency patients. Jack was very tired, and tried to suggest that he see them the first thing the next morning. She insisted and said, "The patients heard you were coming and have been standing in line since three o'clock this afternoon. A couple of them are critically ill." I offered to go with Jack, so he reluctantly agreed. It was a good thing he did, because he said later, "Probably both of the critically ill patients would have been dead by morning." Jack was astonished at how much knowledge about medicine that Ruth had, for being self-taught. There were so many patients waiting that Jack and I agreed that if we could go to bed and get some rest, we would start clinic at six o'clock the next morning. Our bedroom cottage was unbelievable for being isolated so far out in the jungle. We had three beds with good mattresses, a toilet, shower, electricity, screened windows, and a satellite telephone.

The next morning we set up our dental and medical clinics in Ruth's small medical building. Ruth had hand- picked all the patients that she felt should see the doctor, because their problems were beyond her ability to handle. The teeth in this group of Indians were much harder to remove, but I still removed a lot of them. I suspected it was a result of better nutrition. I remember one teenage Indian boy, who had very large scars on his face. I asked him, "How did you get those scars?" He told me that he had been attacked by a mountain lion while hunting in the jungle, and if it weren't for his friends who were with him, he probably would have died.

At lunch I asked Ruth why she had never gone back home in over 60 years? She said, "This is my home, I am needed here." It was easy to see that she was very loved, respected, and needed by her people.

After lunch we said thank you and goodbye to a very special lady, and her unique mission and family. We flew to the remote village of San Ferando. This village also had no road access, except for a couple of months during the dry season when the swamps sometimes dried-up enough for a four-wheel drive vehicle to get through. We worked there four hours. Clinic was busy and successful. There was no place to stay overnight, so we left and I thought we were headed back to Robore, Chi Chi's hometown, where we had spent our first night.

Milton Whittiker had been in contact with Chi Chi by radio several times, begging him to stop and visit them. He had a good place for us to sleep and they would feed us well. He even offered to drive us to Robore the next morning if Chi Chi wanted to fly home to

Robore and spend the night with his family. There was a small airport at which he could land and drop us off in Santiago, near the place where Milton lived. He would pick us up. Chi Chi didn't know if we would have enough time in our schedule, so he did not say anything to us and didn't promise Milton anything. Chi Chi started thinking about it as we were flying back to Robore. In Robore we would have to pay for our hotel and meals, and tomorrow all we had planned was to fly back to Santa Cruz. If Milton could get us back to Robore by noon, we could fly back to Santa Cruz in the afternoon.

So without saying anything, Chi Chi located the village of Santiago, and put the plane down on a small deserted grassy runway. He unloaded our small personal overnight bags and said, "I am going to take off and fly back to Robore. I have been in radio contact with Milton, and he will pick you up shortly, and you can stay with him tonight. He will drive you back to Robore in the morning. This runway is so short that I could not take off with all of you on the plane anyway." He climbed back in the plane, taxied to the end of the runway, and took off, just nicely clearing the trees.

There was no one around. I felt like we had been dumped in the middle of the jungle and abandoned. Suddenly, we saw several uniformed armed men with rifles running rapidly up the two track path that led to the runway. They seemed excited and were yelling and shouting. It was an uncomfortable feeling, especially when I could not understand what they were saying. We just stood there and waited for them.

We found out through Steve, who understood them, that they had heard the plane land, and they didn't know why it took off so quickly. They were in charge of the airport, and they didn't know where it had come from, or where it was going, and they were concerned. Steve talked to them and explained what was going on, and they started to calm down. Just then, Milton came up in his pickup. Milton was the only permanent foreign resident in the village, and had been elected village mayor on several occasions, so everybody knew him and respected him. Milton was a Harvard University graduate that had helped the villagers improve their lives in many ways.

Milton loaded us into his truck and headed to his house, which was only a mile or so away. At his house we greeted his beautiful blonde wife, Kathy, and their three blonde children, Rachel 7, Romona5, and Joseph 3. The reason I mention blondes is because there are none in the native population in Bolivia.

I couldn't believe how excited everyone was to see us. We were strangers. As it turned out, Jack and I were the first Americans that Milton and Kathy had visit them in over 10 years, since they had moved to this village. They had many promises of people coming to visit, and had actually built and furnished a small guest house for visitors, but we were the first. They were really located in the middle of nowhere.

Kathy made us a supper of hamburgers and french fries, since she knew we hadn't had any for a couple of weeks. Then we talked and talked. It seemed that Milton was about to be drafted after graduating from Harvard, but because of his Mennonite faith, he was having problems accepting the bearing of arms, so he fled the country and came to Bolivia a number of years ago.

Kathy was raised on a farm in northern Indiana in a large Mennonite community. She was the only child, so she helped on the farm and milked cows by hand from an early age. She went to college, graduated with a teaching degree, and got a teaching job in her hometown. She lived at home and milked cows in the morning before she taught at school all day. After doing this for several years with no prospect of getting married, she became discouraged. One night she had a dream, which she described as a clear vision. She was to leave home and teaching, and go to Bolivia where she would meet the man she was going to marry. She knew nothing of Milton.

When school was out for the summer, she packed her bags, and went to Bolivia, where she did meet Milton in a Mennonite Church the second week after she arrived. They fell in love, got married and moved to this remote town. They had three children, and had been there a little over 10 years. Milton had no family left. Kathy's mom and dad had never seen the grandchildren. They were getting older, and afraid to come to Bolivia, even though they planned and promised several times. Kathy's parents had told her that they would give them the entire farm, which is quite large and very valuable, if she and Milton would come home.

Milton still had concerns about being arrested and prosecuted as a draft evader, even after 20 years. They had established a good dairy farm in Santiago, which developed into a yogurt business also. Milton had been successful in ordering and receiving some special yogurt cultures from Belgium, which allowed him to develop his new yogurt business. Milton had several employees working for him. Both Milton and Kathy were very happy here, felt well- respected in the village, and felt that they had been able to help the villagers in many ways, and at the same time they were working as missionaries spreading the Gospel of Jesus Christ. They really did not want to return to the U.S., but they sure were lonely. We talked and played with the kids until late into the night.

We had great sleeping facilities in their guest house, with nice soft beds. I slept great. The next morning Kathy cooked us blueberry pancakes, bacon and hot chocolate. Boy, did that taste good for a change! Milton showed us his cows, barns, and yogurt culturing business. We loaded Milton's truck with his weekly milk and yogurt deliveries, and headed to Robore. It was an hour drive on a rather rough dirt road. Chi Chi had planned a typical Bolivian pig roast for us for lunch, but since there were nasty storm clouds on the horizon, Chi Chi had Milton take us directly to the airport. We thanked Milton and bid him farewell, and took off quickly for Santa Cruz. It was a rough and bumpy four-hour ride, but we made it safely.

Ken picked us up and we went to his house, unloaded our baggage, cleaned up and went to SAM headquarters for supper. Every Wednesday night all of SAM personnel that were in town gathered for supper and a prayer meeting. Ken played the guitar for their singing.

They asked Jack and me to share our experiences out in the jungle villages. After the prayer meeting, several people came up to us and asked if we could take their mail and packages with us back to the U.S. and mail the items for them. Bolivia's mail was slow, expensive and unreliable. We were happy to do it, although it amounted to quite a lot.

While we were gone, Ken had an emergency arise. The company, from which they had been renting their airplane hangar and mechanical shop, decided that they needed it back for themselves. They gave SAM 10 days to get out. Ken was in charge of the aviation division, so he had to make some fast decisions. He secured a couple of large metal shipping containers, and put doors in them. He used one for the office, and the other one for the mechanical shop. He also purchased a large temporary portable building which was large enough to hold their three airplanes, and it could be moved if necessary in the future. This was almost completed by the time we returned.

The next morning Placido with his sister, Carmen, picked up Jack, Steve, and me and we headed back to Barrio Bolivar. Placido shared with me in private that Carmen was a senior in dental school, and he had hoped she would be able to help him in his health ministry with the Ayore Indians, but she seemed to totally lack self-confidence. He hoped I could teach her more about extractions so she would gain enough self-confidence to help him. I did work closely with Carmen and tried to teach her many of the so-called tricks of the trade. I had her extract many teeth with my help and guidance. She explained that at school she had only extracted two teeth. She seemed to learn quickly. With some positive encouragement and reassurance, it seemed by the end of the day, she was feeling better about herself.

The next morning all five of us went to Pasa Verda, an Ayore Indian village about one and a half hours east of Santa Cruz. During our drive to this village we came to a long bridge which crossed the large Rio Grand River. We stopped and waited twenty minutes for our turn. It was a one-way railroad bridge. They nailed heavy wooden planks to the railroad ties and placed them in-between and alongside the rails. This allowed for one-way traffic of cars and trucks when there was not a train scheduled. It was the only bridge, crossing this big river for more than 100 miles.

Placido rarely got to visit this village, so the severity of their problems was greater and the number of people needing treatment was larger. Today Carmen was feeling a little more self-confident. She observed the long line of patients that were waiting and begging us to relieve them of their pain by removing their infected teeth. I helped Carmen a little, but soon she started working by herself. We worked great together and were able to finish all our waiting dental patients.

Placido and Jack had more difficult patients and a larger number. They were not able to finish all their patients before we had to stop and leave to get back before dark. We returned home just about dark. Jack and I took Ken and family out for dinner as a thank you for their wonderful hospitality

Saturday morning we were free, so Steve and Rachel took Jack and me downtown to the heart of Santa Cruz. We did a little souvenir shopping and looked around. The thing that amazed me was the traffic. The streets were narrow and the buildings were close to the streets. There were no stop signs or traffic lights. The cars drove through the intersections, both ways, at pretty good speed, even though the intersection was almost completely blind. I waited and watched for an accident, but I never saw one, and I don't understand why. It was absolutely amazing to watch.

We ate lunch at a restaurant, before going to a graduation ceremony at the Santa Cruz Christian Learning Center where Ken and Diana's three children were attending. Ken was president of the school board, and he handed out the graduation diplomas. It was a nice English-speaking school which had several hundred K-12 students. Steve Cubas's sister was one of the graduates.

After graduation we were invited to Dave and Marilyn's home for a wonderful chicken dinner. Then it was back to Ken's to pack for our early morning flight home.

In summary: This was not a typical HTI mission trip, because we did not go primarily to unreached people groups. We were responding to a call for help from Ken, my friend. We helped people with great health needs where they had no healthcare. We were also helping missionaries in many areas to gain respectability and confidence from the local village people, with the hope that their ears and hearts would be more receptive to the Gospel. This was Jack's first mission trip, and I'm sure he will never forget it. I personally had a very satisfying feeling that I had been able to serve my Lord in a very meaningful way.

## And Now the Rest of the Story

We found out after returning home, that the little boy that we flew out of the jungle with his mother, had actually been stepped on by a cow, and it had ruptured his intestines. He had acute peritonitis, and was only a few hours away from death. The doctors at the hospital operated immediately, and successfully saved his life. The boy and his mother had returned to their jungle village.

I received a nice letter from Jack. He was very happy with his experiences, and stated it was one of the highlights of his life.

Ken was promoted to the head of all of SAM's mission operations in Bolivia. Their two oldest girls are now in college in the U.S. Ken felt our mission was so successful he invited me to return to Bolivia for a similar mission a few years later. Memories of that trip are in Chapter 29.

# CHAPTER 21

# NEPAL
# WITNESSING WITHOUT WORDS

Nepal is a land of mystery. Not much news has come from this isolated mountainous country until recent years. Only a few years ago the first road was constructed into Katmandu, the capital. Nepal is nestled in the heart of the Himalayan Mountains where the famous Mount Everest is located.

When we went to Nepal in 1999, it was the only Hindu kingdom in the world that was dominated by a Hindu king. They had a parliamentary government which had limited powers. The country was 99 percent Hindu, with only 2/10 of one percent Christians.

I had heard that Nepal was starting to open to outsiders and that almost everyone there was unreached with the Gospel. I asked Dr. Miller if he had any contacts in Nepal. He e-mailed the Joshua Movement in Colorado Springs and asked them for names of Christian leaders in Nepal. They gave him three names, which he sent to me. I e-mailed all three. Dr. Tirtha Thapa responded first to my offer of free health care, with an enthusiastic, "Yes."

He offered to host our team and make all the necessary arrangements in Nepal. He told me details of how he hoped to use our team. Dr. Thapa, the founder and head of the National Council of Christian Churches, was trying to get all the different protestant churches and missions to unite and to work together to help each other, particularly in trying to control the persecution that the Christians were receiving.

His position sounded important and his goals for our team sounded very realistic, so we started discussing dates and numbers of people for the team. He suggested about 12 dental and medical team members, and suggested the first two weeks of October as the best time. That worked well with me. All I had to do was assemble a team. I put my need for team members in HTI's newsletter that we send to over 2000 Christian healthcare providers and friends. I also made 50 to 100 telephone calls to individuals whom I thought might be interested.

I called a physician named Dr. David Shull. He had recently been put on permanent medical disability because of some physical problems. He had been wondering how he could use his skills to serve the Lord. He had never been on a medical mission and this was exactly what he was looking for. He was excited, and so was I. He said, "No one has ever asked me to help on a mission trip."

I called a Dr. David Colville, who turned out to be a kidney specialist at the Mayo Clinic. He had never been on a mission trip and he agreed to go. I had a Dr. Cherian Samuel phone me from Texas. He was a recently retired Indian physician who had just retired from Great Britain's socialist medical system. He was in the process of starting his own medical mission organization. He was interested in joining us. He had been to Nepal previously and knew the language.

I called a dentist, Dr. Richard Bedinghaus, who was an Oral Roberts University graduate, and a Captain in the Air Force. He wanted to join our team. I had a dental assistant, Tammy McNealy, call me from California, and she also joined. A retired engineer from General Motors, Tom Ruster and his wife Judy,

whom I knew from my church, expressed an interest in joining us after learning that we could use them, following a casual conversation I had with them one evening.

I represented HTI with a display booth in Toronto, Canada, at the International Christian Medical and Dental Association Convention in April, 2009. I had a dentist, Dr. Tom Harle, come to our booth and ask, "What is HTI all about?" After I explained about HTI's purpose and organization, he asked, "What do you have scheduled?" I said, "Several things, but my most urgent need is for another dentist to go with me to Nepal the first two weeks in October. He took a step backward, and was quiet for a moment, and then he said "You've got to be kidding." I assured him I wasn't kidding.

Then he told me this story: Just before leaving for this convention, I marked out the first two weeks of October in my appointment book for a vacation. Just as I was leaving the office, my office manager said to me, "I think it would be nice if you used the first two weeks of October to go on a mission trip to Nepal." I don't know how the Lord could speak to me any clearer. Count me in.

I have always found it exciting to see how the Lord has assembled our teams with different people from all over the U.S. and Canada. Dr. Harle soon asked me if his wife Patty, who was an RN, could join us. I said, "Great, we don't have any nurses committed yet." Next Dr. Harle called and said he had another nurse, Jane Duncan, from his church, that wanted to go, and a helper, Sherrie Falardeau, that would like to go also. I said, "Fine. That makes 12, our exact planned number of team members. We now have three physicians, three dentists, one dental assistant, two nurses, and three helpers."

Then in June, I asked my trusted travel agent, Jill, to book 12 round-trip flights to Katmandu, Nepal, for October 1 through 16. A few days later she called me back and said there were absolutely no flights available to Nepal during those dates or any dates close to it. She said that October was the ideal time of year for people to go backpacking in Nepal's Himalayan Mountains. The government only gave a limited number of trekking permits each year, and there was a one or two year waiting list for permits. As soon as people received their permits, often a year in advance, they would immediately schedule their flights.

I told Jill that we had to go at that time. I already had made many advance arrangements. I told her that I was going to call every travel agent in the country until I got something. She said, "Good luck." I called several other travel agents and got the same answer. I was getting discouraged.

A few days later, Jill called me back and said, "I have 12 round-trip tickets from the West Coast to Katmandu on the exact days you requested." I said, "Great, how did you do that?" Jill said, "I have a friend who is an important official with the Korean Airlines. He owed me a big favor, so I called him and said, "It's time you paid me back the big favor you owe me. This is what I need." He called me back, and said, "The flights are all full, but I got 12 seats anyway." Jill said, "I don't know how he did it, and I didn't ask." That was truly an answer to prayer.

On October 1, 1999, we left for Nepal, after the assembling and packing of medications, supplies, and equipment that we would need. Our packing was complicated. We couldn't send anything to Canada for our four Canadian team members to carry in their luggage, because of customs delays and problems. The U.S. team members had to carry everything. Fortunately, we could each still carry two 70 pound suitcases without being charged extra.

We flew Korean Airlines to Bangkok, Thailand, with a short stop in Taipei. We had a 25-hour layover in Bangkok, which allowed us to get some sleep, and to take some very interesting tours. This was the first visit to Bangkok for everyone on the team. The next morning we transferred to the Nepal Airways and finished our flight to Katmandu.

Dr. Thapa and his wife Esther were at the airport to greet us. We had a problem getting our supplies through customs, and all of our luggage was impounded. Dr. Thapa had called and written to the Nepal Minister of Health, asking for special approval to get our supplies through customs, and he had said, "No problem." Then Dr. Thapa's written request got pigeonholed and the Minister of Health left town on business for a month. After we returned home Dr. Thapa received a letter of apology, but for then we were stuck.

One of our 24 pieces of checked luggage never arrived. It was Dr. David Shull's. We filed a claim, but he never saw the luggage again. It contained a lot of medications and clothes. Since then, I always put on 2 luggage tags, and tape my business card on the top, inside the luggage. I also divide my clothes and supplies and put a little of each in different suitcases. That way if one is delayed, we can still operate our clinics. Dr. Shull's luggage has been the only luggage that I have ever known to be permanently lost. I suspect the reason was because his luggage tag was broken off and there was no other identification.

Dr. Thapa took us to a hotel close to his office and only a few blocks from downtown. We did have our carry-on with us. In those days, we could carry all of our essentials in our carry-on and I always carried an extra change of clothes because I had experienced delayed luggage many times.

The next morning we went back to the airport. We waited for an hour for a friend of Dr. Thapa's to arrive. He was a member of the Nepal Parliament. Dr. Thapa, the Member of Parliament, and I went into a room with two customs officials. They talked for an hour. I understood nothing and said nothing. Finally, everyone shook hands and smiled. We retrieved our luggage and headed out of town. We had a full day's drive ahead of us, but it was close to noon before we left.

We headed west on Nepal's main east-west road, down a river valley with beautiful mountains on both sides. We had a moderate-sized bus with our luggage inside. We had lots of room. I felt a little guilty, observing all the other buses packed with people hanging on the back and sides and sitting on the roof. It was after dark before we turned off the main road and headed north up another valley. The road was small and quickly became dirt. Dr. Thapa told us that the road we were now on was 45 miles long, and had been completed only six months prior. It connected Besishahar, the capital city of Lamjung District, to the outside world.

Lamjung is a District in Nepal similar to a state in the United States. Previously, Besishahar was only accessible by a 45-mile mule trail.

Because it was dark, we could see little except with our bus headlights. On several occasions the bus drove through rivers with flowing water. The ride was very rough. We arrived at Besishahar at 11 P.M. We were supposed to be there before dark. Our hotel people were waiting. Almost immediately upon arrival, we were met by a couple of people who wanted the doctor to come quickly. A lady had been stung many times by a swarm of bees, and she was unconscious. Dr. Shull was an emergency medicine specialist and had worked emergency rooms his entire career. He, along with Jane immediately responded and went to see the patient. The patient was in critical condition. Dr. Shull administered several emergency medications.

Dr. Thapa informed us that a welcoming ceremony with several high officials was planned for 7 the next morning. This meeting was to be held in the building which would serve as our clinic. We unpacked and went quickly to bed.

The night was short. We were up, had breakfast, and had all of our supplies transferred to the clinic building before 7 A.M. The building was about three-quarters of a mile away. The luggage was transported in a vehicle, but we walked.

Dr. Shull had been up and had already checked his patient. She was deteriorating fast, and there was nothing more he could do for her. Dr. Thapa arranged for a vehicle to transport her to the nearest hospital, which was six hours away.

Our opening ceremony consisted of six or eight officials sitting on a raised platform. They requested Dr. Thapa and me to sit on the platform with them. There were about 80 to 100 people gathered. One by one each official made a speech, none of which the team or I could understand a word. Then suddenly, without warning the head man turned to me and said, "It's your turn." I panicked. I thought, "What am I supposed to say?" No one warned me about this. Then Dr. Thapa nudged me to stand up and he stood beside me to interpret.

This is basically what I said, "I bring you greetings from the Christians in the United States and Canada. We have come to help you with your medical and dental problems, because we love you. We are Christians, and we are taught to love everybody, and to help those in need. Thank you." It was short and sweet, and then I sat down. The other officials had each talked for nearly an hour. I was last, and the ceremony ended. We set up our clinic and started working.

Dr. Thapa came to me and apologized. He said, "I should have told you that it's against the law to talk about your religion. You were lucky you were not shot, right on the platform." Then he advised me, and he went to each of the team members and told them, "Please don't say anything about your Christianity, unless somebody asks you a specific question. You can answer a question, but only the question, and then say no more." He continued, "There is a mandatory three-year prison term for anyone sharing their faith, and a six-year prison term if you convert anyone to your faith."

In the two weeks that we were there, Dr. Harle had one person ask him two questions, and he answered both in one sentence. I felt bad because HTI's purpose is to help evangelize. How can we evangelize if we can't say anything? You will be surprised!

Dr. Thapa said, "Don't worry. We know how to get around the law, and we will do a follow-up later. You just show these people Christian love." So we did, and we made that our goal. We showed them we were Christians by our love. We adopted as our theme song, a song that says repeatedly, "They will know we are Christians by our love." We sang this daily, and often in the clinic. Besishahar and the entire valley was 100 percent Hindu. Hinduism does not have any hymns or songs. Consequently, people liked to hear us sing. We were often asked to sing in the clinic.

We could sing our theme song or other hymns, since no one, except our Christian translators that Dr. Thapa brought with him, could understand English.

The second morning when we had our devotions, I asked Dr. Thapa to tell us about his life and testimony. This is the story he told us: He was born and raised in a farming family that lived in a village a short distance from there. He went to a summer camp one year at age 13. At camp he met some Christians. They led him to Christ and he became a Christian. Dr. Thapa's family, as well as the entire Lamjung valley were Hindus. When he returned home and told his parents that he had become a Christian, they disowned him and kicked him out of their house.

He had no place to go, so he just stayed around home and ate scraps of food discarded by the family. As cold weather set in, he would sleep huddled up by the front doorsill trying to stay warm. Finally one cold night his parents let him back into the house.

When his parents did this, the village mayor commanded the villagers to ostracize and disown the entire family. They couldn't talk to them, sell them any food, or buy any of their farm products. They couldn't even look at them. He prevented them from drawing water from the village well. They had to go farther to a stream to get water and then boil it. He kicked all the family's children out of school, and they had to walk two hours up a 2000-foot mountain, to a small village at the top, six days a week, to go to school. The villagers, as directed by the mayor, made life for the whole Thapa family very difficult.

When Thapa graduated from high school, he moved to Katmandu, and worked his way through college. He met Esther. They got married and had two daughters. After they both received their bachelors' degrees, they both felt a strong call to the ministry. They moved to Hong Kong for five years. Esther earned a masters' degree in Christian theology while raising their two daughters. Thapa earned both a masters' and doctors' degree in theology.

They moved back to Katmandu and felt led to try to organize and unify all the Christian churches and missions so they could help each other. Persecution against Christians was sporadic, but severe. Churches and pastors' homes were being burned, and pastors and church leaders were being arrested, tortured, and even killed by police and Hindu government officials. Thapa hoped that if Christians could band together, they might be able to control or reduce this type of persecution.

He sent out invitations to all Christian pastors and missionaries that he could identify throughout the country, inviting them to an organizational meeting. He requested RSVPs, but communication in Nepal was often difficult. He only heard back from 75 pastors. He felt optimistic so he planned for one hundred. On the first day of this organizational meeting of Christian leaders, Dr. Thapa was overwhelmed. He had 350 people who came.

Everyone agreed they needed to work together to stop the persecution, and to work together on many other things. They elected Dr. Thapa as their president and CEO of their new organization which they called The National Council of Christian Churches.

Very shortly after the meeting he got my e-mail offering to help. He knew that the new road to his hometown area of Lamjung was going to be opened in a few months. He knew there were no Christians in the area, and that they had essentially no medical and certainly no dental services in the area. He felt that going in with a Christian medical and dental team might be enough to crack the Hindu stronghold, and start a Christian base of influence in the area, so we were invited.

When our devotions were finished, we had breakfast and walked to the clinic. Dr. Shull, who was still recovering from hip surgery, somehow received a ride each day. We learned upon arrival that the bee sting patient that we had made arrangements to send to a hospital, died en route. A rainstorm during the night washed out the road. As an attempt was being made to fill in the road enough to get through, she died.

An active youth group of 18 to 25 year old young people asked if they could help us. Dr. Thapa said, "Yes" and he gave them the job of organizing the patients. At 6 A.M. the young people started to give out numbers to the patients already standing in line for treatment. They gave only enough numbers for dental and medical that we estimated we could treat in one day. All of the people with their families and curious spectators waited outside on the lawn in front of the clinic all day. Their numbers were called by the young people when we were almost ready for a new patient. They did a great job. We always had an immediate and smooth flow of patients. The young people did a variety of other jobs also. They were great helpers.

The building we were using was supposed to be a hospital. It was fairly large with eight or ten large rooms. The only problem was a doctor had never been at the hospital or anywhere else in town. Occasionally a visiting nurse would pass through. About eight patients were in one room lying on the cool concrete floor, just waiting to die. The townspeople brought their family members there to die. The building was very run down, with large holes in the roof. It was dirty and full of cobwebs. There was no furniture, or supplies.

Since we were prevented from verbally witnessing to the people and our patients, the Lord took over, and turned everything around for us. One of the doctors saw a 70 year-old patient that had been totally deaf for 20 years. He was a highly honored retired military officer. He had lived in town his entire life, except for the years of active duty in the Army. He was a well known and a respected elder of the town.

Through sign language, which his wife interpreted, he asked the doctor if they could fix his hearing. The doctor examined his ears thoroughly and could find no problem. One of the other doctors passed by and was asked to look at the patient's ears also.

He could not see a problem either. They asked this respected elder if it would be okay if they prayed for him. He shook his head, yes. Both doctors and one nurse placed their hands on his head and started to pray. Within a few minutes he began to shake, and then he started screaming, "I can hear! I can hear!" We heard him in the next room. This is as close as I had ever come to personally witnessing a medical healing.

The thing that happened next was also a God thing. After running up and down the hall screaming, this respected elder went out in front of the clinic, held his hands up, and announced to the mass of people out there, "People, we need to listen to their God. He is much stronger than our god. He has cured my hearing. I can now hear!"

Word spread quickly and many more people came to the clinic. We worked harder and longer, sometimes 10 or 12 hours, and occasionally even after dark by flashlight. We started to run out of anesthesia, and had to send someone to travel six hours to a large town to buy more anesthesia. Fortunately, it arrived just in time so that we never ran out. Since we couldn't talk to our patients about Jesus, we were able to see many more of them.

Most of their teeth came out fairly easy, so we accomplished an unusually large number of extractions.

There was a Maoist Communist movement in the country against the government. The Communists called for a one-day national strike. They demanded that all society come to a stop. When we got up that morning, no shops or restaurants were open, and no buses or vehicles of any kind were moving on the roads. The streets looked like a ghost town. Dr. Thapa had been asked to continue to operate the clinic as usual, so we walked to the clinic building, through this eerie ghost town. We found a lot of patients waiting for us. There were also several government armed military men there to protect us if we needed. We never had a problem. My guess was that some of the Maoists needed treatment also.

In the afternoon the Governor of the Lamjung District came to the clinic. We examined and cleaned his teeth, and he received a physical exam. He lingered around the clinic most of the afternoon, often talking with Dr. Thapa. Dr. Thapa was the only Nepalese Doctor of Christian Theology in the entire country of Nepal.

One afternoon Dr. Thapa saw an old sickly-looking man whom he had not seen in over 20 years. He recognized him as the mayor of his family's village. He was the man that had led all the persecution against his family when he was young. He was walking slowly around outside and looking very sad. Dr. Thapa went out and put his arms around him, and asked him how we could help him. He said, "I am very sick and I didn't get here early enough this morning to get a number so that I could see the doctor."

Dr. Thapa said, "Come with me and let's see what I can do." He brought the mayor into the clinic and when there was a little slackness, he worked him in to see the doctor. The doctor was able to diagnose his problem and had the proper medicine. When the doctor gave him his medicine, he said, "I want to see you again tomorrow." Dr. Thapa gave him a number so he could be seen the next day.

Dr. Thapa said the man was visibly crying as he left the clinic, which was very unusual, because Nepalese men never cry. Dr. Thapa said, "I think God is preparing his heart. I plan to get back to him and talk to him about Jesus."

Dr. Thapa told us this story of what had happened with his former mayor during supper. I asked Dr. Thapa, "Didn't you find it hard to treat this man so kindly after he had persecuted you and your family for so many years?"

I will never forget his answer. He said, "I forgave this man a long time ago, and I have prayed for him ever since. I thank God that he gave me the opportunity and privilege to show him true Christian love."

Immediately, Jesus' words as recorded in Matthew, Chapter 5, verse 44, popped into my head. Jesus said, "Love your enemies, bless them that curse you, do good to those who hate you, and pray for those who persecute you." This has to be one of the hardest commandments we as Christians are asked to obey. I can't think of a more perfect example of anyone fulfilling this commandment of Jesus more completely than Dr. Thapa did that day.

One evening toward the end of our stay, the Governor requested Dr. Thapa to join him and the Chief of Police for supper. Dr. Thapa was frightened. He asked the whole team to pray for him continuously while he was gone. We did. He said the Governor had the power to put him in jail, or he could ask the whole team to leave town immediately. He didn't know what to think.

Later that evening when he returned he was smiling. He said, "The Governor is very pleased with our work. He has offered to give me one million dollars worth of land and property, if I would open a Christian mission hospital in Lamjung." I told the Governor, "I would love to do just exactly that, but I will need lots of help."

We had a beautiful, lush green, 2000-foot mountain right behind our hotel. A castle-like building was right at the peak. A bright light shone from it all night. Dr. Thapa told us that the castle was where one of the former kings lived, so that he could see down the mountain over his kingdom.

Our weather every day was perfect, 65° at night and 75° during the day. Each day was bright, sunny and clear. Everything was green and beautiful. We were told that the most famous backpacking trail in the world, the Himalayan Anapurna trail began from this town, and one could backpack into the Himalayas for two or three weeks and end in the town of Pokhara.

Being an adventurer, it came to my mind how wonderful it would be if we could have one of our morning devotions on top of this beautiful mountain behind our hotel.

I mentioned it to Dr. Thapa and he said, "That might be a possibility on our last day. We have only a half day of clinic scheduled. We had planned to have clinic in the morning, but if you wish, we could go up the mountain and have devotions in the morning, and have our clinic in the afternoon. The whole team thought this would be a great idea.

Dr. Thapa asked Dr. Shull if he thought he could ride a horse. He said, "Yes." So Dr. Thapa asked the Chief of Police, if Dr. Shull could borrow his horse to ride up the mountain, and he consented.

We got up before daybreak and had our breakfast. Just as it was getting light, we started up the mountain. One of the hotel employees led the way. The climb was difficult. Part of the trail was so steep that I had to climb on my hands and feet. Dr. Shull started up on the horse, but had to turn back because the ascent was much too steep for the horse. As we neared the top, the land flattened into a plateau. We observed several small fields of a wheat-type grain that was growing. It was still green and not ripe, even in the middle of October. We finally reached the top.

The town of the Besishahar was at the 6000-foot elevation and the air was already a little thin for us. The 2000-foot steep climb was a little tougher than we had anticipated. It took us three hours and we were all winded. One of the youthful male waiters from our hotel, who was a part-time trekking guide, climbed to the top after he finished his morning duties at the hotel. It took him 45 minutes.

The old king's palace that had the bright light at night was currently a Hindu monastery. As we sat in front of the Hindu monastery catching our breath, a priest came out and offered to show us through the old castle. We found it very interesting.

We observed a small clearing at the top of a cliff that looked out over the whole valley. Off in the distance we could see several 20,000-foot snowcapped Himalayan mountains. They surrounded us. It was, for me, the most beautiful sight my eyes had ever seen, and I took a lot of photos to prove it. We sat down and sang God's praises, prayed, read Scripture, and gave testimonies as to how God was touching our lives. God's beauty and majesty just doesn't get any better.

Dr. Thapa and Esther came with us. After devotions, we were ready to start down, when Dr. Thapa said, "Let's take a few minutes and visit the town just over this ridge." We walked up a small ridge, and behold, we saw a little village of about a hundred houses on this small mountaintop plateau. Dr. Thapa showed us the school that he and his brothers and sisters were forced to walk up to each day. This was where he had graduated from high school.

We walked around the village a little. Dr. Thapa saw someone he knew. It was his high school English teacher. The man was older and didn't recognize him, so Dr. Thapa introduced himself. The man's face lit up with a big happy smile. He said, "You are the most famous student I have ever taught. Everyone in the village knows all about you. I never thought I would see you again. Thanks for coming back." He gave Dr. Thapa a big hug.

Esther had never had the opportunity to visit the school and village where her husband had graduated from high school. She was also excited. The descent down the mountain took us less than an hour. We didn't have to stop every few minutes to catch our breath.

After lunch we had a busy last afternoon of clinic. We found it difficult to stop, but the minister of health had a reception party planned for us. At this party, fancy hors d'oeuvres were served and most of the important town officials were present.

A closing thank you ceremony was held in an auditorium after supper. Several hundred people were in attendance. The ceremony lasted several hours and a number of speeches were given. The electricity went out and we had to wait briefly for the generator to be turned on. The government officials called us up, one at a time and gave us various gifts. The young people, who had been helping us, dressed in costumes and did several traditional Nepalese dances and a couple of short plays. They also called us up, one at a time, and gave us gifts and bouquets of flowers.

Our goal was to show them we were Christians by our love. Our biggest gift of the evening was given to us by the Governor. He stated in his speech, "These people have treated us more kindly than any people that have ever visited our valley." Yes! Our goal was accomplished.

However, we still left with a somewhat empty feeling. This trip was the first of several hundred HTI mission trips where we never once had an opportunity to verbalize our faith, nor help lost people receive Jesus into their hearts and lives. We did the best we could, but we never said a word.

We visited Pokhara, a unique and interesting town on our way back to Katmandu. In Katmandu we visited the Temple of the Monkeys, and Dr. Thapa's office. We also shopped downtown. We visited and were very impressed with a Bible school of 50 to 75 students, where Esther was the principal and administrator. It was the only Christian Bible School in Nepal which trained pastors.

Our flight home was long, but uneventful. We stopped in Seoul, South Korea, and had time for a tour. We visited the largest Protestant church in the world. Wow! After we got home, it took about a week to get over the 12-hour jet lag.

In summary: It was a very beautiful, unusually adventurous mission. We had to concentrate on showing real Christian love toward people with whom we couldn't speak to about Jesus. We also witnessed God performing a healing miracle. We all learned from Dr. Thapa an excellent example of loving your enemy. I developed several new personal lifelong friends, some of whom are helping me to carry HTI missions into the future.

## And Now the Rest of the Story

Dr. David Shull became a member of the HTI board of directors the following year. He has been a great administrative help to me. He has been a team member on several additional mission trips, as well as a team leader, organizing and taking his own teams on several missions.

Dr. Tom Harle also became a member of the HTI board of directors. Since Dr. Harle lives in Ottawa, Canada, the board requested that he investigate the possibility of HTI getting a charitable tax status in Canada for Canadian team members. Dr. Harle successfully did just that. He had to incorporate an HTI branch in Canada, of which he is president, and he appointed several helpful hard working officers. He helped to develop a successful fundraising campaign, and was able to purchase supplies and equipment for use with their team members from Canada.

Dr. Harle has organized and led an HTI mission trip every year since our Nepal mission. He helped to recruit team members, and has helped organize and equip several other HTI missions. He has started a free dental clinic in downtown Ottawa to meet the needs of the homeless and poor. He has gotten many of Ottawa's dentists, hygienists and assistants to help him a day or two a month with this clinic. This clinic has become very successful in caring for the dental work of the needy. It has become a model clinic through Canada. Numerous similar clinics have begun to spring up in other Canadian cities. He has become a very valuable, innovative, progressive thinker and hard-worker, whom HTI is honored to have as a board member.

Several weeks after we returned home I received a lengthy e-mail from Dr. Thapa. He reported that they had been back in Besishahar doing follow up work. He stated that the elder that had his hearing miraculously cured, along with his family and many of the young people that helped us and witnessed the miracle had now become Christians. They had started a church and had 45 in attendance on Wednesdays and Sundays. He also reported that the Governor was hosting a Bible study in his home for the Chief of Police, the Minister of Health and other government officials.

Later e-mails over the next few years reported that the Governor did not have the authority to give government property to Dr. Thapa, a private citizen, without the approval of the National Parliament.

The National Parliament had never given property to a private Christian person. The rumors were that there was absolutely no chance the Parliament would approve such a gift of property.

Then the King of Nepal was assassinated. In the transfer of leadership, the Parliament was dissolved. The very last item brought before the parliament was the request of the Governor of Lamjung to give Dr. Thapa the land and buildings to start a hospital. Despite previous negative indications, it passed by a large margin.

Today, ten years later, under the leadership of Dr. Thapa and with the help of many others, there is a full 100-bed Christian Mission Hospital open and operating in Besishahar, Lamjung. They have seven foreign doctors, with several specialty departments including Pediatrics, Obstetrics and Gynecology. They have over 50 Nepalese nurses and assistants.

The hospital has morning Christian devotions, a Wednesday prayer meeting, a Bible study, and Sunday services for all who wish to attend.

The Lamjung Christian Mission Hospital has become so successful that it has become the country's premier model small hospital. Doctors and administrators come from all over the country to observe and study how it is operated.

Dr. Thapa and the organization of specialists he has developed to run the hospital in Lamjung have had requests for them to take over the administration of numerous other small hospitals. They have accepted and they are now administering several small Christian hospitals throughout Nepal.

Dr. Thapa's original goal for asking us to come to Nepal was to try to crack the Hindu stronghold in his home area of Lamjung, and start a Christian base of influence.

With our initial help, I think he has done a fantastic job in more than accomplishing his goal. The most amazing thing to me is that all of our WITNESSING OCCURED WITHOUT SAYING A WORD.

# CHAPTER 22

# CAMEROON 3
# MAROUA

Maroua is the predominantly Moslem Far North Provincial Capital of Cameroon. The area is a hot dry sub-Sahara Desert, except for the four month rainy season in which the people can grow millet and store enough to feed themselves during the dry season. There are over one million people living in this province. They only have one dentist, with a year's training, who provides treatment exclusively for the government officials and the rich people. The area is 99% Moslem.

Before I came home from my second Cameroon mission with the pygmies, our host John Ngoh, requested that I return the following spring with another HTI team. Upon returning home, a personal friend of mine, Ken Krestan, asked if I could come to Bolivia and help him. About the same time, I received a very unique and unusual invitation to bring a HTI team to Nepal that next year also. As I was pondering what to do, Dr. John Hibbert called and informed me he wanted to go to Cameroon next year and bring his wife, Omelda, who is a nurse. When I explained to him about my invitations to Bolivia and Nepal, he indicated that was no problem, he could lead the team back to Cameroon. Dr. Hibbert did lead a team back to Cameroon in the spring of 1999, and had a very successful mission.

After Dr. Hibbert returned from Cameroon John e-mailed me and asked if HTI could send another team in the spring of 2000. I asked Dr. Hibbert if he would lead another team to Cameroon that next year. He indicated that both he and Omelda wanted to go again next year, but he was not able to lead the team. It was a much bigger job than he had expected.

I had teams planned for Bolivia in May and Nepal in Oct. of 1999 and I had numerous other opportunities I was anxious to explore, so I searched hard to find another team leader for Cameroon. John Ngoh was such an excellent host I didn't feel it was that difficult to be a team leader to Cameroon. I was unable to find anyone to lead the team back to Cameroon.

The Lord placed a heavy burden on my heart. We were seeing over 1000 people come to the Lord on each mission. I was concerned that if I didn't accept to lead the team, there might be no team, and there would be over 1000 people who wouldn't get saved and would never have the joy of spending eternity in heaven. This burden was too much for me to carry, so I volunteered to lead the team back to Cameroon in March 2000.

John indicated he wanted to reach the unreached Fulain people in the Far Northern Providence around the capital of Maroua. They were almost 100% Muslim. He requested I bring a larger team.

Dr. Hibbert asked if he could bring Michel, his Air Force medical technician, and an Air Force dentist, Dr. William Nerestant. He also had a pastor and his wife, Rev. Jim and Joan Kidd that wanted to join us. A dentist from British Columbia, Canada, Dr. Jack Ratzlaff, called and asked if he could go.

I had two dental assistants from my office, 21 year old Kelly Burgess and 22 year old Heather Smith, who came to me one day and asked if they could go with me. They were surprised, happy, and excited when I said, "Sure". Heather shared with me that she had always wanted to go to Africa ever since she was a little girl. I ended up with a team of 15, the largest team I had ever taken. I had 2 MDs, 4 dentists, 3 nurses, 3 dental assistants, 1 medical technician, 1 pastor, and 1 helper.

We left in March of 2000. We arrived into Douala on time. We had no problems with customs, so we ended up getting to bed earlier than usual, after our 40-hour trip. Cameroon is a land of contrasts. In Douala our hotel was a very nice four-star hotel, while the remote villages in which we worked were one of the most primitive places on this earth.

Our first day was spent in orientation, resting from our jet lag, sightseeing, and shopping. Fortunately we had no lost luggage to recover. The following morning at daybreak, John assembled his evangelists and translators and we all packed our luggage onto the roof of a small bus, loaded up, and were on our way to Yaounde, Cameroon's capital. We arrived at the train station in Yaounde in mid-afternoon, and unloaded our baggage in an open area across the street from the railroad station. There were masses of people in and around the station. John went to pick up our reserved tickets.

While we were waiting and standing around talking, Pastor Kidd's carry-on bag was stolen, with his reading glasses in it. There were people everywhere, but no one saw it happen. As a result we piled all of our baggage in one pile, and sat on our bags all around the perimeter of the circle. We had 45 pieces of baggage ourselves, plus John's and his helpers'.

Finally John came with our tickets, and several porters with baggage carts. We stayed close together, and weaved our way through the massive crowd. Our luggage had to go in the baggage car, which bothered us a little, because it contained over $100,000 of medications, equipment, supplies, and all our personal belongings. We loaded into a nice cool Pullman car, where each compartment contained four soft seats, which folded out into four nice beds. The rest of the passengers were not as fortunate. They were overloaded into old coach cars for the 18-hour ride.

This was the only train in the entire country. It had been built by the Germans before World War I. The train went from Douala to Yaounde, then from Yaounde to Ngaoundere where it terminated. The road from Douala to Yaounde was good, and we could drive it faster and cheaper than taking the train. The road from Yaounde to Ngaoundere was rough and in very poor condition. It went through woods and hills where highway robbers frequently made the trip very unsafe. The train was cheaper, safer, and faster than driving this section of the country, but it was still very slow with many stops. Some villages had no roads leading into them except for the train. The ride was bumpy, rocky, and noisy, but I slept well. We were fed our meals in our compartments, only eating the well cooked food.

We arrived at Ngaoundere in the early afternoon the next day. Dr. Ratzlaff took some photos of the railroad station and of some interesting people. I guess that was a no-no. The police arrested Jack and ushered him into a room where they took away his camera and passport.

It took more than an hour for our luggage to be unloaded and for us to locate each piece. Fortunately it all arrived safely. Then we loaded everything on top of a small bus again, all 45-plus pieces. This resulted in a stack about 5 feet high which they covered with a tarp and tied down. It was obvious the driver was skilled at doing this.

While we were getting our luggage and loading, John was busy negotiating for Jack. He was finally released with his camera and passport returned, but with the film in his camera removed. I don't know whether John had to bribe them or not. Bribing police is very common in Cameroon. John indicated that often the police would set up road blocks, stop drivers, and hassle them for a long time until the drivers finally gave them some money. Then they would let them go. It was so common that taxi drivers in Yaounde went on strike to protest this abuse.

We drove about 5 miles to a small hotel on the outskirts of Ngaoundere, where we had supper and spent the night. There was a big hill behind the hotel all covered with unusually large rocky boulders. It was the only hill in the area. As we were talking about it the gardener overheard us and said, "There's a nice path from the back of the hotel right to the top of that hill." It was too far and too late to hike it that night, so we asked the gardener, if he would take us to the top at daybreak in the morning. He said, "Yes, I would enjoy doing that."

Near daybreak, before the sun rose, Michael, Heather, Kelly, and I met the gardener, and we took an hour-long climb up to the top of this rocky hill. We saw the sunrise over the city of Ngaoundere. It was beautiful. We then scrambled down, tipped our gardener, which made him very happy, and went to the hotel dining room just in time to join the rest of the team for breakfast. We were always careful what we ate. It had to be well cooked, such as scrambled eggs, or peeled, such as bananas. We had no fruit juices, milk, cereals, jellies, etc.

We loaded our bus, and again they stacked our luggage on top so high that I knew we would never get under any bridges, but as it turned out, we didn't have to worry about that, because there weren't any bridges. The road was paved and in fairly decent shape. It was the only road northeast up the narrow horn of Cameroon. We started on our way shortly after 8 A.M.

Chad, a small landlocked desert country, bordered Cameroon on the north and eastern sides. They used this road heavily with huge trucks. It was Chad's only route to the ocean, and thus to the rest of the world for their imports and exports. The all-day drive was very interesting, hot, and different. It seemed like we were driving back in time. As we left the city and drove further into the country, things became much more primitive.

We observed high voltage electric lines alongside our road all day. They connected the three provincial capital cities of Ngaoundere, Garoua and Maroua. These high-powered electric lines went right over the tops of the villages along this road. Rarely did we see any power lines reaching down to the villages. We were told that most of these villages were without electricity. I saw many things on this drive that I have never seen anywhere else in the world.

We arrived at Maroua, around 6 P.M., and went directly to our hotel, had supper and went to bed. We had been traveling long and hard for two days. We had been 18 hours on the train and 10 hours in the bus.

We had our team prayer, devotions, and daily orientation in my room at 6 A.M. each morning. Breakfast was at 7 A.M. and we tried to be on the road by 8. We drove to small villages 30 minutes to 1 hour outside of Maroua for our clinics.

John had visited Maroua earlier, and had made our arrangements ahead of time. He visited each village and asked the chief if he would like for us to come, and he told him we were Christians and would be sharing our faith. Each chief agreed, so John set a specific date for each village. John could only find and bring four Christian translators who could speak both Fulani and English, so he had to recruit five local Muslims to help us with translation. John didn't know anyone in his part of the country that spoke both languages, so it turned out to be a most interesting project. Our Moslem translators were at the hotel waiting for us when we arrived.

Again rather than describing each day or village separately, I will summarize the highlights. We typically drove through barren sandy desert land to reach these villages. The roads were often two-track sandy paths. We rarely saw other motorized vehicles. People were walking, carrying things on their heads, and sometimes pushing a wheel barrow or a cart in the sand. There were times we saw two-wheeled carts being pulled by cows. We drove through many sandy riverbeds. John said, "When the four months of rains come during the summer, we can't get a vehicle into these villages, because there are no bridges across any of these currently dry rivers."

When we first arrived at a village, the African tradition was to pay a courtesy call to the chief. One of our Muslim translators was the chief's son in one of the villages we visited. The chief designated a specific area for us to set up our clinic. It was usually right in front of his personal dwelling in the center of the village. They often built a sun shelter out of poles and palm leaves to keep the hot sun off of us.

Many of these villages were just like stepping back in time 2000 years. The villagers lived in mud huts, with thatched roofs. They had a hole in the middle of town for a well. The chief told them when to get up, what to do, and when to go to bed. During the rainy season they worked hard in the sand fields to raise millet, which is a type of corn. They hoped to raise enough to last them for 12 months, until harvest time next year. Millet was their main food staple. There was no machinery. It was all hand labor. There were a few cattle and goats in some areas although I'm not sure what they ate.

The marriage tradition was that a young man bought his wife from his future father-in-law, for so many cows and goats. This was negotiated. If your wife didn't produce a child within one year, you had the option of trading her back to her father and getting your cows and goats back.

We had an opportunity to visit the inside of many of these huts. There was no furniture in them, often just a couple of reed mats on the sandy floor, but the people seemed to be happy. Children are children the world around. They were laughing, playing, and always seemed to be happy and having fun with little or nothing, as long as they were healthy.

John had the portable PA system, which I brought him from the U.S. a few years ago. Upon arrival at a village, he would start playing Christian music very loudly. This brought people from near and far to the center of the village to see what was happening. John then proceeded to tell the people why we had come, and gave them a Christian salvation message. I fell in love with the music John played. It was Carman's, "I Surrender All." I purchased it and continue to listen to it often, even ten years later as I am writing these memoirs.

We then started registering patients. We directed them to the physicians and nurses for medical problems, then to spiritual one-on-one counseling, and then to the pharmacy. The dental patients received their spiritual counseling first and then went to the dentist. The dentists gave their patients pain pills and a toothbrush when they finished extracting their teeth, so they didn't need to visit the pharmacy. The pharmacy was so busy it had a hard time keeping up with the prescriptions that the physicians and nurses were writing.

We took turns giving our testimony before John preached each morning. He would randomly call on one of us. Kelly had a Lutheran background and wasn't accustomed to testimonies. One day John called upon her to give her testimony to the crowd of people. She took the microphone and even surprised herself by giving a nice Christian testimony.

It was the first public testimony this 21 year old young girl had ever given in her life. I was proud of her.

It was easy to see from the first day, that the demand for extractions was greater than we dentists could accomplish, so I asked Heather and Kelly if they would help extract teeth. They were scared, but willing. With their dental assisting experience, and a few hours of close personal training, they learned very quickly. In no time, we expanded our four-chair extraction clinic to a six-chair clinic, and significantly increased the number of patients that we could treat. Both girls got along remarkably well, and rarely had to call upon me for help.

These people had large numbers of abscessed teeth which caused them a great deal of pain. I saw two different women who had pus running out of the side of their faces. I asked them how long this pus had been coming out of their cheek. One lady told me 7 years and the other lady told me 10 years. They were both caused by abscessed and infected molars, which took about 10 minutes to numb and remove. One lady told me that she could never remember a time in her life that she didn't have a toothache.

These people had never seen a dentist once in their entire life. They probably would never have an opportunity to receive dental treatment again. We tried to extract all their aching teeth when we saw them, which often numbered 8 to 10 teeth. By training Heather and Kelly to help us, my thinking was, that something was better than nothing, and if I didn't get more help to get these teeth extracted, nothing is exactly what many of them would end up with. There were basically one million people in this province, with not one dentist available to the common people.

One day Kelly came to me and said she had an upper premolar, which is a medium-sized tooth, that wouldn't budge. Kelly was a petite little gal of probably 100 pounds. The tooth was decayed, abscessed, and painful, but the decay was not really that large. It wasn't decayed off level with the gum like many of the teeth. I helped her apply the forceps to the tooth, close to the bone, and we got a real good grip on it. Then I coached her to wiggle, twist, rotate, and to continue to apply more and more pressure. She turned red, her muscles popped out, and tightened up, and she gave that tooth every ounce of strength she had. Finally the crown went "pop," and broke off even with the bone. I knew she had to be applying a lot of force to get that tooth to break the way it did.

I decided it was time for me to step in and take over. I gently pushed the gum back and got another grip on the tooth, and I couldn't move it one single bit myself. I then pulled the gum back farther, and got the hammer and chisel, and with Kelly swinging the hammer, I chiseled the bone away from the entire side of the tooth right to the tip of the root, before I could pry out the root. On very rare occasions, the root will completely fuse to the bone, and will not come out in the usual manner. I'll have to admit this was one of the toughest teeth I have ever had to remove.

I was pleased by the determination which Kelly showed in not giving up on this tooth. I was amazed by the amount of force she was able to generate. I was happy to see her put her whole heart and soul into conquering this tooth, and together we did. I couldn't help thinking how much this one experience may have influenced the rest of Kelly's life. See the rest of the story at the end of this chapter.

One morning after we loaded the bus, and started to travel to one of the remote villages, my translator, who was a Moslem, and seated next to me, leaned over and asked me, "Why can't I become a Christian too?" Our translators had been living with us in the hotel, eating with us, traveling with us, and translating for us, including the Good News of the Gospel. They had witnessed many Moslems who had become Christians. We had actually become fairly close friends.

I asked my translator, "What did you say?" He repeated, "I want to be a Christian." I asked him "Why do you want to become a Christian?" He said, "I want to be happy like you people. There's nothing in the Moslem faith to be happy about." Our team frequently laughed and joked and had a good time together. He asked me, "What do I have to do?" This caught me off guard, and although I had been a Christian since I was a child, and had gone to church all my life, I had never personally led a person to salvation in Jesus. I panicked a bit. John was sitting right in front of me, so I said, "John, my translator wants to become a Christian." He immediately turned around and led him to Christ.

One morning Heather and Kelly were running a little late, and they left some of their clothes on the floor in the hotel. When we returned at the end of the day five items of their clothing were washed, pressed, and neatly lay on their bed. They thought that was nice, until they saw the bill, $45. They argued and said, "I didn't ask to have my clothes washed, or even want them washed." But the local custom was if you wanted your clothes washed, you left them on the floor. All the arguing John did for us was of no avail, because we ended up paying the bill.

One Sunday afternoon after church and lunch, we decided to travel an hour and a half to a park, which had some unique sites. The bus driver wasn't prepared to take us, so we had to stop at a gas station and get some gas. Just as we stopped, the electricity went out. The gas station attendant calmly got a screwdriver, took the front cover off the gas pump, got a special crank, inserted it into the pump, and hand-cranked until we had the gasoline we needed. It was obvious that this problem happened often.

We traveled on a fairly main paved road, heading toward the Nigerian border. As we were passing through a small village, the driver suddenly pulled over, stopped and got out. We had a flat tire and he didn't have a spare. Fortunately we were near a tire repair shop which was just ahead of us. John said, "While they're fixing the tire, let's go to the market they are having in this village today." They only had market day on Sunday in this particular village.

We walked a few hundred yards down a gradual slope to the edge of a dried-up river, where there was a large open-air market. We divided into groups and went in different directions. Heather and Kelly stuck close to me; I think they were still a little intimidated by the 100% black native people. It had been a whole week since we had seen a white person, other than of our own team members.

We came upon a cute little goat tied to a stake. Kelly and Heather were attracted to it. There was no one around, so Kelly petted it for quite awhile. Finally we left, and walked only 20 or 30 steps when we heard this blood curdling scream. We turned around just in time to see a man finish slitting the throat of this cute little goat that Kelly had been petting. Blood was spurting all over. Then I heard another scream. It was from Kelly as she put her hands over her face and started running as fast as she could. When I caught up to her she was sobbing hysterically. It took awhile, but she finally calmed down. Obviously, market day was also the day they slaughtered meat to sell in the market, and that is why the goat was tied to the post.

We walked around the market, and observed things we would never see in our U.S. markets. We noticed people clumped in groups in the center of the large dried up riverbed, so we walked out there to see what they were doing. We found that they had dug several 3-foot deep holes in the sandy riverbed, and had found water. They were dipping it out, filtering it through a cloth, and drinking it. No thanks!

As we were about to leave, a young black man walked up to the three of us and pointed to Kelly, who was an exceptionally beautiful young lady, and in rather broken English he asked, "How much for her?" Obviously he thought I was Kelly's father, and he wanted a bridal price. I was amused, so I casually said, "4 goats and 3 cows." Immediately, Kelly came apart at the seams, and she ran to me screaming, "You wouldn't do that; you wouldn't do that, would you?" I smiled and laughed a little and said, "No." The young man hung his head, turned and walked away. I thought I was being funny, but Kelly's first reaction indicated she didn't think it was very funny. My wife later said, "I expect your assistants don't see you joking or kidding around when they are working in your dental office."

Dr. Hibbert had about 500 pairs of used eyeglasses given to him, shortly before coming to Cameroon. He had room, so he packed them and brought them. He asked Michael if he would try to see if anyone could use these glasses. Michael spread 20 or 30 pairs of glasses out on a table. He took two or three patients at a time that were complaining about not seeing well. He would have them try on different glasses, until they found a pair which allowed them to see clearly the printed material he had put on the table, or until they could clearly see the E chart, that was 30 feet away. It was purely trial and error, and it was amazing how excited the patients got when they put on a pair of glasses and suddenly they could see again. Michael had all 500 pairs of glasses distributed within one week.

The hotel usually packed food for our lunch each day, and we took it with us in the morning. Using this food, we made sandwiches, and had some pop and cookies. One day about 10 A.M., a motorcycle came into the village where we were working. He unloaded a big paper bag, and gave it to John. It was the bread for our sandwiches. We had forgotten it and he brought it to us, special delivery.

We had some bread left over that day, so before we left for our hotel, Michael decided to give it to some of the villagers. Michael was about 30 years old, 6 feet tall, and probably 250 pounds. He had several loaves of bread which he had broken in half. As he started to hand out the bread, instantly there were many people, particularly older children, rushing him from all directions. He was almost crushed in the stampede, but survived. This was another good lesson learned.

The weather was extremely hot and dry. We took a lot of bottled water with us each day and some days I think I drank a gallon of water, but at the end of the day I probably only urinated about a half a cup. I never seemed to sweat. I was told that the humidity was so low, the sweat evaporated as fast as it formed. We had to be careful to protect ourselves against dehydration.

I had brought two small thermometers with me. One day I put them out in the sun next to where we were working. After a little while I checked them. One read 120 degrees which was the top of the liquid in the thermometer, and the other one, which was a digital thermometer, was at its maximum of 125 degrees and was blinking. I really don't know how hot it was in the sun. In the shade the thermometers averaged between 110 to 115 degrees.

The last morning at our 6 A.M. prayer and devotion time, I asked the translators to join us, and to say a few words as to how these last two weeks had influenced their lives. It was absolutely thrilling to hear four out of the five tell us how they had become Christians, and the wonderful changes it had made in their lives. The fifth translator was almost ready to make a decision, but not quite yet he said.

The morning that we were to leave Maroua by bus to get to Ngaoundere to catch our train, we were all packed and in the bus at the scheduled 8 A.M. departure time, but John wasn't there. I checked and he wasn't in his room. Finally I found him in a back room talking with the hotel manager. We waited and waited. Finally he arrived an hour and a half later, and then we departed. John had been bargaining over our room fees, meals, and laundry charges. He had tried to do it the evening before, but the hotel manager insisted on doing it in the morning. John having been born and raised in Cameroon was culturally wise and carefully looked out for our interests.

We were seriously behind schedule, so the driver was pushing it a little. Around noon as we were going through a small village, our driver pulled over under a shade tree at the side of the road and stopped. He jumped out and started walking rapidly away. John jumped out and ran after him. After a short conversation, John came back to the bus while the driver continued to walk away. John announced, "The driver is Moslem, and it is time for his prayers." The driver said, "It wasn't his problem we got a late start." We had shared Jesus with everybody else, but we hadn't shared Jesus with our driver. On our next trip to

Cameroon John shared Christ with our Moslem driver early into our trip, and he became a Christian. That was another lesson well learned.

The train was supposed to leave at 6 P.M. We rolled up to the train station at 5:45 P.M., but the train hadn't even arrived. It was late, and Ngaoundere was the end of the line, so when it did arrive, it had to unload, refuel, and reload. It arrived at 8:30 P.M. and it was well after 11 P.M. before we got loaded and started to roll. We found out that during the two weeks we were in Maroua, the train had derailed, and didn't run for five days. We were just happy that it was back in operation. There wasn't any other safe way out of Ngaoundere with all our luggage.

While we were waiting, we piled all of our more than 50 pieces of luggage into a teepee-type pile on the floor in the center of the station's main room, and took turns sitting and guarding the perimeters. It was very hot, we hadn't had supper, and we were all getting tired. I think riding all day in our small bus was more tiring than working.

Since this was again an overnight train ride, John had reserved sleeping berths for us. Our compartment was so hot we opened our window. When the conductor came around to collect our tickets, he advised us to close our window. He said, "The train has many stops, and in the past when it stopped, robbers would reach in the windows or get in the windows and steal valuables while people were sleeping." It was a very long, bumpy, hot night, but we all were tired enough that I think everyone slept.

The train served us breakfast and lunch in our rooms, for what it was worth. We were scheduled to arrive in Yaounde at 10 A.M., but we didn't arrive until 3 P.M. We unloaded and put our baggage in a pile in front of the station as before, and set our perimeter of guards, because the bus we had arranged to meet us at 10 A.M. was not there.

John got a cab and went to find our bus. We waited patiently several hours, and no word from John. These were the days before cell phones. Around 6 P.M. as the sun was starting to get low in the west, some of the conversation turned to, what we were going to do if John didn't come back. Where would we go to get a hotel? I had confidence that John would return, and I tried to keep the team calm and patient.

John finally did return with a bus, so we loaded up and took off. John explained that our bus driver was there at 10 A.M. and he had waited until noon, but then took the bus back to the bus garage and left. The owner couldn't find him or anyone else to drive us. He didn't want to give back John's deposit, but he finally did refund it. John then found another bus rental service, but had no success. He found a third bus rental service, and the owner finally found a driver who was willing to drive us, but John had to go in his taxi out to the driver's house and get him. When they came back to the bus garage, he had to put gas in the bus before they came to get us. It's wonderful to have a determined, knowledgeable, native host who is street smart, and knows the customs of the country.

John doesn't like to travel on the road with a team at night, because of the potential presence of highway robbers, but he indicated that the roads we needed to travel had very few problems, and the team agreed to go for it. We had a 6-hour drive from Yaounde to Douala, then on to Limbe. Limbe was John's new hometown, where he had made hotel reservations for the team that night. We got to the hotel at 12:30 A.M. and went right to bed.

I delayed our next morning's prayer and devotions until 7 A.M. We had a one-day clinic scheduled at John's church. John's church was actually a one-room warehouse. They had built a platform at one end, and for services they set up folding chairs. For our clinic they furnished us with tables and folded up the chairs, so we had lots of room to work. There were many people waiting when we arrived, so we quickly got started. We saw several hundred people, most of them from outside of John's church from the surrounding neighborhood.

One interesting patient that Kelly saw was a pleasant older lady that had an abscessed tooth. Kelly figured out what tooth it was, numbed the tooth, and extracted it with no problem. Most people in Limbe spoke English. After the tooth was out, the lady started talking with Kelly. Kelly then came and got me. She wanted to introduce her patient to me. Kelly's patient was a widow of the local dentist. He had died a few years ago. She also was the owner of the warehouse that John was renting for his church. She was a member of John's church. I couldn't stop thinking of how ironic it was that Kelly, a dental assistant, had just extracted a tooth for the wife of a former dentist. The patient was very happy, and gave us each a big hug of thanks.

That evening John had a special evening service, in which not only his own church people, but all the patients we saw during the day were invited, especially those who had become Christians that day. John's church service was more of the Pentecostal or charismatic type of service. The music was very up-tempo with a lot of clapping and dancing in the aisles. Praying was done with everyone praying out loud and some in tongues all at the same time. The sermon involved a lot of emotionally raised voices and shouting. At the end of the service John asked everyone to thank our team by praying for us and laying hands on us. Everyone started praying loudly, and they started circling around us, touching the top of each of our heads as they passed by us. For me, I thought it was a very touching thank you gesture. I found out later that Kelly, who rarely ever missed a Sunday in her own church, and who had never been to any other churches except for her conservative Lutheran church, found this to be a frightening and emotional experience. Heather said, "I had to physically restrain Kelly from jumping up and bolting out of the church." It was an experience Kelly will never forget, but it all ended well.

It was rewarding to me that in talking with Kelly on our way home, she admitted that she had learned more about the saving grace of Jesus, prayer, and what it really means to be a true Christian, than she had learned in all 21 years in church. Praise the Lord. I have had many team members over the years tell me they didn't know who benefited the most from our trip, the patients or themselves. They often felt a great strengthening of their own personal faith and felt much closer to God.

The last day in Limbe we relaxed, and drove to a sandy beach, with nice big waves, and warm ocean water. We saw a lava flow from a recent eruption two years ago, from Mount Cameroon. It had flowed completely over the main highway. They hadn't attempted to remove it yet. They just drove around it.

On our last day we packed our bags and left Limbe in the late morning. On our way to Douala, we stopped and walked into the edge of a rubber plantation, and a banana plantation. We did some souvenir shopping in Douala at the Arts and Crafts Market. Our flight home was without any problems.

In Summary: John's final figures indicated that we had treated over 3000 patients, and had over 2000 people, mostly all Moslems, who accepted Christ and became Christians. John only counted the people who made a decision for Christ with one-on-one counseling, and not the people that raised their hands at the end of his morning messages and invitations in the villages. I had been successful in receiving 2000 thirty page scripture tracks in the local Fulani language, from The World Missionary Press. We gave each new Fulani Christian one of these tracks. We gave each village chief a complete Bible. I came home with a good feeling of accomplishment and lots of unforgettable memories.

## And Now the Rest of the Story

Jack Ratzlaff was diagnosed with prostate cancer shortly after returning home. He missed joining the team the following year, but he successfully overcame his cancer, and participated in several mission trips after that, until he was well into his eighties.

Both Heather and Kelly decided after they returned home that they wanted to become dentists. I encouraged them, even though I knew that only 1 out of 20 who wanted to become a dentist ever made it. Heather continued part-time in college on a pre-dental course of studies for a year or two. Then she and her husband, Todd, became proud parents of two beautiful girls. She has continued to work for me as a dental assistant, and has just completed her 11th year.

Kelly finished her pre-dental college training and was accepted at the University of Michigan, School of Dentistry. She graduated with her Doctor of Dental Surgery, D.D.S. degree, and was licensed in 2006. She is practicing dentistry in a city not too far from us.

We were all amazed at the tremendous excitement and appreciation expressed by the patients that Michael was able to fit with our donated glasses. Michael's method of fitting glasses was a very primitive trial and error method. This encouraged me to consider including optical into future missions.

I found out that the Lions Club would give me all the used glasses I needed. They were cleaned, reconditioned, and put in separate plastic bags with the prescription of the glasses written on the bag. I also found portable instruments that would tell us what prescription of glasses the patient needed. I found several people who offered to fit glasses, and could do that very successfully with just a little training.

With this unplanned donation of glasses and our primitive success, a new and valuable beginning in HTI's optical health service began. Today most HTI missions include fitting glasses. Unlike medicine and dentistry, the benefits of glasses are immediate, and result in patients becoming happy very quickly. Again this is something they would never in a life-time ever have the opportunity to receive.

Actually our optical service has become more popular than medicine or dentistry. We have more people wanting to see optical than either medicine or dentistry. Patients will live with a toothache or a sick body, if only they could see again. It has become a very important part of HTI's health care services, and has helped to open the hearts of many unreached people to hear and receive Jesus into their lives.

## HTI President

In September of 2000, we had our annual board meeting of Health Teams International. Dr. Miller, the founder and President of HTI for 14 years, announced that his health no longer allowed him to work as President and CEO of HTI. He was in his late 70s. We had only seven board members. The President and the HTI board are non-paid volunteers. Dr. Miller had been working at it full-time for 14 years.

I was vice-president, and had announced for several years, that I hoped to retire in 2000. I could retire financially, but I enjoyed my family practice so much that I was not ready to retire. The other HTI board members were younger with young families, and right in the busiest years of their practice. Clearly it was out of the question for them to take over HTI.

The board started discussing what we were going to have to do to dissolve HTI. We were a 501-C3 nonprofit corporation, and therefore we had to distribute all of our assets free to another charitable organization.

The Lord laid a heavy burden on my heart. HTI had seen over 30,000 unreached people become Christians in its first 14 years. I didn't think the Lord would be pleased to see that stopped, or for HTI to be disbanded. I had just witnessed one of HTI's most successful years in our history, with over 2000 people giving their lives to Christ and becoming Christians, in Cameroon alone. That didn't count the numerous other healthcare mission trips that HTI had led or sponsored during the past year. I didn't want to see that stop, and I'm sure the Lord didn't either.

I have always spent many hours working hard in my local church. Currently I was chairman of the deacon board; founder, president and coach of the men's church soft-ball league; part-time adult Sunday school teacher; vice president of our West Highland Christian Academy, which I started over 25 years ago. I was busy helping to manage and operate a multimillion-dollar Dental Corporation with 60 employees. I was treating patients at the office 4 days a week. I had four married children and nine grandchildren living very close to us, and they were busy in all types of different activities. I was as busy as a person could be. How could I take over the full-time position as President and CEO of HTI? On the other hand, how could I not do it, and see it disappear?

During our board meeting's lunch break, I went off alone and prayed. I called my wife and asked her if she would help me. She said, "Yes." I called Dr. David Shull, a somewhat new board member, who was not present at the meeting. Dr. Shull was permanently disabled and not working. I asked him if he would help me, particularly with the computer work. He was very good at computers, and I was not. He said, "Yes." I asked Dr. Miller if he would consider being Chairman of the Board of Directors, a new honorary position, and if he would continue as the editor of our HTI newsletter, at which he was very skilled. He agreed. I asked Jan, Dr. Miller's wife, if she would continue as HTI secretary and treasurer. She agreed.

My rationale was, that for all the time and effort I had put into my church work, I had seen little results in people becoming new Christians, whereas with HTI I had seen thousands of people coming to Christ. There are many people in my church that could take over my responsibilities, but there wasn't anyone at present, who could take over the leadership of HTI. I had felt for a long time that one of my spiritual gifts was organizing and managing, and that's exactly what HTI needed.

I accepted the responsibility of president and CEO of HTI. I resigned my position as deacon board chairman at the end of my term which was on January 1, 2001. I reduced my Sunday school teaching responsibility. I reduced my responsibilities as vice President of West Highland Christian Academy. I got someone else to coach the church softball team. I reduced my management responsibilities at the office, and cut my days of work down to 2 1/2 days. I got several other people to help me, particularly in my areas of weakness.

HTI has prospered and grown. We continue to divide the responsibilities of operating HTI, among the 20 board members we now have. I spend an average of 20 hours a week working on HTI business. It's really a pleasure because I feel that I am working for the Lord. Recently we celebrated our 23d HTI anniversary and reported that HTI had helped to reach over 80,000 unreached people who had become Christians. Praise the Lord!

# CHAPTER 23

# CAMEROON 4
# GAROUA & PYGMIES

Garoua is the provincial capital of a remote northeastern Muslim province of Cameroon just south of Maroua. Garoua has a sub -Sahara type of terrain, which is very hot. There is a large river which runs across Cameroon, through the town of Garoua, then north into Nigeria, before emptying into the Atlantic. There are many small and very primitive villages scattered throughout the area. They have no medical, dental, or optical treatment available.

Our host, Reverend John Ngoh, has an important Christian friend in Garoua. He is an army Captain, and a civil engineer who is in charge of a large group of soldiers. During peacetime, he is responsible for building government projects, such as bridges. Captain, as he preferred to be called, was a very strong Christian leader who had started several small churches throughout this predominantly Muslim area.

Pastor John Ngoh asked me before we came home from our Maroua mission, if I could bring a larger team back next year. I immediately started assembling a team when I returned home. It was exciting to see what God was doing through us in Cameroon. I had several previous Cameroon team members including Dora May and me, that wanted to return.

Dr. Kuenzi and his wife Martha, Dr. Hibbert and his wife Amelia, and Dr. Wiklund all asked if they could return to Cameroon with me. Dr. Bill Pratt called me and asked if he and his wife Peggy could join us. Dr. Pratt and Peggy had gone with me to Manchuria, China in 1995. Dr. Pratt had become a HTI board member in charge of China, and had led several teams to China but he desired a change.

Dr. Pratt had a young nurse, Gina Ridgeway, in his church that expressed an interest in going. Gina had been seriously dating a young man, Neil Partain, who had been born and raised in West Africa by missionary parents. He was at Tulane University, studying to be a M.D, specializing in tropical medicine, so that he could return to Africa as a missionary.

Gina's father wisely thought that if his daughter had any serious thoughts of marrying a missionary doctor, who was planning to go back to Africa, she needed to get a reality check, and find out what life in Africa would really be like. So he offered to pay for both Gina and Neil to go on our mission trip with us.

I was requested to speak, and show my slides to a large group of dentists in a city near my home, concerning my dental mission trips. After I lectured, a young dentist, Randy Kovicak, who had been a former student of mine at the University of Michigan, called and asked if he could go on my next dental mission trip. After finding our Christian faith to be similar, and our objectives to be the same, I gladly welcomed him to our team.

Dr. Kuenzi had a young nurse in his church, Julie Hutchcraft, that requested to join us. Dr. David Shull, a M.D., and HTI board member, who had been on several HTI mission trips previously, called and asked if he could join our team. Dr. Bill Rogers, a veterinarian from Montana, called me and asked if he could be used on our mission team. I told him about the success of our dispensing glasses on our last mission, and he said, "I can learn to fit glasses." He said, "I have a good friend who is an ophthalmologist. I will get him to teach me."

This made a team of 16. This was the largest team I had ever led. We had 4 MDs, 4 nurses, 3 dentists, and 1 medical student, someone to fit glasses, 2 dental assistants, and 1helper.

We packed heavily, and left in March, 2001. All of our flights went smoothly, but when we got to Douala we were missing several pieces of luggage. Air France paid us $100 for each missing piece of luggage. This is the first time I had ever been paid for missing luggage.

We stayed overnight in our usual nice Hotel Sawa in Douala, and prepared our luggage that we did have, to be shipped by train at 6 a.m. the next morning. The train went from Douala, through Yaounde, to Ngaoundere. Two of John's trusted helpers traveled with our 28 pieces of luggage. I went to the train station very early the next morning to see them leave. I then returned to the hotel and went back to bed. Our first day was designed for resting, recovering from jet lag, organizing, planning, shopping, and recovering our missing luggage.

On our second day, John had arranged for us to fly to Garoua. It took 2 1/2 hours rather than the two-day trip by bus, train, and again by bus which we traveled last year. Shortly after we arrived in Garoua, John's helpers arrived with all of our baggage intact. The reason we didn't fly last year was because we couldn't get all our luggage on the plane. Cameroon Airlines' domestic weight limits were much smaller than the international limits. This new idea of sending our luggage by train and letting us fly turned out to be great. It saved the team a long tiring two days of travel, and it gave us two more working days that we would have otherwise lost in traveling.

John's friend, Captain, was at the airport to meet us. John had flown to Garoua a few weeks earlier, and had worked with Captain, planning the details for our trip, such as hotels, meals, transportation, translators, and spiritual counselors. They visited and received permission from each of the chiefs in the rural villages that we hoped to visit, and made detailed arrangements. Upon arrival we went immediately to our hotel. When our luggage arrived, we unpacked and then repacked for our first day of clinic which was to be the next morning.

Each morning started at 6 a.m. with prayer, devotions, and details of our day's activity. The Captain gave his Christian testimony that first morning which was most memorable. It would fill many pages if I attempted to repeat it. He was a super dynamic Christian leader. The Army had court-martialed him twice because of activities involving his Christian faith, and they tried to get him discharged. He told us that he hired no lawyer. He just took the Holy Spirit with him to defend himself. He won both court-martials, and got a promise that they wouldn't bother him again. He was the top commanding Army officer in this 95% Moslem area.

Dora May and I were put in a large room in the hotel, since I kept all the dental supplies and equipment. I unpacked after each day's clinic, and then repacked for the next day. I only took a one-day supply at a time to the villages. We were on the third floor, and since there were no elevators, we had a lot of stairs to climb several times a day. This was the first time Dora May noticed one of her knees becoming painful. She ended up having total knee replacement two years later.

After our 6 a.m. daily prayer and devotions, we had breakfast at 7, and we were on the road by 8. The first morning we had an appointment with the Governor of the Province. The six doctors, John, Captain, and I met with the Governor. We introduced ourselves and explained to him how we planned to help his people. He was very friendly and wished us well.

Again, rather than going through the experiences of each village, I will try to summarize the highlights.

The villages were 45 minutes to an hour out of town. It was the dry season. It hadn't rained a drop in six months. The land was dusty, barren, dry, and sandy. We had three mini-buses and about 35 to 40 people with our luggage strapped on top. The villages we visited ranged in size from 200 to 500 people. They knew we were coming, and had informed the people in the surrounding villages.

Many times we drove through dry river beds and across desert sands where we could hardly determine the tracks of the road. We rarely saw another vehicle. John said that during the six month rainy season, these dry river beds filled with water and these villages were inaccessible by motor vehicle.

The villages consisted of many round mud huts with thatched roofs. There was often a small round mud grain bin near the houses that had been built eight to ten feet off the ground. That was where they stored their millet (a corn-like grain). They raised millet in the rainy season and stored enough to last all year until the next year's rainy season harvest. Occasionally there was a small herd of cattle or goats roaming the landscape, but it was hard to see what they could possibly eat.

Each visit to the villages started with a visit with the chief. The village chiefs were the supreme law of the community, and the villagers respected and obeyed their chief. One chief had six men that were around him all the time. I guess they were to make sure that people obeyed. Villages were frequently located in a little oasis, where they had a few trees and a good well.

Usually we set up our dental clinics under a shade tree, or under an open-air shelter that the chief had his people construct specifically for our one-day clinic. The medical team usually needed to work in an area where they could get some privacy, in case they needed to examine a patient's private anatomy.

Upon arriving in the villages, there was always a large crowd of people gathered, just waiting for us. After our courtesy call to the chief, John would hook up his portable battery operated PA system, and tell the people why we had come. He also shared with them a Gospel message. He did this while we spent 30 minutes setting up our clinics.

We would then have each patient register, where we took a brief history and gave them a number and routing slip. Medical patients first went to see the doctor, then to spiritual counseling which was done, one on one, for 10 to 15 minutes, and then to the pharmacy to get their medications. Every one received at least some Tylenol. If they didn't get something, they were unhappy and we had been donated plenty of Tylenol. Most everyone had some aches and pains somewhere.

The routing for dental and optical patients started with spiritual counseling, then to dental for treatment, or optical to get their eyes checked and to be fitted with glasses. That year we took a lot of glasses with us. HTI purchased an optical instrument called a photometer. It was a little bigger than the size of a flashlight. It read the lens of the eye, and greatly helped in determining the strength of glasses that was needed. I sent the photometer to Dr. Bill Rogers several months before the trip, and he got his ophthalmologist friend to teach him how to use it, and how to fit glasses.

We were surprised that Dr. Rogers always had longer lines of patients waiting to see him, than either medical or dental. He did an excellent job in examining and fitting glasses. The results he achieved created instantaneous gratitude and appreciation. He had very happy patients. We never saw one villager in any village with glasses when we first arrived. Because of the intense and continuous sun, no sunglasses for UV protection, very low humidity, cooking inside their smoke-filled huts, and blowing sand, the villagers had a lot of eye problems.

One day I noticed an unusual darkening in the sky, on the northern horizon. It wasn't clouds. We hadn't seen a cloud of any kind in many days. I asked Captain what it was and he told me, "Dust." The darkening area in the sky kept getting larger and rising over us, like a summer thunderstorm. In this case there was no lightening or clouds, but it was a storm, a dust storm. The wind didn't really blow very hard, but we started getting a fine layer of sand all over our dental instruments on our table.

I felt confident that the intense sun would kill any micro-organisms that were in the air or on the sand, so it was like sterile sand being deposited on our instruments. We used a large quantity of gauze, because we would wipe the sand off the instruments before we used them. We were under a shade tree, and there was no place to go inside. The medical team filled the inside of the small school, and they told us that the sand filtered in there also. The sandstorm lasted two days. John said, "Sometimes sandstorms become so bad, blowing south off the Sahara Desert, that airports close for days at a time."

In one village that we visited, the chief, who was about 50 years old, asked Dr. Dan to come into his private quarters to examine him. Upon removing his neck to toe gown, Dr. Dan who is a dermatologist, could immediately see many open sores which were very diagnostic of the terminal stage of AIDS. Dan immediately consulted with John, and together they sat down and told the chief what his diagnosis and prognosis were. They also explained the good news of the Gospel, and how that we Christians had the promise of heaven, and a new body after we die. The chief excitedly accepted Jesus and asked to become a Christian. No one else knew of his condition, as far as we could determine.

When we got ready to leave his 100% Moslem village, we presented the chief and some of his village leaders with Bibles written in their own language. The chief then stood on the front steps of their Moslem mosque, and surprised us by announcing to a large crowd of people that had gathered, over our PA loudspeaker system, "People, we have been worshiping the wrong god. We need to worship Jesus Christ."

In one of our villages we had a young American girl in her 20s, come into our clinic. She lived in a neighboring village and was a Peace Corp worker who was trying to help the people with their agricultural needs. She had been there over a year, and had not seen another white person. She quickly bonded with Gina, Neil, Randy, and Julie, who were all in their 20s. She stayed for lunch and had a good time talking with them.

In one village the Captain told us a short story about a young woman who was exceptionally beautiful. Recently a wealthy British man who was passing through the area saw her. He was convinced that with a little help, she would make an excellent British model. He offered to take her to London, and train her to be a model. This would greatly improve her standard of living, and give her wealth beyond her dreams. She said, "No." He increased his offer, and no matter what he said, she continued to say, "No." She didn't want to leave her family and friends in her village.

When we were in her village the captain pointed her out to me. She was truly beautiful. I had been taking photos of many people without any problem. When I started to take her photo, she turned and ran away. I think I can identify with her. I'm not sure I would trade the love and happiness of family and friends for fame and money.

The Captain's wife did all the cooking for the 35 to 40 people on our team for lunch every day. It was different, safe, and some of it was fairly good. One chief surprised us at lunch one day by having his cook kill a goat and cook it. At lunch time he brought out this whole cooked goat. The cook proudly carved it and gave everyone a big chunk of meat. It was good, I was told. Almost anything is good when you're hungry enough. Personally, I usually ate some cheese crackers, raisins, nuts, and Oreo cookies that I brought with me for lunch, along with a big bottle of Geno that John furnished us.

Geno was a unique fruit-tasting soda pop that I had never seen or tasted anywhere else in the world. Everyone in all of our teams to Cameroon loved the taste of Geno. I often thought that I ought to get a patent on Geno, bottle and sell it in the United States. I think it would be very popular.

One day Dr. Rogers fit one of our translators with glasses. He was a pastor from Garoua who not only translated, but agreed to follow-up on the new Christians in the villages. Early the next morning he came to our hotel expressing great happiness and excitement. He said, "With my new glasses, I can read my Bible again. I haven't been able to read my Bible for 10 years. I was so excited I stayed up all night reading, and never went to bed." I thought to myself, he's going to be a great translator today. He will probably fall asleep. He translated for one of the medical doctors and I was informed that he did well.

The local language in these villages was not French or English, but Fukenel. I was able to get scripture pamphlets in their language, free through World Missionary Press, and I brought enough for every patient. It was about 30 pages of key scriptures. It contained the complete message of salvation. It was excellent.

We went to one village on a Saturday, and had a good clinic with several hundred Muslims accepting Christ. We were not aware that there had been a Cameroon native Christian pastor that had been working in this village for over a year. He had six converts that would meet with him on Sundays for church. Evidently the pastor didn't know we were coming, and was out of town until late Saturday night. Can you imagine his surprise when he had over 200 people show up for church Sunday morning? He finally went out under a big shade tree to hold church. Sunday afternoon he came to our hotel, all excited, to tell us what had happened, and to thank us.

Sunday morning the Captain divided our team, and we went to several small churches around Garoua that had been helping us with translation and spiritual counseling. Gina, Randy, Julie, and Neil went to a small church that was new. They didn't have a roof on their new church yet, and the rainy season was coming soon. Julie had been given $100 from a woman in her church before coming, with instructions to give it to someone or some project that would honor Jesus. Julie presented the hundred dollars to the church, and everyone was exceptionally happy. That was exactly the amount that they needed to roof their church.

Dora May and I went to the Captain's home church, where his wife and 7 children attended. The Captain preached that morning, but on Sundays he would often visit one of several small churches that he had started, and preach there. The Captain's 7 children were between the ages of 3 and 15. He and his wife also adopted a very beautiful young lady, Anna, who was 20 years old. The Captain had led her to the Lord, and her Moslem father kicked her out of the house. She had nowhere to go. She came to the Captain for advice. He took her into his family, and she had been living with them for a couple of years. Anna's goal was to be a nurse, so she was very excited about working with the physicians all week. We even let her extract some simple teeth. She was a very pleasant, but shy, quiet, and reserved young lady.

I was shocked beyond belief, when at the church service she led the singing. She was anything but shy or quiet. She sang loudly, clapped her hands, stamped her feet vigorously, and danced around to the beat of the African-type music. I hardly recognized her as the same person, but it was a pleasant surprise. After church no one wanted to leave. They all stood around and talked and laughed, while we took lots of pictures.

On Sunday afternoon the Captain asked if we wanted to go down and see the big river that ran through the heart of Garoua. We hadn't seen a drop of water in this entire area in over a week, so we thought, why not? While we were walking along the river, a young man asked the Captain if we would like to see the hippopotamuses that lived in the river. The Captain asked us, and we said, "Sure." The young man asked us for a little money, so he could buy some sweet potatoes, which hippos like. We gave him a dollar or two and he was back in a couple of minutes with a bag of sweet potatoes. He went to the river bank and started to call the hippos, and splashed in the water at the edge of the river.

The Captain told us that there were two known hippopotamuses that lived in the river, and they were wild and very dangerous. The newspaper had a story a week or two prior, about a teenage boy that was swimming in the river, and was attacked and killed by one of the hippos. The paper concluded that the boy had swam between the mother and her baby, and that she was just protecting her baby.

It took several minutes, but finally we could see the eyes of the hippo coming toward us. The young man fed the hippo a couple of sweet potatoes, and coaxed him out of the water and back away from the riverbank, by continuing to feed him sweet potatoes. He asked me if I wanted to pet him. I slowly walked up next to him and stuck my hand out and touched him. What a rough, wet, slimy skin it had. I immediately backed away.

The hippo would open his mouth real wide and hold it open waiting for the man to throw in a sweet potato. He had only two teeth on the top and two on the bottom. They were rounded, broken off, jagged canine-type teeth. It was obvious he didn't chew anything with these teeth. I was told they pulled grass and vegetation up with their big heavy lips and swallowed it whole. He didn't eat the boy he killed. He just grabbed him and held him under the water until he drowned, and then let him go. I was told that hippos kill more people in Africa than any other wild animal.

The young man continued to pet the hippo's nose area, and said that he had done this many times, and he was a good friend of the hippos. Nevertheless, the hippo was really wild. By this time quite a large crowd had gathered. They were standing about two hundred feet away, which started to make me feel a little uncomfortable standing so close. The young man actually stuck his head into the hippo's wide-opened mouth. I got a photo of it. After a while the hippo suddenly turned and without warning, galloped very fast, making the ground shake, and he shot off the 3 or 4 foot bank into the water with a big splash. The show was over.

One morning on the way to a village we crossed over a brand-new stone and steel bridge which spanned a sizable dry riverbed. The Captain said, "This is one of the bridges that I designed and my Army Seabees have just finished building." He said it was the only connection between a dozen villages and the capital city of Garoua during the six-month rainy season.

When we arrived at the village right across from the new bridge, we found a semi-conscious seven-year-old boy lying abandoned on a bench. No one around knew who the boy was or where his parents were. The boy was not responding to our talking or shaking him. Dr. David Shull was a specialist in Emergency Medicine. He examined the boy, found that he had a high temperature and was severely dehydrated. They started an IV and gave him a heavy dose of intravenous antibiotics. By the end of the day the boy was up and walking around, and guess what? His parents showed up to claim him.

This village was bigger, and the crowds were much larger. I remember the people forming a long single-file line of 50 or 60 people. They stood out in the hot sun for several hours waiting to be seen. The temperature must have been well over 100 degrees. We closed medical registration, where they gave out numbers, early in the afternoon, so that everyone who was in line would be seen.

We dentists set up clinic under a big shade tree again. We were very busy extracting infected and painful teeth. Our line was not too long, and we finished everyone who had asked for help.

One afternoon in a different village, we also closed registration shortly after lunch, because we had given out all the numbers that we thought the doctors would be able to treat by the end of the day. As one of John's helpers was closing registration, a woman walked up to him and said, "I need to see the doctor. I have been walking since early morning from a distant village." She had three children; a 2-year-old that was walking beside her, holding her hand, a 1-year-old that she was holding in her arms and a very young baby that was strapped to her back. It was a very hot day, and the mother looked like she was ready to collapse. The native Cameroonian registrar took pity on the woman and started filling out the registration slips by asking simple questions. After he had completed the questions about the problems that the one and two-year-old children had, the mother then took the young baby off of her back, only to find that she hadn't made it in time. The baby was dead. The mother started crying hysterically, and turned around and started walking rapidly away. The young registrar panicked, and ran and told one of the physicians. By the time he got back, she had disappeared out of sight into the village. We never found her. The poor registrar was so shook up that it took us quite a while to calm him down.

One day we had a uniformed, armed Army Sergeant around our clinic most of the day. There weren't many trees. Underneath the main tree was where we set up our dental clinic. The Army Sergeant spent a lot of time under our shade tree. Dora May began to laugh and joke with him. When he asked my wife why we had come all the way from America to help them, she had an opportunity to share the Gospel with him. She was able to lead him to the Lord. This was the first person in her entire life she had the privilege of leading to the Lord. All the Christians were very happy at this news, because the predominantly Moslem military often persecuted Christians.

In several of these villages, Dr. Hibbert, a general surgeon, as well as Dr. Dan, a dermatologist, had the opportunity to surgically remove several cysts, fatty tumors, and skin lesions. Dr. Dan even supervised Neil, a medical student, while he surgically removed a couple of cysts.

One afternoon, Dr. Dan had an exceptionally beautiful young lady in her mid-20s come to see him, seeking his help. She was wearing a very pretty long dress, with a large pretty scarf wrapped around her neck right up to her chin in the scorching hot weather. Dr. Dan asked her, "How can I help you?" She started removing the scarf from around her neck and pulled the top part of her dress down to the top of her breasts. She had one huge, wet, raw, foaming, skin lesion that went from the bottom of her chin to the top of her breasts, and from one arm pit to the other. Dr. Dan had been practicing dermatology for over 30 years, and he had never seen anything as large and ugly as this. He asked her, "How long has this been present?" She said, "Several years, and it just keeps getting bigger." Dr. Dan and several of us looked at it and took pictures. Although Dr. Dan had never seen anything exactly like this, he thought he knew what it was, and he gave her a heavy antibiotic treatment. Check the rest of the story at the end of this chapter to see what happened.

In several of the villages, either at noon, or as we were packing at the end of the day, we would attract a large group of curious children. We frequently would sing a song to them, and then encourage them to sing a song back, and they nearly always did. Then we would sing another song, and then get them to sing one, etc. In one village we were shocked when we sang "Jesus Loves Me" to the children, and they turned around and sang it back, with the same tune, but in their own language. This happened several times when we sang Christian choruses with this particular group of children. It was a Moslem village. When we asked how they had learned these songs, we were told that a Christian had been in the area working with the children, and he had taught them these songs. Moslems basically have no songs. We were certainly surprised.

I was amazed and surprised at how easy it was to convert these Moslems to Christianity. Almost everyone, with whom we talked, wanted to become a Christian. We had two village chiefs who became Christians. Most of them had never heard the Gospel of Jesus Christ.

Before we left Garoua, Captain, John, several of the doctors, and I, went back to meet with the Governor. We reported that we had treated almost 4000 patients. We listed the most common diseases and the types of treatments, in a written report. The Governor thanked us, and then made a historic statement. He said, "You Christians aren't really that bad after all. We as a government need to take more steps to prevent persecution of you Christians." Praise the Lord. The Captain said, "That was the first time the Governor had ever made such a statement, and hopefully it would reduce the persecution of Christians, especially by the government, and allow the Christians to better and more freely share the Gospel." The Captain said, "In the long run, that may be the most valuable single aspect of our entire mission."

We finally had to pack our luggage and send it back to Douala, basically the same way it came, by bus and train. We flew back to Douala, and then got on a bus and went south, down the coast a hundred miles to the resort village of Kribi. We checked in at the fairly nice Hotel Framotel. We had a scheduled day of rest and relaxation. There was no sightseeing, because there was really nothing special to see. Visiting museums, cathedrals, temples, mosques, or zoos are not of great interest to me anyway, even if they were in existence. After touring over 137 countries, I had my fill of that type of sightseeing. Meeting and getting to know the people had become the most interesting parts of visiting a foreign country to me.

While we were waiting for our luggage and supplies to catch up with us, we spent a day at a beautiful beach on the Atlantic Ocean. We were the only ones at this large beautiful beach. John had arranged for six or eight young men to furnish us with a lunch while we were at the beach for the day. I had never experienced anything like it. They put a series of small plastic tables together for the 18 of us, including John and our driver. They put on tablecloths, decorated the tables with flowers, and put on nice place settings. They had plastic chairs for each of us, right in the sand, on this big stretch of beach, in the shade under some coconut palm trees. They even got some coconuts from the trees and cut them open so we could drink the fresh safe coconut milk.

The men came early that morning, and caught fresh shrimp out of the river, and cooked them in a large kettle over an open wood fire right on the beach. They had various fresh fruits and a variety of other things to eat. We had cold sodas that John furnished. It was an extremely memorable banquet on this beautiful lonely stretch of beach, with no bugs. We stayed at the beach most all day. The water was extremely warm. When we got back to our hotel, John's two helpers arrived with our luggage and supplies.

The next morning we drove 30 to 40 minutes farther south, down the coast, on a very primitive road. We came to a moderate-sized river, 30 to 50 feet across. We stopped and unloaded our supplies and carried everything a short distance down a bank to the river. Some of the same men that had fed us the day before were waiting with several long dugout canoes, with a motor on the back. We had with us several of John's helpers, and several church leaders from a small church in Kribi with whom John had been working. You could see that John was a fantastic organizer, putting all those details together for us.

We put 10 to 12 people in each boat, and pushed off and headed up the river. This river emptied into the Atlantic Ocean about a half mile downstream from where we left, but right at the mouth of the river there was a 30 to 40-foot cascading falls. We moved quite well through the water. There were a lot of fallen trees in the water that we frequently had to go around. Occasionally we would see a small dugout canoe floating or paddling downriver, loaded with items to be taken to the market in Kribi to sell.

We motored upstream about 2 1/2 hours. We never saw any signs of human life along the river. The river banks contained heavy jungle-like vegetation, including lots of bamboo. Finally we pulled our canoes up to a little clearing along the bank, and unloaded. We then started hiking, carrying our supplies along a winding jungle path. In 10 to 15 minutes we came to a clearing with several small thatched buildings, and several small people.

John had arranged this visit through the church in Kribi. Our boat drivers traveled the river frequently and knew about this village. This was a village that John had not had a chance to visit. This was a pygmy village, deep in the jungle, many miles from the nearest road. The only access was by river.

Our first order of business was to meet with the chief. Actually in this village there were two chiefs, a father 50 years old and a son about 30. John introduced himself and me to the chiefs and asked them if they knew why we had come to visit them. John was shocked, when the older chief said, "You have come to tell us about your great God, and we want to hear." While we set up our clinics, John told the two chiefs about Jesus, and they both eagerly became Christians.

I had my photo taken with these two small new Christian pygmy chiefs, one on each side of me. The tops of their heads were level with my shoulders. At five foot ten inches tall, I looked like a giant. This photo has appeared in several newspapers, newsletters, bulletins, and other literature. It turned out to be my most important photo of all the mission trips I have taken.

Many people gathered before we even got our clinics set up. Fortunately it was cloudy, because our clinics had to be outside in the little clearing. Their houses were very small and made of sticks and palm leaves. There were a lot of trees for shade, but under them was dense jungle, so we stayed in the clearing. We had a very successful clinic. John even led our bus driver, who had come with us, to the Lord. Dr. Bill fit our bus driver with glasses.

288

After putting his new glasses on he said, "Wow! Now I can see a lot better." I'm glad we didn't know he needed glasses earlier.

The pygmies were very open to the Gospel, and with the encouragement of their chiefs, everyone we treated asked to become a Christian. Again these people had never heard of Jesus, not even once in their entire life. I am glad we had several of the church leaders from Kribi with us. They shared that they had been trying to reach these people for a long time, and they assured us that they would follow up and shepherd them.

Dr. Kuenzi had been talking to the editor of the Kansas City Star newspaper. The editor challenged Dr. Kuenzi to take a picture of himself with several of the pygmies, while holding up an old copy of the Kansas City Star newspaper. He guaranteed Dr. Kuenzi that he would publish it on the front page of his newspaper. Dr. Kuenzi had me take the photo, and sure enough, after we got home, it appeared on the front page of the newspaper, along with a nice article.

These pygmies had never seen a doctor or dentist and as a result, we saw a variety of very unusual problems. We had to pack up and leave a little after 4 p.m. so we could get back before dark. We had seen all of the patients who had come to see us. Going down river was a little faster. The different types of vegetation along the banks of this jungle river were very fascinating. We heard many different sounds of birds, and even saw some monkeys.

Since John wasn't sure how our trip up the river to the pygmies was going to work out, he only planned one day. Since it was so successful, he planned more days in our later mission trips.

We arrived back at the hotel without any problems. The next morning we left for Douala to catch our flight home. On the way, our bus got a flat tire, out in the middle of nowhere. Our driver had never changed a tire and really didn't know what to do. Neil, having been raised in the jungle of Africa as a son of missionaries, had changed many flat tires out in the jungle, so he took over, and completely changed the tire while the driver watched. It was a four-hour trip. We stopped at the Arts and Crafts Market in Douala to purchase a few souvenirs. Our flight home was long, but uneventful.

In summary: This was my biggest team ever (16), with half the members being former Cameroon veterans. We had the most successful results of any team in HTI's 15-year history. John reported that we treated over 3551 patients, and saw 2500 of them become Christians, including two Moslem village chiefs, and two pygmy chiefs. In two weeks, I saw more people become Christians than I had seen in my evangelical home church in the last 50 years. This was not accomplished by any one person. It was truly a team effort, which actually involved several hundred people, in one way or another. At one point in time, I wasn't sure that I was supposed to lead another team back to Cameroon, but I'm so glad I did. The great success of this mission helped change the direction of my life.

# Now for the rest of the story

The Captain's daughter, Anna, went on to nursing school, graduated, and is working as a Christian nurse. The Captain's wife had the opportunity to come to the United States to attend an International Women's Missions Conference. After the conference, we had the privilege of having her stay in our home for a couple of weeks.

Many years later, I still hear from Randy. He has started a successful practice in Western Michigan. He got married and has a young family. He is very happy and hopes to go on more mission trips in the future.

I asked Gina, on our plane ride home, what she thought of Africa. She said, "I loved every moment of it, and I can't wait to go back." Neil and Gina were married the following year. Currently, I have lost contact with them.

Dr. Dan Wiklund continued to be haunted by the massive neck and chest lesion of the young lady he had treated. He took his photos to the Medical Library at the University of Washington where he taught, and did some research in tropical medicine. He discovered that he had missed the diagnosis, and his treatment was incorrect and ineffective. He felt so bad that he wrote Captain and sent a picture of the young lady. He told him that if he could locate the girl, take her picture and send it to him, he would send the proper medication to treat the girl, along with a nice gift for Captain's church.

It took the Captain two weeks to find the girl. He was back in one of the villages where we had a clinic, and was showing the picture of the girl to different people. One woman finally said, "I think that is a girl from a distant village." The Captain asked, "Will you take me there?" She did, and the Captain located the young woman. He told her why he had come. He took a picture of her and the lesion had gotten bigger. He sent the photo and information back to Dr. Dan. Dr. Dan bought a full year's supply of medication, at his own expense, and sent it back to the Captain with instructions, and also sent a nice gift for his church.

The Captain located the young lady again, and gave her the medication with instructions. He had the opportunity to sit down with her in private and share the Gospel with her, and lead her to the Lord. Being from a Moslem family, in addition to being unclean and a burden to her family with this infection, when she became a Christian, her father disowned her and kicked her out of the home. The Captain made arrangements for her to live with a pastor and his family in the nearby village.

As her lesion healed, and as she learned more about the Christian faith, she became more excited about being a Christian. It took a full year for the lesion to completely heal. The Captain reported that she had become a very strong Christian and she was sharing her wonderful testimony of how she was healed. She now has become an evangelist and has won many people to the Lord.

This must have also influenced Dr. Dan, because he subsequently went to London, and took the famous three-months Tropical Medicine Course. He has become a tropical medicine special consultant in the Seattle, Washington area. He has also become a valued HTI board member. He eventually replaced me as team leader allowing me the opportunity to open new mission fields for HTI. He has led teams of 20 to 25 team members back to Cameroon the last seven years, and is still going strong.

In 2008 Dr. Dan and his team were invited to the private office of the Prime Minister of Cameroon, where they were honored and given a personal thank you from the Prime Minister. As a result of Dr. Dan's strong leadership and commitment to serving our Lord, there have been an additional 15,000-plus unreached people in Cameroon that have accepted Jesus into their hearts and lives. Praise the Lord!

# CHAPTER 24

# WESTERN CHINA

China is a land of great diversity with nuclear power plants, atomic bombs, space satellites, great industry, and large modern cities like Shanghai, Beijing, and Hong Kong. One fifth of the world's population lives in China. It also has massive poor areas where people live in mud huts with no electricity, no running water, and in very primitive conditions. Western China is a part of China that is undeveloped. China is currently making a big effort to modernize its western area.

Health Teams International was invited to western China by a host, whose name I best not mention, due to the potential of persecution. Dr. Bill Pratt is our HTI board member who volunteered to coordinate HTI's China missions. He decided to accept this invitation, and lead this mission himself. He asked if I would be interested in joining him, so I did. We had a team of seven. We had two physicians, Dr. Dan Wiklund, and Dr. John Brothwell, (a general surgeon from Phoenix, Arizona). There were four dentists, Dr. Bill Pratt, Dr. Karl Furukawa, (a colonel in the Army stationed in Hawaii), Dr. Tara Wilson, (a young Christian dentist who was a new associate in my office), and me. Dr. Bill's wife, Peggy, also went as a dental assistant.

We left in the summer of 2001. This was the first mission trip that I ever went on that I did not serve as the team leader. Dr. Bill asked me to gather and pack all the dental supplies, as well as purchase Dr. Wilson's and my airline tickets. We were to join the team in Vancouver, Canada. These preparations were easy in comparison to being the team leader, but they became complicated very quickly when we arrived at our first airport in Detroit. I had scheduled for Dr. Wilson and me to fly United Airlines to Chicago, transfer with a one hour layover and fly directly to Vancouver.

After we had checked in at the airport and were waiting at the gate, it was announced that our flight would be delayed. The gentleman next to me said, "That's nothing new. I fly this flight every week and it's never on time." I was concerned because of our short layover in Chicago of only one hour. They didn't say how long the delay would be, so after a half hour passed I went up to the desk. The agent looked up at me and said, "You must be Dr. Charlick." Rather surprised I said, "Yes." She said, "I was getting ready to call for you. You're going to miss your connection to Vancouver. There is a direct flight to Vancouver at the next gate on American Airlines that is just starting to board, and they said they would have space for you and Dr. Wilson." I asked about our luggage, which contained all of our supplies, and she said, "It is being transferred now, no problem." This was a big relief, because if we missed the first connection we would miss two more connecting flights all the way to western China.

When we got to Vancouver, we had less than 30 minutes to meet our team, and catch our International Air Canada flight to Beijing. We found Vancouver's airport terminal to be very large and spread out. Dr. Wilson and I ran through the terminal to the gate, where we met Dr. Bill and the rest of the team. They were actually standing up and getting ready to board. This proved to be an excellent lesson for me. When planning multiple flights, plan much longer layovers between flights because of the possibility of delays.

After our overnight flight to Beijing, we were met by Chin, our Chinese tour agent, who took us to the Friendship Hotel. It was a very large excellent hotel right in downtown Beijing. We spent several hours checking out the local area on foot observing such strange places as McDonald's, Dairy Queen, Colonel Sanders, as well as stores for shopping. The next morning Chin picked us up at our hotel, and took us to the airport to catch our domestic Chinese Air flight to Xining, the capital of the large western Chinese province of Qinghai.

At the airport we had a luggage problem. Our international weight limit was 70 pounds, and each piece of our luggage was 70 pounds. Domestic weight limit was 50 pounds. All of our 14 bags of luggage were overweight. This was adding up to be a major expense, like over $1000. Dr. Bill talked with the agent, then his supervisor, trying to explain to him through our interpreter who we were, what was in our luggage and what we were planning to do in Xining. Finally the supervisor gave in, and loaded our entire luggage at no extra charge.

It was an interesting flight west as I sat looking out the window. At first there was dense population, then green farm lands, which gave way to the barren land of the great Gobi Desert. I could easily see where the Yellow River wound through the Gobi Desert, because like the Nile going through the Sahara Desert, there was rich green vegetation on both sides of the river, with everything else being a dull brown. I could frequently see cities along the river. When we flew over Xining I noticed a much larger and wider green area where another major river joined the Yellow River. We landed and were met by the Minister of Health and several other high government officials. They took us to a nice hotel, where we settled in and had lunch.

In the afternoon we were taken to a local hospital. Medical and dental services were provided only in government hospitals. There were no private medical or dental practices.

At that time all medical and dental services were provided free by the Communist government, the cradle to the grave philosophy. The hospital rooms were small, so they divided our dental team into three rooms. Fortunately Dr. Wilson and I were in the same room. Dr. Wilson was young, had only been out of school a few years, and this was her first mission trip. We set our clinics up so we would be all ready to go to work the next morning. They locked our rooms. Dr. Bill set his room up to do fillings. Dr. Karl had a specialty in prosthetics, so he set his clinic up in an area where they were doing prosthetics. Dr. Wilson and I planned to do just extractions.

That evening at our hotel our host had a welcoming banquet for us. Everyone who was anyone was there, including the local Government's Chief Health Officer, the Head of the Hospital, the Chief of the Hospital Surgery, etc. I'll have to admit that after 35 mission trips, and visits to over 137 different countries, I have never been treated with finer hospitality than by our hosts in western China. I was made to feel like I was the King of England, and was there on a royal visit. I don't know how a King could have felt any more welcome.

The only part of their graciousness I was not real excited about was when they got up from the table and came over and put their very expensive delicacies on my plate for me, so that I would be sure to get some. They served snakeskin, frog eggs, and the red comb from the head of a rooster, fish eyes, and many more. I ate it and didn't get sick or die. I was just fascinated by their unusual graciousness and hospitality

In the morning we went to the hospital where there were a lot of patients waiting for us. One of my first patients was a little old lady. When she opened her mouth I saw something I have never seen before or since. She had 30 black stubs of rotten teeth all decayed off level with her gums. Just as I was showing this unusual patient to Dr. Wilson, one of our host doctors came and asked me if I would speak to a group of doctors and nurses who had assembled in the auditorium. I said, "Sure." I turned to Dr. Wilson and said, "Why don't you remove these roots for this lady." Dr. Wilson had never seen teeth like this before either, and she had never before had the opportunity to remove many teeth that were decayed level with the gum. She said, "You've got to be kidding." I assumed the doctors in the auditorium were waiting for me, so I just said, "You can do it. They should come out easy. You can probably scoop them out with one of our surgical spoons." I could see she wasn't wholeheartedly buying my reasoning, so I added, "Dr. Karl's right down the hall if you need any help. Maybe you could just take half of them out today, and have her come back tomorrow for the other half." Then I left. I'm sure Dr. Wilson will never forget this initiation into missionary dentistry.

When I got to the auditorium there were about a hundred doctors and nurses listening to Dr. Dan Wiklund lecturing. Evidently they had found out that both Dr. Wiklund and I were University professors back in the U. S. I asked my host what he wanted me to talk about, and he said, "The medical relationships between dentistry and medicine." I gave a sigh of relief. That's an easy subject I thought to myself, I could talk for hours on that subject. Dr.

Dan's talk lasted about 45 minutes, and then they told me I had 45 minutes to speak. They indicated that we would plan to continue our lectures tomorrow. I had no problem lecturing, especially with the frequent rest periods for translation. I was amazed at the degree of attention and interest that the doctors and nurses displayed. We were told later that they never had a foreign doctor come to lecture or work with them before, and they knew very little about the relationship between dentistry and medicine.

Dr. Wilson successfully removed half of the lady's roots that were decayed off at the gum, and that afternoon the lady came back and Dr. Wilson took out the other half. Dr. Wilson admitted to me that the roots scooped out easily like I had indicated. She had a good feeling of accomplishment at the end of our first day.

We spent all week at the hospital treating patients and were kept very busy. Dr. Bill brought his restorative equipment and he and Peggy were in a different room doing only fillings. We saw very few restorations of any kind in peoples' mouths, and the few we did see were painful and abscessed, and required extraction. We saw a couple of what should have been removable partial dentures, but they were permanently cemented to the teeth and couldn't be removed. Since the patients couldn't take them out for cleaning, they had developed a massive infection underneath the partial denture as well as abscesses in the teeth to which they were cemented. We ended up extracting the teeth as well as the partial denture.

Saturday was the last scheduled day of clinics at this hospital. When we were packing up our supplies, one of the Chinese physicians offered to give me a traditional Chinese back and neck massage. I said, "No, thank you." He insisted, telling me he had spent four years learning this skill, and that he was a specialist. Dr. Bill finally suggested that I let him do it, or I might hurt his feelings. I finally said, "Ok." He sat me down on a stool and started working on my back and neck. The first thing I knew, he was pounding and then hammering on me with both of his hands. It didn't really feel very good. It hurt. After 15 or 20 minutes, which felt like forever, I had to get up and tell him, "Thank You." I have never had such a painful, sore back and neck in my life. The pain lasted almost a week, and he spent four years learning how to do this?

Saturday evening we had a farewell banquet, and it was just as exotic and exciting as our welcome banquet had been. Again all the important people were there. Dr. John, our general surgeon, had developed a very close relationship with the Chief of Surgery. They had done many major operations together. Dr. Dan and I had lectured almost every day. Supper was again a truly great example of fantastic hospitality.

Early Sunday morning we got up and walked to the only Christian Church in Xining, a city of over one million people. It was a church started by Adoniram Judson, with his Southeast Asia missions, over 200 years ago. The church was packed, and already in session. They made us as guests sit in the front row, where they had saved seats for us. After an hour of listening to their beautiful singing, and hearing them talk but not understanding a word, we got up and left. We were told the service would continue for several hours.

After church we walked around town, and did a little shopping. It was unusual to look down the street six or eight blocks in either direction, and see large totally barren sand dunes rising into the sky. I guess the part of the city we were in, was an area where the Yellow River Valley was quite narrow. In the valley everything was green and normal. We passed an old fort that we were told was very active in the days when Marco Polo's caravan stopped on his historic trips to Eastern China.

In the afternoon our hosts offered to take us out into the wastelands to a Great Salt Lake in the foothills of the Himalayan Mountains. We traveled by a small bus with many of our Chinese doctor friends coming with us. We traveled for a couple of hours, driving through barren winding sandy hills, without seeing many signs of life. At one stop at an old fort, there were some vendors. One vendor had a yak all decorated which he would let people ride. Dr. Wilson took a ride, and I got a great picture of her on the yak. When we reached the Great Salt Lake, we observed it from a high vantage point, where our host explained to us about its size. It was over 100 miles long and 10 miles wide. It was huge in size, making our Great Salt Lake in Utah look small. There was no outlet to the lake, and very few people lived around it. It was unusual. I guess it was the only sightseeing attraction they could think to show us.

Monday morning we loaded into a small bus and headed down the Yellow River Valley. The valley as I viewed it from the plane was green and heavily populated, but when the road went a slight way around the inhabited area and into the desert, it very abruptly became nothing but barren sandy hills. Then we would come back into the lush green valley. It was a very rapid and striking contrast.

After a few hours we came to the city of Lanzhou, where the valley widened. Lanzhou had a population of 300,000 to 400, 000 and was much smaller than the capital city of Xining. We were immediately taken to the hospital where we were ushered into a third-story walk-up conference room. The room had a huge circular row of tables which was very nicely decorated with flowers and large bowls of fresh fruit at each seat. There were already 20 to 30 white-coated men and women in the room around the table waiting for us. They ushered us to the empty seats on either side of the Hospital Director, and the welcoming ceremonies started. Dr. Bill, as team leader, was called upon to give a speech. It seemed different, but nice, that it was he, rather than I that had to give the speech. The welcoming ceremony lasted almost an hour with lots of speeches, while hot tea and fresh fruit was being served. Again the quality of hospitality was fantastic.

We checked into our hotel, had lunch, went back to the hospital, and set up for an afternoon clinic. The hospital rooms were fairly large, and it could be locked so our supplies and equipment would be secure overnight, because we planned to work there for several days. The patients were waiting for us in mass. The hospital staff organized and controlled them well, keeping them far down the hall, and away from the clinic. One tooth I extracted had a piece of calculus on it that was bigger than the tooth itself. I saved it for a souvenir, because I knew my hygienists at the office back home, wouldn't believe it unless they saw it.

The dental extractions were routine, but the people and their stories were very unique. One of the head physicians from the hospital brought his wife to me to have a couple of aching teeth extracted. I asked him, "Doesn't your hospital have a dental clinic?" He answered, "Yes, but I wouldn't take my dying mother to that clinic." He asked me, "Have you visited the clinic?" I said, "No." He said, "You should visit it. It is one floor up almost directly above your room."

When Dr. Wilson and I needed a break, we went upstairs to the dental clinic, and this is what we found. There were two young female dentists. We observed one dental chair, a light and equipment like we used in the 1920s in the U.S. They were in the middle of a very large otherwise empty room. Remember, this was a government owned and operated free dental clinic. They had two dental needles in the whole clinic, which they reused when they occasionally gave dental anesthesia, which they said was not very often. The dental hand-piece they used to drill the teeth was actually held together with adhesive tape, which of course couldn't be sterilized. Their sterilization was a hot plate on which they boiled instruments in a pan, which we know is only partial sterilization. They had no dental patients. They were very pleasant, and answered all of our questions, and showed us around. They said they averaged two or three patients a day. They indicated their government requirement was to see eight patients a day, but not that many people requested their services. They were the only dental clinic for an area covering a half million people.

We were told that without anesthesia, the screams from the dental clinic sometimes could be heard all over the hospital. If you think about it, the more they hurt people, the worse their reputation became and the fewer patients they would get, the less they would have to work, while getting paid the same government salary. It was a sad situation, but not uncommon to socialized dentistry. Now I can understand better why the physician made the comments he did.

Dr. Bill worked in a private room doing restorative fillings. One of his patients shared with him, in strictest privacy, that she and her family were Christians. When Dr. Bill asked her how she became a Christian, she said her family had become Christians many years ago when Adoniram Judson of the Southeast Asia Mission came to the area. They had remained Christians ever since. She then shared the tremendous persecution her family had endured over the years, particularly under the Communist regime. She said, "Currently we are keeping our Christianity very quiet and a secret in order to survive." She wanted to invite us to her home, but was afraid to do so. If someone were to see us, they might start to ask questions, and it might cause more trouble.

When we got to this smaller town, our Christian host recommended we share Jesus openly with our patients. He said our translators personally were not allowed to share Jesus with patients, but as interpreters they could interpret whatever we said without fear. Some of our team members hadn't had a lot of experience sharing Jesus with unreached people. Our Christian host and interpreters said, "If you don't feel comfortable sharing the salvation message with your patients, you can say anything you want, and we will share the salvation message with the patients, because no one else will know what you say anyway. Just keep saying something, anything, and we'll share Jesus with them."

There were two patients at this hospital I will never forget. There was one older lady that had several abscessed teeth. We gave her anesthesia, and then asked her, "Do you know why we came all the way from America to help you?" She said, "No." We said, "Because we love you. We are Christians and we are taught to love everyone and to help those in need. Do you know what Christians believe?" She said, "No." We asked, "While we're waiting for the numbing medicine to work, do you want us to tell you what Christians believe?" She said, "Oh yes," with great enthusiasm. We spent 20 minutes or so and explained what a Christian believes, and what you needed to do to become a Christian. All the time we were telling her these things, tears poured out of her eyes, and because she was lying back in the dental chair, they collected in her ears. We continually blotted her ears to keep her tears out of them so she could hear. Finally we asked her, "Would you like to become a Christian?" Her answer changed the direction of my life.

She said, "You know our Communist Government has been telling me all my life that there was no god, but deep down in my heart I knew there had to be a god. I'm getting old, and will be dying soon, and I didn't know how to find God. Finally you came all the way from America, to tell me how to find God through Jesus." She prayed and asked Jesus to forgive her sins, and for Jesus to come into her heart and life. She got up from the chair and hugged us all with cries of joy. She said, "Today I am the happiest person in the world." We all got so excited we almost forgot to extract her abscessed teeth.

Today we have over 6 billion people in the world, and over 2 billion of them have never heard of the name of Jesus. According to a recent survey, 68% of the people of the world have heard of Coca-Cola, but only 62% have ever heard of Jesus. This elderly lady reminded me that there are still over 2 billion people out there, many of them just waiting for someone to come tell them about Jesus.

A couple of days later we had a larger than average man, who was better dressed than most, who brought his wife into our clinic to get some abscessed teeth removed. We gave her anesthesia, and while we were waiting for her to get numb, we went through the same discussion as we had with the elderly lady the day before. We started out asking her if she knew why we came all the way from America to help her, etc. When we asked if she would like to know what Christians believe, she said, "Yes," so we started telling her.

Her husband stood by the side of the chair with his arms folded, and watched and listened. Shortly into our explanation, he interrupted and said, "But I'm a Communist." In order to be a member of the Communist Party you need to sign a sworn affidavit every year that there is no god. We said to the man, "That's all right; we're not talking anything about government. We are talking about what is going to happen to you after you die." We then continued explaining the Gospel to his wife. Again the man interrupted with a sterner and louder voice and said, "But I'm a Communist." We said the same thing to the man assuring him this didn't have anything to do with government. We were talking about what was going to happen to you after you die. And we continued discussing the Gospel with his wife.

The third time the man said, "You don't understand, I am the Secretary of the Communist Party for over a million people in this area." My first thought was, oh boy! We might spend the night in the pokey tonight. In an attempt to improve the situation, we stopped, took off our gloves, and went over to him and put a hand on the man's shoulder, patted him on the back, and congratulated him. We told him "You have a very important job and a lot of people to take care of." He smiled. We assured him that Jesus loves Communists, He loves everybody. We reassured him again that this had nothing to do with government. We were talking about what was going to happen when you die. I'm not sure how it happened, but the Lord gave us strength and courage to continue sharing with his wife. When we got to the end we asked his wife the same question we asked everybody, "Would you like to become a Christian?" Before she had a chance to blink her eyes, her husband, the Secretary of the Communist Party, said in a loud voice, "Yes, I do." We led both of them to salvation in Jesus Christ. He told us afterwards, "You know, I'm 55 years old, and no one has ever told me about Jesus before."

This taught me two important principles to live by. First, everyone deserves to hear about Jesus Christ at least once in their life, even the Secretary of the Communist Party. Secondly, I again realized we don't save anyone. It's only the Holy Spirit working in the hearts of people that changes them. We are simply God's humble messengers. There is no way we could have changed this man's hardened heart. Only God did it, and surprised all of us.

We had a lot of people come to the Lord in our dental clinic in our second week, including several Communist Party members. This included teachers, soldiers, administrators, police, and other government officials. We had some who said they were Communists, and they were afraid to become Christians. I had one old Tibetan Buddhist Monk who said he didn't even want to hear what Christians believe. He is the only person to date who has ever told me that. Many of the non-Communist Party members accepted Jesus without any fear, or at least without any visible fear.

Dr. Wilson worked right beside me, and had an excellent Christian interpreter. They were leading people to Jesus just as fast as I was. This was a new and exciting experience, leading so many people to Christ right in our dental chairs. The follow-up in this area was difficult, but after we left, one of the male translators was planning on staying for a while and following up on as many of the new Christians as he could. We didn't want to tell one person that another person was a Christian, because of the possibility of persecution. There was no church in this entire area. The nearest church was two hours away in the capital, the one which we had attended on Sunday. For lack of anything better, we recommended this church to the new Christians.

We had one patient who was a member of the Communist Party, and when we asked her if she wanted to become a Christian she said very quietly, "Yes." When we prayed with her she didn't repeat the prayer. When we asked her why, she said she was afraid someone might hear her. She was afraid she might lose her job and she had two children to support. She surprised me by saying, "I prayed silently, and no one needs to know that Jesus is in my heart now."

On the last day our hosts divided up our team, and they sent us to different small village clinics. We usually don't divide up our teams, but for one day we agreed. Dr. Dan and I, along with our interpreters, were put in a shiny new black car, and traveled up a populated valley that was a tributary stream to the Yellow River for almost an hour. I couldn't help but marvel at the luxury and smooth ride of this very nice car. I figured it must be a Mercedes or some fancy expensive car. Finally curiosity got the best of me, and I asked, "What make of car is this?" I was told, "It's a Volkswagen, made right here in China, and it is the most popular car in China." Wow! What a surprise!

The clinic to which we were taken had an old dental chair, which didn't work, so I pushed it aside and used a regular straight-backed chair. They had never had any dental supplies or equipment and never had a dentist come to this area. Needless to say, we were kept very busy all day. We were able to lead several people to the Lord that day. The patients were very appreciative and couldn't do enough for us. We were told that the people had no source of transportation to go to Lanzhou for treatment.

On our last day our host wanted to thank us by showing us around the area. They picked us up in the morning with several small vehicles. I rode in a new Jeep Grand Cherokee. Here I was on the other side of the world, and riding in a vehicle that was built 60 miles from where I live, and I hadn't ever ridden in one before. They took us up a different tributary river valley of the Yellow River, for about two hours. The road was under major reconstruction. It was very hilly, and there were dozens of workers that were cutting down the sides of these large hills by hand. I experienced another first in my life. It hadn't rained in many months and where they were cutting the sides of the hills down, it was very dusty. It was like powdered snow. Our car tires sank several inches into the powdery dust. Sometimes the car in front would stir up so much dust that we had to stop, because we couldn't see anything. I have been in a white-out of snow, but this was the first time I had ever been in a brown-out of dust. I will credit the Jeep Grand Cherokee for one thing; there was not one speck of dust that got into the passenger space.

We visited a mountainside Tibetan Buddhist temple. It was very old, ornate and beautiful, but it made my heart sad knowing that most of these Buddhist Monks, who had dedicated their lives to pleasing God, had never had anyone tell them about Jesus. They didn't know any different.

After returning to the city, we had a nice lunch under canopies in the middle of a fruit orchard. We returned to the hotel and packed for our return trip home. We had a little time left before supper, so several of us took a walk. We walked through the area of several beautiful rice paddies terraced up the side of a large hill. I was fascinated by how they channeled water into these rice paddies halfway up this big hill. When we finally got to the top of this hill, we could look down over the entire city, the river, and the whole valley. We met a local young man at the top of the hill and we got into an interesting sign language conversation, in part, using sticks to draw pictures in the dust. We had no translator with us

On our way down the hill, we met the young man we had attempted to communicate with at the top of the hill. He was sitting in front of his living quarters, at a brick factory where he worked. He invited us into his living quarters, and served us tea. He had a one room apartment about 10 feet wide and 25 feet long. It had a bed, a table, a couple of chairs, and that was about all. It made me feel embarrassed because I have a bigger and nicer garage than his house.

When we got back to the hotel we were rushed off to our supper restaurant. We didn't know it, but our host had planned a special thank you banquet for us. Again we experienced some fantastic western Chinese hospitality.

In Summary: My time in western China proved to be very valuable not only to our patients, but to me personally. We probably treated more patients, in Lanzhou and treated them better and safer in one week than the two hospital dentists treated in one year. We had the opportunity to openly share the Gospel with our patients in Lanzhou, and many of them accepted Jesus into their hearts and lives. We even had two of our hotel room maids, and one waitress in the restaurant in which we ate regularly, accept Jesus.

Most of all I learned two valuable principles that have greatly influenced my life. One is that there are millions of people in this world just waiting for someone to come to tell them about Jesus. Secondly, everybody deserves to hear about Jesus at least once in their life, even a Secretary of the Communist Party.

## And Now the Rest of the Story

The great sense of personal satisfaction and fulfillment in serving our Lord on this trip has resulted in all of our team members going on numerous additional mission trips, except Dr. Wilson who currently has the priority of mothering her new young family.

# CHAPTER 25

# CAMEROON 5
# NGAOUNDERE

Ngaoundere is the capital of one of Cameroon's seven provinces. It is a province to which Reverend John Ngoh has never taken one of our HTI teams. John's goal is to share the Gospel with the unreached people in all seven provinces. This will be the fifth province in which John and a HTI team will have worked. It is also the home of the country's Supreme Moslem Chief who has the ultimate authority over all the Moslem Chiefs.

I accepted the challenge to get a team together and return to Cameroon in the spring of 2002. I was able to put together a team of 13. There were six returning team members; Dr. Dan Wiklund, Dr. John Hibbert and his wife, Amelda, Debbie Locher R.N., Dr. Bill Rogers, and me. Dr. Rogers brought his wife, Helen, with him for the first time. I had a dental hygienist from my office, Tammy Jones that asked to join us. I met a pharmacist, named David Worms who agreed to go. I had a neurosurgeon from Toronto Canada, and a nurse, Dottie Staggers, that requested to join us. Dr. Rick Bedinghaus, an Oral Roberts University dental graduate, and a former student and friend of Dr. Miller, asked to join the team. A lady named Betty Woods from Tampa, Florida, called me and asked to join our team as a helper. It's interesting how all these people find out about our mission trips, and how they locate and contact me. They literally come from all parts of the U.S. and Canada.

We packed and left in March of 2002. The same day a big snow storm hit the Midwest. Everyone finally got to Chicago, our meeting place, except Dr. Rick Bedinghaus. He was coming from Kansas City, and they actually closed the Kansas City Airport because the storm was so bad.

The rest of us left Chicago on Air France four hours late. We were afraid the Chicago airport might be closed, because it was snowing very hard, but thank goodness, it wasn't. We only had a four-hour layover in Paris to get our connecting flight to Cameroon, so naturally we were concerned that we might miss our connection. Upon arrival in Paris, the crew called our team to the front of the plane first, and took us down the outside side stairs of the ramp, and put us on a waiting bus. It took us a long distance around the airport. When the bus finally stopped, they had us to go up the outside stairs of the loading ramp, and board our waiting connecting flight. They immediately closed the door and took off. We arrived at Douala on time, and most of our luggage arrived also. I will never know how our luggage made it.

John picked us up and we went to Hotel Sawa for a good night's sleep. We missed one night of sleep, and lost six hours during our traveling. The next morning, at 4 a.m., John, his two helpers, and I took the luggage to the train station. John's 2 helpers went with our luggage all the way to Ngaoundere.

Our first day in Douala was for rest to help us recover from our jet lag, organization, shopping, and receiving the rest of our luggage. We were surprised when Dr. Rick Bedinghaus arrived the next day on the same flight with our missing luggage. Our team was complete.

The next morning we flew to Ngaoundere, the capital of Adamawa Province near the center of the country. This area was 95% Moslem. The Captain and some of our former interpreters were at the airport to greet us. We went to a fairly nice hotel and unpacked. In the afternoon John, the Captain, the doctors, and I went to the capital building and paid a courtesy call on the Governor. He was very friendly and cordial, and insisted on assigning two armed military men to accompany us on all of our trips out of the city. This seemed to be a nice gesture but unnecessary, until we heard why. A foreigner had been robbed and murdered on one of the roads in his province a few weeks ago. It made national and international news headlines. It was a great embarrassment to the Governor.

We then went to visit the Supreme Moslem Chief. He was the head chief over all the local village chiefs in the Moslem northeast one-third of the country. He welcomed us into his large, mud and thatched, guest receiving quarters. There were big cushions around in a circle on the floor where we sat. He was very kind and gracious and served us tea. John and the Captain talked with him for about 45 minutes, while we sat smiling, not understanding a word of what they said. John told him that we were Christians, and told him exactly what we planned to do. He gave us his blessing, and insisted that we take two of his armed guards to protect us. We told him about the Governor's soldiers, but he insisted also.

It's an interesting relationship between the Governor and the Supreme Chief. The Governor is the official government lawmaker for the province, with the police and a national army to back him. The Supreme Chief has the respect and confidence of the people's hearts, and the people will generally do what the Supreme Chief commands, regardless of the Governor's laws. The Governor and the Supreme Chief are routinely conferring and compromising, to make sure that they are in agreement to keep the people happy and controlled. We were told that the Governor was helpless to make new laws without consulting with the Supreme Chief first. It seemed to be working.

The next morning we left for a village an hour and a half away, using three minibuses. We stopped and picked up a local pastor of a Christian church in Ngaoundere and several of his church leaders. They had committed to help with evangelism and to do the follow-up work. Upon arrival, we stopped at that village chief's house, and did our usual courtesy call. He had a deep well in his front yard that had a group of people around it drawing water. We learned that all of the other wells in the village had dried up during this unusually dry season, and that the river was contaminated. This meant that this was the only well for the town of several hundred people. They said the chief's well had never run dry.

We went to the top of the little hill, where there was a nice breeze, to a health center building that the chief had built for his people. There was one nurse there who welcomed us and helped us get set up. The dental team set up their clinic in front of the building under a large shade tree because of the good light and a nice breeze. Medical had to set up inside the building, to get privacy for some of their patients. Some of the Moslem women would only let the female nurses look at their female problems. The nurses often had to go to the doctor and describe the signs and symptoms in order to get a diagnosis and the proper medication. Four of the chief's wives, and 15 of his children, came as a group to see the physicians. The chief sat under the shade tree in the breeze and watched us.

This whole northeast part of Cameroon had at one time become Christian, a hundred years or more ago. The missionaries got after the chiefs who had multiple wives, and told them they could only have one wife. They weren't happy about that. Then the Moslems came along and informed the chiefs that the Moslems worship the same God, and it was all right for them to have up to four wives. The chiefs and the people quickly changed and became 100% Moslem. Cameroon Moslems were not real strict or militant. Women there were treated much better than most Moslem women. They didn't have to wear head or facial cover-ups, although I never saw any of them in blue jeans or shorts.

During a slow period, Tammy offered to clean one of our armed military guard's teeth. He agreed and sat down in the dental chair, keeping his machine gun with him standing up between his legs. We were just using regular chairs. I noticed that the barrel of the machine gun was pointed directly at Tammy's head as she worked. She didn't notice it until I asked her if she were accustomed to cleaning people's teeth with a loaded machine gun pointed at her head. We all laughed and he put it down.

A couple of the villages we visited had no shade trees, or any buildings in which we could work. When John visited these villages before we came, he gave the chief $20 and asked him to have his people build a shelter under which we could work and not be in the direct hot sun. They did great. They put poles in the ground and then put poles and palm branches on top. We were in a different village each day, and the people always welcomed us and were very appreciative.

At the end of each day we had a presentation ceremony, where John and I presented a complete Bible in their own language to the chief, and several New Testaments to other village leaders. Dr. Rick Bedinghaus brought several nice soccer balls with air pumps, and presented one to the chief or to the school teacher, if they had a school. Soccer is the national sport, and really the only sport in Cameroon. Cameroon recently won the World Soccer Championship. The small villages we visited had no soccer ball and I sometimes thought that the people, and especially the young people, were more excited about getting the soccer ball, than they were the Bibles. The people were very open to the Gospel and almost everyone we treated accepted Jesus, including some chiefs. We left a big project for the Ngaoundere pastor and his church leaders to follow-up and disciple. I gave the pastor a video of the Jesus Film in their native language. He said he had a projector to use to show the film and was really happy to receive it.

After four previous missions to Cameroon, there was nothing particularly unusual about our clinics. It was very hot and we were extremely busy, but at least we didn't have any dust storms. Every time I go to Cameroon I am reminded that the black Africans have the hardest teeth in the world to extract. We often worked in our dental clinic with straight-backed ordinary chairs. I often had to bend over and turn upside down to see where I was working. It was interesting that I never went home after a hard, hot, long, busy day of work with a backache. This didn't happen occasionally, it happened every day, no backaches.

In the U.S., in my office, I have a modern computer- operated dental chair, which almost tips the patient upside down for me. I have fantastic lighting, good suction, and a chair side assistant. I have the latest scientifically designed dental stool on which to sit. I don't work nearly as hard or as long, and the temperature is always just right, but frequently I go home with a backache. You explain that! My explanation is, when I am serving the Lord, He takes care of me.

Saturday we flew back to Douala, and went by bus to John's hometown of Limbe. John's two helpers brought our luggage back by train, which took two days. They arrived Sunday evening in plenty of time for our Monday clinic.

Sunday morning we went to John's Church, and after lunch, John took us to a beautiful beach on the Atlantic Ocean.

The hotel where we stayed was on the ocean, but it had no beach. Dr. Dan and I were assigned to stay in separate rooms, in a small cottage close to the water, because the main hotel building was full. The first night we were there, Dr. Dan saw a shadow of a man walk in front of his large screened window and stop, and he appeared to be looking inside. Dr. Dan gave a very loud shout, "Get out of here!" He quickly disappeared. The next morning we heard the story about the night watchman who was patrolling the grounds around the cottage, and almost had a heart attack, because he was scared to death by someone out of nowhere, yelling at him. Dr. Dan just smiled when he heard about it, because he had been rather frightened himself.

Monday, it was back to the same routine; 6 a.m. prayer and devotions, 7 a.m. breakfast, then load up so we could be on the road by 8 a.m. Our morning devotions often proved to be very interesting. All the team members had an opportunity to share, which usually consisted of their testimony. That frequently included an autobiography as to how they met Jesus, how they had grown in the Lord, what they had done for the Lord, and what the Lord had done for them. By the end of the trip you felt like you knew each team member very personally. For instance our neurosurgeon had just lost his wife of 35 years a few months before our trip, after a two-year long struggle with cancer that ended in a very horrible painful death. He was depressed, and knew one of the best ways to treat depression was to get busy helping others, particularly those who are much worse off than yourself.

The second week we worked in the Southwest Province, our sixth Cameroon province, which contained Limbe and Mount Cameroon. Most of the people in this province spoke English. There were several unreached native tribal groups that lived fairly isolated at different elevations on this huge, single pointed, volcanic mountain. Mount Cameroon is the largest mountain in West Africa. It had a somewhat quiet eruption with a major lava flow down the side of the mountain, just three years prior to our trip.

Early in the week John and I went to a radio station studio, and had an interview taped, telling about our work and our upcoming clinic that we were going to have in Limbe, which was open to the public.

John had 15 of his Bible school students come with us each day. These Bible school students were very excited to put into practice what they had been learning in school. They counseled with our patients 15 to 30 minutes, sharing the Gospel with each one of them. They had almost 100% success.

Each morning as we were setting up our clinics, the students would sing upbeat gospel songs as they danced to the beat. This drew a big crowd. John would then share a short Gospel message with the people.

It really worked well when John had trained Christians who could speak the local language and share the Gospel with each patient. That meant that we professionals could stick to doing what we do best, and that is treating patients. With this combination we could see almost twice as many patients. Sometimes the total number of people working together as a team was over 40. This also helps to explain why we have had more people accepting Christ on our Cameroon missions than anywhere else in the world.

Again I will try to summarize the highlights of the four villages in which we worked. One day as we drove up the side of the mountain, we stayed on a very small narrow two-track path, plowing through 10-foot high weeds, before reaching our isolated village.

Dr. Bill and his wife became very skilled at fitting glasses. One patient for whom they were fitting glasses had a swollen cheek. It looked like he had a ping-pong ball in his cheek, and it felt hard to touch, so Dr. Bill sent him to me.

He was an older man, and upon examining him I saw the largest accumulation of calculus, or tartar, that I have ever seen in my life. It was on the outside of his upper back teeth and it was about the size of a half of a medium-sized chicken egg. It surely did make his cheek bulge. The teeth were loose. I asked him how long it had been there, and he said, "It has been growing there for many years." It was not painful at all and he could eat anything he wanted. There was no way that I could remove the calculus without the teeth coming out with the calculus. If not treated, his teeth would eventually get loose enough that they would probably fall out by themselves. Right now he was doing fine, and he strongly indicated he didn't want us to do anything. We just took photos, and gave him a toothbrush and some aspirin in case it became painful.

One day we went to a small village which was the hometown of the current Prime Minister of Cameroon. It was similar to other villages, except that it had a beautiful white cement government health building with eight rooms. It only had one part-time nurse, who was very glad to see us. He helped us a lot.

Dr. Dan, our dermatologist, had a patient come into the clinic that had a tumor on his back about the size of a softball. It wasn't painful or malignant, but it was giving him a lot of problems when he tried to lie down at night to sleep. Dr. Dan numbed it, using our dental anesthesia, and completely removed it, and sutured it up in about 15 minutes. It was a non-malignant fatty tumor. Needless to say, the man was very happy.

John heard that the Prime Minister was in town. John had a shipping container of supplies from the U.S. on which he was paying monthly rent. It had been tied up in customs for over a year. He knew that with one word from the Prime Minister, the problem would be solved. John walked into town to find the Prime Minister. In a short time he returned, saying, "Yes, he is in town, but his bodyguards wouldn't let me anywhere near him."

In the middle of the afternoon, the Prime Minister and his wife came strolling down the road, and walked right up to our clinic without any visible bodyguards around. He just wanted to tell us thank you for coming and helping his people. He told us we were welcome in his country anytime. We all had our pictures taken with him. John gave him one of his business cards and told him of his problem with customs. The Prime Minister said, "Consider it done," and it was. John got his container of supplies released from customs very quickly. The Prime Minister and his wife were extremely cordial and nice, and repeatedly thanked us for coming. He spoke very good English. That was a pleasant surprise.

In one village we had two visiting village chiefs whom John won to the Lord, within an hour after we had arrived.

An older patient came with a very large burn scar involving most of his arm. He had burned it many years ago. He also had a large number of weeping deep ulcerated lesions in the scar. Dr. Dan said, "The ulcerated lesions were cancer, squamous cell carcinoma." He told us that this type of cancer is very common in old burn scar tissue. There was nothing that could be done for the man, short of amputating his arm, and he probably wasn't healthy enough to survive that type of operation, which we couldn't do anyway. Either way, it would be fatal. The best thing we could do was to tell him about Jesus. We did, and he gladly became a Christian. We treated and helped a lot of patients, but there was the occasional patient that we could not treat, and it always broke our hearts.

These villages were all near the Atlantic Ocean, where it was not only hot, but very humid. I often would observe two puddles of liquid on the floor by my feet. At first it puzzled me, but then I realized that my hands were sweating underneath my gloves so much, that sweat was running down my arms and dripping off my elbows and forming the puddles on the floor.

There were frequent rain showers near the coast, which helped make the vegetation very green. We usually had to find an area inside in which to work, because of the possibility of rain.

In one village we were directed to a school which was in session. Upon our arrival, the students were all sent home for the day, and we took over and worked in the small school. I felt bad but we were told that it was the only place large enough in this town for us to have our clinics. I specifically remember this day because it rained torrents and I was amazed to see so many native people just walking around out in the rain like nothing was happening.

One village we worked in, dental and optical were put in a separate building from medical, which was a little different type of structure. Upon inquiring, we found out that it was the courthouse for a rather large area. Obviously, court wasn't in session.

The last day of clinic was held in John's church. We had an unusually large number of people, probably because of the radio broadcast. John's church was still in the large one-room warehouse. During the week, John divided the room into sections and used it as a Bible school where he taught 15 to 20 students, enrolled in a one-year program, studying to be pastors.

Over the years we had come to know several of the graduates from John's Bible School who had become very successful pastors. One graduate, Emmanuel, with the help of John, had opened a branch Bible school for John, in another town, and he had 15 students. Emmanuel had been my personal interpreter on one of my earlier Cameroon missions when he had been a student. We became very good friends. On our last clinic day at John's church, Emmanuel and his new wife traveled a long way and came to see us. We enjoyed visiting with them.

On my earlier trip when Emmanuel interpreted for me, I had an old aluminum folding lounge chair that I had brought and used for my dental chair. The fabric tore and the aluminum broke to the point I knew it was irreparable. When I started to throw it away, Emmanuel asked if he could have it. During Emmanuel's visit he told me that he had successfully repaired my old dental chair and it was now a proud piece of his living room furniture. I noticed that he was still wearing my old tennis shoes that I had given him several years ago. I gave him a lot of my current clothes, a flashlight, and a variety of other things that I thought he could use.

That evening we met a man at our hotel from the U.S., who was traveling through the area, acting as an adviser to the people managing Zoos. He mentioned that the zoo in Limbe had a gorilla which had a very bad eye infection and he was concerned that it would probably kill him. Dr. Bill Rogers, being a veterinarian said, "Why don't we surgically remove the eye?" The adviser agreed that would probably be the only way to save the gorilla's life.

We talked with this adviser for quite some time that evening, sharing some of our experiences, and he in turn shared one of his most unusual experiences with us. He was swimming in a river when he was attacked by a hippo, which grabbed him by the waist and took him down, under the water. Fortunately, being an African animal expert, he knew his only chance of survival. He reached around and stuck his fingers up the hippo's nose. This opened the valve which let water into the hippo's lungs. The hippo immediately discharged him and headed for the surface. Needless to say, he swam away in the opposite direction and got away safely.

Early the next morning before we were to leave for Douala, Dr. Rogers, Dr. Dan, along with several of our team members who wanted to observe, and I went to the zoo. The adviser already had the gorilla asleep, and had him on a table. Dr. Rogers with Dr. Dan assisting took the gorilla's eye out with the group of spectators observing. Then they sutured his eyelids together and we left. The next year Dr. Rogers and Dr. Dan visited the zoo and found the gorilla alive and doing well.

Saturday afternoon we packed up and took a small bus ride of about an hour to Douala. We made a last minute stop at the Arts and Crafts Market, and then we went to the airport, where we had our long flight home. Everyone arrived home at a decent hour on Sunday.

In summary: John reported that we treated 4040 patients, and we had over 3500 become Christians. We had been able to treat both the physical and spiritual needs of many unreached people in eight villages in two different provinces. We now have only one remaining province in Cameroon in which we haven't had the opportunity to serve.

## And now for the rest of the story

Two years later John got a letter from the Supreme Moslem Chief in Ngaoundere. He asked John if he could bring a team back to his area and treat more of his people, especially the people in Ngaoundere and his personal compound. John answered him, and told him we would be glad to come, but he needed to understand that we were Christians, and we needed to share the Gospel of the Good News of Jesus to anyone who wanted to hear, and that some people would probably want to become Christians. John got a surprising letter back from the Supreme Moslem Chief saying, "Thank you, I understand about your Christianity, and I still want you to come."

Unfortunately the Iraq war broke out about that time, and John thought it might be better to wait on this unusual invitation for a little while for safety reasons. Seven years later we still haven't gotten back there.

Again we broke a record in having more people accept Christ than in any mission HTI has ever conducted, 3500. How exciting! Life just doesn't get much better. I have been accurately quoted in several writings as saying, "HTI has had more success in reaching the unreached with the love and Gospel of Jesus Christ in Cameroon than in any other nation in the world that HTI has ever served." Praise the Lord!

# CHAPTER 26

# TIBET

Tibet is a large southwestern province of China. It has one of the world's highest elevations, located in the heart of the Himalayan Mountains. Nepal is just to the south, with Mt. Everest very near the Nepal and Tibet border. Lasia is the capital of Tibet, and is at an elevation of over 13,000 feet.

Tibet had been part of China for thousands of years, but became an independent country many years ago, with the Dalai Lama ruling the country, which consisted primarily of Tibet Buddhists. Communist China invaded Tibet several years ago and made it again part of China. China has poured a lot of money into Tibet, improving its infrastructure and standard of living. The Dalai Lama was forced to flee into exile into India, along with many other Tibet refugees that fled into India and Nepal. It has been the goal of the Dalai Lama and the refugees to take back their country, but it appears now that they have given up on this hope.

Dr. Bill Pratt and Chris, our China host, had tried to get permission for our HTI team to go into Tibet last year, but permission was not granted. Instead we went into Western China to Xining, near the Tibet border. This year permission was granted for us to take our HTI team to Tibet, so Dr. Pratt got busy and recruited a team of nine people, including five from the previous year. The returnees included Dr. Dan Wiklund, Dr. John Brothwell, Dr. Bill and his wife Peggy, and me.

We had four new team members. Dr. Dan's wife, Ulrike, agreed to join him for her first mission trip. Lisa my former dental assistant, called me out of the blue one day, and asked if I had any dental mission trips coming up. I told her about the upcoming Tibet trip, and she immediately asked, "Can I go?" Lisa had accompanied Dora May and me on our second Cameroon mission trip to the pigmies. She left my employment to become a highly paid professional model. She returned to the University of Michigan and earned a four-year degree in dental hygiene. She was currently practicing dental hygiene as well as doing professional modeling.

We had a young female dentist, Dr. Thuha Vuong, from the Seattle, Washington area that Dr. Pratt personally knew and invited. She gladly agreed to join us. Dr. Vuong was originally from South Vietnam. Her dad was an important government official. She and her dad were airlifted off the top of the American embassy in Saigon on the second to last helicopter to evacuate personnel, before the North Vietnamese took over the city, and ended the war. Her mother was supposed to be evacuated with her dad, but she sent her teenage daughter in her place. Her father would have been killed if he had been captured. Her mother was able to blend in with the common people, and later escaped, and joined the family in the U.S. Dr. Vuong had worked her way through college and dental school living part of the time with Dr. Pratt and his family. She currently had a private dental practice in Seattle, and had become a strong Christian.

Our ninth member was Dr. Dale Christophe, a dentist from British Columbia. He had somehow heard about HTI's trip to Tibet, so he called Dr. Pratt and asked if he could go. Dr. Pratt questioned him in detail about his Christian faith. He finally admitted, his wife was a strong Christian, and he went to church every week with her, and was active in the church, but wasn't sure he believed all that stuff. Dr. Pratt said, "I'm sorry, we only take Christians." Dr. Pratt sent him a Bible, with all the steps to salvation properly outlined. He read them all, and sat down and had a long talk with his wife. Dr. Dale told us later, he came to the conclusion that either Jesus was the greatest liar of all times, or he was truly the Son of God and was speaking the truth. He decided he couldn't sit on the fence any longer. He had to decide one way or the other. On his own, one evening he decided he was going to believe that Jesus spoke the truth. He went through the steps of salvation that Dr. Pratt had sent him, and asked for his sins to be forgiven, and invited Jesus into his heart and life. Dr. Dale said, "I immediately felt a great feeling of peace." He told his wife, and together they told his pastor. Dr. Dale went forward the next Sunday in church during the invitation call. Dr. Dale called Dr. Pratt and thanked him for his help in becoming a Christian, and he told him how it happened. He asked if it were too late to join the Tibet mission. Dr. Pratt was happy to add him to our team.

Dr. Vuong and Lisa had not been to China. They decided to go three days early so that they could tour the sites in and around Beijing. They were scheduled to fly different flights to Beijing, so Dr. Vuong asked Lisa, "How will I identify you at the airport in Beijing?" Lisa asked her if she had ever seen the movie "Pocahontas". She said, "Yes." Lisa said, "Just look for somebody that looks exactly like Pocahontas, and you'll find me." Dr. Vuong said she had no problem finding Lisa at the airport.

Our other 7 members assembled in Vancouver, in the summer of 2002, and we flew together to Beijing. We were met by Chin and again transferred to the Friendship Hotel, where we joined Dr. Vuong and Lisa. The next morning we flew to Xining again. Dr. Pratt and Chris had received many repeated requests from several different officials, asking us to return to Xining, where we had been last year. Dr. Pratt and Chris thought we should go there for a few days at least, before we continued on to Tibet. It was on our way.

We were met at the Xining airport by the same Minister of Health along with several of the doctors that we had worked with last year. We went to a different but nice hotel. We were again treated to a wonderful welcoming banquet, with the world's best hospitality. We found out that the Communist Government's policy of cradle to grave free health care had been eliminated during the past year. All health care had become privatized, with each patient paying his own way. Most of the people had very little money, and health insurance hadn't been developed. Things were greatly different. Hospitals that partnered together under last year's system were suddenly competitors.

We went to a different hospital this year, set up our clinics, and started working. Dr. Dan and I lectured again, but this time we came better prepared with more slides. Dr. John, our general surgeon from Phoenix, brought along several instruments to do laparoscopic surgery. They were good expensive working instruments, but the hospital where he worked had bought newer models, and had planned to throw these out. Dr. John felt they could probably use them in Xining, where he had become good friends with the Chief of Surgery last year. Dr. John located his Chief of Surgery friend, and presented him with the laparoscopic instruments. He was rather surprised when the Chief of Surgery asked, "What is laparoscopic surgery?" He had never heard of it before, but was very anxious to learn all about it. Dr. John started teaching the Chief of Surgery and his staff how to do simple laparoscopic surgery, such as taking out gall bladders. The best way of teaching is to do the actual surgery. They did many operations together, but when our team was ready to go to Tibet, Dr. John didn't feel the doctors were ready to do laparoscopic surgery on their own. He stayed behind and continued to teach them until he felt comfortable that they were ready to operate without his help.

Dr. John joined us three days later in Tibet. He told us he had worked with the surgeons on 29 successful laparoscopic operations, and he felt they were capable of continuing on their own. When we got back to Beijing as we were leaving China, some of Chris's friends showed us a copy of the Chinese National Newspaper. It had a picture of Dr. John and the Chief of Surgery with the headlines saying, "Laparoscopic surgery reaches Western China," and there was a nice article with it.

While we were in Xining, we worked in the hospital four days. We were exceptionally busy, particularly since ours was the only free service left. The Minister of Health asked us to go an hour or so outside of Xining, to a small village hospital, and help them for a day. That we did, all except for Dr. John, who kept teaching laparoscopic surgery.

The village hospital was small, only three stories high with 10 to 15 rooms per floor. They knew we were coming so there was a welcoming committee of 50 people out front to welcome us. Most of them were wearing white coats. Dr. Pratt set up for his restorative clinic in a small private room. Dr. Dale, Dr. Vuong, Lisa, and I set up our extraction clinic in a large long narrow room. Lisa was cleaning teeth and doing hygiene work.

Our host Chris felt it would be good to start sharing Jesus with our patients. So we did, and we had most all of our patients wanting to become Christians. Chris had brought his 13-year-old daughter with him, and she was translating for Lisa. They were also getting great results with their salvation message.

Lisa worked right beside me. She was from a Lutheran background, and was not used to this type of evangelism, but with lots of help from her 13-year-old translator, she started sharing Jesus with all her patients. At first her patients were mainly the hospital nurses and staff. She had several of the hospital nurses accept Christ. She even personally led them in the prayer of salvation. I was amazed, surprised, and at the same time very pleased. One nurse whom Lisa shared with for a long time while cleaning her teeth, asked to become a Christian. Lisa prayed with her and she accepted Christ into her heart and life. It turned out this was the head nurse of the hospital.

Later in the afternoon I had a doctor who was the chief of staff, the head doctor of the hospital, come to see me. He wanted his teeth examined, so I did, and found them healthy. He then said to me, "My wife tells me that she has become a Christian." I asked, "Who is your wife?" He told me "She is the head nurse." I remembered that this was the lady Lisa had led to the Lord that morning. I asked him "Would you like to know what Christians believe," and he answered, "Yes."

My translator was a young excited new Christian, and a very sharp evangelist. We spent 20 minutes or so sharing the good news of Jesus with this doctor. I asked him, "Would you like to become a Christian like your wife and several other people on your staff? Dr. Dale had been listening from a distance, and before the doctor had a chance to answer my question, he popped over and spontaneously said "I have only been a Christian for a few weeks, and it is the best thing that has ever happened to me in my life. I have true peace and happiness now." Dr. Dale sure said the right thing at the right moment, but I was also happy to hear for the first time how Dr. Dale felt about his newfound faith. It hadn't become Dr. Dale's turn to share in our morning devotions, so I hadn't heard his personal testimony.

The doctor, who was the chief of staff of the hospital, asked to become a Christian. We prayed with him and he asked Jesus to come into his heart and life. I asked him if he wanted a Bible, and he said, "Yes." I gave him one of the few Chinese Bibles that we had with us. Then I said to him, "As a leader of this hospital, and with your wife, several nurses, and staff becoming Christians today, you should start a church in your home to praise God, and to help teach each other how to become better Christians using your Bible. He shook his head positively, but didn't say anything. We plant seeds, and pray for their growth. There was no Christian Church, or other known Christians in the area to help them.

When we got ready to leave the hospital and head back to Xining, all the staff came out in front of the hospital, and gave us a very warm and gracious thank you. It was certainly another day that I will always remember.

That evening back in Xining our host had a big thank you farewell banquet for us, because the next morning we were leaving to fly to Tibet. The team was presented with a large burgundy colored cloth banner, about 4' x 6' in size. On the banner in large gold letters was a thank you in English. When Chris looked at it, he was shocked. Among other things, it said, "Thank You American Missionaries." Chris said, "In Eastern China the word missionary could either get you thrown in jail, or kicked out of the country." But there it was, so we just said thank you.

The Minister of Health was a 40-year-old doctor who had been our official host on both trips. She was frequently with us and had overheard the good news of the Gospel many times when we shared it with our patients. She never stopped us or interfered in any way. On the way to the airport the next morning, one of the doctors asked her directly, what she thought about Christianity. Her answer was unique. She smiled and said, "I am the only one who knows what is in my heart, and I can't share that with you or anybody." As a high government official she was a member of the Communist Party and sworn to atheism. If anyone knew she was a Christian, she might lose her job, her respect, and everything. Some day we will know.

At the airport we were overweight again, and China Airline was going to charge us a lot. The Minister of Health walked up to the agent, and said a few words, and they checked our luggage without any charges. I received a window seat on the plane, and was awed at the sights, as we flew into the heart of the Himalayan Mountains. There was a huge range of white snowcapped mountains, even in the middle of the summer, separated by deep green valleys with a river at the bottom. We landed at the small, simple Lhasa airport. Lhasa is the capital city of Tibet. We had to drive up the river several miles, across a bridge, and then drive back several miles again to reach Lhasa. There weren't many flat areas in these mountains for an airport. Lhasa was over 13,000 feet in elevation. I noticed the elevation most when I was going up a flight of stairs. I lost my breath real fast.

A little bus brought us to a small hotel, which proved to be adequate. We found out there were 80 rooms in this hotel and 60 of them were permanently occupied by Tibetan Buddhist Monks. We unpacked and settled in. I was asked to room with our host, Chris, which I found to be most enjoyable. It was Saturday afternoon so we spent the rest of the day walking around downtown markets, and the main central Buddhist temple. There were masses of people in the streets, and many sidewalk vendor booths all around the temple.

On Sunday morning we had our own church service, since we couldn't find any Christian Churches in Lhasa. After church we went to the Internet Café where Dr. Dan wanted to check his e-mails, and to send some. I went along even though I was not at that time skilled at e-mail. While waiting for Dr. Dan, he called me over and said, "Dick I have an e-mail for you from Reverend John Ngoh in Cameroon." It was an e-mail he sent me, with a copy to Dr. Dan, asking about our next year's Cameroon mission trip. It completely amazes me that I could sit in Lhasa, Tibet, and read today's mail sent to me in the U.S, from Cameroon, West Africa.

Sunday afternoon we took a walking tour of the Dalai Lama's great Petola. The city of Lhasa is located on a flat plateau, not too far from the river. The Petola was the residence of the Dalai Lama, from which he ruled Tibet for many years. It was built on top of a huge rocky outcropping right in the middle of this flat plateau. It was about 50 to 75 stories tall, about four or five city blocks long, and two or three blocks wide. The Petola was built of stone on top of this massive irregular rock. It looked like the biggest castle I had ever seen. It must have had several hundred rooms in it.

When China conquered Tibet a few years back, the general that led the Chinese troops into Lhasa had orders to tear down the Petola. It was so massive, and so beautiful, that he refused his orders and did not tear it down. The general was later disciplined for disobeying orders, but it would be like tearing down the pyramids in Egypt. What a beautiful massive world landmark it was!

Today the Petola has become the main tourist attraction of Western China, and has been turned into a Museum and Buddhist Temple. We had to climb several hundred steps carved out of the side of the rock, to reach the bottom floor. It was slow going, because at that altitude, we had to stop and catch our breath frequently. Once we got into the bottom floor there were several additional floors to climb. It was exceptionally interesting, and took us most of the afternoon.

In one of the small museum rooms there was a young Buddhist monk guarding the artifacts, and helping to explain the meaning of them. He could speak moderately good English, and as we talked to him he said he was desperately searching to find the one true God. We didn't say anything, but if I could ever relive that moment, I would have told him that I had found the one true God, and would have asked him if he would like me to tell him about Him. To this day, I regret missing that golden opportunity!

Coming down was a lot easier. In front of the Petola was a large city square. We stopped to get a can of soda from a street vendor. The street vendor was a lady, and she had a real cute four-year-old daughter running around her stand. Several of the doctors started playing with the child. The mother asked if we wanted to buy her. We asked her if she were joking, and she said, "No, she is for sale for $3000." We didn't buy.

Dr. Bill Pratt had been to Lhasa several years earlier and was asked to set up his clinic next to a Chinese dentist in the main hospital. He said he ran into two problems. One was the screaming from the patients of the Chinese dentist, because it got on his nerves. The Chinese dentist didn't have and didn't want to use anesthesia to extract teeth, so there was a lot of screaming and verbal unhappiness expressed right next to him. When Dr. Pratt used anesthesia the patients quickly caught on, and no one would go to the Chinese dentist any more. This made the Chinese dentist very jealous and angry, and he expressed his anger so strongly that Dr. Pratt left and found another location to extract teeth, where he could work by himself.

On this trip Dr. Pratt had requested we go to villages outside of Lhasa. The government wouldn't allow us to go to a much higher elevation, because of the fear that the higher elevation, for people not used to it, could cause air embolisms in the lungs. This could cause rapid death to a person before he could be brought down to a lower elevation. That advice sounded wise to me.

Our first clinic was about four hours away, up a side valley to the main river, but only about 1000 feet higher in elevation. The Chinese government had built a nice three-story 40-room new health clinic and small hospital. The only problem was that it had never been used. Tibet had no medical or dental schools, so they had to rely on Chinese doctors. The change in policy of the Communist Chinese Government to eliminate cradle-to-grave free healthcare, and make the patients pay for their health services, caused two problems. One was that the patients couldn't afford to pay, and secondly, it resulted in no doctors wanting to come to the area since they now had some choices.

We checked in at a hotel, and went to the government clinic and set up. They knew we were coming, so we had an instant crowd of patients. One of the first patients Dr. Dale saw was a 14-year-old boy who came with his mother and father. He had several abscessed teeth which Dr. Dale numbed for extraction. While he was waiting, Dr. Dale offered to tell them what a Christian believes. The father explained that they were Tibetan Buddhist, but he was very interested in knowing what Christians believe, so Dr. Dale, with the help of his translator spent 20 minutes, and shared the Gospel with them. When he finished he asked them if they would like to become Christians, and he was a bit surprised by their answer. The dad said, "You mean we can become Christians like you? Of course, we want to become Christians." Dr. Dale led all three of them to the Lord. They were very excited and thanked him, and thanked him. As they left the room they were overheard telling the people waiting, "We have become Christians just like the doctors." This was an exciting time for Dr. Dale especially because his faith was so new.

The first afternoon went fine. The second day the crowd was much bigger, and there was a concern that everyone might not be able to be treated. At lunch time we left the clinic, locked it up, and went back to our hotel. When we came back after lunch there was a massive crowd of around two hundred people pressing up to the front door. It was obvious that we could never get through that packed crowd, so our local host took us around to the back door. There were about 20 people gathered around that door also. We pushed through the crowd and when our host unlocked the door and started to open it, the whole crowd stampeded and rushed the door, forced it open and almost trampled us as they poured in and started running down the hall toward the registration desk. We went to the rooms where our clinics were and started to work.

After we had been working for a while, I could hear a lot of loud voices in the hall. When I opened our door and looked out, I saw that our local host had positioned the registration desk so that it totally blocked the hall. He was standing on top of the desk with a long switch trying to beat the people back, but it was of no use, because the people were packed solidly down the hall and down the stairway, and they were pushing from the back.

I suggested to our host that we call the police to help restore order. He said, "I don't think that will help. The chief of police is in the middle of the crowd out there right now, trying to get treatment for himself." Remember this town had no medical or dental care. For any health services they needed to travel four hours by bus to Lhasa, wait a long time to be treated, and then pay for it, and to make it worse they were treated by a Chinese healthcare person. They were still bitter about the Chinese invasion and takeover of their land, including the killing of many of their family and friends. Today they had American healthcare, free, and in their own town, with free medications, but it wouldn't last long. It was obvious that everyone was not going to be treated. The people were desperate.

After looking down the hall at the chaos, I closed the door to our dental clinic, and decided to let the locals deal with the problem themselves. I was told that at one point, a group of patients got past the desk, and crowded into Dr. Dan's office pushing and shoving. He told them that he wouldn't treat anyone until every person had left his office. He sat at his desk and folded his arms and waited. It took a while, but finally they left.

We were scheduled to work until noon the next day, and then drive back to Lhasa in the afternoon. Our host advised us to pack up at the end of the second day, and plan to leave very early the next morning, because he said the crowd had become uncontrollable, and he was fearful of a riot. We took his advice, and were packed, ate our breakfast, and were starting to load the bus at 7 A.M. Somehow the word got out, and people started crowding into the hotel lobby, asking questions, and wanting medicines. Dr. Dan handed out some medicines, but finally had to push his way to the bus. We quickly finished loading and drove away. I have never been in an area anywhere in my 35 mission trips where the people were so desperate to receive health care treatment.

As we were coming down the valley we observed a massive project where the Chinese were building electric towers to take electricity up the valley. We also observed the beautiful green crops growing on the narrow flood plain of the tributary river. Otherwise everything we saw was barren and rocky.

The other three villages we visited were only a 1 or 2 hour drive out of Lhasa, so we returned each night to our hotel. I started to let Lisa our hygienist do more and more extractions, because the demand was so great, and she was capable. I worked very closely with her. Usually I saw the patients first and diagnosed which tooth or teeth needed to be extracted. I would tell Lisa exactly which one to extract, and she would give the anesthesia and extract it. One older man I saw, I just turned to Lisa and said, "You take care of this one." She said, "What tooth am I supposed to extract?" I said, "This time you figure it out."

She got a little apprehensive look on her face and said, "You've got to be kidding." She had the patient open his mouth and he took his finger and wiggled the only tooth left in his mouth. Lisa smiled and said, "You had me a little concerned for a moment." She didn't have a very hard time figuring out which tooth needed to come out. She took care of him with no problem.

One morning I extracted a lower molar from a man, and had no particular difficulty. Later that morning he came bursting into the small room where we were holding our clinic. He was bleeding excessively and had blood all over him. I quickly sat him down, cleaned the blood out of his mouth with gauze, and applied pressure over the extraction area with new gauze. Applying pressure over the bleeding area normally stops the bleeding in 99% of the cases. I held it tight for a while and it seemed to stop. When I let go, it instantly started bleeding excessively again. I put new gauze on the area, and held it longer. When I took the pressure off, I had the same problem, heavy bleeding. I got some sutures out and sutured the extraction site with six or eight sutures, which usually solves the problem, but it didn't slow the bleeding down one bit, and it was bleeding a lot. I started to get a little concerned. I have never had a patient that didn't stop bleeding with pressure and sutures. I knew we were a good hour and a half away from Lhasa, and he would never make it at the rate he was bleeding. I asked myself, what could they do, that we couldn't do. We were supposed to be the experts. I knew I had to solve this problem here and now.

I consulted with Dr. Dale who had become quite interested in what was happening. He had never seen such a situation either. The bleeding seemed to be coming from the inside of the lower jaw bone under his tongue. Dr. Dale suggested we put a suture in the gum on the inside of the jawbone, so I did. Nothing happened. It still seemed to be bleeding the same, and from the same area. I was getting more concerned. Dr. Dale suggested we put another suture in the same area but further back in the mouth, so I did with his help, because it was in a very difficult area to get access. Immediately 100% of the bleeding stopped. I had never put a suture in this area before in anyone's mouth. Remembering my anatomy, this is the area where the lingel (tongue) artery is located. Obviously it had ruptured, and we had finally gotten a suture around it, and tied it off. It wasn't bleeding when the patient left after the extraction in the morning. What caused it to rupture and start bleeding is a mystery to this day, and I will probably never know. I sure hope I never see a situation like that again.

This experience taught me a good lesson. Never be afraid to ask for help from another dentist, even if he is half your age. It was Dr. Dale's idea to put the suture in this unusual area. I was also reminded of the cardinal rule of dentistry; never panic, stay cool and calm, and reason your way through problems. This is an experience I will never forget.

One morning when we arrived at a village, there were about a hundred people gathered around a gate in a large stone wall fence. We stopped, got our equipment in hand, and worked our way through the crowd to the gate. The gate keeper opened the gate and in we went. Inside was a large grassy area a little larger than a basketball court. It had buildings around the edge of this grassy area. There was a long porch about 5 feet high in front of the main building. It was a cool 65° with no wind and full sunshine; it felt great, so I decided to set up our dental clinic outside on the porch.

Our clinic went well, but boy, did we get a good sunburn before the end of the day. We had many patients, and had a good opportunity to share the Gospel. Many of our patients asked to become Christians. We saw all the dental patients initially at the extraction clinic. Dr. Bill was inside a small room doing fillings. We selected teeth with small decayed areas that he could easily fill, and sent the patients to him for a filling.

In mid to late afternoon, voices started to become louder at the registration desk, which was blocking the front gate. Suddenly the desk got tipped over, the gates opened wide and a mass of people poured in the front gate. I thought, oh boy here we go again. They spread out all over the grassy area, and just stood there looking around. Slowly they walked back out the front gate and the registration desk was set back up. Registration continued with no more problems. I guess the curiosity of what was going on inside the gates, and the possibility of not being seen, had become too great for them. When their curiosity was satisfied and cooler heads prevailed, everything returned to normal.

Dr. John joined us in Lhasa after we got back from our first three-day trip. He worked with us in our last three villages. It was a good thing he came when he did. Dr. Dan had become good friends with a local physician in Lhasa. He invited Dr. Dan to his home for dinner one evening. The next morning Dr. Dan didn't show up for breakfast. Dr. John went to his room and asked if there was any problem. There certainly was! His wife said he had been up all night with severe gastrointestinal problems. Dr. Dan admitted he probably had gotten food poisoning at his dinner at the doctor's house the evening before. He said he was taking some good strong medication, so he hoped for a fast recovery. Dr. John saw all the medical patients in the clinic that day. Dr. Dan recovered quickly and was his usual self the next day. Another lesson learned; anyone can get food poisoning, even a physician. You can't be too careful about what you eat.

Our host offered to treat us one evening by taking us to an American-style restaurant, where they had hamburgers. I ordered a yak burger. It was so tough and full of gristle that I only ate a little of it, and just counted it as another unique experience.

On our last day some government officials planned a farewell thank you banquet in our honor. They invited several government officials and several doctors. We had a very nice banquet. The one thing that made Dr. Bill and Chris excited was that the head official said in his thank you speech that we had an open invitation to return to Tibet anytime we wished. Dr. Bill and Chris thought of all the effort it took over several years time to get our team into Tibet this first time, and now we had an open invitation to return anytime.

When we got to the Lhasa airport to start our trip home, our luggage was still over-weight. Dr. Bill, Chris, or no one could talk our way out of it this time, so we got charged almost $1000 for our overweight luggage. Fortunately, they accepted Dr. Bill' visa. Each of us gave Dr. Bill $100 each to divide up the cost. In Beijing we stayed overnight in the Friendship Hotel. Our flight wasn't until the next afternoon, so early in the morning Chris took us to the famed Beijing Silk Market to shop. It had everything. I found some beautiful handmade silk neckties that would normally sell in the U.S. for $30 or $40 each. When I priced them, they were one dollar each. I was so excited I bought 45 of them, enough to last me a lifetime, and some to give away as gifts. I still have 25 of them in my closet that have never had the tags removed. Our flight home was uneventful, but long.

In summary: I was extremely impressed at the extensive amount of time and detailed work that went into planning this mission, and also the large number of people who were directly involved in helping. It seemed so good not to be the team leader, and to carry the awesome responsibility for putting it all together. We had seven professionals treating patients, but I believe that there were probably several hundred people who helped us in one way or another in order to make this trip successful.

After returning from Cameroon where we saw 3500 unreached people come to the Lord, I was initially a little disappointed after we counted only 125 people that we saw come to the Lord. I mentioned this to Chris, and his answer was, "Adoniram Judson was in Burma for many years before he saw his first conversion and Hudson Taylor was in India for several years before he saw his first conversion. Your team has been doing similar mission work by introducing Jesus into a culture that has never heard of Jesus before. Your team has been in Western China and Tibet for just two weeks, in a land where there are no Christians, and in a country where it is technically illegal to share your faith, and you saw 125 conversions. I don't think you should feel bad about that at all."

With that perspective I just thank the Lord for being with us, and for touching the hearts of as many people as He did. It was a fantastic experience and I came home with great peace and joy in my heart.

# CHAPTER 27

# CAMEROON 6
# YAOUNDÉ & PYGMIES

Yaoundé is the national capital of Cameroon, and the provincial capital of a large central area of the country. Rev. John Ngoh had taken our HTI teams, along with his very successful evangelical teams, to six of the seven provinces in Cameroon. The province around the capital was the only area we hadn't served.

The city of Yaoundé is reasonably modern in places, for a third world country, but 20 or 30 miles out of the city, people are living a thousand years in the past. They have absolutely no healthcare available, and most of them have never heard the good news of Jesus. This was John's challenge for us on this mission.

I was able to put together a team of 17, my largest team ever. We had 5 physicians, 4 dentists, 3 nurses, 2 people to fit glasses, 2 dental assistants, and one EMT (emergency medical technician). Ten of them were returning team members. Eight of them had been with me 3 or more times. They came from 8 different states of the U.S, and 2 Canadian provinces. Dr. Dan Wiklund agreed to help me again by heading up the medical team.

We left in March of 2003, and had excellent flights with no lost luggage. This time instead of flying to the large port city of Douala, we flew directly to Yaoundé. It had the only other international airport in the country. We settled into our hotel, and were ready for our first village clinic by noon the next day.

We were taken by bus to a different primitive village each day and received a wonderful welcome in each one. Unlike the last three Cameroon missions, none of these villages were Moslem. They consisted of a variety of African religions but were mainly nature and ancestor worshipers.

On our last Cameroon mission, John had several of his Bible school students come and help us with evangelism. This really worked great, so John brought several of the students with him again to work with us. It was good practical experience for the students. All patients had a personal counselor that spent 20 to 30 minutes sharing the Gospel with them. Again we had almost 100% of the people accept Jesus into their hearts and lives.

We had no highly unusual dental, medical, or optical patients. This being our sixth mission trip, what may have been unusual before was just becoming routine. Medically, malaria and worms continued to be our two most common problems, both which were easily treatable. Dentally, we extracted many abscessed teeth, and they continued to be the most difficult teeth that I have ever removed anywhere in the world. Their bone structure was just like concrete. Optically, we fit several hundred pairs of glasses.

One day dental was working outside in the open air under a shade tree. Several hundred people had gathered around and were watching. When it came time for lunch, John informed us that we had to walk down the road several hundred yards to a location where lunch was all prepared. Everyone left, but I didn't feel comfortable leaving the many thousands of dollars of dental instruments and equipment unprotected, and out in the open with so many people around. I was personally responsible for all of the equipment. I got a big bottle of pop out of John's cooler, and sat by the equipment. I got out my usual lunch of cheese and crackers, M&Ms, peanuts, raisins, and cookies. I started eating my lunch, while watching the instruments. This was probably safer and tastier food than the African food that the team members were eating.

I was very content and happy except for one thing. The several hundred people all around me sat down and stared at me with every bite I took. I quickly developed a very guilty feeling. None of them had any lunch, and they probably needed food worse than I did. I couldn't start handing out my few packages of food. It wouldn't go very far and I might create a small riot.

I had seen a near riot on a previous mission trip when one of our team members attempted to hand out some leftover pieces of bread. One time I attempted to hand out some used toothbrushes at the end of the day. It got very scary with people just mobbing me from all directions and almost crushing me. I finally felt so guilty eating lunch in front of all these people who were staring at me that I just put my lunch away and found something to read.

We had several pastors and local church leaders from Yaoundé that traveled with us each day to these remote villages. They not only helped us with sharing the Gospel, but they committed to do follow-up work with the large number of people who were becoming Christians. It was a very exciting time, which appeared to be a win-win situation all the way around.

When we finished working in the villages that John had scheduled, we checked out of our hotel, and loaded all our luggage and supplies on the top of our small buses. On our way out of town, we stopped at the main government hospital in Yaoundé. We were given a nice tour of the hospital. For the biggest and best hospital in the country, it had much to be desired.

This was the hospital where John, as a young man, sat helplessly at the bedside of his mother and watched her die. She had pneumonia, which developed an excessive amount of mucus. John sat and watched his mother gasp for breath and eventually drown in her own mucus. The hospital had only one suction machine, and it was being used by someone else. John never forgot this tragedy.

When John was in the states, he collected several used suction machines from different charitable organizations. He also received a new, several thousand dollars, oxygen condensing machine. It could produce condensed oxygen from the air for patients to breathe. He had the machines shipped to Cameroon in one of his shipping containers. He brought the machines with him to give to the hospital. The hospital authorities were aware of this, and they planned a nice presentation ceremony, during which John officially presented the several machines, worth thousands of dollars, to the hospital administration.

After the presentation ceremony we loaded into our bus and headed toward Douala. Just before reaching Douala, we turned south and headed toward the town of Kirby. On the way, we passed many small roadside stands displaying and selling mangoes. Several of the team had never tasted a mango, so John stopped and bought us some, so that everyone could get a taste of a tree-ripened mango.

We arrived at Kirby late Saturday afternoon, and checked in at our hotel. It was actually several groups of rooms spread out over several acres. On Sunday we went to a local church. John had arranged for the pastor and leaders of this church to work with us again in our next outreach to the pygmies.

After a nice, but very different Sunday morning service, we went to a lonely stretch of Atlantic beach coast, and had a fresh shrimp dinner with all the trimmings, similar to the one we had on our trip two years ago. They had set up a nicely decorated table with chairs, right in the sand on the beach. This was done by the same group of men that were going to take us up the river to reach the pygmies. They cooked over an open fire, and the shrimp they served were caught fresh out of the river that morning. It was an unusually outstanding dining experience. We spent much of the afternoon swimming and sunning on the beach. On our way back to the hotel late that afternoon, we stopped at one of the local markets and did some souvenir shopping.

Monday morning we packed only the things that we thought we would need for the day. We drove south along the coast to the river we had traveled two years before, in which we had a very successful experience in locating and helping a village of pygmies.

Our boatmen were there waiting for us with long dugout canoes with motors in the rear. We loaded all of our team, along with our supplies and translators, into three longboats and headed upstream. We traveled for 3 1/2 hours without stopping. This was much farther than we had traveled last time. There were no seats in these dugout canoes, so we just sat on boards in the bottom. Believe me; they got pretty hard after 3 1/2 hours. The ride was pretty interesting with dense jungle on both sides of the river. I can guarantee, you would never see anything like it in the U.S. or on a scheduled travel tour anywhere in the world. This was truly off the tourist track. We saw no signs of human life on the river, except for a few small canoes loaded with firewood, which were being paddled down the river to take the wood to the Kirby market to sell.

We finally reached an area where our riverboat captain said there was a pygmy village located nearby. John had not been able to visit these villages ahead of time like he usually had done. We unloaded and packed our supplies for a walk into the jungle, down a path to the village. Surprise! When we got to the village, all the primitive stick and leaf houses were still there, but the village was completely empty. There were no signs of life anywhere. We turned around and headed back toward our boats.

When we reached the boats, a pygmy, who was headed downstream with a load of firewood, stopped to check us out. We asked him if he knew where all the people from the village had gone. He told us they were downstream a short distance on the other side of the river. Pygmies are somewhat nomadic. They frequently move to new places where they can find better food or hunting.

We loaded our longboats and found our hard boards on which we sat, and headed downriver, following the new directions we had been given. Each boat had at least 10 people in it. When one of the boat captains located the area, which looked like all the rest of the river bank to me, we beached our longboats, packed our supplies and hiked into the jungle along another path. This path I remembered well, because we hiked through the biggest grove of bamboo trees that I had ever seen.

Why the pygmies never lived near the river, I was never told. I suppose, like in Zaire or the Congo, they were trying to get away from all the waterborne mosquitoes and other insects that carried so many different diseases. We finally reached a fairly good-sized pygmy village. After our traditional meeting with the chief, we set up clinic and started treating patients.

We asked the chief why they had moved, and he said to find better hunting grounds. Hunting was their primary source of food.

We set up our dental clinic under a big shade tree, which worked out well. There were no tables, so we put our instruments and equipment on top of our supply trunks. Since there was no place to put our dental trays, we had our patients hold the trays, which contained our instruments, on their laps. This was the first time in my life I ever did this, and it worked fine. These pygmies had a lot of dental problems, so we were very busy. None of them had ever seen a dentist.

We actually started seeing patients faster than the spiritual counselors could counsel them. With the help of our translators, we started sharing the Gospel with our patients who were seated on stools, which we were using for dental chairs. It was encouraging, because almost every patient we talked to asked to become a Christian, once they heard for the first time, the good news of Jesus Christ.

Both the medical and optical teams had to work under shade trees also, with very little in the way of tables and chairs. They also started sharing the Gospel directly with patients, and received the same exciting results. We worked until about three o'clock in the afternoon. We then packed up, said our goodbyes and headed toward the river for our long journey back. We arrived at the bridge, where the bus was waiting, just before dark.

The next morning we headed upstream again. This time they promised not to go quite so far, only a couple of hours. We took more spiritual counselors from the local church. We found the pygmy village the first try this time. Again we had a short hike into the rain forest, away from the river. We had our traditional meeting with the chief, set up our clinics and started to work. This village was large, so we had more patients. The spiritual counseling was great, and kept ahead of medical, dental, and optical. This allowed us to do more healthcare treatment, while at the same time making sure that all our patients heard the good news of the Gospel. In the afternoon we had a hard time finishing all the patients that were waiting.

It was about 4:30 before we finally got packed, said our goodbyes, and headed to the river. We saw the sunset traveling down the river. Then it got jet black very quickly. We were located very near the equator, and I am told, the closer you get to the equator, the less twilight time there is, after the sun goes down, and before it gets totally dark. There was no moon that night and no reflected light from any neighboring villages. It got so dark I couldn't see my hand in front of my face.

I knew the river was full of fallen trees, branches, and rocks, including a few rapids. We went from one side of the river to the other, going upstream. Our boat captains kept right on motoring at the same speed. We were heavily loaded and the sides of the canoe were only a few inches out of the water. I have tipped over in a canoe before and it happens very fast. I was just waiting for our long dugout canoe to run upon a downed tree limb and flip over any moment. Our boat captains must have had eyes like an owl's. I don't know how they could see where they were going, but they did, and got us all back safely to the bridge.

Our three boat captains' degree of fear was expressed, when they told John that they would not take us up the river again the next day unless we agreed to leave early enough so that we would get back before dark. That wasn't hard for John to agree to, because I think we were all a little frightened.

The next day we went up the river, and located a different pygmy village, where we had a very successful ministry and clinic. In the middle of the afternoon, we had to leave some people untreated, but we left early enough to get back before dark.

I must have been riding in a different canoe going up the river, because this canoe had water seeping through the side of the canoe. It was heavily loaded and sat unusually low in the water. There were about 3 or 4 inches of water in the bottom of the boat, so we had to keep our feet uncomfortably propped up on the side of the canoe to keep them out of the water. The captain had a young man in the back of the boat that was bailing as fast as he could, but it became obvious that he wasn't keeping up. Finally the captain gave us several cans and we each took turns bailing.

Some of the team members got the idea to stick some Kleenex into the small holes that were leaking the most. That seemed to slow down the leaks. There was a leak next to me up near the water line, and it seemed to be getting worse. I didn't have any Kleenex, but I had some dental gauze, so I tried to stuff the gauze into the leak when suddenly my finger went right through the side of the rotten wood. I then had a finger-sized fountain that spurt water all the way across the canoe. I quickly put the palm of my hand over the hole and held it there for the last hour of the trip. I was real glad to see the bridge. I didn't feel bad about breaking the boat, because it was rotten. I could see a dozen areas where they had patched the canoe previously. I was rather happy that this was our last scheduled day on the river. We had only three longboat type canoes for 40 people and I wasn't sure our canoe could make another 4-hour trip up and back on the river.

The next morning we drove about three hours to Douala, had lunch, did a little shopping, and then continued two more hours to the town of Limbe. Limbe was where John and his family lived. He found it very beneficial to his ministry for our team to finish up our last day with a clinic in his church. We had many unreached townspeople who became Christians, and hopefully joined his ministry. Without John's strong ministry and his great hosting abilities, HTI wouldn't have the privilege of helping him reach the unreached with the Gospel of Jesus Christ in his country.

Dr. Dan and Dr. Bill Rogers, our veterinarian, stopped by the zoo to check on the gorilla whose eye they had removed last year, and found him doing well.

In summary: According to John's records, we treated over 3500 patients, and almost 3000 of them accepted Jesus as their Savior. This was a total team effort, including the 20 to 30 people who worked directly with us, as well as the hundreds of people back home that supported us in so many different ways. Our trip home was uneventful.

## Now the Rest of the Story

Dr. Dan Wiklund, a valuable HTI board member, had participated in our last four mission trips to Cameroon as my medical director. After this trip I asked him if he would consider leading next year's team to Cameroon, and he said, "It would be a privilege." I certainly would not want to see our missions to Cameroon stop, because we have had greater success in Cameroon than in any other country in which HTI has ever worked.

Dr. Dan has led teams of up to 24 people back to Cameroon for the last six years. He has developed such a love for Cameroon that he took time off from his practice to take the famous three-month Tropical Medicine Course in London a few years ago. Dr. Dan has had greater success with larger teams with more experience, than I did with my earlier teams. Dr. Dan is a very intelligent, lovable, dynamic leader who has done a fantastic job in leading teams to Cameroon. To date, we have seen over 32,000 unreached people accept Christ and become Christians in our joint 12 Cameroon missions.

With Dr. Dan taking over leading our teams to Cameroon, this has given me the opportunity to evaluate other invitations HTI continually receives from missionaries, pastors, and evangelists from all around the world. If they share the same goals as HTI, trying to reach unreached people groups in their countries with the Gospel, then I am interested. The opening of a new country to accept HTI teams often takes a lot of extra time, experience, and effort, but it is something I really enjoy doing.

I was able to locate an excellent evangelical pastor in the country of Myanmar, formerly called Burma. I have been successful in opening the country of Myanmar to HTI teams, with the great help of our in-country pastor host. We have seen over 3000 people who have never heard of the name of Jesus, very excitedly accept Jesus and become Christians, including numerous Buddhist monks. I have now trained new team leaders to lead some of our Myanmar missions.

With the help of Pastor John Ngoh, I led the first HTI team into the Voodoo dominated country of Benin, West Africa. I am currently planning our first HTI team to enter Equatorial Guinea, Africa.

I had 10 returning team members on this mission to Cameroon. Dr. Dan reported he had 20 team members on his 2008 mission trip to Cameroon, and at the completion of that mission, all 20 members asked to return on the next year's mission trip.

These people have to stop working in their busy practices for two weeks, during which they earn no income, and most of their office expenses continue. They pay several thousand dollars to come, and the loss of income from their practices is many times more than that. The food, accommodations, and working conditions are poor. It is extremely hot, humid and uncomfortable, and they probably work harder and longer than they would at home.

You may well ask yourself, why do these people want to come back again and again? I have asked myself the same question, and I have come to the following conclusions. Basically, serving people in this way makes them feel good.

Why? There are several reasons. Many of the people are suffering great pain and discomfort from treatable infections and diseases. They probably would continue suffering for the rest of their lives because there would be no chance for them to get help. Many of these people are extremely grateful and show their appreciation with great emotion.

I think the biggest reason our people keep returning is because they feel a great sense of satisfaction in being part of a team that is introducing so many lost people to Jesus Christ for the first time. Everybody deserves to hear about Jesus at least once in there lifetime. Knowing that your efforts have been pleasing to our Lord gives great joy. Seeing lives changed both physically and spiritually for now and forever gives a sense of personal happiness. Try it; I know you will like it.

## CHAPTER 28

# EXPLORING MYANMAR (BURMA)

In 2001 I received an e-mail from a Reverend Dr. Robin Seia from Yangon, Myanmar. I had to get out the world atlas, and even then I couldn't find Myanmar until I found a newer atlas. The name had been changed from Rangoon, Burma, to Yangon, Myanmar, a few years previously. I remembered having a young couple from our church, when I was young, that were missionaries in Rangoon, Burma. I also remembered during World War II hearing about the U. S. airlift they called "Flying the Burma Hump." Then there was the book, "On the Road to Mandalay," and the movie, "Bridge over the River Kwai." That was a long time ago. I hadn't heard anything about Burma or Myanmar for a long time.

Reverend Seia introduced himself as a former Buddhist, who was now a Christian evangelist. He was the founder and president of the Myanmar Christian Evangelistic Association. With Myanmar being 92% Buddhist, and less than 2% Christian, Reverend Seia's stated goal was to reach the unreached for Christ. He had been attending an International Missions Conference on World Evangelism in Amsterdam, Netherlands. Someone gave him a reference book on missions that contained a description of HTI, with my name and e-mail address. He observed that HTI's purpose was to help evangelize unreached people of the world with the ministration of short-term Christian healthcare teams. Our goals matched perfectly. He knew that healthcare was very poor in his country, with many areas having none at all, especially in rural areas that were 100% Buddhist. He felt, as we did, that free healthcare could open the hearts of people, so that they would be more receptive to the Gospel.

After introducing himself, Reverend Seia asked me if I could send a HTI team to Myanmar, to help him reach some unreached people groups. He also asked me for more details as to how HTI operated. During the next year and a half we sent over 100 e-mails back and forth getting better acquainted.

Reverend Seia sounded too good to be true. I remembered the old saying, "If it sounds too good to be true, it probably is." I know I continually get a lot of e-mails offering to give me millions of dollars, if I will just help some rich widow with her financial problem. Many of these e-mails sound real good, too good to be true and they are not true. I kept waiting for Reverend Seia to ask me to send him $10,000 to help him set up our mission trip, and I was concerned that I might never hear from him again, but he never asked for a penny.

To put a team together, and get all the medications, supplies and equipment, and to get 5 or 10 doctors to give up their practice for 2 weeks, pay their own airfare, and other travel expenses, would cost well over $100,000. I couldn't risk the possibility of this being a hoax.

Dora May and I were due for a winter vacation, so I contacted Jill, my friend and travel agent, and asked her to check for a vacation to Myanmar. She called me back a few days later and said, "There are almost no tours that go to Myanmar. They don't really welcome tourists." She did find a United Airlines Vacation Package that had a five day stop in Myanmar. It also went to Thailand and Cambodia. The price was reasonable. There was one catch. United Airlines' policy was that they would only take a minimum group of 10 people, and we were the first to sign up. I e-mailed Reverend Seia and asked him if he would be available to talk with me. I gave him the dates I would be in Yangon. He responded with an enthusiastic, "Yes." We booked our vacation for February 2003 to go on a Southeast Asian Vacation Package with United Airlines, if they could get the minimum of 10 people.

I started to study the recent history of Myanmar. It was formerly a British colony called Burma that won its independence from Britain in 1948. They set up a democratic British form of government, and elected a prime minister. A few years later, in 1962, there was a military coup, and the military leader set up a dictatorship that ruled by force. He socialized the country, with the government forcibly taking over the ownership and operation of most private properties and businesses; including trains, buses, hotels, hospitals, schools, universities, and a lot of the bigger businesses. The government expelled all foreigners from the country, including all missionaries.

Geographically, Myanmar is the largest country in Southeast Asia with a population of over 50 million. It has a large central fertile valley, with mountains making up its borders with Bangladesh, India, China, Laos, and Thailand. The people in the central valley, where the majority of the population is located, are mainly Buddhist. The mountainous border areas of the country contain minority groups of Hindus, Muslims, and Christians, who do not want to be part of Myanmar's brutal Buddhist military dictatorship. Many of them want their own independence. So there has been an ongoing civil war raging in the mountainous areas for almost 50 years, making it one of the longest civil wars in recent history.

There are no roads into the mountains, and the war has been a smoldering, sporadic, guerrilla-type warfare. On various occasions, the much larger and stronger Burmese Army has gone into mountain villages and killed every man, woman and child, and burned their villages to the ground. This has caused many of the persecuted Burmese to flee into refugee camps in Thailand. Reports of these horrible atrocities, far beyond normal warfare, have frequently occurred, and it has included many Christian villages. On occasions the Burmese Army has crossed the border into Thailand and raided the refugee camps. This has made political tension between Myanmar and Thailand, with lots of threats being exchanged. Thailand is currently building up its military and buying jet fighters from the U.S. to strengthen its Air Force. Myanmar has moved its government out of Yangon and into an area near the center of the country in a large mountainous valley, where they are putting all their important government offices underground. The valley offers much better protection than they had in the middle of Yangon. Myanmar has vastly increased the size of its Army.

Foreign governments have tried to put pressure on the military dictatorship to hold elections, so in 1990 they finally held elections. The granddaughter of the first Prime Minister, Aung San Suu Kyi, ran against the military dictator and won a very high majority of the vote. The military dictator declared the elections invalid, and took Aung San Suu Kyi, and put her in jail. Later they changed it to house arrest, where she remains today. In 1991 she won the Nobel Peace Prize.

After reading all this about Myanmar, I kept asking Reverend Seia, "Is it safe for us to come?" He continually assured me that everything was safe and had been safe and quiet in the cities and main valley. The only safety problems were scattered on the borders, deep in the mountains.

In February of 2003, Dora May and I took off on our Southeast Asian Vacation, with our primary goal to meet Reverend Seia in Yangon, Myanmar. After spending a couple of days touring Bangkok, Thailand, we flew to Yangon. It turned out that Dora May and I were the only two on this United Airlines Vacation Package, and for some reason they didn't cancel the trip. The vacation package included everything, such as guides, transfers, hotels, meals, fees to enter different tourist attractions, and everything was super first-class. We were met at the airport in Myanmar by our guide, who was to guide us during our stay in Yangon. We quickly found out that he was also a government agent, assigned to keep us under very close scrutiny.

Our guide took us to our assigned hotel, which turned out to be the best hotel in the country, a super five-star hotel, right in the heart of downtown Yangon. I had e-mailed Rev. Seia, and asked him to meet us at our room in the Traders Hotel at noon the day we arrived. We got to our room at 11:45 A.M., and started to unpack. At exactly noon, there was a knock on the door. It was Reverend Robin Seia. We invited him in, and talked a little. We then invited him to join us for lunch in the hotel restaurant and we talked more.

Reverend Seia asked if we would like to visit his orphanage and Bible School. We said, "Great." This was Saturday. I asked Reverend Seia, "What time is church on Sunday, and could we join you?" He said that church was scheduled at 1 p.m. and we would be welcome.

Suddenly I remembered that our tour guide was waiting for us in the lobby, so I found him and asked him if he would show us around town Sunday morning, but we wanted to be back to the hotel by noon. He said, "Fine, I'll pick you up at eight." He then took off for the day. I asked Reverend Seia if we could invite our guide to join us for church tomorrow, and he said, "Please do not. He is no more than a government spy, and could cause our church big trouble."

Reverend Seia called on his cell phone, and his son, Charles, picked us up, and took us about an hour to the outskirts of Yangon to a walled compound containing three buildings. One was the orphanage, one was the Bible School, and the other was Charles' house.

Charles had come to the U.S. for college, and he had graduated from Taccoa Falls Bible College in Georgia. He returned home, got married, had two children, and was helping his father by taking over the day-to-day management of the orphanage and Bible School. First we visited the orphanage, where they had about 30 orphans between the ages of 3 and 15, living in one large house, with a house mother.

We then went over to the Bible School, which had about 25 students who lived at the school. Charles had gathered them together on Saturday afternoon in the main lecture room to meet me. Reverend Seia, who asked me to call him Robin, turned to me and asked, "You will speak to the students, won't you?" I asked him, "What do you want me to speak about and how long?" He said, "Your testimony, or about HTI, or anything about Scripture, but please hold it to an hour or so." I was a bit surprised and to be frank, I was rather shocked, but I stood up in front and talked to them for about 45 minutes. Unlike most groups that I talk to in the U.S., they were extremely attentive. Afterward I had a chance to meet and talk with the students informally. Charles and Robin had taught the students English, so all my communication was in English. Robin and Charles then took us out for supper. On our way back to the hotel Robin asked if we would like to stop at one of his house churches. Since we had never been to a house church, of course we were interested.

We turned down a small residential street, and stopped at a house where20 to 30 people were packed into a living room. Robin introduced me to the group, and asked me, in front of the group, "You will speak to the group, won't you?" I asked how long, and he said, "30 to 45minutes." Fortunately I had my New Testament in my pocket with pages identified and verses underlined that I had used in previous talks back home, and some that I used at the Bible School, so I shared with them for about 40 minutes. These people spoke Burmese, which was the primary and official language of the country, so Robin had to interpret everything I said. I liked this better, because it gave me more time to think about what I was going to say next. It was after 9 p.m. before we got back to the hotel.

Reverend Seia said, "I will pick you up at noon for church". I asked him, "Do you expect me to speak at church tomorrow?" He said, "Yes, would you please?" I asked, "How long," and he said, "One hour." Well, at least this time I had a little warning, and I had some time to get prepared.

At 8 a.m. the next morning our guide picked us up, and we toured around Yangon. We went to Shwedagon Pagoda, the largest Buddhist Stupa in the world. It is 326 feet tall containing several tons of gold, 80,000 diamonds and precious jewels, and eight original hairs of Buddha. It is 2500 years old, although it has been rebuilt and improved over the years. We also went to a museum and a few other places. We got back to the hotel about 11:30, and had a few minutes to freshen up before we met Robin in the lobby, ready to go to church.

Rangoon was the name of the capital city, and Burma the name of the country when it was a British colony. After the military dictatorship took over, they immediately asked all foreigners to leave the country. To help erase any remnant influence of foreigners, they changed the name of the capital to Yangon, and the name of the country to Myanmar. They outlawed the use of English in any advertisements or signs.

Under British rule, there were many missionaries that came to Burma, and a variety of Christian churches were started in Rangoon. The present policy of the dictatorship government was to tolerate other religions, but certainly not to encourage or help them in any way. The government was 100% Buddhist. They had taken over all Christian Schools, Christian Universities, Christian Hospitals, and made them government-owned and operated and 100% Buddhist. There were no K-12 private schools, and the first hour, every school day, was set aside for mandatory Buddhist prayer and study. If you were a Christian and a government employee, it was understood that you would never get promoted. Christian churches that requested a building permit, were usually delayed a year or two before one was granted. They had many ways to discourage Christians, but they were allowed to meet and worship, but only inside their own buildings.

When we arrived at the church, we learned that it was a Nazarene Church. Reverend Seia was the founder of all Nazarene churches in Myanmar and the field superintendent, or head man. He was also the senior pastor of this church, and was grooming his son-in-law, Jubilee, who was currently the assistant pastor, to become the senior pastor. The service and songs were in Burmese, but the order of service was similar to that which we were accustomed back home. There were probably about 150 to 200 people in church, with a large children's church going on simultaneously.

I ended up having the sermon for the church service, and spoke for an hour, primarily on the theme of loving one another. After church it was their custom for the pastor and guest, to go to the front door, and shake hands and greet each person in the congregation, which we did. We also had a chance to tour the remaining church facilities.

We met the rest of Robin's family, including his wife, Mi Mi, Charles, their son and his wife and children. We also met Robin's and Mi Mi's two daughters. Their oldest daughter was Shanda, and she was married and had children. Their youngest daughter was Mo Mo, and she was married to the assistant pastor, Jubilee. Robin's entire family was active in his ministry in some way.

I invited Robin's family to join Dora May and me for supper at the hotel that evening. Because of the late hour, Shanda and her young children couldn't make it. Robin, Mi Mi, Charles, Jubilee, and Mo Mo were able to join us. We talked and became better acquainted. It was a long and most enjoyable supper. After supper when most everyone had gone home, I sat down with Robin in the corner of the lobby and we discussed 101 details concerning my bringing a HTI team. We discussed what equipment and supplies we could bring, and how we could get them through customs. We talked about how we usually set up our clinics, what kind of space we would need, and how many translators would be needed. We also discussed how we would need him to help us in making hotel reservations, furnish transportation, help keep our food safe, furnish us with bottled water, and many other details. I told him that our team would not be a financial burden to him or his team, and that we would pay for all of our expenses, but it usually worked best if he would pay for the expenses initially and we would reimburse him. We would send most of the money before we arrived, and we would pay him the remainder at the end of the mission. He needed to keep track of all of our expenses, and give us an accounting.

Robin assured me that he could handle all our needs, and asked me to bring a team of around 10 people. He thought January and February were the best months to come, because the weather would be drier and cooler. We agreed and planned two weeks with specific dates set for the end of January and the beginning of February, 2004. We spent a good two hours of uninterrupted, one-on-one conversation, working out the many details. I thought afterward that this would have been one big and almost impossible task to accomplish by e-mail.

The next morning we left by plane for Bagan, one of the three areas the government allowed tourists to travel. Bagan was interesting because of the hundreds of Buddhist pagodas and stupas, built over several hundred years. We then flew to Mandalay where we toured more Buddhist temples and monasteries, before returning to Yangon for overnight, before we left Myanmar the following morning. We had a final opportunity to meet with Robin, and say goodbye, with the hope we would see him in one year. We left Myanmar and flew to Siem Reap, Cambodia, for three days, where we visited Angkor Wat and several other ancient remains, before returning home.

In summary: I was very excited and pleased to meet Reverend Robin Seia and his family, and to learn about his many ministries. He was a much stronger and dynamic Christian leader than I had expected. I was pleased that we had an opportunity to make adequate preparations so that we could anticipate a successful future HTI mission trip. I was surprised and honored that Robin asked me to preach three times within the first 26 hours that I was in the country. I came home with a good feeling of accomplishment. Praise the Lord.

# And Now the Rest of the Story

HTI has now had nine successful mission trips to Myanmar and I have had the privilege to lead six. We have seen several thousand unreached people invite Jesus into their hearts and lives. It has also helped Robin's ministry to grow greatly. Currently, we have even more mission trips planned to Myanmar.

# CHAPTER 29

# BOLIVIA – 2

Our first mission to Bolivia was so successful that Ken Krestan e-mailed me, and asked if I would return and bring a physician. Ken had been promoted and was in charge of all SAM, South American Missions, in Bolivia. He proposed a plan for us of first driving west into the foothills of the Andes to help a missionary friend, and then flying to remote villages in the eastern and northern parts of the country.

I found a Christian pediatrician, Dr. Peter Davenport, from Pensacola, Florida, who was semi-retired and taught part-time at the University of Florida. He agreed to join me.

This time instead of paying someone to do our trip planning, I did it myself, since I usually did it for all my trips anyway. I secured all of the medications, equipment, supplies, then packed, and flew to Miami, May 2, 2003. There I met Dr. Pete. We had a good overnight flight to Santa Cruz, Bolivia.

Ken met us early in the morning at the airport and took us to the guest house at the SAM headquarters compound. It was a group of several buildings surrounded by a tall security wall. We went to church with Ken, Diana and family. After lunch we unpacked and repacked our supplies. Ken picked us up in a four wheel drive vehicle and we headed west into the foothills of the Andes. Near dusk we arrived at the small village of Samaipata. After asking around, we received directions to the house of Dr. Bruce and Katie Kniegge, who were the U.S. missionaries with whom we planned to work.

Dr. Bruce was a Christian chiropractor with a tremendous zeal for the Lord, and a great love for the people. He and his wife, Katie, were independent missionaries, who had been serving in Bolivia for many years. They had become good friends with Ken, Diana and family, through the American Christian School where they both sent their children. One day, Dr. Bruce asked Ken if he knew of a good physician and dentist that could help him with some of the local healthcare problems that he couldn't treat. That was one of the reasons why we were invited to help.

Dr. Bruce had rented a neighboring cottage in which we were to stay. We had supper and all of our meals with them, in their house next-door. Katie loved to cook and was a great cook. In the morning we drove to a rural village and set up our clinics. Katie translated for Dr. Pete, while Ken translated for me.

Dr. Bruce set up a portable metal chiropractic table and worked vigorously on people complaining of muscle and back pains. I don't understand the physical principles of chiropractic treatment, but it sure was interesting to see the physical effort that he put into his work. He worked up a sweat in no time.

We held clinics in three different villages. They were all accessible by road, and were not anywhere near as primitive as the jungle villages in eastern Bolivia. We had no unusual problems in any of our clinics. The people we treated were very poor and without any healthcare. We were able to help a lot of people out of their sickness and pain.

They knew that we were Christians, and that we were working for them because of the love of Jesus. We usually didn't take time to do evangelism with our patients. That's something I probably would do differently today, but this was primarily Dr. Bruce and Katie's mission field. Tuesday morning we bid them farewell and drove back to SAM's headquarters.

Ken had planned and scheduled for us to go to two isolated tribal villages in eastern Bolivia for the next two days. He introduced us to Rob, who was to be our pilot. We had seen Rob around the guest house and at meals. He was an American missionary pilot, who had been taking over some of Ken's responsibilities, since Ken had assumed the responsibilities of SAM's head administrative officer. Rob was a veteran SAM pilot who was just a few weeks away from taking his pregnant wife and family back to the U.S. for their scheduled furlough.

Right after lunch we packed and headed to SAM's small private airport. We admired the new portable hangar that SAM had built. We also checked out the two steel ocean-shipping containers that they had made into their office and mechanical shops. They had really fixed up things quite nice.

Rob, Dr. Pete and I flew east over the massive farms of soybean fields, which had been cleared out of the jungle by U.S. Mennonite farmers, who had emigrated there from the U.S. We flew several hours east to Robore, the town I had flown into on my last mission trip to Bolivia.

We landed on Robore's grassy runway and saw no one around. We parked the plane next to SAM's gas storage depot, and walked to the same hotel as we had on our last mission. We had a nice supper and a good night's sleep.

Early the next morning we returned to the airport, and took off for the rural village of San Fernando. Our clinic set-up was a little different in this village. I was asked to set up my dental clinic on the edge of the village under a small shelter, which had a good breeze and good light. They requested that Dr. Pete go into the village center, and set up his clinic in a private hut, again for some patients' privacy needs.

This would have been fine except Rob was our only translator, and he spent all day with Dr. Pete. This left me alone, without a translator. I quickly learned a combination of sign language, charades, and a smile, to communicate. It worked out surprisingly well. I usually was able to figure out what tooth was hurting, by tapping the teeth, and when the patient flinched with pain, I knew I had the right tooth. I was able to extract a lot of painful teeth. It was the only time in my 35 mission trips that I have been totally without a translator all day, but it worked surprisingly well.

There was no place for us to stay overnight, so we left in the late afternoon and flew to Candelaria, which was our next scheduled village. Although Ken had made arrangements for us to spend the night, our host was not in the village when we arrived, and no one else knew that we were coming. A couple of village men showed us to a large building which had open sides with a roof on it. It was the community center. They thought that this would be the best place for us to have our clinic. They indicated that we could stay overnight in a small building which was back of the community center.

We checked the building, and found it had 3 1/2 walls, a roof, and a dirt floor. We got our sleeping bags and food rations out of the plane, and had supper. Rob had purchased some bread in town, but I guess sitting in the hot plane was too much for it, because it was moldy. Rob said, "Bread mold is good for you. It even contains penicillin." He ate a couple of slices of the moldy bread for supper, and didn't even bother to pick off the moldy spots. We just watched. He didn't seem to have any ill effects from it. We opened our sleeping bags, and put them on some boards that we had found, and crawled inside. I didn't sleep well that night.

The next morning, our biggest problem was finding a bush to go behind to use as a bathroom, because there were people everywhere. For a village that didn't know we were coming, there certainly were a lot of people gathering around. We started at daybreak, just like the villagers. In the jungle they don't have clocks or watches, so our day started with sunrise and stopped at sunset.

We got busy and set up our clinic, and had long lines of patients waiting before we were ready to start. Clinic was busy, but nothing unusual. Dr. Pete and I worked closely together, so that Rob could stand between us and translate for both of us. Everything worked well. We saw and helped a lot of people. About 4 p.m. we packed up and headed back to Robore for overnight.

Dr. Pete told us that his patients' most common complaint that day was that their urine was yellow, and they wanted him to fix it. He had several patients urinate into a white paper cup, and sure enough, it was yellow, a normal yellow. He spent quite a lot of time trying to convince his patients that yellow urine was normal, but he wasn't sure he was successful convincing very many, until he urinated into a white paper cup and showed them his urine was the same yellow color. We never did see our host in this village, but it worked out fine.

The next morning, Friday, we fueled the plane, using some of SAM's gas reserves, and flew back to Santa Cruz. We transferred to SAM headquarters, had a good lunch, took a welcomed shower and had a nice rest.

Early Saturday morning Dr. Placido and Dr. Toni picked us up to take us out to Barrio Bolivar, the suburban slum encampment of the Ayore Indians.

Before leaving town we stopped at a pharmacy across the street from the hospital. Dr. Toni got out, went into the pharmacy, and then ran over to the hospital. One of the Ayore Indians had gotten so sick he ended up in the hospital. The government hospital treats the native Bolivian Indians free, but the doctors just write prescriptions for medicine. It is the responsibility of the sick patient, or the family, if they have any, to go outside the hospital and buy the medicine, if they have the money and when the pharmacy is open. Dr. Toni had visited this man the evening before and got his prescription, but the pharmacy was closed.

This hospitalized Ayore Indian had no family, and had no money, so Dr. Toni bought his prescription for him, and took it upstairs to the nurses' station. The nurses would administer it to the patients if it were given to them. Unfortunately, this is the way hospital healthcare works in many countries of the world, especially in the so-called socialized medical systems. I asked Dr. Toni, "What would happen if the patient couldn't get the medicine?" She said, "The doctors and nurses would just stand there and watch him die. It happens all the time."

We drove about 30 minutes to reach the suburban Ayore Indians group of small temporary houses built with cardboard and scrap building material, and placed closely together. This was the area where Dr. Placido and Dr. Toni brought me on my last visit to Bolivia. They had built a church out of cinder blocks, which doubled as a clinic. They had a small room in the back where they kept their supplies and equipment locked. They tried to get out there every other Saturday for a medical clinic, and every Sunday to lead the church service.

We treated patients all day. Dr. Pete's pediatric training came in really handy, because there were a lot of children needing treatment. Dr. Placido and Dr. Toni were constantly consulting with Dr. Pete. I'm sure they learned a lot from him because they were both recent graduates. We closed around 4:30, and returned to SAM headquarters for supper, a shower, and a good night of sleep.

Early Sunday morning Dr. Placido and Dr. Toni picked us up again, but this time they were taking us to Posa Verde. This was the village where we went on our last mission to Bolivia in 1999. We traveled by Land Rover, for an hour. Again we had to drive across the Rio Grand River on the unique one-way modified railroad bridge. After some bumpy, small, dirt back roads, we arrived at the Ayore Indian village of Posa Verde. The people were excited to see us.

We set up clinic and started to work. We had a very busy long hot day with nothing highly unusual, except one child with two well-developed thumbs on one hand. We did nothing but observe it. It was difficult closing clinics because our waiting lines were so long, but at four-thirty we had to close and head back to Santa Cruz. It was slightly after dark when we finally made it back to SAM's headquarters.

Monday morning Ken picked us up and we went to SAM's airport. Ken had a couple of isolated jungle villages he planned for us to visit. It was a beautiful, cool, refreshing morning. Ken was our pilot this time. After the routine of carefully weighing the three of us and our luggage, we took off and headed north. We landed at the village of Surusubi. We were met by Antonio, one of SAM's native trained missionaries. Ken had helped to train him and they had become good friends. SAM helped him build a home for himself and his family. We went to his house and met his wife, Santo, and their family. They had several children. Santo had a nice lunch prepared and waiting for us. Ken must have been talking on the radio to Antonio while we were in the air. This area was isolated with no roads near it.

After lunch, we set up our clinic in the shell of a building that they were currently still building and using as their church. We immediately had many patients and worked until nearly dark. Santo fed us supper and we sat around and talked until late in the evening. Finally Antonio showed us to our sleeping quarters. We laid out our sleeping bags, with no pillow, and turned in.

My room was upstairs and was about five feet by seven feet. There was only a single bed in the room with a few boards on top of the frame. It had a large open window, with no glass or screens. I guess it was one of the children's rooms. I didn't know where they put the child. There was an eerie dead silence as the full moon shown in the window directly onto my bed. I felt like I could reach out my hand and touch God. Unfortunately, I didn't sleep well that night, and when I did, my dreams were not pleasant. I was glad when morning came.

After a nice breakfast we set up clinic and started to work again. I am continually amazed when I see a pretty smiling teenage girl sit down in my chair, and when she opens her mouth, I find a half-dozen infected teeth which are decayed to the gum. You would think after over 28 mission trips that I wouldn't be so surprised. These people must suffer an incredible amount of pain, and they don't even have an aspirin or anything to dull the pain. It is a good thing that dental infections rarely kill people, but I suspect that when the pain gets very intense, with little chance of it going away, probably some people wish they could die.

Since Ken had planned for us to stay overnight again, we worked until dark and finished all our waiting patients. We didn't solve all health problems. I couldn't replace the teeth I removed or fill decayed teeth. Dr. Pete couldn't treat heart murmurs, diabetes, high blood pressure, eye cataracts, or many other conditions. But this one thing I am sure, we helped a lot of patients by eliminating infections and relieved a lot of pain and suffering.

After a pleasant evening and a good night's sleep, we took off and flew to the Ayore Indian village of Zapaco. Ken and I had visited this village in 1999. Pedro was at the grassy air strip, along with 75 other villagers, mainly children, to meet us. Pedro was also a native young man that was trained by SAM. He was set up in this village by SAM to replace retired American missionary Bill Pencil.

We went to the health building that was built by Bill Pencil many years ago, but had since been boarded up and no longer used. Pedro had opened it up and cleaned it out for us. He had some of the natives take our personal overnight bags to his house, while we started to set up clinic.

I think, when the natives first heard the airplane coming, they must have started lining up, because when we arrived at the health building, there was already a good-sized waiting line. We had a busy, but good day treating many patients which were very appreciative and thanked us repeatedly.

We had supper and stayed overnight with Pedro and his family. They lived quite primitively, with no electricity, no bathroom, no running water, and they cooked over an open fire, but we felt very welcomed and comfortable. It was easy to see why I couldn't have brought a bigger team.

Pedro's wife had been stocked by SAM with some general basic supplies, like fish hooks, pails, soap, pots and pans, etc. She sold them to the villagers at no profit. The nearest village with a store was a long day's walk from there. She did that to help the villagers and to show them love in a meaningful way.

Thursday we had an all-day clinic and finished all the villagers who were requesting help by late afternoon. We stayed overnight at Pedro's again. Pedro's wife fed us all of our meals and they were good, particularly considering we were a long way from home cooking. They were excellent hosts and couldn't do enough for us. They really made us feel welcomed.

Friday Ken flew us back to Santa Cruz, after a short stop in Concepcion. We went to the guest house at SAM's headquarters and picked up all our belongings. Evidently they had more guests coming in, than they had rooms for, and Ken knew we were flexible.

We transferred to Ray Rising's home. Ray and his wife were home on furlough, and a young SAM airplane mechanic was living in their home, for safety purposes, while they were gone. It was a beautiful home. We felt like kings.

I met Ray, and his wife, in 1988 and 1989 while we were in Columbia, South America, at Loma Linda, working with Wycliffe Bible Translators. Ray was an electronic genius. My wife, Dora May, did secretarial work for Ray for two weeks when I was out in the jungle. We had dinner at their house a couple of times, and grew fond of them.

In the early 1990's Ray was kidnapped by the Communist guerrillas and held captive, without much communication, in the jungle for two years. Evidently they needed his electronic expertise. Suddenly he was released for unknown reasons and he returned to the United States to reunite with his family. I lost track of Ray after that.

Evidently no one could stop a good man from working for the Lord. Ray was working as an electronic advisor for several Christian missions in Bolivia. I am just sorry that I missed seeing him again.

Saturday was our free day. We went to the market, looked around town, including downtown, had lunch in town, and shopped at a great souvenir store. In the evening we started packing for our return home. Very early Sunday morning Ken picked us up and took us to the Santa Cruz International Airport. Dr. Pete and I transferred in Miami and went different ways. We both returned home to our families later the same day.

In summary: We had a good two weeks. We were able to help a lot of people out of their sickness and pain. We had the opportunity to share the Gospel directly with some of our patients, who were very receptive to the good news. We were able to help several missionaries who were trying to evangelize those people. Hopefully the love we showed, by giving free health services helped give the missionaries more respect among the people, so that their hearts would be more receptive to the Gospel of Jesus.

## Now the Rest of the Story

After returning home, I stopped to reflect. Having just returned home from Myanmar and Southeast Asia in February, Cameroon in March, and then Bolivia in May, I had been on exactly a total of 40 flights in less than four months. That is a lifetime record that I will probably never break, and it was all for the glory of our Lord.

Having just finished three mission trips, I was ready to stay home for a while. Although, I will admit, that being a part of seeing over 2500 people come to Christ in the last four months gave me much to rejoice about, and to thank our Lord. I am happiest when serving our Lord.

# CHAPTER 30

# INDIA
# UDAIPUR

I think of India as a land of wall-to-wall people, and women dressed in beautiful bright colored saris. One out of every six people on the face of the earth lives in this Asian sub-continent, approximately half the size of the U.S. The people of India are more than 80% Hindu, and claim to worship over 55 million gods. Christianity is a minority. Most people have never heard of Jesus.

After being introduced several years ago to Dr. David Inderjet, and getting to know him, we asked him to join our Board of Directors of HTI. Dr. David is a native of India and received his medical degree there. He then went to England and received a specialty degree in ophthalmology. It was there he met his wife. She was also a medical doctor, but studying anesthesiology. They were both Christians, and felt called to the mission field.

They went to the Middle East, to various Moslem countries in the Arabian Peninsula. Dr. David came to the U.S. to get additional training, including degrees in laser eye surgery. He did eye surgery while his wife did the anesthesia. They had three children, which they raised on the mission field.

When Dr. David's children got ready for college, they had little money. Oral Roberts University gave his children scholarships. Two of his children received medical degrees and all of his children married and stayed in the United States. Dr. David's wife died on the mission field after 30 years as a missionary doctor. A few years after that, Dr. David retired and came to the U.S. to be near his children and grandchildren.

While helping with the marriage of his physician daughter, Daphne, who married another physician, Dr. David met his son-in-law's widowed mother, Pat. They fell in love and got married. Dr. David had no retirement pension, no U.S. Social Security, and although a brilliant experienced eye surgeon, he wasn't allowed to practice in the U.S. Pat had a job with the school system, and Dr. David's children sometimes helped support them financially.

Dr. David and Pat have an energetic active zeal for sharing the Gospel with unreached people. He has a special concern for the lost in his own country of India. HTI put him in charge of all our India missions. Dr. David can speak five languages, and has many contacts in India. He and Pat offered to go to India for six months, and continually host HTI teams every few weeks. He had many invitations and places for our HTI teams to serve.

Dr. David had a wealthy friend in Delhi, who offered to let him use one of his large homes as a home base for our mission teams. Dr. David asked me to help him get teams for all of his anticipated missions. He was especially concerned about his first mission to Udaipur, which was to help a good friend and great evangelist, Reverend Thomas Matthews.

I volunteered to recruit and help lead his first team. Dr. Dan Wiklund and Dr. David Shull were my first volunteers. Dr. David Inderjet's daughter, Dr. Daphne Thomas volunteered and she asked if she could bring two female physician friends, Dr. Marlena Edwards, and Dr. Diane Traficante. Gail Dawson, a nurse, and HTI's first female board member, agreed to go. A dentist, Dr. Earl Young, his wife, Floy, and his adult daughter, Leslie, asked to join our team. Tom and Judy Ruster, friends from my church agreed to go.

It didn't take long to get a real good team put together. We had 6 physicians, 1 nurse, 2 dentists, and 5 helpers, including Dr. David and Pat.

We left November 9, 2004, and flew directly to Delhi with one short refueling stop in Europe. We arrived late Sunday evening. We had no problems with customs, which was unusual, because the Indian customs are frequently difficult. Dr. David and Pat met us at the airport, and took us to the large donated house. It was large enough to sleep all 14 of us. Our luggage was picked up early the next morning, and driven to Udaipur by truck, a 24-hour drive. The weight of our luggage was more than the domestic airline allowed.

Pat prepared a nice breakfast for us at the house. After breakfast, we all headed to Delhi's Domestic Air Terminal, where we caught a flight to Udaipur. Reverend Matthews picked us up at the Udaipur airport, and drove us 30 minutes to his mission compound.

Dr. Matthews and his wife were the first Christian missionaries to come to Udaipur, 35 years ago. When we think of missionaries, we often think of Americans working overseas, but Dr. Matthews and his family are Indian missionaries, who work in India. Udaipur was mostly all Hindu. Dr. Matthews and family have undergone severe persecution in the past, and still some today.

Starting from nothing, he has built a big beautiful church with over 600 members. He has a moderately large Bible School, where he trains students to be evangelist and pastors. The Bible School includes dormitories, dining hall, library, and etc. He has guest rooms where we stayed. He operates a sizable printing shop, where he prints books, and all types of gospel literature, for use in his ministry.

Reverend Matthew's son is helping to take over pasturing the church, and helping with many other parts of their ministry. His daughter-in-law is a nurse, and was in charge of our health mission. The main thrust of Reverend Matthew's ministry was reaching out into the many surrounding rural villages to unreached people with the Gospel, and starting new Christian church in the areas. Often his Bible School graduates would pastor these new churches. He has started over one hundred churches. He wanted us to reach other unreached villages, which still had not heard the Gospel, and where they didn't have much Christian witness.

We were assigned rooms in their guest house, followed by supper with his family, and many of the Bible School students in their large dinning hall. There were so many villages that Dr. Matthews wanted to reach, some days we divided our team in half and went to two different villages. We traveled to 15 different villages in nine days of clinics. I will summarize some of the highlights of our experiences. We usually got started early in the morning, and drove for an hour or two to reach the prearranged villages. We set up clinic, and worked in a lot of different type of facilities, often in small buildings where they were trying to start a church. We also set up in homes, community centers, and one day in a Hindu girl's school.

The drive to these villages was often interesting, and sometimes challenging. The roads often were very narrow, and sometimes wound around, up and over some pretty big hills. One morning as we came around a sharp blind curve, a small car suddenly came around the corner directly at us. The driver was going to fast, and came over on our side of the road and hit us head-on. No one was hurt. Reverend Matthew's son was driving. Fortunately we were driving a big Land Rover, and the other car was a very small cheap car which was completely totaled. It didn't seem to damage our vehicle too much, so after much discussion, we continued on without any significant problems. The other driver admitted he was wrong, because he was obviously on the wrong side of the road. This is the only accident I have ever been involved in, with over a total of a year and a half of extensive mission traveling, often in very remote parts of the world.

On occasions we would pass groups of Gypsies, who were camping along the side of the road in the barren hills. Often there would be groups of 50 to a 100 Gypsies at one time. We were told that they move from village to village earning their living by entertaining the villagers with their talents. At one point we stopped and went into their encampment and talked with some of the Gypsies. They seemed like real nice people and our host indicated that most of them were good people, and they were well liked by the villagers.

I saw and extracted a lot of badly abscessed teeth. Fortunately the Indians bone was quite soft, and the teeth generally come out very easy. Since we didn't have a pharmacist with us, and had six physicians, every evening after supper most all the team would gather in a room where we kept the medications. We prepackaged the medications that the doctors anticipate they would need the next day, so they would be ready for the doctors to hand out.

The weather cooperated beautifully. It was in the 70s and 80s with no rain, and a pleasant breeze. I frequently set up our dental clinic outside in the shade where we had good light and a nice breeze.

We joined Reverend Matthew's church service Sunday morning, and were surprised and pleased by the large number of enthusiastic and excited people. They sang and clapped with all their heart and lungs. Reverend Matthews's son preached the sermon, and although we couldn't understand any of it, he sure held their attention, and seemed to do a good job.

Sunday afternoon they showed us around some of the interesting historical places in town. In the evening Rev. Mathew's son took a few of us to a Christian friends home who was a jeweler. He showed us several types of jewelry including Indian rubes. I bought 5 nice small ruby rings for the 5 girls in my life, my wife, 2 daughters and 2 daughter-in laws. They were extremely reasonable in cost, and I hadn't bought any Christmas gifts yet. They were all surprised and real happy.

On our last day we stayed at the mission compound, and worked on family, staff, students, and many people from the surrounding neighborhood. By this time we had developed good organization, and our team had become quite efficient. We treated a lot of patience that day. Dr. David and Pat work next to us the last day, and I was amazed at their energy, enthusiasm, efficiency, and teamwork. The demand for glasses was great, and they saw all the patients that were waiting.

We needed to leave for Delhi on Friday morning, even though our flight back to the U.S. didn't leave till midnight Saturday. The reason was there were no flights to Delhi on Saturday. This gave us a day to visit the city of Agra, and the Taj Mahal. We expressed our thanks and said farewell Friday morning, and flew to Delhi. Friday afternoon we shopped, and did a little sightseeing in Delhi.

Saturday morning we left at daybreak, in two big taxis for our 4-hour drive to the city of Agra, and the Taj Mahal. It was truly spectacular. After shopping, and a late lunch we returned to Delhi in the early evening. Our all day cab fare was eight dollars each. We picked up our luggage and went to the airport, where we had a non-eventful flight home.

In summary: Although we didn't keep exact records, the number of patients we treated had to be well over 2000. The Hindus were not as receptive to the gospel as the Buddhist are in Myanmar, but most listened, and many accepted Jesus and became Christians. I feel our biggest benefit was generating greater respect for the native Christian pastors and evangelists, in these small villages. In our visit we treated many people and showed them great love, which should significantly give them more credibility when sharing the Gospel. As I returned home, I had a good feeling that all of my time and effort was valuable, and hopefully would please my Lord.

# And Now the Rest of the Story

I was able to recruit numerous additional team members for Dr. David Inderjet, so he continued with five additional HTI missions. Dr. Tom Harel, the president of HTI Canada, took a mostly Canadian team of 12 to India in March of 2004. This was the final mission of Dr. David's continuous series of six different missions.

HTI has sent teams back to Udaipur for the last four years to help Reverend Matthew's Ministry. One year ago the Lord suddenly took Reverend Tom Matthews home to be with Him with a heart attack. His son and family are successfully carrying on his Ministry.

Dr. David has developed health problems which have limited his ability to travel and personally lead teams to India. He is still organizing and sending HTI teams without him being able to go. His daughter Dr. Daphne Thomas is now leading some of his teams.

# CHAPTER 31

# MYANMAR 1

The newspaper, USA Today, recently listed the dictator of Myanmar as the third worst dictator in the world. How can Health Teams International, HTI, a Christian evangelical healthcare organization, get into a closed Buddhist dictatorship? The Christian Medical Dental Society, the Christian Dental Society, and other Christian organizations have not been able to get into Myanmar, no matter how hard they have tried. Note, HTI does not have Christian in its name, and we did not have a website. This helped us to get into a lot of countries that have been closed to Christians.

Our host, Reverend Dr. Robin Seia, whom I will refer to as Robin, has lived in downtown Yangon for 35 years with many of the top government officials as neighbors. He knows the right people in the right positions, and has their respect. For the usual expected donation of appreciation, bribery to us, we were allowed into the country to help the poor, widowed, and orphans with their healthcare. We were watched, and monitored very closely. I asked Robin, "Is bribery the best way to go?" He answered, "That is the normal, usual, and only way this government operates."

I talked to one doctor who had tried to get into the country with a team two years earlier, without understanding how the system worked. They had all their supplies and equipment taken away from them at customs at the airport, and were put in a hotel and told not to leave. They were escorted to the airport two weeks later, and put on their scheduled flight out of the country. They never got any of their supplies or equipment back.

A single physician, Dr. Joel Holcombe, who was on this ill-fated mission, met a young single pharmacist, Scarlet. They fell in love and were married. They heard I was taking another health team to Myanmar, so they phoned me. After they heard about our host, Robin, and how he planned to get us into the country, they asked to join Dora May and me. They said, "This will be like a second honeymoon."

I had a physician from the mountains of North Carolina, Dr. Bill Johansen, request to join us. A retired Christian dentist, Dr. Earl Young, and his dental assistant wife, Floy, agreed to join us. Robin was anxious for us to keep the team small, so hopefully, we would be less visible, and less threatening to the paranoid government. We only had seven on this team, consisting of two physicians, a pharmacist, two dentists, and two dental assistants.

We left in late January, 2004. We met for the first time in the Thai Airways waiting area of the Los Angeles airport, where we had a chance to start to get acquainted. We flew directly to Bangkok, Thailand, where we overnighted inside the airport terminal in an airport hotel. We paid for our rooms by the hour. We only had six hours before we had to get up and catch our Thai Airways flight to Yangon, Myanmar, which was formerly called Rangoon, Burma. The six hours of sleep felt real good after having been up for 36 hours straight. Thank goodness we were able to check our luggage all the way from our U.S. home city, to Yangon, and it all arrived safely with us.

We had no problems with customs. We found out later, that Robin had negotiated an appreciation of $2000, to the right person before we arrived, in order for us to get through customs. Robin, Charles, Jubilee, Mi Mi, and Mo Mo, were all there to meet us. They had rented a small bus with a driver. We loaded up and they took us, and our 21 pieces of luggage, to a very nice four-star hotel. That afternoon, Robin, Jubilee, and Mo Mo, took us to the very large city central market, where they had everything you could think of, and for a relatively cheap price, including souvenirs and jewelry. The market was so large that we only got through a small portion of it.

Our first evening, Robin and his family took us to the Royal Barge for supper. This was a very beautifully decorated Buddhist dinner restaurant. It was one of the main tourist attractions in Yangon. They had a typical Burmese buffet, and an excellent stage show with several colorfully costumed dancers performing various Burmese traditional dances, with a typical Burmese Orchestra. Everyone enjoyed the evening immensely. The food and entertainment certainly reminded us that we were in a most unique foreign country.

The next morning Robin picked us up and moved us to another hotel. Our new hotel was only a three-star hotel, but it was very adequate and located much more conveniently. Robin negotiated $30 per night with breakfast, rather than $70 per night without breakfast at our first hotel. Our new hotel also had 24-hour electricity. Electricity in most of the city was very intermittent.

Robin then had us repack our luggage to the domestic airline limit of 50 pounds. That afternoon we went to the airport and boarded one of Myanmar's seven government-owned and operated aircraft. We flew to Kalemyo, home of the Chin people in the northwest part of the country. Actually the plane was a nice U.S.-made Boeing 727. Myanmar had no international planes, and they allowed very few international air carriers into the country. The main ones were Thai Airways, Singapore Air, and Indian Airways.

The flight was good. Most passengers were military officials, and men in white shirts, ties and suits. We felt a little out of place, and I guess we were. Usually seats on planes were reserved for military and government officials. Robin had to pull strings to get us on board. The government only allowed Robin and Charles to come with us, saying two translators were enough. Jubilee had gone 10 days earlier to make all the detailed arrangements for us. Jubilee was a Chin, who had been born and raised in Kalemyo where his parents still lived.

When we arrived at the Kalemyo Airport, we put our luggage on airport carts, and pushed them out of the airport and across the street to the hotel. Robin indicated that this was the government hotel where we were required to stay. It looked nice from the outside, but it had a lot to be desired on the inside. We found out later it was the best hotel in town. The next day Robin's wife, Mi Mi, and Jubilee's wife Mo Mo, were able to get a flight to Kalemyo, so they could join us and help with translation.

The next morning we were up at 5:30 to get ready for our 6 o'clock devotions. There was no electricity and consequently no lights. We learned that the hotel only furnished electricity from 6 to 8 a.m. and from 6 to 10 p.m. When the city electricity wasn't available during those periods, which was frequent, the hotel had its own generators which they used. It was the same every morning. We got up and got ready by flashlight.

At our first morning devotions I asked Robin to give his testimony, share his call to the ministry, and his walk with the Lord. After a time of prayer, Robin shared the following story with us: "I was born in Yangon, to devoted Buddhist parents. When I was in college, I had a friend who kept asking me to attend an evening church meeting with him. I told him no, and that I was Buddhist, but he kept asking me every night. Finally one evening I broke down and said, "Okay." We sneaked into the church while they were singing, and sat in the very last row, hoping no one would see me. After I listened to the salvation message, an invitation was given for those who wanted to believe in Jesus to come forward. I am not sure how it happened, but the next thing I knew, I was walking down the aisle, and I gave my life to Jesus, and became a Christian. I got a Bible and started reading it.

Eventually I had to tell my mother why I didn't want to go to the Buddhist Temple with her and worship Buddha. Once I told my parents that I had become a Christian, they asked me to leave home. I moved in with my friend, and finished working my way through college. I maintained a good relationship with my parents and continued to show them love. It wasn't long before I won my mother to the Lord, and then my father.

After college I wanted to study more about Christianity. There were no Christian schools in Myanmar, so I walked many days over the mountains into India. I caught a bus, and went to Southern India where I found a Bible College. I worked my way through college again. By chance, I received an opportunity to go to the United States, and I landed in Southern California. I had heard about the Fuller Theological Seminary. I got a cab and went as far as my remaining money would take me. I found a hotel and asked at the desk if they knew where Fuller Theological Seminary was. They said it was within walking distance, but since it was Sunday, there would be no one there. I explained my situation and they were kind enough to let me sleep in a soft chair in the lobby. The next morning I walked to Fuller and went to the admissions office. I explained my dream of getting a better Christian education, so that I could go back to Myanmar and help save my people. Fuller had never had a student from Myanmar. They gave me a scholarship and I studied hard for several years, and eventually received a doctorate degree.

I returned to Myanmar with the help of several area churches which helped sponsor me. I became a traveling evangelist. At one of the churches where I was holding evangelistic meetings, I met my wife, Mi Mi. We got married and had three children. I continued to be an evangelist and helped to start many churches. I became pastor of the Nazarene Church in Yangon, and eventually became overseer of all the Nazarene churches in Myanmar. I founded and became president of the Myanmar Christian Evangelistic Association, which included many different churches, all committed to the same goal of nationwide evangelism. I started an orphanage and a Bible School with one, two, and four year diploma and degree programs. My family has all stayed active in my ministry." Wow! What a story and what a man of God.

After breakfast we loaded into a small bus, and drove 20 minutes to a suburban community center, where Jubilee had arranged for us to set up our clinics. We couldn't set up outside, because the government wouldn't allow any outside gatherings of people. Jubilee had to schedule a limited number of patients at a time. He asked them to come at different times, so we wouldn't attract a large crowd. He did a great job, because we always had patients, and it never really got crowded.

Jubilee found a young Christian man named Peter, who knew some English, and asked him to be my translator. Peter was a traveling pastor of several small house churches in the rural area surrounding Kalemyo.

Kalemyo is one of the largest cities in the Chin State. Myanmar is divided into seven states, mainly by the areas occupied by different people groups. Myanmar has seven major people groups and over 100 smaller groups that have different languages, traditions, and customs. The people in Kalemyo were mainly Chin people. Jubilee had a special burden for his Chin people.

Getting our first clinics started was a little difficult, because we didn't have enough translators. To begin with, I shared Peter with Dr. Young. Peter worked fairly well, considering his English wasn't fluent, and that he had never translated for anyone. Our first few patients were Christians, but then we had mostly Buddhist patients, who had never heard of Jesus, or what Christians believed. We didn't have the time or adequate personnel to share Jesus with our patients.

In Cameroon, we had a large team of evangelists that worked with us. In China, we had adequate translators who were excellent evangelists and helped us a great deal. Here, I had no one to help me share the good news of the Gospel. I started feeling very uncomfortable. I was relieving my patients' pain and infection, and sending them right out the door to go straight to hell. They probably would never have another chance to hear about Jesus. I personally was uncomfortable about leading people to Christ; because I had never really done it by myself. I always had help.

After our first day of clinic, I went back to the hotel and tried to sleep, but I couldn't. All I could think about was all the people that I had sent out the door to hell, without telling them about Jesus. This really upset me. I prayed and asked the Lord for help. After all, I had gone to church one, two, or three times a week for over 60 years. I should know by now, how to put together a salvation message, although no one had ever sat down and told me the one, two, threes of how to do it. I didn't want to pressure people, and make them think they had to become Christians in order to get their teeth pulled.

I laid awake most of the night with my mind racing back over 60 years of teaching, trying to put together a simple message of salvation for the non-educated Buddhists, who had never heard of the name of Jesus. I felt strongly that everyone ought to have an opportunity to hear what a Christian believed, if they wanted to, at least once in their life. I felt that everyone should have a voluntary choice to become a Christian, or not, and that they shouldn't feel pressured, as if they were being backed into a corner.

By morning I came up with a sequence of what Christians believe, and a simple message of how to become a Christian. I had it fairly well memorized. I promised God that everyone who wanted to would have the opportunity to hear about Jesus.

We had clinic in the same building for four days. People came from many miles away to our clinic. I held true to my promise to God. After telling people that we were Christians and that we loved them, I asked them if they would like to know what Christians believed. I was surprised that everyone said, "Yes," so I told them in simple terms what Christians believe. I'm sure it was rather poorly done at first. But when I asked them if they wanted to become a Christian, again I was shocked, that almost everyone said, "Yes."

I was excited, because I was doing something more important than just extracting teeth. The relief of pain was only temporary because other toothaches would likely occur, but salvation through Jesus was eternal. The first afternoon after I started sharing about Jesus, a woman came to me, in her mid-30s, and requested the removal of a couple of painful teeth. I numbed her, and started to share with her. She asked to know what Christians believe, so I told her. She seemed unusually interested, so I spent some extra time with her. She was very excited to receive Jesus into her heart and life, and she became a Christian.

The next morning, the same lady came back. She brought a friend, about her same age. Her friend had some painful teeth also. I thought she must have been happy with the teeth that I took out for her yesterday, because she was bringing her friend. After I numbed her friend, I told her that we were Christians and we loved her, and asked if she knew what a Christian believed. She said, "Oh yes, my friend told me all about Jesus last night. He has forgiven my bad deeds, and I have invited him into my heart and life, so now I'm a Christian also." She told me this with great enthusiasm and excitement, smiling from ear to ear.

Two things flashed through my mind. First I had a great sense of humility. I had been a Christian for 60 years before I led my first person to Christ. This woman had been a Christian only a few hours before she led her first person to Christ. Secondly, HTI considers itself seed planters. We plant the Gospel in people who have never heard of Jesus. Jesus tells us, not all seeds will fall on fertile ground. But that seed I planted yesterday must have landed on real fertile ground, because the results were good, and quick.

HTI doesn't often get to see the results of the seeds of the Gospel that we plant. Seeing this rapid multiplication of the Gospel, was one of the biggest rewards I could have received for all the efforts that I put into mission trips and HTI. This was only the second day that I had shared the Gospel of Jesus by myself, and it was already multiplying. I was also getting excited because almost everybody I shared the Gospel with wanted to pray and to invite Jesus into their heart, and become Christians. This motivated me even more.

I shared at our morning devotions the conviction that God had given me about sharing the plan of salvation to anyone who wanted to hear, and the fantastic success I was getting. I also shared the story of how this one patient had led her friend to the Lord only hours after she had become a Christian. This was encouraging to all of our team. Some asked me how I was doing it, so I told them the exact sequence of what the Lord had laid on my heart to share. See Chapter 38 for details.

I even shared with patients who just requested an exam or advice, and they became Christians. When I treated children, I invited the parents into the clinic, and shared with them. When we had families; husband, wife, sisters, mother and daughters, and such, we shared with them together. The result was all the same. Everyone wanted to become a Christian.

The way our family sharing actually got started, was when we had a young lady in her 20s that brought her very old grandmother to us for dental pain. The grandmother didn't understand the Burmese language, and only spoke Chin. The granddaughter translated grandma's Chin into Burmese, and then Peter would translate the Burmese into English. Everything I said had to be double-translated and the reverse when she said something. She asked to know what Christians believed, so I told her. When I asked if she would like to become a Christian, the granddaughter spent a lot of time talking to her. Finally, the granddaughter came back with this answer, "I'm not sure that grandma understands all of what you're saying, but I want to be a Christian. Can I be a Christian?" We led her to Christ. She had only been the translator, and we mentally had been talking only with grandma. From then on, we included all the family members in our discussion of what Christians believe, and in our invitation to become a Christian. Many times we would have two and three family members who became Christians together.

One evening after supper, I noticed Robin in the lobby of the hotel busily writing. He had filled a whole page with writing. Curiosity got the best of me, so I asked him, "What are you writing." He said, "My daily report to the government. I have to fax the government's intelligence department a detailed description of our daily activities every day." I thought they sure are keeping close track of us. We were located well out of the areas that tourists were allowed.

When we were packing up on our last day of clinic, I gave Peter, my faithful translator, a few small gifts, and I thanked him for his help. Peter surprised me by saying; "I am the one who should be thanking you. You have taught me so much about how I should be telling people what Christians believe, and then telling them how to become Christians. I am going to make this the central theme of my ministry."

Saturday morning before we left to return to Yangon, Jubilee took us to the local market. The market had no souvenirs, because tourists weren't allowed in this part of the country. Jubilee introduced us to his mother, who was sitting on a raised wooden platform with hundreds of bolts of material all around her. Jubilee indicated that she sat there six days a week for the last 20 years selling material. There were about 10 stalls selling fabric all around her, and very few people in the market. Jubilee's dad was an auto mechanic. After Robin had become a Christian, He led his mom, dad, and his whole family to Christ. I thought as I left Jubilee's mom, how blessed I am. I would be bored out of my mind, spending six days a week for 20 years, sitting on the floor with little to do, except bargain and haggle with occasional customers.

We had a good flight back to Yangon. Sunday morning we went to Robin's church. He had some of our team give greetings and a short testimony. He asked me to deliver the main sermon. After church we went out for dinner.

In the afternoon we went to the largest and most important Buddhist Pagoda in the world. A Buddhist Pagoda is a place of worship. This place was called Shwedagon Pagoda. It consisted of a very tall golden cone-shaped structure on a hill right in the middle of Yangon, with 20 or 30 Buddhist temples surrounding it. You could see it from most parts of the city, and it was lit up all night. There has been a pagoda on this site for 2500 years. It is said to have eight hairs of Buddha buried underneath the pagoda. It is 326 feet tall, contains many tons of gold and has 80,000 diamonds and precious jewels located at the very top. This is a massive wealth for a country where most of its people are in great poverty.

It was a most interesting place to visit, but at the same time it broke my heart to see all those people bowing down and worshiping a stone image of a man, who lived 2500 years ago. Buddha himself said many times in his writings that he was not God. These people were trying so hard to find and please God, but no one had ever told them that it was only through Jesus that they could find God. In spite of all their efforts, they were headed to hell. What a heartbreak that was! These were beautiful loveable people that Jesus loved very much, but they had no one to tell them about Jesus.

That evening we packed for our next week's clinic. The next morning we were up, had breakfast, had our bus loaded, and were on the road by 6 a.m. Robin wanted to get out of town before the morning rush hour traffic. We left Yangon and headed north on the Road to Mandalay. We had a six-hour drive, on Myanmar's main road right up the middle of the country's large fertile valley, located between the surrounding mountain ranges.

We passed several large trucks loaded with huge teakwood logs, which had been cut in the mountains. They were headed to Yangon for export. Teakwood was the country's most valuable export, followed by rice. The valley was flat and filled with bright green rice fields as far as you could see in all directions. Occasionally we saw rice thrashing floors, which were hard, packed dirt circles around a center post, where oxen slowly walked around the center post and tramped out the rice. That was the same type of thrashing that Jesus talked about back in the Bible times 2000 years ago. It was amazing to see the contrast between the 2000 year-old thrashing floor, beside a paved highway with trucks and buses moving along at 50 miles an hour.

The road traffic consisted of about 5% trucks and buses, with extremely few cars, 5% ox carts, 20% motorcycles, 50% bicycles, and 20% of people just walking. That was quite different from our main highways in the U.S. The road was being resurfaced in several places. There was 200 foot-long sections where men would heat up barrels of tar, with wood fires, until it melted. They then put it in small buckets and poured it onto the road. The women would work on piles of rocks which had been dumped alongside the road. They broke the rocks into small pieces with hammers. They put the small stones in a basket, carried them to the road, and sprinkled them onto the hot tar. Needless to say, there were 10 times more women workers than men. I figured if they did 200 yards a day, they would be doing well, but it would take a long time to go 600 miles, which was the full length of the road.

Our ride on the Road to Mandalay was an education in itself. We actually went only half-way to Mandalay. The vehicles drove on the right-hand side of the road just like in the U.S., but the driver and the steering wheel were on the right side. That meant when you came up behind a truck, the driver would have to pull all the way out into the oncoming traffic, on the two-lane road, before he could see if it were safe to pass. That would have been suicide, so the driver had an extra person that stayed on the far left-hand side of the vehicle, and told the driver when it was safe to pull out and pass.

We arrived at the town of Taungoo, which was the capital of the Karen State. This state contained predominantly the Karen people, who had their own language and customs. The official language of the country was Burmese, which was being taught in all the schools. Most of the Karen people spoke both their native Karen language and Burmese.

We turned off the main road and drove east. We crossed over the main river of the central valley and went a mile or two out of town. We arrived at a small Nazarene Church which had a group of people around it. There were 12 young ladies all dressed in brightly colored traditional Karen dresses lined up to greet us. They all had fresh flower leis, which they put around our necks as we got off the bus. This was not a place where tourists were allowed, and most of these people had never seen a foreigner come to their area.

Again, Jubilee came before we did and made arrangements for our team. The church building was just one room, so Jubilee had arranged for ropes to be tied across the ceiling area, over which blankets were hung to divide the dental, medical and reception areas. Tables were already there, so it didn't take a lot of effort, to set up and start operating. A public health nurse from town came to help us. We quickly trained her in the method we used to sterilize our dental instruments. This was a big help. We had a busy and profitable clinic.

There was a military road control outpost at the edge of the town of Taungoo, which we had to come through to get to the church. Jubilee had checked with them, and they said there had been some guerrilla activity 30 or 40 miles down the road at the edge of the mountains. They were stationed there to make sure that no guerrillas came into town. They requested that we return to town before dark, because they closed the road after dark. About 30 minutes before dark, around 6:30 p.m., we closed the clinic, locked our supplies in the church, and headed back to town.

Jubilee had made arrangements for us to stay in the best hotel in town, again the government required hotel. There weren't many hotels around, with no tourists allowed, and most people being poor. At our devotions the next morning, someone asked Robin how the church got started, and how he knew about it. Robin told us this story: "I was traveling through this area in my car, about three years ago, while I was going to another town to do some evangelistic outreach work. The Lord suddenly came to me in my thoughts, and said, "Where are you going? These people need Jesus also, stop!" I pulled off the road and stopped the car. After praying, I got out and went up to the nearest house and knocked on the door. A big man came to the door and asked me what I wanted. I introduced myself and he invited me in, and we talked. He was a recently retired Myanmar Army Colonel. After talking for a while, I led him and his wife to the Lord. The Colonel got excited. He told me, "Stay right here, I'm going to get some of my friends." He came back with three other men, and the Colonel asked me to share Jesus with them. I did, and all three of them became Christians. I told the four men that they needed to start a church here in the Colonel's home. They agreed. I gave them some literature and went on my way, promising to check back with them.

On the way through the area several months later, I stopped to see how they were coming along. They were doing well, but they wanted to build a church. The Colonel said that they could use his land, where the church is today. I furnished some plans and financing, and the men built the church themselves. They built the walls out of mud and sticks, and put on a metal roof. They finished about two years ago. I visit and preach for them every few months. Otherwise, the Colonel or one of the other three men conducted the services. I felt your team would not only help care for their health needs, but also be a significant growth potential for their new young church. The church people have committed to follow up on any new Christians and to love and teach them."

Tuesday, Wednesday, and Thursday we had big all-day clinics. People came from all around the area. I guess news of our rather unusual visit traveled fast. We treated several very sick people, some that were brought by ox cart from the foothills of the mountains. On Tuesday one of Robin's former Bible School students, who was now pastoring a church in the Mon state, a good 10 hours away, arrived by bus to help us with evangelism. He shared the Gospel mainly with the medical patients, because the doctors were swamped with patients. Dental had less patients and more time, so we continued to share Jesus with each of our patients, and we had almost100% success.

I did have one patient that Jubilee advised me to not share the Gospel. The patient, a young man in his 20s, who had an abscessed tooth, told us that he was a government intelligence agent. He was sent to spy on us, and he had to make a report on us when he left. He was the only one, after the first day with whom I did not share the Gospel. I felt bad, but I respected Jubilee's wisdom. We were in an area where tourists were not allowed, and we were engaging in some activities that would probably displease the government.

For lunches, we went next door to the Colonel's house. Mi Mi had supervised the cooking, with the help of the Colonel's wife, and a few other women. They cooked our lunches over open wood fires in the back yard of the house. We had outstanding lunches. The Colonel had a beautiful teenage daughter that had the longest hair I had ever seen. It hung down her back well below her knees.

I had about 300 pairs of glasses donated to me. I had cleaned them, put them in plastic sandwich bags, and brought them with me. I didn't take them to Kalemyo because of the airline weight restrictions. I put them out on a table in the reception area, with a reading chart. Mi Mi saw the need, so she decided to help the people who were interested in glasses, to find the right pair, simply by using a trial and error method. She had them try on different glasses until they could read the fine print on the bottom of the reading chart. She became very popular and used every single pair of glasses I brought.

The Colonel, Robin, and Jubilee had planned evening evangelistic services in the church, but because of the military restrictions we couldn't do it. They decided to have a short service right after lunch before we started clinic. Tuesday afternoon the church was about half full. Wednesday afternoon there was a full church. They had an electronic keyboard which somebody had learned to play, and that was a big help to the service. The people sang loudly and with enthusiasm and clapping their hands. Robin gave a short evangelistic message each day with significant results.

I had one lady that received a pair of glasses before she came to get her aching tooth extracted. She was excited and happy. She could see much better and could now read. I shared the Gospel with her and she became a Christian. In the course of our conversation she said, "I'm so glad that I skipped work today so that I could come and get my glasses, have my tooth pulled, and become a Christian." I asked her, "Where do you work?" She said, "For the government. I help resurface roads." Yes, her job was breaking the stones into small pieces with a hammer, carrying them in her basket, and sprinkling them into the hot tar. I asked her, "How much do you get paid?" She said, "The same as everybody else, ten cents an hour." She was very happy and proud of her job. I don't know if she earned enough money in a week to buy enough rice to eat.

We were told that glasses cost over $100 in Myanmar. I guess that's one reason she was so excited about receiving her new glasses. That also explained why we never saw anyone in the rural areas wearing glasses.

I had a mother and dad bring their 10-year-old daughter for help with a toothache. I numbed her, and the parents wanted to know what a Christian believed, so I told them. All the time that I was telling them, the young girl looked straight into my eyes and listened intently. When I finished I asked the parents if they wanted to become Christians, and they both said, "Yes." Just before we started to pray, the young girl burst out and said, "What about me? I want to become a Christian too." I had the privilege to lead all three of them to the Lord. It is sometimes difficult to tell when children understand, or when they are ready to make a decision. After that experience, I decided that in the future, if there were any question at all, I would ask the child, "What about you?" Several children surprised me by accepting the Lord.

On our morning drive to the clinic on our last day, we stopped at the military roadblock. Jubilee told the Army guard that this was our last day and we might be a little late leaving. We had our closing service after we finished with all our patients, packed our supplies, loaded the bus, took down the blanket dividers, and put the bench back in the church. The church was totally packed with people sitting on the benches, sitting on every square inch of floor, standing in the doorways, and hanging in the windows. A church this size in the U.S. would probably hold 30 or 40 people. That evening we probably had nearly 200 people in and around the church. The singing was fabulous. Robin, Jubilee, the Colonel, several other church leaders, and I all shared a few words.

We then presented each of the church leaders with a complete Bible, which they didn't have. The Government did not allow Bibles to be brought into the country, and as a result they were very hard to find. I gave the public health nurse a gift for helping in dental. I also gave the Colonel the watch which I was wearing. I had bought several five dollar nice-looking gold watches at Wal-Mart before I came, and I had put this one on special that morning. This went over real big because watches were a luxury item. They thanked us, and we thanked them, for their part in setting everything up, organizing, feeding us, and everything else that they had done. The success of a venture like that involved many people helping in many different ways.

It was an hour after dark before we said our final goodbyes, loaded on the bus, and started leaving. It was really hard to say goodbye. These people were so lovable and appreciative. Everyone wanted to shake our hand and pat us on the back. Children were hanging on my legs. We finally got going and when we got to the army checkpoint, the gate was closed. There was a uniformed soldier with a gun standing in front of the gate. Our bus driver stopped 50 feet away from the gate. I thought we could be in for trouble. Jubilee jumped out and went up and talked with the soldier at the gate for quite a while. I was wondering where are we going to sleep tonight. Finally, Jubilee came back smiling, and the soldier opened the gate, and we went through. Jubilee explained to us that the soldier was waiting for us because he wanted to be sure we stopped, so he could thank us for the great pair of glasses he received at our clinic that morning. He was seeing so much better. That was just another reason to praise the Lord.

Friday morning we drove back to Yangon with no problems. After lunch we went to the Central market again and did our final shopping. That evening we went to a nice restaurant with most of Robin's family for a farewell banquet.

Saturday morning Robin promised he would have our final bills all added up, and could tell us what we owed him. Robin had paid for all our expenses while we were in the country. Originally when I discussed cost with Robin many months ago, he estimated our in-country expenses would probably be around $2800. I told Robin that was unacceptable. HTI never had our expenses run over $1500 for a two-week mission anywhere in the world. He really didn't know, because he had never done this before, so he started getting some estimates from hotels, buses, etc. He came back with an estimated cost of $1600-$1800. I told him we could live with that, but that we would need a final accounting.

Two months before we came, Robin e-mailed me and said that the U.S. government had just imposed a financial embargo on Myanmar, and the U.S. dollar could not be exchanged into Myanmar currency or the Myanmar currency into U.S. dollars. Credit cards could not be used. The U.S. government, as well as other governments, was trying to put pressure on Myanmar's military dictatorship.

Robin had a plan because he needed some money before we arrived. He had a friend who was a Chinese businessman, who did business in both Myanmar and the United States. In fact he had a house in California where he lived part-time. Robin arranged for me to send the Chinese businessman $1000 for each team member, or a total of $7,000 to his bank in California by a wire transfer. The businessman was going to transfer our funds into Chinese currency, and then transfer the Chinese currency into Myanmar currency. The businessman would then give the money to Robin, so he could make our advance reservations. This sounded good. Robin gave me the name of the man, the name of the bank, and the bank account number, where I was to transfer the money. He also gave me a phone number, if I had any questions.

I was a little uncomfortable, so I called the phone number and asked for the Chinese businessman. I was told, "He is not here." I asked a lot of questions, and got a lot of vague answers. I talked with several people with heavily accented English. I asked, "When will the businessman return?" They didn't know. I asked, "Have you ever heard of Reverend Robin Seia?" They answered, "No." I asked, "Are you Christians?" They answered, "No, we are Buddhist." I was getting more uncomfortable. I told them, "I have been asked to wire $7,000 and I gave them the bank name and account number." They said, "No don't do that, send it to us in a check." That was the final straw. I said, "Thank you," and hung up the phone.

I e-mailed Robin, and told him what had happened. I got an e-mail back saying his Chinese businessman friend had not talked to his family, and they were unaware of the arrangements he had made with Robin. Robin indicated he had the problem solved. I was to call Sue and talk only with her. I called Sue and she had been told about the agreement between Robin and the Chinese businessman, and said, "It is okay to send the money to the bank as directed." I wired the $7,000 and Robin reported that he received the money very shortly thereafter. Everything finally worked as planned.

Saturday morning Robin presented me with a final bill, and it totaled $1625 per person. The biggest expenses were $4500 for the appreciation he needed to pay to many people along the way, and the airline tickets we had purchased to fly to Kalemyo. Airline tickets for foreigners were three times as expensive as they were for Myanmar citizens. I collected the balance from everyone and gave it to Robin and everybody was happy.

In summary: We treated just over a thousand patients, and saw 125 Buddhists become Christians. I had the conviction, determination, and courage to develop and organize a commentary on what a Christian believes, and how you can become a Christian. As a result I had the wonderful opportunity and pleasure of leading my first 45 people to salvation in Jesus, completely by myself. That was almost 100% of every Buddhist with whom I talked. I also had the unique privilege of seeing some of the fruits of my efforts multiply, when the one lady led another lady to the Lord only a few hours after she had become a Christian. This certainly had been for me my most rewarding mission to date, and the beginning of greater things to come.

## And Now the Rest of the Story

This was Dr. Bill Johansen's first HTI mission. He has gone on several additional HTI missions. He was invited to join HTI Board of Directors and is currently vice president. In early 2007 he led his first HTI mission team to Myanmar, which was very successful. He has led two successful teams since.

The significant interest in our eye glasses distribution on this mission, has led to a much more technically sophisticated distribution method of fitting glasses. Currently, eye glasses have become one of our most requested healthcare services.

Robin was very pleased with the results of our joint efforts and asked me before we left to go home, "You will bring back another team again next year, won't you?"

# CHAPTER 32

# MYANMAR 2

The Buddhists in Myanmar were so open to the Gospel that I couldn't wait to return. I haven't been anywhere in the world where every person I talked to about Jesus wanted to become a Christian. Reverend Dr. Robin Seia was anxious for us to return also. His goal is also to reach the unreached. Our team led more people to Jesus in two weeks, than his Ministry usually did in a year.

Dora May and I were the only two members of our first team that could return in January 2005. Perry and Penny Sherwood from our church, who had gone with us to Cameroon a couple of times, agreed to join us. I requested that they take charge of fitting glasses. A dentist, Dr. Dale Christophe, from British Columbia who went with me to Tibet, phoned me and asked to join us on this trip. Dr. Dale had previously committed to go on our first Myanmar mission, until he found out his wife was pregnant, and due to deliver the same time as we were scheduled to be gone. Due to that, he said, "Plan on me for next year." Dotty Staggers, a nurse who had gone to Cameroon several times with me, called and asked to join the team. Dr. Dale Lewis, a retired dentist from Colorado, and his wife Mary Ann called and asked to join us.

I had 8 team members signed up by mid-summer, but not one physician. I was starting to get a little concerned. I got an invitation to display our HTI booth at a Health Missions Conference at a church in St. Louis, Missouri, on a Saturday in early November. I usually get a lot of invitations that I cannot accept, so I didn't think seriously about it and just set it aside. In early October, Dora May and I took our motor home and went to New England to see the fall colors, and to visit a former pastor. One night when I was praying, I asked God what I was going to do about finding a physician for our Myanmar mission. The Lord seemed to rather clearly tell me, that He had sent me an invitation to go to the Health Missions Conference in Missouri, but I hadn't done anything about it. As soon as we returned home, I called and made arrangements to display our HTI booth at the St. Louis Conference.

I marked that Friday off my dental office schedule, and Dora May and I left very early and drove nine hours to the St. Louis area. We found the church and set up our HTI booth, because they planned to open the conference Friday evening. One of the conference organizers came by our booth, and during our conversation I told him of my need and concern for getting a physician for our scheduled Myanmar mission in January. He said to me, "That's the whole purpose of this conference, to get the Christian healthcare providers to start doing short-term mission work." Then he said, "I will give you 10 minutes during our opening session tomorrow morning to share your need with everyone attending the conference."

Saturday morning I told the 75 to 100 professionals in attendance, about my need for a physician to go to Myanmar. I told them that when I was invited to go on my first mission trip, I couldn't think of a good excuse not to go, that would satisfy God. I then said, "I would like to invite you to go to Myanmar with me in January, and if you think you have an excuse not to go, see if God is willing to accept your excuse." It was short and sweet, but to the point!

After the opening session there was time for the participants to visit the exhibits. I had two physicians come to me and say that they were interested, so I told them the details. Dr. Brian Andrews was an OB GYN specialist and hadn't done general medicine for many years. He was sure that his wife would not agree to let him go, but he really wanted to go. Guess what? I phoned his wife and talked with her for over an hour. He went, and did fine.

The other physician was a Pediatric Emergency Room Physician, Dr. Cora Orphe. She had planned to go to Haiti, but the door was closing there because of the violence and safety problems. She also agreed to go with us. The Lord answered my prayers about getting physicians, but I almost missed the opportunity. About a month before we were to go, Dr. Dale from British Columbia called, and said his best, friend a physician, Dr. Noel Grisdale, from Calgary, Canada, wanted to join us. Now we had 11 team members, including three physicians and three dentists.

We all met in the Thai Airways waiting area at the Los Angeles Airport, on a Friday evening on January 28, 2005. We flew to Bangkok, where we stayed overnight, and then flew to Yangon Monday morning. We lost Sunday crossing the International Date Line.

Customs in Yangon was a little different this time. Robin wasn't allowed into the customs area. The customs officers started opening our luggage. Then what appeared to be the head customs agent started raising his voice and getting very upset. Robin heard him and came into the customs area anyway. He went up to the man and asked what the problem was. The man got very angry, and started screaming in Robin's face nonstop for several minutes. Robin stayed cool, and when he got a break, he told the man he had already seen the top customs officer, and made the necessary arrangements for us. The man suddenly smiled, and said, "Okay, sign here, and you're free to go." In reality what Robin had said was, "I have already shown my appreciation to your boss, sorry you didn't get the word."

Robin and family took us to our hotel. In the afternoon we went to visit the orphanage and Bible school. The house mother assembled the 30 some children and they sang songs and repeated scripture for us. They sang with great gusto and enthusiasm. The children were ages 4 to 16, and from several different people groups from all parts of the country. The song that I will never forget was one they sang in English, "I Have Decided to Follow Jesus." Robin said they had all made a profession of faith, and that some of the former orphans were currently in his Bible school.

That evening Robin and his family took our team to the Royal Barge again for a great buffet and a Myanmar cultural show. The next morning we went to the private home of one of Robin's church members. It was about an hour's drive from the hotel and in a poor residential suburb. The street was barely wide enough for our small van to maneuver. The host family had taken all the furniture out of their ground floor, except for the tables that we needed for our clinic. We set it up for dental, medical, and pharmacy inside the house, but Perry and Penny had to set up outside to do the optical. This time we had brought over a thousand pairs of glasses along with a photometer. The photometer was a small telescopic instrument that the patients could look through, and adjust it until the chart 20 feet away was in focus. Then we could read the markings on the side of the photometer, similar to the f-stops on a camera lens. This told us what strength of glasses the patient needed. It worked quite well, but you needed good light, and a distance of 20 feet to the eye chart.

We had lots of patients waiting, so we got right to work. At our devotions that morning, I went over what I said to my patients when they wanted to know what Christians believe, and how I led them to salvation. Shortly after our clinics started, I went to check and see how our new glasses program was working with Perry and Penny. As I was walking by medical, I overheard Dr. Brian praying the sinner's prayer and leading his patient to Jesus. I stopped and waited for them to finish. I then asked Brian, knowing the patient didn't understand English, "Is this your first one this morning?" He smiled broadly and said, "Not only the first one this morning, but the first one in my life." I said, "Good feeling isn't it?" He beamed with happiness and said, "It's great."

I continued my promise to God, to tell all my patients who wanted to hear what Christians believe and how to become a Christian. They all wanted to hear, and they all wanted to become Christians. Dr. Christophe, Dr. Lewis and Mary Ann were doing the same thing right beside me, and having the same results. You may remember that Dr. Dale had just given his heart to the Lord one and a half years ago, just before going on our Tibet mission.

When I asked one lady if she knew what Christians believed, she said rather firmly, "No, I am a Buddhist." I asked her kindly how she became a Buddhist. She paused for a moment, and then said, "I don't know, I guess I was just born a Buddhist." I asked her if she would like to know what Christians believe, and she said, "Yes." After 30 minutes I asked her if she would like to become a Christian, and she really got excited and said, "Yes," and she prayed to become a Christian. When I told her she was now a Christian, she got even more excited, and told me this story: She said, "Several years ago some American Baptist missionaries helped my daughter to become a Christian. My daughter has been trying to tell me about Jesus ever since, but I just didn't understand." She said, "Now I understand, and I can go tell my daughter that I am a Christian too, and I will be able to spend forever with her in heaven someday." She beamed with a big smile of happiness, and literally danced out of the clinic.

The Mayor of the community came into our clinic. Robin showed him around, and explained what we were doing. After a few moments, he said to Robin, "You Christians aren't so bad after all. I will lift my ban on showing your film in the community center." Later when Robin asked our host what the mayor meant, he told him that they had been trying to show the Jesus Film in the community center for a long time, but each time they asked the mayor for permission, he said, "No." They were very excited about his change of heart.

I was very excited and really pumped up because every patient I treated was accepting Christ. Around noon Robin came and said, "We need to close the clinic and go to a local restaurant for lunch." I really wasn't hungry and I didn't want to go. I started thinking; there were more patients here than we would be able to see. If I went to lunch there would be two or three patients I wouldn't be able to share Jesus with, and they would probably end up in hell, just because I had to go eat lunch. My strong guess was that most of the people waiting in line wouldn't go home for lunch. I was starting to feel very guilty about this, and told Robin. He said, "If you don't eat and take care of yourself, and you get sick, there will be a lot of people who won't get to hear about Jesus." I was the team leader, the boss, but I was in Myanmar. I guess I was under the authority of Robin, my host. I finally gave in reluctantly and went to lunch with the rest of the team.

In the afternoon I had a spry lady in her mid-30s come in and sit down in my chair. When I asked how I could help her, she said, "I don't have any dental problems, but my friends told me that you are telling people about Jesus. I just want to hear about Jesus." She also accepted Jesus into her heart and life.

The local Burmese pastor, who was translating for me, just shook his head in amazement. He said, "You don't understand how hard it is to convert these Buddhists to Christianity." He said, "Sometimes I will work a whole year and only two or three people will be converted. Here everyone who is sitting down is becoming a Christian. People are even begging you to tell them about Jesus. I don't understand and can't believe what's happening." I told him, "I don't understand it either, but I know one thing, I have never saved anyone, only the Holy Spirit can change a person's heart. We are just His messengers."

After we closed the clinic at the end of the day, we gathered around and sang our Myanmar theme song, "This Is the Day That the Lord Has Made." After singing, Robin thanked our hosts and presented them with one of the Bibles I had brought. They didn't have a Bible. It's illegal to import them. I brought several with me, and we gave them as gifts. I gave the man of the house my watch off my wrist as a thank you. Again the watch was a five dollar Wal-Mart special that looked real expensive and worked fine. He was extremely happy.

Robin had hoped to take our team back to Kalemyo, to the Chin people. He couldn't buy our tickets ahead of time. They only scheduled a day or two in advance and there were some political problems as well as mechanical airplane problems that were complicating the situation. He had hoped we could fly to the Chin people the first day, but he couldn't get tickets, so at the last minute he scheduled this house clinic. I was happy and felt we had a great first day clinic.

Robin spent much of our first day on his cell phone. He still couldn't get airline tickets for us, and it didn't look good for the future. He called a former student who was now a pastor of a church in the Mon state, and asked if he could bring our team to his church. This pastor was the one who came by bus for eight hours, to work as an evangelist last year when we were in Taungoo, with the Karen people. He was very excited that we would consider coming to his church.

At 6 a.m. the next morning, we loaded the bus and headed for the Mon state. The Mon people are the most unreached people group in Myanmar. It was a good six-hour drive. We stopped after five hours in a small town, where Robin went into a hotel and left a deposit on the rooms he had booked for us by phone the previous day. After another hour of riding, we came to a small Nazarene Church. We had passed many Buddhist temples, but this was the first church we had seen. Robin indicated it was the only Christian church in this whole area.

The pastor had cleared out the church furnishings, and it was ready for us to set up our clinic. The pastor's wife and some helpers provided us with a quick lunch before we started. Perry and Penny set up outside again, with their eye clinic.

Some government army officers visited us, and asked "What's going on and why so many people?" The pastor had led the local retired Chief of Police to Christ and had him there helping with the registration of patients. Between the Chief of Police, the pastor, Robin, and a little appreciation, they finally left and caused no problem.

They did inform us that a big new bridge, the largest one in Southeast Asia, which crossed the bay into the neighboring town of Moulamein, was going to be dedicated in a day or two. It had been bombed twice during construction by terrorists. Security was very tight. Convoys of government officials that were coming to the dedication would be traveling on the road. When the convoys were coming, the road would be closed.

We had noticed how neat and clean the side of the road was when we came. We found out later that it was a strict government mandate that each home owner clean his section of the road side, so that it would be nice looking when the government officials traveled by.

We closed the clinic about 5 p.m., and headed one hour back, on the road we had just come, to our hotel. Robin couldn't get reservations anywhere in the big nearby city of Moulamein, because they were all booked by the government officials. Robin didn't want to be on the road after dark, because of safety concerns.

When we reached our hotel, we received our room assignments. Our rooms were minimally adequate, probably a one-star rating. Much of the time there was no electricity. We had supper in the hotel restaurant, which left a lot to be desired. The next morning we had breakfast there also, and got on the road very early hoping to beat the road closure for the government officials. We beat them. Shortly after our arrival at the church, the road was closed for most of that day.

Perry evidently ate some bad food at the hotel restaurant, because he became quite sick with diarrhea and high fever. The doctors gave him some strong medicine, and put him to bed in the pastor's house for the day. By evening he was feeling better, and by the next morning he was back to normal.

Early that morning a mother brought her sick baby into the clinic. Dr. Cora, our Pediatrician was asked to see the baby. The baby looked six to eight weeks old, but the mother said the baby was a little over a year old. The baby was skin and bones, very lethargic, running a high fever, and having difficulty breathing. Dr. Cora was alarmed. She said, "This baby could die any moment." She started an IV on the baby and slowly dripped in several different medications. They put the baby in a makeshift bed, and asked the mother to stay with the baby all day. By the end of the day the baby was doing much better. Dr. Cora asked the mother to bring the baby back the next day.

I had two Buddhist monks in their orange robes come into the clinic. One sat in my chair, and the other in Dr. Dale's chair. I had promised God to share the Gospel with everyone who wanted to hear, because I believe everyone deserves to hear about Jesus at least once in their life. I wondered what I should do under such circumstances as these. Jubilee, who was translating for me, checked with the local pastor. He said, "It's okay to share with them, if they want to hear." I went through the same presentation, as is described in Chapter 38, and they both said they would like to hear what Christians believe. I sat the two monks together and shared with them with Jubilee translating for me. Jubilee had done his Masters Thesis in Theology on comparing Christianity with Buddhism, so he knew what they were thinking. Jubilee added a lot of additional information to what I said, because he took much longer to translate than normal.

When I finished my explanation, I asked them the same question I asked everyone else, "Would you like to become a Christian?" They both surprised me by saying, "Yes." I led them in prayer, asking them to repeat the words after me. I didn't hear them repeating my words. When I finished praying, I asked Jubilee if they had repeated the prayer to invite Jesus into their hearts and lives. He talked to them, and they told him with a smile, that they had said it in their hearts. They didn't want to upset anyone around them that might be listening. I looked at the Buddhist monks and smiled. They smiled back with a big smile. Buddhist monks are not supposed to smile at any time. They work hard when first becoming a monk to learn not to smile at anything. I concluded that their smiles meant that Jesus had truly changed their hearts.

The two Buddhist monks shocked us by telling Jubilee how happy they were, and they wanted to know if I would come to their monastery and tell all the monks about Jesus. After talking with the local pastor and Robin, we regretfully agreed that this would not be wise. Sharing the Gospel one-on-one was okay, but preaching to a temple full of monks was definitely not. That could be dangerous in many ways, since the government was very strong and strictly Buddhist.

Due to the very poor hygiene at our hotel restaurant, and Perry's sickness, and the road being closed so much of the time, we ate all the rest of our meals at the pastor's house with the pastor's wife and several other women cooking and serving us, under Mi Mi's supervision. Everything had to be cooked over an open wood fire. They had a good well, but no running water and no dependable electricity. It was quite an interesting process. They fixed jackfruit for us one day for dessert. It was the consistency, color and size of a soft peeled peach, but was much sweeter, with a very large clingstone in the center. I had never had jackfruit before, and it was very good. It was growing on their trees in the back yard where the pastor had a fairly large garden. They fed us really well, and when we were eating the women would walk behind us and fan us, because it was very hot. I felt like a king.

One evening around 10 p.m., when we were in bed sleeping, Robin got a knock on his door. Two military officers came in, and wanted to know who all those white people were with him, and what they were doing here. Again tourists were not normally allowed in these areas. Robin gave the officers copies of our passports and visas, and explained who we were, and what we were doing, and showed them a little appreciation, and they left with no problem. Robin had already called the authorities in the area and received permission for us to come, but the officers knew this would be easy income for them. Ten dollars each was more than they got paid in an entire week.

One morning at devotions I had Jubilee give his testimony. He was born into a Buddhist family in the Chin State, near Kalemyo. He was introduced to Jesus and became a Christian at a Christian summer camp. He then came to Yangon to live with his aunt so he could go to high school and eventually the university. He met Robin, and Robin mentored him in his new Christian faith. He started attending Robin's church, where Robin's daughter Mo Mo was in the same young people's class. They were mutually attracted to each other. After graduating from the University, Jubilee wanted to study more about Christianity. Robin got him into a good theological university in the Philippines, while Mo Mo went to the United

States to Taccoa Falls Bible College in Georgia. Their romance continued to blossom via long distance. One school break when they were both back in Myanmar, they were married. Jubilee went back to school in the Philippines, and Mo Mo went back to school in the United States. Jubilee graduated first and came home and started to work with Robin. After Mo Mo graduated, she was accepted into nursing school. Before nursing school started she came home for a surprise short visit. It happened to be the Christmas after 9/11. She could never get her visa renewed to return to the U.S. They now have two beautiful children. Jubilee would like to go to the U.S. to get his doctorate in Theology, like Robin, but the U.S. Embassy will not issue Jubilee a visa. He has tried several times.

On Friday, our final day, we closed the clinic early, and had a church service with singing, testimonies, thank yous, and gifts. I gave the pastor my watch, and we presented a Bible to the retired Chief of Police, who had helped us a lot. The pastor gave each of us a gift. The men received a longye, a bright colored cloth that the men traditionally wrap around them and wear like a skirt in place of trousers. Many Burmese men wear them, including Robin and Jubilee.

We had supper, and as we were loading the bus, a woman brought a young baby into the yard with a large cleft lip and palate. Dr. Cora held the baby and her heart was broken. She knew there was nothing that she could do, and probably there was nothing that could be done anywhere in Myanmar. It was starting to get dark and we had an hour to drive. We had a difficult time separating Dr. Cora from the little baby, and getting her into the bus. We said good-bye and left. The road closure had just been lifted. It was well after dark before we arrived safely at our hotel.

Early the next morning we traveled back to Yangon, and went directly to Charles's house, which was next to the orphanage and Bible school. Charles' wife had prepared a beautiful lunch for us. After lunch we set up clinic and treated the orphans and Bible School students.

There was a very pretty 16-year-old orphan girl that was the oldest child in the orphanage. She was very hard of hearing, and couldn't go to school, or get a job, and didn't have any other place to go. Someone had given me a cheap Sears hearing aid that just fit into any average ear. I was busy but Perry was free. I asked Perry if he could figure out how this thing worked, and to please see if he could fit it into this girl's ear. It was worth a try, and I didn't want to take it home. He got it to work and fit it into her ear. We had 20 or 30 extra batteries that we gave her.

When we returned a week later, the house mother reported the hearing aid work wonderfully. The girl was not the same girl she had been before. She had self-confidence, was back in school, happy, helping her with the rest of the children and they could talk to each other now.

Sunday we went to church with Robin, and he requested I preach again. I suspected he might want me to preach, so this time I had prepared. I shared the success of our clinics with the church people, and then challenged them to help us reach the unreached. They knew who they were, and could speak their language. I made a deal with them. Our team would set up our medical, dental, and optical clinics in front of the church after the service, and would be glad to treat anyone who would commit to sharing our Christian Gospel with at least one unreached person this week. After church we had a busy clinic for a couple of hours, with each patient promising to share with at least one unreached person the Gospel of Jesus.

Later in the afternoon as it started to get cooler, we went to Shwedagon Pagoda, the world's most important and very beautiful Buddhist stupa. Again it was bleeding heart time for me, seeing thousands of beautiful people that God dearly loves, sincerely trying to find and please Him, so they would have a better life after death. To accomplish this, all that they knew how to do was to worship a stone statue of a dead man. They had no one to tell them about Jesus.

Very early the next morning we headed out in our bus on the Road to Mandalay heading to Taungoo, the capital of the Karen State. We stayed in the same hotel, and went to the same church that we worked in last year. Again the church people did a great job getting things ready, organizing and registering the people. Consequently we had some excellent clinics. In dental, Dr. Dale, Dr. Lewis and Mary Ann, and I shared the Gospel with every patient, and had great acceptance.

After they became Christians, Dora May took a Polaroid photo of them with the Dr. and translator beside them. We gave this to the patient as a gift for them to remember the most important day in their life, the day they decided where they were going to spend eternity. Watching their faces as they gradually saw the picture develop in front of them on this white piece of paper was interesting to see. Most of them had never seen or had a photo of themselves. Then we gave them a 30-page booklet of Scripture, as well as a toothbrush, Tylenol, a sticker that says "Jesus loves you," and a cloth bracelet that said, "I have Jesus in my heart." When they left they were very happy people.

Perry and Penny saw many people who needed glasses, including some Buddhist monks. The monks had a problem. They were supposed to study their Scriptures six to eight hours a day and they couldn't see to read. They had no money or material possessions. They were 100% beggars, even for their daily food. They begged glasses from Perry and Penny so they could read. They were treated with respect and kindness, and were given some Scripture tracts.

This is the first time we had three physicians and three dentists in Myanmar, and together we saw a lot of patients. Dottie, our nurse, was kept busy dispensing medications. For lunch Mi Mi found a restaurant that sold carry out food, so she went with our bus driver and brought back our lunches. We stopped and ate right in the clinic. The food was good and it was much quicker, simpler, and cheaper.

We had several patients brought in from the mountains by oxcart. People came from all over. The clinic went very smoothly allowing us to see a lot of patients. A little experience the previous week made a big difference in our efficiency. On our way back to the hotel one evening, Jubilee located a store that had interesting Karen traditional clothing and other items. They had no souvenir stores in town, because tourists were not allowed in this section of the country. We stopped and all the women got a traditional type dress of the Karen people. Some even had them tailor-made. We picked them up the next evening. They were very cheap and very pretty. Several of the women wore them to supper one evening.

We left for Yangon early Friday morning, and got back in the early afternoon, in time for everyone to shop at the city market. I never saw so much jewelry, especially rubies, which were mined in Myanmar. They were reasonably priced, but you had to learn to bargain for everything.

Later that afternoon, I went with Jubilee to the American Embassy, with the hope of talking to the U.S. Ambassador or some important official about getting Jubilee a visa to study in the United States. The Embassy was very heavily guarded with U.S. Marines. We went through several security chambers and halls, to get to the reception room. It cost Jubilee 100 U.S. dollars every time he submitted an application for a visa. He had submitted three over a period of time, and he had been turned down all three times with no refund. I was unsuccessful in getting to talk to anyone except the receptionist. I was told by the receptionist to write the Ambassador a letter, which I later did, and mailed it directly to him on University of Michigan stationery signed as a Professor Emeritus, and so far nothing has helped, not even letters from U.S. Congressmen.

On our last evening, Robin and Mi Mi invited the whole team to their apartment for supper. They lived on the second floor, over retail shops, right downtown where they had lived and raised their children for over 30 years. Many of the government officials lived in this area, and as a result they had electricity 100% of the time. The rest of the city, had electricity less than 50% of the time. Electricity was especially important for Robin, with his computer work and all his e-mails. He has also written many books using his computer. Over the years Robin became friends and gained respect with many of the politicians, who were his neighbors.

Mi Mi and her two daughters fixed a nice supper, and put it on a table in the living room. All of Robin's family was there. We filled our plates, and sat around the living room with our plates on our laps and ate while Robin and his family watched us. When we had all finished they collected our plates and took the serving dishes off the table. We sat around talking. Then I realized that Robin and his family were not with us. I wandered out to the kitchen, and Robin's whole family of 10, were sitting on the floor, where the table used to be, and they were eating our leftovers on paper plates with their fingers. They were very happy, laughing and joking as they ate. I felt very guilty. I guess that's their custom; guests eat first, and hosts eat what is left.

After supper Robin and his family gave each of us a small thank you gift, a decorated harp of the traditional Burmese style. It was very kind and a nice souvenir gift. Our only problem was its size. It was fragile, and came in a box about 18 inches square. We were due to leave for the airport early the next morning, so we were all packed to the maximum. When we got back to the hotel, everyone scrambled to repack, and tried to get it in their luggage. Some ended up carrying it separately, and the airlines didn't object.

I also presented Robin with an official certificate, making him an Associate Director of Health Teams International, in charge of HTI's missions to Myanmar. Our HTI Board of Directors had agreed to this earlier, but this was the official certificate, and it was very important to him. He certainly had worked hard caring for all the details of our mission.

Early the next morning Robin had the final total of all of our in-country expenses. I had forwarded him $1000 per person, by the same route as before. Our total per-person cost was just $1150. Our cost was much less than last year's, because there were no in-country air fares, and he was able to negotiate only half as much appreciation cost. Everyone was happy.

We flew to Bangkok and arrived around noon. We had prearranged for a group tour of Bangkok by canal boats. Bangkok has many waterways and canals. Oftentimes you could get around faster by the canal taxis than you could by roads, because of the heavy traffic. In the evening we enjoyed a dinner show. Early the next morning we flew home.

In Summary: we treated over 2000 patients, mostly Buddhists. We saw over 250 people become Christians, twice as many as on our first mission trip there. I personally saw five Christian dental patients, and 75 Buddhist patients. I spent 30 to 40 minutes with each of the Buddhist patients telling them what Christians believed and how to become a Christian. All 75 patients, including two Buddhist monks, became Christians. Introducing Jesus to these 75 Buddhists has been one of my greatest thrills, and certainly a highlight of my life. I thank God for this unique opportunity.

## And Now for the Rest of the Story

Robin and Mi Mi had an unusual opportunity to come to a large International Missions Conference in Indianapolis, Indiana, in the last week of June 2005. Surprisingly Robin and Mi Mi had no problem getting U.S. visas. Robin had only been to Fuller Theological Seminary in Southern California, and Mi Mi had never been to the U.S. Robin e-mailed me and asked if he could come and visit me after the convention, and he also asked me if I would help him visit around the United States. Their visas were good until mid-August.

The problem I had was that I had reservations to leave with 15 of my family for a three-week vacation in Colorado and Montana. I planned to leave the first of July, which was the same day Robin's Missions Conference ended. This vacation had been planned for eight months. I got on my cell phone and started making calls.

After a week or so, I worked out a schedule. Since we were scheduled to go by Indianapolis, the same day and time that his convention finished, I offered to pick Robin and Mi Mi up in our motor home, and drive them to St. Louis, where I had arranged a four-day stay, over the Fourth of July, with Dr. Brian Andrews and family. We dropped them off at Dr. Brian's, and I continued with my family out to a Christian family dude ranch nestled in the Rocky Mountains of Colorado.

On the fifth of July, Dr. Brian put Robin and Mi Mi on a plane and sent them to Denver, Colorado. Dora May and I picked them up and took them to the dude ranch, where they spent the rest of the week with us. Although Robin had never been on a horse, he rode many times with us in the mountains and had a great time. Mi Mi was fearful of horses and just sat on a horse long enough to get her picture taken.

At the end of the week, I took part of my family to the Denver airport and they went home, and I took Robin and Mi Mi to Dr. Dale and Mary Ann Lewis's home near Denver, Colorado. They stayed with Dr. Dale and Mary Ann for a week while 8 of our family went to the mountains of Montana to an ATV (all terrain vehicles) ranch. We enjoyed riding our four wheelers up into the Rocky Mountains each day for a week, while staying in our motor homes at night.

We went back to Denver, and picked up Robin and Mi Mi at Dr. Dale's and Mary Ann's, and we took them on a tour with us as we drove back to Michigan. We went through the Black Hills, Mount Rushmore, the Badlands, Wall Drugs, the Corn Palace, etc. We arrived in Chicago where we had arranged for Robin and Mi Mi to stay with friends for the weekend. They toured around Chicago, and then were put on a train for Michigan. We picked them up, and they stayed with us for a few days. They spent the next weekend with Perry and Penny. They stayed with us a few more days and we were able to show them around Detroit and southern Michigan.

We put them on a bus to Buffalo, New York, where Dottie met them, and they stayed in her home for several days. Dottie showed them around the area, including Niagara Falls, before putting them on another bus to Germantown, Maryland, where Mi Mi had a married sister whom she hadn't seen in many years. They stayed with them for a week, before getting on a bus to go back to Indianapolis to catch their international flight home. They got home the exact day that their visa expired. They saw a lot of the United States in two months. They enjoyed and appreciated everything. Between all of us we were able to care for their entire expenses. I felt that Robin's and Mi Mi's sacrifices and hard work for our Lord deserved some help from us. They had earned a good vacation. I was thankful that we were able to help them.

## CHAPTER 33

# BENIN
# THE DEVIL'S STRONGHOLD

Benin, West Africa, is the birthplace of Voodooism. Currently 70% of the population is still actively practicing Voodooism. There is no question in my mind, but that Benin is one of the Devil's largest, most active strongholds in the world today. It was a former French colony that won its independence in 1960. A Communist Marxist Military Dictatorship soon took over control of the country. In 1989 with the worldwide fall of Communism, Benin established a democratic government. In the early 2000's the people elected their first Christian president. Christians are a small minority in the country. The new Christian president recently opened Benin's borders and welcomed outside help for the first time.

Reverend John Ngoh is an associate board member of HTI and has agreed to oversee our African missions. He has hosted 12 highly successful HTI missions in his country of Cameroon, which has seen 40,000 unreached people become Christians.

Rev. Ngoh met a Christian pastor, Rev. Sam Aco at an International Missions Conference in Cameroon. They became friends. Reverend Aco, who was from Cotonou, Benin, heard about HTI and their successful missions in Cameroon. He begged Rev. Ngoh to make arrangements for a HTI team to come to Benin. Rev. Ngoh traveled to Benin and met again with Rev. Aco. He checked out the safety of the area and researched the many details of bringing a mission team to Benin.

Rev. Ngoh then e-mailed an official invitation to me to bring a HTI team to Benin, and personally offered to be our host. This was a new country and I felt the opportunity was great. I didn't have anyone available to lead the team, so I agreed to do it myself.

It wasn't difficult to get volunteer Christian healthcare providers interested in going to peaceful, but unknown Benin, West Africa. But when they, or their spouses, did a little research on Benin, and found that it was the birthplace and world center of Voodooism, most of them changed their minds and said, "No way, I don't want anything to do with Voodooism."

There's no question in my mind that Voodooism is 100% satanic. Hal Lindsay's book, "Satan is Alive and Well on Planet Earth", describes numerous instances in which Satan has demonstrated miraculous powers. I have talked with several people who have personally witnessed the satanic powers of Voodooism. I think people are wise to be concerned about Voodooism, but if you read and believe what God has told us in His Bible, then there is no reason to fear Voodooism.

The Bible assures us, that greater is He that is in us, than he that is in the world. The Bible is full of promises of God's being with us. The last phrase of the great commission at the end of Matthew says, "Lo, I am with you always, even to the ends of the earth". The Bible instructs us to flee from evil. In other words, don't participate in satanic or voodoo activities or customs. After reviewing my Bible and God's promises, I felt perfectly safe going into Satan's stronghold, because I knew that my God is stronger than Satan. If we don't participate in evil things, He will always be with us and protect us. After I started sharing that with potential team members, I started getting those people who were really solid Christian believers to agree, and to join our team.

The Lord helped me to assemble a team of 13, which consisted of three physicians, two nurses, three dentists, one dental hygienist, one dental assistant, one person to fit glasses, and two helpers. Dr. Dale Louis, a retired dentist, and his wife and assistant, Mary Ann, who had gone with me to Myanmar in February, were the first to sign up. Dr. David Shull, a physician and HTI board member, signed up and brought four others with him; Miki, his wife of a few months, who was a nurse, and three others from his church. They were; Patrick Murphy, a nurse, Dr. Robert Sigworth a physician, and Brett Pharo, the chairman of their church mission committee.

I was driving my motor home with nine of my family in it, through the hot plains of Kansas, as we were going on our summer vacation, when my cell phone rang. It was Elizabeth Martins, a dental hygienist from California. She wanted to join us. Dr. Gerry Rouse, HTI's executive director, offered to join us. He was trained and experienced in fitting glasses. Dr. Bill Johanson, a physician, offered to join us. I had an oral surgeon, Dr. Frank Greskovich ask to come. Dr. Frank was the first and only oral surgeon that has ever offered to go on a mission trip with me in over 35 trips.

Reverend John Ngoh's wife, Kathy, was in an airport killing time between flights. She was admiring some jewelry in a showcase, when a woman from behind said, "Nice piece isn't it? Why don't you buy it?" Kathy said, "I can't afford it, I'm a missionary's wife." The lady, who was a solid evangelical Christian, started asking Kathy a lot of questions, which led to our upcoming Benin mission. The lady, Cathy Tankersley, bought Kathy the jewelry. She then hurried home and called me to ask if she could go to Benin with us as a helper. I am continually amazed at the way the Lord puts our teams together. I could write many pages of interesting stories about how the Lord worked things out for willing servants, in their lives, their jobs, their families, and their finances, to allow them to come.

We met in Detroit on October 1, 2005, and we took a new discounted Air France flight from Detroit, to Paris, then on to Cotonou, Benin. We all arrived fine, but we were missing 8 of our 26 pieces of luggage. That is exactly the reason that when we pack, we put a little of each medication, supplies, and equipment in different pieces of luggage, so that if our luggage is delayed, we can still start our clinics. That was the way we had packed this time and we had a little of everything to get started.

Our luggage dribbled in one or two pieces at a time over the next week. Air France reimbursed us several hundred dollars for the delays, and apologized to us. They were having a baggage handler's slowdown in Paris, because of delays in union contract talks.

Our HTI host, Reverend John Ngoh, whom I'll refer to as John, met us at the airport. He took us to the nicest hotel in Cotonou, which was a four-star hotel. This country had been relatively closed to outsiders and tourists for a long time, and as a result there was little in the way of hotels. When we arrived at the hotel, there was a big iron gate at the entrance, with several armed guards. We were each inspected before we were allowed into the hotel grounds. Even though the hotel was on a beautiful Atlantic Beach, there was a high barbed wire fence completely around the hotel, with armed guards patrolling the fences. There were uniformed armed guards at the doors of the hotel, as well as in the lobby, in the stairwells, and in the hallways on each floor. We were warned not to try to go to the beach, because it was not safe. What a great welcome!

It was comforting to know that we would be safe in the hotel, but I wondered why all the security, and what about when we had to leave for our clinics. John explained to us that Benin was the poorest country in all of Africa and there were many people unemployed, hungry, and desperate. Although there was very little personal violence, there was a high rate of robbery. There was no value in the native people robbing their own countrymen, because none of them had any money. But they thought all white people were rich, and that they were the ones that had money and were worth robbing.

It was a nice hotel with air-conditioning, swimming pool, and a restaurant with good food. We ate and slept there daily, until we left to return home. We went right to bed upon arrival, after being up for over 36 hours. The next day was a day of rest, recovering from jet lag, unpacking, repacking for our first day of clinic, getting organized, and being indoc-trinated into our new and quite different country.

John introduced us to our local host, Reverend Sam Aco, who stopped by the hotel to visit with us. He was pastor of a large evangelical Christian church in Cotonou, and president of an Evangelistic Association of 12 Christian churches in Cotonou. The French started Christianity in Cotonou many years ago. Cotonou is the largest city in Benin, and the only port city in the country. Christianity was a small minority, and had not really spread much outside the big city.

Rev. Sam Aco's goal was to reach out into the unreached villages surrounding Cotonou with the Gospel. His evangelical group of Christian churches was working together to try to do that. They had actually trained several pastors and were supporting them financially. They had sent them out into various voodoo villages to bring the Gospel to the people. They had been living out in the villages for a year, but the results were disappointing. They hadn't been able to get many converts and they hadn't been able to start one church in any of the villages in which they had been working.

Rev. Aco had hoped that if we took healthcare into the villages, that maybe the people would start to listen, and hopefully we would have the same good results that HTI teams had been having in Cameroon. Rev. Aco had assembled a team of 25 to 30 people from 10 different churches to work as organizers, translators, evangelists, and helpers.

Each morning we were up shortly after 5. At 6 our team gathered for our daily time of prayer, devotions, testimony, and instructions for the day. At 7 we had breakfast and by 8 we were packed and on our minibus. We met two other minibuses, which had picked up our local helpers from all over town.

The first morning we traveled east for a little over an hour, approaching close to the border of Nigeria. We turned off the main road and wound our way south toward the ocean, down a two-track trail with grass growing between the tracks. We traveled slowly for several miles, before coming to a clearing that had a long building at one end. We drove up to the building, almost getting stuck in the sand. It was a six-room school which was not in session. Someone had built us a large shelter for shade in front of the school, out of sticks and palm leaves. There were very few people around when we arrived. Suddenly they started coming from everywhere, until we had several hundred people around us, watching us set up our clinics.

John and Rev. Sam Aco, whom I will refer to as Sam, gathered the people together and told them who we were, and why we had come, using a good battery operated PA system. Then they shared a short evangelistic message with an invitation, while we were setting up our clinics. I saw a lot of hands go up during the invitation, but that wasn't good enough, because each person was going to receive one-on-one personal counseling. We had a team of 45, and many were trained and assigned to be spiritual counselors.

Everyone received an invitation to return to the school yard when it got dark, to see a movie. Some of our local native team planned to return with a generator and a PA system which would first play music to assemble the people. Then they planned to show the Jesus film, in their tribal language, followed by a message, invitation and counseling. I'm sure most of these people had never seen a movie. They didn't have any type of electricity in their village. We planned to spend two days in this village, as well as two days in three additional villages.

After the morning message we started registration, counseling, and then they sent the patients to medical, dental, or the glasses clinic. Dental set up outside under the shady palm leaf shelter, to get better light and a breeze. My translator was a young man named Christian. He was about 20 years old and had been going to college in Accra, Ghana, studying computer programming. He had returned home between classes. His classes wouldn't start again until they had a minimum number of students enrolled. They promised to call him when his classes were ready to resume.

I explained to Christian about my personal conviction of the need to share the Gospel with anyone who wanted to hear. I realized that all of the patients would have had personal spiritual counseling, but I wanted to share more. He understood and was happy to help. He was a solid Christian himself.

It wasn't long until we were all busy with lots of patients. I was once again quickly reminded that these young black Africans had the hardest teeth in the world to extract. Sugarcane was abundant and almost everyone who sat down in my chair had multiple abscesses. When I asked them how long their teeth had been aching, several of them told me, that they couldn't ever remember not having a toothache. They had always ached.

I anesthetized several aching teeth for one lady, and had to leave her for a few moments. When I came back she was probably already numb and her pain was gone. I started sharing with her. My first statement was usually a question. It makes them start to think. I asked her, "Do you know why we have come all the way from America to help you?" She looked me right in the eye and said with all sincerity, "You must be angels sent by some god." She caught me by surprise. Most people just say, no. It took me a minute to refocus my thoughts. She eventually asked to hear what Christians believed, so I told her the whole story, and she committed her life to Christ.

When I took enough time, and explained things to my patients thoroughly, as I have recorded in chapter 38, almost every patient wanted to become a Christian. Different doctors share different parts of the Gospel with their patients, but none of them were anywhere as thorough as I was. Fortunately I had more time than most of the other doctors. My thinking was; most people would be reluctant to seriously change the whole direction of their beliefs and spiritual life with just 5 or 10 minutes of information. I felt it would probably take a lot more convincing information than that.

When I finished sharing the Gospel with them, I would extract their teeth, give them pain medication, instructions, and a toothbrush, because most of them had nothing for hygiene. I brought many 30-page booklets written in their own language, with key scriptures that pointed out the steps they had just taken for their salvation. I was shocked at the number of people who tried to give the booklets back to me. Some simply admitted that they couldn't read. 100% of the women and 80% of the men were illiterate. Women were never allowed to go to school in the past, and even men had little motivation or opportunity to learn to read or write.

I have read statistics from time to time about the percentage of illiteracy in different countries, but after visiting 137 different countries, this was the first time I had ever personally met a large number of adults that were totally illiterate. I never met one woman in this village who could read or write. I would ask the patients if they knew someone who could read it to them. I figured this might be a good way to get the Gospel to additional people. The answer that frequently came back was "Yes, I will get my children to read it to me. They are going to school now and learning to read." I brought a thousand of the Scripture booklets, which were designed for children, with simpler language and pictures. I located them and started handing them out to my illiterate patients.

Sam had been working with a 50-year-old single Dutch missionary, named Annie. She had been commissioned by a European Mission Society to come to Benin to survey the religious beliefs of the people in all parts of the country. The country had just been opened to outsiders and missionaries hadn't arrived yet. We were told that we were the first health-care mission group to come to Benin since the new Christian president had opened the country to outsiders.

When Annie heard that we were coming to Benin, she asked Sam how she could help. He asked her to fix our daily lunches, so it would be safe for our delicate foreign stomachs. She not only cooked for the HTI team, but also for the 30 native Christian young people that were helping us. She served lunch in one of the empty classrooms.

Annie had been in Benin over a year without seeing or talking to an English speaking foreigner. I perceived that she was a little lonely. I stayed with the dental equipment during lunch, to keep an eye on it, and ate my lunch snacks which I had brought with me. It tasted better to me than Benin food anyway.

Late the first afternoon when we were about ready to close and pack up our clinics, a lady came in the clinic carrying a three-year-old girl, who was having a very difficult time breathing. Dr. Shull was a specialist in emergency medicine. He quickly diagnosed her as having an acute asthmatic attack. The mother said that her daughter had never had this much trouble breathing. Dr. Shull took the little girl and held her in his arms and wouldn't let her go. We had no medication to treat her and he was feeling helpless. It was almost as if he were waiting for her to gasp her last breath and die in his arms, because she was gasping so severely. We were all packed up and waiting to go as it was getting late in the day. Finally Dr. Shull said, "We need to take this little girl back to town and find her some medicine or she might not make it." We took the girl and her mother with us. It was an hour drive back to Cotonou. We stopped at the first pharmacy we saw. Dr. Shull went in and bought the needed medications and some extra, and immediately administered it to her. We took the mother and child back to our hotel, to observe her until she improved. After her breathing was nearly normal, we hired a taxi to take the mother and little girl back to their village, carrying with her additional medication, in case she had another serious attack.

The second day we returned to the same isolated voodoo village. It started to get cloudy late in the morning. I could see a fairly black cloud rolling up. The palm leaves we were under were not waterproof. I started covering up our supplies and equipment on the table with large plastic shower curtains that we had brought with us. Dr. Dale and I finished our patients and just waited a little before starting another one. Dr. Frank had one of those tough teeth that had broken off, and he was starting a surgical removal. Suddenly there was a big flash of lightning, and a very loud quick crash of thunder. The native people all started to scream and run in every direction. I thought to myself, surely these people have experienced lightening and thunder before. I quickly found out they had, and they knew what they were doing, because almost instantly after the thunder, the wind started blowing hard and the sky opened up and it poured rain like I have seldom seen. I scrambled a few steps to get under the school's porch roof.

Dr. Frank continued to work. Usually this was where I would be called in to bailout a dentist. I usually had the most experience with a hammer and chisel, removing difficult teeth, but Dr. Frank was an oral surgeon, and many times more qualified than I. It still took him time and a lot of effort. I felt a little guilty just standing there watching them get soaked in the downpour. Elizabeth, (Liz,) stayed right with him, with a flashlight, and located additional supplies or equipment from under the plastic shower curtain as he needed. The patient had his head tipped back, and I noticed a couple of times that he had to stop and spit out the rainwater that was collecting in his mouth. It took them about 20 minutes to finish, and they were totally soaked. Thankfully it was warm, probably in the high 80s.

It continued to rain very hard for about an hour. As we all huddled together out of the rain, packed tightly together on the porch, a young man in his mid-20s came running toward us in the rain. He was covered with blood from head to toe. He ran right up to Dr. Frank. He was bleeding severely from an extraction earlier in the day. Dr. Frank said later, that his initial running to get out of the rain had probably increased his blood pressure so much, that he popped the blood clot out, and he made it even worse by running more when coming back to see us. I don't think I have ever seen anyone bleeding as much from an extraction as he, and to make things worse, he was a very frightened young man. His blood pressure was probably increased further because of his fear and anxiety.

Again this is a problem I normally would have been responsible to solve, and I was even frightened a little myself. This was a great trip to have my first oral surgeon with me. Dr. Frank was completely soaked but he quickly took over with soaked Liz right at his side to assist him. He went through a large number of gauze pads, putting a lot of pressure on the bleeding site, before the patient's blood pressure finally lowered a little, and the bleeding slowed. Then he put in several tight sutures, and the bleeding stopped. He instructed the patient not to do any more running or heavy exercise for the rest of the day.

There were probably a hundred people packed on the porch, and they had nothing else to do but to watch. The man bled heavily and there was blood everywhere before Dr. Frank finally got it under control. My curious mind made me wonder, what possibly could be going through the minds of all these people watching. I know one thing; it didn't slow the number of patients that lined up to get their teeth removed after the rain stopped.

The team members took advantage of the down time during the rain to go to lunch. I stayed and watched the equipment. The porch was packed with people all around me. I had my bag with all my lunch snacks in it, but I felt guilty taking it out and eating it in front of them. They looked like they needed the food much more than I did. So I fasted for lunch that day, and you know, it didn't bother me at all. After an hour it started letting up, and within another hour it stopped completely. It took us 30 minutes to clean up, sterilize all the equipment again, and to start working. Even the school classrooms experienced a lot of leaking and build-up of water. I had put a metal cup on the table on top of the plastic shower curtain before it rained to hold it down. It was about 3 inches deep, and it was full and overflowing.

After the rain stopped, some vendors from the village came around selling food for the natives' lunch. One lady had several 5-foot long stalks of sugarcane. When someone asked her for some, she would take a big machete, and put one end of the sugarcane on a block of wood, and chop the thick skin off the outside. This wasn't an easy task. She put a lot of muscle and skill into her chopping. She would then chop off a ten-inch length of sugarcane and hand it to her customer. They in turn would suck on the stalk, not eating it, but just sucking out the sugar. This was their lunch. No wonder we saw so many decayed and abscessed teeth.

We had several patients that came to see us the second day from a neighboring village that was actually in Nigeria. As we started packing up at the end of the second day, Patrick gathered a group of children together, and performed a couple of simple magic tricks for them. Then he started singing to them, and he got them to sing a song back to him. John, Sam, and I got together and presented a Bible to the village chief in his own language. We also gave the missionary that Sam's group had trained and sent to this village, several New Testaments and scripture booklets. We had many people accept Christ and become Christians. The missionary hoped that he could now get a church started.

We always took two uniformed soldiers carrying machine guns, with us. We picked them up at the gates of the hotel each morning. They stayed with us at all times every day. I'm sure our team paid them something. We never had a problem. Their purpose was primarily just to prevent problems.

I sat by an open window in the back of the minibus as the team loaded up to leave. The two military soldiers escorted a man across the clearing and right up to me. He looked at me right in the eye. I wondered what this was all about. I felt a twinge of apprehension. The man then talked to me while John interpreted. He was the government's public health representative for this village, and he just wanted to thank us. He said, "No one has ever come to our village to help us with our health. You are the very first ones."

Sam had made arrangements for us to visit the nearby village. We stopped in the middle of the village and got out of our minibus. We could see the voodoo priest's temple, and where he performed some of his voodoo deeds. We didn't go near it.

John talked with a lady standing out in front of her typical village house. Then John told us that she had agreed to let us go inside her house and look around. Talk about being primitive, it had mud walls, thatched roof, a dirt floor, a pile of smoldering wood at one end where she cooked, and mats on the ground at the other end where they slept. She had no furniture, no table or chairs, no electricity or lights, no windows or screens, no bathroom or running water. She seemed quite proud of her house.

We left and headed back to our hotel, because we needed to get there before dark. Even our armed guards agreed to that. As we left the village, the two-track trail went through a swamp area which was now quite wet. The ground was very soft, and the vegetation was so thick and jungle-like that it scraped both sides of our minibus. We just barely got through the swamp and made it back to the hotel before dark.

The third and fourth days we went to our second village. Again it was a very isolated place, where Sam's trained missionary had not made much progress in overcoming the stronghold that voodooism had in controlling the people. There was a community-type building that Sam had received permission for us to use. While we were setting up, Dr. Shull preached to the crowd that had gathered, for about 20 minutes, and had a good response. Medical set up inside again, because some patients required privacy with their problems. The dental and optical clinics set up outside. Again they had built a shelter from the sun for us with palm branches held up by sticks and poles. It worked well.

I observed a fifty year old lady waiting in the medical line, and she had no nose. She had a hole in the front of her face about the size of a quarter. She let me take her picture, and then I talked with her. She told me that she developed an infection in her nose. She didn't have any money, or any way to go to a doctor or hospital. It happened 10 years ago, and she was just happy that the infection only destroyed her nose and not her life. It didn't seem to bother her at all, even though I could see a green layer of mold growing inside the hole on the floor of her nose. Then she told me something that surprised and pleased me. She said to me, "I don't mind not having a nose, because I am getting old, and when I die, Jesus has promised me a whole new body in heaven." She was the only Christian we met in this entire village.

Gerry had a continuous long line of people waiting to get checked for glasses. Every 10 to 15 minutes, he would quickly go through the line, and weed out the people with obvious cataracts. Glasses really wouldn't solve their problem and there was no use for them to wait in line just to have him say, "I'm sorry I can't help you." With the damage caused by many years of bright tropical sun, and having no eye protection, almost 50% of the patients wanting to see Gerry had cataracts.

We observed a variety of unusual medical and dental conditions in this village. We saw one lady with a softball sized goiter in the front of her neck. It didn't bother her, and it wasn't why she was waiting to see the doctor. We had a dental patient who had a cyst-like growth on her knee, about the size of a softball. It had been there 15 years and didn't bother her, so she didn't plan to see the doctor about it.

It was quite common for a dental patient to have six or eight abscessed teeth, but they only wanted one or two removed, because those were the only ones that were currently hurting. We just took out those that they requested. We usually showed them the other abscessed teeth which were often just black roots, level with the gums. We advised them and occasionally they would ask us to take them out also, after they found out it didn't hurt.

One morning a mother came into our dental clinic and went right to the front of the line, and sat in one of our empty dental chairs. She was holding a six-year-old girl, who was whimpering and partially delirious. The left side of the child's face was about the size of a half of a softball. She had pus coming out of the corner of her mouth and the corner of her eye. She had two holes under her chin with pus running out there also. She had a high temperature. Her mother said that the child had not eaten or drunk anything in three days. She didn't respond to our talking to her, and only responded slightly with a groan when we touched the swollen area. I had never seen anything like that in my life and I was at a loss to know what to do. She wouldn't even open her mouth. Now I know why God in his wisdom had brought Dr. Frank, an oral surgeon, along.

Dr. Frank took over. He pried the child's mouth open. She had a large piece of calculus, about the size of a silverware knife handle, and about an inch and a half long on the cheek side of her lower jaw. Dr. Frank pried it off, and there was no soft tissue under it. It exposed a big area of raw jawbone. She had several abscessed baby molars, which he removed. Dr. Frank said that the abscessed teeth had probably been painful, so she had stopped eating on that side, and that caused the calculus to accumulate in such a large amount.

Then Dr. Frank opened the two holes under the child's chin, and drained as much of the pus as he could. The little girl moaned and squirmed a little, but was generally not responsive. Dr. Frank injected some very strong antibiotic into the girl, and told her mother she had to get some fluids into her. He said, "I need to see her tomorrow." Tomorrow came and went and we didn't see her. The next day we moved to a different village several miles away. In the afternoon the mother brought the youngster into the clinic, and she was skipping along and smiling, and we were all relieved and happy. That is as close as I have ever come to seeing anybody die because of a dental infection. Thankfully, the little girl was making a fantastic recovery, thanks to Dr. Frank's years of training and experience in treating these kinds of infections.

We had one lady come into the dental clinic and we noticed several hundred half-inch long raised scars close together down her arms. We inquired as to what caused the scars, and she said, "I have headaches, and I go to the voodoo witch doctor, and he makes cuts in my skin and packs cow manure in the cuts." We asked her, "Did it help?" She answered, "Eventually the headaches went away, but they always came back." I know that eventually most all headaches go away sooner or later. Then she said, "First he started on my back, but he ran out of room, so then he started down my arms." She quickly took her blouse off her back, and it was obvious she was used to doing that. Every square inch of her back was covered with raised scars. We asked her, "Did it hurt?" She said, "Oh yes, it was painful for several days." She was otherwise a very nice looking young lady in her 30s. We shared the Gospel with her and she was excited and happy to become a Christian.

In the evenings, after we got back to the hotel, we would shower, have supper, and then go to Dr. Shull's room. There we would package the medications that the medical doctors thought they might use the next day. Many times we would work until 11 or 12 o'clock at night. Miki, Patrick, and sometimes Cathy worked in the pharmacy. If the medications were prepackaged, they would have more time to share the Gospel with the patients. We called Cathy our evangelist. Coming from a Pentecostal background she was very anxious and excited to share the Gospel with anybody she could. She did a good job and was very successful.

During lunch one day, I asked my translator, Christian, how he had become a Christian and he pointed to another dental translator, Joel, and said, "Ask him." I got our dental team together, and asked Joel to share with us how he and Christian had become Christians. He told us this story: "One evening when I was a teenager, a friend invited me to a YWAM, Youth with a Mission meeting, where I was introduced to Jesus, and I became a Christian. I joined Sam's church and became active, and right now I am the church's youth leader."

"Christian was a good friend of mine, so I shared the Gospel with him, and he accepted Jesus and started going to church with me. We studied the Bible together. One day as Christian and I were studying, we felt challenged to win our families to Christ. I won my mother to Christ first, but my dad was a high voodoo priest, and it took a little longer, but he also became a Christian and gave up voodoo.

Christian then told us, "My mother was a voodoo priestess, and I was able to win her to Christ. My dad was a doctor of veterinary medicine, and it took a little longer to win him to Christ, but I did, along with all my brothers and sisters."

On Friday Christian announced that he had just received notice that his university classes were going to resume on Monday, and he needed to leave Saturday morning by bus. It would take two days to travel across Benin, and go through the country of Togo, to reach Acura the capital of Ghana, where his college was. No computer courses were offered in Benin. It was hard to say goodbye, because in just four days we had grown very close, and had won a lot of people to Christ together. After I got home I received several e-mails from Christian. Sam got busy and found another translator for me for the remaining five days of clinic.

On Friday, our long hours from 5 a.m. in the morning until midnight, caught up with Miki, and she was too exhausted to come to clinic. On Saturday both Miki and Dr. Shull were too exhausted to make clinic. We changed rooms where we packed and labeled our medications, and shortened our hours, so everyone was finished by 10 p.m. No one had any further problems after that.

On Saturday we went to a different village. We were shocked when we arrived, around 8:30 A.M., to find several hundred people standing around waiting. While we set up our clinics, Brett, with John translating, gave a good salvation message to the people and again had a good response. This was the Saturday that Dr. Shull and Miki didn't make it to clinic. Patrick and Cathy handled the pharmacy okay. There was a local Christian physician who heard we were going to be there, and since he didn't have office hours on Saturday, he dropped in, and asked if he could help. Dr. Bill talked to him a little, and put him to work in the room planned for Dr. Shull.

The waiting line for our dental clinic got long and had over 50 people in it, so we started making some changes. Hygienists in California are trained in diagnosis and administering local anesthesia. We asked Liz, our hygienist, if she would diagnose which teeth needed to be removed, and numb the patients for us. Liz diagnosed and numbed the patients for both Dr. Dale and Dr. Frank. This greatly increased their efficiency.

I still diagnosed and numbed my own patients, but I started taking them two or three at a time and shared the Gospel with them in a small group. This increased my efficiency. One time Liz got ahead of Dr. Dale and Dr. Frank, and she had no place to put her numbed patient, so she just picked up a forcep and extracted the tooth herself. She chose a tooth that was loose and very easy to extract. We kidded her, and told her we were going to report her to the State Board of Dentistry in California, but she did a fine job, and ended up extracting several other easy teeth.

One time when the physicians were backed up, they had a patient with two swollen pussy abscesses under his chin, not related to his teeth, but they needed to be lanced and drained. They asked Dr. Frank if he would lance and drain the abscesses. That's something that I wouldn't have felt comfortable doing, but Dr. Frank had no problem.

About 4:30 in the afternoon just before we were ready to close, I had a pleasant gentle lady sit down in my chair. I asked her how long she'd been waiting. She said, "Since 6 a.m. this morning." This made me feel sad, but it also told me that these teeth must really hurt for her to wait all day to get them removed.

Gerry was very popular with his glasses clinic. In the late afternoon, it became obvious that not everyone was going to be able to be seen. Gerry was taking time to share the Gospel with each patient. The waiting patients started pushing and shoving and arguing in the waiting line. Finally our two machine-gun toting army men, tried to restore peace, and in the process one of the soldiers got accidentally pushed to the ground, with a thud, right in front of me. For an instant I feared that his temper might flare, and we could have a bigger problem, but he just got up and continued successfully settling down the crowd.

On Sunday we all went to Sam's church. They held church in a rented conference center, since they had outgrown their church, and were in the process of building a bigger church.

They requested us as guests, to sit in the front row. There were several hundred people there. When I stepped to the side to take a photo, my eye caught sight of a beautiful young blonde white lady, dressed in a pretty white dress, against a background of black people all dressed in dark clothes. What a contrast that was. The gal was our own Liz. Probably nobody else noticed the contrast but me, but it showed up dramatically in the pictures.

Rev. Sam preached, and Rev. John translated into English, because Rev. Sam wanted us to hear what he was saying. He asked the congregation how many people worked from five in the morning until midnight, like our mission team. They did something a little different in the service. When it came time to greet one another, which many churches do, he asked his people to find somebody they didn't know, had never met, take 15 minutes, and get acquainted.

Their church service was much longer than ours in the U.S. We arrived at 10 a.m., and the service was already in progress. They had a praise band to accompany the singing, with a piano, electronic keyboard, a couple of electric guitars, and some heavy drums. I asked myself if they got the praise band idea from us, or did we get it from them? We left at 12 noon during some singing, but the service was still going on.

After church we went to the suburbs to a home of a member of Sam's church. It had a tall wall around the property. Inside the gate was a beautifully landscaped house with a large gazebo in the yard. It was the nicest house I had seen anywhere in Benin. It felt like I just stepped into a different world.

I asked what type of business the owner was in, and was told he was a middleman in an import-export business. I always had a gut feeling that the middleman in our society received more than his fair share, especially when dealing with farm products. They had tables and chairs set up for lunch under the large gazebo. Sam had invited all the pastors of the various churches that were providing helpers for us. Annie, our Dutch missionary, purchased all the food and cooked dinner for us. We had to wait a while for all the pastors to arrive after their church services. We then had a several course cafeteria style dinner, and a great time visiting.

Monday we finished our second day of clinic in the third village. On Tuesday we went to our fourth and last village. We only drove about 30 minutes before stopping at the shore of a big lake. There were about 50 to 75 people milling around a dock area. Some were coming with a catch of seafood from the lake, and some were going, but all had small boats. We loaded all of our gear and 40-some people into two big longboats. We took off and headed out into the lake, powered by a good sized outboard motor. We rode for an hour through that large inland lake, which was 25 miles long and 10 miles wide. It had a river which entered at one end, and went out the other, and eventually emptied into the ocean at Cotonou. The maximum depth of the lake was 9 feet with an average depth of 3 to 4 feet.

We were told that there were 25,000 people actually living on this lake in houses built on poles. We went into the village of Ganvie in which there were several hundred houses.

We also observed restaurants, hotels, and stores all built on poles in this large lake. There was a floating market of 10 to 15 small boats selling vegetables and fruits. We eventually pulled up to a dock near a moderate-sized concrete building. Sam said that the government had built this Community Center for the villagers in 2 feet of water on concrete pillars.

There was a 75-yard-long concrete elevated walkway that led from the dock to the community center. Sam had received permission for us to use it, but it was still locked and nobody was around. With a little bit of ingenuity, we got in and started to set up our clinics. By the time our clinics were ready, there was a crowd of people. The dental and optical clinics set up on the five-foot-wide outside porch that surrounded the building. After a short Gospel message, we started our clinics.

We saw a lot of patients. Dr. Frank had one patient that had a sore in his mouth. Upon examination he found a raw mass of tissue about the size of an egg. Dr. Frank concluded that it was a fast growing cancer that already involved most of his nose and eye and that it was not treatable. The best thing we could do was give him some medication to help keep him comfortable, and introduce him to Jesus, which we did. This is the only cancer we saw in our clinics. In Africa, cancer is often considered the white man's disease, because it is so rare.

I had a 50-year-old lady who had 10 raised scars in a symmetrical pattern on her face. I asked her how she got the scars. She said, "When I was young it was considered a sign of great beauty in our tribe." It reminded me of tattoos that some of our young people get because they think they are beautiful. We had to close our clinics a little early that afternoon, because we had a long ride to get to our hotel before dark.

The second day we traveled the same route. On the lake we saw several interesting things, such as fishermen with huge unique nets, fish farms, small boats containing entire families in them, rowing for miles. Some of the canoes had a pole in the middle with different colored scraps of cloth, rigged as a sail.

In the village of Ganvie we saw several boats, with large porcelain jars, collecting water from a 3-inch black plastic pipe. The government had furnished this water pipe for the village, so the people would have safe drinking water. We saw people swimming, bathing, washing their clothes, and going to the bathroom in the lake. Our physicians said, one of the biggest infections they saw were eye infections from people going to the bathroom in the same water in which they bathed and swam. They treated the infection, but they didn't have an easy solution for the problem affecting 25,000 people.

When we arrived at the community center, there were 50 little boats around the dock with about two hundred people waiting on the five-foot-wide elevated walkway. It was packed. I didn't think we were going to be able to get through to the community center, but people parted and we went right down the middle. Then the pushing and shoving started. Some people were accidentally pushed off the walkway and fell 4 feet down into 2 feet of grassy water. No one was hurt, or got mad. They just climbed back onto the walkway.

Mary Ann gave the morning's Gospel message and invitation. It took much effort to get the patients organized, registered, and sent to the right clinics. I saw one man coming to our clinic just walking through the 2 feet of grassy water. We could also see children walking to school slowly in foot deep water. It was just a way of life.

The spiritual counselors shared the Gospel with every patient before being seen by the doctors. I still took time to share more completely, and had excellent success with almost everyone asking to become a Christian. I wondered how the crowd would have acted if we had returned the third day. When we had finished and were packing up our longboats, I observed a young teenage boy standing on the dock. He was wearing a maize and blue T-shirt with the University of Michigan printed on it. It is a small world sometimes. The ride back across the lake was cooling after a long hard hot day.

Thursday we had our clinic at the hotel. We worked on all our helpers and their families, and some of the hotel employees and their families. We did have a little problem at the start. Although the hotel manager told us it was okay for us to have our clinics at the hotel, the security guards at the gate refused to let our native team members and their families into the hotel compound. Finally we got them in, but then the hotel manager was afraid a large number of black natives in the hotel would frighten their white guests. We compromised and only let them into the hotel one at a time to go to the doctor's room for consultation and treatment. The hotel manager asked the dental clinic to set up in a staff dining room off the kitchen which was off-limits to guests. All patients had to be let in the kitchen's back door, one at a time, but we made it work, treated a lot of people, and didn't upset any of the guests.

On our last day of clinic in the lake, when we were packing up, one of our native helpers threw out our sterilizing solution, thinking it was just waste water. Annie brought in her hot plate and pressure cooker, so we could boil our instruments under pressure. This is really the best method of sterilization, but it is much slower, and you need electricity, which we didn't have in any of the villages. Everyone was appreciative that we remembered to help those that had helped us. It was our way of saying thank you, because it took a whole team to succeed.

Friday, our last day, Sam offered to take us to look around the area. Since Benin didn't usually have tourists, they didn't have any of the typical tourist things to see. They didn't even have souvenir stores. We went to one interesting village called Ouidah, which is known as the voodoo center in Benin, with the largest concentration of voodoo priests. It also had an ancient Portuguese Fort that they had turned into a museum.

In the Fort Museum there was a small Christian chapel, located right over the dungeon holding area. That was where the Portuguese held up to 500 slaves at one time, in unbelievably poor conditions, waiting for ships to arrive to take them to America. I couldn't stop thinking about what the Bible tells us; love one another, love your neighbor as yourself, and do unto others as you would have them do unto you. These early Christian Portuguese traders and soldiers worshiped Jesus right on top of these slave-holding dungeons. The slaves' treatment was so poor that only 50% lived long enough to arrive at their destinations. These human beings, whom God loved, had done nothing to deserve this fate. It was a sad and disgraceful period in human history.

The morning we were there, the chapel was full of people. Sam was shocked. He had never seen the chapel in use because it was a museum. He figured it must be just a historical meeting. He asked a man that was coming out of the chapel, "What is going on in there?" The man happened to be the one in charge of the group. He said, "We have gathered together local Christian leaders, including several former voodoo priests, who have become Christians, to make plans on how we are going to get the Gospel of Jesus to our people in this area." Then the man asked Sam, "Would you like to talk to the group and encourage them?" Sam said, "I think Dr. Charlick would be better talking to the group." He turned to me and said, "Would you do that?" How could I say no?

I spent 10 minutes telling them how God had led hundreds of people to Jesus in the two weeks we had been sharing the Gospel. I assured them that everyone deserves to be told about Jesus and his offer of salvation and eternal life, at least once in their life. I told them that because they could speak the same language, they had an advantage over us, but Jesus asked all of us to go and tell people about him. I praised them for their strong belief in Jesus, and all their efforts in trying to be used by God.

We were told; the Portuguese landed here in the 1700's and made friends with the coastal natives, giving them pots and pans, hoes and rakes, and things that made their life easier. Then the Portuguese got into the slave trading business, and they hired and armed the coastal natives to go into the interior and capture rival tribal people, and bring them back to be sold as slaves. The slave ships couldn't dock, so they anchored offshore, and sent small boats to pick up the shackled slaves.

The Portuguese built a big arch on the beach that they traditionally took all the slaves through before putting them into the small boats and taking them to the mother ship. They had rebuilt this huge arch. The museum said that there were over 3 million slaves taken through this arch for shipment to the new world, mainly to Brazil. Slave trading was mostly stopped in 1890 with the worldwide Emancipation Proclamation.

The voodoo priests would bless the native coastal warriors before they went to the interior to capture rival tribes people, but they always warned the warriors never to go into water to capture an enemy. That is why so many of the natives went into the shallow lake, and built their houses and lived in the lake. Even though the emancipation of slavery was in 1890, after living, growing and harvesting their food in the lake for over a hundred years, living in the lake had just become a way of life. There was plenty of land, and the government offered to relocate them, but their life and livelihood was in the lake, and they didn't want to leave.

In summary: Our goal was to reach the unreached. We had over 2000 unreached people become Christians. Our goal was also to help the missionaries, who were already in these villages, to start churches, and to become a better respected Christian witness in these pre-dominantly voodoo villages. Before we left Benin, they had three churches started, one in each of our first three villages, with between 50 and a 100 people in each church. The last village we visited, which was the one in the lake on stilts, reported getting a church started shortly after we left. I had the pleasure of personally leading over 75 people to Christ. It was a large team effort with around 50 people directly involved, and many hundreds helping behind the scenes.

To put it bluntly, we barnstormed the Devil's stronghold and came out winners.

## And Now the Rest on the Story

This mission was exceptionally rewarding and fulfilling, and it has influenced the lives of several of our team members. Dr. David Shull has accepted the responsibility of leading several successful HTI missions.

Dr. Bill Johanson has gone on several more HTI mission trips, and he is now leading mission trips also. He has become a HTI board member and was elected vice president two years ago. He is my right hand helper.

Dr. Dale and Mary Ann Louis are averaging over five mission trips a year, and both of them have joined our HTI board of directors. Mary Ann is currently working on a Masters Degree in Theology.

Elizabeth Martins has gone on several additional HTI mission trips and she also has joined our board of directors.

Rev. Sam Aco has invited HTI to return again for another mission. This is under current evaluation.

# CHAPTER 34

# MYANMAR 3

Not much had changed in Myanmar since our last visit a year ago, except Dr. David Shull had taken a team of 10 in March of 2005, and had great success. I was anxious to return because the Holy Spirit was changing so many peoples' hearts, and they were so anxious and happy to hear about Jesus. I had an additional reason for wanting to return. Karen, my daughter, and her 13-year-old daughter, Morgan, agreed to go with Dora May and me.

Morgan had been asking to go on a mission trip with us for years. When she finally became a teenager, she asked her mom and dad, "Can I go with Grandma and Grandpa on a mission trip, now that I'm a teenager?" One of their problems was school. We were going in the middle of the school year. So Karen talked with Morgan's teachers, and since Morgan was a straight-A student, they gave her their blessings. She missed two weeks of school, and still got straight A's.

I had taken all three of my other children with me on mission trips in the past, but Karen never had had a chance to go with us. Although Karen had been my dental assistant for almost 30 years, I asked her if she would take charge of our most requested healthcare service, that of fitting glasses.

As I was trying to put my team together, I got a phone call from Dr. Larry Black. I had known Larry professionally from a dental study club we had attended several years ago. He had since retired and moved to Florida, and I had lost contact with him. Larry said to me, "Hey, Dick, are you still going on those mission trips?" I said, "I sure am. In fact, I'm in the process of putting a team together to go to Myanmar in February." His next words were, "Can I go?" I said to Larry, "I didn't know you were a Christian. What led you to call me now?" He then told me, "I just finished reading Rick Warren's book, "The Purpose Driven Life," and it has convicted me. I need to be serving the Lord with the talents He has given me."

Dottie Staggers, a nurse who went with us previously, called and asked if she could go again. Dr. Joel and Scarlet Holcomb, a physician and a pharmacist, who went with us on our first mission to Myanmar, called and asked if they could go. Dr. Donald Kuenzi, a physician, a HTI board member, and a fellow team member on several Cameroon missions, volunteered to join us with his wife, Martha. This made a good solid Christian team of nine; two physicians, two dentists, one nurse, one pharmacist, one dental assistant, and Karen to fit glasses, with Morgan and Martha to help her. This would be a great team and I was excited.

Dora May and I exhibited our HTI information booth at the world's largest missions health conference, called "Global Health Missions Conference," held annually in Louisville, Kentucky, every November. I met a man at this conference named Holland Kendall. He was a retired engineer and computer expert, who had great interest in eye problems, and wanted to serve the Lord with his skills and interests. Holland took a portable auto refractor and connected it to a computer. He then entered the prescription of a few thousand pairs of glasses into the computer, and developed a unique program. The portable auto refractor would read the lens of the eye, enter that reading into the computer, and the computer would select the best pair of glasses, in the inventory that most closely fit the patient's eye needs. With this method you didn't need to be an optometrist or an ophthalmologist to fit glasses. Not being an eye doctor, we couldn't diagnose or treat eye diseases, or cataracts, but we could greatly improve the vision of about 75 to 80% of the people who came to us, by fitting them with glasses. The auto refractor and Holland's special computer program did all the work.

Holland Kendall has developed a charitable organization called Kendall Optometry Ministries. The equipment was donated to his ministries. Holland went on mission trips to Central America a couple of times each year and personally used this equipment to fit glasses. When he wasn't using the equipment he allowed others to use it, if they used it to honor our Lord. This was the only known program of its type in the world at that time. The equipment was valued at over $12,000, and he let Karen and I, under the sponsorship of HTI, use it free of charge. Karen and I went down to Louisville one Saturday to Holland's church, where he gave us personal instructions on how to connect the equipment, properly use it, and care for it.

The Wisconsin Lions Club gave me seven thousand pairs of good used glasses. They were all cleaned and bagged, with the prescriptions of the lens written on the clear plastic bags. We entered these prescriptions into Holland's computer program before we left on our mission trip. The glasses were neatly numbered and filed in special cardboard boxes that fit into heavy cloth bags that Holland designed and had constructed to the exact size and weight to meet airline luggage requirements. Holland also designed two special durable hard plastic cases for packing and carrying the auto refractor, batteries, cords, a printer and other miscellaneous optical equipment. These cases were just the right size to use as carry-ons on the airplane, so there wasn't any chance of losing them.

Our travel agent Jill, had problems trying to get Thai Airways, which we had successfully used on our last two mission trips to Myanmar, to commit to a price or schedule. We eventually learned that Thai Airways was in bankruptcy, and they had to wait for court instructions. Jill then booked us with Singapore Airlines, which gave us a better price, and schedule. Singapore Airlines had been rated for years as the best airline in the world.

We left January 27, 2006, and met in the Singapore Airlines waiting area in the San Francisco airport. We flew to Singapore, and then with only a three-hour layover, we flew to Yangon. Robin and his family met us at the airport, and transferred us to a new hotel, Hotel K. Paradise. It was a much nicer hotel, about the same price, better food, good location, and electricity 24 hours a day. The first day we rested, after being up 46 hours straight while traveling exactly half-way around the world. There is a twelve-hour difference in time. We also unpacked, reorganized, and repacked for a one-week trip to the Mon state. Our first evening Robin and his family took us out to the Royal Barge again for a typical Burmese buffet dinner with the traditional Burmese floor show. After supper while we were watching the dancers, Dora May fell sound asleep in her chair. We were all still very tired from jet lag, so we went back to the hotel and turned in early.

Early Tuesday morning we packed our small bus and headed for the Mon state. It continues to be the most unreached state in Myanmar. Last year we visited the only known Evangelical Christian Church in the Mon state. Robin had help set up a Mon student who had graduate from his Bible school as pastor. He wanted to go back and evangelize his own people. Robin helped him buy a home for his family on the only main road in the Mon state. They built a small Nazarene Church in front of his home, with good visibility to the road. We spent three very successful days there last year, and this was where we planned to work again this year.

The longest bridge in Southeast Asia was now open, and we could cross it and go into the large town of Manlamyini. It was a very beautiful new bridge, engineered by the Chinese. Security was very heavy, and every time we crossed it Robin had to give the security officers a copy of our visas and passports. Robin had made 30 copies because he knew they would be required in many places, like our hotels, bridges, state borders, and just plain road security checkpoints. Remember, this was an area where tourists were not allowed. We arrived at Manlamyini in the late afternoon and stayed at the best hotel in town, which was chosen and required by the government. It was a big improvement over our hotel last year, but still only about a two-star hotel.

Wednesday morning we had a well-cooked breakfast at the hotel, and went to the Nazarene church for clinic. One of the first things I noticed was that the church was bigger. Last year they had about thirty people in attendance, in a church building that would seat a hundred people. After we left last year they didn't have enough room for all the new people that came, so they had to expand the church to seat a hundred and fifty people. We greeted the pastor and his family that had hosted us so well last year. There were people already waiting when we arrived, so we got busy and set up our clinic.

All optical had to do was to hook everything up, seat the patient, hold the auto refractor close to the lens of one eye, click the trigger, and the auto refractor accurately read the lens of the eye. Karen did the same for the patient's other eye, and then transferred these readings into the computer. Kendall's special computer program automatically and instantly told her which pair of glasses best fit the patient, and printed out the prescription on a small printer. It also told her where the glasses were located in our inventory. Morgan's job was to find the glasses in our inventory boxes. Both Morgan and Martha fit the glasses to the patient, and then double-checked the accuracy, using various charts. It worked great and was an absolutely fantastic new and accurate method of fitting glasses.

One of my privileges has been to counsel and teach other Christians how to lead people to Jesus. Dr. Larry Black had never had the opportunity to lead anyone to Christ, especially a person who had never even heard of Jesus. Larry's dental chair was close to mine, and he regularly heard the results I was getting when I shared Jesus with my patients, and led them to the Lord. Larry decided to try to share Jesus with his patients. His first attempt was with an older man. He agreed that he would like to know what a Christian believed. While Larry was sharing with him, tears started streaming down the man's face. When Larry finished and asked him if he would like to become a Christian, he said, "Oh, yes." He asked Jesus to forgive his sins, and invited Him into his heart and life. He then told Larry, "I have been worried all my life as to what was going to happen to me after I died. Now I have more peace and happiness in my heart than I have ever felt before in my whole life. I now know for sure where I will go." This motivated and excited Larry so much that he led every patient that sat down in his chair to the Lord after that.

One of my first patients was a pretty young lady that I recognized from last year. I had extracted some of her teeth last year, and she had become a Christian. I asked her, "How is your faith holding up?" She said, "Great, I have led all my family to the Lord." I extracted her currently aching tooth, and she went over to see Karen. She had traveled over an hour to get to our clinic. After Karen and Morgan fit her with glasses, she thanked them and said, "I'm so happy! I can read again. Now I can go back to college."

A lady came into our dental clinic with an abscessed tooth. I shared Jesus with her and she accepted Him into her heart and became a Christian. I noticed a yellow string around her neck. I inquired about the string. She told me, "I was apprehensive about coming into a Christian church to your clinic, so I went to the head Buddhist monk at the temple. He tied the string around my neck to protect me from the evil spirits that you foreigners might curse on me." She then said "Since I now have Jesus in my heart, I don't need this string anymore. You can cut it off," and we did. By the end of the day we had a pile of about 12 different colored, Buddhist, evil spirit, collar protectors, which our new Christians were willing to give up.

Karen did really well operating the auto refractor and computer. She kept Morgan, Martha, and even Mi Mi very busy locating the glasses, fitting, and then double-checking the accuracy. The team worked very efficiently together. It was interesting to see Morgan, a small 13-year old girl fitting glasses to adults that were not only several times her age, but some were important officials. If the glasses had metal frames, she would take them and bend them until they fit comfortably. If they were plastic and needed adjustment, Morgan lit a small propane torch that we brought with us, and warmed the plastic, and using a washcloth, to avoid burning her hands, she would bend them to the right size. She developed good self-confidence in doing this, and the patients really appeared to respect her.

Patients' demands for glasses were greater than for either medical or dental services. Patients would go to the glasses clinic before coming to medical or dental, in case there wasn't enough time for both. They would rather suffer with a toothache or a painful sickness if only they could get glasses and see again. We observed that there were almost no Burmese people with glasses, because they were priced totally out of their range.

Fitting glasses was very rewarding for our team members. Seeing their patient's face burst into a smile, when suddenly their whole world came into focus, was very exciting. Glasses were an excellent way for people to instantly see God's love in action. Treating sick people and extracting teeth don't give the same instantaneous gratifying results that glasses do. My hope for our next mission trip is to get more team members to work in the glasses clinic.

The pastor brought his five-year-old son to me and said, "My son is tongue-tied and is having trouble speaking properly." I examined the child and he did indeed have a cord, (lower lingual fraenum), which was attached to the underside of the front of his tongue and to the back of the gums of his front teeth, in such a way as to severely restrict the movement of his tongue. I immediately knew that this cord needed to be cut, (called a fraenectomy). I had studied about this in dental school, and had read about this minor operation. It seemed everybody recommended doing it a different way, so I always referred those patients to the oral surgeon. In this case there was no specialist. I was the specialist. This condition is rare, and I had never done this type of surgery. My heart started racing. I had to do something. This boy couldn't talk right and his future was in jeopardy.

I gave him lots of local anesthesia, and took a sharp pair of scissors and quickly cut the cord, just like cutting a piece of string. It was over in a fraction of a second. There was no pain and the little boy didn't even flinch. Then his mouth instantly filled with blood, much more blood than I had ever seen in any extraction. My heart started racing again. What have I done? I applied pressure to the cut area with gauze but it kept bleeding. I changed the gauze repeatedly. It took a long time, but it gradually slowed down and finally stopped.

I didn't know what was going to happen for a few moments. It really got my adrenalin flowing.

The pastor brought his son back late that afternoon. The boy was not bleeding and appeared to be in no pain. The pastor couldn't stop thanking me enough and said, "My son is already starting to talk much better." I was suddenly transformed from a panic-stricken dentist, to a hero, at least in the pastor's eyes. I saw this boy the following year and he was doing great. His father told me, "His speech is normal." Everything ended well. Praise the Lord!

Our days at the Nazarene Church clinic were very busy. In dental we had time to share Jesus with all of our patients, and 100% of them became Christians. We had lunch in the pastor's house again, and it was very good. While we were eating, the women who helped prepare our meal, stood behind us and fanned us, to cool us, because the temperature was hot. It made us feel like we were kings and queens.

Last year there was a man, named Max, who somehow heard about our clinic. He traveled two hours by bus, to come to our clinic to have a painful abscessed tooth removed. I also introduced him to Jesus and he became a Christian. I challenged him, as I do all new Christians, to share Jesus with his family and friends. This year Max returned to our clinic and reported to Robin that he had introduced his whole family and two neighboring families to Jesus. He then begged Robin to bring our team for at least one day to his area, and he would host us. He indicated that some of his other neighbors wouldn't believe him, and weren't becoming Christians, but he was sure that if we would come, they would listen to us and become Christians.

After Jubilee investigated the area, checked the facilities, and negotiated the proper amount of appreciation with the government officials, we went to Max's home. It was located right in the middle of a rubber plantation, with rubber trees as far as you could see in all directions. There was a shell of a building they called a community center, right across the street from his house. It was adequate for us to use for our clinics. Max fed all the U.S. team members' lunch in his home. He also fed our 17 Burmese translators and helpers.

Before we went to this area Robin asked about a toilet facility. Max said, "No problem." Max constructed one for us. He dug a small hole in the sand, put two boards over the hole, and left a space between the boards. He then put four poles in the sand around the boards, and wrapped dark plastic around them. It was primitive, but it worked.

I had a lady come in and sit in my dental chair with an aching tooth. I asked her if she knew what a Christian believed, and she sat straight up in the chair and said proudly, "I am a Christian. I am the only Christian in the area where I live, which is about one hour from here." I asked her, "How did you become a Christian?" She answered, "Have you ever heard of Adoniram Judson?" I said, "Yes." She then told me the following story: "Adoniram Judson landed right off the shore in this area many years ago, and he led my family to the

Lord five generations ago. Our whole family is still Christian today, but it hasn't been easy. We are the only Christians in a totally Buddhist community. When my son wanted to get married, there were no Christian girls around, so he married a Buddhist girl. It took us three years to convert her to Christianity, but now our whole family is Christian again."

Children's glasses are hard to fit. One morning a mother brought her three-year-old boy into the clinic. He was squirming and thrashing around. His mother said, "He never stops, except when he is asleep." The child's eyes were moving erratically back and forth. Karen had a hard time using the auto refractor to get a reading of the lens of his eyes, because of his body and eye movements. Finally she got a reading, and found the correct small children's glasses and put them on him.

Immediately the child stopped thrashing, and his eyes stop moving. He looked at his mother and a big smile lit up his face. She grabbed her little boy and hugged him. She couldn't stop crying and her expressions of joy were overwhelming. She thanked Karen many times and left with a totally different little boy, who was just looking all around at his new world.

I challenged an older lady that I had just introduced to Jesus, to find some good Christian friends who would love, help and teach her. Just then, I saw Max walk by, I called him over. I told my patient, "Max is a Christian, and he will be your friend. Max smiled and told me, "I have been telling this lady about Jesus for a long time, but she wouldn't believe me, but now when you tell her, she finally believes. They hugged and were both very happy brothers and sisters in Jesus. That's the exact reason why Max asked us to come. We had many other people with whom Max had shared Jesus that accepted Him into their hearts and lives for the first time.

Our dental clinic finished a little early, so I left Larry to finish up any patients that might arrive later. I went over to the glasses clinic to help Karen, Morgan, Martha, and Mi Mi, because they still had a long line. I had brought 500 new reading glasses, in addition to the large number of more complex prescription glasses. I put to work some of the training that Holland had given me. I was actually able to take new patients, who only needed reading glasses, and find out what line on the reading chart they could see clearly. The reading chart had 10 lines, with 10 different sized lettering on each line. It also listed the strength of the reading glasses the patient would need according to which line they could see clearly. For those who just needed reading glasses, I was able to fit quite rapidly. Together, we were able to get glasses for everyone that was waiting, by the end of our clinic day.

One of our last medical patients was a young lady that was carried into the clinic, near death, from advanced AIDS. Medically we had no cure, but we gave her medicines to help make her more comfortable. More importantly, we shared Jesus with her and her family. They all accepted Jesus as their personal Savior, so that everyone knew where they were going when they died.

This was one of our biggest and busiest days. We treated 324 patients and 70 of them became Christians. Max was very happy with all the new Christians. He agreed to follow up and minister to them. We observed that he was rapidly becoming a strong Christian leader. We gave him a Bible as well as a watch. Robin and Jubilee returned to this area several times to help him with his follow-up and teaching.

On Saturday we had to return to Yangon. On our way we stopped at a house right in the middle of a small town. It was still in the Mon state, and it was located between two Buddhist temples. The house was called Community Fellowship House. One of Robin's female Mon Bible School graduates, Florin, wanted to come back and evangelize her people. Robin found this house on the main road that was run-down, and the well was dry. It was for sale, but no one would go near it, because it was rumored to be full of evil spirits and demons. Robin was able to buy it very cheaply about a year ago. He wanted to prove to the whole community, that our God was stronger than all the evil spirits and demons. Florin, a beautiful young Christian girl, was able to move in, clean everything up, and live in this house without any evil spirits or demons bothering her. She got the well cleaned out, and now, during the dry season, it was the only well in the area that didn't run dry. She invited the neighbors to come and draw water from her well.

Robin was reluctant to call it a house church, because of the potential persecution from the Buddhists. Florin has gained great community respect, and now it is generally known as The Christian Center. She conducts Bible school for the children and a Bible study for adults. She has a Sunday morning worship service with about 15 people in attendance.

After Florin's dad died, her mother moved in with her. She was a Buddhist. Florin led her to Jesus and now she is a big help to her daughter in her ministry. They served us hot tea and cookies, and were very encouraged by our visit. We were the first outsiders to ever visit them.

On our way back to Yangon we stopped at the only decent restaurant on the whole six-hour trip, to have lunch. It is the only time that I have stopped at a restaurant where the hostess comes out with an umbrella and holds it over your head, while you walk into the restaurant, to shield you from hot noonday sun. We also stopped at a very beautiful, well kept, British World War II Cemetery, on the outskirts of Yangon, before enjoying a little late afternoon shopping at the Central market.

Sunday we went to Robin's church. Actually Jubilee is now the senior pastor. Jubilee asked me to preach and to report on our mission, and to challenge his people to share Jesus with people around them who had never heard of Jesus. After church, we had a nice lunch at a Western-style restaurant, and visited the Shwedagon Pagoda. It was only two blocks from the hotel in which we were staying this year.

On Monday morning we were scheduled to take our bus and go eight hours north on the road to Mandalay, to Taungoo. This was the church in which we had ministered on our last two trips, among the Karen people. When we got back to the hotel Sunday evening and as we started packing, we received a message. Sunday afternoon Jubilee received a phone call from the pastor in the Taungoo church. He said there had been several terrorist bombings in Taungoo overnight, and things were in panic and turmoil. He had consulted with the chief of police, and he suggested that now was not a good time for us to come, and that he couldn't guarantee our safety.

Some team members were disappointed, but God works everything for good for those who love Him. We did not know where our team was going the next day. Robin and Jubilee got busy and we had a great clinic every day, including the two days of clinic we would have missed, if we had been traveling eight hours each way to Taungoo. Dr. David Shull was planning to bring another HTI team next month. Maybe they would be able to go north to the Karen people.

One of the areas where our team went to was in the suburbs of Yangon. The neighborhood was 100% Buddhist, with no church, and no previous Christian witness, except for one Christian family that Robin had led to the Lord several years ago. This family invited us to come and have clinic in their home. Robin and Jubilee spent many hours checking with all of the local government and police authorities before we went. The Christian widow lady, with the help of Jubilee and team, moved all her furniture into one room, and we set up our medical and dental clinics in her house. The optical team set up in the side yard, which they partitioned off with tarps. The government was very paranoid about any groups gathering outside.

We had our busiest day at this house, and treated 349 patients, and introduced 82 people to Jesus. It was the day we had planned to spend eight hours on the road. Proof again, that the Lord knows best.

One lady came into the clinic very upset and depressed. She was seven months pregnant, in midlife, and her youngest child was 20 years old. Ever since she got pregnant she said the demons had been giving her all types of problems. She asked our doctors to abort her baby. After 45 minutes of counseling she became a Christian. It was pointed out to her, that the devil tried to kill Jesus by getting King Herrod to kill all the babies, because the devil knew that Jesus would be great. Maybe the devil was trying to get rid of her child also, because he knew her child would be great among their people, and win many people to Jesus. With Jesus in her heart she promised to love and care for her baby. She indicated she had great peace in her heart and thanked God for the baby within her.

The next two days we worked in the old Bible school building at the orphanage compound, where Charles and family lived. The orphanage was located in suburban Yangon in an all-Buddhist neighborhood. The orphans, about 30 of them, sang for us and quoted scriptures in English. Again, I was personally touched when they sang, "I Have Decided to Follow Jesus," in English. We presented them with a couple of suitcases full of new and used clothes. Dottie brought one complete suitcase full of new children's clothes.

It was Robin's and Jubilee's hope that by opening our clinic to their Buddhist neighbors, they would not only make more friends in the area, but that they might actually introduce some of their neighbors to Jesus. The children's house mother was a fantastic evangelist, and worked hard sharing Jesus. She was also going to be there after we left to help follow-up on her new Christian neighbors. Again in the dental clinic, we had 100% conversions with everyone who sat in our chairs becoming a Christian. We had so many conversions that they decided to start a Bible study and a house church after we left. I had one neighbor lady who became a Christian, and got so excited that she offered to help start the Bible study.

A few people that we asked, if they knew what Christians believed, said they had a Christian friend, or one lady said, she went occasionally to a Catholic church, but they all wanted to know more about what Christians believed. We shared about God and Jesus, and they all became Christians. It was what several said, after they became Christians, that bothered me. They said, "Why didn't any of my Christian friends tell me about Jesus?" I could not help but think of how many friends I have in the U.S. that know I am a Christian, but I have never offered to take the time to sit down and to share with them about Jesus, and what Christians really believe. How about you?

A lady sat down in my chair and requested to have a couple of abscessed teeth removed. I noticed an area where two other teeth had been recently extracted. I asked her where she had had these teeth removed. She said, "The other dentist took them out," and she pointed to Larry. "He removed them a few days earlier at the other clinic." I asked her if she had become a Christian, and she said, "Yes, that's the main reason I came back. I wanted to hear more about Jesus."

On our last day and a half, we worked in the dining hall of the Bible school that Robin not only started, but taught in, and supervised. They had moved out of the old smaller building next to the orphanage, and moved into a new school building that was attached to Robin's and Jubilee's new Church. They had been building it for several years and it was finally finished. They had been able to increase the number of students, and start a library. In addition to the one-year course, they were able to add a two-year course, and a four-year degree program. Again we opened up the clinic to the surrounding Buddhist neighborhood.

One young lady came to me with bleeding gums. During our discussion I found out that she was a Christian, and a Bible school student. When I asked her how she became a Christian, she told me this story: "Last year when you ministered in the Karen State, my father came to you with an abscessed tooth. You led him to Jesus. You challenged him to tell his family and friends about Jesus. My dad, with the help of the 30-page scripture booklet that you gave him, led our whole family to Christ, and started sharing Jesus with his neighbors and friends. He sent me to Robin's Bible school so that I could learn how to more effectively help him evangelize our Karen people. When I finish school, I plan to return home and help my family introduce our people to Jesus." Again this reminded me that there is no way of knowing the influence that one new Christian may have in introducing others to Jesus.

One morning a young, bright, intelligent, female college student asked to hear what Christians believe. I shared with her for about 30 minutes like I did with most patients. She asked a lot of questions. She was very excited to accept Jesus, and prayed to become a Christian. I challenged her that if she wanted her family or friends to go to heaven, she had the responsibility of telling them about Jesus.

Early the next morning I had a young female patient who came to me with no dental problem. She sat down in my chair and said "My sister, the college student who accepted Jesus yesterday, called me last night and told me I needed to come and see you right away, and that you would tell me about Jesus." She lived several hours away and had gotten up in the middle of the night and had taken several buses to get here early enough so that she could be sure to be seen by me. She asked me if I would tell her about Jesus. I did, and she happily prayed and became a Christian.

The new Christian college student worked part-time in sales at the vegetable market. She started telling her customers in the market that they needed to come and see us. Several came and they all became Christians. One of the new Christians told me that the college student told her that she had never been treated so kindly by anyone in her entire life, and we surely must be angels sent by God.

One afternoon a middle aged lady came to me for removal of an abscessed tooth. She also said she wanted to know what Christians believe. After 30 minutes or so, I asked her if she would like to become a Christian. She said, "Yes," and then she started to cry a lot, and she became very emotional. Jubilee said to me "We just need to wait and be patient." It took her several minutes to control herself so she could pray with us. Jubilee told me after she left, "This lady is Mi Mi's sister and the whole family has been witnessing to her and praying for her for many years, and finally the Holy Spirit touched her when you shared with her, and she accepted Jesus and became a Christian." The whole family rejoiced. A year later, her faith remained strong, and she was volunteering as the church custodian.

Late one afternoon, a well built, strong, middle-aged man who spoke with authority to those around him, and obviously was respected, sat down in my chair. He had several abscessed teeth. While waiting to get numb, I asked him if he would like to know what Christians believed. He said "Yes, I have no idea at all." As I was sharing with him he asked many questions. All the time I was talking to him, even when Jubilee was translating, he continually stared straight into my eyes. It actually made me feel a little uncomfortable. When it came time that I asked him if he would like to become a Christian, he very enthusiastically said, "Yes," and he repeated the sinner's prayer very loudly and boldly.

I gave him a 30-page scripture booklet. He hung his head and shook it, no. Jubilee quickly found out that he was sad because he couldn't read it, because his eyes were bad.

I immediately thought, I will send him to Karen and maybe she can get him some glasses. It was already late in the day and the eye clinic waiting line was very long, so I knew he would never be seen. Using my one day of training that I had received a couple of weeks earlier from Holland Kendall, I got the glasses reading chart with various size lettering on it. I pointed to the largest print, but he shook his head, no. He couldn't even see that clearly. So I went to our glasses supply and got one of the strongest pair of reading glasses I could find.

I will always remember his expression when I put the glasses on him. His face lit up like a Christmas tree, and he started smiling from ear to ear. He could now read the smallest print on the bottom of the reading chart. He hugged me and thanked me over and over, and wouldn't stop shaking my hand. When he finally left, he went outside to a window, and while wearing his new glasses, he waved and smiled at me every time I looked up for about 15 minutes. I'm sure he was very happy, but for me it was another rewarding, memorable, life-changing experience.

One young man came to me and asked if he could become a Christian. I said, "Yes," and led him to the Lord. When I asked him why he wanted to become a Christian, he said, "I have been watching your team for several days, and I saw that you were very happy people. I want to be happy like you, and there is nothing in Buddhism to be happy about."

We usually don't know how our actions, words, and deeds may be influencing nonbelievers watching us. We had a wonderful mission team that was happy, got along great, and had a good time enjoying each other.

In summary: We treated 2500 patients, which were mostly all Buddhists. We gave out over 3000 prescriptions, treated 1337 in medical, extracted over a thousand teeth, and fit almost a thousand pairs of glasses. Most importantly, we had 402 Buddhists become Christians. I had 96 Buddhists who sat in my dental chair. When I gave them the opportunity, they all wanted to hear what Christians believed. The Holy Spirit convicted their hearts, and allowed me to lead every single one, all 96 of them, to salvation through Jesus Christ. Dora May took Polaroid pictures of each new Christian in our dental clinic. We underestimated the number of patients that we would lead to Jesus, and we ran out of film in the early morning of the last day. You can be sure that will never happen on any future mission trip. It was especially encouraging to see some of the positive results from our previous year's mission trips starting to multiply. I feel the Lord has blessed our efforts in Myanmar greatly, and I am already looking forward to returning in the near future.

## And Now the Rest of the Story

David Shull, M. D., and a HTI board member, had asked to go with me on this trip. I told him he was welcome, but that I felt it would be more valuable for him to lead his own team to Myanmar in March. He had never led a team. I promised to help him. Robin had been asking for a second team. Dr. Shull agreed and took a team of 10, a month after our team had gone, and had very successful results. They also had several hundred people who became Christians. Robin and Jubilee have been kept very busy following up on all the new Christians.

This was Dr. Larry Black's first mission trip. He was so excited and fulfilled about the trip and leading so many people to Jesus that he asked to return again. Even though it strained his retirement finances, he returned in 2008, and has signed up to go with me again in 2010. There is no question; it is a very rewarding experience.

# CHAPTER 35

# MYANMAR 4

My excitement about returning to Myanmar was rewarded when Robin and I were able to agree on a date in late November 2006, only nine months after my last visit. In June I started to assemble our team. The success of our trips is always very dependent upon the quality of our team members. Even after 35 mission trips, I still find it exciting to see how the Lord leads people to join our mission teams. They come from many walks of life, and from all over the U.S. and Canada.

I called Tom and Judy Ruster and asked if they would be interested in joining Dora May and me in our November mission trip to Myanmar. Tom and Judy were close friends from our church, who had accompanied me to both Nepal and India on previous mission trips. Neither Tom nor Judy had any healthcare training or skills. Tom was a retired GM Engineer, and I knew both he and his wife were very skilled in the use of the computer. So I asked Tom and Judy if with a little training, they would take charge of our glasses program. They were both excited and agreed with enthusiasm. Tom and Judy went to Holland Kendall's six-hour course and learned how to operate the auto refractor and work his optical program on his laptop computer. I ordered a lot of glasses from the Lions Club, and helped them put the glasses into Holland's Computer Inventory Program before we left.

I called Dr. Gary Moberg, a dentist, former HTI board member, who had also been a former dental student of mine at the University of Michigan, and asked if there were any possibility that he could join us on our Myanmar mission. He had asked if he could go with me the previous year, but something came up that hindered his going. Gary had sold his dental practice a few years ago and moved to Minneapolis, where he attended a Bible College full-time, working on a Master's Degree in Theology, which specialized in missions. I knew he was scheduled to graduate in June, so I called him shortly thereafter. He told me that after three years of school, the person who had bought his dental practice had given it back to him. So financially he had to return to his dental practice, rather than go into full-time missions. He wanted to do mission work, but for the moment he was limited to part-time and this Myanmar mission would work perfectly. He said, "Yes, both Lyndell and I would be delighted to join your Myanmar mission team." Lyndell was his wife. I talked with her and asked if she would be willing to help Tom and Judy with glasses, and she said, "Fine." She was actually a dental hygienist. Since glasses had become our most popular healthcare service, I was committed to increasing the personnel in this program.

I met a dental assistant, Kathy LeBarron, at a dental seminar in Hawaii six years ago. She heard of my work with HTI at that time, and expressed a desire to join me sometime. We exchanged addresses and phone numbers. I tried to phone her several times, but could never reach her. One day six years later Kathy called me and said, "My last child will be going to college, and I am ready to join you on one of your mission trips. What do you have coming up?" I explained to her our upcoming mission trip to Myanmar, and she said, "Great, I want to go". I asked her if she would be willing to work with Tom and Judy in our glasses program, and she said, "Great, anyplace you need me."

Dr. David Shull was having health problems, so I asked Dr. Bill Johanson if he would lead a second team back to Myanmar in March, one month after our trip. Bill was a HTI board member, and had been with me to Cameroon twice and to Myanmar twice. He said, "Good, I am ready to lead a team." When I was talking to him, I expressed my concern about not being able to find a physician for my November team. Bill said, "If you can't find anyone, I'll go with you in November and still lead the March team." Dr. Brian Andrews an OB/GYN, who had gone with me on our second Myanmar mission, called me and expressed an interest in going. He wasn't comfortable being the only physician, so he said he would go if Bill would go also. So we had our two physicians.

Gail Dawson, a nurse, and HTI board member, who had gone on several different HTI missions, called and offered to join us and act as our pharmacist. Gail completed our team of 10. We had two physicians, two dentists, one nurse, one dental assistant, and four to work with glasses. Again we had all solid Christians. I was pleased about the quality of our team, and particularly excited about learning new things from Dr. Moberg, since he had just graduated with a Masters Degree in Theology.

In mid-November 2006 we met in Los Angeles in the Singapore Airlines waiting area. We flew directly to Singapore, and then onto Yangon the same day. Robin and family met us. This time Robin was able to come into the customs area. He asked us to check our luggage with one particular female customs agent. Bill had already started through her line before Robin had told us. She opened his luggage and started searching it. Robin walked over and winked at her, and she had him close his luggage and go right through. All the rest of us followed, without ever slowing down. She didn't check anything in our bags. This was the result of Robin getting there ahead of time and making the appropriate arrangements and showing proper appreciation.

We went directly to our hotel, and after having been up and traveling for 46 hours, we quickly went to bed. The first day we rested, unpacked, repacked to leave town for a week the next day, and we generally got organized. That evening we went to the traditional Burmese buffet dinner and show at the Royal Barge, and came back to the hotel early and went to bed. The next morning Robin had the hotel fix us a special early breakfast. We ate, packed our small bus, and were on the road by 6 a.m. We beat the morning rush hour out of Yangon, and headed toward the Mon state.

Robin and Jubilee had been working with Max, the man in the rubber plantation, and had been following up on the new Christians from last February. Max was very anxious for us to come back again, and he offered to personally host our whole clinic in his home and yard. Robin thought this would be an effective area in which our team could work again. We went across the big new bridge and into Manlamyini, and stayed in the same government hotel.

We drove an hour to Max's home early the next morning. He had put up tarps on poles around the outside of his house so we could work in the shade. He roped off special areas, and had adequate tables and chairs ready for us. There were people already waiting, so we set up and started to work. Max had some of his neighbors help with registration, organization, and routing of patients. In general, things worked quite smoothly.

I continued my philosophy that everyone should have an opportunity to hear about Jesus, at least once in their lifetime. When I asked my patients, they all asked to hear what a Christian believed. I was pleased and grateful that Gary shared the same philosophy, and spent 20 to 30 minutes sharing with his patients also. We both had 100% of our patients ask to become Christians, and we had the privilege of leading each one of them to the Lord. I did have one man on the second day, when I asked if he wanted to become a Christian, he said, "This is all so new to me, I need a little time to think about it." We didn't apply any pressure. He was the only person in my last three mission trips that didn't ask to become a Christian. We saw lots of children, and again we had the whole family come and sit around the chair, and we were able to lead entire families to Jesus.

The first day I had a 78-year-old monk, in his orange robe, come in and sit down in my chair with an abscessed tooth. I went through the same presentation with him and he was quite anxious to hear what a Christian believed. I asked him "Do you know what is going to happen to you after you die?" He said, "No, but I sure would like to know." I told him, "I know what is going to happen to me." After my presentation he was anxious to become a Christian, and he did. He was relieved to finally know what was going to happen to him after he died.

He then told me this story: Fifteen years ago his wife had died, and all of his children had died. He had no family to help take care of him and he was growing old. He had no money or job. He was in his late sixties, and in the Burmese society he was too old to work. So he became a Buddhist monk. They provided a room and a bed. He begged for his food, as all monks do, and people provided him with food because he was a monk. He had developed a lot of new friends. Life was fairly comfortable for him. He had been able to get a Bible, and had read part of it, but he didn't understand it. He was going to get his Bible out and secretly read it more completely. I advised him to start with the Gospels. He said he wasn't going to tell the other monks that he was a Christian until he could find another place to live. He said he would keep Jesus and his new faith in his heart.

Jubilee was my translator, and he was one sharp, personable, knowledgeable, persuasive young man. For his Master's Thesis in Theology, he compared Buddhism to Christianity. He told us that Buddha had lived 500 years B.C. at the time of Jeremiah and Micah. In his many writings he stated many times that he, (Buddha), was not God. He was only a human teacher. He prophesied that God would send a God-man to earth, who would be born of a virgin, and that He would be a great teacher. He also prophesied that this God-man would have nail scars in his hands and feet. The Buddhist military dictatorship in Myanmar had removed these prophecies of a God-man from Buddha's writings, because it sounded too much like Jesus. They didn't want their Burmese Buddhists to become confused and to become Christians. Buddha's God-man prophecies are in his writings in every other Buddhist country in the world today, except Myanmar.

Buddha taught reincarnation, and claimed he had been reincarnated many times. You could be reincarnated either up or down in the animal kingdom. You could be reincarnated as a better or wealthier person or as a cow or insect. Reincarnation was really the center of everyone's daily thoughts and activities. Everyone was trying to be good and please God, so they would have a better life when they were reincarnated. Their ultimate goal was to reach Nirvana, or what we know as heaven. That is partly why the Burmese people are so friendly. They are the friendliest people I have ever met in the world. This is also why they are so passive, patient, and can tolerate a military dictatorship. Jubilee said if you were to walk down the street, and go up to any house and tell them you were hungry, they would feed you, even if it were their only food that they had for the day.

Buddhists don't know where they are going after they die, and that is their life's biggest concern. Then I came along, and they heard for the first time in their life, that they could know for sure where they were going after they die. I know where I am going. Jesus has promised me that I will go to heaven, (Nirvana), and it's a much better place. They can go there too, if they want. It is simple and it's free. Needless to say, everyone from this insecure Buddhist cultural background was interested in becoming a Christian.

Max's wife and several of the neighborhood women spent all morning cooking lunch for us. They cooked over open wood fires out in a small kitchen building separate from the house. They cooked a fantastic buffet of 8 to 10 dishes. They then stood behind us, while we were eating, and fanned us to keep us cool. They fed all the helpers also.

While eating lunch, Max told Robin about the fate of some Korean Christian missionaries. They came into a nearby area with a health team. Two hours after they started their clinic, the police came and told them they were not welcome, and forced them to leave. I asked Robin, "Why were they asked to leave and we are having no problems?" Robin said, "They didn't understand the customs of our country. They didn't go to the right people before they came, as we did, and show the right amount of appreciation."

Then Robin said to me, "See those two men sitting over there laughing and having tea? They are local military officers, and they have come to check on us. Even though we have gone to their bosses, and showed the proper appreciation, they have come around with the authority to close us up. Really, they just want a little appreciation shown to them also. I gave them five dollars each. With their monthly wages amounting to $20 to $30, it doesn't take much to make them happy. This is simply the way our country operates and has operated for generations."

I shared my salvation presentation, as recorded in chapter 38, with our team during our morning devotions, and encouraged everyone to share the Gospel with every patient. I gave each person a written copy of the presentation. At lunch time, Kathy, who has a big heart for evangelization, asked Jubilee if he could come and help her in their glasses clinic. They had a long waiting line, and although they were treating many patients, they were not adequately sharing the Gospel with their patients. Their particular translators were not helping them as much as they wanted with evangelism.

Jubilee was happy to go and translate for Kathy. They were seeing so many patients in the glasses clinic, that Kathy and Jubilee started sharing the Gospel in groups of 10 to 15 people gathered in a small circle. Kathy shared and Jubilee translated. Their success was so great with everyone wanting to become a Christian that it greatly impressed and touched Kathy. I think that it may have been an influence that helped to change the direction of her life. See "The Rest of the Story", at the end of this chapter. She was very thrilled to observe lives being changed.

I got along fine with my new translator and we continued to have 100% success. My translator was a relatively new Christian, and a helper at the Mon Nazarene Church in which we had worked the last two years. After a couple of hours, my translator turned to me and said, "I like the way you are sharing Jesus with these people. This gives me a lot of good ideas as to how I can better share Jesus with the people in my ministry." Dora May took Polaroid pictures again of all of our new Christian patients, so they would have something to remember the most important day of their life, the day they decided where they were going to spend eternity.

We also gave each new Christian a 30-page booklet in Burmese containing selected important Bible scriptures. Both Robin and Jubilee, who had been doing follow-up with our new Christians, commented that the new Christians were having trouble understanding many of the Scripture verses. They were written in the King James Version. They wondered if we could get something simpler to give them. Then Jubilee suggested, "Why don't we write up your salvation message and print our own booklets? I know a person who could draw some simple creative illustrations for our booklet."

I had already written copies of my presentation and handed it to all of our team members to guide and encourage them in sharing the Gospel. Dr. David Drake who came with Dr. Shull's team last March used my presentation fairly intact. He reported that over a hundred people, without exception, every Buddhist patient with whom he had shared the message of salvation, accepted Jesus and had become a Christian.

I thought to myself, I have encouraged every new Christian to share Jesus with their friends and family, but I'm sure they didn't remember everything that I told them. They probably would appreciate reviewing a written copy of what I had said. They could use this information in helping lead their family and friends to Jesus, by telling them exactly what they had to do to become Christians. So I told Jubilee, "Yes, let's do it. We will make our own booklet." Jubilee wisely suggested that we make the author unknown, so I could get back into the country next year, in case it fell into the wrong hands.

When we arrived at Max's house the next morning, and were starting to set our clinic up, Jubilee came to me and said, "I have five Buddhist monks that want you to tell them what a Christian believes." They were standing in a group huddled off to the side of the crowd. Jubilee said, "They never mix with people and always stay to themselves." I asked Gary and Dora May to please finish setting up our clinic. My heart was starting to pound.

What happened in the next 50 minutes, I will never forget as long as I live. I asked Jubilee "Where would be a good place for us to share?" He indicated that we would need to find a private place. Jubilee checked around and received permission to use a neighbor's house that I had just led to the Lord the day before. It was near our clinic. Jubilee, the five robed monks, and I went to the house, and went upstairs to the living quarters. The ground floor was for the animals. I asked Jubilee, "Should I use the same presentation?" He said, "Yes."

In the upstairs living quarters was a huge vacant room, with a mat on the floor at one end, and no furniture. There was one trunk on the side, and since I don't sit well on the floor, Jubilee and I pulled it over and put it in front of the mat. The five monks quickly sat down on the mat, 4 or 5 feet in front of me. I asked Jubilee if he wanted to sit on the trunk with me, and he said, "I think it would be better if I were to sit on the floor next to you." My heart was really pounding now.

I started with the same presentation I had been regularly using. The five monks were exceptionally attentive, and it became obvious that the slightly older monk in front was the head monk. All the men were in their 30s and 40s. When I asked them questions, they would answer loudly in unison, and frequently nod their heads as I was talking. They never once interrupted me. I thought I might get into an argument or debate, but it never happened. Often my one or two sentences would take Jubilee three or four times longer to translate. I assumed that Jubilee, with his wisdom about Buddhism, would add appropriate additional explanations to my presentation.

When I finally got to the important question and asked them if they would like to be sure, that when they died, they could go to heaven, they all shook their heads, yes, and answered in a loud voice, "Yes." I then told them how, and asked them to pray and repeat after me. A couple of years ago when I asked two monks to repeat the sinners prayer after me, I never heard them, but I sure heard these five monks. I wouldn't have been surprised if they heard them praying back at the clinic. They prayed louder and with more vigor and enthusiasm than any patients I had ever had.

When I finally told them, "If you believed what you prayed, you are now a Christian." They all broke out in big smiles. I remembered that Buddhist monks were trained never to smile. As I described what it meant to be a Christian, they again listened very intently. I taught many students at the University of Michigan for 30 years, but these men listened more intently to every word I said than any student I can remember.

When I finished, they all shook my hand and with a big smile said, "Thank you." We went back to the clinic. I got them together and had Dora May take our picture as a group, and then individually. She took individual Polaroid pictures of each of them with Jubilee and me, which we gave to them. Everyone knew what it meant to get a Polaroid picture taken. These men were smiling, mixing with the people and shaking everyone's hand. They were very obviously changed people. When they were getting their pictures taken, one of the monks, or should I say, new Christian, put his arm around me and squeezed me quite hard. I knew he was different, because for monks this was a no-no, because monks were not allowed to touch anyone. I could tell he was quite excited.

We fit three of the monks with glasses. One saw the physician and received medications. I extracted a tooth for one of them. I often wondered if the 78-year-old monk, who accepted Christ the day before, had talked to them and sent them to see me. Jubilee said, "They asked specifically to see you, and they had walked quite a distance from two different Buddhist monasteries." I will probably never know, and I guess it really doesn't make much difference. These men were unquestionably leaders and now Christian ones at that. Jubilee told me that they would now need to stop being monks, leave their Buddhist monasteries, and integrate back into society. Jubilee said, "This is not a big deal. Monks join and leave every day but rarely because they have become a Christian." I read that over 2% of the population in Myanmar are Buddhist monks.

In the afternoon I had a lady sit down in my chair with a toothache. When I asked if she knew what a Christian believed, she said that her neighbor, Max, had been telling her about Jesus. I asked her if she would like for me to tell her more about what Christians believe while we were waiting for her to get numb, and she said, "Yes". I shared with her the full presentation. While I was sharing with her, she continuously glanced to one side. When I asked her if she wanted to be a Christian she said, "Yes", and prayed with me, but she continually glanced to the side. Jubilee saw my curiosity about this distraction, and told me that the man standing 20 feet away helping with the medical patients was her husband. He was a neighbor and best friend of Max, and had been working tirelessly with medical in organizing and moving patients around. Although Max had shared the gospel with him several times, he remained a Buddhist. His wife hadn't asked for permission from her husband to become a Christian. Fortunately, there was no indication that her husband was aware of what was going on, and the wife elected not to have a Polaroid picture taken. I will be eager to find out the next time we return what has happened to this family since our last visit.

We had an older gentleman sit down in my chair the last afternoon with several abscessed teeth. I numbed him and went through the same presentation. When I got to the place where I asked him if he knew what a Christian believed, he said, "Oh yes. I was here yesterday and got glasses. This young man," as he pointed to Jubilee, "told me all about Jesus and now I am a Christian." He also said, "I was up most all night sharing Jesus with my wife," as we encouraged them to do, "and now she is a Christian, too."

When Jubilee had been sharing with optical, he shared with groups of 10 to 15, and he didn't recognize the man from the day before. This man's story reminds me of two things. First, HTI considers itself as seed planters of the Gospel. We often don't know what seeds may land on fertile ground and multiply. Secondly, people who are sick and have painful abscesses, often go to optical and get glasses first, before seeking medical or dental treatment, because they think getting glasses is more important. I considered our three days spent at Max's house, in the middle of the rubber plantation, extremely worthwhile.

Max believed that with the number of new Christians, he could now start a church. If you remember, all this started two years ago when Max traveled two hours by bus, to get an aching tooth removed, heard about Jesus, became a Christian, and accepted the challenge to share Jesus with his family and friends. This was another encouraging example of a Gospel seed that landed on fertile ground and multiplied.

Robin had found a new location in a different rubber plantation where he thought our clinic would be of value. All arrangements had been made, officials had received their appreciation, and we were ready to start in the new area the next morning. As we were eating supper in a local hotel, Jubilee came into the restaurant. He had been driving the truck with our equipment and translators. On his way back to town he had gone by the area where we were scheduled to go the next day, just to make sure everything was ready.

Our local host there told Jubilee that he had just heard that a big government official was planning to come to the exact area where we had planned to work the next day. He recommended strongly that we not come at this time. After a little discussion, we decided to head back to Yangon the next day, and to do clinics around the Yangon suburbs.

On our drive to Yangon the next morning, we stopped at the Community Fellowship House that I described in our third mission trip. It was interesting and good for our new team members to see the miracles that were happening in this Buddhist village. It broke up our long drive. It also was an encouragement to Florin, the young lady who was a former graduate of Robin's Bible school, and her mother, who were ministering in this isolated Buddhist village.

Florin reported that their Sunday morning church service had grown from 10 to 15 last February to 60 or 70 people in November. She shared other encouraging improvements in her ministry. Florin explained one of her problems currently was that they didn't have enough chairs, and most people had to sit on the floor. I asked what she needed, and she said, "We need fifty light plastic stackable chairs at a cost of two dollars each." Dr. Bill and I gave her the funds to buy the chairs. They served us tea and cookies again. It will be interesting to see what has happened since, if we have the opportunity to return again.

We got back into Yangon in the early afternoon, and spent the rest of the day shopping in the big central market. It had everything.

Charles, Robin's son, had obtained a visa to go to the U.S., and was currently in the states working on a doctorate degree in Theology. We spent the next six days in and around Yangon. You don't have to go far to find unreached people with 95% Buddhists in the Yangon area.

Sunday, we went to church with Robin and Jubilee. They asked me to preach again, so I reported the great success we had in introducing people to Jesus. Then I spent the rest of the time going over the presentation that we used, and exactly how they could share what Christians believed, and how to lead people to Christ.

I wish someone had told me how simple it was, many years ago. After church we toured through the new Bible school facilities which were attached to the church. We ate lunch at a nice western restaurant, and then for the seven new team members, we visited Shwedagon Pagoda, the largest gold pagoda in the world, containing many tons of gold. It was two blocks from our hotel.

We went back to the same two houses that we had clinics in on our previous mission trips. We were very busy and just as successful as before.

One day I had a lady come in asking to have some aching teeth removed, so I numbed her and started with the presentation. As I started, she looked at me and said, "You don't remember me, do you? You removed these two teeth for me last year." She pointed to an area in her mouth where the teeth were missing. I asked her, "Did you become a Christian?" and she answered, "Yes." I then asked her if she had been able to share Jesus with her family or friends. She said, "My family is now all Christians, and we have found a good church. I have become the leader of our woman's Bible study, and I tell many women about Jesus every week."

We spent a day at the orphanage, not only treating the orphans, but mainly the Buddhist neighbors in the surrounding community. I am repeatedly thrilled with the orphans' enthusiastic singing, particularly the song, "I Have Decided to Follow Jesus." We presented them with lots of clothes again which we had brought in our suitcases.

We spent our last day and a half at Robin's and Jubilee's church working in some of the Bible school classrooms. We saw a few Bible school students, but in general they were young and healthy. We had several pairs of designer sunglasses left, so we gave each student an opportunity to pick out their favorite designer sunglasses. They were donated to us back home, and the students were really excited about getting them.

I saw one middle-aged man who had a bad tooth which I removed. In the process, he accepted Jesus and became a Christian. Just as we were finishing, Mo Mo walked by, and stopped and talked with him. Smiling happily, he told her that he had just become a Christian. Mo Mo told me later that he was the owner of a small local grocery store where she usually shopped. She had seen his swollen jaw and had invited him to come to our clinic. She was particularly happy with his decision to become a Christian, because she had been witnessing to him for a long time. Mo Mo indicated that he was a very influential person in the community.

Jubilee and I played a little game with our patients. The classroom in which we were working was too small to allow patients to wait in the room, so we had them come in one at a time after we finished with our previous patient. They needed to come down a short hall before entering the classroom. From where our dental chair was placed we could see clearly right down the hall. We were seeing a few Christian patients. I would tell Jubilee before the patients got into my chair whether they were a Christian or a Buddhist, and 9 out of 10 times I was correct. This puzzled Jubilee greatly. I observed that the Buddhists were very somber and serious, and often walked with their heads down. The Christians usually had a big smile on their face and walked with their heads up. It wasn't long before Jubilee caught on and was just as successful at recognizing the Christians by their facial appearance.

We finished our clinic about 1 p.m. on Friday, and had a final closing ceremony in the dining hall during which we showed our appreciation with financial gifts to all of our translators and helpers. We gave them other gifts as well. It was easy to get personally attached to our translators after working with them closely for two weeks.

Dr. Dale Lewis, on one of our previous mission trips had a translator who taught in the Bible school. His goal was to go to the Philippines and get a Masters Degree in Theology, like Jubilee had done. He wanted to be a better teacher in the Bible school. Dr. Dale felt so close to him that he financially supported him to go to school in the Philippines for the past two years. He has now graduated and is back teaching at the Bible school. Jubilee and Mo Mo had become very close to Dora May and me, and we tried to help them in several ways also.

Friday afternoon we finished our shopping at the market, and the girls picked up their Burmese dresses that they had tailor-made for them from our earlier visit. They were very beautiful and unbelievably cheap. We tried to get Mi Mi a new dress but she insisted we only buy her material, because she preferred to make it herself. We bought her the material and later she sent us a photo of the dress she made.

That evening we went to Robin and Mi Mi's second-floor apartment over the retail shops, right in the middle of downtown. Several of the girls wore their Burmese dresses. Mi Mi and her daughters prepared a wonderful supper for us. This time we persuaded Robin's whole family to eat with us.

After dinner we had the final report of our mission activities for the two weeks. We exchanged speeches, gifts, and our expressions of appreciation. This time I was successful in getting Robin and Mi Mi to get us smaller, simpler, cheaper gifts so that we could more easily pack them to take home. This was a pleasant way to officially end our mission efforts.

When we got back to the hotel, we had to inventory our leftover supplies, which comprised quite a large amount. The purpose was to inform the next team what they needed to bring. We packed everything and got ready for an early-morning departure.

Early Saturday morning Robin presented us with a final bill of all our land expenses. It totaled $1200 per person for our two weeks, including all of our hotels, food, transportation, appreciation payments, and everything. We felt that Robin had cared for us very well, and that the cost was very reasonable. This was much less than we expected. Everyone was happy. Many of us left Robin a financial thank you gift.

We had no problem getting out of the country, although the airport was rather old, primitive and inefficient. We arrived in Singapore about 3:30 p.m., and our next flight home wasn't until 9 a.m. the next morning. Singapore Airlines put us up in the Hilton Hotel right in the middle of downtown. The cost of the room was listed on the door as $250 per night but we only had to pay $60. Saturday night the town was jumping with people. They had the most fantastic Christmas street lights and decorations that I had ever seen. We had a pizza dinner together, and enjoyed walking around, observing everything, and yes, shopping. We could use our credit cards here. The next morning we had a long and non-eventful flight home.

In summary: We treated 2715 patients, the most ever. We fitted 1431 pairs of glasses, and had 369 Buddhist who accepted Christ as their personal Savior and Lord. I had the privilege, with the help of the Holy Spirit, of leading almost 100 people to Jesus. It was especially encouraging to see some positive results of our previous year's efforts starting to multiply. We again had a most exciting and rewarding experience in serving our Lord. I know the Lord has greatly blessed our efforts in Myanmar, and I am already looking forward to returning in the near future.

# And Now the Rest of the Story

When Kathy returned home, she quit her job and enrolled in a mission school, where she was trained to be a full-time missionary. She has since spent full-time working for our Lord in missions and currently is working in Thailand.

Dr. Bill Johanson led his team of 10 back to Myanmar in March, and Robin reported it was very successful. I immediately began the process of getting a team together to return in late January 2009. The Holy Spirit continues to touch many lives in Myanmar. It is thrilling to experience.

Jubilee e-mailed me after Christmas. He said they tried using some of HTI's principles, and my presentation in a different situation. He took a team from his church into the hospital just before Christmas. They visited patients and gave them small Christmas gifts, and showed them lots of love. Then they offered to tell them what Christians believed, if they wanted to hear. Many of them wanted to hear, and many of them became Christians. It was exciting for both Jubilee and me to see our principles and presentation applied successfully in a different situation. I feel it is important to show people that you love them, before most are willing to listen to the Gospel.

Jubilee and I got together by e-mail, and refined my presentation on what a Christian believes, and what you needed to do to become a Christian. Jubilee proceeded to get the presentation illustrated and printed in Burmese. He printed 2000 copies initially, with the $500 I sent him. The booklets are 25 pages long and written in a very simple language which should be a great extension of our ministry. These booklets were so successful we printed several thousand more and have used them in all our future missions. Currently other churches and evangelistic outreaches are requesting copies to use in there ministry to the unreached. Praise the Lord.

# CHAPTER 36

# MYANMAR 5

Iwas delighted again by Robin's invitation to bring another HTI team to Myanmar. I got busy and started to search for quality team members, early in the summer of 2007. Dr. Larry Black, a dentist friend who went with us on our third Myanmar mission, was the first to call and ask to go.

I asked Dr. Jim Okamoto, M.D., to join us and take charge of medical and pharmacy. Jim had gone on more than 40 mission trips with HTI and other Christian organizations. He planned to go to Vietnam in October 2007, Sudan in December, and Myanmar in January 2008 with us and to Cameroon in March. He was single, around 40 years old, and had a big heart for missions, both helping people physically, as well as sharing the Gospel. He also joined the HTI Board of Directors in November of 2007.

Dr. Brian Andrews, a physician and OB/GYN, offered to join us for the third time. Susan Jacob, a pharmacist from Seattle, called and asked to join us for her first mission trip. Our new pastor at my church, Reverend Tom Roberts, asked to join us. He agreed to take charge of our glasses program. Pastor Tom, who was around 60 years old, had never been out of the United States. Gretchen Bettcher, a widow who had recently retired, was our part-time adult Sunday school teacher at our church. She offered to join us and help Pastor Tom with the glasses. Both Pastor Tom and Gretchen went to Holland Kendall's one-day course and learned how to operate the auto refractor and Holland's unique computer glasses program.

I had a dentist, Jim, from California, and a nurse, Gloria, from Colorado ask to join us. I had my team of 10, which included my wife Dora May, all formed by the beginning of September.

In late September 2007, Burmese Buddhist monks started a peaceful march in the streets of Yangon, to protest the military dictatorship and its doubling of the price of gasoline. That increased the price of many essentials, and severely hurt the masses. The monks were highly respected leaders in Myanmar's predominantly Buddhist Society.

After a few days of peaceful marches by the monks, the army surrounded the Buddhist monasteries where the monks lived. They arrested the monks that were leading the marches and refused to let any of the other monks out of their monasteries.

Many of the Burmese citizens were angered, not only at the increase in gas prices, but at the army's treatment of their revered monks. The citizens then took to the streets and started marching. They were met by severe violence from the military. Many people were killed, and many others were arrested and imprisoned.

Myanmar's last government protests occurred in the early 1990s. In 2007 communications had changed, and by using cell phone cameras and the Internet, daily reports and TV pictures were flashed around the world. The violence ended in a week or two with the army using heavy brutal force. This resulted in worldwide headlines, and international disapproval.

Needless to say, this caused my team and me considerable concern about Myanmar's future, and our scheduled January 2008 mission trip. Robin advised me just to put a hold on our trip, wait and see what happened, but not to cancel it. I was in the process of finalizing our Singapore Airlines tickets with a large deposit, when all this occurred. Singapore Airlines offered to hold our reservations until 30 days before we were to leave, without any deposits. The Myanmar Government closed the Internet in their country for several weeks and I lost communication with Robin for almost a month.

Due to all the negative media coverage, we lost two of our team members. Dr. Jim, the dentist from California was okay to hold, but his wife was near a nervous breakdown worrying about her husband's safety, so he had to cancel. Gloria, our nurse from Colorado, wrote me a letter, and said she was frightened and needed to cancel.

This left us on hold with 8 team members. We had two physicians, one pharmacist, two dentists, one dental assistant, and two people to fit glasses. I felt this was a good variety of health providers and prayed that we had no further cancellations. As the fall progressed, things quieted down in Myanmar, and Robin started feeling more comfortable about our safety.

In the late fall I received a phone call from Dr. Bill Hill, a dentist from Alberta, Canada, and he asked to join our team. He had hoped to go to the Sudan with Dr. Jim Okamoto in December, which didn't work out, so he asked to join us. Dr. Hill was originally from England, and he had been a staunch atheist for 38 years, until the Holy Spirit convicted him, and he became a Christian. Like many Christians that get converted later in life, he was on fire for our Lord. He had a wife and four young children. He had never been on a mission trip before, but felt convicted to share his faith along with his dental skills.

In early December, Singapore Airlines called Jill, our travel agent, and informed her that they had canceled our flight. They were no longer flying on Saturdays, which was our scheduled date of departure. I thought to myself, the devil is putting all types of obstacles in our path to prevent us from going. This increased my determination to overcome the devil's roadblocks. I had Jill tentatively book us for Friday, which was one day earlier. Then I called all my team members and they made special arrangements to leave on Friday.

We met in the waiting area of Singapore Airlines in Los Angeles, and flew directly to Singapore, and then onto Yangon, Myanmar, after a three-hour layover. We arrived Sunday afternoon and Robin and family met us. We were surprised to see that Myanmar had built a new airport terminal in Yangon which was very nice. We had no problems with customs, and Robin took us straight to our hotel, where we quickly crashed.

I calculated that from Detroit we had been up 49 hours straight, and that we were actually in the air flying 27 hours. Most of us caught naps on the plane, but Pastor Tom could not sleep at all. He told us that he had never been so tired in all of his life. A good full night's sleep put us all in much better shape.

On Monday morning we unpacked, reorganized, and repacked. When packing before coming, we divided our clothes, supplies, equipment, medications, and gifts, and put some in each of our suitcases. This was done in case some of our luggage got lost or delayed, which had happened many times. That way, if we lost some luggage, we could start our clinics and work for several days, while trying to recover our luggage. This time we received all of our luggage upon arrival. We also had a lot of supplies, medications and particularly glasses that had been left from our previous trips. Robin had them all waiting for us when we arrived at the hotel. It was a big reorganization project. Medical probably had over 1500 bottles of medications, and optical had almost 3000 pairs of glasses.

Monday afternoon we went to Robin's orphanage. We met with the orphans, listened to their fantastic singing again, and gave them lots of clothes that we had brought especially for them. A Girl Scout troop, near where I live, had collected and sent me several hundred small soft stuffed animals. We were able to give each orphan a stuffed animal. It was probably the first and only one they ever had in their life. We then set up clinic, and treated the orphans, staff, and several selected neighbors.

Charles, Robin's son, who had been living at the orphanage and managing it, was still in the U.S. studying for his doctorate. Charles' wife and three children still lived in the house at the orphanage during Charles' absence. Monday evening we went to the Royal Barge, for our Burmese buffet dinner and show.

I shared with all of our team at morning devotions the presentation I had been using, with great success, to share Jesus with the Buddhist people. I gave them a written copy and told them that the booklet we gave each patient contained the same presentation.

The next two days we returned to the orphanage and treated people from the surrounding Buddhist neighborhood. Everyone wanted to hear what a Christian believed, and everyone asked to become a Christian.

The optical clinic was set up in a neighboring room. Shortly after we started treating patients, Gretchen came bursting into our dental clinic yelling and sobbing quite hard. Dora May ran over to see what was the matter. She burst out and said, "I just led my first person to Jesus." She was just crying for joy. Both Gretchen and Dr Hill had the pleasure and excitement of leading their first person in their lives to Jesus, followed by many more.

After a patient asked to hear what a Christian believes, it usually took 30 minutes to do a good basic explanation, especially with translation time. I strongly held the view that if you expect a person to change his or her whole life's purpose and beliefs, you needed to spend more than 5 minutes with them and especially if they had never heard of the name of Jesus.

In the afternoon our dental waiting line got so long that Jubilee and I started sharing Jesus with three people at a time, and that worked equally well. It only took five minutes in the dental chair to numb a person and extract a tooth. We were actually spending 80 to 90% of our time sharing with them. Toothaches are temporary, but salvation through Jesus is eternal.

Robin had made all the arrangements for us to go to Taungoo, to work with the Karen people again. We had great success working with them on our first and second mission trips, but we had missed going there our third year because of terrorist bombings, the night before we were to go.

This time, shortly before we were to go, Robin got a phone call from a military officer who was second in command in Taungoo. It seemed that the Colonel, with whom Robin had made the arrangements, and had been given the necessary approval, had been unexpectedly called to the capital. He was to meet with a special U.N. Envoy that had just arrived, to discuss Myanmar's human rights violations, resulting from the violent putdown of the protesters in September 2007. We were told we would have to wait a few days until the Colonel returned. As it turned out, the Colonel didn't return until after we had left the country, so we missed going to Taungoo again.

Robin and Jubilee got busy, and found other great places for us to work around Yangon. As it worked out, instead of spending a day traveling to Taungoo, and another day returning, we had two extra days to have our clinic. These two extra days resulted in more than 150 people becoming Christians. So what looked like another devil's roadblock turned out to be a blessing.

We spent several days holding clinic at the widow's house, where we had had great success several times before. Her home was where we had our largest number of decisions for Christ. It was located in a suburb of Yangon that was almost 100% Buddhist.

One day Pastor Tom had the community's Mayor come in, and he fit him successfully with glasses, and led him to the Lord. The Mayor then left and returned with his daughter to get glasses. The Mayor stayed around and helped with organizing the waiting patients. He said his job was to look after the welfare of his people, and he felt this was the best way he could serve. Actually he was a big help, and a good person to have around in case of any problems, which thankfully never happened.

Gretchen fit reading glasses, while Pastor Tom used the auto refractor to fit more complex glasses including bifocals. One day Gretchen and her translator had 30 decisions for Christ, which was a new one-day record. This was quite a change for a person who had never led one person to Christ in her entire life.

Susan got along great, and was kept busy in pharmacy. Bill, Larry, and I always kept busy in our dental clinic, but we went slower than optical or medical, because we spent more time sharing the Good News of Jesus. Dental was able to take care of all our registered patients each day, so we didn't have to turn anyone away who had been waiting.

I had one patient whom I had seen last year in this area, and she had become a Christian. She said her faith was still strong. When I asked her, "Have you been able to lead any of your family to the Lord?" she said, "Yes." She had led all of her children to the Lord including her 19-year-old son, and they had found a church in Yangon, and were attending regularly. Her only problem was her husband. He remained a Buddhist and she asked me to pray for him, which I did. We gave her one of our new pamphlets hoping that it might help her in explaining Jesus to her husband.

I had one middle-aged woman bring in her elderly mother, who had an abscessed tooth. The daughter requested that I talk with her mother about Jesus. She said that she was a Christian, but her mother wouldn't listen to her when she tried to tell her about Jesus. I went through my usual presentation, and the mother said she wanted to hear what a Christian believed. By the time we finished, her mother asked to become a Christian and she accepted Jesus into her heart. Her daughter was so happy that she began hugging her mother and crying. I finally had to separate the two for a few minutes, so I could take the mother's tooth out. We had numbed her 40 minutes prior. They left as one happy family. We have seen this happen several times, where people won't believe their own family members when they tell them about Jesus, but for some reason, they believe us.

We couldn't stay too long in the same place, because the word of our free clinic spread quickly. Each day the crowds kept getting bigger. When we arrived the third day at the widow's house, the complete road in front of her house was blocked with a large crowd of people. We were told that some people had been waiting since 4 a.m. The police were unhappy and paranoid about the gathering of such a large crowd. Fortunately, the neighbor across the street invited the crowd to wait in her front yard, and this calmed the authorities' concerns. Three days seemed to be as long as we could stay in any one place before the crowd got too big.

Sunday we went to Robin's and Jubilee's church. Jubilee is now the senior pastor, and Robin is the overseer of all Nazarene churches in Myanmar. I suggested to Robin that he have Pastor Tom preach, rather than me, because he is much better. Robin asked Pastor Tom, and told him to speak about 45 minutes. Pastor Tom preached and Robin interpreted.

Pastor Tom had never preached using an interpreter, so his sermon only lasted 35 minutes. After church we all went to the back door area, and greeted and shook hands with every person in the church as they were leaving.

After church we toured the attached Bible School, and the small built-in apartment where Jubilee, Mo Mo and their two children lived. On our way to lunch Pastor Tom commented that this was the first time he had ever preached in a foreign country using a translator, and it was also the first time in his life he was ever criticized for not preaching long enough. Evidently many of the people enjoyed his sermon, and expressed that they would have liked for him to have preached longer.

We had lunch at a Western-style restaurant near the main city market. After lunch we shopped in the market. It was so large that it would take days to see everything. Most people knew what they wished to purchase, so with the help of Robin, Jubilee, and Mo Mo, we were finished by 4:30 p.m.

We then proceeded to Shwedagon Pagoda, hoping that the sun and the temperature would start to cool as evening came. Foreigners had to pay to go into the temple complex, but we did get an elevator ride up, a fair distance, to the temple grounds. The main golden stupa along with the surrounding 20 or 30 huge decorated ornate temples were on the top of the hill. This helped to make the tall central golden stupa visible from many parts of town.

We needed to take our shoes off and leave them in the lobby before getting on the elevator. This meant we walked barefoot for an hour and a half but it was on nice polished marble floors. When we got ready to come down, the elevators were closed for security purposes. A foreign head of state was scheduled to visit. This meant that we had to walk down on rough cobblestone steps, and then walk through a gravel parking lot to recover our shoes. For a tenderfoot like me, who rarely goes barefoot, this was pure torture, but I survived. We went to a very nice fancy restaurant for supper and finally back to our hotel. I think we were more exhausted at the end of this day, than when we worked all day in the clinic.

On Monday we went to another suburban house. It was one of Robin's church members, where we had gone with great success in previous years. We worked three days there with lots of patients, and many came to the Lord.

We spent a considerable amount of time, especially with all our dental patients, teaching and encouraging our new Christians to be evangelists to their own families and friends. From the feedback we have received, I am convinced that our new Christians over the years have led more people to Jesus than we have.

Jubilee had completed editing and printing our 25-page illustrated pamphlet of my presentation. See chapter 38 for its contents. Each patient we saw in our clinics, plus some extra people, received a copy of this very simple language pamphlet, "What Christians Believe and How to Become a Christian." I can't help but conclude that this pamphlet is a major extension of our ministry, in leading unreached people to the Lord. We handed out so many of the pamphlets that we didn't have enough for Dr. Johansen's team, which was to follow us in two weeks. I gave Jubilee some more money, and he was going to have additional copies printed right away.

World Missionary Press gives out scripture pamphlets that are about 30 pages long, and they contain only Bible scriptures. They have these pamphlets printed in almost every written language. I have worked with them for years. They give the pamphlets out free by the thousands to any missionary who agrees to distribute them directly to the people.

I asked them for a simpler illustrated children's scripture booklet, which I hoped would be easier for these people to understand. They didn't have any in their warehouse in Burmese, so they asked their printer in Yangon, just down the street from Robin, to print several thousand copies for us. I made arrangements to pick them up when we got to Yangon, which we did.

This eliminated our having to carry the heavy booklets in our luggage, which gave us more room for supplies, toothbrushes, stuffed animals, clothes for the orphans, etc. Every patient we saw also received a copy of the simplified scripture booklet. Bibles are very hard to find in Myanmar, and are only available on the black market, so the scripture booklets are a helpful beginning. Burmese Bibles are also hard to find in the U.S. When a few become available, I usually buy three and take them, even though they cost thirty dollars each. We give them to our various hosts as thank-you gifts.

I had one patient come to me to get a tooth extracted. She reminded me that I had removed a tooth from her last year and had led her to the Lord. When I asked her if her Christian faith was still strong, she said, "Yes." When I asked her if she had led any of her family to the Lord, she said, "I would like to, but I don't know how." I asked her, "Would you like for me to teach you?" She said, "Yes."

I basically went through the whole presentation again, answering questions as we went along. This time I gave her our new pamphlet that contained exactly what I had just told her. I asked her to take it home and use it to help share Jesus with her family. I asked her if she were ready to share Jesus with her family now, and she said, "Yes, I'm ready."

Our last day and a half, we again spent at Robin's Bible School where they had 45 students now enrolled. We treated a few students and a few people from the church, but mainly Buddhist people from the surrounding neighborhood.

Thursday evening, Robin and all of our team were invited by our hotel owner, to a rooftop dinner and celebration of their Chinese New Year. We arrived on the eighth floor rooftop just as the sun was setting. The whole area was decorated beautifully, and the weather was perfect, 70°F with no wind.

We could see the tall golden stupa of Shwedagon Pagoda all beautifully lit up, two blocks away, with the sun setting behind it. We took some fabulous photos. Our team sat around one big table that they had prepared especially for us. The owner came around and personally greeted each of us. Robin said we were the seventh HTI team that had stayed at his hotel for two weeks each, and he really appreciated our business.

We had a fabulous buffet dinner. There were probably 150 people present. After supper two very prettily dressed young ladies came around and had each of us take a slip of paper out of a big bowl. On the paper was a number that represented a gift from the owner. The ladies went and retrieved our gifts, which were quite nice and useful things. The gifts for our table alone, probably came to well over $100. Then they had a floor show with various types of music, dance, and drama.

I couldn't help but ponder as we sat there in the peace, luxury, and tranquility of that beautiful evening, with all the great food, gifts, and entertainment, that the country of Myanmar was currently engaged in an ugly 50-year civil war. Also within a few miles of where we sat, there were hundreds of thousands of people who lived in severe poverty. Many of them were sick, in pain, hungry, without jobs, or glasses. They had no hope, and no one to tell them about Jesus. It was a heavy burden on my heart as we returned to our beautiful comfortable rooms.

We closed clinic at noon on Friday. I don't remember one person that I saw, that I didn't have the privilege of leading to the Lord, because every patient asked to become a Christian. I have never had this degree of success in leading people to Christ anywhere else in the world. Bill and Larry had almost 100% success also. Pastor Tom and Gretchen didn't report anyone they had shared with, that didn't want to become a Christian.

Our translators this year were especially helpful in sharing the Gospel. Many of them were teachers at the Bible School. Robin taught all his Bible School students English. The few people in Myanmar who could speak English received much greater respect. That helped to create a good position from which a new pastor could start.

At noon on Friday, we had a short closing service. Some of the Bible school students sang beautifully for us. Robin showed our appreciation to all the translators and helpers in the form of a monetary gift. I gave away a couple of my remaining watches and a couple of the complete Bibles that I had brought from home.

Gretchen had someone find Bibles for her on the black market, so she bought several for eight dollars each, and handed them out to the Bible School students, whom the Dean of Students said didn't have a personal Bible of their own. I gave out 30 new ballpoint pens I had brought, and we sang, prayed, and just had a great time of celebration.

We took all of our equipment and supplies back to the hotel to sort, organize, inventory, and pack to go home. We left all of our supplies, glasses, medications, and most of our equipment for Dr. Johanson's team, as they were arriving in two weeks. Our luggage was much lighter going home.

Friday evening we all went to Robin's apartment for supper. Mi Mi and her daughters not only fixed supper for the nine of us, and their whole family, but also for 15 Bible school students that Robin had invited to come and sing for us. Their voices were spectacular.

Robin shared the statistical results of our two weeks of work. Pastor Tom was asked to give a short devotion and prayer, and we all sang, prayed, and exchanged gifts.

Early Saturday morning Robin presented us with our total cost of all of our land expenses, which was only $1350 per person. Again that was much less than we had anticipated, and everyone was happy.

Robin, Jubilee, and Mo Mo accompanied us to Yangon's new airport terminal where we bid them farewell until next time. We flew to Singapore and stayed overnight in the downtown Hilton Hotel, before proceeding the rest of the long way home the next morning.

Again, I feel fantastically happy and satisfied in my heart that we had a very successful two weeks, regardless of all the roadblocks the devil threw at us. This mission was a good example of why we need to be patient and not get discouraged and give up when the devil throws roadblocks in front of us. Not only did we treat a lot of patients, medically, dentally, and optically, but the Holy Spirit worked through us in changing a lot of people's hearts and brought them to salvation in Jesus Christ. That's what it's all about.

I think that Susan, Pastor Tom, Gretchen, and Dr. Hill, who each experienced their first overseas mission, had a fantastic experience, with a lot of good positive memories that they will never forget. I was particularly happy and excited to see Gretchen and Dr. Hill have the experience of leading their first person to Christ. I'm sure they will never forget it as long as they live. As I think back, there were literally hundreds of people who all worked together to make this mission possible. Praise the Lord.

In summary: We treated 2718 patients, a new record. Medically we treated 1200 patients, extracted over 1000 teeth, and fit 1036 pairs of glasses. Most importantly, we saw 608 people accept Christ as their personal Savior and Lord. That was a glorious new record for Myanmar. I think we were all filled to overflowing with joy and just praised the Lord.

## And Now the Rest of the Story

I received a letter from Dr. Bill Hill shortly after returning home. He thanked me for giving him the opportunity to serve the Lord on this mission. He said that this was the most memorable and enjoyable two weeks he could remember, and he was ready to return anytime.

Dr. Bill Johanson reported that something went wrong when his team attempted to go through customs upon their arrival in Yangon two weeks later. The customs officials took away all their supplies and equipment, and they never returned any of it. Fortunately, we had left a large number of supplies, and all of our equipment. Dr. Johanson used all of our leftover supplies and equipment, purchased a few medications locally, and wasn't slowed down at all. He reported having a very successful two-week mission, with several hundred more people coming to the Lord.

# CHAPTER 37

# MYANMAR 6

Before leaving Myanmar in February, 2008, we made arrangements with Robin to return in November that same year. I was so pleased and excited about the number of people we were able to lead to the Lord that I couldn't wait to return. The feedback we were receiving as to the success of many of our new Christians leading their families, neighbors and friends to the Lord was also exciting.

Dr. Bill Hill told me he was ready to go back. He asked if he could bring his 19-year-old daughter, Fiona, who was very interested in missions and was looking for a short-term mission. She did not have any health skills but was willing to work anywhere that she was needed.

Kathy LeBarron also telephoned and said she was available and would like to join us again. Kathy was excited about a new I-pod-sized recorder speaker that had just been developed that had the Jesus story and message of salvation on it, in the Burmese language. She felt this would be especially good for those people who were not literate. She offered to raise money to help purchase several of those recorders to take with us.

My only concern was customs. The Myanmar government had been known to be paranoid about people bringing in unknown electronic instruments into the country. I told Kathy, "Let's go for it anyway, and we will trust the Lord for protection."

When Dr. Moberg heard we were returning to Myanmar, he called me and said both he and his wife, Lyndell, were available and anxious to return. I couldn't have been happier. Both Lyndell and Kathy offered to work in optical, but neither one felt qualified or comfortable in operating the auto refractor. Both were unavailable to attend Holland Kendall's training class.

Doreen Crockett, a close friend from our home church, indicated that her daughter, Stephanie, had expressed an interest in going with us on one of my mission trips. Stephanie was a senior in high school in our church academy. She was a straight-A student, and her goal was to be a medical doctor. Stephanie had been talking with Pastor Tom and Gretchen, who were instrumental in creating great excitement for her, as a result of sharing their experiences about working in the optical clinic on our last mission trip. Doreen and Stephanie talked with her teachers at the academy and they encouraged her to go and agreed that it would probably be the best time in her schooling to go.

Stephanie was an exceptionally mature young lady and a strong leader in her youth groups. She, like most young people these days, was very proficient in using the computer. I asked Stephanie if she would consider going to Louisville, Kentucky, to be trained by Holland Kendall to operate the auto refractor and his computer program. She agreed and was actually pleased about the opportunity. Doreen went with Stephanie and took the course with her. Stephanie received the auto refractor and laptop computer a week before we left, which gave her time to practice.

Physicians always seem to be the hardest team members to recruit. It must be hard for them to leave their sick and hospitalized patients for 2 weeks to go on a mission. I had my team nearly completed, but again, no physicians.

One night late after I was in bed, I received a phone call from Dr. Samuel Cherian, who had gone with me to Nepal in 1999. He had heard of my need and the Lord was leading him to go. His wife, Molly, who was a pediatrician, also wanted to go. I knew them both to be strong devoted Christians. Presto! My prayers were answered and I slept really well that night.

I had 2 MDs, 3 dentists, 1 dental assistant, my wife, Dora May, 3 to work in optical and Fiona. I asked Fiona if she would work as a pharmacist and help our physicians dispense medications. She was excited about that and asked me to send her a list of the medications. She said that she would get her sister who was a nurse, to help teach her about the medications. That sounded great to me.

I was in the process of assembling a team, when in May of 2008, the severe Nargis Cyclone (in the U.S. it would be called a hurricane) hit Myanmar. The government estimated that there were 60,000 lives lost. Most agencies and people estimated the loss of life to be over 300,000. The number of people left homeless, injured, sick, and without food or water was much larger. The cyclone also hit Yangon and I lost e-mail communication with Robin for several weeks.

The military dictatorship in Myanmar refused to accept any aid or to let any aid workers into the country. They claimed there were only a few people in need and they were caring for them adequately themselves. With modern air and satellite photos, cell phones, and a CNN reporter secretly videotaping the disaster from the hardest hit area, information quickly leaked out of the country. The whole world was shown and told that the number of people killed and left homeless was much greater than the government had reported, and that their needs were not being met. Massive aid was immediately made available, but the government continued to refuse to accept any help, which created world-wide condemnation of Myanmar's military dictatorship.

The U.S. had naval ships off the shore of the Irrawaddy Delta where the destruction had been the worst. They offered to have helicopters drop desperately needed supplies into the area, but the government refused to let them fly into any of Myanmar's air space. The International disapproval and criticism was great and increasing.

Finally the government allowed a few select countries to bring a few supplies into the Yangon airport. There were a lot of rumors about the misuse of the aid supplies. One common rumor was that the military took the aid supplies and used them to stock their warehouses. Then they took some of their old and rotten rice and gave it to their people in need. It also became obvious that if you were not a Buddhist, you weren't considered for any help.

The cyclone was in May and we were scheduled to return to Myanmar in late November. With all the severe restrictions as to whom the government was allowing into the country, we were not sure we would be able to get a visa. We waited and prayed.

International disapproval slowed when the government finally allowed a little aid into the country. An article in the paper in mid-August indicated that Myanmar was complaining that their small tourist income had come to a complete stop.

I submitted Dora May's and my application for a tourist visa in late August. I was surprised when it was quickly approved. Then I had the rest of the team submit their applications, and they were all approved also. Praise the Lord.

With our visas approved, we more aggressively continued to assemble our supplies and equipment. Dora May and I have always felt that taking a Polaroid picture of a new Christian, along with the interpreter and person who led them to Christ, was important. We gave them their picture, so that every time they looked at it, they would be reminded that they were now a Christian, and had accepted Jesus into their heart. Since this was probably the first and only picture that most of these people had ever had of themselves, it would be likely to be prominently displayed for a long time.

A problem occurred when Dora May and I tried to buy Polaroid film. We couldn't find it anywhere. We e-mailed the Polaroid Company, directly, asking for film. Their response was that they did not sell film, and they referred us to their retail outlet stores. None of their suggested outlet stores had any, except one "Staples" store, which had three packages. Upon checking the expiration date on the film, I found that it had expired four years ago, and it cost over two dollars a picture. Then we found out what was happening.

Polaroid had come out with a new printer and it attached directly to most digital cameras. It was battery-operated and about the size of a wallet. It printed any selected picture in good color in 90 seconds and didn't use a printer cartridge. It printed using a new laser technique that required no maintenance. The cost of the printer was less than $100, and the special paper was less then fifty cents each. The paper was much more durable and was water resistant.

What really happened was that Polaroid cameras had become outdated and obsolete, therefore no film. They had been replaced by a much better and newer technology. We bought Polaroid's new photo printer, used it, and it worked great.

We met in the waiting area of Singapore Airlines in San Francisco on November 22, 2008. Kathy brought several small recorder speakers that had the Gospel message on them in Burmese, in her carryon, as I had advised her. We divided them up and we each took 2 or 3 and put them in our pockets, purses, or carryons. Customs didn't usually check our pockets or purses and one recorder speaker in our carryon shouldn't create a big concern.

We flew directly to Singapore and 3 hours later, onto Yangon. Robin and family were there to meet us. Robin was able to get into the customs area and he instructed us which customs agent to check with. We had no problem. We received all our luggage and none was opened by customs.

After Dr. Johanson's equipment and supplies were all taken away in customs last March and never returned, I was concerned about our $12,000 auto refractor and computer. I found special insurance that would totally protect me if I had lost the auto refractor in customs. Fortunately, we had no problem. Dr. Johanson did not have the auto refractor with him last March, thank the Lord.

On the way to our hotel we observed evidence of damage from the cyclone in Yangon. There were a lot of tree stumps where trees had been blown down, and trees with half their limbs missing. It was 6½ months after the cyclone and most downed trees had been removed. We saw a lot of repairs that had been made to houses, especially roofs, porches and windows. There were still tarps over some of the roofs. Robin told us that the cost of repair materials had skyrocketed and some materials were completely gone and not available, such as nails.

Upon arriving at the hotel we went directly to bed, after being up for 45 to 50 hours. The next morning we unpacked and reorganized. Robin took us to the orphanage in the afternoon. We were informed that the new proper name was the Children's Home.

We stopped at a restaurant, called "The Million Coins," for lunch. This was a high quality, somewhat western restaurant that was frequented heavily by foreigners. Robin believed that the food was safe for us to eat in this restaurant. We had stopped there many times on previous missions and the food was always good.

This time we observed something different. We were the only ones in the restaurant. Robin explained that Burma's tourist business had almost completely stopped. Many of the hotels and restaurants that catered to foreigners had closed or were going bankrupt. He did not know what the future was going to be.

When arriving at the children's home we met the same house mother who had continued to care for the 30 children for many years. In addition to providing their food, clothing and shelter, she taught them English, Bible and led them to the Lord. The children were exceptionally well-behaved and responded to her slightest command. She cooked for them and saw that they had all their individual needs met. They appeared happy and sang with gusto and quoted by memory lengthy sections of the Bible in English.

Robin told us this story about the house mother: One day many years ago she came to me and said, "My husband has died and my children have all left home. I want to serve the Lord with the rest of my life. How can I help you in your ministry?" Robin said "I currently am in need of a house mother for my children's home." She immediately answered, "I love children. I will take it and do my best."

These children came from all parts of the country, initially speaking different languages. She had taught and cared for these children, like her very own, for over 10 years, mostly by herself.

The beautiful young lady we had fit with a hearing aid five years ago was now 20 years old. She had stayed in the children's home to help the house mother care for the children. The house mother now had a little freedom to travel with our team whenever we were in the Yangon area. She helped the team with evangelism, food or wherever she was needed. She always had such a joyful spirit and a radiant big smile. Put yourself in her position. How would you like, after reaching 50 years of age, to raise 30 children all under one roof, by yourself? I continue to be amazed every time I see her or meet any of her well-behaved, polite children.

Robin offered to take us to the Royal Barge for our traditional Burmese buffet dinner and show our first night. Lyndell wisely suggested that Robin wait a few days until we could recover from jet lag so that we could enjoy it more. We waited and really did enjoy it more.

We spent the entire second day at the children's home working mainly with Buddhist neighbors. The children's home was in an extremely poor section in the Yangon suburbs. Many years ago the government gave Robin the land for the children's home. The area was mostly swamps and not good for much of anything.

As we were driving less than a block away from the children's home, Robin pointed out a one-room dwelling about 15-feet-square on poles in the swamp. The house was made of scraps of bamboo and miscellaneous building materials with palm leaves for the roof. There was a widow who lived there with 3 young children and had no job. Myanmar's government had no form of welfare. When the cyclone came, her house was totally blown away. None of them lost their lives but they had absolutely nothing. Robin, Jubilee, some of Jubilee's church men and the older boys from the children's home helped to rebuild her house. They used scraps of building materials that had blown off other people's houses and had scattered in the swamp. They gave her food to feed her children and herself, which kept them alive.

While driving to the children's home we frequently commented to each other about the amount of destruction and new repairs we observed in these poorly constructed, slum-type homes. Actually, even the children's home that was built of cement blocks had lost a significant part of its metal roof during the cyclone.

Immediately after the cyclone Robin e-mailed me and asked for help. He assured me that we couldn't get into the country and said the best way we could help was to send money. HTI is not a disaster relief organization. I had several former team members call and ask how they could help.

I set up a special fund within HTI and notified all previous team members how they could help if they felt led to, by sending money to this special fund. We collected over $6000 which was sent to Robin by wiring it to a bank in a third country where it could be changed into Burmese money and forwarded to him. Robin said that he used some of this money to help the widow in the swamp rebuild her house, as well as to repair the roof on the children's home. He also used some of the money to help repair the roofs and other damages to the two houses in the Yangon suburbs that we had successfully used for many of our clinics in previous years.

On our second day I had a neighbor lady come to see me with severely aching teeth. I anesthetized all of them that were aching and started with my presentation. She said she wanted to hear what a Christian believed, so I continued. When I asked the question, "Have you ever heard of Christmas?" she said "No". This is the first and only person I can remember anywhere in the world that had never heard of Christmas.

In Myanmar where the population is 95% Buddhist and almost no one has ever heard the name of Christ or Jesus, Christmas is a National Holiday. All businesses close and families gather to exchange gifts. Even though it was late November, the stores and streets were all decorated and lighted Christmas trees were everywhere, very similar to the U.S. I asked my patient, "Haven't you seen any of the Christmas decorations or lights in town?" She answered, "I have never been in Yangon. I have never left this area in my whole life." Wow! – Hard to believe.

I continued and when I got to the place where I asked her if she wanted to be a Christian, she said, "Yes, but God wouldn't want me. I am too bad." I asked her what she meant. She told me this story: "I married very young and had several children. I never went to school, so I do not know how to read or write. My husband died and left me with 4 children. I have never had a job. None of my children have gone to school. (School is free but you have to buy uniforms, books, and there are other expenses.) We eat essentially garbage or other people's leftovers. My oldest daughter got pregnant at age 16. We have no money so we couldn't afford a doctor. I tried to help deliver my daughter's baby at home 2 weeks ago. We had problems and both my daughter and her baby died. I am just no good. God wouldn't want me."

It took Jubilee and me some extra time to explain to her that no one is too bad for Jesus. He loves everybody, regardless of what they have done or who they are. We used the example of the thief on the cross. She finally believed us and prayed to become a Christian. After many verbal instructions, she agreed she would like for her children to go to heaven also, and would tell them about Jesus and teach them how to become Christians. We told her if she ever had any questions, to come and ask the house mother and she would help her.

Our dental waiting line was not too long, so Robin suggested early on the second day that Dr. Gary Moberg and his interpreter, who was the Dean of Students at Robin's Bible School, go and help share Jesus with the waiting medical and optical patients. Their clinics were so busy that it was difficult for them to stop and share for very long.

After a while Gary came back into the dental clinic with a big smile on his face and a tear in his eye. He said, "This is so wonderful! I have groups of 10-15 people all accepting Jesus and becoming Christians. They are so hungry for the Good News of Jesus. This is what I have dreamed and prayed about for many years."

This method of having Gary share Jesus with groups of waiting medical and optical patients worked so well that we continued doing it for the rest of our trip. I don't think he extracted another tooth. We had improved our method of sharing Jesus and our results showed it. We had a large number of patients who became Christians.

Kathy gave one of her recorder speakers to the house mother at the children's home that contained the Jesus story in Burmese. The children gathered around and listened intently and were very excited.

The third, fourth and fifth days, we went to a house in the suburbs of Yangon, where we had gone several previous times. The owners were good members and leaders in Robin's and Jubilee's church, and one of the houses our HTI cyclone fund helped to repair.

Optical set up under a large tarp covering the small front yard again this year. When the sun was shining, it was so bright the auto refractor did not work accurately. After getting a towel, putting it over Stephanie and her patient's head to make it darker, it worked perfectly.

Stephanie worked great operating the auto refractor, and computer and printing out the patients information. She kept Lyndell, Kathy and occasionally Mi Mi very busy finding the glasses in the inventory, fitting them to the patient and then double-checking the accuracy.

Holland Kendall advised me where I could purchase good, new reading glasses from a wholesaler in Montana. I called the person that Holland recommended and ordered 1000 pairs of mixed-strength new reading glasses. The wholesaler was excited and happy to sell them to me at 42 cents each. I knew he was making a profit. They arrived in brand new packages all labeled for retail sale with the price of $12.95 on each pair of glasses. I have often wondered how a retailer could sell products at a 70% discount and still make a profit;

now I know. If these glasses were sold at a 70% discount the retailer would still be making over a 900% profit.

About 50% of our patients only needed reading glasses, so Kathy and Lyndell were kept extremely busy and were able to please a lot of patients.

Stephanie reported that one older gentleman was led to her chair with one person on each side guiding him. Stephanie read his lens and Lyndell fit him with an unusually strong pair of glasses, one that was designed for extremely poor eyes. When Lyndell put his glasses on, a big smile appeared on his face. He then stood up, waved his helpers away, and walked out of the clinic all by himself.

Gary continued to share Jesus with groups of 15-20 people with great success in a private room in the house. Bill and I were kept busy and finished all our dental patients. We were able to share the Gospel with everyone in our dental clinic, and all of them asked to become a Christian.

The house behind the one where we were holding our clinic had two walls that had been destroyed by the cyclone. The residents were living in one small, intact room at the other end of the house. They did not have money to repair it.

Jubilee said we could not do clinic at the widow's house this year, because the severe damage to her house from the cyclone was still being repaired, with the help of some of our HTI donations. The widow lady came to our clinic at this house and wanted to help. She recognized Dora May and gave her a big hug.

Saturday we went to a new location 30 miles southeast of Yangon, near the restricted border of the Irrawaddy Delta. It had been six and one half months since the Nargis Cyclone and still no one was allowed into the Delta area except residents and United Nation trained and certified Burmese rescue workers, which were few.

The pastor of the church where we went was one of Robin's former Bible School students that Robin had helped to get started. It was in a rural, farming community. The officials, from whom we received permission to come, had an unusual requirement. No foreigner was allowed to leave the church property at any time. The cyclone damage was moderately severe in this area, but the biggest problem that they had was that their rice crop had been destroyed.

I was not aware that Kathy and Lyndell had some funds given to them before coming to help the cyclone survivors. They had their interpreters buy two 100 pound bags of rice. During our lunch break, they gave out several quarts of rice to 60-70 families that the pastor had designated as the families with the greatest needs. The pastor told us that the amount we gave them should feed their families for a month. Needless to say, they were very thankful and happy.

Our clinic at this new church went very well. We were able to treat a lot of people and many came to the Lord.

One lady from the church asked me to pray for her teenage son who was the only one in her family who was not a Christian, so I did. I then asked her if he was at home, and she said "Yes." I asked her to go get him and I would give him a free dental exam and talk to him. In a little while she brought him back. I examined his teeth. They were in great shape. I then started through my presentation. He agreed that he would like to hear what Christians believed. By the time I finished, he asked to become a Christian and prayed with me to have Jesus forgive his sins, and he invited Him into his heart and life. He indicated he never really understood what Christians believed or the advantage of becoming a Christian. Needless to say, his mother was one happy lady. She had a hard time controlling her tears and emotions of joy.

On our way back to our hotel we stopped at a pharmacy to purchase more vitamins, medication for scabies, and several pediatric medications. The experience of purchasing local Myanmar medications taught us several things. The medications were cheaper than we could purchase at special mission discount prices in the U.S. It also reminded us that we could not always tell what types and what numbers of different medical diseases we were going to encounter. By purchasing them locally we did not have to worry about customs taking them away, and we could more accurately buy only what was needed. This may change our future strategy concerning a lot of the medications we take to Myanmar.

Sunday we went to church with Robin, Jubilee and their families. Robin asked me to preach. I suggested he ask Dr. Gary Moberg since he had recently graduated from college with a Masters in Theology. So Robin asked Gary. He preached, did a great job and was excited to do it.

Sunday afternoon we had lunch, shopped in the central market, visited Shwedagon Pagoda, had supper, returned to the hotel, and packed to leave Yangon for the Mon state early Monday morning.

We had an early breakfast, were packed and on our way by 6:00 A.M. The Nazarene Church where we planned to go had one of Robin's former students as the pastor. It was the only known evangelical Christian church for several million people. We had been there a couple of times previously and had had great success.

It was a long, hot drive. The road had become extremely rough, in part due to the cyclone. We stayed in the same hotel in the big city of Manlamyini.

After arriving and unpacking we went to a nice restaurant for supper. The weather was perfect so we decided to eat outside. As it was getting dark, I looked up in the sky and saw something I had never seen before and probably will never see again. It was a huge smiley face looking down at us. There was a sliver of a moon that was horizontal, rather than vertical like we usually see it in the U.S. It formed a big smiling mouth. Then there were two equally bright stars, that I later found out were planets. They were located exactly where you would expect to find eyes in a smiley face. It was not very dark, so there were no other stars visible. We took several good photos of that unusual phenomenon.

Suddenly there were lots of sirens blaring. A lot of the people went to one side of the restaurant, so we followed. The sky was a bright orange with billows of smoke filling the sky. It was only about six blocks away behind some tall buildings. We watched the orange smoky sky until our supper came. Since there was nothing we could do about it, we went back and ate our supper.

Upon returning to our hotel, the people at the front desk told us the city's central market was on fire. We had shopped at the central market on previous trips. It was a huge sprawling market covering several blocks. It was made up of several hundred, small, family-owned stalls selling everything you could imagine. The small stalls and shops were single-story and constructed out of wood and bamboo, with many having thatched roofs. As I thought about it, everything was constructed of extremely flammable material.

The next morning we drove about thirty minutes to the church. They were ready for us. There were several patients already waiting, so we set up clinic and started to work. Shortly after we started, a couple of plainclothes officials arrived to talk with Robin and the pastor. They were the officials from whom Robin had received authorization for us to have our clinic, and he had shown them monetary appreciation.

They told Robin that the central market had burned completely to the ground. There were a lot of rumors as to how it had started, including terrorists, foreigners, and the government. Everything was in turmoil. The central government was sending several big government officials to investigate the fire, and they would be driving right by the church and our clinic. If some of the government officials found out that a group of foreigners were allowed into an area, where they were not supposed to be, there could be big trouble, especially because of the fire. The two officials appeared fearful for their jobs. They didn't want us to leave because we would probably meet the officials on the road, and it would look like we were running from something.

After much discussion it was decided that we could continue our clinic, but we had to hide the bus behind the church. All our patients that were waiting needed to wait behind the house. No team members, who were dressed in medical scrubs, were allowed outside the church, where we could be seen from the road. We even had to close some of the church windows, so it wouldn't look as if it were in use.

Despite the restrictions, we had a very successful clinic. I had one lady come to me and ask me to remove an aching tooth. I found out her house was located right next to the church, about ten feet away. She said she could hear the people singing, but she had never been inside the church, because she was a Buddhist.

I went through my presentation and she became a Christian. I found the pastor and introduced him to his new Christian neighbor. He was delighted. He said, "I have witnessed to her many times, but with no success." As for the lady, she was anxious to share her new faith with her husband. She was definitely excited about her new faith and showed it. She said, "Now I can come and sing the songs with all the other Christians. I have heard them so many times that I know them by heart."

The two officials came back in the late afternoon, and talked to Robin and the pastor. After they had collected information all day as to what was happening, they strongly recommended that we leave town and return to Yangon very early the next morning.

It was getting nearly dark when we returned to Manlamyini. We asked Robin if we could go by the burned down central market. Robin was not happy about the idea, but he finally agreed, only if we went to the hotel first and changed out of our scrubs. He said, "They make you stick out as foreigners, even in the bus."

After we changed into our street clothes, we drove by the burned market on our way to supper. It had burned totally to the ground. There were still some red embers and a few small flames coming up from the ashes. It was sad to think of the hundreds of people that lost their entire life savings.

We had supper and very early the next morning, we headed back to Yangon. We had no problems or questions leaving town. We stopped after a couple of hours to visit and encourage Florin again with her house ministry. She had purchased the 50 stackable plastic chairs with the money we had given her on our last visit. She reported they were all full each Sunday morning for church services. It appeared she was continuing to do well.

Thursday and Friday mornings we held clinic at Robin's Bible School, and worked primarily on his Buddhist neighbors around the church and school.

One Buddhist middle-aged lady asked to hear what a Christian believes, and then very excitedly became a Christian. I told her what it meant to be a Christian, and challenged her to share Jesus with her family and friends. Dora May took her photo with Jubilee and me and printed a copy for her. I extracted her tooth. We gave her our two booklets, a toothbrush, Tylenol, stickers, and a colorful cloth bracelet that said, "I have Jesus in my heart." We do this routine for all of our patients, but then something happened with this lady that I will never forget. She knelt down on the floor right in front of me, and put her hands together in front of her. She started bowing repeatedly; face down in front of me, just like I had observed the Buddhists doing in front of the gold statue of Buddha at Shwedagon Pagoda. I told Jubilee, "Make her stop, and tell her I am not a god." He talked with her and then told me, "Be patient, just sit there and let her go." She bowed from a kneeling position and put her face on the floor with her hands folded together in front of her. She did this 12 times. I really felt uncomfortable. When she finished, she got up, smiled, shook my hand and left.

I asked Jubilee, "What was that all about?" He said, "The woman knows that you are not a god and she was not worshiping you. She couldn't speak English and she just wanted to personally thank you for telling her about Jesus and how she could go to heaven. This was the only way she knew how to say thank you." It was certainly the most unusual, memorable, and humbling thank you I have ever received.

I treated a middle-aged man who was in the Irrawaddy Delta when cyclone Nargis hit. He said they had no warning. Fortunately his wife and two children were in Yangon visiting relatives at the time. He lost two brothers and a sister in the storm. Eighty five percent of his village had completely disappeared. I led him to the Lord. We instructed him on how to be an evangelist and gave him our two booklets. He expressed excitement about going home and telling his wife, children and relatives about Jesus.

Jubilee, Robin and several Bible School students went to a special course taught by UN personnel on how to be a rescue worker. They were then allowed to go into the Irrawaddy Delta. Only residents and trained Burmese people were allowed into the Delta. Even most UN personnel were not allowed to enter.

Robin, Jubilee and the six Bible School students had made three trips into the Delta. Jubilee took many photos, with the promise he would never publish them. Thursday after clinic we stayed at the Bible School late and Jubilee showed us his pictures on his laptop computer, and told us of some of his experiences.

Their first trip was 30 days after the cyclone. They had to go by boat because the roads were impassable. The government newspaper announced a few days after the cyclone that they had removed all the dead bodies. Jubilee showed us pictures of many dead bodies still along the banks of the river 30 days later. He indicated that they really smelled terrible.

They went to a designated village and took rice, pots and pans, mosquito netting, drinking water, and a variety of medications. They found a large group of people gathered at the bank of the river, sick and half-starved, when they arrived. Jubilee's group was the first to reach them with any help. Needless to say they were happy to see them arrive.

There was almost nothing left of their village. The typical home in the delta was made on poles, 4 to 6 feet above the ground, constructed of bamboo and palm leaves, tied together with vines. It was easy to understand why there was so much destruction with 150 mile-per-hour winds and repeated waves and water surges 8 to 12 feet high. Jubilee showed us photos of the small remaining trees with grass and debris that was 12 feet high where the waterline once was. How anyone survived is hard to understand.

Some of the supplies they took were furnished by the UN and some were purchased by the donations of our former HTI mission team members. Jubilee and team stayed there for quite a while, and had the opportunity to lead many people to Jesus. They had been back to the same village several times and planned to return again.

We closed clinic at noon on Friday and had a gathering of the whole team. We sang songs and Robin presented monetary gifts to our translators and helpers. The team presented a variety of other gifts to them, along with many thank yous. Kathy gave her audio recorder speaker instruments to our translators and several of the Bible School students. They were excited about receiving them and immediately had to try them.

We had lunch, did a little last minute shopping at the central market, and went back to our hotel. We started reorganizing and inventorying our supplies and equipment that we were planning to leave for Dr. Johanson's team, that was scheduled to arrive in late February, 2009. We also packed for our trip home.

Friday evening Robin and family had the team over to his small apartment for a very nice supper and a final evening together. Robin gave us a copy of the statistics of our two weeks work, along with some very nice thank you gifts.

I gave Robin a gift from Dora May and me the evening we went to the Royal Barge for supper. Robin had been asking for a portable DVD projector for several years so that he could show the Jesus Film, as well as other Christian DVD's in various places where he traveled. Originally when we started shopping years ago, the lowest cost was about $2000. I finally found one and bought it for my personal use for $1200.

When we were at the Global Health Missions Conference, one of the missionary suppliers had a portable DVD projector that he was selling for $220. It was small and compact with a nice padded carrying case. It had a light bulb with lots of power and a life expectancy of 10,000 hours, more than needed. It could be operated with either 110V or 220Vs and Robin needed 220V. It included all the cords to hook to a laptop computer. I could hardly believe my eyes. It was just what Robin had been wanting, so, I purchased it, and tried it out at home before taking it to Myanmar.

I gave it to Robin early, so that he could check it out and make sure it was working and that it would meet his needs, before we left. Sunday morning Jubilee used it during the morning worship service and it worked perfectly. Needless to say, everyone was happy.

Six o'clock Saturday morning Robin arrived at our hotel with the final accounting of our land expenses. Our final cost was $1500 per person, which was lower than we had anticipated, considering the post cyclone inflation that Myanmar had experienced. Everyone was delighted.

Robin and family took us to the airport, and we flew to Singapore. We stayed overnight in a major downtown hotel. We had supper, shopped, and enjoyed viewing the fantastic Christmas street lights and decorations. Our return home the next day was long, but uneventful.

In Summary: This trip was somewhat different from our previous trips. There was a greater sense of tension as we observed plainclothes government officials visiting our clinic every day. They often would hang around and watch us. They never gave us any problem. We treated 1759 patients. The medical team treated 600, the optical team fit 836 pairs of glasses, and the dental team removed over 800 teeth. Most importantly, we had 544 people accept Jesus as their personal Savior and Lord.

Dr. Gary Moberg spent all of his time sharing Jesus with small groups of waiting medical and optical patients, which worked exceptionally well. We had a higher percentage of our patients become Christians this trip than any previous trip. Dental had one hundred percent of their patients become Christians. Our results were exciting and almost unbelievable. Fiona worked hard and did a great job organizing and dispensing medications, considering she was neither a nurse nor pharmacist.

## And Now the Rest of the Story

Dr. Bill Johanson led HTIs 9th team to Myanmar in February, 2009. They had no problems with customs, and reported a very successful mission, with many people coming to the Lord.

All of Stephanie's expenses were paid by family, friends, and our church.

Robin and I have agreed on a return HTI mission, which I hope to lead in late January, 2010. Already, almost a year ahead of time, Dr. Larry Black, Dr. Bill Hill as well as other former team members have expressed a desire to return. Fiona wanted to return, but she was accepted into a Bible College and decided she needed to get a better Christian education, so she would be more valuable on future mission trips. It was a very rewarding and fulfilling experience. People who are serving the Lord are happy people.

# CHAPTER 38

# WHAT CHRISTIANS BELIEVE
# HOW TO BE SAVED

On a mission trip to Myanmar (Burma), a few years ago, (Chapter 31), I unexpectedly discovered that I had absolutely no one to help me share the good news of Jesus. I knew my patients had never heard of Jesus, and if I didn't tell them, they might never have the opportunity to hear about Him in their lifetime. I thought I was doing good, by extracting teeth and relieving pain. Then I realized that I was allowing my patients to walk out the door and go to an eternity in hell, because I was too proud, ignorant, or stubborn to tell them about Jesus. The Holy Spirit convicted me, and I had such an uncomfortable heavy feeling in my heart. I felt terrible.

I started thinking. I had gone to church at least twice a week all my life and I had been a Christian for over 65 years. I should know how to share a salvation message with people, but no one had ever told me exactly how to do it. I laid in bed that night, and asked the Holy Spirit to help me put together a message for my totally unreached Buddhist patients, that would cause them to want to know what a Christian believed, and to help me to tell them how to become a Christian. I didn't get much sleep that night. The Holy Spirit did help me to draw on a lifetime of hearing the Gospel and reading my Bible, to put together a presentation to share with my patients.

I started sharing this presentation with my patients. I was surprised and pleased when almost everybody wanted to know what a Christian believed, and wanted to become a Christian. It worked so well that I started sharing it with the other dentists working with me. They started using it and had the same exciting results. Eventually I refined it and wrote it down as an outline for my other team members. I gave it as a suggestion to other teams going to Myanmar, and they reported great success. In time, we published this presentation in Burmese in a 30 page illustrated booklet, and we gave it to all of our patients. Now other churches and evangelical teams are asking for copies of this booklet.

I knew that most of the people that became Christians would not have a church to attend, because in most areas there were no Christian churches. I needed to reassure them that they were now a Christian, then give them some instructions, and challenge them to share their faith with others.

I don't claim to have all the answers. I also am sure that each individual Christian would make the presentation a little differently. This is a presentation that works for me, and if it will challenge your thinking on how you could do better in presenting the Gospel, then it will have been of value. There are differences in various denominations, and in different people's beliefs, but I think the central theme of salvation is the same in all Christian faiths. Each individual may need to modify this presentation to fit specific beliefs of the people he is presenting it to, while not compromising the main foundations of Christianity. It is my hope that the following presentation and information will be a helpful guide for introducing unreached people to Jesus.

## The Presentation

The spaces between the sentences in the following presentation are to give the translator time to repeat what you have said into the local language.

For my dental patients, I diagnose the problem, give them dental advice, recommendations, and options for treatment. Most frequently they require extractions, so I will give them local anesthesia and say;

"We have to wait for the medicine to work." (I pause a few moments and then activate their mind by asking them a question.) (If they don't require anesthesia, I skip this step and just ask the following :)

"Do you know why we came all the way from America to help you?"

"Because we love you." (Most people have never had a stranger tell them that they loved them.)

"We are Christians and we are taught to love and to help people in need."

"Do you know what Christians believe?"

"Would you like for me to tell you while we are waiting?"

"Christians believe that there is one God." (I hold up one finger.)

"Christians believe that a long time ago, God created the whole world. He created the sky, stars, moon, sun, earth, water, all the plants, and animals, and everything."

"We believe that God makes the sun come up in the morning, the wind, the clouds, and the rain, and makes everything grow. He controls all of nature."

"God created man and woman a long time ago to be friends with Him, like a family, and He gave them freedom to make their own choices."

"But God was disappointed with people, because they disobeyed Him. They argued, lied, cheated, fought and did bad things."

"So God decided 2010 years ago, to send his only Son, Jesus, down to earth to teach people how to live good and please God." (Use current date.)

"Have you ever heard of Christmas?" (I have only had one person say no.)

"Everyone in the world has heard of Christmas. It is Jesus' birthday. It is when God sent Jesus down to earth to help us."

"After Jesus grew up to be a young man, He taught people how to be good and please God. All of His teachings are recorded in a book called the Bible."

"The Bible has become the most important book in the entire world. More people have bought it and read it than any other book in the history of the world."

"Today there is over 6 billion people in the world."

"There are over 2 billion people in the world that have already become Christians. One out of every three people in the world is a Christian." (I hold up one finger on one hand and two fingers on the other hand.)

"There still are 2 billion people in the world that have never heard of Jesus. We believe everyone should have the opportunity to hear of Jesus and understand about Jesus, at least once in their life, so they can make a decision for themselves."

"After Jesus taught people how to live right and please God, God was again disappointed. People still disobeyed by lying, cheating, arguing, fighting, and doing bad things."

"So Jesus volunteered to die and to be killed on a cross, as a sacrifice before God, so we could have all of our bad deeds forgiven by God."

"After three days, God brought his Son, Jesus, back to life, and He continued to teach His followers."

"One day He rose up into the sky in front of many people, and went back up into heaven to be with His Father, God and he lives there today."

"I am75 years old. I am getting old, and will be dying soon, but I'm not afraid to die."

"Jesus promised me that when I die, I will go to heaven, and will be with Him and God, and all my Christian family and friends forever."

"Jesus teaches us that heaven is a good place, where we will get new bodies, and there will be no more sickness or pain, no more fighting or sorrow, and everything will be good forever and ever."

"Would you like to go to heaven when you die?"

"Jesus teaches us that we only have to do two things, and they are simple and free." (I hold up two fingers.)

"First, you need to ask Jesus to forgive you for all the mistakes you have made, or bad things you have done, in your whole life." (I hold up one finger.)

"Second, you need to ask Jesus to come into your heart and life, and believe He is the one true God." (I hold up two fingers.)

"If you'd like to do this, I will teach you how. We do this by talking to God. He can hear us, and He can understand all languages because He made us. We call it prayer." (They will often sit up and fold their hands.)

"Please repeat after me."

"Jesus, please forgive me for all the bad things that I have done in my whole life."

"Jesus, please come into my heart and into my life, and help me believe you are the one true God."

"Amen." (Pause)

"Did you believe what you just said?"

"You are now a Christian, like us."

"We are all part of God's family, no matter where we live."

'Jesus promised us that once we invite Him into our heart and life, He will never, never leave us, and no one can take Him away."

"Jesus also teaches us that He is the only way to God or to heaven. There is no other way in the whole world." (This is meant to tell our new Christians in a positive way that they do not need to continue to worship Buddha.)

"Jesus teaches us, that when we die, we will meet God one-on-one, face to face, and it won't make any difference what our family or anyone else in the world believes. It is only what is in your heart and what you believe that counts."

"I am very happy for you. Christians are usually happy people, because they don't have to worry about where they are going after they die. They know they are going to heaven."

"Christians are usually happiest when they are with good Christian friends that will love them, teach them, and help them."

"You don't have to go to church to be a Christian. You just need to have Jesus in your heart and life and believe in Him.

"Usually Christians are happy when they go to church because they find Christian friends that will love and help them. I hope you can find some good Christian friends."

"This is the most important day in your entire life, because it's the day you decided where you are going to spend forever and ever after you die, which is in heaven."

"I have some gifts I want to give you so that you can always remember this important day."

At this point, I ask my wife to take a Polaroid picture of the patient with the translator and me. Originally we gave the undeveloped photo to my patient, and they watched it develop. It really excites them. It is probably the first and only picture they have ever had taken of themselves. It is a good memory object so they can remember the most important day of their life. This step, of course, is optional. On our last few missions we couldn't find any Polaroid film so we bought the new pocket sized laser Polaroid printer. It will print a picture from any digital camera quicker, much cheaper, and of better quality.

No one has objected to having their picture taken. We also found it was an easy way to keep track of the number of people who had accepted Jesus, by counting the number of prints we had made. We give them a 30-page tract that contains 100% scriptures of key Bible verses of Jesus' teachings.

We also give each person the booklet we printed which contains all of the above presentation. It contains the exact steps they went through to become a Christian, and hopefully they will use this to help lead their family and friends to Jesus.

I extract the tooth, or sometimes many teeth, and give them pain medication with postoperative instructions. We also give them a toothbrush, a colorful cloth bracelet that says, "I have Jesus in my heart," and I take a sticker off my scrub and put it on them. The sticker has "Jesus loves me," printed on it. They are cheap little gifts I get on line from Oriental Trading Co., but I have observed that this simple expression of my love to them is important.

I asked them "May I pray for you before you leave." (I do this for all patients.)

"Jesus, I pray these wounds will heal with no problems or complications."

"Jesus, I thank you that this (lady, man, girl or boy) has become a Christian today and invited Jesus into (his or her) heart and life." (This is a reinforcement of their commitment.)

I pray that this (man or lady) will have courage to tell (his or her) family and friends about Jesus.

"Jesus, I pray this (lady, man, girl or boy) will be able to find some good Christian friends who will love (him or her), teach (him or her), and help (him or her)."

"Jesus I pray that you will give this (lady or man) peace in (his or her) heart, and happiness in (his or her) life."

"Amen."

"Do you have a family?"

"Would you like for your family, (usually children) to go to heaven to be with you, when they die?"

"You have an important job as (mother, father, head of the family) to teach your (children, family) about Jesus."

"This booklet will help you, but if you need more help, ask a church pastor or Christian friends to help you."

I put my hand on their shoulder and say, "God bless you my new Christian (brother or sister)," and I motion for them to leave by my standing up at this time. I always shake their hand and say, "Thank you," as they are leaving. It is not customary in the Buddhist culture to hug, especially those of the opposite sex.

If the patient does not need an extraction, just a consultation or an exam, I ask them if they know why we have come to help, etc. Then I ask if they have a few moments for me to tell them what a Christian believes. They have always said yes. Burmese people never seem to be in a hurry.

•
•
# • **Comments on the Presentation**
•
•

I have made a personal resolve that everyone deserves to hear about Jesus, so I offer to share the Gospel with everyone who sits down in my dental chair. In several trips to Burma, 100% of my patients have asked to hear what Christians believe, and 100% have prayed to become Christians, even eight Buddhist monks. I have seen some fantastic fruits of the Holy Spirit. Several hundred people have accepted Jesus in my dental chair, but I always remember that I have never saved anyone. Only the Holy Spirit can change people's hearts. I am only the messenger.

Notice, in my presentation I have kept it very simple, with none of the religious Christian terminology such as sin, saved, born-again, salvation, hell, eternity, etc. I purposely repeat Jesus' name several times. I repeat in my prayer that they are now Christians, that they need to find good Christian friends, and that they need to tell their family and friends about Jesus. I feel these three things are important and worth reinforcing.

Notice, I did not criticize or preach against any other religion, which I feel is not necessary, and it may just create anger, defensiveness, and bitterness. I just present the good news of the Gospel.

Many of the comments and wording of this presentation have been tailored to the Buddhist cultural beliefs, and potential problems. Some new Christians could be thrown out of their homes if the family, usually the father, found out that they are Christians.

I try to sound enthusiastic. I ask questions to keep their mind from wandering. I look him or her in the eye when talking, and use motions or gestures including holding up fingers.

I pray for all patients before they leave my chair. Depending upon the interpreter, the total presentation, prayer, etc. usually lasts 25 to 30 minutes.

We need to remember that most of these people have never heard of the Bible, Jesus, or what Christians believe. Example: most of them have never even heard of heaven, or what it is.

Buddhists have no church services and basically have no literature for the common person, and have basically no one to teach them except family. When asking several Buddhists how they became Buddhist, they said they didn't know. "I guess I was just born Buddhist," they would say.

Our local pastors and translators were repeatedly astonished that everyone we saw wanted to become a Christian. They said to me, "You don't know how hard it is to convert a Buddhist to Christianity. Many times we work a whole year and only get a handful of converts." After thinking about it, we came to these conclusions: most of the team was older and white-haired. White hair is almost nonexistent in their society, and they greatly respect age and white hair. We were also white-skinned Doctors from America, and that commanded great respect also. Their society does not have a caste system, but the rich and educated almost never sit down and talk with the common people concerning anything. If commoners or poor people went to a physician, they were never allowed to ask a question. Although over 2% of the population is comprised of Buddhist monks, they never sit down and talk to the common people. There are no church type services, scripture study times, or courses for the common people. There is no Buddhist literature for the common people to read.

Then all of a sudden, here came a respected, older, white-haired, white-skinned, educated, American doctor, who would take the time to sit down and talk to a common person one-on-one, ask questions about his job and family, and show a genuine concern about his happiness and his future welfare, even after death. That just absolutely blows their minds. No one had ever done this before, nor shown a sincere interest in them as an important individual person. Then the doctor would take care of their health care problem free. The pastor said they respected us almost like we spoke with the authority of God. Maybe that is why some have called us angels, sent by God.

At first we did not understand our fantastic success in sharing the Gospel, but when you put it into their cultural perspective, we started to understand. What a great opportunity we have as old white-haired, educated, foreign, white professionals, to present the good news of Jesus Christ to these people, who have never before heard the name of Jesus. We need to take advantage of this unique and fantastic opportunity.

Over 90% of the population in Myanmar is Buddhist. In the areas where we worked, it was almost 100% Buddhist. Christians, Hindus, and Muslims were in the minority.

In many areas where we worked, there were no Christian churches, and sometimes not even a Christian home fellowship.

Although sharing Jesus takes more time, we have been able to finish most of our dental patients every day. When our dental waiting line got long, I took two or three patients at a time, anesthetized them, and shared Jesus with two or three huddled together. This worked very well also.

I try to reinforce several times that they are now Christians, and to make sure they know that they are Christians.

I had a lady come to me and ask to have two abscessed teeth extracted. I anesthetized her and started my usual presentation. She looked at me and said, "You don't remember me, do you? You took out these teeth last year," as she pointed to an edentulous area, "and you told me all about Jesus." I asked her if she accepted Jesus into her life, and she said, "Yes." I always challenge new Christians to tell their family and friends about Jesus, so I asked her if she had been able to tell other people about Jesus. She indicated her whole family was now Christians. She reported they had found a good church, and now she was in charge of a woman's Bible fellowship, teaching and telling a lot of women about Jesus every week.

Members of Health Teams International consider themselves as seed planters of the Gospel in areas of unreached people groups. Jesus told us that some seeds will fall on rocky ground only to wither and die, some will be choked out by weeds and thorns, but some will fall on fertile ground. The seeds of the Gospel for this lady had fallen on fertile ground. Most of the time we never know how many of our seeds will grow and multiply, but that's okay. Our job is to plant seeds of the Gospel the best way we know how.

This lady also pointed out another important principle. People without dental care will likely have another toothache, but I fear that most of them, especially in Myanmar, may never have another opportunity to hear the Gospel before they die. Which is more important, eliminating a toothache, or introducing a person to Jesus and saving their life for eternity?

For 65 years I kept telling myself that my gift was not as an evangelist. I couldn't do that. I didn't know how. Now, I know how, and so do you. I'm sure you could do it, if you want to. Ask the Holy Spirit for help and courage.

One of my greatest joys has been to teach people how to effectively share Jesus with the unreached, and then to experience their personal joy that comes when they introduce a person to believe in Jesus, especially their very first time.

On one of our last trips to Myanmar, a dentist whom I taught and encouraged to use my presentation shared the Gospel of Jesus with an older man. As he shared the good news of Jesus, tears streamed down the old man's face. After the man invited Jesus into his heart, he told the dentist he was getting old, and that he had worried all his life about what was going to happen to him after he died. Now he had a greater sense of peace in his heart than he had ever felt before in his entire life, because he finally knew for sure what was going to happen to him after he died. Not only was the patient one happy man, but the dentist, who had never before had the privilege of leading a person to Jesus, was equally happy, and so was I.

**Try it, you'll like it. Jesus commands us to do it. I will guarantee it will change your life and make you one very happy person**